D1085213

PSYCHOPATHOLOGY AND THE FAMILY

PSYCHOPATHOLOGY AND THE FAMILY

EDITED BY

JENNIFER L. HUDSON and RONALD M. RAPEE

Macquarie University, Sydney, New South Wales, Australia

ELSEVIER

Amsterdam – Boston – Heidelberg – London – New York – Oxford
Paris – San Diego – San Francisco – Singapore – Sydney – Tokyo

ELSEVIER B.V.
Radarweg 29
P.O. Box 211, 1000 AE
Amsterdam, The Netherlands

ELSEVIER Inc.
525 B Street, Suite 1900
San Diego, CA 92101-4495
USA

**ELSEVIER Ltd
The Boulevard, Langford Lane
Kidlington, Oxford OX5 1GB
UK**

ELSEVIER Ltd
84 Theobalds Road
London WC1X 8RR
UK

First edition 2005

Library of Congress Cataloging in Publication Data
A catalog record is available from the Library of Congress.

British Library Cataloguing in Publication Data
A catalogue record is available from the British Library.

ISBN-10: 0-08-044449-0
ISBN-13: 978-0-08-044449-9

♾ The paper used in this publication meets the requirements of ANSI/NISO Z39.48-1992 (Permanence of Paper).
Printed in The Netherlands.

To my parents, for their truly
unconditional love and nurturing.
Jennifer Hudson

To my fabulous girls, Alice and Lucy,
and my beautiful parenting support, Wendy.
Ron Rapee

Contents

SECTION III

Contributors

Shelli Avenevoli	National Institute of Mental Health, National Institutes of Health, Department of Health and Human Services, Bethesda, MD, USA
Kevin P. Conway	National Institute on Drug Abuse, National Institutes of Health, Department of Health and Human Services, Bethesda, MD, USA
Mark R. Dadds	School of Psychology, The University of New South Wales, Australia
Frank M. Dattilio	Department of Psychiatry, Harvard Medical School, Boston, MA, USA
Thalia C. Eley	Social, Genetic and Developmental Psychiatry Center, Institute of Psychiatry, King's College London, UK
Caitlin Ferriter	Department of Psychology, Harvard University, Cambridge, MA, USA
Natalie S. Gar	Macquarie University, New South Wales, Australia
Judy Garber	Vanderbilt University, Nashville, TN, USA
Gemma L. Gladstone	School of Psychiatry, The University of New South Wales and Black Dog Institute, Prince of Wales Hospital, New South Wales, Australia
David J. Hawes	School of Psychology, The University of New South Wales, Australia
Jill M. Hooley	Department of Psychology, Harvard University, Cambridge, MA, USA

Jennifer L. Hudson	Department of Psychology, Macquarie University, New South Wales, Australia
Charlotte Johnston	Department of Psychology, University of British Columbia, Canada
Jennifer Y. F. Lau	Social, Genetic and Developmental Psychiatry Center, Institute of Psychiatry, King's College London, UK
Katharina Manassis	Department of Psychiatry, Hospital for Sick Children, Toronto, Ontario, Canada
Eric J. Mash	Department of Psychology, University of Calgary, Alberta, Canada
Catherine McMahon	Psychology Department, Macquarie University, New South Wales, Australia
Joel Paris	McGill University, Montreal, Canada
Gordon B. Parker	School of Psychiatry, The University of New South Wales and Black Dog Institute, Prince of Wales Hospital, New South Wales, Australia
Alan Ralph	Parenting and Family Support Centre, School of Psychology, The University of Queensland, Brisbane, Australia
Ronald M. Rapee	Macquarie University, New South Wales, Australia
Kathleen Ries Merikangas	National Institute of Mental Health, National Institutes of Health, Department of Health and Human Services, Bethesda, MD, USA
Matthew R. Sanders	Parenting and Family Support Centre, School of Psychology, The University of Queensland, Brisbane, Australia
Judy Ungerer	Psychology Department, Macquarie University, New South Wales, Australia
Tracey Wade	School of Psychology, Flinders University, Adelaide, Australia
Kristen A. Woodberry	Department of Psychology, Harvard University, Cambridge, MA, USA

Preface

On a recent Sydney radio programme a heated debate raged between the announcer of the popular daytime programme and a caller. The debate was about the importance of "good" parenting to raise healthy and well-adjusted children. The announcer ended the debate by stating, "My mother always said that you can tell the quality of the parents by the behaviour of the children".

In current Western society there is perhaps no topic that generates debate and stimulates the emotions as much as the role of the family in children's adjustment. From Bejamin Spock's early books to current television programmes such as "The Super Nanny", there are few topics that generate this degree of popularity and passion.

From among this morass of popular opinion, hearsay, and misguided welfare, an entire population of scientists has attempted to study and develop theories about the role of family interactions in the development of psychopathology. Perhaps, unsurprisingly, the scientific literature has been almost as polarised as the popular. John Bowlby stimulated decades of research and theory with his descriptions of the role of the parent–child relationship in the onset of a range of psychological disorders. The attachment literature has continued to apply scientific enquiry and careful observation to examine the psychological influence of specific styles of parent–child interactions. On the opposite side of the ledger lies the highly controversial paper by David Rowe (1990) titled *As the Twig is Bent: The myth of child-rearing influences on personality development*. In this paper Rowe marshals empirical data from behaviour genetic studies into a range of psychopathology that demonstrates that the variance in symptoms of disorder and personality accounted for by shared environmental variables (such as parenting styles, socioeconomic factors, family disruption etc.), is negligible. He concludes that parents need to stop berating themselves for ruining their child's life, since the evidence clearly exonerates them from any influence on their child's personality.

The purpose of this book is to draw together scientifically based information on the role of the family in the development and maintenance of psychopathology. We have assembled a wonderful group of authors, each of whom is an international authority in their field and have asked them to provide an up-to-date synopsis of the evidence. The chapters provide scientifically balanced, careful, and critical appraisals of the literature, drawing together what is known and highlighting what is yet to be shown, in terms of the extent of the influence of family factors on psychopathology.

We begin the book with a chapter on behaviour genetics by Thalia Eley and Jennifer Lau. Statistical methods and understanding of interactions has improved since the paper by Rowe and Dr Eley provides a thorough and balanced introduction to the methods used in behaviour genetics as well as an overview of the limitations and implications these methods hold for our understanding of family influences. Emma Gladstone and Gordon Parker provide the next methodological chapter, summarising decades of research into one of the most influential self-report measures of parenting styles, the Parental Bonding Instrument. This is followed by a chapter by Judy Ungerer and Catherine McMahon reviewing the wealth of observational data on the construct of attachment and its influence on child behaviour. The first section is completed by Jennifer Hudson's chapter reviewing perhaps the most emotional topic of the role of family conflict and violence in the development of psychopathology.

Following these early chapters that overview areas and methods of research into family factors, we then include eight chapters reviewing the role of family functioning in specific areas of psychopathology. Each chapter provides a critical appraisal of the evidence and draws conclusions about the extent of our knowledge to date as well as pointing to areas that require further investigation.

Finally, the book concludes with three chapters outlining the implications of the family for various aspects of clinical practice. Katharina Manassis provides a careful and systematic review of the empirical literature, while Frank Datillio describes the more subtle issues to consider in including the family in clinical practice. Finally, Mathew Sanders and Alan Ralph draw on their experience with *Triple P* to describe the implications that family factors may hold in implementing programmes to prevent the development of psychopathology.

It is only by drawing together empirical evidence and critical appraisal in a book such as this that we will begin to overcome the misinformation and emotional intensity associated with discussion of family influence. In turn it is only by moving away from blame and innuendo that we can develop a real understanding of those family factors that may be important in the development of psychopathology and those that are not. Ultimately, such improved understanding will help us to either focus interventions onto factors that are influential or to redirect resources to areas of greater impact. This book will be of value to researchers in psychopathology and mental health as well as to practitioners who deal with families on a daily basis and hopefully also to policy makers whose role it is to decide where the most appropriate expenditure of mental health resources lies.

Jennifer L. Hudson and Ronald M. Rapee,

10th May, 2005

SECTION I

Chapter 1

Genetics and the Family Environment

Thalia C. Eley and Jennifer Y. F. Lau

One could be forgiven for asking why there is a chapter on behavioural genetics in a book on the family environment. Those somewhat familiar with the behavioural genetic literature may already know that within this discipline, in addition to estimating the level of genetic influence on any measure, we also look at environmental influences — divided into those that are shared between family members (shared environment) and those that are individual-specific (non-shared environment). A second, and related thought that many may have therefore is that this chapter must be about the "shared" environment, as surely this is where the influence of the family environment will be most strongly seen? As it turns out, this is not the case. The family environment operates in a far more child-specific fashion (i.e. making children within the same family different from one another) than was ever imagined previous to the work of behavioural geneticists. The field is also now starting to address the complexity of the dynamics of the family environment, which is made up also of indirect genetic effects and interactions between genetic and environmental effects. We hope that this chapter will give some insight into the valuable contribution made by behavioural genetics to the understanding of the family environment.

Behavioural Genetic Methodology

There are three main types of behavioural genetic study. The first, and historically the most broadly applied of which is the family study. It has long been recognised that family members resemble one another for a wide variety of characteristics ranging from cognitive ability or personality to emotional and behavioural symptoms. This resemblance may be due to shared genetic influence, and thus can be taken as a maximum level of potential genetic effect. However, this resemblance can also be due to the shared environment that family member's experience, but the family method is unable to distinguish between these two. This limitation means that results from family studies are best considered in combination with other behavioural genetic designs.

Twin studies make use of the natural experiment provided by the existence of two types of twins: monozygotic (MZ) twins who share all their genes and dizygotic (DZ) twins who

Psychopathology and the Family
Edited by J. L. Hudson and R. M. Rapee
Copyright © 2005 by Elsevier Ltd.
All rights of reproduction in any form reserved
ISBN: 0-08-044449-0

share on average half their segregating genes (those that vary in the human population: *A*). As with other family members they share their family environment. Aspects of this environment that make twins (and other family members) resemble one another are defined as shared environment (*C*). Aspects of the environment (including family and non-family influences) that make family members different from one another are termed non-shared environment (*E*). MZ twins therefore share all their genes and all their shared environment (i.e. rMZ = A + C). In contrast, DZ twins share just half their genes, but again all of the effects of shared environment (i.e. rDZ = ½ A + C). The difference in correlation between a group of MZ and DZ twins therefore provides a rough estimate of heritability (i.e. A = 2(rMZ − rDZ)). Shared environment is the difference between MZ resemblance and heritability (i.e. C = rMZ − A). Non-shared environment or *E* is calculated as the difference between the MZ twin correlation and 1 (i.e. E = 1 − rMZ). Thus, this approach allows the variance in a trait to be divided into that due to each of these three factors. Model-fitting analyses allow the estimation of precise variance components, i.e. the contribution to variance in the measure of genes, shared environment and non-shared environment, along with confidence intervals. Furthermore, such models can be extended to examine more sophisticated hypotheses such as the role of genes, shared and non-shared environment on the covariation between two measures, or on continuity over time.

However, there are limitations to the twin study, and these include the equal environments assumption, chorionicity, assortative mating and generalisability. The equal environment assumption states that both MZ and DZ twin pairs experience shared environment to the same degree. However, some authors question this assumption on the basis that twins who resemble one another more closely physically are more likely to be treated alike, inflating their experience of shared environment. In fact, studies exploring the equal environments assumption have found that for most aspects of psychopathology it holds true, and that although MZ twins are treated more similarly, this is because they behave in a more similar fashion and thus elicit more similar responses from others, an effect that is thus due to their genes (and therefore accurately modelled as such) rather than the environment (Martin, Boomsma, & Machin, 1997). Chorionicity refers to the number of chorions, the sack within which, in singletons, the foetus develops. In all DZ twins there are two chorions, but in two-thirds of MZ twins there is just one chorion, thus leading to the possibility that increased MZ resemblance may be due to chorion sharing. There is little data on this issue as it requires skilled work, but that which there is indicates that monochorionic MZ twins may be a little more similar to one another than dichorionic MZ twins, an effect which would slightly inflate heritability estimates (Plomin, DeFries, McClearn, & McGuffin, 2001; Martin et al., 1997). Assortative mating refers to the well-replicated finding that "birds of a feather flock together" or that individuals mate with those similar to themselves. This leads to an increase in genetic variance in the population, and in increased genetic resemblance in DZ twin-pairs and a resultant decrease in genetic estimates (Plomin et al., 2001). Finally, there is the question of the degree to which twins are representative of the non-twin population. Extant data indicate that with the exception of a slight initial delay in language development, which disappears by school-age, twins are largely indistinguishable from non-twins (Rutter & Redshaw, 1991). These limitations mean that values of, for example, heritability, from twin studies should not be regarded as absolute, but as an indication of the approximate role of genes on the measured trait. The best way to validate data from a twin study is to utilise a method which has different strengths and weaknesses, i.e. the adoption design.

In adopted families the parent–child resemblance and sibling resemblance (if adopted from separate families) is assumed to be due to shared environment only. In contrast, the resemblance between the adopted offspring and biological parents is assumed to be due to genetic influence. Thus, these two types of relationship provide very clean, direct estimates of genetic and shared environmental influence. Of course, there are assumptions here too (Plomin et al., 2001). Aspects of the uterine environment may be important, but will get included in the estimate of genetic effect as they are provided by the biological mother who in all other ways only shares genes with her adopted away offspring. Also, both those who have their offspring adopted and those who adopt may not be representative of the total population. Finally, there is sometimes matching on some characteristics such as physical looks, or even perceived IQ, between the biological and adoptive parents, which may lead to genetic similarity between the adoptive family and adopted offspring. However, as with the twin design precise estimates should not be taken as "gold standard" but rather used as indicators of rough levels of genetic and environmental influence. The combination of similar findings from studies using both the adoption and twin designs provides the surest evidence for any finding.

Behavioural Genetic Studies of Development Psychopathology: Shared versus Non-Shared Environment

As noted earlier, an initial reflection on the contribution of behavioural genetics to a book on family environment might be taken to be referring to what is termed the shared environment. In fact, one of the most startling findings from the research of the late 1980s and 1990s was that shared environment accounts for little of the variance in most aspects of psychopathology, and that it is non-shared environment that is found to be substantial and significant (Plomin, Chipuer, & Neiderhiser, 1994a). An early study illustrating this effect asked adoptive and biological siblings to report on their differential experiences with regard to sibling interaction and parental treatment (Daniels & Plomin, 1985). The study found that children report high levels of differential experience, indicating that aspects of the family environment tend to be child-specific (i.e. children do not receive or perceive their family environments in the same way). Child-specific aspects of the family environment make up the factor described "non-shared" environment within behavioural genetic models. A study set up specifically to examine this issue — The Non-shared Environment and Adolescent Development study (NEAD) — has gone on to explore child-specific aspects of the environment in considerable detail since this time (Plomin et al., 2001). The data from this study consistently show that the environmental influence of the family is non-shared, even when observational ratings are used. For example, parent–child interaction ratings including warmth, communication, anger, coercion, and involvement are all more influenced by non-shared environment factors than any other (proportion of variance ranging from 61% to 80%). These findings do not negate the role of the family environment, but indicate that these influences act in a far more child-specific fashion than was previously imagined.

The two main exceptions to this pattern of findings are some aspects of antisocial behaviour, notably non-aggressive antisocial behaviour (e.g. Eley, Lichtenstein, & Stevenson, 1999) and aspects of anxiety, including separation anxiety disorder (Feigon, Waldman, Levy, & Hay, 2001; Silberg, Rutter, Neale, & Eaves, 2001), separation anxiety symptoms (Silove, Manicavasagar, O'Connell, & Morris-Yates, 1995; Topolski et al., 1997), and fear symptoms (Lichtenstein & Annas, 2000; Rose & Ditto, 1983; Stevenson, Batten, & Cherner, 1992), although there are exceptions to this pattern of results (Silberg et al., 2001; Eaves et al., 1997). For antisocial behaviour there are many candidates for this shared environmental influence including sibling or shared peer effects, socio-economic status (SES), and education — all of which may operate to make two members of the same family similar to one another. For separation anxiety, this effect may be due to the possibility that the behaviour of the mother is a significant component of the problem, and that this is likely to affect more than one child in a family. The role of shared environment in fear symptoms may result from learning or modelling effects.

The finding that environmental influences on the development of psychopathology are largely child-specific was itself something of a surprise to many. However, there are even more interesting questions that can be answered regarding the family environment using a behavioural genetic approach. For example, what are the relative roles of genes, shared and non-shared environment on measured aspects of the family environment? How do genes, shared and non-shared environment impact on the links between measured aspects of the family environment and psychopathological traits? It is to these two questions that we turn next.

Behavioural Genetic Studies of Family Environment and Developmental Psychopathology

Behavioural genetic studies of family environment largely rely on questionnaire measures, although there are data on observational measures. Of note, almost every study to date has found genetic influence on measures of family life including family connectedness (Jacobson & Rowe, 1999), parent–child interaction as assessed by questionnaire (Plomin, Reiss, Hetherington, & Howe, 1994b), observation (O'Connor, Hetherington, Reiss, & Plomin, 1995) or both (Pike, McGuire, Hetherington, Reiss, & Plomin, 1996a), sibling interactions assessed by questionnaire alone (Plomin et al., 1994b) or combined with observation (Pike et al., 1996a), parental divorce (O'Connor, Caspi, DeFries, & Plomin, 2000) and life events (Thapar & McGuffin, 1996; Thapar, Harold, & McGuffin, 1998; Silberg et al., 1999). This astonishing array of family environment variables on which there is significant genetic influence indicates that there is far more complexity to the origins of the family environment than had previously been thought.

An even more interesting area of research is that regarding the origins of the links between family environment and psychopathology, which have all found that not only are there genetic influences on these measured aspects of the environment, but that these overlap to some degree with the genetic influences on psychological outcomes in the child. For example, genetic overlap has been identified on the associations between parenting and both aggression and depression (Pike et al., 1996a), parental divorce and many aspects of child adjustment (O'Connor et al., 2000), and between life events and depression (Thapar et al., 1998; Rice,

Harold, & Thapar, 2003; Silberg et al., 1999). These results reveal that the same genes are involved not only in the aetiology of aspects of the child's environment, but also in the development of their symptoms. This means that the child may in some way be driving their own environments more than has previously been thought (e.g. their behaviour influencing the way they are disciplined), or that the genes the child has inherited from the parent that influence the development of symptoms, also impact on the parents own life choices (e.g. divorce).

A powerful behavioural genetic tool for examining purely non-shared environmental impact (i.e. independent of genetic influence) of specific measured aspects of the environment is the MZ differences design. The strength of this design lies in the fact that, like the adoption design, it can give you a clean estimate of one type of effect — non-shared environment. As the similarity between MZ twins is due to genes and shared environment, any differences are solely due to non-shared environment. Thus, the extent to which MZ twins differ on measured aspects of the family environment indicates the level of non-shared environmental influence of that variable. Similarly, the extent to which MZ twins differ on behavioural and emotional ratings is assumed to be due to non-shared environment only. Thus, the association between MZ twin differences on family environment and child outcomes indicates the degree of influence of the non-shared environmental route between the two (as compared to genetic or shared environmental). For example, early work on this method identified MZ differences for both parental negativity and adolescent adjustment using a combination of parent-report, observation and adolescent-report (Pike, Reiss, Hetherington, & Plomin, 1996b). MZ difference scores in parental negativity correlated significantly with relative differences in adolescent antisocial behaviour. In other words, the twin that parents were more negative towards was also the twin that had higher antisocial behaviour scores. As MZ twins are genetically identical, this association must be environmental in origin. Thus, there is an environmentally mediated association between the child's antisocial behaviour and the parental negativity.

Similarly, in a more recent study, MZ differences in parent-reported harsh discipline and negative parental feelings were correlated with MZ differences in parent-reported anxiety, conduct, hyperactivity and prosocial behaviour (Asbury, Dunn, Pike, & Plomin, 2003). Significant links were found between harsh parental discipline and both hyperactivity and conduct problems, and prosocial behaviour (negative association). Significant links were also found between all four child outcomes and negative parental feelings. In all cases, the child for whom the more negative discipline or feelings were reported had the poorer outcome (high anxiety, conduct or hyperactivity symptoms and lower prosocial behaviour). Thus again, there is an environmental link between parental discipline and negativity and child emotional and behavioural symptoms. Unfortunately both these studies used cross-sectional data, which means we are unable to talk about any direction of effect, but these data do indicate that these associations are environmental in origin. Thus, they are consistent with the interpretation that children who experience parental negativity develop more emotional and behavioural symptoms as a result. However, they are also consistent with the explanation that children with emotional and behavioural symptoms lead their parents to be more negative.

In order to extend these findings to examine both sequelae and maintaining factors of adolescent depression, we collected data at two time-points 6 months apart (Liang & Eley, press). Depression *per se* predicted subsequent negative and constructive parenting, negative life events (dependent and independent), peer group (antisocial and prosocial) and depression scores. When examining MZ twin differences, differences in depression scores predicted subsequent differences in depression, aspects of parenting (maternal negative and paternal constructive discipline) and dependent life events. Thus, the adolescent with higher depression scores at time one, reported higher depression, poorer parenting and greater numbers of dependent life events at time two, findings which can only have been mediated via non-shared environmental routes. When we predicted time two differences in depression taking into account earlier depression (i.e. examined maintaining factors), we found that only dependent life events played a non-shared environmental role in the maintenance of depression over time.

In summary, there are substantial genetic influences on many aspects of the family environment. Furthermore, to the extent that these "environmental" variables act through non-genetic routes, the effects tend to be child-specific (i.e. non-shared environment). Evidence from the MZ differences design has revealed environmentally driven links between aspects of the family environment and emotional and behavioural symptoms. Moreover, these links are due to child-specific environmental effects in that they lead to differences within twin pairs. Thus, there are both genetic and non-shared environmental influences on most aspects of family environment. The latter effect is clear to understand, but how exactly might genetic influences on the environment come about?

Specifying Gene–Family Environment Correlations in Developmental Psychopathology

Genetic influence on measured aspects of the environment is described by the term "gene–environment correlation". There are three routes by which gene–environment correlations may arise. First, biological family members share both genes and environment. So, for example, antisocial parents are likely not only to pass on genes related to such behaviours to their children, but are also likely to expose the children to such behaviours which may then be modelled and learned. This is called a passive gene–environment correlation (Scarr & McCartney, 1983). Evocative gene–environment correlations refer to the fact that the behaviour of a child will evoke certain reactions from others, thus influencing the experienced environment. For example, a sociable smiley baby will evoke positive responses from those around it, whereas one with high irritability and low soothability will elicit quite different responses from others. This can have the effect of producing a vicious cycle whereby the more positive or negative a child's behaviour, the more their environment reflects that, and thus the better or worse their chances of optimal psychological development. Finally, active gene–environment correlation refers to the fact that as children grow, and particularly once they enter adolescence or adulthood, they make choices about their worlds. For example, a child who is bright may choose to join after-school clubs of an educational nature, thus increasing their learning and potential. A child who is struggling may not feel comfortable with any extra exposure to learning situations and will thus lose out on this opportunity to help their development. For an illustrative figure of gene–environment correlation, i.e. the effects of genetic influence on the family environment see Figure 1a. This figure simply illustrates the typical pattern of effects of moderate

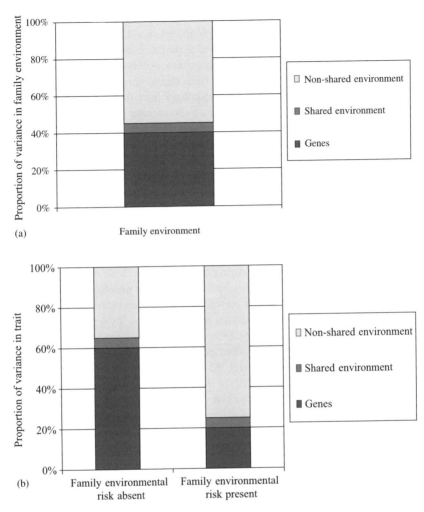

Figure 1: (a) Gene–environment correlation. (b) Gene–environment interaction.

genetic effects (40%), minimal shared environmental effects (5%), and substantial non-shared environment (55%) on a measured aspect of the environment.

It is fairly difficult to distinguish between the three types of gene–environment correlation, and often all that can be said is that the overall effect is present. However, some studies have been able to use specific approaches to tackle this question. One approach is to use the children of twins design, which has recently been described as being able to resolve passive and evocative/active gene–environment correlation (Silberg & Eaves, 2004). This method utilises information about not only parent–offspring correlations, but MZ and DZ twin aunt–offspring correlations. The correlation between mother–child pairs and MZ versus DZ twin aunt–child pairs are influenced by differing levels of genetic and shared environmental resemblance. For example, genetic sharing is 0.5 for mother–child and MZ twin aunt–child pairs, but only 0.25 for DZ twin aunt–child pairs. In contrast, shared environment sharing is 1.0 for mother–child pairs compared to zero for either MZ or DZ twin aunt–child pairs. These differences can be used to partition inter-generational associations between parental variables and child outcomes into genetic and environmental factors. Although there is clearly much to be learned from this method, to date, no studies of family environment and developmental psychopathology have used this approach. However, there is one example of this method being used to examine the nature of the association between maternal smoking and child birth-weight. Three mechanisms that could account for the association between maternal smoking and subsequent child birth-weight were explored: direct environmental causality, shared genetic influences (passive gene–environment correlation), or shared environmental influences (D'Onofrio et al., 2003). Thus, in addition to a direct causal environmental route between smoking during pregnancy and low birth weight, the possibility that the association may be accounted for by genetic factors or another shared environmental factor influencing both the parental variable and characteristics of the child was also investigated. This possibility can arise if maternal smoking during pregnancy is a marker of other "social" circumstances related to child outcome, such as low SES and difficult rearing conditions. As these circumstances may not be purely environmental, but may also be influenced by genetic factors, mediated by mother-characteristics such as mother personality, this route represents a test of passive gene–environment correlation. However, the results of this study lent support to the claim that smoking during pregnancy, despite being genetically influenced, has direct environmental effects on birth weight, rather than being associated through a common genetic route. It is possible that inadequate power led to these negative findings.

The adoption design is the perfect tool for examining evocative gene–environment correlations. In one such study, biological risk in adopted children, as indexed by the frequency of psychopathology in the birth parent, including alcoholism, substance abuse and antisocial problems, was found to predict harsh disciplinary parenting style in adoptive parents (Riggins-Caspers, Cadoret, Knutson, & Langbehn, 2003). Furthermore, this relationship was mediated by adolescent problem behaviours, a result signifying evocative gene–environment correlation. In other words, behaviours in the children influenced by genes inherited from their biological parents, evoke certain parenting practices in their adoptive parents.

In addition, a combined evocative and active gene–environment correlation effect was detected in a study of the links between life events and depression in a child and adolescent sample (Rice et al., 2003). The aim of the study was to explore the origins of the increase in heritability of depression in adolescence as compared to children. The association between "dependent" life events (i.e. those that are likely to arise through one's own behaviour) and subsequent depression symptoms was decomposed into genetic and environmental components, for two age groups (8–11 and 12–17 years). Not only was there a genetic contribution to this relationship, but, as hypothesised, the magnitude of the effect was much greater in adolescents compared to children. Thus, the role of genes in the link between depression and dependent life events grows over the child and adolescent period. These findings are important in demonstrating that gene–environment correlations may play a role in developmental trajectories.

Finally, one study has explored personality as a possible mediator of genetic influences on life events (Saudino, Pedersen, Lichtenstein, McClearn, & Plomin, 1997). The study found that genetic influences on controllable, desirable and undesirable life events were all shared with those on personality, indicating that the genetic influence on life events is likely to be mediated by personality.

Interactions between Genetic Influences and Family Environment on the Development of Psychopathology

Another major area in the study of gene–environment mechanisms is the analysis of gene–environment interactions. In contrast to gene–environment correlations, here the heritability of the phenotype of interest varies as a function of the level of the environmental risk variable (see Figure 1b), whereas for gene–environment correlations, the pertinent issue is the genetic influence on the environmental variable itself. In this figure, it can be clearly seen that the heritability of the outcome measure (or trait) varies as a function of the presence or absence of a specific measured environmental risk. In this example, when the risk is absent, the genetic influence on the trait is 60%, substantially greater than that seen for the group for whom the risk is present (heritability = 20%). The reverse effect is also found, whereby genetic influence is greater in the group of higher environmental risk. The illustrated example can be thought of as genetic factors being maximised given the relatively free situation of the environmental risk being absent — or that at the high environmental risk end, that genetic factors are "swamped" by these greater environmental risks. The reverse position can be thought of as an additive interaction in which having the environmental risk increases the effects of any risk genes present in the population.

The first stage of work in this area has been to explore interaction effects between differing types of risk on psychopathology within the family design. For example, one study found that the offspring of adult women with depression who also had chronic inter-personal difficulties were more depressed than the offspring those with depression but no inter-personal difficulties or of non-depressed women (Hammen, Shih, Altman, & Brennan, 2003). Another recent study used a composite index of parental familial vulnerability to anxiety, depression, and neuroticism, to predict depression scores in their adolescent offspring (Eley et al., 2004a). The composite index of vulnerability was previously created using quantitative genetic modelling techniques that maximised familial liability to depression, anxiety and neuroticism in an adult sample of siblings (Sham et al., 2000), and is likely to reflect the effects of shared genes among family members. A significant interaction was found between this parental familial vulnerability composite and parental educational level on self-reported symptoms in the adolescent offspring. Specifically, individuals whose parents lacked educational qualifications and who displayed high levels of familial risk were the most likely to have high depression scores. This implies that adolescents in families with a high rate of depression are particularly at risk for depression themselves if their parents lack qualifications. This effect may be mediated by coping strategies and ability to seek help, as these may all be improved in families where educational qualifications have been obtained.

While these findings are both interesting and provocative, they do not enable us to disentangle the familial influence into that due to genes and that due to shared environment. For this other approaches are necessary, one of which is the adoption design. As described earlier, biological (including genetic) risks are indexed by psychopathology in the birth parent, while the adoptive family home represents purely environmental influence. Using this paradigm, interaction effects were examined between genetic risk (negative emotionality in the biological parent), and environmental risk (separation of adoptive parents), on several areas of child adjustment (O'Connor, Caspi, DeFries, & Plomin, 2003). Gene-environment interactions were identified for adoptive parent-reported externalising symptoms and for an observer-rated social competence measure. A non-significant trend was also found for internalising symptoms. Interaction effects were also tested for negative emotionality of adoptive parents and adoptive parental separation for comparison, with no significant effects. Thus, these results suggest that children who possessed both genetic and psychosocial risks exhibited the highest level of behavioural difficulties. However, it should be noted that this may reflect gene–environment correlation, with genetic risk in the offspring leading to greater family discord and eventually parental discord.

An adoption study, which considered the role of both gene–environment correlation and interaction found that exposure to adversity in the life of the adoptive parents (environmental risk) moderated the effects of genetic risk (biological parental psychopathology) on the child's environment (Riggins-Caspers et al., 2003). Under conditions of low psychosocial risk, there was no evidence for an association between biological risk and harsh parental discipline (a gene–environment correlation, see above). On the contrary, individuals whose adoptive parents were faced with adversity were more likely to elicit harsher parenting practices. These results highlight the importance of jointly considering gene–environment interactions and correlations.

As with simpler hypotheses, it is important to gather evidence from as many types of design as possible. Data from a large epidemiological study of 5-year-old twins revealed a "double whammy" of genetic and environmental risks for conduct problems, transmitted from biological fathers (Jaffee, Moffitt, Caspi, & Taylor, 2003). Information on parental antisocial behaviour, child conduct problems, and the degree of father presence in the family home was collated, and used in a regression framework that had traditionally been designed to assess the effects of genetic and shared environmental variance. The interaction between father's antisocial behaviour and his presence in the home explained a significant proportion of variation in children's conduct problems independent of the transmission of genetic effects. From these findings, both gene–environment correlation and interaction effects can be inferred. When highly antisocial fathers reside at home, their children tend to experience both the risk effects transmitted through shared genes as well as the rearing environment provided.

Subsequent analyses from the same sample subdivided the twins into four groups varying in genetic risk for conduct disorder (Jaffee, Caspi, & Moffitt, 2004). Having first established that conduct disorder was heritable (72%) within the sample, groups were devised based upon co-twin diagnostic status and the pair's zygosity. Group 1, the highest risk group, consisted of children whose MZ co-twins manifested the disorder. Given that MZ twins share all of their genes, both members of the pair possess the same susceptibility genes. In contrast, for group 2 individuals who had an affected DZ co-twin, the level of risk is attenuated, due to the lower degree of genetic sharing within pairs. Similarly, genetic risk is lower among individuals with unaffected DZ co-twins (group 3) and lowest in those with unaffected MZ (group 4) co-twins. The results revealed that maltreatment was associated with a much greater increase in the probability of a conduct disorder among children of high genetic risk (24%) compared with children of lower genetic risk (2%). These findings are consistent with two interpretations. First, the effects of exposure to an adverse environmental stressor, such as maltreatment was exacerbated in the presence of genetic risk for conduct disorder, and second, there may be a protective role of genotype on children's risk for conduct problems.

An alternative modelling technique was used to test for interaction effects between several birth and pregnancy complications and genetic risk on subsequent problem behaviours in childhood and adolescence (Wichers et al., 2002). In this approach, the magnitude of genetic and environmental influence on a phenotype can be compared across groups under different environmental conditions (for example, those exposed and not exposed to birth complications). Where significant differences are found between the groups, this represents a gene–environment interaction. Using this approach, exposure to harmful birth practices (mode of delivery, mode of induction of ovulation and foetal presentation) were examined, with no significant differences in the size of genetic effects between environmental strata. A conceptually different modelling technique was applied to birth weight, a continuously distributed variable that cannot easily be dichotomised according to exposure status. Instead, the model needs to take into account that genetic effects may increase or decrease as a linear function of the environmental moderator (Purcell, 2002). To specify this, the genetic parameter is partitioned into a basic component independent of the measure of the environment and a part that is a linear function of the environmental measure (the interaction term). The level of significance of this term implicates gene–environment interaction. Applying this method, results were consistent with a negative gene–birth weight interaction, such that the effects of genes on problem behaviours were greatly reduced in individuals who were small for gestational age, with a corresponding increase in the influences of the environment.

While most of these findings appear supportive of gene–environment interaction effects, many of them fail to recognise that their results may reflect correlations between genes and environments rather than interactions. For example, in the study of gene–environment interaction for conduct disorder described above (Jaffee et al., 2005), the results are also consistent with the explanation that the genetic risk for conduct disorder somehow leads to the maltreatment of the children, perhaps mediated by their personality, a gene–environment correlation. True interaction effects are premised on the assumption that genotypes are randomly distributed over the range of environmental conditions (Eaves & Erkanli, 2003). As such, a violation of this assumption arises when allele frequencies are higher in individuals exposed to certain environmental factors (i.e. gene–environment correlation) or when the environmental measure is influenced by genes that also contribute to the phenotype. In other words, it must be absolutely clear that the environmental variable being examined could not be influenced by genes that are also associated with the outcome — if that were the case this would signify a gene–environment correlation (Rutter & Silberg, 2002). Although some authors have acknowledged this eventuality, most have not considered it.

One approach to this issue has been to examine environmental stressors that have been shown to be free of genetic influence. One study utilising this method found evidence for an interaction between genetic risk and a composite measure of three life events on depression in adolescent females (Silberg et al., 2001). However, the requirement that the life events not be genetically influenced led to an odd selection of events for the composite scale (new step-sibling, sibling leaving home, father losing job — all of which should surely apply equally to both members of a twin pair). A more sophisticated approach is to model gene–environment correlation alongside gene–environment interaction (Purcell, 2002). This approach has been used to examine the role of gene–environment interaction in the presence or absence of gene–environment correlation for adolescent depression (Lau & Eley, 2004). The environmental measures were parental negative disciplinary style and life events, and both were found to be influenced by a combination of gene–environment correlation and gene–environment interaction. Thus, genetic influences on adolescent depression are not only shared with those on negative disciplinary style or life events, but they were also moderated by the presence of negative discipline or life events. In both cases, the variation in depression increased substantially with higher levels of the moderator, and genetic differences were important in this increase. In other words, there was a greater range of depression scores in those at the "at-risk" end of the environmental distribution, and this was partly due to a greater "expression" of genetic influence on those individuals. This indicates that when individuals experience high levels of life events or negative parenting, the genes they have that are influential on depression have a greater opportunity to show their effect.

The most precise way to examine gene–environment interactions is to obtain specific measures not only of the environment but of individual sources of genetic risk, in other words to identify specific candidate genes and to include these in the analysis. Results from this new and exciting research area are considered in the next section.

Molecular Genetics, Developmental Psychopathology and the Family Environment

Molecular genetics has taken off over the last decade and will, without doubt, play an ever-increasing role in research in developmental psychopathology. In this approach, specific sections of DNA called markers, usually within but sometimes just close to genes are examined. For markers to be informative they need to vary across the population, leading to different variants called "alleles" in different individuals. These markers are also called polymorphisms reflecting the different versions identified within and across populations. The most useful markers are those where the different alleles have an effect on the function of the gene, so-called "functional polymorphisms" as it is these that give the most direct information about the action of the gene. However, it is also common to use more anonymous markers in the hope that they are linked to (very close to and therefore almost always inherited with) the gene of interest. There are several different sampling approaches that can be taken within molecular genetics, but for the studies described here the approach is one of case-comparison, in which genetic polymorphism frequencies are compared between the two groups, similar to any other type of risk factor.

One of the first exciting studies in this field examined the joint impact of a functional polymorphism in the monoamine oxidase A (MAOA) gene and childhood maltreatment on the development of subsequent antisocial behaviour in a large longitudinal birth cohort study (Caspi et al., 2002). The MAOA gene is responsible for encoding an enzyme that metabolises several neurotransmitters, some of which may be involved in stress regulation

(Shih, Chen, & Ridd, 1999), thus it may be relevant to short- and long-term responses to maltreatment (Pine, 2003). Two allelic forms associated with high and low levels of MAOA enzyme activity were studied. No significant main effect of genotype was found, however a significant gene–environment interaction emerged for a range of antisocial outcomes, including adolescent conduct disorder, criminal record, self-rated dispositions and antisocial personality disorder at age 26, when exposure to maltreatment status was included as an environmental variable in the analyses. Individuals with the high MAOA activity variant were less likely to develop antisocial problems in response to childhood maltreatment, implying that MAOA status has a protective (or negative) impact following a severe physical and emotional stressor.

Using a similar design, the moderating effects of a functional polymorphism in the serotonin (5-HT) transporter promoter region on the effect of life events, in relation to depression symptoms was examined (Caspi et al., 2003). The 5-HT transporter gene is involved in regulatory processes during stress (Hariri et al., 2002) making it an excellent candidate for interaction with environmental stress. The polymorphism exists in two forms a "long" and a "short" form. The short allele is less efficient than the longer allele, thus leading to differences in available serotonin in the brain (Lesch et al., 1996). The study sample comprised the same birth cohort as the MAOA study, including data from both males and females. Analyses revealed another significant interaction between the 5-HT transporter gene and self-reported life events over the last 5 years on depression symptoms. The effects of stressful life events were significantly stronger among individuals carrying one or two copies of the short form of the allele *s*, as shown by an increase in symptom frequencies and severity. Furthermore, this allele also moderated the longitudinal prediction from childhood maltreatment to adult depression. A subsequent study produced similar results in an adolescent sample but in the females only, with an interaction between the same serotonin transporter regulatory region and a family-based measure of environmental risk (including social adversity, family life events and parental employment level) (Eley et al., 2004b). The effects of family-based environmental risk were significantly stronger among female adolescents who possessed at least one short allele. Together, these findings suggest that, like MAOA, this allelic variant is involved in augmenting the effects of stress on emotional and behavioural symptoms.

Conclusions

In summary, much has been learned about the origins and mechanisms of impact of the family environment from behavioural genetic studies. Notably, environmental influences are generally found to be child-specific in their effects. Thus, for example, negative parenting, while being a potential risk factor for all members of a family, is found to be individual specific. In other words, the effects of parenting are different for each child, and indeed within any one family negative aspects of parenting may apply to only one child. Furthermore, the family environment is strongly influenced by genetic factors, that also impact on child outcomes. This has led to new developments: first, the use of MZ differences designs to obtain estimates of purely non-shared environmental impact of family environment, and second, studies of the degree and type of genetic influence on family environment and developmental psychopathology outcomes. Designs are starting to be developed that can differentiate between different types of gene–environment correlation. A final complexity in this arena that has come to the fore in recent years is the presence of gene–environment interactions, and most recently, the need to consider these in conjunction with potential gene–environment correlations such that one does not contaminate and thus lead to biased estimates of the other. Perhaps the most exciting area of all will be the incorporation of molecular genetic methods, and directly assessed genotypes into studies of family environment and developmental psychopathology. The ever-increasing ease with which such techniques can be applied, from the simple use of cheek swabs to extract DNA (Freeman et al., 2003), to the constant reduction in genotyping costs and the recent publication of the entire human genome, make this an area ripe for expansion within child psychology.

It is clear that in order to gain an accurate picture of the family environment genetic influences must be taken into account. This will lead to greater understanding of the processes linking parental psychopathology, social adversity, parent–child interaction, parental disciplinary style and other elements of the rearing environment to child psychopathology. In the same way that genetic research has quashed the long-held prejudicial view that cold and harsh parenting leads to child autism, understanding how genetic factors fit into the links between family environment and psychopathology has the potential not only to increase understanding and awareness but also to alter stigmatism, and to highlight potential avenues for prevention and intervention.

References

Asbury, K., Dunn, J., Pike, A., & Plomin, R. (2003). Non-shared environmental influences on individual differences in early behavioral development: An MZ differences study. *Child Development, 74*, 933–943.

Caspi, A., McClay, J., Moffitt, T. E., Mill, J., Martin, J., Craig, I. W., Taylor, A., & Poulton, R. (2002). Role of genotype in the cycle of violence in maltreated children. *Science, 297*, 851–854.

Caspi, A., Sugden, K., Moffitt, T. E., Taylor, A., Craig, I. W., Harrington, H., McClay, J., Mill, J., Martin, J., Braithwaite, A., & Poulton, R. (2003). Influence of life stress on depression: Moderation by a polymorphism in the 5-HTT gene. *Science, 301*, 386–389.

Daniels, D., & Plomin, R. (1985). Differential experience of siblings in the same family. *Developmental Psychology, 21*, 747–760.

D'Onofrio, B. M., Turkheimer, E. N., Eaves, L. J., Corey, L. A., Berg, K., Solaas, M. H., & Emery, R. E. (2003). The role of the children of twins design in elucidating causal relations between parent characteristics and child outcomes. *Journal of Child Psychology & Psychiatry & Allied Disciplines, 44*, 1130–1144.

Eaves, L., & Erkanli, A. (2003). Markov Chain Monte Carlo approaches to analysis of genetic and environmental components of human developmental change and G × E interaction. *Behavior Genetics, 33*, 279–299.

Eaves, L. J., Silberg, J. L., Meyer, J. M., Maes, H. H., Simonoff, E., Pickles, A., Rutter, M., Neale, M. C., Reynolds, C. A., Erickson, M. T., Heath, A. C., Loeber, R., Truett, K. R., & Hewitt, J. K. (1997). Genetics and developmental psychopathology: 2. The main effects of genes and environment on behavioral problems in the Virginia twin study of adolescent behavioral development. *Journal of Child Psychology and Psychiatry, 38*, 965–980.

Eley, T. C., Lichtenstein, P., & Stevenson, J. (1999). Sex differences in the aetiology of aggressive and non-aggressive antisocial behavior: Results from two twin studies. *Child Development, 70*, 155–168.

Eley, T. C., Liang, H., Plomin, R., Sham, P., Sterne, A., Williamson, R., & Purcell, S. (2004a). Parental vulnerability, family environment and their interactions as predictors of depressive symptoms in adolescents . *Journal of the American Academic of Child and Adolescent Psychiatry, 43*, 298–306.

Eley, T. C., Sugden, K., Gregory, A. M., Sterne, A., Plomin, R., & Craig, I. W. (2004b). Gene–environment interaction analysis of serotonin system markers with adolescent depression. *Molecular Psychiatry, Lilly-Molecular Psychiatry Award Winner, 9*, 908–915.

Feigon, S. A., Waldman, I. D., Levy, F., & Hay, D. A. (2001). Genetic and environmental influences on separation anxiety disorder symptoms and their moderation by age and sex. *Behavior Genetics, 31*, 403–411.

Freeman, B., Smith, N., Curtis, C., Huckett, L., Mill, J., & Craig, I. W. (2003). DNA from buccal swabs recruited by mail: Evaluation of storage effects on long-term stability and suitability for multiplex polymerase chain reaction genotyping. *Behavior Genetics, 33*, 67–72.

Hammen, C., Shih, J. S., Altman, T., & Brennan, P. A. (2003). Interpersonal impairment and the prediction of depressive symptoms in adolescent children of depressed and nondepressed mothers. *Journal of the American Academic of Child and Adolescent Psychiatry, 42*, 571–577.

Hariri, A. R., Mattay, V. S., Tessitore, A., Kolachana, B., Fera, F., Goldman, D., Egan, M. F., & Weinberger, D. R. (2002). Serotonin transporter genetic variation and the response of the human amygdala. *Science, 297*, 400–403.

Jacobson, K. C., & Rowe, D. C. (1999). Genetic and environmental influences on the relationships between family connectedness, school connectedness, and adolescent depressed mood: Sex differences. *Developmental Psychology, 35*, 926–939.

Jaffee, S. R., Caspi, A., & Moffitt, T. E. (2005). Nature × nurture: Genetic vulnerabilities interact with physical maltreatment to promote conduct problems. *Development and Psychopathology, 17*, 67–84.

Jaffee, S. R., Moffitt, T. E., Caspi, A., & Taylor, A. (2003). Life with (or without) father: The benefits of living with two biological parents depend on the father's antisocial behavior. *Child Development, 74*, 109–126.

Lau, J. Y. F., & Eley, T. C. (2004). Gene environment interactions and correlations on adolescent depression. Submitted.

Lesch, K. P., Bengel, D., Heils, A., Zhang Sabol, S., Greenburg, B. D., Petri, S., Benjamin, J., Müller, C. R., Hamer, D. H., & Murphy, D. L. (1996). Association of anxiety-related traits with a polymorphism in the serotonin transporter gene regulatory region. *Science, 274*, 1527–1531.

Liang, H., & Eley, T. C. (press). Non-shared environmental influences of parenting, life events and peers in the prediction and maintenance of depressive symptoms in adolescents: A monozygotic twin study. *Child Development*.

Lichtenstein, P., & Annas, P. (2000). Heritability and prevalence of specific fears and phobia in childhood. *Journal of Child Psychology & Psychiatry, 41*, 927–937.

Martin, N., Boomsma, D. I., & Machin, G. (1997). A twin-pronged attack on complex trait. *Nature Genetics, 17*, 387–392.

O'Connor, T. G., Hetherington, E. M., Reiss, D., & Plomin, R. (1995). A twin-sibling study of observed parent–adolescent interactions. *Child Development, 66*, 812–829.

O'Connor, T. G., Caspi, A., DeFries, J. C., & Plomin, R. (2000). Are associations between parental divorce in children's adjustment genetically mediated? An adoption study. *Developmental Psychology, 36*, 429–437.

O'Connor, T. G., Caspi, A., DeFries, J. C., & Plomin, R. (2003). Genotype–environment interaction in children's adjustment to parental separation. *Journal of Child Psychology and Psychiatry, 44*, 849–857.

Pike, A., McGuire, S., Hetherington, E. M., Reiss, D., & Plomin, R. (1996a). Family environment and adolescent depressive symptoms and antisocial behavior: A multivariate genetic analysis. *Developmental Psychology, 32*, 590–603.

Pike, A., Reiss, D., Hetherington, E. M., & Plomin, R. (1996b). Using MZ differences in the search for nonshared environmental effects. *Journal of Child Psychology and Psychiatry, 37*, 695–704.

Pine, D. S. (2003). Developmental psychobiology and response to threats: Relevance to trauma in children and adolescents. *Biological Psychiatry, 53*, 796–808.

Plomin, R., Chipuer, H. M., & Neiderhiser, J. M. (1994a). Behavioral genetic evidence for the importance of nonshared environment. In: E. M. Hetherington, D. Reiss & R. Plomin (Eds), *Separate social worlds of siblings: The impact of non-shared environment on development* (pp. 1–31). New Jersey: Lawrence Erlbaum Assoc. Inc.

Plomin, R., Reiss, D., Hetherington, E. M., & Howe, G. W. (1994b). Nature and nurture: Genetic contributions to measures of the family environment. *Developmental Psychology, 30*, 32–43.

Plomin, R., DeFries, J. C., McClearn, G. E., & McGuffin, P. (2001). *Behavioral genetics* (4th ed.). New York: Worth Publishers.

Purcell, S. (2002). Variance components models for gene–environment interaction in twin analysis. *Twin Research, 5*, 554–571.

Rice, F., Harold, G. T., & Thapar, A. (2003). Negative life events as an account of age-related differences in the genetic aetiology of depression in childhood and adolescence. *Journal of Child Psychology and Psychiatry, 44*, 977–987.

Riggins-Caspers, K. M., Cadoret, R. J., Knutson, J. F., & Langbehn, D. (2003). Biology–environment interaction and evocative biology–environment correlation: Contributions of harsh discipline and parental psychopathology to problem adolescent behaviors. *Behavior Genetics, 33*, 205–220.

Rose, R. J., & Ditto, W. B. (1983). A developmental-genetic analysis of common fears from early adolescence to early adulthood. *Child Development, 54*, 361–368.

Rutter, M., & Redshaw, J. (1991). Annotation: Growing up as a twin: Twin–singleton differences in psychological development. *Journal of Child Psychology and Psychiatry, 32*, 885–895.

Rutter, M., & Silberg, J. (2002). Gene–environment interplay in relation to emotional and behavioral disturbance. *Annual Review of Psychology, 53*, 463–490.

Saudino, K. J., Pedersen, N. L., Lichtenstein, P., McClearn, G. E., & Plomin, R. (1997). Can personality explain genetic influences on life events? *Journal of Personality and Social Psychology, 72*, 196–206.

Scarr, S., & McCartney, K. (1983). How people make their own environments: A theory of genotype –> environmental effects. *Child Development, 54*, 424–435.

Sham, P. C., Sterne, A., Purcell, S., Cherny, S. S., Webster, M., Rijsdijk, F. V., Asherson, P. J., Ball, D., Craig, I., Eley, T. C., Goldberg, D., Gray, J., Mann, A., Owen, M., & Plomin, R. (2000). GENESiS: Creating a composite index of the vulnerability to anxiety and depression in a community-based sample of siblings. *Twin Research, 3*, 316–322.

Shih, J. C., Chen, K., & Ridd, M. J. (1999). Monoamine oxidase: From genes to behavior. *Annual Review of Neuroscience, 22*, 197–217.

Silberg, J. L., & Eaves, L. J. (2004). Analysing the contributions of genes and parent–child interaction to childhood behavioural and emotional problems: A model for the children of twins. *Psychological Medicine, 34*, 347–356.

Silberg, J., Pickles, A., Rutter, M., Hewitt, J., Simonoff, E., Maes, H., Carbonneau, R., Murrell, L., Foley, D., & Eaves, L. (1999). The influence of genetic factors and life stress on depression among adolescent girls. *Archives of General Psychiatry, 56*, 225–232.

Silberg, J., Rutter, M., Neale, M., & Eaves, L. (2001). Genetic moderation of environmental risk for depression and anxiety in adolescent girls. *British Journal of Psychiatry, 179*, 116–121.

Silove, D., Manicavasagar, V., O'Connell, D., & Morris-Yates, A. (1995). Genetic factors in early separation anxiety: Implications for the genesis of adult anxiety disorders. *Acta Psychiatrica Scandinavica, 92*, 17–24.

Stevenson, J., Batten, N., & Cherner, M. (1992). Fears and fearfulness in children and adolescents: A genetic analysis of twin data. *Journal of Child Psychology and Psychiatry, 33*, 977–985.

Thapar, A., & McGuffin, P. (1996). Genetic influences on life events in childhood. *Psychological Medicine, 26*, 813–820.

Thapar, A., Harold, G., & McGuffin, P. (1998). Life events and depressive symptoms in childhood-shared genes or shared adversity? A research note. *Journal of Child Psychology and Psychiatry, 39*, 1153–1158.

Topolski, T. D., Hewitt, J. K., Eaves, L. J., Silberg, J. L., Meyer, J. M., Rutter, M., Pickles, A., & Simonoff, E. (1997). Genetic and environmental influences on child reports of manifest anxiety and symptoms of separation anxiety and overanxious disorders: A community-based twin study. *Behavior Genetics, 27*, 15–28.

Wichers, M. C., Purcell, S., Danckaerts, M., Derom, C., Derom, R., Vlietinck, R., & van Os, J. (2002). Prenatal life and post-natal psychopathology: Evidence for negative gene–birth weight interaction. *Psychological Medicine, 32*, 1165–1174.

Chapter 2

The Role of Parenting in the Development of Psychopathology: An Overview of Research Using the Parental Bonding Instrument

Gemma L. Gladstone and Gordon B. Parker

Importance of Parental Influences

The emotional bond between a parent or caregiver and a young child defines a core and continuing human experience. This primary parent–child union constitutes the strongest and most important attachment for a young child, and serves as an essential ingredient for a child's growth and development, both physically and psychologically.

The process of attachment as a developmentally geared protective function first gained considerable recognition when experiments conducted by psychologist Harry Harlow (e.g. Harlow & Zimmerman, 1959) in the 1950s and ethologist Konrad Lorenz (1935/1957) sought to test Freud's earlier postulated drive reduction theory. These researchers moved the focus away from the role of feeding as the central factor responsible for infant attachment and instead, highlighted its protective/survival function and also the importance of emotional and physical security as a vital component in adaptive infant development. Harlow's (Harlow & Harlow, 1962) studies of maternal deprivation in infant rhesus monkeys were particularly poignant illustrations of the negative consequences of inadequate or aberrant parenting.

Bowlby (1969) proposed that infants build, what he coined 'internal working models' of self (i.e. loveable or unloveable) and others (i.e. emotionally reliable, trustworthy) and that these somewhat 'fixed' models served to guide subsequent interpersonal bonding. Exposure to rejecting or ambivalent care-giving was said to lead to a sense of insecurity that may then lead to deviations in personality development. Thus, childhood experiences of insecure parental attachments (Radke-Yarrow, Cummings, Kuczynski, & Chapman, 1985) and parental loss (Bowlby, 1988) have been traditionally considered risk factors for later depression. The work by Bowlby and others (Ainsworth et al., 1978) in the field of human attachment has sparked tremendous interest as well as controversy, and has provided the impetus

Psychopathology and the Family
Edited by J. L. Hudson and R. M. Rapee
Copyright © 2005 by Elsevier Ltd.
All rights of reproduction in any form reserved
ISBN: 0-08-044449-0

for much of the research into parental influences on later development, which followed in subsequent decades.

The Parental Bonding Instrument

Although parenting styles clearly are multifaceted, research using factor analytic techniques (Arrindell et al., 1986; Parker, Tupling, & Brown, 1979; Roe & Siegelman, 1963) to examine core dimensions of parenting (i.e. parental attitudes and behaviours) has consistently identified two qualitative constructs responsible for most of the variance. The first has been an 'affection/warmth' dimension contrasted with 'rejection/antipathy', and the second, an 'autonomy' dimension contrasted with 'over-control/over-protection'. Further, other psychological research (Hinde, 1979) suggested that all interpersonal relationships (e.g. romantic partners) probably possess two fundamental dimensions akin to 'affection–rejection' and 'psychological autonomy–dominance'.

Research interest in the role of parental bonding styles as psychological diatheses for mental health problems of children later in life, has grown considerably in the last few decades. The relationship between parenting experiences and adult adjustment and psychopathology, has been studied predominately using self-report measures of parental behaviours. The most widely used and extensively validated measure of this type is the Parental Bonding Instrument or PBI developed by Parker and colleagues (Parker et al., 1979). The PBI was developed in response to a need for empirical data to broaden the study of parental influences and as a research tool to examine the influence of aberrant parenting on the psychological and social functioning of recipients. The PBI is completed for the respondent's first 16 years of their life, thus, it represents an overall view of parent–child bonding during these years of development. Mothers and fathers are rated separately on the 25 items that make up the instrument, with scores generated for two parental bonding scales. The first is a 'care' scale (12 items), defined at one pole by emotional warmth, acceptance and empathy, and by emotional coldness and rejection at the other. The second is an 'overprotection' scale (13 items), with one pole defined by parental allowance of autonomy and independence of the child, and the other defined by items that suggest parental over-control and intrusion.

In addition to generating care and protection scores for each scale, PBI scores allow parents to be 'assigned' to one of four quadrants (i.e. 'optimal parenting' = high care and low protection; 'affectionate constraint' = high care and high protection; 'affectionless control' = high protection and low care; and 'neglectful parenting' = low care and low protection). The assignment to 'high' or 'low' categories is based on the following cut-off scores — for mothers, a care score of 27.0 and a protection score of 13.5; for fathers, a care score of 24.0 and a protection score of 12.5.

Determinants of Parenting

While it is beyond the scope of this chapter to provide a comprehensive overview of the determinants of parenting, we provide a broad overview here. Any discussion of the role of parenting in the development of psychological problems in offspring first deserves some attention given to the forces that shape that parenting behaviour.

Parenting is a complex set of behaviours and psychological processors which are determined by multiple factors. Some salient factors include those such as the parent's own personality or the presence of parental psychopathology (Parker & Lipscombe, 1981), parental neurobiological factors (Maestripieri, 1999), intergenerational influence of child-rearing practices (Miller, Kramer, Warner, Wickramaratne, & Weissman, 1997), cultural and religious influences (Luft, 1987), the child's temperament (Kendler, 1996), the quality of the marital relationship (Maccoby & Martin, 1983), as well as a host of potentially influential social factors (e.g. social support networks, employment, economic resources).

Two studies using the PBI to examine parental determinants warrant attention. The first was a report by Kendler (1996), which sort to disentangle the genetic and environmental determinants of parenting. Kendler used a reduced 16-item version of the PBI (described shortly) modified for multiple informants — a sample of adult female twin pairs and their parents. In sum, Kendler (1996) found that the display of 'warmth' (or 'care') by parents was influenced by characteristics of the parent's temperament (which are partly determined by genetics), and that the degree of warmth provided to a particular child was also partly determined by genetically based characteristics of that individual child (i.e. the child's temperament). However, genetic influences were less relevant in the determination of other parenting characteristics. Parental 'protectiveness', as well as the tendency to be 'authoritarian', were only minimally influenced by genetic factors in parents, but instead, likely to be shaped by a parent's own upbringing and family of origin influences, such as cultural and other social norms common to that family. Although genetically mediated aspects of a child's temperament were somewhat influential in the elicitation of parental protectiveness and authoritarianism, such influences were considerably less important than they were for the elicitation of parental warmth. Although this study sampled only female twins, it is important in that it highlights potential differences in the degree to which genetic and environmental factors influence certain parenting styles.

In a second study, Kendler, Sham, and MacLean (1997) further examined the predictors of three parenting dimensions ('warmth', 'protectiveness' and 'authoritarianism') derived from the same 16-item version of the PBI previously used (Kendler, 1996). Their sample included adult female–female twin pairs (who reported on the parenting both they and their co-twin had received), and their parents (who reported on the parenting they had provided to their twins) — a total of 828 twin families. They investigated the influence of numerous variables on reports of parenting, including socio-demographic, parental personality and childhood vulnerability factors. In sum, they found that parental 'warmth' was predicted by personal qualities of both parents and offspring, and that low perceived warmth from parents was associated with higher levels of parental neuroticism, as well as depressive and anxiety symptoms. Parental education level and religious orientation were important predictors of 'protectiveness', with lower education and more fundamentalist religions predictive of over-protectiveness. Not surprisingly, anxiety-prone parents were also more protective of children, and neurotic and hyperactive traits in children also predicted parental protectiveness. These results are consistent with a collection of studies indicating the significant influence of culture, religion and educational factors on the degree to which parents exercise control over their children (Luft, 1987; Parker &

Lipsombe, 1979, 1981). For example, Parker (1983) previously found that the tendency for mothers to be 'overprotective' was significantly influenced by both social (less education, religious) and psychological (anxiety and anxiety disorders) determinants. Returning to the Kendler et al. (1997) study, a similar pattern of associations was found for 'authoritarianism', although additionally, older parents tended to display a more authoritarian parenting style, perhaps reflecting broad social shifts in parenting norms. Authoritarianism was however less influenced by parental anxiety levels.

Both studies reported provide important information about parenting determinants, particularly in highlighting the role of genetic factors for each dimension (to varying degrees). Overall, parental warmth (i.e. care, empathy) was found to be more strongly influenced by parental traits, which are under at least modest genetic control (i.e. personality, vulnerability to psychological disorders), while both dimensions relating to parental protectiveness and control were seen to be more significantly influenced by characteristics of parents shaped by their exposure to environmental (common and unique) input (i.e. religion, social and cultural norms and education level).

Reliability and Validity of the PBI

The original data (Parker et al., 1979) for the PBI were generated from 150 subjects including students and nurses and 500 general practice attendees. Numerous other populations have been studied since then, generating a corpus of research attesting the psychometric properties of the PBI. The PBI has been found to have good reliability and validity based on several studies. Scores on the PBI have been shown to be mostly independent of respondents' sex and social class or education and age (Parker, 1990). One study found particularly good concordance between sibling ratings (Parker, 1990) — suggesting that the PBI provides a valid assessment of actual, rather than simply perceived parenting.

Scores on the PBI have shown consistency over testing periods. In the original study (Parker et al., 1979) the PBI possessed good internal consistency and re-test reliability, and in a prospective community study, scores on the PBI were remarkably stable over time (Mackinnon, Henderson, Scott, & Duncan-Jones, 1989). Data will be published shortly showing high PBI scores consistency over a 25-year test–retest period.

PBI scores have also been differentiated from the more non-specific effects of neuroticism or negative affect (Cubis, Lewin, & Dawes, 1989; Duggan, Sham, Minnie, Lee, & Murray, 1998). A study by Parker (1979), for example, first, identified an association between both PBI scores and depression and PBI scores and neuroticism, and then re-examined the association between PBI scores and depression while controlling any effect of neuroticism scores. The result was that the association between depression and PBI scores remained, with only mild attenuation.

Several studies using the PBI have examined remembered parental qualities in adults with depressive disorders (current mood disturbance). Use of the instrument in such samples (and other clinical samples) had sparked concerns regarding the validity of depressed individuals' subjective reports of their parents, not only because of the retrospective recall involved, but because of the potential influence of altered (i.e. negative) mood states. To date however, there is consistent evidence that PBI responses are not affected by current depressive symptoms (e.g. Gotlib, Mount, Cordy, & Whiffen, 1988; Parker, 1981). Furthermore, Brewin, Andrews, and Gotlib, 1993, in a review of the relevant literature, concluded that recall of significant past events was not significantly affected by mood state, and that depressed subjects' perceptions of parents tend to remain predominately consistent after recovery from a depressive episode (Brewin, Andrews, & Furnham, 1996).

Factor Structure of the PBI: Two or Three Parenting Dimensions

One area of uncertainty regarding the PBI is whether or not the underlying factor structure of the instrument is better defined by the two original factors (Parker et al., 1979) or by three factors. In the accumulated literature, there is a general consensus for a robust dimension of parental care, while there is less support for a single dimension of parental over-protectiveness. Parker (1989) has previously noted that, in addition to 'care', two factors emerged in several analyses, one defined as 'overprotection', the other as 'encouragement of independence and autonomy'. Since then, other studies have suggested that the original over-protection scale might best be viewed as two separate dimensions, and that the use of two dimensions may yield more specific information about the link between parenting and psychological disorders (Cubis et al., 1989; Gomez-Beneyto, Pedros, Tomas, Aguilar, & Leal, 1993; Murphy, Brewin, & Silka, 1997). For example, Murphy et al. (1997) factor analysed PBI scores from a sample of 583 US and 236 UK students and found that a 3-factor solution provided more insight into the different qualities of overprotection, arguing that 'discouragement of behavioural freedom' was specifically linked to depression in females. In the study by Kendler et al. (1997) examining parenting determinants, the three factors identified (using 16-item version of the PBI) were defined as 'warmth' (a 'care' factor), 'protectiveness' and 'authoritarianism'. While the 'protectiveness' factor reflected an over-controlling parenting style, the 'authoritarianism' factor possessed items more relevant to the discouragement of a child's sense of autonomy and independence — thus warranting the recognition of two factors belonging to a more global 'over-protectiveness' factor. Others have since replicated this 3-factor structure, arguing for the validity of the two scales of 'protectiveness' and 'authoritarianism' (Cox, Enns, & Clara, 2000; Sato et al., 1999; Lizardi & Klein, 2002).

Parental Bonding and Adult Psychopathology

While there is no doubt that deprivational or abusive parenting constitutes harm for a developing child, the extent to which parenting styles in general might influence the development of psychopathology in offspring is less lucid, and unlikely to constitute a linear or singular causal process. Parent–child relations, like any other, are moulded by reciprocal interpersonal dynamics. Furthermore, individual differences, such as temperament and human environmental experiences will always serve as influential mechanisms shaping how people internalise these relationships, and how these internal representations then manifest. Before reviewing some of the more recent literature on the relationship between parenting and common psychological disorders, it is important to highlight the notion that any treatment by parents may constitute both direct and oblique channels of influence on development, and to that end, the risk for subsequent psychopathology.

The association between parental bonding (as measured by the PBI) and adult adjustment and psychopathology has been examined in a large number of studies (Parker & Gladstone, 1996). At the broadest level, these studies suggest that low levels of parental care and high levels of parental control are linked to an increased risk of developing common emotional disorders (particularly depression and anxiety), but that such parental styles are less distinctly over-represented in those who develop more biological psychiatric disorders, such as schizophrenia and psychotic depression (Parker, 1983).

Many of the earlier studies employing the PBI focused upon the relevance of parental bonding in depressive disorders, with most studies detecting specificity with low care and high control being associated with non-melancholic, but not with melancholic or bipolar depression (Joyce, 1984; Parker & Hadzi-Pavlovic, 1992; Parker, Kiloh, & Hayward, 1987). Other clinical research using the PBI has highlighted the relevance of low parental care and/or high control in the childhoods of patients with anxiety disorders (Silove, Parker, Hadzi-Pavlovic, Manicavasagar, & Blaszcynski, 1991), substance abuse (Torresani, Favaretto, & Zimmermann, 2000) and eating disorders (Gomez, 1984).

In a study examining specificity among depressed groups, Lizardi et al. (1995) assessed PBI scores in patients with early onset dysthymia (EOD), episodic major depression (EMD) and non-depressed controls. They found that patients with EOD were significantly more likely to report a poorer relationship with parents (low care, high control) than both EMD patients and controls.

Lizardi and Klein (2002) then re-analysed their data based on the 3-factor structure reported by Kendler (1996) and found evidence of greater sensitivity in examining links between parenting and these types of depression. Specifically they found that 'authoritarianism' scores (a component of the original 'overprotectiveness'), rather than 'protectiveness' scores, significantly distinguished between their subject groups. Subjects with EOD reported the most maternal and paternal authoritarianism, followed by those with major depression, compared with normal control subjects.

Enns, Cox, and Clara (2002) examined the association between parental bonding and 13 common psychological disorders using data from the US National Comorbidity Survey (Kessler et al., 1994). The relationship between parental bonding and psychopathology was examined separately for men and women ($N = 5877$). Disorders included: unipolar non-melancholic depression; post-traumatic stress disorder; dysthymia; panic disorder; agoraphobia; social phobia; simple phobia; generalised anxiety disorder; alcohol abuse and dependence; drug abuse and dependence and antisocial personality disorder (APD). Disorders such as endogenous depression, bipolar disorder and schizophrenia were not considered. Parental bonding was assessed using abbreviated 8-item versions of the PBI–father and PBI–mother scales, which each generated a robust 3-factor structure: 'care', 'overprotection' and 'authoritarianism'. Enns et al. (2002) used logistic models while controlling for any potential influence of socio-demographic variables. Based on significant odds ratios, parental scale scores were associated with a wide range of disorders for both men and women, however, lack of care was the parenting variable most consistently associated with psychological disorders. In fact, 'overprotection' and 'authoritarianism' were not more significantly linked to any of the disorders than was 'care'.

Such associations reporting the superior relationship between low care and common psychological disorders have also been reported recently by others (e.g. Duggan et al., 2000). Enns et al. (2002) also found that associations were much stronger for perceptions of maternal bonding than for paternal bonding — for both male and female respondents — suggesting the greater impact of perceived mothering for respondents generally. Among the disorders considered, they found little evidence for specific links between parental bonding and different expressions of psychopathology. However, they did observe a differing pattern relevant to externalising disorders (i.e. substance abuse and APD) in male subjects, whereby paternal overprotection and authoritarianism was associated with reduced risk for these disorders. In contrast, higher maternal overprotection and authoritarianism were related to increased risk in male subjects. These results do suggest some specificity depicting such a parental style in fathers as providing some 'protection' against these externalising disorders in males.

Child and Adolescent Respondents

The PBI was originally designed as a retrospective instrument for completion by adults, however there are now some studies employing the PBI as a measure of parent–child bonding in child (Capelli et al., 1988) and adolescent (Chambers, Power, Loucks, & Swanson, 2000) respondents.

Stein et al. (2000) examined the relationship between parent–child bonding and depression in a sample of youngsters age 6–17, who were either depressed, non-depressed children of a depressed parent (i.e. 'high risk') or non-depressed children with neither parent depressed (i.e. 'low risk'). They used the original version of the PBI and also considered the four bonding quadrants described earlier. Children with depression perceived both their mothers and fathers as significantly less caring, and mothers as significantly more overprotective, than those in the 'low risk' group. Depressed children also rated mothers (but not fathers) as more overprotective than those in the 'high risk' group. There was no difference between the high- and low-risk groups in reports of both paternal and maternal care and protection. Children's PBI scores did not appear to be significantly affected by parental depression. Compared to the low-risk group, children with depression were significantly more likely to score mothers as belonging to the 'affectionless-control' quadrant, but interestingly, high-risk (non-depressed) children tended to rate both parents as belonging to this quadrant when compared to the low-risk (non-depressed) group. These finding were also not accounted for by parental depression. The results suggest that, in children considered to be at risk for developing depression, the influence of parental over-involvement and rejection may provide a key stressor in determining the development of a depressive disorder.

Parenting Styles and Childhood Abuse

Parental influence as measured by the bonding dimensions assessed by the PBI may exert an array of indirect influences upon adult adjustment and later psychopathology, such as depressive and anxious disorders. One example of this relates to the association between parental bonding styles and experiences of childhood abuse.

For example, a lack of parental care or neglectful parenting, by creating greater vulnerability, is often associated with child maltreatment and abuse occurring either within the home (Bifulco & Moran, 1998) or at the hands of extra-familial perpetrators (Elliott, Browne, & Kilcoyne, 1995; Gladstone, Parker, Wilhem, Mitchell, & Austin, 1999). The occurrence of childhood sexual abuse (CSA), for example, is sometimes highly correlated with other forms of abusive parenting such as physical abuse (Bifulco & Moran, 1998), as well as parental conflict and domestic violence (Bowen, 2000) and parental alcoholism (Gladstone et al., 1999; McLaughlin et al., 2000). CSA is also frequently corelated with psychological and emotional abuse from parents (Bifulco & Moran, 1998) — patterns of parenting often defined by enduring expressions of low care and antipathy.

Hill et al. (2000) determined that low levels of parental care probably increased the risk of CSA by non-relatives in young children (based on women's reports of CSA before the age of 11), while abuse by a relative was strongly predicted by both low care (from mothers and fathers) and high control from fathers. They then determined that fathers who perpetrated the abuse were perceived by women as also being highly controlling.

Strong evidence for the relationship between CSA and neglectful parenting was also found in a large Australian twin study (McLaughlin et al., 2000) using the PBI with both male and female respondents. They found that subjects who reported sexual abuse, also reported having experienced emotionally cold parenting, and that this negative and rejecting style was also recognised by twin siblings who did not themselves report a history of sexual abuse.

Two further studies assessing family dysfunction and parental representations in women with CSA histories used the Measure of Parental Style or MOPS (Parker et al., 1997), which is a modified version of the PBI. The MOPS is a 15-item self-report instrument, which generates three dimensions of parental behaviours: (1) 'indifference' (i.e. lack of care, leaving child alone, neglect); 'over-control' (intrusiveness and control) and 'abuse' (i.e. physical and verbal abuse, and making the child feel in danger). In a sample of women with major depression, Gladstone et al. (1999) found that women with CSA reported considerably more pervasive dysfunction in their family of origin (parental indifference, lack of protection, alcohol abuse), and that the tendency to self-injure in these women was significantly predicted by both CSA and also by reports of maternal indifference. A parental style of over-control was not linked to CSA in this sample.

More recently, Gladstone et al. (2004), studying a second group of women with depression, found that the relationship between parental 'emotional abuse and neglect' and CSA, was not direct, but mediated by the presence of physical abuse by parents. Thus, because most of the perpetrators of sexual abuse in the study were reported to be non-family members, lack of care and physical abuse in the home appeared to significantly increase vulnerability to sexual abuse for such individuals. They found that 'parental conflict' (severe arguments, violence) was directly linked to both CSA and physical abuse, underscoring the highly dangerous potential for this family risk factor upon children's welfare.

Pathways to Adjustment Problems and Emotional Disorder

Accumulative evidence from studies using the PBI suggests that sub-optimal parenting, particularly low parental care, does increase an individual's chance of developing common psychological disorders, such as non-melancholic depression and anxiety disorders. Overall, neglectful and rejecting parental styles most likely act to instigate primary psychological vulnerabilities (e.g. low self-worth, abandonment concerns), which in combination with temperament traits, lead to psychological distress, either generally, or in response to salient environmental triggers. As previously mentioned, direct causal relationships between parental bonding styles and formal psychopathology are unlikely, particularly given the multiple channels of influence, which render an individual vulnerable to emotional disorder, and the often complex correlations between such determinants.

As outlined, determinants of how individuals parent their offspring are vast, largely grouped under biological/genetic factors (both parental and child) and broad environmental factors. Negative parenting, whether that be in the form of pervasive or chronic noxious patterns (e.g. emotional abuse or neglect) or overt victimisation (e.g. sexual or physical abuse), constitute exposure to harmful 'stress' (with differing severity), with potential threat to normal psychological and physical development, and healthy, functional well-being. 'Stress', or exposure to stressful life events (acute or chronic), is a central concept in any discussion of vulnerability to emotional disorder, and paramount when considering the variable 'pathways' from early life experiences to later psychopathology. Such formulations are readily taken up by conceptualisations of stress (e.g. Cicchetti & Cohen, 1995) and stress-diathesis theories (e.g. Abramson, Metalsky, & Alloy, 1989). The influence of parenting, or one's exposure to negative parental aspects, albeit important, is one of many potential environmental 'stressors'. Others include, trauma (e.g. non-parental CSA, natural or man-made disaster); loss (e.g. death of family member); peer victimisation (e.g. bullying, peer rejection); learning difficulties; consequences of personal illness or disability; and the accumulation of daily hassles.

In our discussion of parental influences in this chapter, we have focused predominately on the contribution made by parenting styles, the quality of perceived parent–child bonds and more 'direct' parent-to-child behaviours. However, of equal importance to a child's development, are a host of other more indirect influences, also constituting sources of acute or chronic stress. Some of these include parental hardship in the form of unemployment or poverty, parental conflict and violence and the chronic illness of a parent (Worsham, Compas, & Ey, 1997), including mental illness.

The relationship(s) between 'stress' and emotional adjustment and disorder is complex and highly influenced by a host of moderating and mediating factors, including 'fixed' characteristics such as age and gender (Parker & Brotchie, 2004). Age is an important factor when considering any allowance for environmental moderators of harmful stress created by parents. For example, for very young children and infants, the pathway from neglectful or abusive parenting is fairly clear, with research demonstrating direct negative outcomes (Field, 1995; Perry, Pollard, Blakley, Baker, & Vigilante, 1995). The moderators and mediators directly influencing infant adaptation to negative (or deprivational) parenting are limited, and include the child's innate temperament qualities and any existing genetic liability to disorder (which may or may not require environmental or developmental 'activation'). Any moderating effects of environmental influences such as social support or other positive influences may be less available or perhaps detectable for very young children. The well-studied role of cognitive mediators (e.g. schemas, cognitive appraisals) in theories of psychological vulnerabilities to disorder (Lazarus & Folkman, 1984), is not a valuable concept applicable to young children because they do not as yet possess the necessary cognitive capacities (Nolen-Hoeksema, Girgus, & Seligman, 1992). Stress-diathesis models (Gladstone & Parker, 2001 for a review), provide some important insight into the potential role of personal beliefs and other cognitive appraisals as key mediators in the pathway from 'stress' (e.g. negative parenting), with several studies of adolescents identifying the important vulnerability status of 'depressogenic' cognitive mediators (e.g. Alloy et al., 1999).

Conclusion

The very primacy of parental influences for children, underscores their vital importance in influencing early physical and emotional development, and subsequently in shaping early psychological constructs (e.g. self-beliefs, views about others and the world), personality development and behaviours. Effects of early parental influences (which are sometimes deeply ingrained in an individual's sense of self), are however subject to subsequent environmental moderators (e.g. psychological interventions; positive interpersonal relationships), which may provide beneficial ameliorating influences, or mediators (e.g. stressful events; poor coping, unresolved emotional pain), which may precipitate or fuel pathways to disorder.

The focus of future research and practice needs to further address effective approaches to reducing the vulnerability to psychological disorders in individuals who have experienced detrimental parenting, and perhaps identifying more novel therapeutic approaches in working with those whose adult adjustment or psychopathology has its origins in deprivational or abusive experiences with primary care-givers.

References

Abramson, L. Y., Metalsky, G. I., & Alloy, L. B. (1989). Hopelessness depression: A theory-based subtype of depression. *Psychological Review, 96,* 358–372.

Ainsworth, M. D. S., Blehar, M. C., Waters, E., & Wall, S. (1978). *Patterns of attachment: A psychological study of the strange situation.* Hillsdale, NJ: Lawrence Erlbaum.

Alloy, L. B., Abramson, L. Y., Whitehouse, W. G., Hogan, M. E., Tashman, N. A., Steinberg, D. L., Rose, D. T., & Donovan, P. (1999). Depressogenic cognitive styles: Predictive validity, information processing and personality characteristics, and developmental origins. *Behaviour Research and Therapy, 37,* 503–531.

Arrindell, W. A., Perris, C., Perris, H., Eisemann, M., Van der Ende, J., & Von Knorring, L. (1986). Cross-national invariance of dimensions of parental rearing behavior: Comparisons of psychometric data of Swedish depressives and healthy controls with Dutch target ratings on the EMBU. *British Journal of Psychiatry, 148*, 305–309.

Bifulco, A., & Moran., P. (1998). *Wednesday's child: Research into women's experience of neglect and abuse in childhood, and adult depression.* London: Routledge.

Bowen, K. (2000). Child abuse and domestic violence in families of children seen for suspected sexual abuse. *Clinical Pediatrics, 39*, 33–40.

Bowlby, J. (1969). Attachment and loss. *Attachment* (Vol. I). New York: Basic Books.

Bowlby, J. (1988). *A secure base:* Parent–Child Attachment and Healthy Human Development.

Brewin, C. R., Andrews, B., & Gotlib, I. H. (1993). Psychopathology and early experience: A reappraisal of retrospective reports. *Psychological Bulletin, 113,* 82–98.

Brewin, C. R., Andrews, B., & Furnham, A. (1996). Self-critical attitudes and parental criticism in young women. *British Journal of Medical Psychology, 69*, 69–78.

Capelli, M., McGrath, P. J., MacDonald, N. E., Boland, M., Fried, P., & Katsanis, J. (1988). Parent, family and disease factors as predictors of psychosocial functioning in children with cystic fibrosis. *Canadian Journal of Behavior, 20*, 413–423.

Chambers, J. A., Power, K. G., Loucks, V., & Swanson, V. (2000). Psychometric properties of the parental bonding instrument and its association with psychological distress in a group of incarcerated young offenders in Scotland. *Social Psychiatry and Psychiatric Epidemiology, 35*, 318–325.

Cicchetti, D., & Cohen, D. (1995). Perspectives on developmental psychopathology. In: D. Cicchetti & D. Cohen (Eds), *Developmental psychopathology: Vol.1. theory and methods* (pp. 3–20). New York: Wiley.

Cox, B. J., Enns, M. W., & Clara, I. P. (2000). The parental bonding instrument: Confirmatory evidence for a three-factor model in a psychiatric clinical sample and in the national comorbidity survey. *Social Psychiatry and Psychiatric Epidemiology, 35*, 353–357.

Cubis, J., Lewin, T., & Dawes, F. (1989). Australian adolescents' perceptions of their parents. *Australian and New Zealand Journal of Psychiatry, 23*, 35–47.

Duggan, C., Sham, P., Minnie, C., Lee, A., & Murray, R. (1998). Quality of parenting and vulnerability to depression: results from a family study. *Psychological Medicine, 28*, 185–191.

Elliott, M., Browne, K., & Kilcoyne, J. (1995). Child sexual abuse prevention: What offenders tell us. *Child Abuse and Neglect, 19*, 579–594.

Enns, M. W., Cox, B. J., & Clara, I. (2002). Parental bonding and adult psychopathology: Results from the US National Comorbidity Survey. *Psychological Medicine, 32*, 997–1008.

Field, T. (1995). Infants of depressed mothers. *Infant Behavior and Development, 18*, 1–13.

Gladstone, G., & Parker, G. (2001). Depressogenic cognitive schemas: Enduring beliefs or mood state artefacts? *Australian and New Zealand Journal of Psychiatry, 35*, 210–216.

Gladstone, G., Parker, G., Wilhelm, K., Mitchell, P., & Austin, M.-P. (1999). Characteristics of depressed patients who report childhood sexual abuse. *American Journal of Psychiatry, 156,* 431–437.

Gladstone, G., Parker, G., Mitchell, P., Malhi, G., Wilhelm, K., & Austin, M.-P. (2004). Childhood trauma and its implications for depressed women: An analysis of pathways from childhood sexual abuse to adult self-harm and revictimization. *American Journal of Psychiatry, 161,* 1–9.

Gomez, J. (1984). Learning to drink: The influence of psychosexual development. *Journal of Psychosomatic Research, 28*, 403–410.

Gomez-Beneyto, M., Pedros, A., Tomas, A., Aguilar, K., & Leal, C. (1993). Psychometric properties of the parental bonding instrument in a Spanish sample. *Social Psychiatry and Psychiatric Epidemiology, 28*, 252–255.

Gotlib, I. H., Mount, J. H., Cordy, N. I., & Whiffen, V. E. (1988). Depression and perceptions of early parenting: A longitudinal investigation. *British Journal of Psychiatry, 152*, 24–27.

Harlow, H. F., & Harlow, M. K. (1962). Social deprivation in monkeys. *Scientific American, 207*, 137–146.

Harlow, H. F., & Zimmerman, R. (1959). Affectional responses in the infant monkey. *Science, 130*, 421–432.

Hill, J., Davis, R., Byatt, M., Burnside, E., Rollinson., & Fear, S. (2000). Childhood sexual abuse and affective symptoms in women: A general population study. *Psychological Medicine, 30*, 1283–1291.

Hinde, R. A. (1979). *Toward understanding relationships*. London: Academic Press.

Joyce, P. R. (1984). Parental bonding in bipolar affective disorder. *Journal of Affective Disorders, 7*, 319–324.

Kendler, K. S. (1996). Parenting: A genetic-epidemiological perspective. *American Journal of Psychiatry, 153*, 11–20.

Kendler, K. S., Sham, P. C., & MacLean, C. J. (1997). The determinants of parenting: An epidemiological, multi-informant, retrospective study. *Psychological Medicine, 27*, 549–563.

Kessler, R. C., McConagle, K. A., Zhao, S., Nelson, C. B., Hughes, M., Eshleman, S., Wittchen, H. U., & Kendler, K. S. (1994). Lifetime and 12-month prevalence of DSM-III-R psychiatric disorders in the United States: Results from the National Co-morbidity Survey. *Archives of General Psychiatry, 51*, 8–19.

Lazarus, R. S., & Folkman, S. (1984). *Stress, appraisal and coping*. New York: Springer.

Lizardi, H., & Klein, D. N. (2002). Evidence of increased sensitivity using a three-factor version of the parental bonding instrument. *The Journal of Nervous and Mental Disease, 190*, 619–623.

Lizardi, H., Klein, D. N., Crosby-Ouimette, P., Riso, L. P., Anderson, R. L., & Donaldson, S. K. (1995). Reports of the childhood home environment in early-onset dysthymia and episodic major depression. *Journal of Abnormal Psychology, 104*, 132–139.

Lorenz, K. Z. (1935). Der kumpan in der umwelt des vogels. *Journal of Ornithology, 83*, 137–413.

Schiller, C. H. (Ed.). (1957). Translation in *instinctive behavior*. New York: International Universities Press.

Luft, G. A. (1987). Parenting style and parent–adolescent religious value consensus. *Journal of Adolescent Research, 2*, 53–68.

Maccoby, E. E., & Martin, J. A. (1983). Socialization in the context of the family: Parent–child interaction. In: P. H. Mussen (Ed.), *Handbook of child psychology* (pp. 1–101). New York: Wiley.

Maestripieri, D. (1999). The biology of human parenting: Insights from nonhuman primates. *Neuroscience and Biobehavioral Reviews, 23*, 411–422.

McLaughlin, T. L., Heath, A. C., Bucholz, K. K., Madden, P. A. F., Bierut, L. J., Slutske, W. S., Dinwiddie, S., Statham, D. J., Dunne, M. P., & Martin, N. G. (2000). Childhood sexual abuse and pathogenic parenting in the childhood recollections of adult twin pairs. *Psychological Medicine, 30*, 1293–1302.

Miller, L., Kramer, R., Warner, V., Wickramaratne, P., Weissman, M. (1997). Intergenerational transmission of parental bonding among women. *Journal of the American Academy of Child and Adolescent Psychiatry, 36*, 1134–1139.

Murphy, E., Brewin, C. R., & Silka, L. (1997). The assessment of parenting using the parental bonding instrument: Two or three factors? *Psychological Medicine, 27*, 333–342.

Nolen-Hoeksema, S., Girgus, J. S., & Seligman, M. E. P. (1992). Predictors and consequences of childhood depressive symptoms: A 5-year longitudinal study. *Journal of Abnormal Psychology, 101*, 405–422.

Parker, G. (1979). Reported parental characteristics in relation to trait depression and anxiety levels in a non-clinical group. *Australian and New Zealand Journal of Psychiatry, 13*, 260–264.

Parker, G. (1981). Parental reports of depressives: An investigation of several explanations. *Journal of Affect Disorders, 3*, 131–140.

Parker, G. (1983). Parental affectionless control as an antecedent to adult depression. *Archives of General Psychiatry, 40*, 956–960.

Parker, G. (1989). The parental bonding instrument: Psychometric properties reviewed. *Psychiatric Developments, 4*, 317–335.

Parker, G. (1990). The parental bonding instrument: A decade of research. *Social Psychiatry and Psychiatric Epidemiology, 25*, 281–282.

Parker, G., & Lipscombe, P. (1979). Parental characteristics of Jews and Greeks in Australia. *Australian and New Zealand Journal of Psychiatry, 13*, 225–229.

Parker, G., & Lipscombe, P. (1981). Influences on maternal overprotection. *British Journal of Psychiatry, 138*, 303–311.

Parker, G., & Hadzi-Pavlovic, D. (1992). Parental representations of melancholic and non-melancholic depressives: Examining for specificity to depressive types and for evidence of additive effects. *Psychological Medicine, 22*, 657–665.

Parker, G., & Gladstone, G. (1996). Parental characteristics as influences on adjustment in adulthood. In: G. B. Sarason & B. R. Sarason (Eds), *Handbook of social support and the family* (pp. 195–218). New York: Plenum Press.

Parker, G., & Brotchie, H. (2004). From diathesis to dimorphism: The biology of gender differences in depression. *The Journal of Nervous and Mental Disease, 192*, 210–216.

Parker, G., Tupling, H., & Brown. (1979). A parental bonding instrument. *British Journal of Medical Psychology, 52*, 1–10.

Parker, G., Kiloh, L., & Hayward, L. (1987). Parental representations of neurotic and endogenous depressives. *Journal of Affective Disorders, 13*, 75–82.

Parker, G., Roussos, J., Hadzi-Pavlovic, D., Mitchell, P., Austin, M.-P. (1997). Development of a refined measure of dysfunctional parenting and assessment of its relevance in patients with affective disorders. *Psychological Medicine, 27*, 1193–1203.

Perry, B. D., Pollard, R. A., Blakley, T. L., & Vigilante, D. (1995). Childhood trauma, the neurobiology of adaptation, and 'use-dependent' development of the brain: How 'states' become 'traits'. *Infant Mental Health Journal, 16*, 271–289.

Radke-Yarrow, M., Cummings, E. M., Kuczynski, L., Chapman, M. (1985). Patterns of attachment in two- and three-year-olds in normal families and families with parental depression. *Child Development, 56*, 884–893.

Roe, A., & Siegelman, M. (1963). A parent–child questionnaire. *Child Development, 34*, 355–369.

Sato, T., Narita, T., Hirano, S., Kusunoki, K., Sakado, K., Uehara, T. (1999). Confirmatory factor analysis of the parental bonding instrument in a Japanese population. *Psychological Medicine, 29*, 127–133.

Silove, D., Parker, G., Hadzi-Pavlovic, D., Manicavasagar, V., & Blaszczynski, A. (1991). Parental representations of patients with panic disorder and generalised anxiety disorder. *British Journal of Psychiatry, 159*, 835–841.

Stein, D., Williamsom, D. E., Birmaher, B., Brent, D. A., Kaufam, J., Dahl, R. E., Perel, J. M., & Ryan, N. D. (2000). Parent–child bonding and family functioning in depressed children and children at high risk and low risk for future depression. *Journal of the American Academy of Child and Adolescent Psychiatry, 39*, 1387–1395.

Torresani, S., Favaretto, R., & Zimmermann, C. (2000). Parental representations in drug-dependent patients and their parents. *Comprehensive Psychiatry, 41*, 123–129.

Worsham, N., Compas, B., & Ey, S. (1997). Children's coping with parental illness. In: S. Wolchik & I. N. Sandler (Eds), *Handbook of children's coping: Linking theory and intervention. Issues in clinical child psychology* (pp. 195–213). New York: Plenum Press.

Chapter 3

Attachment and Psychopathology: A Lifespan Perspective

Judy Ungerer and Catherine McMahon

Attachment Relationships — Early Development and Individual Differences

Many presentations of Bowlby's attachment theory begin by describing the evolutionary context in which the theory is set. This is not merely an academic exercise, but rather serves to highlight Bowlby's unique contribution to our understanding of attachment by emphasising the functional adaptiveness of attachment relationships for infants, and more generally, for the human species. Attachment refers to the intimate emotional bond that infants form with their caregivers and that develops during the infant's first year of life (Bowlby, 1988a). Bowlby (1969/1982) proposed that infants from birth are biologically pre-adapted to interact with and form attachment relationships with the parents who provide them with care. Interaction is ensured through the infant's expression of attachment behaviours like approaching, clinging, crying, following and smiling. Parents, for their part, are biologically pre-adapted to respond with caregiving behaviour to these infant signals and provide the feeding, soothing and other care that will ensure that the infant's needs are met. The infant's attachment behaviours serve as a protective function (Carlson, Sampson, & Sroufe, 2003) by making it more likely that the parent will be physically close to the infant and, therefore, available when the infant is in need. In this sense, the parent has been described as a "safe haven" for the infant, that is, "a source of comfort and protection in the context of extreme arousal or environmental threat" (Carlson et al., 2003, p. 3). In a complementary fashion, a parent who is experienced as a "safe haven" by the infant will also function as a "secure base" from which the infant is comfortable to go out and explore the environment, since the infant can be certain of the parent's availability if he or she encounters trouble or is in need. In this way, attachment relationships not only impact the physical survival of the infant, but can influence the extent to which infants are able to engage and learn from their broader physical and social environment as well.

Psychopathology and the Family
Edited by J. L. Hudson and R. M. Rapee
Copyright © 2005 by Elsevier Ltd.
All rights of reproduction in any form reserved
ISBN: 0-08-044449-0

While attachment relationships are critical to the physical survival of the infant, their impact on development also extends to domains that can be seen as important for children's broader personality and social–emotional development. In order to understand these broader sequelae of attachment relationships, it is necessary to acknowledge the changing nature of attachment relationships over the first few years of the child's life. These changes are largely driven by two main factors: the increasing developmental competence of the child and the individual caregiving experiences that the child encounters within his or her own specific attachment relationships. Let us first examine the developmental nature of changes in children's attachment relationships.

Developmental Changes in Attachment Relationships in the Early Years

Bowlby (1988a) described four phases in the development of attachment relationships, three of which occur in the first year of life. Between birth and 2–3 months of age, infants respond to their human caregivers in ways that increase the likelihood that interaction will occur. In particular, they visually orient to human faces and follow their movement, and they are attentive to human voices. They also signal their physiological needs, for example, by crying when distressed. However, they do not show a clear preference for one caregiver over another. Caregivers, on their part, respond to these infant signals with social interaction and the provision of care, thus providing the external support that very young infants need to engage with their environment and to maintain a well-modulated physiological state.

Over the remainder of the first year, the infant's increasing developmental competence underpins specific changes in the nature of their attachment relationships (Marvin & Britner, 1999). First, the infant's repertoire of attachment behaviours becomes expanded and better organised into coherent behavioural systems that are integrated with each other. On a simple level with very young infants, this involves, for example, the integration of vision and reaching, such that infants will reach out to grab onto the mother when she comes into view. On a more complex level with older infants, it involves the emergence of new attachment behaviours like crawling that are used very intentionally to follow and maintain proximity to a caregiver who is seen to be moving away. Overall, this greater developmental competence enables the infant to exert more control over interactions with caregivers and to initiate rather than simply respond to attachment, caregiving and social interactions.

Second, there is a move away from indiscriminate responding to caregivers to an hierarchically organised preferential responding to specific attachment figures (Marvin & Britner, 1999). Most infants are cared for by more than one person, be it another parent, a grandparent, or a professional carer like a child care worker or nanny. It is common for infants to form attachment relationships with these caregivers if their experience with them is sufficiently frequent for such a relationship to become established. However, by the end of the first year most infants will have identified one caregiver, usually the mother if she is the primary caregiver, as their preferred attachment figure whom they will seek out in times of need. The preferred attachment figure will be the person to whom the infant is most likely to direct social smiles and cries for attention, and that person is also the adult who is most effective in terminating the infant's attachment signals, that is, in soothing the distressed infant and enabling the infant to return to a calm state.

Third, as infants mature cognitively during the first year and develop a basic knowledge of object permanence, they are able to understand the continued existence of the attachment figure even when he or she is not physically present (Marvin & Britner, 1999). This involves the formation of what Bowlby (1988a) termed an internal working model (IWM) of the attachment relationship. The IWM is like a cognitive schema or mental representation of the attachment relationship. It includes the infant's concept of the caregiver and of itself in relation to the caregiver, based on the infant's actual experiences of care in that attachment relationship. Importantly, the IWM is influenced by the extent to which the infant has received sensitive and responsive care from the attachment figure, and underlies the infant's expectations regarding interactions with future attachment figures. Thus, the IWM becomes the mechanism by which earlier attachment relationships can influence the child's expectations and actual interactions with subsequent attachment figures and other social partners. While the nature of the IWM can be modified by subsequent attachment experiences, the longer a model has been in place, the more resistant to change it becomes (Bowlby, 1988a).

The IWM has implications for the child's more general personality and social–emotional development in two ways. First, the IWM is a core component of the child's self-concept. In relationships where caregivers are sensitive and responsive to a child's needs, this self-concept is positive as the child will view itself as being valued and "worthy" of care. In relationships where caregiving is less sensitively attuned to the child's needs, the child's self-concept will be correspondingly less positive. Second, the IWM is the child's first model of social relationships, and the child uses this model to guide its interactions with other social partners, including other caregivers and peers. When the child's experience in the primary attachment relationship has been one of responsive care, the child will approach new relationships with a sense of trust that any communications will be attended to and bids for interaction will receive a positive response. In contrast, when the child's experience in the primary attachment relationship has been less than optimal, the child will carry forward more negative expectations that are likely to make future social relationships more difficult to manage successfully (Bowlby, 1988a).

Changes in attachment relationships continue to occur beyond the first few years of life. During the preschool period as children's language skills become more developed, children become less reliant on actual physical proximity and contact to manage their attachment needs. They are more likely to rely on simple physical orientation to the caregiver, eye contact, non-verbal expressions, and direct conversation with caregivers to communicate their needs (Cassidy & Marvin, 1992). Ultimately, this sets the stage for a developmental transition in the attachment relationship to what Bowlby (1988b) has termed a "goal-corrected partnership" which emerges gradually between 2 and 4 years of age (Marvin & Britner, 1999). The hallmark of the goal-corrected partnership is the ability of children to understand their own mental states and those of others, and to use this understanding to guide interactions with them. The emerging ability to talk about feelings, desires and motives with a caregiver, demonstrates the ability to identify and label their own internal states. When this understanding gradually extends to being able to identify and label internal states in others, children are able to engage in more complex relationships where mutual goals can be set and plans and strategies can be developed which take account of the needs and desires of all involved. From an attachment theory perspective, the critical achievement of the goal-corrected partnership phase is the child's development of the ability to reflect on the internal state of another. This capacity is essential for the establishment of healthy attachment and other social relationships across the lifespan, and in adulthood it is the competence central to the establishment of sensitive and responsive caregiving relationships with infants and young children (Fonagy, Steele, Moran, Steele, & Higgitt, 1991).

Individual Differences in Attachment Relationships

One of the most important contributions of attachment theory, particularly as it relates to the significance of early attachment relationships for children's longer term healthy psychological development, is the identification of individual differences in the quality of attachment relationships. As Weinfield, Sroufe, Egeland, and Carlson (1999) note, an initial distinction between "the presence of an attachment relationship and the quality of an attachment relationship is important" (p. 68). Infants, due to their biological evolutionary heritage, will form an attachment relationship to a caregiver as long as that person is sufficiently available to fill the role of an attachment figure. This biological propensity is sufficiently strong that an attachment relationship will form regardless of the quality of care received. Infants form attachment relationships even to caregivers who maltreat or abuse them, and these attachments are equally strong as attachments to more sensitive and responsive caregivers. It is only in cases of extremely unreliable care, for example, in some institutional settings where care is provided, but there is little predictability as to who will provide that care, that infants will fail to form attachment relationships with their caregivers. However, not all attachment relationships are the same in a qualitative sense; they vary specifically as a function of the quality of the caregiving received by the child, and they differentially influence the child's developing sense of self and his or her ability to effectively manage or regulate emotional responses, particularly in social–emotional contexts (Cassidy, 1994).

The research of Ainsworth, Blehar, Waters, and Wall (1978), and Main and Solomon (1990) has been central to advancing our understanding of these qualitative differences in children's early attachment relationships. Two approaches have been found useful in characterising these early differences. First, attachment relationships are characterised as either secure or insecure. In secure attachment relationships, children experience the caregiver as reliably available and effective in responding to their attachment needs. So, for example, the secure child who falls and grazes a knee while playing in the park knows that crying out will quickly bring mother who will pick the child up, give a warm hug, and attend to the injury, and the child will experience the physical contact with the mother and her administrations as comforting. Such sensitive and responsive care fosters the development in the child of a positive sense of self who is "worthy of care", and supports the child's development of skills for managing distressing feelings based on the experience of effective holding and containing by the caregiver. In contrast, in an insecure attachment relationship, the child experiences the caregiver as unpredictably available or even rejecting of their attachment needs, and contact with the caregiver is less effective in providing comfort. In the extreme, contact with the mother can even be experienced as a source of fear rather than comfort. A child in such an attachment relationship is likely to develop a more negative sense of self as "not worthy of care", and develop emotion regulation strategies that defensively exclude or fail to contain feelings of distress (Cassidy, 1994; Weinfeld et al., 1999).

The second approach characterises attachment relationships as either organised or disorganised. In the attachment context, organisation refers to the strategies children in different attachment relationships use to manage their distressing feelings (Main & Solomon, 1990). Organised strategies are coherent, integrated patterns of behaviour that children use reliably when interacting with their caregivers in order to get their attachment needs met. Secure attachment relationships are characterised by organised strategies, but some types of insecure attachment relationships are considered to involve organised strategies as well. A secure, organised attachment strategy is defined by the open and direct expression of affect to the caregiver (Cassidy, 1994). The secure child who is distressed, cries, looks directly to the caregiver, and approaches the caregiver for comfort. The child's signals are clear and easy to read. Positive emotions are expressed as openly and directly as negative emotions. Furthermore, the child's expression of affect is "well-modulated". Distress builds gradually rather than abruptly, and the child's return to a calm state also occurs in a gradual, seemingly controlled way. The overall sense is of a child who is emotionally in control. Secure children learn these strategies as a result of the way they are responded to by their caregivers. Distress is quickly and reliably responded to, and children are held and comforted until they are in a calm, settled state and ready to venture on their own into the environment again. Secure caregivers are sensitive to their children's signals and respond in a calm, containing way that promotes the development of the children's own self-regulatory skills.

In contrast, two types of organised insecure attachment strategies have also been described. These are the avoidant and the ambivalent/resistant attachment strategies. The avoidant strategy involves the minimisation or inhibition rather than direct expression of negative feelings to the caregiver, and is linked to a history of having these feelings repeatedly ignored or rejected by the caregiver (Cassidy, 1994). Avoidant infants are least likely to cry when left by their mothers, and when their mothers return they typically fail to approach them for comfort. Instead, they engage in exploration and play, presumably as a way of redirecting their attention away from the mother and dampening down their attachment needs. Regarding modulation of affect, these infants would be described as relatively flat in affect expression, and this extends to positive feelings as well as to negative feelings like anger or distress. In terms of the significance of such a strategy for later personality functioning, the avoidant affect minimising strategy has been linked to defenses like idealisation (that is, avoiding thinking about negative aspects of experiences or relationships) and repression (an inability to easily access memories of early attachment relationships) (Bowlby, 1980; Hesse, 1999). These defenses will be discussed in more detail later in the chapter.

Opposite to the avoidant minimising strategy is the maximising strategy used by ambivalent/resistant infants. This strategy involves a heightened expression of negative feelings presumably as an attempt to maximise the possibility that they will gain the attention and nurturance of caregivers who have a history of being inconsistently responsive to their attachment needs. These infants have been described as possibly expressing more negative affect than they actually feel in order to gain the attention of their unresponsive caregivers (Cassidy, 1994), and they typically show abrupt affect changes. Their distress tends to build very quickly and go to extreme levels, and they are correspondingly difficult to soothe. When left by the mother, intense crying can quickly ensue. However, this distress can also be just as abruptly turned off when the child is picked up when the mother returns, but the actual return to a calm state is difficult to achieve. If these children are put down by the mother who interprets their cessation of crying as a cue that everything is alright, they are just as likely to abruptly start crying again and get entrenched in a negative cycle of heightened negative affect expression (Ainsworth et al., 1978). While these children have a coherent and predictable maximising attachment strategy, they lack the well-modulated emotion regulation of secure children or the inhibitory control of avoidant children. The ambivalent/resistant maximising strategy has been linked conceptually and in cross-sectional studies to heightened anxiety and a tendency to ruminate extensively on unmet attachment needs in children and adults (Dozier, Stovall, & Albus, 1999; Shamir-Essakow, Ungerer, & Rapee, 2005).

The final attachment strategy is both insecure and lacking organisation. It characterises a group of children originally identified by Main, and Solomon (1990) who are known as the disorganised attachment group. These children do not have a clear and coherent strategy that they are able to use with a caregiver to get their attachment needs met. Instead, their behaviour towards the caregiver reflects what appears to be an approach-avoidance conflict, that is, attempts to approach the caregiver are blocked by behaviours that keep the child at a distance. The child can appear confused and disoriented, and even frozen in space for periods of time. Such behaviours have been linked to dissociative symptoms in the early adult years (Carlson, 1998). The absence of an organised attachment strategy is believed to result from caregiving behaviours that elicit fear in infants and young children (Main & Hesse, 1990). This includes abusive or threatening interactions where the behaviour of the caregiver is actually frightening to the child. However, this fear response also appears to be elicited by caregivers who themselves are frightened by being in the caregiving role, and who may themselves experience periods of confusion or even dissociation when interacting with their children. The parents of disorganised children have been described as effectively abdicating the caregiving role in a way that appears to place these children at greatest risk for later maladaptive social–emotional functioning and psychopathology (George & Solomon, 1999).

Thus, attachment theory provides a dynamic explanatory model indicating how childhood caregiving experiences contribute to vulnerability to stress and psychopathology across the lifespan. Carlson et al. (2003) note that individual differences in attachment have a lasting influence on an individual's capacity to develop and utilise internal and external resources to manage stress and challenging situations. With respect to internal resources, there is emerging interest in the extent to which different patterns of caregiving in infancy may have lasting effects on the developing brain that may impact a child's capacity to develop effective self-regulatory skills (Carlson et al., 2003). Secondly, the attachment relationship may provide a foundation for stable patterns of self-regulation (including defenses that involve minimising or maximising negative affect) that may have an ongoing impact on the way an individual responds to stress. With respect to capacity to utilise external resources, it is believed that an infant's capacity for social interaction develops as a result of their experiences with an attachment figure, and determines their later capacity to utilise support from others. Finally, representational models derived from early attachment experiences guide the infants' expectations, attitudes, and feelings regarding themselves and others and, thereby, influence the nature of the attachment relationships they develop later in life (Carlson et al., 2003).

While there is some research evidence to support each of the above assertions, most studies are cross-sectional in design, and results from long-term, longitudinal prospective studies are still only emerging. What seems clear from the available research, however, is that for most infants, attachment variations do not represent pathology or even directly cause pathology. Rather, varying patterns of attachment represent "initiating conditions" that play a dynamic role in the development of pathology and resilience. The enduring effects of early experiences may derive, firstly, from the way the environment supports early tendencies or dispositions in the child (Green & Goldwyn, 2002). For example, children with difficult temperaments are known to be at greater risk for developing insecure attachment relationships, particularly in the context of other risk factors, like chronic maternal depression or marital conflict, that may make it difficult for their caregivers to respond sensitively to their needs (Vaughn & Bost, 1999). Other biological vulnerabilities that have been linked specifically to an increase in insecure disorganised attachment include pervasive developmental disorder (Willensen-Swinkels, Bakermans-Kronenburg, Buitelaar, & van IJzendoorn, 2000), delayed cognitive development in infancy (Lyons-Ruth, Easterbrooks, & Cibelli, 1997), and Down syndrome (Atkinson et al., 1999). Thus biological vulnerabilities may increase the risk of insecure attachment, which in turn may continue to support the negative impact of these risk factors on children's development.

In a complementary way, the enduring effects of early experience may also derive from patterns of caregiving that impair the development of children's biological regulatory systems. For example, Spangler and Grossman (1999) have reported associations between disorganised attachment in the Strange Situation in infants at 12 months of age and increased cardiac activation during separation episodes and following the occurrence of specific disorganised behaviours in the presence of the caregiver. These same infants also showed an increase in cortisol levels, indicating heightened adrenocortical activation. Both heart rate and cortisol responses indicate that disorganised infants "experience more intense alarm and negative emotional arousal on a physiological level…(and) have difficulties or indicate more effort to organize an effective coping response" (Spangler & Grossman, 1999, p. 105). While there is some longitudinal data indicating that the effects of these early attachment experiences may be enduring, replication and extension of these findings is clearly needed. Furthermore, both theory and data indicate that "although the capacity for developmental change diminishes with age, change continues throughout the life cycle" (Bowlby, 1988a, p. 136). In this sense, attachment relationships are no different from other experiences, like maternal depression or economic hardship, which can significantly impact a child's development. The unique characteristic of attachment, however, is that it is something that impacts all infants, and in this sense the likelihood of maladaptive attachment experiences being a significant influence on population outcomes is correspondingly enhanced.

Attachment and Psychopathology: Beyond Infancy

Reports of inadequate caregiving during childhood are associated with a diverse range of psychopathology later in life (Dozier et al., 1999). For example, adverse childhood caretaking experiences (e.g. loss of a caregiver, and/or harsh or abusive parenting) are associated with vulnerability to depression in adulthood (Bifulco, Brown, & Harris, 1994), and Bowlby (1973) proposed that family environments characterised by excessive parental control and overprotection are likely to engender anxiety disorders. According to Bowlby (1980), the management of anxiety, anger and sadness through the healthy use of secure base figures and mature defenses is a major protective factor against psychopathology throughout life. In contrast, the relatively stable defensive strategies for processing attachment-related thoughts and feelings acquired in the context of suboptimal early caregiving continue to compromise the developing individual's capacity to draw effectively on both internal (self-regulatory) and external (relationship) resources in times of stress (Bowlby, 1980; Carlson et al., 2003).

Despite the importance attributed to early experiences in setting up adaptive or maladaptive pathways, attachment theory also acknowledges the possibility for change in a positive direction, and thus provides a model for psychological resiliency. Since working models of attachment are dynamic, they can be revised and reformulated in the light of corrective attachment experiences during childhood or later in life. This, of course, is the assumption underpinning all psychotherapy and dynamically oriented interventions.

In this section, we first discuss prospective studies that examine relations between individual differences in attachment behaviours identified in infancy and early childhood and psychological adaptation and psychopathology during childhood and adolescence. Next, we examine methodologies for assessing the working model of attachment in adolescence and adulthood and consider the cross-sectional empirical evidence linking attachment state of mind and psychopathology. We then consider the extension of this methodology to the investigation of attachment representations in children and discuss an emerging body of research that examines links between attachment representations and behaviour problems in children. Finally, we consider the contribution of attachment theory in explaining the inter-generational transmission of both risk and resiliency and the implications of attachment theory for therapeutic interventions.

Attachment and Psychopathology: Prospective Longitudinal Research

Much of the evidence for relations between individual differences in infant attachment and later maladaptation comes from the Minnesota longitudinal study conducted by Alan Sroufe and colleagues, who have followed a high-risk sample of teenage mothers and their offspring for almost 30 years (Sroufe, Egeland, Carlson, & Collins, 2005). The study provides evidence that composite measures of early experience, including attachment, predict risk of behaviour problems in the preschool years and predict middle childhood and adolescent adaptation according to teacher emotional health ratings. More specifically, this group of researchers have shown that avoidant attachment identified in infancy (in the context of other life-stress and risk factors) was related to aggression in middle childhood and aggression and antisocial behaviour in adolescence, while ambivalent attachment in infancy was shown to predict anxiety disorders, even after controlling for maternal anxiety and child temperament (Warren, Huston, Egeland, & Sroufe, 1997), and depressive symptoms in adolescence. In contrast, in this high-risk sample, secure attachment in infancy predicted later resiliency, including greater social competence with peers and less negative reaction to periods of high family stress as adolescents. These findings clearly support a cumulative risk model and suggest that insecure attachment combined with family adversity places children at risk of later psychological difficulties (Weinfield, Sroufe, & Egeland, 2000), while secure attachment appears to be protective. No long-term main effects for infant attachment status have been found in low-risk samples where the majority of children are secure and rates of psychopathology are very low (Greenberg, 1999).

Green and Goldwyn (2002) note that the identification of disorganised attachment has greatly improved the predictive validity of the attachment construct with respect to psychopathology in childhood. Disorganisation in infancy has been powerfully associated with externalising and internalising behaviour problems in the early school years (see Lyons-Ruth & Jacobvitz, 1999, for a review), as well as poor peer interaction and unusual or bizarre behaviour in the classroom (Jacobvitz & Hazan, 1999). Moss, Cyr, and Dubois-Comtois (2004) and Moss, St-Laurent, and Parent (1999) reported that disorganised attachment assessed at 5–7 years of age was associated with concurrent teacher reports of internalising and externalising problems as well as later child-reported poor academic self-esteem. Furthermore, children disorganised in infancy in the Minnesota longitudinal study showed higher levels of teacher-rated dissociative symptoms and internalising symptoms in middle childhood and higher levels of overall psychopathology at 17 years (Carlson, 1998). A meta-analysis of studies linking disorganised attachment with externalising behaviour problems has revealed effect sizes ranging from 0.17 to 0.54, with a mean of 0.29 (van IJzendoorn, Schuengel, & Bakermans-Kranenburg, 1999).

Working Models of Attachment: Assessment in Adolescence and Adulthood

An adult's state of mind (or working model) with respect to attachment is a product of both their early experiences with their caregivers and their reformulation of those experiences over time. In 1984, Main and Goldwyn (1984, 1998), using a language-based methodology, were able to identify individual differences in current processing of attachment-related memories in adults that paralleled the patterns of infant behaviour identified in the Strange Situation procedure. This well-validated measure has enabled the empirical study of concurrent associations between attachment representations and psychopathology in adolescence and adulthood, differential responsiveness to supportive interventions, and the inter-generational transmission of resilience and vulnerability to stress.

The Adult Attachment Interview.   The Adult Attachment Interview (George, Kaplan, & Main, 1985, 1996) is a disarmingly simple interview regarding early attachment experiences that aims to elicit specific semantic and episodic memories of childhood experiences with parents and evaluations of the ways in which these experiences influence current functioning. Any reports of loss or abuse are systematically probed regarding reactions to the event, changes in feeling over time, and effects upon adult personality. Because there are ample opportunities for speakers to contradict or fail to support their portrayals of their early experiences during the hour-long interview, the methodology is unique in its capacity to capture unconscious defensive processes (Main, 1996), in particular avoidant defenses such as idealisation, that are not able to be detected by other self-report measures (Stein, Jacobs, Ferguson, Allen, & Fonagy, 1998).

Verbatim transcripts are analysed in detail, and four states of mind with respect to attachment are identified based on the coherence of the account (in particular, the capacity to support descriptions of relationships with episodic memories) and the degree of collaboration with the interviewer (particularly a flexible capacity for reflection about attachment-related experiences) (Main & Goldwyn, 1985, 1998). Attachment state of mind is classified as secure-autonomous, irrespective of life history, in adults who value attachment experiences, whose presentation and evaluation of attachment experiences is internally consistent, and who are freely able to evaluate the impact of these experiences on their later functioning. Thus, secure-autonomous adults demonstrate relatively undefended behavioural and psychological integration of their earlier attachment experiences, allowing them to function flexibly in goal-corrected partnerships with others that contribute to a sense of safety and wellbeing (George & West, 1999). Consistent with secure infants and young children, secure-autonomous individuals are able to express their feelings openly and have incorporated models of the self as worthy of protection and care and others as reliable and helpful, which enables them to draw effectively on supportive relationships in times of need.

Individuals are classified as avoidant-dismissing if they are actively derogating or dismissive about their attachment experiences or the impact of them, and/or present highly positive idealised accounts of early childhood relationships that are not supported by episodic memories. Dismissing adults, like avoidant infants, engage in what Bowlby (1980) described as the defensive exclusion of affect laden information about attachment that would lead to anxiety, suffering and pain if it were fully processed. Dismissing states of mind incorporate working models of the self as invulnerable and unlovable and others as probably rejecting, and are believed to be associated with externalising disorders such as personality disorder, substance abuse, and hostile forms of depression (Dozier et al., 1999).

Individuals are classified as ambivalent/pre-occupied if they appear to be currently angrily or passively pre-occupied with their earlier attachment experiences. This classification, like the infant ambivalent/resistant classification, reflects a defensive strategy of maximising or exaggerating attachment needs and negative affect to elicit responsiveness from an unpredictable caregiver.   Theoretically, pre-occupied attachment reflecting absorption with negative affect, a fruitless rumination over negative experiences in the past, and a working model of self as unlovable and others as unloving or unsupportive is believed to predispose individuals to internalising disorders.

Transcripts are judged unresolved/disoriented if lapses in discourse or reasoning suggest mental disorganisation or disorientation with respect to prior experiences of loss, abuse or trauma. These lapses, like the lapses in behaviour identified in disorganised infants, are believed to reflect a momentary breakdown of defenses that results in dysfunctional, dysregulated behaviour and emotional flooding (Solomon & George, 1999a). Such dysregulation places the individual at risk for mental and behavioural disintegration and helplessness (George & West, 1999) and is believed to predispose individuals to dissociative disorders.

The classifications based on the Adult Attachment Interview have been shown to be relatively stable, independent of intelligence, memory and personality (Bakermans-

Kranenburg & van IJzendoorn, 1993), and to reliably predict attachment classification in offspring (van IJzendoorn, 1995; van IJzendoorn et al., 1999).

Attachment State of Mind and Psychopathology in Adolescents and Adults

While there appear to be clear links between insecure unresolved/disoriented states of mind and psychopathology (Fonagy et al., 1996), providing empirical support for the specific theoretical links between pre-occupied and dismissing states of mind and internalising and externalising disorders, respectively, has proven challenging. A few small studies with adolescent inpatients have provided some evidence linking a dismissing state of mind with eating disorders (Cole-Detke & Kobak, 1996) and conduct disorders (Allen, Hauser, & Borman-Spurrell, 1996; Rosenstein & Horowitz, 1996). There is also some evidence that a pre-occupied state of mind regarding attachment is more prevalent in individuals with internalising disorders such as unipolar depression (Cole-Detke & Kobak, 1996; Fonagy et al., 1996; Rosenstein & Horowitz, 1996), anxious and dysthymic personality traits (Rosenstein & Horowitz, 1996), anxiety disorders (Fonagy et al., 1996) and suicidality (Adam, Sheldon-Keller, & West, 1995). However, an over representation of dismissing (avoidant) attachment has also been reported in depressed individuals (Patrick, Hobson, Castle, Howard, & Maughan, 1994), and in the case of anxiety disorders, the unresolved/disoriented classification has been shown to best discriminate individuals with anxiety disorders from other clinical groups (Fonagy et al., 1996).

These mixed findings may be due, in part, to the heterogeneous clinical profiles noted in both depression and anxiety (subsuming individuals who are self-focused and withdrawn as well as those who are outward focused and hostile), and also to study differences with respect to exclusion criteria for co-morbid diagnoses (Dozier et al., 1999).

Consistent with the research regarding disorganized attachment in childhood, the evidence is strongest for an association between psychiatric disorders in adolescence and adulthood and an unresolved/disoriented state of mind with respect to loss and abuse (Dozier et al., 1999), particularly for those mental health disorders that have relational difficulties as one of their hallmark features, including partner violence, borderline personality disorder, dissociation and suicidal behaviour (Fonagy et al., 1996; George & West, 1999; Holmes, 2004). The links between disorganised attachment in infancy and later dissociative symptoms in childhood and adolescence have already been described. However, studies have not yet systematically examined attachment states of mind in adults with dissociative disorders (Dozier et al., 1999). More recently, studies exploring relations between attachment state of mind and affective functioning in non-clinical community samples have reported that pre-occupied attachment status was linked to higher levels of psychiatric distress in a low-income community sample (Pianta, Egeland, & Adam, 1996), to more suicidal ideation in a population of expectant parents (Riggs & Jacobvitz, 2002), and to more psychological problems in college women (Creasey, 2002).

Working Models of Attachment in Younger Children

Based on the adult attachment interview, researchers have begun to develop comparable age-appropriate techniques for assessment of IWMs and attachment state of mind for use with preschool and school age children. These measures have generally taken two forms (Solomon & George, 1999b): a series of photographs depicting a child separating from parent attachment figures where the child is asked to describe the feelings and behavioural responses of the depicted child to the separation (e.g. Kaplan, 1987; Klagsbrun & Bowlby, 1976; Slough & Greenberg, 1990), and doll-play techniques where children are asked to respond verbally and/or with doll play to distressing events acted out with family doll figures, like a child falling off a rock and grazing a knee, or a child finding a monster in the bedroom (e.g. Bretherton, Ridgeway, & Cassidy, 1990; George & Solomon, 1994; Green, Stanley, Smith, & Goldwyn, 2000).

Security versus insecurity of attachment is judged in different ways depending on the specific measure used, however, some commonalities, specifically with respect to the secure and disorganised attachment groups are apparent. The representations of secure children typically characterise adults as trustworthy, competent, and willing to provide protection and care, and their stories are well-organised and coherent. In contrast, the representations of disorganised children are chaotic and bizarre, and include violent actions and unresolved story endings. Characteristics of representations differentiating the other insecure attachment groups have not been consistently reported (Gloger-Tippelt, Gomille, Koenig, & Vetter, 2002).

Research literature validating these measures is limited and largely based on samples of normal children, although some results with clinical or at-risk samples have been reported. In normal groups, children's attachment representations have been shown to be associated with maternal attachment states of mind assessed with the Adult Attachment Interview (AAI) (Gloger-Tippelt et al., 2002; Goldwyn, Stanley, Smith, & Green, 2000; Miljkovitch, Pierrehumbert, Bretherton, & Halfon, 2004), and representational indices of disorganisation have been linked to teacher-reported behaviour problems (Goldwyn et al., 2000). In addition, insecure attachment representations have been shown to differentiate 8 to 12-year-old children with Attention Deficit Hyperactivity Disorder (ADHD) from matched controls (Clarke, Ungerer, Chahoud, Johnson, & Stiefel, 2002) and to contribute to the prediction of anxiety symptoms in behaviourally inhibited preschool (Shamir-Essakow et al., 2005) and typical school-aged (Warren, Emde, & Sroufe, 2000) children.

Overall, representational measures of attachment in preschool and primary school-aged children show potential to provide useful information about attachment state of mind in these groups, although further development and validation of these measures is needed. Specifically, validation of the representational measures against interaction-based measures of attachment security is critical. The extent to which children's responses can be influenced by their cognitive and language competence also needs to be determined, so that measures and scoring systems appropriate to the developmental level of the child can be established (Solomon & George, 1999a). With adequate development and validation, representation measures may provide access to children's "view about painful emotions and experiences" (p. 106) that have proven difficult to access in other ways (Warren et al., 2000).

Attachment State of Mind and Parenting: Intergenerational Transmission of Vulnerability and Resilience

We began this chapter by considering Ainsworth's seminal work linking individual differences in observed parental sensitivity to infant attachment classifications. In a similar way, the Adult Attachment Interview has provided a means for empirically exploring how individual differences in state of mind regarding attachment may be related to parenting quality, and how both vulnerability to psychopathology and resiliency may be transmitted from one generation to the next. An impressive body of research now confirms that a mother's state of mind regarding attachment, derived from her own early caretaking experiences, is a powerful determinant of parent–child attachment (see van IJzendoorn, 1995, for a meta-analysis). Importantly from a clinical perspective, there are also strong intergenerational links between an unresolved/disoriented maternal state of mind and disorganised attachment in the infant. The consistency and strength of this association between inferences from a language-based assessment in adults and the observed behaviour of their infants in response to moderately stressful separations is quite remarkable. Indeed the concordance between parent state of mind and child attachment (75% across studies) is much stronger than that between observed parenting behaviour and child attachment (12% across studies), leading van IJzendoorn to coin the phrase "transmission gap" to reflect the gap in our knowledge of the mechanisms through which a mother's own attachment experiences influence her infant's attachment security.

We have referred in some detail to the Minnesota longitudinal study. As well as exploring prospectively the transmission of risk, the study was able to examine, through observation of second-generation parenting, what characterised those individuals who, although they had grown up in harsh or abusive caretaking environments, were able to provide a supportive frame for their own infants. Study findings (Egeland, Jacobvitz, & Sroufe, 1988) showed that where a vulnerable child experienced a corrective attachment experience (with an alternate caregiver, a mentor or a professional counsellor who was able to provide them with a "secure base"), they appeared to be able to revise their working model of attachment. Subsequently, they were able to provide a secure base for their own children. The Adult Attachment Interview includes a classification of "earned secure" to describe such individuals, who, despite adverse childhood caretaking experiences, achieve a coherent and secure state of mind regarding attachment. Empirical studies (e.g. Pearson, Cohn, Cowan, & Cowan, 1994) have demonstrated that while individuals classified "earned secure" are as vulnerable as others from adverse family backgrounds to experiencing depressive symptoms in adulthood, they are nonetheless able to provide sensitive, responsive care for their infants.

Implications of Attachment Theory for Psychological Interventions

An attachment theory framework is useful for clinicians, irrespective of their particular therapeutic model, in a number of ways. Firstly, central to the theory is the understanding that attachment histories and patterns constitute an aetiological framework with which to approach mental distress (Schwartz & Pollard, 2004). Secondly, the theory suggests that a critical component of any therapeutic intervention is the provision of a secure base experience for the client (Holmes, 2004) and recognition that a core aspect of change is the achievement of an increase in mentalising ability or reflective functioning (Fonagy et al., 1991).

Attachment theory also provides a systematic framework for the exploration of defenses and the way in which these may contribute to individual differences in engagement and compliance with treatment (Dozier, 1990; Dozier, Lomax, Tyrrell, & Lee, 2001; Fonagy et al., 1996; Harris, 2004) and countertransference (Harris, 2004; Slade, 1999). Individual differences in attachment state of mind may require different approaches and different therapeutic tasks (Dozier et al., 2001; Fonagy et al., 1996; Holmes, 2000). Stronger avoidant tendencies have been associated with a denial of the need for help, greater rejection of treatment providers and less self-disclosure, while those with pre-occupied states of mind may present as needy and dependent in therapeutic contexts (Dozier, 1990). Thus, it has been suggested that individuals with avoidant strategies may benefit from more treatment approaches that allow more interpersonal distance, while those using pre-occupied strategies may benefit from treatment involving more interaction and supervision (Dozier, 1990). Subsequently, the task for the clinician with avoidant clients may be to challenge or break-open the somewhat clichéd (defended) narratives they bring to therapy, while for ambivalent patients the therapist may need to "introduce punctuation and shape into their stories — a making rather than a breaking function" (Holmes, 2000, p. 169).

In a recent meta-analysis of interventions designed to increase maternal sensitivity and promote secure attachment, Bakermans-Kranenburg and colleagues (2003) concluded that the most effective interventions used a moderate number of sessions and a clear-cut behavioural focus to promote parental sensitivity. Interventions that were successful in improving sensitivity were also more effective in promoting secure attachment. Further research evaluating attachment-based interventions will confirm the legacy of attachment theory and its continued relevance in both theoretical and applied contexts.

References

Adam, K., Sheldon-Keller, A. E., & West, M. (1995). Attachment organization and history of suicidal behaviour in clinical adolescents. *Journal of Consulting and Clinical Psychology, 64,* 264–272.

Ainsworth, M. D. S., Blehar, M. C., Waters, E., & Wall, S. (1978). *Patterns of attachment: A psychological study of the strange situation.* Hillsdale, NJ: Erlbaum.

Allen, J. P., Hauser, S. T., & Borman-Spurrell, E. (1996). Attachment insecurity and related sequelae in severe adolescent psychopathology: An eleven year follow-up study. *Journal of Consulting and Clinical Psychology, 64,* 254–263.

Atkinson, L., Chisholm, V. C., Scott, B., Goldberg, S., Vaughn, B. E., Blackwell, D. S., & Tam, F. (1999). Maternal sensitivity, child functional level, and attachment in Down syndrome. In: J. I. Vondra, & D. Barnett (Eds), *Atypical attachment in infancy and early childhood among children at developmental risk* (pp. 45–66). *Monographs of the Society for Research in Child Development, 64*(3, serial no. 258).

Bakermans-Kranenburg, M., & van IJzendoorn, M. (1993). A psychometric study of the adult attachment interview: Reliability and discriminant validity. *Developmental Psychology, 29,* 870–880.

Bakermans-Kranenburg, M., van IJzendoorn, M., & Juffer, F. (2003). Less is more: Meta-analysis of sensitivity and attachment interventions in early childhood. *Psychological Bulletin, 129,* 195–215.

Bifulco, A., Brown, G., & Harris, T. (1994). Childhood experiences of care and abuse (CECA): A retrospective interview measure. *Journal of Child Psychology & Psychiatry, 35,* 1419–1435.

Bowlby, J. (1969/1982). *Attachment and loss (Vol 1): Attachment.* New York: Basic Books.

Bowlby, J. (1973). *Attachment and loss (Vol 2): Separation.* New York: Basic Books.

Bowlby, J. (1980). *Attachment and loss (Vol 3): Loss.* New York: Basic Books.

Bowlby, J. (1988a). *A secure base.* New York: Basic Books.

Bowlby, J. (1988b). *Clinical implications of attachment theory.* London: Routledge.

Bretherton, I., Ridgeway, D., & Cassidy, J. (1990). Assessing internal working models of the attachment relationship: An attachment story completion task for 3 year-olds In: M. T. Greenberg, D. Cicchetti & E. M. Cummings (Eds), *Attachment in the preschool years* (pp. 273–308). Chicago: University of Chicago Press.

Carlson, E. A. (1998). A prospective longitudinal study of attachment disorganization/disorientation. *Child Development, 69,* 1107–1128.

Cassidy, J. (1994). Emotion regulation: Influences of attachment relationships. In: N. Fox (Ed.), The development of emotion regulation: Biological and behavioural considerations. *Monographs of the Society for Research in Child Development, 59* (2–3), 228–249.

Cassidy, J., & Marvin, R. S, with the MacArthur Working Group. (1992). *Attachment organisation in preschool children: Procedures and coding manual.* Unpublished manuscript. University of Virginia.

Clarke, L., Ungerer, J., Chahoud, K., Johnson, S., & Stiefel, I. (2002). Attention deficit hyperactivity disorder is associated with attachment insecurity. *Clinical Child Psychology and Psychiatry, 7,* 179–198.

Cole-Detke, H., & Kobak, R. (1996). Attachment processes in eating disorders and depression. *Journal of Consulting and Clinical Psychology, 64,* 282–290.

Creasey, G. (2002). Psychological distress in college-aged women: Links with unresolved/preoccupied attachment status and the mediating role of negative mood regulation expectancies. *Attachment and Human Development, 4,* 261–277.

Dozier, M. (1990). Attachment organization and treatment use for adults with serious psychopathological disorders. *Development and Psychopathology, 2,* 47–60.

Dozier, M., Lomax, L., Tyrrell, C. L., & Lee, S. W. (2001). The challenge of treatment for clients with dismissing states of mind. *Attachment and Human Development, 3,* 62–76.

Dozier, M., Stovall, K., & Albus, K. (1999). Attachment and psychopathology in adulthood. In: J. Cassidy & P. Shaver (Eds), *Handbook of attachment: Theory, research, and clinical applications* (pp. 497–520). New York: Guilford Press.

Egeland, B., Jacobvitz, D., & Sroufe, L. A. (1988). Breaking the cycle of abuse. *Child Development, 59,* 1080–1088.

Fonagy, P., Leigh, T., Steele, M., Steele, H., Kennedy, G., Mattoon, M., Target, M., & Gerber, A. (1996). The relationship of attachment status, psychiatric classification and response to psychotherapy. *Journal of Consulting and Clinical Psychology, 64,* 24–31.

Fonagy, P., Steele, H., Moran, G. S., Steele, M., & Higgit, A. (1991). The capacity for understanding mental states: The reflective self in parent and child and its significance for security of attachment. *Infant Mental Health Journal, 13,* 200–217.

George, C., Kaplan, N., & Main, M. (1985, 1996). *Adult attachment interview.* Unpublished manuscript. University of California at Berkeley.

George, C., & Solomon, J. (1994). *Six-year attachment doll play procedures and classification system.* Unpublished manuscript. Mills College, Oakland, CA.

George, C., & Solomon, J. (1999). Attachment and caregiving: The caregiving behavioural system. In: J. Cassidy & P. R. Shaver (Eds), *Handbook of attachment: Theory, research, and clinical applications* (pp. 649–670). New York: Guilford Press.

George, C., & West, M. (1999). Developmental vs. social personality models of adult attachment and mental ill health. *British Journal of Medical Psychology, 72,* 285–303.

Gloger-Tippelt, G., Gomille, B., Koenig, L., & Vetter, J. (2002). Attachment representations in 6-year olds: Related longitudinally to the quality of attachment in infancy and mothers' attachment representations. *Attachment and Human Development, 4,* 318–339.

Goldwyn, R., Stanley, C., Smith, V., & Green, J. (2000). The Manchester Child Attachment Story Task: Relationship with parental AAI, SAT, and child behaviour. *Attachment and Human Development, 2,* 71–84.

Greenberg, M. T. (1999). Attachment and psychopathology in childhood. In: J. Cassidy & P. R. Shaver (Eds), *Handbook of attachment: Theory, research and clinical applications* (pp. 469–497). New York: Guilford Press.

Green, J., & Goldwyn, R. (2002). Annotation: Attachment disorganization and psychopathology: New findings in attachment research and their potential implications for developmental psychopathology in childhood. *Journal of Child Psychology and Psychiatry, 43,* 835–846.

Green, J., Stanley, C., Smith, V., & Goldwyn, R. (2000). A new method of evaluating attachment representations in young school-age children: The Manchester Child Attachment Story Task. *Attachment and Human Development, 2,* 48–70.

Harris, T. (2004). Chef or chemist? Practicing psychotherapy within the attachment paradigm. *Attachment and Human Development, 6,* 191–207.

Hesse, E. (1999). The adult attachment interview: Historical and current perspectives. In: J. Cassidy & P. R. Shaver (Eds), *Handbook of attachment: Theory, research and clinical applications* (pp. 395–433). New York: Guilford Press.

Holmes, J. (2000). Attachment theory and psychoanalysis: A rapprochement. *British Journal of Psychotherapy, 17,* 152–172.

Holmes, J. (2004). Disorganized attachment and borderline personality disorder: A clinical perspective. *Attachment and Human Development, 6,* 181–191.

Jacobvitz, D., & Hazan, N. (1999). Developmental pathways from infant disorganization to childhood peer relationships. In: J. Solomon & C. George (Eds), *Attachment disorganization* (pp. 127–159). New York: Guilford Press.

Kaplan, N. (1987). *Individual differences in six-year-olds' thoughts about separation: Predicted from attachment to mother at one year of age.* Unpublished doctoral dissertation. University of California at Berkeley.

Klagsbrun, M., & Bowlby, J. (1976). Responses to separation from parents: A clinical test for young children. *British Journal of Projective Psychology, 21,* 7–21.

Lyons-Ruth, K., Easterbrooks, A., & Cibelli, C. (1997). Infant attachment strategies, infant mental lag, and maternal depressive symptoms: Predictors of internalising and externalising problems at age 7. *Developmental Psychology, 33,* 681–692.

Lyons-Ruth, K., & Jacobvitz, D. (1999). Attachment disorganization: Unresolved loss, relational violence and lapses in behavioural and attentional strategies. In: J. Cassidy & P. R. Shaver (Eds), *Handbook of attachment: Theory, research, and clinical applications* (pp. 520–554). New York: Guilford Press.

Main, M. (1996). Introduction to the special section on attachment and psychopathology: 2. Overview of the field of attachment. *Journal of Counselling and Clinical Psychology, 64,* 237–243.

Main, M., & Goldwyn, R. (1984, 1998). *Adult attachment scoring and classification system.* Unpublished manuscript. University of California at Berkeley.

Main, M., & Hesse, E. (1990). Parent's unresolved traumatic experiences are related to infant disorganized attachment status: Is frightened and/or frightening parental behaviour the linking mechanism? In: M. T. Greenberg, D. Cicchetti & E. M. Cummings (Eds), *Attachment in the preschool years* (pp. 161–182). Chicago: University of Chicago Press.

Main, M., & Solomon, J. (1990). Procedures for identifying infants as disorganized/disoriented during the Ainsworth Strange Situation. In: M. Greenberg, D. Cicchetti & E. M. Cummings (Eds), *Attachment in the preschool years: Theory, research, and intervention* (pp. 121–160). Chicago: University of Chicago Press.

Marvin, R. S., & Britner, P. A. (1999). Normative development: The ontogeny of attachment. In: J. Cassidy & P. Shaver (Eds), *Handbook of attachment: Theory, research, and clinical applications* (pp. 44–67). New York: Guilford Press.

Miljkovitch, R., Pierrehumbert, B., Bretherton, I., Halfon, O. (2004). Associations between parental and child attachment representations. *Attachment and Human Development, 6*, 305–327.

Moss, E., Cyr, C., & Dubois-Comtois, K. (2004). Attachment at early school age and developmental risks: Examining family contexts and behaviour problems of controlling-caregiving, controlling-punitive, and behaviorally disorganised children. *Developmental Psychology, 40*, 519–532.

Moss, E., St-Laurent, D., & Parent, S., (1999). Disorganised attachment and developmental risk at school age. In: J. Solomon & C. George (Eds), *Attachment disorganisation* (pp. 160–186). New York: Guilford Press.

Patrick, M., Hobson, R. P., Castle, D., Howard, R., & Maughan, B. (1994). Personality disorder and the mental representation of early social experience. *Development and Psychopathology, 6*, 359–373.

Pearson, J. L., Cohn, D. A. Cowan, P. A., & Cowan, C. P. (1994). Earned-and continuous-security in adult attachment: Relation to depressive symptomatology and parenting style. *Development and Psychopathology, 6*, 359–373.

Pianta, R., Egeland, B., & Adam, E. (1996). Adult attachment classification and self-reported psychiatric symptomatology as assessed by the Minnesota Multiphasic Personality Inventory–2. *Journal of Consulting and Clinical Psychology, 64*, 273–281.

Riggs, S. A., & Jacobvitz, D. (2002). Expectant parents' representations of early attachment relationships: Associations with mental health and family history. *Journal of Consulting and Clinical Psychology, 70*, 195–204.

Rosenstein, D. S., & Horowitz H. A. (1996). Adolescent attachment and psychopathology. *Journal of Consulting and Clinical Psychology, 64*, 244–253.

Schwartz, J., & Pollard, J. (2004). Introduction to the special issue: Attachment-based psychoanalytic psychotherapy. *Attachment and Human Development, 6*, 113–117.

Shamir-Essakow, G., Ungerer, J. A., & Rapee, R. M. (2005). Attachment, behavioral inhibition, and anxiety in preschool children. *Journal of Abnormal Child Psychology, 33*(2), 131–143.

Slade, A. (1999). Attachment theory and research: Implications for the theory and practice of individual psychotherapy with adults. In: J. Cassidy & P. Shaver (Eds), *Handbook of attachment: Theory, research, and clinical applications* (pp. 575–595). New York: Guilford Press.

Slough, N. M., & Greenberg, M. T. (1990). Five-year olds' representations of separation from parents: Responses from the perspective of self and other. In: I. Bretherton & M. W. Watson (Eds), *New directions for child development: No. 48. Children's perspectives on the family* (pp. 67–84). San Francisco: Jossey Bass.

Solomon, J., & George, C. (1999a). The measurement of attachment security in infancy and childhood. In: J. Cassidy & P. Shaver (Eds), *Handbook of attachment: Theory, research, and clinical applications* (pp. 287–316). New York: Guilford Press.

Solomon, J., & George, C. (1999b). The place of disorganization in attachment theory: Linking classic observations with contemporary findings. In: J. Solomon & C. George (Eds), *Attachment disorganization* (pp. 3–31). New York: Guilford Press.

Spangler, G., & Grossman, K. (1999). Individual and physiological correlates of attachment disorganization in infancy. In: J. Solomon & C. George (Eds), *Attachment disorganization* (pp. 95–124). New York: The Guilford Press.

Sroufe, L. A., Egeland, B., Carlson, E., Collins, W. A. (2005). *The development of the person.* The Minnesota Study of Risk and Adaptation from Birth to Adulthood. New York: The Guilford press.

Stein, H., Jacobs, N., Ferguson, K., Allen, K., & Fonagy, P. (1998). What do adult attachment scales measure? *Bulletin of the Menninger Clinic, 62*, 33–82.

van IJzendoorn, M. (1995). Adult attachment representations, parental responsiveness and infant attachment: A meta–analysis on the predictive validity of the Adult Attachment Interview. *Psychological Bulletin, 117*, 387–403.

van IJzendoorn, M., Schuengel, C., & Bakermans-Kranenburg, M. (1999). Disorganized attachment in early childhood: Meta-analysis of precursors, concomitants, and sequelae. *Development and Psychopathology, 11*, 225–249.

Vaughn, B., & Bost, K. (1999). Attachment and temperament: Redundant, independent, or interacting influences on interpersonal adaptation and personality development? In: J. Cassidy & P. Shaver (Eds), *Handbook of attachment: Theory, research, and clinical applications* (pp. 198–225). New York: The Guilford Press.

Warren, S. L., Emde, R., & Sroufe, L. A. (2000). Predicting anxiety from children's play narratives. *Journal of the American Academy of Child and Adolescent Psychiatry, 39*, 100–107.

Warren, S. L., Huston, L., Egeland, B., & Sroufe, L. A. (1997). Child and adolescent anxiety disorders and early attachment. *Journal of the American Academy of Child and Adolescent Psychiatry, 36*, 637–644.

Weinfield, N. S., Sroufe, L. A., & Egeland, B. (2000). Attachment from infancy to early adulthood in a high-risk sample: Continuity, discontinuity and their correlates. *Child Development, 71*, 695–702.

Weinfield, N. S., Sroufe, L. A., Egeland, B., & Carlson, E. A. (1999). The nature of individual differences in infant–caregiver attachment. In: J. Cassidy & P. R. Shaver (Eds), *Handbook of attachment* (pp. 68–89). New York: Guilford Press.

Willensen-Swinkels, S., Bakermans-Kronenburg, M., Buitelaar, M., & van IJzendoorn, M. (2000). Insecure and disorganised attachment in children with a pervasive developmental disorder: Relationship with social interaction and heart rate. *Journal of Child Psychology and Psychiatry, 41*, 759–769.

Chapter 4

Interparental Conflict, Violence and Psychopathology

Jennifer L. Hudson

There has been considerable research establishing a link between interparental conflict and child adjustment (Cummings & Davies, 2002; Fincham, Grych, & Osborne, 1994). Although spousal relationships can frequently bring conflict to the family environment, not all children develop psychological difficulties, suggesting that certain factors such as the content, history and degree of resolution of the conflict may alter the effect of conflict on a child's psychological functioning (Grych & Fincham, 1990). Research has also established a clear link between interparental violence and child adjustment with studies consistently showing higher levels of psychopathology in children from violent homes (Fergusson & Horwood, 1998; Kitzmann, Gaylord, Holt, & Kenny, 2003; McCloskey, Figueredo, & Koss, 1995). Children exposed to interparental violence are also more likely themselves to be at risk of being exposed to physical abuse and other forms of maltreatment such as sexual abuse, neglect and emotional abuse (Saunders, 1994; Straus & Gelles, 1990). Clearly, children exposed to interparental conflict and violence are at greater risk for negative psychological outcomes.

Recently, there have been an increasing number of process-oriented studies that have attempted to understand the mechanisms behind the detrimental effects of interparental conflict (Crockenberg & Langrock, 2001; Davies & Windle, 2001; Grych, Harold, & Miles, 2003). The possible pathways towards maladjustment resulting from a child's exposure to interparental conflict and violence are complex. Some theorists have proposed that exposure to conflict impacts on the child's emotional security and this in turn impacts on the child's adjustment (Cummings & Cummings, 1988). Others have suggested that marital conflict has a direct impact on the parenting skills/style and it is the deficit in parenting that impacts on the child's adjustment (Fauber, Forehand, Thomas, & Wierson, 1990). Children's poor adjustment has also been hypothesised to result from modelling of the parent's aggression or dysfunctional conflict tactics (Bandura, 1973).

This chapter will review the evidence for the impact of interparental conflict and violence on the psychological outcome of the child. Focus will be given to the presence of psychopathology such as anxiety, depression, oppositional defiance, conduct problems and

Psychopathology and the Family
Edited by J. L. Hudson and R. M. Rapee
Copyright © 2005 by Elsevier Ltd.
All rights of reproduction in any form reserved
ISBN: 0-08-044449-0

substance abuse. Rarely is psychopathology assessed using structured diagnostic interviews to determine the presence of specific DSM-IV (American Psychiatric Association, 1994) disorders. Instead much of the research focuses on symptoms, most notably the categories of internalising (e.g. anxiety and depression) and externalising (oppositional defiance, conduct disorder) symptoms. Research also relies heavily on parent, teacher and child report measures such as the Child Behavior Checklist (CBCL: Achenbach, 1991); Revised Behavior Problem Checklist (RPBC: Quay & Peterson, 1987), the Child Depression Inventory (CDI: Kovacs, 1981) and the Revised Children's Manifest Anxiety Scale (RCMAS: Reynolds & Richmond, 1979). Thus, much of the research reviewed in this chapter will focus on symptoms of psychological disorders rather than diagnostic categories.

The methods used to assess parental conflict and violence will first be reviewed, followed by a review of the empirical evidence supporting the link between conflict and psychopathology and violence and psychopathology. The research that has attempted to explain these links will also be examined. The research reveals the importance of considering variables such as the degree of resolution of the conflict, the parent's conflict resolution style (e.g. engagement vs. withdrawal) as well as the child's cognitions regarding the conflict (self-blame, experience of threat). These issues must be addressed when exploring the pathways predicting child psychopathology.

Measurement of Conflict and Violence

Interparental conflict has been defined broadly as an interaction between parents involving a difference of opinion, positive or negative (Cummings, Goeke-Morey, & Dukewich, 2001). Disagreements between parents can obviously vary significantly in the severity, frequency and importantly in the tactics used to express and resolve the conflict. Interparental conflict may also be resolved through aggression and physical violence.

The measurement of interparental conflict and violence most frequently occurs through the use of parent-report questionnaires. Frequently used measures include the Conflict Tactics Scale (CTS: Straus, 1979) and the O'Leary–Porter Scale (OPS: Porter & O'Leary, 1980). For example, the CTS includes items assessing the frequency of verbal reasoning, verbal aggression and physical aggression. The physical aggression scale from the CTS is often used as a measure of interparental violence. Participants report specific conflicts over the past year indicating the frequency of certain behaviours on a 0 (never happened)–7-point (happened more than 20 times) scale. The CTS and the OPS have demonstrated average to good internal consistency and test–retest reliability (Porter & O'Leary, 1980; Straus, Hamby, Boney-McCoy, & Sugarman, 1996).

Parental conflict is also measured via child report. For example, the Children's Perception of Interparental Conflict Scale (CPIC: Grych, Seid, & Fincham, 1992) asks children to respond with "true" "sort of true" or "false" on items measuring the frequency of conflict ("I often see my parents arguing"), intensity ("When my parents have an argument, they yell a lot"), resolution ("even after my parents stop arguing they stay mad at each other") and content ("my parents' arguments are usually about something I did"). Another example of a child report measure is the "Things I've Seen and Heard" questionnaire that includes specific domestic violence items (Richters & Martinez, 1993). Some studies assessing family violence have also employed records from child protection services as a way of recording frequency or severity of the violence (English, Marshall, & Stewart, 2003).

Recently, more sophisticated measures of parental conflict have been developed. The use of methods such as daily records, observational coding systems, and analog audio/video methods allow for a more detailed analysis of interparental conflict. For example, the Marital Daily Record (MDR: Cummings, Goeke-Morey, Papp, & Dukewich, 2002) is a diary checklist for couples to separately report on their spousal conflicts (that is, any major or minor interaction that involves a difference of opinion, negative or positive) over a 15-day period. Partners report on the tactics used in the conflict such as calm discussions, humour, support, physical affection, verbal hostility, defensiveness, physical distress, threat, pursuit, personal insult, physical aggression towards an object, physical aggression towards a person, and/or withdrawal. Parents record the content of the conflict (e.g. children, work, finance) as well as their own, their partner's emotional response (e.g. positivity, anger, fear and sadness) and their child's aggressive responses. In a number of studies by Cummings and colleagues (Cummings, Goeke-Morey, & Papp, 2004; Cummings et al., 2002) composite scores were created from frequency counts of conflict to provide a measure of Destructive Tactics (e.g. nonverbal hostility, defensiveness, aggression) and Constructive Tactics (e.g. calm discussion, problem solving). Convergent validity has been established by comparing MDR scores with results from self-report questionnaires including the CTS, OPS and the Short Marital Adjustment Test (SMAT: Locke & Wallace, 1959). The MDR has also been used in observational assessment of interparental interactions (Du Rocher Schudlich & Cummings, 2003). For example, a couple would be observed interacting while an observer counts the frequency of conflict and the use of conflict tactics using the MDR. Mean alphas for the inter-rater reliability based on trained raters to identify the conflict strategies range between 0.86 and 0.91.

Cummings et al. (2004) have examined children's direct responses to marital conflict using video clips of everyday marital conflicts involving different conflict tactics employed by both a maternal and paternal figure. In this study, children were asked to imagine that the people in the videos were their parents. After each 5–10 s clip, children were asked "What would you do if you were in the room with your parents?" Children's aggressive responses (not constructive responses) were then coded. Excellent inter-rater reliability ($\kappa = 0.98$) was obtained for the children's response categories.

Observational techniques provide a more objective view of interparental relationships. A number of coding systems have been developed to specifically examine parent-to-parent conflict. For example, the Specific Affect Coding System (Gottman, 1989) has been designed to measure marital interactions using codes for both the speaker and listener during an interaction. Codes include contempt, belligerence, criticism, interest, affection, validation, humour, stonewalling, and listening. Judgements are based on facial expression, voice tone, verbal content and bodily gestures. Inter-rater reliability ranges from adequate ($\kappa = 0.63$–0.64) to excellent (0.86–0.97: Katz & Gottman, 1993).

In summary, a number of reliable measures of interparental conflict and violence are available. The use of multiple methods of assessment is recommended to obtain the most comprehensive account of severity, frequency, tactics and content. The use of multiple informants is also encouraged, as conflicts particularly domestic violence may be extremely difficult for victims to report (Sternberg, Lamb, & Dawud-Noursi, 1998). Reliance on one informant to assess both conflict/violence and child psychopathology also leads to problems with shared-method variance. Thus, a multi-method, multi-informant approach is recommended to assess the impact of interparental conflict and violence on child psychopathology (Sternberg et al., 1998).

Conflict and Psychopathology — Review

The abundance of research examining the impact of interparental conflict on children has led to a number of review papers and meta-analyses (e.g. Buehler, Anthony, Krishnakumar, & Stone, 1997; Cummings & Davies, 2002; Davis, Hops, Alpert, & Sheeber, 1998; Emery, 1982; Fincham et al., 1994; Grych & Fincham, 1990; Reid & Crisafulli, 1990). The link between marital conflict and psychopathology is clear. Children are at greater risk of psychopathology if they have been exposed to interparental conflict. In fact, one population level study concluded that the elimination of parental verbal conflict and mood problems would result in 20% less child mental health problems (Dwyer, Nicholson, & Battistutta, 2003).

In 1997, Buehler and colleagues conducted a meta-analysis estimating small-to-moderate effect sizes of interparental conflict on child externalising problems (0.39), internalising problems (0.31) and on comorbid internalising and externalising problems (0.21). These effect sizes were larger than that reported in a previous meta-analysis (measuring externalising problems only) but consistent with narrative reviews of the literature (Grych & Fincham, 1990; Reid & Crisafulli, 1990). Clearly, interparental conflict is significantly associated with both child externalising and internalising symptoms. Initially, the impact of interparental conflict on child's internalising symptoms was largely ignored with the major focus being on externalising or behaviour problems such as oppositionality and conduct disorder. Cummings and Cummings (1988) called for researchers to also focus on the often ignored internalising symptoms and highlighted a number of studies showing that conflict between parents can also produce problems such as anxiety and depression that are perhaps less overt but just as interfering. Since then, numerous studies have supported the notion that interparental conflict is associated with higher levels of both internalising and externalising symptoms (e.g. Davies & Lindsay, 2004; Katz & Gottman, 1993).

In the meta-analysis, Buehler et al. (1997) reported significant differences in effect sizes based on symptoms, time since separation/divorce, SES and educational attainment. For example, effects were stronger for externalising symptoms (compared to comorbid internalising and externalising), recently separated families, samples including predominately middle-class or predominately lower-class participants (compared to samples that included a range of respondents), and parents with low educational attainment. Studies reported in the meta-analysis also varied on their use of single or multiple informants and on their use of questionnaire methods versus other more comprehensive reports of conflict such as observation or daily records of conflict. Buehler et al. (1997) reported greater effect sizes when mothers or primary care givers were the reporters of conflict and behaviour and when child adjustment was measured by questionnaires compared to observation.

The studies reviewed above are primarily associative in nature, that is, they have established that marital conflict is associated with increased child internalising and externalising symptoms. Longitudinal research can add to this body of research by testing the notion that interparental conflict is associated with increased internalising and externalising problems later in life. Such findings imply, although not conclusively, that exposure to conflict leads to increased child psychopathology. In line with this, a handful of longitudinal studies have shown a causal relationship between interparental conflict and child psychopathology over time (Fincham et al., 1994; Katz & Gottman, 1993). For example, in a one-year longitudinal study of 178 adolescents, parent- and child-reported interparental conflict predicted teacher-rated internalising and externalising symptoms at both the baseline and follow-up assessments (Wierson, Forehand, & McCombs, 1988). Similarly, in another longitudinal study of families following divorce involving a custody battle, Johnston, Gonzalez, and Campbell (1987) showed that verbal and physical aggression at baseline significantly predicted parent-reported total CBCL scores as well as withdrawn, depressive and aggressive symptoms two and half years later. A number of other studies have also employed longitudinal methods to investigate mediating and moderating variables of the relationship between interparental conflict and child outcomes. These will be discussed later in the chapter.

Interparental Violence and Psychopathology — Review

In addition to research on interparental conflict a number of studies have specifically examined the impact of interparental or domestic violence on children (e.g. Grych, Jouriles, Swank, McDonald, & Norwood, 2000; Jouriles, Norwood, McDonald, Vincent, & Mahoney, 1996). In strong support of the association between violence and child adjustment, one study showed that interparental violence accounted for 56% of variance in symptoms of psychopathology reported by the child's mother in a structured diagnostic interview (McCloskey et al., 1995). Similarly, a meta-analysis by Kitzmann et al. (2003) reported a significant, moderate effect size when comparing outcomes for children who had witnessed domestic violence compared to non-witnesses ($d = -0.40$). The authors concluded that 63% of children exposed to domestic violence were worse off than children not exposed to such violence. The study showed that effect sizes were equivalent for both internalising and externalising problems indicating that violence increases a child's risk for a range of psychological problems. In fact, the authors argued that exposure to physical violence between parents may produce stronger effects than exposure to other destructive conflicts. In contrast, one study showed that after accounting for verbal aggression, physical violence (as reported by the CTS) did not make a unique contribution to externalising and internalising child symptoms (Jouriles et al., 1996). This result suggests that when physical violence is present, it is important to also be aware of other forms of destructive conflict that may impact on the child's outcome.

Importantly, when studying a sample of violent families a number of confounding variables may be present such as shared genes, SES, parental psychopathology and other familial or social contexts. For example, the association between interparental violence and child psychopathology may purely reflect shared genes between parent and child rather than a causal effect of violence on child psychopathology. A number of studies have shown a link between domestic violence and child psychopathology even after controlling for these confounding variables (Fergusson & Horwood, 1998; Jaffee, Moffitt, Caspi, Taylor, & Arseneault, 2002). For example, in a large twin study ($n = 1,116$), Jaffee et al.

(2002) showed that after controlling for latent genetic and environmental effects domestic violence accounted for 2% of the variance in internalising symptoms and 5% of the variance in externalising symptoms.

In a very large study of interparental violence and child outcome that controlled for a number of confounding variables, Fergusson and Horwood (1998) examined the presence of specific psychological disorders using a structured diagnostic interview in a birth cohort of 1,265 children at age 18 years. This is one of the only studies to have used diagnostic interviews to ascertain the presence of specific disorders. Violence was assessed using the CTS with almost 40% of children reporting mild to severe levels of interparental violence. Children exposed to the highest levels of violence (top 5% in the sample, that is exposed to high rates of all types of violent behaviour) were between 2 and 6 times more likely than children not exposed to violence to meet criteria for a psychological disorder. Of children exposed to severe violence exhibited by the father, 60.4% met criteria for major depression, 43.4% met criteria for an anxiety disorder, 32% met criteria for alcohol abuse/dependence and 17% met criteria for conduct disorder. After accounting for contextual factors (such as SES, divorce, alcoholism), interparental violence significantly predicted anxiety disorders, conduct disorders, alcohol abuse/dependence and property crime in the offspring. Father-initiated violence was associated with a greater range of child psychological disorders (anxiety, conduct and property crime) than mother-initiated violence (alcohol abuse). In this study, parental violence was assessed retrospectively at age 18 and hence cannot provide information about the causal link between conflict and violence, but does show clear evidence of an association between dramatically increased risk of psychopathology in children from violent families.

In a large longitudinal study that showed a clear causal link between interparental violence and behaviour problems, Litrownik, Newton, Hunter, English, and Everson (2003) examined 682 children at 4 years of age and again at 6 years of age. Interparental violence witnessed by the child was measured using child report ("Things I Have Seen and Heard" questionnaire: Richters & Martinez, 1993) and a parent-report adapted measure. The CBCL was used to measure aggressive behaviour and anxious/depressed symptoms. After controlling for behavioural problems at 4 years of age, subsequent exposure to interparental violence (reported by both the mother and the child) predicted aggressive and anxious/depressive problems at age 6.

Factors Influencing the Impact of Interparental Conflict/Violence and Psychopathology

A number of contextual and demographic variables may impact on the relationship between interparental conflict/violence and child psychological functioning (e.g. English et al., 2003). These factors, including resolution and history of the conflict, gender, age, and family status will be examined.

Resolution of the conflict   Several empirical studies have demonstrated that the child's reaction to interparental conflict is dependent on the degree of resolution of the conflict (e.g. Cummings, Vogel, Cummings, & El-Sheikh, 1989). Cummings, Ballard, El-Sheikh, and Lake (1991) examined the responses of 98, 5–19 year old children to video-clips of friendly, resolved, partially resolved and unresolved conflicts. Children reported more anger, fear and sadness in response to the unresolved conflicts compared to those that were more resolved. Similarly, Shiflett-Simpson and Cummings (1996) again using video-taped interactions, showed that 5–7 and 9–12 year old children were more likely to exhibit emotional distress when the video-clips showed continued fighting compared to a compromise. Similarly, conflict endings elicited more child distress than friendly interactions.

To further examine the impact of conflict tactics on the child's response to conflict, Cummings et al. (2004) compared the diary records of 108, 8–16 year old children and their parents using the MDR to record interparental conflicts in the home. The results showed that exposure to destructive conflict tactics (such as verbal and non-verbal hostility, threat of physical aggression, withdrawal) increased the likelihood of child aggression. In comparison, mothers' and fathers' use of constructive conflict tactics (calm discussion, humour, support, affection and problem solving) decreased the likelihood of a child's aggressive response. Further, child aggressive responses to interparental conflict at home predicted child externalising problems as measured by the CBCL (mother-report). This study also examined the responses of children to an analogue marital conflict in the laboratory. Ninety six per cent of all aggressive responses occurred in response to video-clips showing destructive conflict tactics. Cummings et al. (2004) also showed that conflict topics that were threatening to the child such as child or marital-related topics increased the likelihood of aggressive responses compared to conflict about work or social activities.

Taken together, these findings indicate that children respond more negatively to destructive, unresolved, and child-relevant conflict compared to more constructive, resolved, and less child-relevant conflict. Although Cummings et al. (2004) showed that immediate aggressive responses to interparental conflict in the home were associated with increased externalising problems, the majority of these studies have primarily focused on the child's immediate responses to conflict in the home or video-taped interactions of actors and have less focus on more long term consequences. A number of studies have gone beyond the examination of immediate responses and examined the link between conflict resolution tactics and child psychopathology. The results from these studies have identified that a child's response to the conflict is dependent on the parent's style of destructive conflict resolution. For example, Katz and Woodin (2002) showed that children of parents observed to be hostile and detached (i.e. attacking and withdrawing) had a greater number of externalising problems as measured by the CBCL compared to children of couples who were positively engaged in the conflict or who were only hostile. Further, Katz and Gottman (1993) in a 3-year longitudinal study showed differential patterns for externalising and internalising child outcomes at age 5 and 8 years. In this study, mutually hostile patterns of interparental conflict at age 5 predicted teacher-reported externalising symptoms at age 8. Interparental conflict predicted internalising symptoms at age 8 in families in which the husband was angry and withdrawn. A number of limitations exist within this study making it difficult to draw conclusions about causality. For example, this study did not control for the child's internalising and externalising symptoms at baseline and did not control for parent personality.

In addition to attacking, angry conflict resolution tactics, avoidant styles of conflict resolution have also been linked to later child adjustment problems, primarily internalising problems. Marchand and Hock (2003) examined parental conflict resolution strategies and internalising and externalising symptoms in a sample of 51 families from the community. The study showed that mothers' and father's reports of avoidant conflict resolution strategies were linked to higher rates of child internalising symptoms but not externalising problems. Mother's avoidance strategies and the combination of avoidance strategies from both the mother and the father significantly predicted internalising symptoms. This study again provides evidence for a differential pathway for internalising and externalising symptoms from family conflict styles.

A major limitation within this body of research is the absence of appropriate controls for potential confounds such as genetics or parent personality or psychopathology. The associations between parental conflict resolution styles and child psychopathology could simply reflect shared genes, that is, aggressive parents have aggressive children and withdrawn parents have withdrawn children. In contrast to this possible explanation, Dadds, Atkinson, Turner, Blums, and Lendich (1999) showed an opposite effect with results indicating that internalising problems in boys were associated with more aggressive maternal conflict resolution while internalising problems in girls were associated with paternal aggressive resolution styles. Regardless, genetic and parent factors were not controlled for in this study and it is possible that the results reflect an inherited increased risk for psychopathology in general. Further research is needed in this area to provide a more thorough understanding of these potential differential pathways, after controlling for possible confounding variables.

Previous experience with conflict   A number of studies have shown that history of exposure to interparental conflict impacts on the child's response to new conflict by increasing aggression (Cummings, Zahn-Waxler, & Radke-Yarrow, 1981; Davies, Myers, Cummings, & Heindel, 1999; El-Sheikh & Cummings, 1995; Garcia O'Hearn, Margolin, & John, 1997). For example, Cummings, Pelligrini, Notarious, and Cummings (1989) showed that children who reported a history of physical conflict between their parents evidenced greater distress. In a laboratory study, Davies et al. (1999) examined the responses of 108, 5–21 year olds after watching video clips of a series of either destructive (hostile, unresolved) or constructive conflicts (mild, resolved) followed by a new conflict with the same couple. Consistent with a sensitisation hypothesis, children who had witnessed the history of destructive conflicts reported more negative responses (e.g. increased anger, sadness) to the new conflict. A number of other analog studies have also shown that children are more likely to evidence a negative response to repeated angry and unresolved conflicts (Cummings et al., 1981; El-Sheikh & Cummings, 1995).

One study showed the effects of repeated exposure to adult conflicts on peer aggression (Cummings, Iannotti, & Zahn-Waxler, 1985). In this study, children exposed to two prior angry conflicts between two adults in a laboratory displayed more aggressive behaviours towards a peer than those who had been exposed to just one angry inter-adult conflict. Rather than children becoming de-sensitised to repeated conflict, the opposite occurs. With repeated exposures, children become sensitised to conflict responding with increased aggression, sadness and fear.

Gender   The differential impact of marital conflict on girls and boys has yet to be adequately determined with results from a number of studies producing conflicting results. Some studies have shown that boys and girls have an increased risk of externalising problems following exposure to interparental conflict (Reid & Crisafulli, 1990) and girls have a greater risk of internalising problems than boys (Davies & Lindsay, 2004). In contrast, a number of other studies (including two large meta-analyses) have shown no differential gender effects, with exposure to conflict or violence emerging as a significant predictor of externalising and internalising problems in girls and boys (Buehler et al., 1997; Davies & Lindsay, 2004; Fergusson & Horwood, 1998; Johnson & O'Leary, 1987; Kitzmann et al., 2003; Litrownik et al., 2003). Although some differential effects have been identified these findings are not consistent. Children, regardless of gender respond negatively to interparental conflict.

Age   Does marital conflict have a greater impact on younger or older children? Studies addressing this question have produced conflicting results. The majority of studies have found no age effect, indicating that hostile conflict at any age will result in an increased risk for psychopathology (e.g. Buehler et al., 1997). In contrast, a handful of studies have shown that at certain ages (particularly pre-school age) conflict is more damaging. For example, Mahoney, Jouriles, and Scavone (1997) showed that preschool children were more at risk from marital conflict. Similarly, Kitzmann et al. (2003) provided some evidence that preschool children were at greatest risk from interparental violence. In contrast, Sim and Vuchinich (1996) showed a stronger effect of conflict on adjustment for adolescents. Further research examining possible age effects is needed.

Divorce   Divorce is frequently associated with increased marital conflict. Interestingly however, it is not the presence of divorce that is associated with poor child outcomes but the presence of discord between the parents. Long, Slater, Forehand, and Fabuer (1988) showed that adolescents from recently divorced families with high levels of parental conflict (prior to and after the divorce) had higher rates of anxiety and withdrawal than adolescents from families with reduced conflict post-divorce and a comparison group of intact families. This finding clearly shows that continued conflict post-divorce produces poorer outcomes for children.

Hetherington, Cox, and Cox (1982) conducted a longitudinal study of children following divorce in comparison to children from intact families. In the first year following divorce, children from divorced families exhibited higher levels of externalising problems compared to high-conflict intact families. However, 2 years after the divorce, boys from high-conflict intact homes exhibited more externalising problems than boys from low-conflict divorced homes. Two years after divorce, girls from high-conflict homes, displayed significantly greater problems such as attention-seeking, demandingness, and whining compared to low-conflict homes. Taken together these findings suggest that the presence of conflict is more damaging to the child than divorce itself and gender differences in the long-term manifestations of persisting difficulties for the child.

Explaining the Link between Interparental Conflict/Violence and Child Psychopathology

Several factors that help to explain the relationship between interparental conflict/violence and child psychopathology have been identified. The relationship between conflict and adjustment is a complex one that is not easily explained by a single pathway. The empirical evidence in support of these possible processes will be discussed.

Parenting   Some authors have argued that the influence of interparental conflict on child adjustment occurs via the influence on parenting practices, that is, conflict may lead to more negative parenting practices such as decreased consistency and increased critical parenting (Fauber, Forehand, Thomas, & Wierson, 1990). In support, several studies have shown that parenting styles mediate the relationship between interparental conflict and child adjustment (Gonzales, Pitts, Hill, & Roosa, 2000; Kitzmann, 1997; Mann & MacKenzie, 1996). For example, Webster-Stratton and Hammond (1999) observed 120 children interacting on a problem-solving task with a peer and at home with their parents. Parents too were observed interacting during a family problem-solving task with each other and with their children. Critical parenting and low emotional responsive parenting mediated the relationship between negative interparental conflict and child externalising problems (In this study, internalising problems were not measured). That is, interparental conflict influenced child externalising problems via its impact on parenting.

In examining both internalising and externalising problems in two samples of 11–14 year olds from intact or divorced homes, further support for the mediational role of parenting was found (Fauber et al., 1990). More specifically, in both samples, parental psychological control and parental rejection/withdrawal mediated the relationship between conflict and internalising problems. Parental rejection/withdrawal also mediated the relationship between conflict and externalising problems in the divorced sample but not the intact sample. In the intact sample, a direct relationship between interparental conflict and externalising problems also occurred.

A recent study has shown a specific mediational role for Psychological Control and Warmth in separately predicting internalising and externalising symptoms (Doyle & Markiewicz, 2005). In this study, psychological control (that is, intrusive, manipulative, low-autonomy granting parenting) mediated the link between interparental conflict and internalising symptoms and parental warmth mediated the relation between conflict and externalising symptoms.

Taken together, these studies provide strong evidence that parenting problems are associated with increased interparental conflict and it is these maladaptive parenting behaviours that are associated with increased child problems. Some of the research has indicated that specific parenting strategies have a separate mediational role in predicting externalising and internalising symptoms.

Modelling   Much less is known about the possible role of modelling in the link between interparental conflict and child outcomes. Evidence for the role of modelling can be seen when a direct relationship between conflict and child outcome provides a better explanation than indirect relationships. That is, child adjustment is directly linked to interparental conflict. In such a case, child behaviour would mirror parent behaviour. Other pathways could explain such a direct link (e.g. genetics) but modelling is one possible explanation. Children model their responses to conflict and their behaviour from observing their parent's (maladaptive) styles of conflict resolution (Bandura, 1973). Thus, based on this model, children with parents who use avoidant conflict strategies would also use avoidant conflict strategies. Similarly attacking styles in parents would be associated with attacking conflict resolution styles in the child. One study which has attempted to examine this question was conducted by Dadds et al. (1999). In this study, parent's conflict resolution strategies were used to predict adolescent's conflict resolution tactics with siblings in a sample of 10–14 year olds. In this study, boys' use of avoidant strategies was associated with their fathers' use of avoidance in interparental conflict. Similarly, girls' use of avoidant strategies was associated with increased maternal avoidant strategies. Further, girls' discussing style of conflict resolution with a sibling was significantly predicted by her father's discussing style. This study provides preliminary support for the modelling hypothesis. Further research examining the impact of modelling is essential to understand the link between interparental conflict and child psychopathology.

Children's appraisals   Accumulating evidence suggests that there a number of child factors that influence the impact of interparental conflict and violence. The variable that has received a great deal of attention in recent years is the child's appraisal of the conflict (Dadds et al., 1999; Grych et al., 2003; Harold & Conger, 1997; Jouriles, Spiller, Stephens, McDonald, & Swank, 2000; Rogers & Holmbeck, 1997). Grych and Fincham (1990) proposed a cognitive–contextual model that uses cognitive process to explain the relationship between conflict and child adjustment. In this model, the relationship between interparental conflict and child maladjustment is mediated by the children's understanding of the conflict. In support of this model, Jouriles et al. (2000) examined 154 children (aged 8–12 years) showing that the degree to which children blamed themselves for their parent's conflict was correlated with mother's report of externalising symptoms (based on the CBCL), and self-reported anxiety and depression (measured by the RCMAS and CDI, respectively). Internalising problems (anxiety and depression) were also associated with the degree to which the child felt threatened by the conflict and the degree to which the child feared being abandoned by their parents as a result of the conflict. Correlations between appraisals and child symptoms were stronger for older children.

A number of other studies have also shown a mediating role for self-blame and threat with some studies showing differential effects for internalising and externalising problems (Cummings, Davies, & Simpson, 1994; Dadds et al., 1999; Grych, Fincham, Jouriles, & McDonald, 2000; Grych et al., 2003). For example, Grych et al. (2000) showed that for boys and girls, perceived threat mediated the relationship between interparental conflict and internalising problems but not externalising problems. Self-blame showed some inconsistent results across two different samples. In a sample of children from a battered women's shelter, self-blame mediated the relationship between conflict and internalising problems for girls and boys, but in a community sample, self-blame mediated the relationship between conflict and internalising problems for boys only. In this study no significant mediation effect was found for perceived threat and self-blame on externalising problems suggesting that self-blame and threat-perception were more important in understanding internalising symptoms. In addition, Dadds et al. (1999) showed different results for internalising and externalising problems. Self-blame and perceived threat were significant predictors of internalising problems for both boys and girls. For externalising problems, self-blame was the only significant predictor for boys and conflict severity was the only significant predictor for girls.

Taken together the mediating effects of self-blame and threat appear to be stronger and more consistent in predicting internalising problems than externalising problems. These studies provide evidence that the child's interpretations of the interparental conflict are integral in understanding a child's subsequent adjustment.

Coping   Research into the influence of coping strategies on the child's response to inter-parental conflict is inconsistent.   Some evidence suggests that although children may attempt to regulate their exposure to their parent's conflict by either avoiding or by attempting to intervene in the conflict, strategies of avoidance and intervention are associated with psychopathology (Jenkins, Smith, & Graham, 1989; O'Brien, Margolin, & John, 1995). For example, O'Brien et al. (1995) showed that children who intervened in their parent's conflict had higher rates of self-reported anxiety, hostility and lower self-esteem than children who did not intervene. On the other hand, children who distracted themselves or distanced themselves from the conflict showed decreased anxiety. O'Brien et al. (1997) also showed that intervening in interparental conflict was associated with increased levels of child depression. In this study the opposite effect was shown for avoidance of conflict. Avoidance accompanied by worry regarding loss of parental love was associated with increased depression. This inconsistent result, along with numerous studies that have failed to replicate these findings (e.g. Davies, Forman, Rasi, & Stevens, 2002), suggest that further research understanding the possible mediational role of coping strategies is needed.

Emotional security   Another child factor that might help to explain the relationship between conflict and child adjustment is the child's emotional security. Cummings and Cummings (1988) proposed that the relationship between interparental conflict and child adjustment was mediated by the child's emotional security regarding the parent–parent subsystem and the parent–child subsystem. Davies and Cummings (1998) measured emotional insecurity by assessing the child's (a) emotional reactivity in response to a simulated conflict between the researcher and the mother, (b) regulation of exposure to parent affect (coping) and (c) internal representations of parental relations. Although some direct effects on internalising symptoms were evident, it was clear that marital conflict was associated with decreased emotional security which in turn was associated with the child's adjustment, most notably the child's internalising symptoms. The authors note that emotional security explained less than half of the variance in the relationship between destructive interparental conflict and child psychopathology suggesting that this pathway is but one that explains the link between conflict and child outcomes.

More recently, Cummings and Davies (2002) have proposed a process-oriented multi-causal model to explain the relationship between marital conflict and child adjustment problems. Cummings and Davies propose a complex interplay between destructive interparental conflict, parenting practices, emotional security and child outcomes. Marital conflict is proposed to have both direct and indirect effects on children's adjustment. Cummings and Davies propose that the relationship between interparental conflict and child adjustment is mediated by effects on parenting (parenting practices, parent–child attachment). The model also emphasises individual child differences in reactions and coping such that children's reactions to the conflict mediate the impact of marital conflict on child adjustment. Interparental conflict is hypothesised to impact on a child's emotional security and then in turn, emotional security impacts on adjustment. Possible moderating variables are also considered in the model such as parental adjustment problems, family-level characteristics, previous history with marital conflict, age and gender of child. This model is based on empirical research to date, combining empirical evidence to provide a theoretical framework with which to understand the link between interparental conflict and child adjustment.

Summary and Future Directions

The findings clearly support a link between children who witness interparental conflict and violence and child psychopathology. This finding has received support from cross-sectional as well as longitudinal studies suggesting a causal link. A number of variables that influence the relationship between conflict and child psychopathology have been identified. Children repeatedly exposed to conflict that is unresolved, aggressive and hostile demonstrate increased rates of internalising and externalising symptoms. There is some suggestion that physical aggression is more consistently linked with more negative child outcomes.

As suggested by Cummings and Davies (2002), the pathways that predict child psychopathology from interparental conflict are complex and are not likely to be explained by one single mediating variable. The evidence to date suggests that there is an important role for the parent's conflict resolution style, the child's perceptions of self-blame (particularly for internalising symptoms), the child's perception of threat, the child's coping response and the child's emotional security. Furthermore, interparental conflict appears to be associated with deficits in parenting and these parenting deficits appear to mediate the relationship between conflict and child outcome.

Future research that employs multi-method, multi-informant assessments is important. Much of the research suffers from shared-method variance when the child's symptoms and interparental conflict are assessed by a single informant. Importantly, some studies above do not show consistent results across reporters. The knowledge regarding symptoms of psychological disorders resulting from interparental conflict is abundant. Few studies have employed structured diagnostic interviews to assess the presence of psychopathology. Thus, to obtain the most comprehensive and accurate understanding of the relationship between conflict and child outcome, future studies need to employ multiple-methods of assessment (questionnaire, observation and structured diagnostic interviews) as well as multiple informants (parents, teachers, children and clinicians).

Since Fincham, Grych and Osborne's call for longitudinal research on conflict and adjustment in 1994 a number of longitudinal studies have been conducted. Further longitudinal research, employing large sample sizes and controlling for possible confounding variables, is needed to test a more complex array of mediating and moderating variables. Such research will be important in understanding the causal role that parental conflict resolution strategies, children's appraisals of the conflict, coping styles and parenting styles play in the development of psychopathology in children who have witnessed interparental conflict and violence.

References

Achenbach, T. M. (1991). *Child behavior checklist.* Burlington: University of Vermont.
American Psychiatric Association. (1994). *Diagnostic and statistical manual of mental disorders* (4th ed.). Washington, DC: American Psychiatric Association.

Bandura, A. (1973). *Aggression: A social learning analysis.* Oxford, England: Prentice-Hall.

Buehler, C., Anthony, C., Krishnakumar, A., & Stone, G. (1997). Interparental conflict and youth problem behaviors: A meta-analysis. *Journal of Child & Family Studies, 6*, 223–247.

Crockenberg, S., & Langrock, A. (2001). The role of specific emotions in children's responses to interparental conflict: A test of the model. *Journal of Family Psychology, 15*, 163–182.

Cummings, E. M., Ballard, M., El-Sheikh, M., & Lake, M. (1991). Resolution and children's responses to interadult anger. *Developmental Psychology, 27*, 462–470.

Cummings, E. M., & Cummings, J. S. (1988). A process-oriented approach to children's coping with adults' angry behavior. *Developmental Review, 8*, 296–321.

Cummings, E. M., & Davies, P. T. (2002). Effects of marital conflict on children: Recent advances and emerging themes in process-oriented research. *Journal of Child Psychology & Psychiatry, 43*, 31–63.

Cummings, E. M., Davies, P. T., & Simpson, K. S. (1994). Marital conflict, gender, and children's appraisals and coping efficacy as mediators of child adjustment. *Journal of Family Psychology, 8*, 141–149.

Cummings, E. M., Goeke-Morey, M. C., & Dukewich, T. L. (2001). The study of relations between marital conflict and child adjustment: Challenges and new directions for methodology. In: J. H. Grych & F. D. Fincham (Eds), *Interparental conflict and child development: Theory, research, and applications* (pp. 39–63). New York, NY: Cambridge University Press.

Cummings, E. M., Goeke-Morey, M. C., & Papp, L. M. (2004). Everyday marital conflict and child aggression. *Journal of Abnormal Child Psychology, 32*, 191–202.

Cummings, E. M., Goeke-Morey, M. C., Papp, L. M., & Dukewich, T. L. (2002). Children's responses to mothers' and fathers' emotionality and tactics in marital conflict in the home. *Journal of Family Psychology, 16*, 478–492.

Cummings, E. M., Iannotti, R. J., & Zahn-Waxler, C. (1985). Influence of conflict between adults on the emotions and aggression of young children. *Developmental Psychology, 21*, 495–507.

Cummings, E. M., Vogel, D., Cummings, J. S., & El-Sheikh, M. (1989). Children's responses to different forms of expression of anger between adults. *Child Development, 60*, 1392–1404.

Cummings, E. M., Zahn-Waxler, C., & Radke-Yarrow, M. (1981). Young children's responses to expressions of anger and affection by others in the family. *Child Development, 52*, 1274–1282.

Cummings, J. S., Pellegrini, D. S., Notarius, C. I., & Cummings, E. M. (1989). Children's responses to angry adult behavior as a function of marital distress and history of interparent hostility. *Child Development, 60*, 1035–1043.

Dadds, M. R., Atkinson, E., Turner, C., Blums, G., & Lendich, B. (1999). Family conflict and child adjustment: Evidence for a cognitive-contextual model of intergenerational transmission. *Journal of Family Psychology, 13*, 194–208.

Davies, P. T., & Cummings, E. M. (1998). Exploring children's emotional security as a mediator of the link between marital relations and child adjustment. *Child Development, 69*, 124–139.

Davies, P. T., Forman, E. M., Rasi, J. A., & Stevens, K. I. (2002). Assessing children's emotional security in the interparental relationship: The security in the interparental subsystem scales. *Child Development, 73*, 544–562.

Davies, P. T., & Lindsay, L. L. (2004). Interparental conflict and adolescent adjustment: Why does gender moderate early adolescent vulnerability? *Journal of Family Psychology, 18*, 160–170.

Davies, P. T., Myers, R. L., Cummings, E. M., & Heindel, S. (1999). Adult conflict history and children's subsequent responses to conflict: An experimental test. *Journal of Family Psychology, 13*, 610–628.

Davies, P. T., & Windle, M. (2001). Interparental discord and adolescent adjustment trajectories: The potentiating and protective role of intrapersonal attributes. *Child Development, 72*, 1163–1178.

Davis, B. T., Hops, H., Alpert, A., & Sheeber, L. (1998). Child responses to parental conflict and their effect on adjustment: A study of triadic relations. *Journal of Family Psychology, 12,* 163–177.

Doyle, A. B., & Markiewicz, D. (2005). Parenting, marital conflict and adjustment from early to mid adolescence: Mediated by adolescent attachment style? *Journal of Youth and Adolescence, 34,* 97–110.

Du Rocher Schudlich, T. D., & Cummings, E. M. (2003). Parental dysphoria and children's internalizing symptoms: Marital conflict styles as mediators of risk. *Child Development, 74,* 1663–1681.

Dwyer, S. B., Nicholson, J. M., & Battistutta, D. (2003). Population level assessment of the family risk factors related to the onset or persistence of children's mental health problems. *Journal of Child Psychology & Psychiatry, 44,* 699–711.

El-Sheikh, M., & Cummings, E. M. (1995). Children's responses to angry adult behavior as a function of experimentally manipulated exposure to resolved and unresolved conflict. *Social Development, 4,* 75–91.

Emery, R. E. (1982). Interparental conflict and the children of discord and divorce. *Psychological Bulletin, 92,* 310–330.

English, D. J., Marshall, D. B., & Stewart, A. J. (2003). Effects of family violence on child behavior and health during early childhood. *Journal of Family Violence, 18,* 43–57.

Fauber, R., Forehand, R., Thomas, A. M., & Wierson, M. (1990). A mediational model of the impact of marital conflict on adolescent adjustment in intact and divorced families: The role of disrupted parenting. *Child Development, 61,* 1112–1123.

Fergusson, D. M., & Horwood, L. (1998). Exposure to interparental violence in childhood and psychosocial adjustment in young adulthood. *Child Abuse & Neglect, 22,* 339–357.

Fincham, F. D., Grych, J. H., & Osborne, L. N. (1994). Does marital conflict cause child maladjustment? Directions and challenges for longitudinal research. *Journal of Family Psychology, 8,* 128–140.

Garcia O'Hearn, H., Margolin, G., & John, R. S. (1997). Mothers' and fathers' reports of children's reactions to naturalistic marital conflict. *Journal of the American Academy of Child & Adolescent Psychiatry, 36,* 1366–1373.

Gonzales, N. A., Pitts, S. C., Hill, N. E., & Roosa, M. W. (2000). A mediational model of the impact of interparental conflict on child adjustment in a multiethnic, low-income sample. *Journal of Family Psychology, 14,* 365–379.

Gottman, J. M. (1989). *Specific affect coding manual.* Unpublished manuscript. University of Washington.

Grych, J. H., & Fincham, F. D. (1990). Marital conflict and children's adjustment: A cognitive-contextual framework. *Psychological Bulletin, 108,* 267–290.

Grych, J. H., Fincham, F. D., Jouriles, E. N., & McDonald, R. (2000). Interparental conflict and child adjustment: Testing the mediational role of appraisals in the cognitive-contextual framework. *Child Development, 71,* 1648–1661.

Grych, J. H., Harold, G. T., & Miles, C. J. (2003). A prospective investigation of appraisals as mediators of the link between interparental conflict and child adjustment. *Child Development, 74,* 1176–1193.

Grych, J. H., Jouriles, E. N., Swank, P. R., McDonald, R., & Norwood, W. D. (2000). Patterns of adjustment among children of battered women. *Journal of Consulting & Clinical Psychology, 68,* 84–94.

Grych, J. H., Seid, M., & Fincham, F. D. (1992). Assessing marital conflict from the child's perspective: The children's perception of interparental conflict scale. *Child Development, 63,* 558–572.

Harold, G. T., & Conger, R. (1997). Marital conflict and adolescent distress: The role of adolescent awareness. *Child Development, 68,* 333–350.

Hetherington, E., Cox, M., & Cox, R. (1982). Effects of divorce on parents and children. In: M. E. Lamb (Ed), *Nontraditional Families*. Hillsdale, NJ: Erlbaum.

Jaffee, S. R., Moffitt, T. E., Caspi, A., Taylor, A., & Arseneault, L. (2002). Influence of adult domestic violence on children's internalizing and externalizing problems: An environmentally informative twin study. *Journal of the American Academy of Child & Adolescent Psychiatry, 41,* 1095–1103.

Jenkins, J. M., Smith, M. A., & Graham, P. J. (1989). Coping with parental quarrels. *Journal of the American Academy of Child & Adolescent Psychiatry, 28,* 182–189.

Johnson, P. L., & O'Leary, D. O. (1987). Parental behavior patterns and conduct disorders in girls. *Journal of Abnormal Child Psychology, 15,* 573–581.

Johnston, J. R., Gonzalez, R., & Campbell, L. E. (1987). Ongoing postdivorce conflict and child disturbance. *Journal of Abnormal Child Psychology, 15,* 493–509.

Jouriles, E. N., Norwood, W. D., McDonald, R., Vincent, J. P., & Mahoney, A. (1996). Physical violence and other forms of marital aggression: Links with children's behavior problems. *Journal of Family Psychology, 10,* 223–234.

Jouriles, E. N., Spiller, L. C., Stephens, N., McDonald, R., & Swank, P. (2000). Variability in adjustment of children of battered women: The role of child appraisals of interparent conflict. *Cognitive Therapy & Research, 24,* 233–249.

Katz, L. F., & Gottman, J. M. (1993). Patterns of marital conflict predict children's internalizing and externalizing behaviors. *Developmental Psychology, 29,* 940–950.

Katz, L. F., & Woodin, E. M. (2002). Hostility, hostile detachment, and conflict engagement in marriages: Effects on child and family functioning. *Child Development, 73,* 636–651.

Kitzmann, K. M. (1997). *The effects of marital conflict on parenting: Observational ratings of the quality of family interactions directly following pleasant and conflictual marital interactions.* University of Virginia, US.

Kitzmann, K. M., Gaylord, N. K., Holt, A. R., & Kenny, E. D. (2003). Child witnesses to domestic violence: A meta-analytic review. *Journal of Consulting & Clinical Psychology, 71,* 339–352.

Kovacs, M. (1981). Rating scales to assess depression in school aged children. *Acta Paedopsychiatrica, 46,* 305–315.

Litrownik, A. J., Newton, R., Hunter, W. M., English, D., & Everson, M. D. (2003). Exposure to family violence in young at-risk children: A longitudinal look at the effects of victimization and witnessed physical and psychological aggression. *Journal of Family Violence, 18,* 59–73.

Locke, H. J., & Wallace, K. M. (1959). Short marital adjustment prediction tests: Their reliability and validity. *Marriage & Family Living, 21,* 251–255.

Long, N., Slater, E., Forehand, R., & Fauber, R. (1988). Continued high or reduced interparental conflict following divorce: Relation to young adolescent adjustment. *Journal of Consulting & Clinical Psychology, 56,* 467–469.

Mahoney, A., Jouriles, E. N., & Scavone, J. (1997). Marital adjustment, marital discord over childrearing, and child behavior problems: Moderating effects of child age. *Journal of Clinical Child Psychology, 26,* 415–423.

Mann, B. J., & MacKenzie, E. P. (1996). Pathways among marital functioning, parental behaviors, and child behavior problems in school-age boys. *Journal of Clinical Child Psychology, 25,* 183–191.

Marchand, J. F., & Hock, E. (2003). Mothers' and father's depressive symptoms and conflict-resolution strategies in the marriage and children's externalizing and internalizing behaviors. *Journal of Genetic Psychology, 164,* 227–239.

McCloskey, L. A., Figueredo, A. J., & Koss, M. P. (1995). The effects of systemic family violence on children's mental health. *Child Development, 66,* 1239–1261.

O'Brien, M., Bahadur, M. A., Gee, C., Balto, K., & Erber, S. (1997). Child exposure to marital conflict and child coping responses as predictors of child adjustment. *Cognitive Therapy & Research, 21*, 39–59.

O'Brien, M., Margolin, G., & John, R. S. (1995). Relation among marital conflict, child coping, and child adjustment. *Journal of Clinical Child Psychology, 24*, 346–361.

Porter, B., & O'Leary, K. D. (1980). Marital discord and childhood behaviour problems. *Journal of Abnormal Child Psychology, 8*, 287–295.

Quay, H. C., & Peterson, D. (1987). *Manual for the revised behavior problem checklist*: Unpublished manuscript.

Reid, W. J., & Crisafulli, A. (1990). Marital discord and child behavior problems: A meta-analysis. *Journal of Abnormal Child Psychology, 18*, 105–117.

Reynolds, C. R., & Richmond, B. D. (1979). Factor structure and construct validity of What I Think and Feel: The revised children's manifest anxiety scale. *Journal of Personality Assessment, 43*, 281–283.

Richters, J., & Martinez, P. (1993). The NIMH community violence project: Children as victims of and witnesses to violence. *Psychiatry, 56*, 7–21.

Rogers, M. J., & Holmbeck, G. N. (1997). Effects of interparental aggression on children's adjustment: The moderating role of cognitive appraisal and coping. *Journal of Family Psychology, 11*, 125–130.

Saunders, D. G. (1994). Child custody decisions in families experiencing woman abuse. *Social Work, 39*, 51–59.

Shifflett-Simpson, K., & Cummings, E. M. (1996). Mixed message resolution and children's responses to interadult conflict. *Child Development, 67*, 437–448.

Sim, H.-O., & Vuchinich, S. (1996). The declining effects of family stressors on antisocial behavior from childhood to adolescence and early adulthood. *Journal of Family Issues, 17*, 408–427.

Sternberg, K. J., Lamb, M. E., & Dawud-Noursi, S. (1998). Using multiple informants to understand domestic violence and its effects. In: G. W. Holden, R. A. Geffner & E. N. Jouriles (Eds), *Children exposed to marital violence: Theory, research, and applied issues.* Washington, DC: American Psychological Association.

Straus, M. A. (1979). Measuring interfamily conflict and violence: The conflict tactics (CT) scales. *Journal of Marriage & the Family, 41*, 75–88.

Straus, M. A., & Gelles, R. (1990). *Physical violence in American families: Risk factors and adaptations to violence in 8,145 families.* New Brunswick, NJ: Transaction.

Straus, M. A., Hamby, S. L., Boney-McCoy, S., & Sugarman, D. B. (1996). The revised Conflict Tactics Scales (CTS2): Development and preliminary psychometric data. *Journal of Family Issues, 17*, 283–316.

Webster-Stratton, C., & Hammond, M. (1999). Marital conflict management skills, parenting style, and early-onset conduct problems: Processes and pathways. *Journal of Child Psychology & Psychiatry, 40*, 917–927.

Wierson, M., Forehand, R., & McCombs, A. (1988). The relationship of early adolescent functioning to parent-reported and adolescent-perceived interparental conflict. *Journal of Abnormal Child Psychology, 16*, 707–718.

SECTION II

Chapter 5

Oppositional and Conduct Problems

David J. Hawes and Mark R. Dadds

The contemporary media suggests a popular fascination with the nature and origins of antisocial behaviour. Investigative journalism concerning violent criminals is largely made up of speculations as to what drives a person to commit such offences, while ubiquitous crime-focused television series (e.g. Law & Order; Wolf, 1990) parade characters who are virtually defined by the suggested origins of their behaviour. Two contrasting explanations for antisocial behaviour are encountered repeatedly in the popular media. The first describes an individual who grows up in an environment of adversity and hostility, gradually indoctrinated into an antisocial lifestyle. The second describes an individual who is born a 'bad seed', inexplicably motivated by cruel and sinister impulses. Interestingly, both stereotypes implicate causal processes beginning in childhood. While such depictions have acquired clichéd status in their popular use, the developmental sciences have much to say about the underlying processes they suggest.

Notions of causality have changed fundamentally over the course of contemporary research into the development of antisocial behaviour. Research and causal models in the literature of recent decades have focused largely on risk associated with environmental variables such as poverty, poor parenting and family adversity. As this research has advanced, an expanding array of factors have been implicated, prompting repeated calls to integrate a large and diffuse body of knowledge (Dodge & Pettit, 2003; Rutter, 2003; Shaw, Bell, & Gilliom, 2000).

This chapter focuses on the role of the family in pathways to antisocial outcomes. In order to discuss family processes in a broader context however, we will begin by focusing on non-family variables. In doing so, we will address evidence of risk associated with child factors (e.g. genetics, biological factors, temperament), and socio–cultural context. Robust findings pertaining to parent and family factors will then be reviewed, followed by an overview of theory and evidence regarding parent–child dynamics that have dominated explanations of antisocial behaviour. Recent innovations in models of antisocial behaviour will then be discussed, focusing on explanations of the interactive processes through which child and parent factors combine in pathways to antisocial behaviour.

Psychopathology and the Family
Edited by J. L. Hudson and R. M. Rapee
ISBN: 0-08-044449-0

What are Conduct Problems?

Findings from research into conduct problems are inherently determined by the definition of conduct problems used, and the methods by which the construct is measured. The definitions predominantly found in the psychological literature are those presented in the Diagnostic and Statistical Manual of Mental Disorders (DSM-IV; APA, 1994), which introduced formal criteria for both Oppositional Defiant Disorder (ODD) and Conduct Disorder (CD) in its third edition (American Psychiatric Association, 1980). Changing conceptualisations of conduct problems are reflected in the successive editions of the DSM; however this diagnostic nomenclature represents only one approach to defining and classifying antisocial behaviour. The literature of the last century has presented a rich language for describing antisocial behaviour in children and adolescents, which has variously been denoted as deviant, aggressive, disruptive and externalising. The terms juvenile delinquent and juvenile offender are also commonplace. The diversity in this language reflects not only historical trends, but also conceptual distinctions between and within disciplines.

It is also important to recognise that in recent years the antisocial literature has become increasingly inclusive of theory and evidence from diverse fields of research (e.g. personality, developmental psychology, forensic psychology) that use constructs different to those in the clinical literature. In keeping with this theoretical diversity and the ongoing redefinition of these constructs, we will use general terms such as conduct problems and antisocial behaviour in place of specific diagnostic or forensic labels.

What is a Family?

It is also worth commenting on the use of the term 'family' before proceeding. Ideas of what constitutes a family have changed markedly over recent decades. The structure and function of a family are not static, but transformed over time through changes in individual members and the impact of both normal and disruptive events. While the concept of family can thus encompass the full complexity of an extended system of multiple generations and relations by cohabitation and marriage, it can also be reduced to the dual components of a care-giving system (e.g. parents, guardians) and a child system. This is the conceptualisation found in much of the family-focused research on antisocial behaviour, which has accordingly studied family processes predominantly in terms of parent–child relationships. Consistent with much of the literature to be presented, references to family processes in this chapter will largely focus on interactions between parental and child systems.

Contemporary Models of Etiology and Risk

While no single risk factor has been found to predict a high proportion of variance in conduct problems, modest risk has been associated with a number of characteristics seen in children, parents, and family environments (Rutter, Giller, & Hagell, 1998). The trend in recent years has been toward an emphasis on the more complex interactive and transactional relationships between risk factors (Greene & Doyle, 1999). Interactive models are based on the premise that risk factors only function to increase risk in the presence (or absence) of other particular risk factors. Alternatively, the magnitude of risk associated with one factor may vary across levels of another (Dodge & Pettit, 2003). For example, parental monitoring and supervision of child behaviour have been found to moderate the effects of family disadvantage on adolescent conduct problems (Pettit, Bates, Dodge, & Meece, 1999), indicating that the close involvement of parents in children's and adolescent's activities may mitigate some of the risk associated with socio–economic adversity.

Such interactive effects however may also involve transactional processes. Such processes are typically seen in reciprocal influence between an individual and his or her environment, in which factors in both spheres are correlated with each other, as well as mediating the effects of each other on conduct problem outcomes (Dodge & Pettit, 2003). Patterson's coercion model (1982) (Reid, Patterson, & Snyder, 2002) is one of the most enduring and clearly articulated examples of this. Based on early observational studies of moment-to-moment family interactions conducted at the Oregon Social Learning Centre, this model describes the reinforcement traps through which deviant child behaviour elicits ineffective parental responses, which in turn reinforce the behaviour. The potential for reciprocal influence between parenting and child factors such as temperament has also been addressed in recent literature (e.g. Dadds & Salmon, 2003; Greene & Doyle, 1999).

Efforts to articulate interactive and transactional relationships between risk factors have also been accompanied by an emphasis on the heterogeneity of conduct problems. Current explanatory models of antisocial behaviour promote the idea that different factors and processes might relate uniquely to distinct groups of individuals exhibiting distinct antisocial outcomes (e.g. Dodge, 1991; Moffitt, 1993; Frick, O'Brien, Wootton, & McBurnett, 1994). For example, a range of evidence indicates that the aggressive versus non-aggressive conduct problem subtypes have different ages of onset, and genetic origins. It is well established that aggressive conduct problems, typically emerging in early childhood, appear to be more highly heritable than the non-aggressive conduct problems usually associated with adolescent onset (e.g. Edelbrock, Rende, Plomin, & Thompson, 1995).

Child Factors

Child factors associated with the development and course of antisocial behaviour are typically grouped into three broad domains. Behavioural factors have received the most attention in this literature, and emphasise characteristics and patterns of the observable behaviour (e.g. timing of onset; number of contexts in which the behaviour is displayed). Biological and psychophysiological factors have also been a major focus of this research in recent years; however are addressed here only in passing due to the focus on family in this chapter (Raine, 2002, for a review). Finally, child temperament has become the subject of a growing body of literature demonstrating the importance of individual differences in early childhood to the development of later antisocial behaviour.

Normative data from large scales longitudinal studies of child development (e.g. The Dunedin Multidisciplinary Health and Development Study; Moffitt, Caspi, Rutter, & Silva,

2001) have allowed researchers not only to study antisocial behaviour as an outcome, but also a predictor of future behaviour. Dimensions of this behaviour found to be most predictive of persistent antisociality include: (1) early age of onset, (2) the generalisability of the behaviour across multiple home school and community settings, and (3) the versatility of the antisocial individual, with those exhibiting both overt and covert forms of deviant behaviour likely to display a particularly severe and chronic pattern of antisocial behaviour (Loeber & Hay, 1997; Moffit, 1993). Overt typically describes antisocial behaviours involving direct confrontation with victims, while covert describes non-violent forms of delinquency such as theft or fraud, involving concealment rather than confrontation (Loeber & Stouthamer-Loeber, 1998).

Findings from twin studies, adoption studies, and behavioural-genetic studies have provided clear evidence of genetic influences on antisocial behaviour (Raine, 2002; Rutter, 1997). Meta-analytic findings of such research indicate that approximately 50% of the variance in the measures of antisocial behaviour in these studies may be attributed to heredity (Mason & Frick, 1994). New evidence pertaining to genetic factors is helping to clarify the differential outcomes resulting from developmental contexts of abuse. Using a birth cohort of 1,037 participants followed from birth to age 26 as part of the Dunedin Multidisciplinary Health and Development Study, Caspi et al. (2002) tested the hypothesis that MAOA genotype could moderate the influence of childhood maltreatment on neural systems implicated in antisocial behaviour. A gene × environment interaction was reported for males, in which the impact of early childhood maltreatment on antisocial outcomes was moderated by a functional polymorphism in the MAOA gene. While requiring ongoing investigation, such interactions help to explain why child abuse leads to antisocial behaviour in some children but not others.

While temperament has been implicated broadly in theoretical explanations of antisocial development, the notion that temperamental factors underlie and drive behavioural manifestations remains controversial (Bates, Pettit, Dodge, & Ridge, 1998; Dadds & Salmon, 2003). Caspi, Henry, McGee, and Moffitt (1995) investigated the importance of temperamental differences in early childhood to externalising and internalising outcomes in late childhood. Participants from the Dunedin Multidisciplinary Health and Development Study (n = 800) were assessed at ages 3, 5, 7, and 9. The study utilised measures of temperament and behaviour problems based on independent reports and observations, and examined the relations between specific temperamental characteristics and specific behaviour problems. Factor analyses revealed temperamental dimensions common to existing models of temperament (e.g. Bates, 1989; Rothbart, 1989). Three such dimensions were revealed at each age: Approach (i.e. extreme friendliness, self-confidence, and self-reliance), Sluggishness (i.e. reacts passively to changing situations, withdraws from novelty, fails to initiate action), and Lack of Control. This final dimension is consistent with typical descriptions of 'negative emotionality', or 'distress proneness', a dimension thought to influence both future levels of conduct problems (Owens & Shaw, 2003), and future trajectories of child–caregiver relationships (Clark, Kochanska, & Ready, 2000).

For both genders, lack of control in early childhood was the best predictor of conduct problems in late childhood. Furthermore, individual differences in early Lack of Control showed predictive specificity in relation to two trajectories of externalising behaviour delineated in Moffitt's (1993) taxonomy. These findings indicated that while an early Lack of Control foretold an early-onset trajectory suggestive of a 'life-course persistent' pattern, antisocial behaviour with an onset during adolescence was not associated with such temperamental factors. These findings are consistent with the theoretical tenets of Moffitt's (1993) taxonomy, in which adolescent-onset conduct problems are thought to represent normative processes of socialisation, while an early-onset trajectory implicates neuropsychological factors.

Dodge and colleagues (Dodge, 1991; Dodge, Lochman, Harnish, Bates, & Pettit, 1997) propose a distinction between subtypes of chronic antisocial children and adolescents based on the nature of the aggression exhibited (reactive versus proactive). The reactive aggression group is characterised by retaliatory hostility, while the aggression exhibited in the proactive group is instrumental in nature, driven by the expectation of reward. It is proposed that the developmental histories of these two groups implicate distinct causal factors and processes. Aggression in the reactive group is thought to develop through processes associated with early experiences of physical abuse and harsh discipline, a temperament characterised by emotional dysregulation, and deficits in social information processing. Alternatively, the aggression observed in the proactive group is suggested to develop primarily through social learning processes related to exposure to aggressive and coercive role models, and the development of a style of social information processing which favours the instrumental use of aggression. The reactive and proactive subtypes are therefore associated with distinct forms of child temperament, as well as implicating distinct family processes.

It is important to recognise that temperament has traditionally been conceptualised as part of an interactional process. Central to the seminal work of Thomas and Chess (1977) is the idea that temperament itself does not lead to behavioural outcomes, but that such outcomes result from the goodness of fit between child temperament and the expectations and resources of the child's family and social environments. Subsequent research has demonstrated the importance of such conditions in shaping divergent outcomes related to a host of child risk factors, including biological variables (Raine, 2002). Consistent with this premise, research is focusing increasingly on the interaction of child factors and parenting in the development of antisocial behaviour.

The Family in Context

An extensive body of epidemiological and longitudinal evidence (e.g. Moffitt, 1993; Dodge & Pettit, 2003) has established links between antisocial behaviour and socio-cultural family context. Ecological models of the family (e.g. Bronfenbrenner, 1986) acknowledge the diversity of risk and protective factors located in the family, community, and cultural systems. One of the most well established of these is socio-economic status at birth, as indexed by income, occupation, and education of parents (Bradley & Corwyn, 2002). Other contextual risk factors in the family system include parental divorce (Amato, 2001), intra-family conflict (Davies & Windle, 2001), and being born to a teenage (Morash & Rucker, 1989) or single parent (Ackerman, D'Eramo, Umylny, Schultz, & Izard, 2001).

Factors associated with socio-cultural context have been implicated in some of the most robust interaction effects in the conduct problems literature. Evidence that the relationship between poverty and conduct problems is mediated by parenting practices has been reported in diverse samples, using diverse measures. In a longitudinal sample followed by Dodge, Pettit, and Bates (1994), for example, parenting practices were found to account for at least half of the direct pathogenic effects of social adversity on conduct problems. Consistent with this research is the idea that characteristics of a child's family environment can function as protective factors. As noted, parental monitoring and supervision (Pettit et al., 1999) appears to buffer the risk for antisocial behaviour associated with socio-economic adversity.

While the environmental-mediation hypothesis is appealing from a social learning perspective, alternative explanations should not be discounted. Dodge and Pettit (2003) have speculated, for example, that factors such as socio-economic adversity, parenting practices, and child conduct problems, may all be influenced also by a separate variable (e.g. parent genes), rather than simply being causally related. It has been suggested that research into preventive interventions may provide the experimental manipulations necessary to test such predictions (Dodge & Pettit, 2003). Clearly, socio-cultural conditions in isolation cannot provide causal explanations for antisocial behaviour. Rather, they appear to function as risk factors that are associated with and perhaps magnify the effects of individual and family levels risk factors.

Parent Factors

Some of the most robust risk factors for conduct problem outcomes involve parent or caregiver characteristics. Parenting practices represent one of the first major focuses of scientific investigations into pathways to antisocial behaviour, and feature prominently in current models. The three strongest predictors of child and adolescent conduct problems to come from this research have been lack of parental involvement, poor monitoring and supervision, and harsh and inconsistent discipline (Dishion, Patterson, Stoolmiller, & Skinner, 1991; Frick, 1992; Strassberg, Dodge, Petit, & Bates, 1994).

While the causal mechanisms associated with these parenting practices remain largely theoretical, a number of interpretations are available. It has been suggested that parents lacking in involvement and providing limited supervision and monitoring will be less aware of problem behaviours in their children and therefore less able to provide appropriate consequences (Patterson, Reid, & Dishion, 1992). Harsh discipline practices may increase conduct problems through parental modelling of aggressive responses to interpersonal conflict. Alternatively, inconsistency in discipline practices has been suggested to contribute to experiences of unpredictability in the child's social environment, thought to negatively affect the development of behavioural control in children (Wahler, 1997).

Parenting has also been examined in terms of the more general styles with which parents respond to children, typically during infancy and early childhood. A number of studies examining such aspects of parent behaviour have identified dimensions that may protect against the development of later conduct problems. One empirically supported dimension that has been a focus of this research is maternal warmth, characterised by positive attention (Gardner, 1994).

Consistent findings have been reported for the conceptually related constructs of maternal responsiveness to infants' bids for attention, and maternal acceptance of child behaviour. Such constructs have also been associated with low levels of conduct problems (Wolchik, Wilcox, Tein, & Sandler, 2000), with protective effects also suggested to come from the positive influence of these parent characteristics on the parent–child relationship, or child self-esteem. Alternatively, the construct of maternal negative control has been associated with increased risk for externalising behaviour in preschool and school age children (Spieker, Larson, Lewis, Keller, & Gilchrist, 1999).

Psychopathology in parents is known to increase risk of antisocial behaviour in their offspring. The earlier discussion of heredity and genetic risk factors suggested the risk associated with parental antisocial personality disorder and related psychopathology (e.g. substance abuse). While maternal depression has been associated with risk for child externalising behaviour (Goodman & Gotlib, 1999), evidence indicates that this relationship is at least partially accounted for by parenting practices (Shaw & Bell, 1993). That is, depression impacts negatively on parenting behaviours, the parent–child relationship, and other aspects of the family climate.

Parent–Child Dynamics

There is broad consensus that the interpersonal dynamics occurring in parent–child dyads are critical to behavioural outcomes in children, both directly and in mediating the effects of other risk factors such as poverty (e.g. Shaw et al., 2000).

The advent of Patterson's (1982) coercion model was associated with both conceptual and methodological advances in the application of social learning theory to explanations of antisocial development. In an effort to collect objective behavioural data concerning family processes, Patterson, Reid and colleagues developed coding systems for recording the moment-to-moment interactions between parents and children during innovative naturalistic–observational studies (Reid et al., 2002 for detailed descriptions). These studies revealed that compared to families of non-conduct problem children, families with conduct problem children were more likely to initiate and reciprocate aggressive behaviour, and to persist in aversive behaviour once they had initiated it. Such families were described as highly coercive social systems, in which all family members contributed to bilateral and systemic coercion in relation to the target child (Snyder & Stoolmiller, 2002).

Patterson (1982) proposed that two main processes were operating in such families, which could be explained using operant conditioning principles. The first of these is the parental modelling of antisocial or aggressive behaviour. The second process involves 'reinforcement traps', which can occur in a variety of ways. A common chain of actions would involve a parent making an intrusive request of a child, the child protesting with aversive behaviour, and the parent then capitulating. In such an example, the child's aversive behaviour is positively reinforced by the parent's capitulation, which in turn is negatively reinforced by the termination of the child's aversive behaviour. In an alternative reinforcement trap, the more a child engages in conduct problems, the less likely the child will be reinforced for positive behaviours.

Parents who develop aversive associations with child interactions due to experiences related to problem behaviours will avoid involvement with the child and therefore be less attentive to positive child behaviours. Evidence in support of these processes has been reported in decades of observational studies (see review by Snyder & Stoolmiller, 2002), and a range of efficacious behavioural interventions have directly flowed from this model (McMahon & Forehand, 2003; Sanders & Dadds, 1993; Webster-Stratton & Hancock, 1998). The application of operant principles to parent–child interactive therapies must be considered one of the most potent innovations of the mental health sciences.

Attachment

While the construct of attachment represents a relatively minor focus within the antisocial development literature, the contributions of attachment theory have received growing attention in recent years, and the integration of such theory with broader social learning-based models appears to be an emerging trend. In a review of recent attachment-related studies of aggressive child behaviour, Lyons-Ruth (1996) comments that many of the family related correlates of such behaviour can be identified in infancy, prior to the onset of coercive cycles. In contrast to the micro processes of family dynamics addressed in Patterson's (1982) coercion model, attachment models are concerned with parent–child relations at a more global level. While studies of middle-class samples have found association between externalising behaviour and avoidant attachment patterns (e.g. Erickson et al., 1985), it appears that disorganised attachment patterns are more strongly related to aggressive behaviour in populations characterised by broader risk factors. Infants with disorganised attachment patterns may exhibit unpredictable alternations of approach and avoidance, and a range of helpless, depressed, or conflict behaviours (Lyons-Ruth, Alpern, & Repacholi, 1993).

While the integration of attachment theory into social learning models of antisocial behaviour represents a relatively new idea, their similarities can be traced back to classic experiments in psychology. Dadds (2002) pointed out that a largely forgotten series of animal experiments conducted by the Harlows (Harlow & Harlow, 1962) elucidate the role that attachment may play in relation to processes such as those in Patterson's coercion model. In these experiments, comfort and food (as well aversive stimuli) was delivered to an infant monkey through a mechanical mother monkey. The authors described 'approach-avoidance' conflicts in these dyads, with the delivery of aversive stimuli from the mother resulting in increased clinging rather than avoidance. Such infant behaviour in the real world would in some cases alternately elicit comforting behaviours and displeasure in mothers. Reactions of displeasure would be associated with further rejecting behaviours, which in turn would increase the likelihood of further aversive clinging behaviour from the infant. It makes theoretical sense that such attachment processes will play a role in the hostile escalations observed in coercive dyads. For example, the emotional reactivity observed in such dyads suggests a strong degree of closeness (albeit ambivalent) that would not be expected in dyads who mutually avoid such aversive exchanges.

While attachment studies of fathers have been rare, they have contributed to knowledge of the role that fathers play in the development of conduct problems. Consistent with findings for infant–mother attachment, insecure attachments with fathers have been associated with peer problems at age 5 (Youngblade & Belsky, 1992), as well as increased likelihood of referral for early-onset conduct problems (Deklyen, Speltz, & Greenberg, 1998). Other evidence indirectly supports the possibility that father–son attachments may be important in protecting against antisocial outcomes than specific learning processes such as observational modelling. Studies examining the relationship between father–son contact and conduct problems in boys have consistently failed to support a modelling hypothesis in explaining the intergenerational transmission of antisocial behaviour (see Frick, 2002, for a review). Alternatively, it appears that closer relationships are associated with fewer conduct problems, even when the father himself is antisocial.

Innovations in Interactive Models

The coercion model (Patterson, 1982; Reid et al., 2002) and the body of research upon which it is based, have made some of the most significant contributions to knowledge of antisocial behaviour of the past three decades. This model was the first to articulate specific transactional processes occurring in the parent–child relationships of children with conduct problems, and led to a range of behavioural family interventions, the most efficacious treatment for conduct problems currently available. Despite the rich complexity captured in this model however, the limitations of its current form are becoming increasingly evident. While Patterson (1982) recognises that individual differences in infants place particular parent–child dyads at risk for developing coercive relationships, child factors and the distinct ways they interact with parenting processes in the development of antisocial behaviour have been given little attention in this research. Various models involving the interaction of child factors with parenting processes have emerged in recent years, some key examples of which will now be discussed. From this research it can be predicted that models articulating the role of child factors in relation to social learning processes occurring in parent–child relationships will become a focus of antisocial research over the next decade.

As discussed earlier, it has been proposed that antisocial children displaying predominantly reactive versus proactive aggression represent distinct groups, involving distinct causal pathways (Dodge, 1991). Importantly, these two groups are proposed to exhibit distinct styles of social information processing, thought to be impulsive in the reactive group, and more deliberate in the proactive group. While cognitive processing is best conceptualised as a child factor, growing evidence is indicating the role that family processes play in influencing these processing styles. For example, while early experiences of abuse have been linked with hypervigilence to hostile cues and a tendency toward hostile attributions (Dodge, Pettit, Bates, & Valente, 1995), findings indicate that important contributions to such biases may also come from less conspicuous family processes. In a study by Barrett, Rapee, Dadds, and Ryan (1996), oppositional, anxious, and nonclinic samples were individually asked to interpret and provide plans of action for ambiguous social scenarios. The task was then repeated, this time with the child and parents discussing the situation together. Consistent with Dodge (1986), both the anxious and oppositional groups made more interpretations of hostile threat than the nonclinic group, with the oppositional group exhibiting the most biased interpretations. As would be expected, the action plans pro-posed individually by children in the two groups where characterised by aggression in the oppositional group, and avoidance in the anxious group. Interestingly, the responses of parents in each of these groups were consistent with those of their children. For example, parents of the oppositional children made more threat interpretations than parents in the other groups. This finding suggests that such biases may be learned by children through parental modelling of aggressive interpretations and responses in social contexts. Of par-ticular interest, however, are the findings regarding the effects of family processes on child responses. While family discussion resulted in a decrease in aggressive and avoidant responses in the nonclinic group, for the oppositional children, the proportion choosing aggressive solutions increased following the family discussions. A similar pattern was observed for anxious children, who were more likely to choose avoidant solutions after discussion with their parents (Barrett et al., 1996). Analyses of the moment-to-moment interactions between the parents and their child showed that parents were instrumental in shaping the direction of the child's preferences for avoidant versus aggressive responding (Dadds, Barrett, Rapee, & Ryan, 1996). These findings indicate that family communica-tion processes may enhance social information processing biases toward aggression or avoidance in the direction of vulnerability in the child.

Predictions for how child temperament may interact with parenting practices in the development of conduct problems can be also be found in Kochanska's (1993, 1995) work on the development of conscience during childhood. For Kochanska, two temperamental processes are central to the development of conscience. The first involves the child's fear-fulness and vulnerability to affective discomfort when planning or engaging in forbidden behaviour. The second involves the child's ability to inhibit the impulse to commit the transgression, and perform a desirable response. The later is analogous to the dimension of effortful control, with this temperament found to be associated with externalising behaviour (Kochanska, Murray, Jacques, & Koenig, 1996), and indicators of empathy in children (Rothbart, Ahadi, & Hershey, 1994).

Kochanska proposes that these traits moderate the impact of parental socialisation. Specifically, it is predicted that children with a fearful temperament will respond well to gentle discipline, as such practices create an optimal level of discomfort and promote inter-nalisation. For children high in fearlessness however, the same methods may fail, as they elicit insufficient discomfort (Kochanska, 1993, 1995). Support for these predictions has been reported in studies measuring these traits using parent report (Kochanska et al., 1997), and psychophysiological indices (electrodermal reactivity) (Fowles & Kochanska, 2000). This research has indicated that for children high in fearfulness, conscience forma-tion was best predicted by gentle discipline, while for highly fearless children, attachment security appeared to play a greater role. While Kochanska's model has received limited evaluation with clinical samples, the author has speculated that parents of highly impulsive children (presumably those high on fearlessness and low on effortful control) are likely to use increasingly power assertive discipline methods, the effectiveness of which will be compromised by escalating anger and frustration. Such parents may then be likely to make external attributions for the child's behaviour.

In recent years, the study of early indicators of "psychopathy" in children has provided further predictions concerning the interaction of child temperament with parenting processes in pathways to antisocial behaviour. Recent research has investigated the characteristics of conduct disordered children who exhibit a temperamental style characterised by limited empathy and guilt, a manipulative use of others, and constricted emotionality (Frick, Cornell, Barry, Bodin, & Dane, 2003). In children with conduct problems, these callous-unemotional (CU) traits have been associated with a more severe and chronic pattern of antisocial behaviour, beginning during the preschool years (Christian, Frick, Hill, & Tyler, 1997). While few studies have examined such traits in young children, a growing body of evidence from studies of adolescent clinical and forensic samples indicates that a number of the well established correlates of adult psychopathy can be identified during this developmental period. Consistent with the adult literature, adolescent males exhibiting CU traits exhibit low levels of anxiety (Frick, Lilienfeld, Edens, Poythress, & McBurnett, 2000), diminished pain sensitivity (Seguin, Pihl, Boulerice, Tremblay, & Harden, 1996), and a reward-dominant/punishment-insensitive style (Blair, Colledge, & Mitchell, 2001).

Emerging evidence indicates that CU traits may interact with parenting practices in the development of conduct problems. Wootton, Frick, Shelton, and Silverthorn (1997) examined correlations between measures of parenting and conduct problems in a clinical sample of 6–13 year olds. The association between ineffective parenting and conduct problems in the sample was found to be moderated by the presence of child CU traits. Ineffective parenting was associated with greater conduct problems only for children lacking in CU traits, while those high in CU traits exhibited high rates of conduct problems regardless of the quality of parenting received.

The clinical implications of this finding were investigated in a recent clinical trial conducted by Hawes and Dadds (in press). A sample of young boys ($n = 55$, aged 4–8 years) was treated using a 10-week behavioural parent training intervention. As predicted, boys with high-stable levels of CU traits exhibited the poorest outcomes at 6-month follow-up, even when controlling for severity of conduct problems. Consistent with the punishment-insensitive temperament associated with CU traits, these boys were also found to be less responsive to time-out than boys without CU traits, and demonstrated less negative affect in response to time-out. The effects of CU were not found to be related to poor implementation of treatment by parents. These findings present important implications for the role of child temperament in the treatment of conduct problems, and provide evidence that conduct problems in children with CU traits are less responsive to changes in parenting processes.

Dadds and Salmon (2003) proposed a transactional model addressing the theoretical construct of punishment insensitivity (PI), which makes predictions about the way children with particular traits respond to, as well as influence, parenting practices. Originally introduced in research concerning adult psychopaths (Lykken, 1957) the construct of PI broadly refers to sensitivity to aversive stimuli, and cues predicting such stimuli. Individuals characterised by high levels of PI exhibit deficits in passive avoidance learning, that is, learning to change behaviour in order to avoidant punishment. The concept of punishment here also encompasses a broad range of events, spanning legal consequences such as imprisonment, to internal aversive states associated with cues of negative affect in others. As noted by Dadds and Salmon (2003), the communication of negative consequences is often achieved through the communication of emotions by facial expressions. Biases in the processing of emotional cues can therefore be presumed to impinge on a child's experience of parental discipline attempts, and data are emerging to indicate that adolescents with high levels of antisocial behaviour may have deficits in their ability to process the facial emotions of others (Blair, Colledge, Murray, & Mitchell, 2001).

Given that Patterson's coercion model emphasises the role of punishment in reinforcement traps, explanations for divergent pathways differentially associated with PI are theoretically appealing. While PI has generally been conceptualised as a stable personality-like trait in the adult literature, Dadds and Salmon (2003) have proposed that the transactional processes seen in Patterson's model may interact with child temperament to shape a child's responsiveness to parental use of punishment over the course of child development. It is suggested that the same ineffective applications of punishment posited to escalate conduct problems in children (e.g. inconsistency punishment, non-contingent punishment, gradual increases in severity of punishment), will, in children characterised by temperament high in fearlessness, also diminish their sensitivity to punishment. While not yet tested, it is proposed that PI will exacerbate coercive cycles, and therefore consolidate a punishment insensitive style even further (Dadds & Salmon, 2003). This model is presented in Figure 1.

In summary, a wealth of work has indicated that certain parenting styles and child characteristics are interactive risk factors for antisocial behaviour. Contemporary approaches are developing methods for modelling how these risks interact to produce outcomes at different developmental stages for the child and the family. The state of the art can be exemplified by three studies that explicitly model the interacting nature of parent and child variables.

Granic and Lamey (2002) used a problem-solving paradigm to observe the interactions between parents and children in a sample of clinic-referred conduct problem boys (mean age 10 years) with and without concurrent anxiety/depression problems. The study included a number of unique design and methodological features, intended to reflect important principles in child development theory. The authors point out that the traditional use of global ratings in observational studies of parent–child interactions may fail to pick up temporal processes important to relationship dynamics. In order to better examine such processes, the authors utilised a methodological strategy based on dynamic systems (DS) theory, a mathematical language that can describe the internal feedback processes of a system in adapting to new conditions. The application of DS principles to parent–child observations allowed for multiple dyadic-interaction patterns to be analysed concurrently, and their relation to one another explored. A combination of case-based and multivariate analyses were employed in this process. In order to examine the role of context changes on these dyadic interactions, a 'perturbation' was used, in which a knock on the laboratory door signalled that the allotted time for the problem-solving discussion was almost over, and a resolution was needed. The rationale for this perturbation included the developmental premises that individual differences are most apparent under stressful situations, and the DS premise that only by perturbing a system can the full range of behavioural possibilities by identified.

Consistent with their predictions, Granic and Lamey (2002) found that parent–child interactions in the two groups (conduct problem children with and without comorbid internalising problems) differed only after the perturbation. Specifically, it was found that during the initial period of the problem-solving discussion, parents in both groups exhibited a

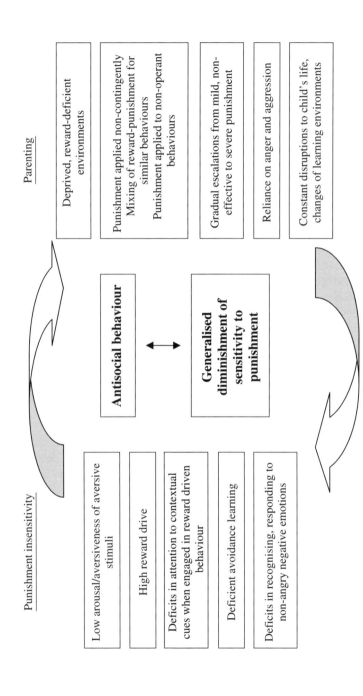

Figure 1: Aspects of punishment insensitivity and likely interactions with parenting.

permissive style in responding to aversive behaviour in their children. Following the perturbation however, only the dyads involving children with comorbid internalising problems shifted to a style of interaction characterised by mutual and escalating criticism and hostility. The findings from this study are of particular interest, as they provide evidence of how subtypes of conduct problem children differ in terms of the transactional processes occurring with their parents, and demonstrate that contextual conditions are important in determining the processes occurring at any given time.

Another example is the Caspi et al. (2002) study showing that genotype moderates the effects of child abuse on adult antisocial outcomes. This study examined the interaction between a particular child factor and parenting practices using an epidemiological sample followed longitudinally from infancy to adulthood. This was one of the first behaviour genetics studies to examine the role of a specific genotype (MAOA) in interaction with parenting practices, providing important evidence of genetic–environmental interactions in a sample that was representative of the general population and studied developmentally over the life course.

A final example is the Barrett et al. (1996) and Dadds et al. (1996) work showing that family processes may enhance aggression in the cognitive styles of aggressive children. The research questions integrate information processing and family-based social learning models of psychopathology. These questions were addressed using moment-to-moment observational measures of family processes and cognitive responses, and examined child and parent behaviours separately, as well as in combination. Such an approach allowed the researchers to determine that processes involved in the parent–child communication enhanced avoidant versus aggressive child responses according to an interaction of the child's vulnerabilities and family processes.

Conclusions and Future Directions

Much is known about the characteristics of parents, children, and family contexts that increase the risk of a child developing antisocial behaviour relative to their peers. From this research, we know that chronic antisocial behaviour is likely to first appear in early childhood, with such children also more likely than their peers to have antisocial parents. During infancy, children with increased risk for antisocial behaviour will exhibit a range of personal characteristics that interact with the parenting they receive to diminish or enhance risk. As noted, one of the most influential models to articulate causal processes important to antisocial behaviour is Patterson's (1982) coercion model. This model has largely defined current understanding of how both parents and children contribute to reciprocal cycles that maintain and exacerbate conduct problems over time. The weakness of this model however is the limited attention given to child factors, which in recent years have been used to distinguish subtypes of antisocial behaviour with distinct symptom profiles, proposed to differ with regard to developmental history and etiological processes.

We have seen that the best current studies simultaneously model interactive processes whereby individual and family characteristics represent more than simply additive risks. It is clear that such models must account for the role of multiple sets of risk factors associated with parents, children, and parent–child relations, including transaction relationships between such factors. Models must account for the heterogeneity of conduct problems, and the distinct causal pathways associated with divergent outcomes, and present clear indications for the treatment of antisocial behaviour. Further, models will have to be responsive to the developmental points at which various risks switch in and out. While family interventions for young conduct problem children have a considerable pedigree, they have been largely insensitive to differences in the presenting characteristics of children and the particular parenting challenges they present. The next decade should witness increasing sophistication in interactive models through which programs of treatment and prevention will be improved, and the societal impact of antisocial behaviour reduced.

References

Ackerman, B. P., D'Eramo, K. S., Umylny, L., Schultz, D., & Izard, C. E. (2001). Family structure and the externalizing behavior of children from economically disadvantaged families. *Journal of Family Psychology, 15*(2), 288–300.

Amato, P. R. (2001) Children of divorce in the 1990s: An update of the Amato and Keith (1991) meta-analysis. *Journal of Family Psychology, 15*(3), 355–370.

American Psychiatric Association. (1980). *Diagnostic and statistical manual of mental disorders* (3rd ed.). Washington, DC: Author.

American Psychiatric Association. (1994). *Diagnostic and statistical manual of mental disorders* (4th ed.). Washington, DC: Author.

Barrett, P. M., Rapee, R. M., Dadds, M. M., & Ryan, S. M. (1996). Family enhancement of cognitive style in anxious and aggressive children. *Journal of Abnormal Child Psychology, 24*, 187–203.

Bates, J. E. (1989). Concepts and measures of temperament. In: G. A. Kohnstamm, J. E. Bates & M. K. Rothbart (Eds), *Temperament in childhood* (pp. 3–26). New York: Wiley.

Bates, J. E., Pettit, G. S., Dodge, K. A., Ridge, B. (1998). Interaction of temperamental resistance to control and restrictive parenting in the development of externalising behaviour. *Developmental Psychology, 34*(5), 982–995.

Blair, R. J. R., Colledge, E., & Mitchell, D. G. V. (2001). Somatic markers and response reversal: Is there orbitofrontal cortex dysfunction in boys with psychopathic tendencies? *Journal of Abnormal Child Psychology, 29*, 499–511.

Blair, R. J. R., Colledge, E., Murray, L., & Mitchell, D. G. V. (2001). A selective impairment in the processing of sad and fearful expressions in children with psychopathic tendencies. *Journal of Abnormal Child Psychology, 29*, 491–498.

Bradley, R. H., & Corwyn, R. F. (2002). Socioeconomic Status and Child Development. *Annual Review of Psychology, 53*, 371–399.

Bronfenbrenner, U. (1986). Ecology of the family as a context for human development: Research perspectives. *Developmental Psychology, 22*, 723–742.

Caspi, A., Henry, B., McGee, R. O., & Moffitt, T. E. (1995). Temperamental origins of child and adolescent behaviour problems: From age three to fifteen. *Child Development, 66*, 55–68.

Caspi, A., McClay, J., Moffitt, T. E., Mill, J., Martin, J., Craig, I. W., et al. (2002). Role of genotype in the cycle of violence in maltreated children. *Science, 297*, 851–854.

Christian, R. E., Frick, P. J., Hill, N, L., & Tyler, L. (1997). Psychopathy and conduct problems in children: II. Implications for subtyping children with conduct problems. *Journal of the American Academy of Child and Adolescent Psychiatry, 36*, 233–241.

Clark, L. A., Kochanska, G., & Ready, R. (2000). Mothers' personality and its interaction with child temperament as predictors of parenting behaviour. *Journal of Personality and Social Psychology, 79*(2), 274–285.

Dadds, M. R. (2002). Learning and intimacy in the families of anxious children. In: R. J. McMahon & R. D. Peters (Eds), *The effects of parental dysfunction on children* (pp. 87–106). New York, NY: Kluwer Academic.

Dadds, M. R., Barrett, P. M., Rapee, R. M., & Ryan, S. (1996). Family process and child anxiety and aggression: An observational analysis. *Journal of Abnormal Child Psychology, 24*(6), 715–734.

Dadds, M. R., & Salmon, K. (2003). Punishment insensitivity and parenting: Temperament and learning as interacting risks for antisocial behaviour. *Clinical Child and Family Psychology Review, 6*(2), 69–86.

Davies, P. T., & Windle, M. (2001). Interparental discord and adolescent adjustment trajectories: The potentiating and protective role of intrapersonal attributes. *Child Development, 72*, 1163–1178.

DeKlyen, M., Speltz, M. L., & Greenberg, M. T. (1998). Fathering and early onset conduct problems: Positive and negative parenting, father-son attachment, and the marital context. *Clinical Child and Family Psychlology Review, 1*(1), 3–21.

Dishion, T. J., Patterson, G. R., Stoolmiller, M., & Skinner, M. I. (1991). Family, school, and behavioral antecedents to early adolescent involvement with antisocial peers. *Developmental Psychology, 27*, 172–180.

Dodge, K. A. (1986). *A social information processing model of social competence in children.* In: M. Perlmutter (Ed.), *Minnesota symposium on child psychology* (pp. 77–125). Hillsdale, NJ: Erlbaum.

Dodge, K. E. (1991). The structure and function of reactive and proactive aggression. In: D. J. Pepler & K. H. Rubin (Eds), *The development and treatment of childhood aggression* (pp. 201–218). Hillsdale, NJ: Lawrence Erlbaum Associates.

Dodge, K. A., Lochman, J. E., Harnish, J. D., Bates, J. E., & Pettit, G. S. (1997). Reactive and proactive aggression in school children and psychiatrically impaired chronically assaultive youth. *Journal of Abnormal Psychology, 106*, 37–51.

Dodge, K. A., & Pettit, G. S. (2003). A biopsychosocial model of the development of chronic conduct problems in adolescence. *Developmental Psychology, 39*(2), 349–371.

Dodge, K. A., Pettit, G. S., & Bates, J. E. (1994). Socialisation mediators of the relation between socio-economic status and child conduct problems. *Child Development, 65*, 649–665.

Dodge, K. A., Pettit, G. S., Bates, J. E., & Valente, E. (1995). Social information-processing patterns partially mediate the effect of early physical abuse on later conduct problems. *Journal of Abnormal Psychology, 104*, 632–643.

Edelbrock, C., Rende, R., Plomin, R., & Thompson, L. A. (1995). A twin study of competence and problems behavior in childhood and early adolescence. *Journal of Child Psychology and Psychiatry, 36*, 775–785.

Erickson, M. F., Sroufe, L. A., & Egeland, B. (1985). The relationship between the quality of attachment and behaviour problems in preschool in a high-risk sample. In: I. Bretherton & E. Waters (Eds), *Growing points of attachment theory and research, Monographs of the Society for Research in Child Development, Vol. 50*(1–2, Serial No. 209), (pp. 147–167). Washington, DC: University of Chicago Press.

Fowles, D. C., & Kochanska, G. (2000). Temperament as a moderator of pathways to conscience in children: The contribution of electrodermal activity. *Psychophysiology, 37*, 788–795.

Frick, P. J. (1992). Familial risk factors to oppositional defiant disorder and conduct disorder: Parental psychopathology and maternal parenting. *Journal of Consulting and Clinical Psychology, 60*(1), 49–55.

Frick, P. J. (2002). Understanding the association between parent and child antisocial behaviour. In: R. J. McMahon & R. D. Peters (Eds), *The Effects of Parental Dysfunction on Children* (pp. 105–126). New York, NY: Kluwer Academic.

Frick, P. J., Cornell, A. H., Barry, C. T., Bodin, S. D., & Dane, H. E. (2003). Callous-unemotional traits and conduct problems in the prediction of conduct problem severity, aggression, and self-report of delinquency. *Journal of Abnormal Child Psychology, 31*(4), 457–470.

Frick, P. J., Lilienfeld, S. O., Edens, J. F., Poythress, N. G., & McBurnett, K. (2000). The association between anxiety and antisocial behaviour. *Primary Psychiatry, 7*, 52–57.

Frick, P. J., O'Brien, B. S., Wootton, J. M., & McBurnett, K. (1994). Psychopathy and conduct problems in children. *Journal of Abnormal Psychology, 103*(4), 700–707.

Gardner, F. (1994). The quality of joint activity between mothers and their children with behaviour problems. *Journal of Child Psychology and Psychiatry, 35*, 935–948.

Goodman, S. H., & Gotlib, I. H. (1999). Risk for psychopathology in the children of depressed mothers: A developmental model for understanding mechanisms of transmission. *Psychological Review, 106*, 458–490.

Granic, I. & Lamey, A. V. (2002). Combining dynamic systems and multivariate analyses to compare the mother-child interactions of externalising subtypes. *Journal of Abnormal Child Psychology, 30*(3), 265–283.

Greene, R. W., & Doyle, A. E. (1999). Toward a transactional conceptualisation of oppositional defiant disorder: Implications for assessment and treatment. *Clinical Child and Family Psychology Review, 2*(3), 129–148.

Harlow, H. F., & Harlow, M. (1962). Social deprivation in monkeys. *Scientific American, 207*, 136–146.

Hawes, D. J., & Dadds, M. R. (in press). The treatment of conduct problems in children with callous-unemotional traits. Journal of Consulting and Clinical Psychology.

Kochanska, G. (1993). Toward a synthesis of parental socialisation and child temperament in early development of conscience. *Child Development, 64*, 325–347.

Kochanska, G. (1995). Children's temperament, mothers' discipline, and security of attachment: Multiple pathways to emerging internalisation. *Child Development, 66*, 597–615.

Kochanska, G., Clark, L. A., & Goldman, M. S. (1997). Implications of mothers' personality for their parenting and their young children's development outcomes. *Journal of Personality, 65*(2), 387–420.

Kochanska, G., Murray, K., Jacques, T. Y., & Koenig, A. (1996). Inhibitory control in young children and its role in emerging internalisation. *Child Development, 67*, 490–507.

Loeber, R., & Hay, D. (1997). Key issues in the development of aggression and violence from childhood to early adulthood. *Annual Review of Psychology, 48*, 371–410.

Loeber, R., & Stouthamer-Loeber, M. (1998). Development of juvenile aggression and violence: Some common misconceptions and controversies. *American Psychologist, 53*, 242–259.

Lykken, D. T. (1957). A study of anxiety in the sociopathic personality. *Journal of Abnormal and Social Psychology, 55*, 6–10.

Lyons-Ruth, K. (1996). Attachment relationships among children with aggressive behavior problems: The role of disorganized early attachment patterns. *Journal of Consulting and Clinical Psychology, 64*, 64–73.

Lyons-Ruth, K., Alpern, L., & Repacholi, B. (1993). Disorganised infant attachment classification and maternal psychosocial problems as predictors of hostile-aggressive behaviour in the preschool classroom. *Child Development, 64*, 572–585.

Mason, D. A., & Frick, P. J. (1994). The heritability of antisocial behavior: A meta-analysis of twin and adoption studies. *Journal of Psychopathology and Behavioral Assessment, 16*(4), 301–323.

McMahon, R. J., & Forehand, R. L. (2003). *Helping the noncompliant child: Family-based treatment for oppositional behavior*. New York, NY: Guilford Press.

Moffit, T. E. (1993). Adolescence-limited and life-course-persistent antisocial behaviour: A developmental taxonomy. *Psychological Review, 100,* 674–701.

Moffitt, T. E., Caspi, A., Rutter, M., & Silva, P. A. (2001). *Sex differences in antisocial behavior: Conduct disorder, delinquency, and violence in the Dunedin longitudinal study*. Cambridge, UK: Cambridge University Press.

Morash, M., & Rucker, L. (1989). An exploratory study of the connection of mother's age at child-bearing to her children's delinquency in four data sets. *Crime and Delinquency, 35,* 45–93.

Owens, E. B., & Shaw, D. S. (2003). Predicting growth curves of externalising behaviour across the preschool years. *Journal of Abnormal Child Psychology, 31,* 575–590.

Oxford, M., Cavell, T.A., & Hughes, J.N. (2003). Callous-unemotional traits moderate the relation between ineffective parenting and child externalizing problems: A partial replication and extension. *Journal of Clinical Child and Adolescent Psychology, 32,* 577–585.

Patterson, G. R. (1982). Coercive family process. Eugene, OR: Castalia Press.

Patterson, G., R., Reid, J. B., & Dishion, T. J. (1992). *A social learning approach: Volume 4. Antisocial boys*. Eugene, OR: Castalia.

Pettit, G. S., Bates, J. E., Dodge, K. A., & Meece, D. W. (1999). The impact of after-school peer contact on early adolescent externalising problems is moderated by parental monitoring, neighbourhood safety, and prior adjustment. *Child Development, 70,* 768–778.

Raine, A. (2002). Biosocial studies of antisocial and violent behaviour in children and adults: A review. *Journal of Abnormal Child Psychology, 30,* 311–326.

Reid, J. B., Patterson, G. R., & Snyder, J. J. (2002). *Antisocial behaviour in children and adolescents: A developmental analysis and model for intervention*. Washington, DC: American Psychological Association.

Rothbart, M. K. (1989). Temperament and development. In: G. Kohnstamm, J. Bates & M. K. Rothbart (Eds), *Temperament in childhood* (pp. 187–248).Chichester, ENG: Wiley.

Rothbart, M. K., Ahadi, S. A., & Hershey, K. L. (1994). Temperament and social behaviour in childhood. *Merrill-Palmer Quarterly, 40,* 21–39.

Rutter, M. L. (1997). Nature-nurture integration: The example of antisocial behaviour. *American Psychologist, 52,* 390–398.

Rutter, M. (2003). Commentary: Causal processes leading to antisocial behaviour. *Developmental Psychology, 39,* 372–378.

Rutter, M., Giller, H., & Hagell, A. (1998). *Antisocial behaviour by young people*. New York: Cambridge University Press.

Sanders, M. R., & Dadds, M. R. (1993). *Behavioral family intervention*. Needham Heights, MA, USA: Allyn & Bacon.

Seguin, J. R., Pihl, R. O., Boulerice, B., Tremblay, R. E., & Harden, P. (1996). Pain sensitivity and stability in physical aggression in boys. *Journal of Child Psychology and Psychiatry, 37,* 823–834.

Shaw, D. S., & Bell, R. Q. (1993). Developmental theories of parental contributors to antisocial behaviour. *Journal of Abnormal Child Psychology, 21,* 493–518.

Shaw, D. S., Bell, R. Q., & Gilliom, M. (2000). A truly early starter model of antisocial behaviour revisited. *Clinical Child and Family Psychology Review, 3,* 155–172.

Snyder, J., & Stoolmiller, M. (2002). Reinforcement and coercive mechanisms in the development of antisocial behavior. The family. In: J. Reid, G. Patterson & J. Snyder (Eds), *Antisocial behavior in children and adolescents: A developmental analysis and model for intervention* (pp. 65–100). Washington, DC: American Psychological Association.

Spieker, S. J., Larson, N. C., Lewis, S. M., Keller, T. E., & Gilchrist, L. (1999). Developmental trajectories of disruptive behaviour problems in preschool children of adolescent mothers. *Child Development, 70*, 443–458.

Strassberg, Z., Dodge, K., Petit, G. S., & Bates, J. E. (1994). Spanking in the home and children's subsequent aggression toward kindergarten peers. *Development and Psychopathology, 6*, 445–461.

Thomas, A., & Chess, S. (1977). *Temperament and development*. New York: Brunner/Mazel.

Wahler, R. G. (1997). On the origins of children's compliance and opposition: Family context, reinforcement and rules. *Journal of Child and Family Studies, 6*, 191–208.

Webster-Stratton, C., & Hancock, L. (1998). Parent training for young children with conduct problems: Content, methods, and therapeutic processes. In: C. E. Schaefer (Ed.), *Handbook of parent training* (pp. 98–152). New York, NY: Wiley.

Wolf, D. (Producer). (1990). *Law and order* [Television series]. New York: NBC.

Wolchik, S. A., Wilcox, K. L., Tein, J. -Y., & Sandler, I. N. (2000). Maternal acceptance and consistency of discipline as buffers of divorce stressors on children's adjustment problems. *Journal of Abnormal Child Psychology, 28*, 87–102.

Wootton, J. M., Frick, P. J., Shelton, K. K., & Silverthorn, P. (1997). Ineffective parenting and childhood conduct problems: The moderating role of callous-unemotional traits. *Journal of Consulting and Clinical Psychology, 65*(2), 292–300.

Youngblade, L. M., & Belsky, J. (1992). Parent-child antecedents of five-year-olds' close friendships: A longitudinal analysis. *Developmental Psychology, 1*, 107–121.

Chapter 6

Attention-Deficit/Hyperactivity Disorder (ADHD) and the Family: A Developmental Psychopathology Perspective

Eric J. Mash and Charlotte Johnston

Attention-deficit/hyperactivity disorder (ADHD) is a severe and often long-lasting condition affecting approximately 4–6% of children (American Psychiatric Association, 2000), and associated with a variety of co-occurring disorders and impairments (Barkley, in press). Although many advances have been made in understanding the biological underpinnings (e.g. Heiser et al., 2004; Levy & Hay, 2001) and cognitive deficits of ADHD (e.g. Barkley, 1997a; Sergeant, 2000), far less is known about its psychosocial aspects, particularly how ADHD characteristics interact with the family environment.

Families of children with ADHD have been studied for some time (e.g. Battle & Lacey, 1972). However, the importance of this research has diminished in the wake of a growing view of ADHD as a predominantly genetic/neurobiological disorder, an emphasis on its behavioral and cognitive deficits, and findings that family-focused interventions often are not as powerful as stimulant medications (Smith, Barkley, & Shapiro, 2006). We argue that the prevailing focus on genetic/neurobiological influences in ADHD has impeded our understanding of the ways in which family factors may operate on the development and expression of ADHD and, in a transactional sense, how the disorder impacts on important family subsystems such as parent–child, marital, and sibling relationships, the relationships among these subsystems, and the family as a whole (Parke, 2004). As a result, many questions concerning the interplay between family influences and ADHD remain unanswered, and the potential for a greater understanding of ADHD and its treatment is lost. Nor do we fully understand the extent to which family difficulties are specific to ADHD or related to frequently co-occurring disorders such as child conduct problems or parent psychopathology.

Even more disconcerting than the lack of descriptive knowledge regarding families and ADHD, developmental conceptualizations of how family factors are related to ADHD have been neglected. The developmental mechanisms that underlie the associations between ADHD and family factors, or the pathways through which child and family characteristics transact to exert their influences over time on the development and maintenance of ADHD and related problems have yet to be elaborated. Further, little is known about

Psychopathology and the Family
Edited by J. L. Hudson and R. M. Rapee
Copyright © 2005 by Elsevier Ltd.
All rights of reproduction in any form reserved
ISBN: 0-08-044449-0

possible moderators of the relationship between ADHD and family factors, for example, gender, culture, adversity, and ADHD subtype, and even less about possible mediators. Importantly, an explicit conceptual framework(s) for understanding the interplay between family factors and ADHD has yet to be proposed, although several implicit theories can be extracted from current research.

We begin this chapter by highlighting several frameworks that have been suggested or implied for understanding the role of family influences in ADHD. This is done using a developmental psychopathology (DP) framework (Rutter & Sroufe, 2000) that suggests several pathways through which family factors may be linked to ADHD, and is consistent with a recent trend to integrate a DP approach with a family systems perspective (Davies & Cicchetti, 2004). We see such an overarching framework as a needed tool for integrating existing research and for advancing research to a more sophisticated level that incorporates developmental and dynamic features in explaining the associations between family factors and childhood ADHD. This is followed by a selective review of findings regarding the associations between ADHD and family characteristics, where we briefly consider evidence that speaks to particular pathways of influence within a DP framework. Next, we comment on the role of the family in the treatment of ADHD. We close the chapter with conclusions and recommendations for future research.

Conceptualizing ADHD in the Context of the Family

A DP framework for conceptualizing ADHD in the context of the family is grounded in key concepts related to family socialization processes and development. Among these are the need to view the family as a social system, the role of direct and indirect family influences, affect and cognition as central processes in family relationships, and the need to examine different units of analysis (e.g. parent–child, sibling, marital, whole family) (Parke, 2004). A DP framework provides predictions of how ADHD characteristics develop over time, and how multiple risk and protective factors, including biology and family environment, transact to impact this development (Johnston & Mash, 2001; Rutter & Sroufe, 2000). Such a model allows for the possibility that, across children and time, various influences weigh differently in the development of the disorder. At one extreme, there may be children for whom ADHD is predominantly determined early in development by genetic/neurobiological factors, with a relatively lesser role for subsequent contributions from family or environmental influences. At another extreme, a high-risk family environment may function as the primary determinant of ADHD symptoms, when combined with minimal child predisposition. In either case, the child's nature and the family environment are likely to exert interactive influences.

The individual characteristics and circumstances of each child will result in unique patterns and strengths of mutual influence operating in the development and expression of ADHD symptomatology. Indeed, most experts agree that the heterogeneity of ADHD suggests multiple causal pathways, with genes and environment interacting in a multitude of ways to produce the behavioral profile characteristic of the disorder (Campbell, 2000; Nigg, Goldsmith, & Sachek, 2004; Sonuga-Barke, 2002). Within this DP framework several specific pathways are suggested in which family factors play a somewhat different role.

The Family as a Carrier of a Biological Predisposition to ADHD

Many suggest that the most common pathway to ADHD development is one in which children are born with a genetic, or perhaps congenitally acquired, predisposition to ADHD (e.g. Gillis, Gilger, Pennington, & DeFries, 1992; Milberger, Biederman, Faraone, Guite, & Tsuang, 1997). The genetic predisposition is seen as relatively strong, with heritability estimates averaging about 70–80% (e.g. Levy & Hay, 2001; Thapar, 2003). However, most agree that genetics are seldom the sole cause of ADHD as MZ twin concordance rates do not approach 100% (Faraone & Biederman, 2000; Kuntsi & Stevenson, 2000) and up to 50% of children with ADHD do not show the biological abnormality presumed to be inherited (Swanson et al., 1998).

With respect to prenatal/congenital factors, the strongest and most consistent support has been found for an association between maternal cigarette smoking during pregnancy and child ADHD (Kotimaa et al., 2003; Linnet et al., 2003). Maternal alcohol consumption before birth may also lead to inattention, hyperactivity, impulsivity, and associated impairments in learning and behavior (Mick, Biederman, Faraone, Sayer, & Kleinman, 2002), but it is less reliably documented as a risk factor for child ADHD than maternal smoking (Linnett et al., 2003). It is important to keep in mind that exposure to these risk factors is not randomly assigned and therefore could be related to ADHD or other confounding factors in the parent or child, which are both environmentally and genetically mediated. For example, mothers of children with ADHD use more alcohol, tobacco, and drugs than control parents, even when they are not pregnant (Mick et al., 2002). In addition, since parental substance use is often associated with a chaotic home environment both before and after birth, it is difficult to disentangle the influence of substance abuse and other factors that occur prior to birth, from the cumulative impact of a negative family environment that occurs during later development.

The Family as a Repository of Shared Genetic Risk

In another pathway linking child predispositions and family risk factors, ADHD may represent a shared genetic risk among family members. This framework receives support from studies showing a familial aggregation of the disorder (Epstein et al., 2000; Faraone et al., 2001). In this case, the dynamics between family variables and child ADHD are influenced not only by the child's predisposition and the stress it places on the family, but also by shared genetic characteristics of parent, child, and other relatives (Biederman et al., 1995a). Sorting the relative contributions of such shared versus non-shared genetic and environmental risks within the families of children with ADHD requires a level of methodological sophistication seldom encountered in existing research.

Family Experience as a Biological/Developmental Programmer of ADHD

Most often the effects of parenting and family environment are assumed to manifest at the level of changes in the child's phenotype or behavioral display. However, characteristics of the family environment may also, during windows of development, function to create changes in the child's biological make-up in brain regions identified to be important in genetic/neurobiological models of ADHD. Referred to as biological or developmental programming, biological systems are presumed to adapt to environmental input during sensitive periods of development (O'Conner, 2003). For example, in the case of ADHD, Taylor (1999) has speculated that not only is the effect of experience seen at the level of the child's psychological or cognitive processing, but that such experience also is inevitably represented in the structure, function, and organization of the neurological processes that underlie the behavioral manifestations. In light of possible associations between early parenting, prefrontal cortex regulatory deficits characteristic of ADHD, and behavioral manifestations of ADHD, it has also been postulated that parenting may serve to moderate and mediate the relation between prefrontal regulation and later ADHD (Morell & Murray, 2003), possibly by producing direct changes in the underlying neurological processes.

Although biological programming during prenatal development has been considered as a source of environmental influence in ADHD, the literature has been silent or rejected a pathway based on post-natal family experience. As yet there are no data that speak directly to this pathway in the realm of ADHD, however, research in other areas of child psychopathology, for example depression (Dawson et al., 1999) and child maltreatment (Teicher, Anderson, Polcari, Anderson, & Navalta, 2002), suggests that early family experiences may impact on stress and emotion regulating systems during sensitive periods in ways that create an ongoing biological risk for later disorders. Whether family experiences also impact directly on these or other brain systems to reduce or increase risk for ADHD has not yet been studied.

Family Disturbances as Secondary to ADHD

Even in a pathway that assumes a strong biological predisposition to ADHD, family environment may play an important role in the development, manifestation, and outcome of the disorder. The stressful, demanding, and intrusive nature of the child's ADHD characteristics are likely to evoke negative reactions from other family members, and exert a disruptive influence on family relationships and on the psychological functioning of parents, which may in turn negatively affect the child's development. This type of disruptive influence of ADHD on the developing parent–child subsystem is suggested by findings of an association between child ADHD and insecure attachment (Clarke, Ungerer, Chahaud, Johnson, & Stiefel, 2002). Thus, in this commonly accepted path, difficulties in families of children with ADHD are seen as originally driven by, and secondary to, characteristics of the disorder (Mash & Johnston, 1990).

The Family as a Mediator/Moderator of ADHD Outcomes

Even if family difficulties are seen primarily as the result of shared genetic vulnerabilities, or as consequences of ADHD, it is inevitable that family circumstances will interact in a transactional and ongoing manner with child characteristics. Here, there is less common ground in the assumptions made about the pathways these reciprocal transactions trace over development. In one possible route, family dysfunction, whether evoked by the child or perhaps related to the parents' own ADHD symptoms, may serve as a risk factor that interacts with child predisposition to exacerbate the presentation and continuity of ADHD symptoms. In this pathway, family factors become linked to ADHD, not as an original cause, but as an amplifying and maintaining influence over the course of development. In some instances, a child may have relatively little predisposition to the disorder, but an inconsistent, disorganized, chaotic, or unresponsive family environment associated with parental ADHD or other forms of parental psychopathology, extreme poverty, or adverse environmental circumstances (e.g. maltreatment, institutional upbringing) would serve to exacerbate inattentive, impulsive, and hyperactive child behaviors to a clinically significant level (e.g. Kreppner, O'Connor, Rutter, & the English and Romanian Adoptees Study Team, 2001; Litt, 2004; Roy, Rutter, & Pickles, 2004; St. Sauver et al., 2004).

To the extent that responsive, sensitive parenting behaviors form the foundation for the development of child self-regulation skills (e.g. Greenberg, Speltz, & DeKlyen, 1993; Kochanska, 1993), parental difficulties in tracking child behavior and synchronizing their actions to the child's needs may be the mediating mechanisms that account for the development of disinhibited, poorly regulated behavior in some children. Obviously, child and family characteristics operate in tandem as it is the difficult infant temperament antecedents of inattention and impulsivity that are most likely to create or exacerbate parents' difficulties in reading and responding sensitively to the infant (Putnam, Sanson, & Rothbart, 2002). It is also the case that the parent's own ADHD symptoms may be associated with such parenting difficulties even in the absence of a challenging infant temperament. In support of this, some studies have found that family adversity during infancy (and the likely disruptions in parenting that are known to accompany it) is a better predictor of later childhood symptoms of ADHD than a difficult infant temperament (Becker, Holtmann, Laucht, & Schmidt, 2004). If insensitive or unresponsive parenting is confirmed to be a better predictor of later symptoms of ADHD than early child temperament, it is possible that the heritability of ADHD is much lower during infancy than at later ages, and that environmental influences play a greater role at this younger age (Morrell & Murray, 2003). However, the current lack of information about ADHD during the first few years of life makes testing these hypotheses quite difficult. Further study of early risk factors for ADHD will be necessary if this pathway is to be investigated.

In an alternate pathway, it is possible that there are extremely responsive, sensitive, and resilient family environments that serve as protective factors that facilitate the child's development of self-regulation and may attenuate or even terminate ADHD symptoms in children with a biological predisposition for the disorder. For example, in one study, maternal warmth was found to moderate the association between low birth weight and ADHD symptoms at age 5, but not the association between low birth weight and IQ (Tully, Arseneault, Caspi, Moffitt, & Morgan, 2004). Interestingly, given the age at which ADHD is most commonly identified (when the child begins school), children in this developmental pathway will not be represented in clinical or even community samples of children who are identified on the basis of ADHD symptomatology. As such, this developmental pathway, while offering the most promise for prevention or early intervention, remains only a hypothetical possibility.

The Family as a Mediator/Moderator of Co-Occurring Conduct Problems and other Difficulties

Other authors have emphasized that family environments exert their influence, not on ADHD symptoms *per se*, but on the development of co-occurring conduct problems (Moffitt, 1990). Here, pathways are proposed whereby the child's ADHD interacts with family factors and parenting practices to create, or prevent, the development of conduct problems (Loeber, Green, Lahey, Frick, & McBurnett, 2000). These pathways predict links between family factors and conduct problems, with ADHD placed in the role of a risk factor or vulnerability (Hawes & Dadds, this volume; Taylor, Chadwick, Heptinstall, & Danckaerts, 1996). ADHD may pose this risk through at least two mechanisms, probably operating simultaneously: (1) the presence of impulsivity and inattention make the child more susceptible to the less than optimal parenting practices associated with conduct problems (e.g. inconsistent discipline, poor monitoring of child behavior), and (2) the child's ADHD acts as the stressor that triggers a breakdown in appropriate parenting and the use of more harsh or reactive forms of discipline.

In summary, a DP framework reveals a number of different pathways through which family factors may be associated with the development of ADHD and other accompanying problems. Distinctions among the pathways rest on a variety of assumptions regarding the genetic versus environmental etiology of ADHD, the primacy of ADHD versus other problems (e.g. conduct problems), the presence or absence of an influence of family environment on ADHD presentation, and the point in time and mechanisms through which family influences may operate. With these various pathways and assumptions in mind, we next consider research on the family characteristics of children with ADHD.

Family Relationships and ADHD

Parent–Child Relationships

A number of studies have used parent reports to assess aspects of family functioning such as communication or conflict (Mash & Johnston, 1996) and to describe parenting practices including discipline and child-rearing attitudes (Johnston, Scoular, & Ohan, 2004). Across community and clinic-referred samples of preschool and school-aged boys and (to a lesser extent) girls, parents of children with ADHD report more stressful and conflicted family environments (e.g. Biederman et al., 1999; Burt, Krueger, McGue, & Iacono, 2003; DuPaul, McGoey, Eckert, & VanBrakle, 2001; Edwards, Barkley, Laneri, Fletcher, & Metevia, 2001), poorer parenting practices (Shelton et al., 1998), more parental criticism (Daley, Sonuga-Barke, & Thompson, 2003; Peris & Hinshaw, 2003), and less authoritative parenting beliefs (Hinshaw, Zupan, Simmel, Nigg, & Melnick, 1997) as compared to parents of non-problem children. However, such differences are not always found (e.g. Byrne, DeWolfe, & Bawden, 1998; Cunningham, Benness, & Siegel, 1988; Cunningham & Boyle, 2002) and the correlational and cross-sectional nature of these studies provide little evidence as to the developmental pathways that may underlie the linkages.

The importance of considering conduct problems as distinct from ADHD has been recognized since Paternite, Loney, and Langhorne (1976) reported that family variables such as SES and parenting style were more strongly associated with child aggression than with symptoms of ADHD. Although these findings have been replicated (e.g. Seipp & Johnston, 2005; Taylor, Schachar, Thorley, & Wieselberg, 1986), not all studies are consistent. For example, Stormont-Spurgin and Zentall (1996) compared clinic-referred children with ADHD, aggression, and children with no problems. Although ADHD was associated with disturbances in family functioning (i.e. in both ADHD groups, mothers used more punishment and fathers were more permissive than parents of non-problem boys were), differences between the comorbid and ADHD-only groups were not significant. Longitudinal designs assessing ADHD symptoms in community samples do suggest alternate pathways, whereby family difficulties, particularly in the early to middle school years, contribute to the development or continuation of conduct problems, but are unrelated to ADHD symptoms. For example, August, Realmuto, Joyce, and Hektner (1999) found mothers' discipline methods (as well as parental psychiatric history and general family adversity) to be predictive of the continuation of child oppositional defiant disorder (ODD), even with initial levels of ADHD and ODD controlled. However, these family factors were not predictive of the continuation of ADHD. Whether the discrepancy in findings across studies is due to the continuous versus categorical approach to ADHD, clinic versus community samples, or cross-sectional versus longitudinal designs, or some combination of these factors remains unknown.

Speaking to the potential interaction of child predisposition and family factors, August, MacDonald, Realmuto, and Skare (1996) found that family functioning was most important in predicting outcomes for children who were initially low on conduct problems, an interaction that did not emerge for child hyperactivity. In contrast, already established, more severe conduct problems and ADHD symptoms appear to override family influences in determining the child's outcome at a later age (Colder, Lochman, & Wells, 1997). Clearly, more longitudinal research is needed to test the mutual influences of family factors, ADHD, and conduct problems over time and to trace differences in developmental pathways for children with different symptom profiles. Such research will need to begin tracking development at as early an age as possible, in order to clarify the contributions of family functioning to the onset versus the maintenance of these child problems.

Parent–child interaction difficulties in families of children with ADHD have been observed from preschool age through adolescence. In general, compared to controls, mothers of children with ADHD are more directive and negative and less socially interactive, and children with ADHD are less compliant and more negative (e.g. Barkley, Karlsson, & Pollard, 1985; Campbell, Breaux, Ewing, Szumowski, & Pierce, 1986; Cunningham & Barkley, 1979). These difficulties are particularly pronounced with younger children (Mash & Johnston, 1982). Conflicted interactions have been observed for both boys and girls with ADHD (Befera & Barkley, 1985) and in interactions with both mothers and fathers (Tallmadge & Barkley, 1983). Other observational studies have focused on more molar aspects of parenting behavior. For example, compared to mothers of non-problem boys, Winsler (1998) rated mothers of boys with ADHD as having poorer quality of scaffolding during a teaching task, including a failure to modify task demands and assistance to be appropriate to the child's skill. Extending observations to include triadic mother–father–child interactions, Buhrmester, Camparo, Christensen, Gonzalez, and Hinshaw (1992) observed more aversive discussions of common child-rearing problems in families of sons with ADHD versus non-problem sons. In summary, observational studies consistently find high levels of negative and controlling behaviors in both parents and their children with ADHD. Although these difficulties have been observed across a range of child ages, there is some evidence that the interaction problems are most severe for young boys interacting with their mothers. However, in the absence of longitudinal designs, this cross-sectional evidence of diminishing problems across child age is at best suggestive of a developmental pathway where, as the symptoms of ADHD, particularly high impact behaviors such as overactivity and impulsiveness, lessen with age (Hart, Lahey, Loeber, Applegate, & Frick, 1995), parents may respond with less directive and controlling interactions. Alternately, it also is possible that a history of unsuccessful parental efforts to control child behavior leads to a reduction of parental control efforts and a disengagement from parent–child interactions, a strategy that may have short-term benefits for the parent but long-term costs for both the parent and the child.

Observations of parent–child interactions in children with ADHD with and without comorbid conduct problems yield somewhat mixed findings. Both Johnston (1996) and Gomez and Sanson (1994) observed mother–child interactions in school-aged children with ADHD, ADHD+conduct problems, and non-problem groups, and found, as predicted, the highest levels of negative child behavior in the comorbid group, followed by the ADHD group, with the control children showing the lowest levels of negative behaviors. However, in the Johnston study, neither mother nor father behavior differed across the three groups, and parents in both ADHD groups reported poorer parenting strategies than parents of non-problem children. In contrast, in the Gomez and Sanson study, mothers in the comorbid group were the most directive and negative and least rewarding, and control mothers and mothers of ADHD-only children did not differ. Similarly, among boys with ADHD, Johnston, Murray, Hinshaw, Pelham, and Hoza (2002) found that observed maternal responsiveness and sensitivity to the child were negatively associated with child conduct problems but not with child symptoms of ADHD. Finally, using a longitudinal design and a community sample of high-risk children, Shaw, Owens, Giovannelli, and Winslow (2001) found that boys at age 6 who had comorbid ADHD+ODD/conduct disorder (CD) had mothers who were observed to be more rejecting (as well as depressed and aggressive) when the child was 2 years old than the mothers of children with ADHD or no problems.

Findings from these and other studies of ADHD children with and without conduct problems suggest a continuum of disturbance, with the highest levels of parent–child conflict in the presence of child conduct problems, but with ADHD alone also being associated with elevations in parent–child difficulties. However, cross-sectional observational assessments of parent–child interactions offer limited insight into how and when child ADHD, conduct problems, or both may be linked to these interactions. The few longitudinal studies that have been reported are most consistent with a developmental pathway through which family problems contribute more to the development of child conduct problems than to ADHD symptomatology. However, the heterogeneity of results across studies suggests that multiple pathways are operative in the relationships between ADHD, conduct problems, and parent–child interactions, and it remains to determine the characteristics of the children and families who follow the different pathways.

Sibling Relationships

Although research is limited, siblings of children with ADHD have been found to be at high risk for psychopathology and functional impairments (Biederman, Faraone, & Monuteaux, 2002; Faraone, Biederman, Mennin, Gershon, & Tsuang, 1996). In addition, Mash and Johnston (1983b) found that interactions between children with ADHD and their siblings were characterized by greater conflict than those of non-problem sibling dyads, and that conflict in ADHD child/sibling interactions was associated with greater parenting stress in the mothers of these children (Mash & Johnston, 1983c). In qualitative studies, siblings of children with ADHD report being negatively affected by their ADHD sibling, and feeling victimized, displaced in their home, and constantly on guard (Kendall, 1999). Further study of sibling relationships will help to broaden our understanding of the impact of ADHD across family members and settings, and comparisons of parents' interactions with children with ADHD and their non-affected siblings may offer insight into the transactional effects that are unique to interactions with ADHD children. In addition, a better understanding of sibling relationships may provide more effective ways of helping parents manage the sibling conflict that occurs in families of a child with ADHD (Johnston & Freeman, 1998). Since siblings of children with ADHD carry a genetic risk for ADHD themselves (Levy, Hay, McLaughlin, Wood, & Waldman, 1996), the extent to which their difficulties are related to their own ADHD, or to the indirect effects of growing up with a sibling with ADHD, or to some combination, is not known.

Marital Relationships

Marital conflict has the potential for both direct (e.g. modeling) and indirect (e.g. inconsistent parenting) influences on children (Emery, 1992) and has been investigated as a correlate of childhood ADHD. Parents of children with ADHD report less marital satisfaction and more marital conflict than those of non-problem children, across a range of child ages and levels of severity (e.g. Befera & Barkley, 1985; Brown & Pacini, 1989; Murphy & Barkley, 1996). Further, in families of children with ADHD, parental disagreement about childrearing has been found to be associated with more child behavior problems, greater marital conflict, and lower levels of marital adjustment (Harvey, 2000). Marital functioning also has been found to be impaired in families where a parent has ADHD, regardless of the gender of the parent (Minde et al., 2003). However, not all studies have reported marital difficulties in families of children with ADHD. For example, Szatmari, Offord, and Boyle (1989) found that, in a community sample, parents of children who met criteria for ADHD did not report more marital problems than controls. Similarly, although Camparo, Christensen, Buhrmester, and Hinshaw (1994) found that parents of sons with ADHD blamed their sons more for family problems, reports of marital functioning did not differ between these families and controls. Thus, although most evidence suggests a link between ADHD and marital dysfunction, the findings are not entirely consistent.

Can the inconsistencies in the link between marital functioning and child ADHD be accounted for by co-occurring conduct problems? Suggesting that they can, Barkley, Anastopoulos, Guevremont, and Fletcher (1992) reported poorer marital adjustment in parents of adolescents with ADHD and ODD than in parents of children with ADHD alone or controls. Similarly, Lindahl (1998) found that, in general, parents of boys with ODD and ADHD+ODD had more marital difficulties than parents of non-problem boys, who did not differ from parents of boys with ADHD. In contrast to these studies, others have not found differences in marital variables between ADHD and comorbid groups (e.g. Barkley, McMurray, Edelbrock, & Robbins, 1989; Johnston, 1996; Schachar & Wachsmuth, 1991). Inconsistent findings in this area preclude firm conclusions regarding associations between either ADHD or conduct symptoms and marital difficulties in families of children with ADHD. These inconsistencies also suggest caution in assuming that marital dysfunction is exclusively related to comorbid conduct problems in families of children with ADHD. Further studies incorporating longitudinal designs are needed to inform our understanding of how this aspect of family functioning interacts with ADHD over development.

Associations between Family Relationships and ADHD

Although the preponderance of evidence suggests relationship disturbances in the families of children with ADHD, particularly those with comorbid conduct problems, findings are far from conclusive. Beyond this problem of limited evidence regarding the degree and dimensions of family functioning that are problematic in families of children with ADHD, important questions remain regarding the mechanisms and developmental processes that operate to determine the differential associations that exist. Below, we highlight research that has investigated the direction of influence in the association between family relationships and child ADHD.

Studies of the early influence of families and parenting on ADHD have used longitudinal designs to examine the relationship over time. Carlson, Jacobvitz, and Sroufe (1995), in a sample of lower socioeconomic status (SES) families, found that maternal insensitivity and over-stimulating or non-responsive physical intimacy during infancy predicted both distractible and hyperactive child behavior during the early school years, even with the effects of early child temperament controlled. Interestingly, the influence of parenting on ADHD was greatest at the youngest ages, suggesting a developmental pathway where family influences on ADHD may diminish over time. These findings replicated previous reports that boys who experienced enmeshing boundary disturbances (mothers turning to their children for intimacy) at 24 and 48 months were more likely to develop inattentive, overactive, and impulsive symptoms of ADHD in kindergarten and grade school (Jacobvitz & Sroufe, 1987; Sroufe & Jacobvitz, 1989). In another longitudinal study, mostly middle class families of non-problem children were observed interacting at home during a series of everyday tasks (Jacobvitz, Hazan, Curran, & Hitchens, 2004). Enmeshed patterns at 24 months were found to predict ADHD symptoms at age 7 for boys, but not girls (for girls, enmeshment was associated with later symptoms of depression). In addition, hostile family interactions (e.g. demeaning, overly critical, sarcastic comments) at 24 months predicted the child's teacher-rated symptoms of ADHD at 7 years. Also supporting the relation between early family factors and later ADHD symptoms, Becker et al. (2004) found that both negativity in the mother–infant interaction and family adversity at 3 months of age predicted later symptoms of ADHD during childhood.

Longitudinal studies by Campbell and colleagues also provide information regarding the temporal ordering of parenting and child ADHD and conduct problems (Campbell, 1994; Campbell, Breaux, Ewing, & Szumowski, 1986; Campbell & Ewing, 1990; Pierce, Ewing, & Campbell, 1999). Following two groups of parent-identified problem preschoolers to age 13, these reports indicated that, with a few exceptions, family adversity (e.g. social class, maternal depression, parenting stress) and more negative and directive maternal behavior when the child was 3 predicted the continuation of both hyperactive and aggressive symptoms in the children, independent of the initial level of the child's symptoms. Interestingly, family problems also predicted the emergence of both hyperactive and aggressive symptoms in the control sample of initially non-problem children. In contrast to these findings, Wakschlag and Hans (1999), in a high-risk sample of African American children followed to age 10, reported that a lack of maternal responsiveness in mother–infant interactions predicted the child's subsequent ODD and CD, but not ADHD, after controlling for concurrent parenting and a variety of biological and family risk factors. Finally, using a prospective design, Morrell and Murray (2003) investigated early processes involved in the development of hyperactivity and CD from 2 months to 8 years. Two developmental trajectories were identified, one in which emotional dysregulation at 9 months predicted conduct problems at 5 and 8 years, and another in which delayed object reaching times predicted hyperactivity at 5 years. These different pathways were strongly influenced by different patterns of early parenting and infant gender, and continuity between early infant behaviors and later childhood symptoms was partially mediated by parenting for conduct problems, but not for hyperactivity.

In sum, longitudinal studies support the role of parenting in the origins of both ADHD and conduct problems, although findings are inconclusive regarding whether or not ADHD and conduct problems share the same or different interactive patterns with parenting and family factors. In addition, these studies remind us that family problems confer a universal risk for the development of child problems and are not specific to children identified as having ADHD.

Studies of the effects of behavioral parent management training (PMT) also speak to the influence of parenting behavior on ADHD. As we will discuss in a later section, changing parenting behavior reduces conduct problems among children with ADHD (e.g. Pollard, Ward, & Barkley, 1983; Strayhorn & Weidman, 1989); however, this treatment appears less likely to alter ADHD symptoms (e.g. Pisterman et al., 1989). Even when effects on ADHD symptoms are found, they are typically weak (e.g. MTA Cooperative Group, 1999a). Thus, although changes in parent behavior can exert an effect on both conduct problems and ADHD symptoms, these studies are most consistent with a pathway in which parenting factors are most influential in altering the course of child conduct problems. Although informative, these treatment outcome studies do not speak to the origin of conduct problems in children with ADHD, and few have focused on the treatment of very young children where changes in parenting styles may play a larger role in altering symptoms of ADHD.

Turning to the influence of child ADHD on family functioning, there are several demonstrations of the effects of medicating the child with ADHD on parenting behavior. Studies have found that children with ADHD are more compliant and mothers are less directive when the children are medicated compared to on placebo (e.g. Barkley, 1988, 1989; Barkley & Cunningham, 1979; Barkley, Karlsson, Pollard, & Murphy, 1985; Barkley, Karlsson, Strzelecki, & Murphy, 1984). Demonstrated with both school-aged and preschool boys and girls, these findings provide support for a child-to-parent effect. Although influential, the importance assigned to these studies must be tempered by methodological and theoretical limitations. Concerns include the short-term nature of the child's medication status (typically 1–2 weeks), the artificial nature of the laboratory inter- actions and child confederates, the relatively small sample sizes, the failure to differenti- ate changes in ADHD versus conduct problem symptoms, and the inconsistency of the effects across measures and situations. Further research is needed to address questions of ecological validity, such as whether the same medication-induced changes in parent–child interactions would appear in more naturalistic settings and would maintain over longer periods. Conceptually, it must also be remembered that the demonstration of a causal effect from child to parent behavior does not necessarily speak to the original cause of parent–child interaction problems in families of children with ADHD (Carlson et al., 1995). Nor does the demonstration of such an effect speak to the existence of other causes, or to the interactive effects of child and parent behavior over the course of time.

Family/Parenting Stress

In light of difficulties in family relationships, it is not surprising that parents of children with ADHD report more stress than comparison parents. Research in this area has relied heavily on the *Parenting Stress Index* (Abidin, 1986), which assesses stress across domains of child, parent, and interaction characteristics, and, in some versions, general life cir- cumstances. More than two decades ago, Mash and Johnston (1983a) reported that par- enting stress in all domains was significantly elevated in mothers of children with ADHD, particularly in mothers of preschool-age children. Similar elevations in parenting stress associated with ADHD have been demonstrated across child ages, for both boys and girls, for children with different levels of symptoms, and generally for both mothers and fathers (e.g. Beck, Young, & Tarnowski, 1990; Byrne et al., 1998; DuPaul et al., 2001; Shelton et al., 1998). Among mothers of children with ADHD, Harrison and Sofronoff (2002) found that, over and above the effects of demographics, the strongest predictors of parent- ing stress were: greater severity of child behavior problems and lower perceived control over child behaviors.

In addition to stress specific to the parenting role, studies have also examined general life stress or psychosocial adversity in families of children with ADHD (Overmeyer, Taylor, Blanz, & Schmidt, 1999). Although Murphy and Barkley (1996) found no differ- ences in negative life events between families of children with ADHD and controls, Biederman et al. (1995b) found that the odds ratio for ADHD increased significantly with increases in general family adversity (e.g. maternal psychopathology, low SES). In addi- tion, a longitudinal study by Becker et al. (2004) found that general family adversity in early infancy predicted later ADHD symptoms during childhood, more so than multiple infant regulatory problems.

Thus, in general, research has linked parenting stress and child ADHD, although the precise nature of this linkage and its specificity to ADHD has not been addressed. Few studies have examined the extent to which parenting stress is linked to ADHD versus co-occurring conduct problems. Anastopoulos, Guevremont, Shelton, and DuPaul (1992) reported that child aggression, severity of ADHD symptoms, child health status, and maternal psychopathology all accounted for significant variance in mothers' reports of parenting stress. However, subgroup analyses found higher levels of parenting stress in mothers of ADHD+ODD children than in mothers of ADHD children. Similarly, Podolski and Nigg (2001) compared ADHD and non-ADHD children and also found that children's conduct problems, hyperactivity, and inattention were all uniquely and positively related to parenting stress, and that both mothers and fathers were distressed by conduct problems over and above the distress related to ADHD severity. In addition, mothers but not fathers were distressed by their children's inattention, over and above the effects of conduct problems. Symptoms of hyperactivity did not, however, contribute to reports of distress over and above those related to conduct problems.

Parenting a child with ADHD in the context of family adversity, low income, and low levels of education presents special challenges and stressors (Litt, 2004). In the realm of general life stress or family adversity, much evidence suggests that in samples of children with ADHD these family factors are not exclusively tied to the presence of conduct problems. Neither Johnston (1996) and Leung et al. (1996) nor Barkley et al. (1989) reported differences in life stress between mothers of aggressive and non-aggressive children with ADHD. Although both Schachar and Tannock (1995) and Schachar and Wachsmuth (1991) found that families of CD and ADHD+CD children experienced more psychosocial adversity (e.g. poverty, unemployment, mental health problems) than pure ADHD or control groups, the latter study also found that families of children with only ADHD had more adversity than controls. However, in a longitudinal study of boys aged 5–13, Moffitt (1990) found that boys with ADHD+delinquency had greater family adversity than boys with ADHD only or controls, and Tiet et al. (2001) found that most adverse life events were related to childhood ODD and CD, but not to ADHD.

Associations between Family/Parenting Stress and ADHD

Despite knowledge of an association between child ADHD and parenting or family stress, our understanding of how this link functions is far from perfect. More than 10 years ago, Fischer (1990) and Mash and Johnston (1990) concluded that the most parsimonious explanation was that ADHD child characteristics led to parenting/family stress. This conclusion appears to stand, as do the acknowledgments that some association may result from a shared genetic substrate of parental and child psychopathology, that parental/family stress may exacerbate existing child problems, and that some of the effects of child behavior on stress may be indirectly mediated via marital discord.

However, there are also inconsistencies and weaknesses in the existing data. For example, Mash and Johnston (1983a) reported increased parenting stress among parents of younger compared to older children, which would seem to argue against a cumulative child effect. Also contrary to a child-effect explanation, Pisterman et al. (1992) reported that although parenting stress decreased following parent training, this decrease was not correlated with improvements in child behavior. Similarly, Wells et al. (2000) reported no differences in the effects of medication, behavioral, medication + behavioral, and community care treatments on parenting stress in families of children with ADHD, a surprising find-ing, given that the treatments differentially reduced difficult child behavior. Again, we would argue that a transactional conceptualization that acknowledges bidirectional links between child ADHD and family stress that unfold over time is needed. The challenge remains to design and conduct studies that will adequately test such a conceptualization and illuminate the pathways linking stress to both ADHD and conduct problems.

Parental Psychological Functioning

Depression and Anxiety

In general, both affective and anxiety disorders are more common in mothers of children with ADHD compared to those of non-problem boys (e.g. Befera & Barkley, 1985; Brown, Borden, Clingerman, & Jenkins, 1988; Cunningham & Boyle, 2002; Cunningham et al., 1988; Faraone et al., 1995). Results for fathers have been variable. Some studies have reported elevated levels of depression in fathers of children with ADHD, compared to those of children with developmental and learning disorders or non-problem controls (e.g. Brown et al., 1988), whereas other studies have reported no differences in paternal depres-sion across ADHD and non-problem groups (Cunningham et al., 1988). Thus, findings regarding the links between both maternal and paternal affective disorders and child ADHD are inconsistent. However, in a review of family studies of parental depression and child ADHD, Faraone and Biederman (1997) concluded that there is reasonable evidence for a familial association of parental depression and child ADHD. Although the link appears strongest in families of children with comorbid ADHD and CD (e.g. Chronis et al., 2003; Nigg & Hinshaw, 1998), most evidence also reveals an elevated risk of depression associated with ADHD alone.

Parental Alcohol Abuse and Antisocial Behavior

With regards to links of parental alcohol abuse to ADHD, findings are again mixed. In com-munity samples, Cadoret and Stewart (1991) did not find a relationship between alcoholism in the biological fathers and child ADHD, and neither did Szatmari et al. (1989) report more alcohol problems in families of children with ADHD versus controls. However, Martin et al. (1994) and Kuperman, Schlosser, Lidral, and Reich (1999) both found elevated rates of aggression, inattention, and impulsivity in the children whose father's histories were posi-tive for alcoholism, but no differences in hyperactivity. In addition, Cunningham et al. (1988) and Gadow et al. (2000) found that parents of ADHD children self-reported higher rates of alcohol consumption than parents of controls, although Gadow et al. found this only among parents of children with ADHD-combined subtype. With regards to comorbidity, an elevated risk for substance abuse among relatives of children with ADHD+CD, compared to children with ADHD+ODD, ADHD only, and normal controls has been reported (Faraone, Biederman, Keenan, & Tsuang, 1991), and in community samples, the associations between parental alcohol abuse and child ADHD appear weaker than those between alcohol abuse and conduct problems (Carbonneau et al., 1998). Looking beyond rates of alcohol use, Molina, Pelham, and Lang (1997) compared alcohol consumption and expectations for the effects of alcohol between parents of boys with ADHD and parents of non-problem boys. They found no differences in consumption or general expectancies for alcohol effects, however, mothers of children with ADHD believed that drinking would increase their negative interactions with their children and these expectancies accounted for significant variance in reports of alcohol consumed. This study also found that SES accounted for much of the difference in drinking behavior between the clinic and control groups, demonstrating the importance of controlling for demographic characteristics in this research.

Investigating the causal links between parental alcohol consumption, parenting behavior, and child ADHD and ODD/CD symptoms, Pelham et al. (1997) found that interacting with a child confederate trained to show both ADHD and CD symptoms increased stress and alcohol consumption, particularly for fathers and single mothers of non-problem children, although the same effects were not found in a sample of parents of children with ADHD and/or ODD/CD (Pelham et al., 1998). *Post hoc* analyses of findings from the latter study suggested that the failure to find effects was not due to child comorbidity, but that the effect was limited to parents with a family history of alcohol abuse. Finally, this group of investigators (Lang, Pelham, Atkeson, & Murphy, 1999) has demonstrated that alcohol consumption reduces parental attending, and increases commands, indulgences, and off-task comments. These studies strongly suggest a reciprocal pattern of effects whereby interacting with children with ADHD/conduct problems can induce higher levels of alcohol consumption in parents, at least among parents at risk for drinking problems. And, alcohol consumption leads to ineffective parenting behaviors that might elicit or exacerbate inattentive, impulsive, or hyperactive child behavior. Despite the elegance of these studies, ADHD and conduct problems in the children are confounded and further work is needed to examine the external validity of these analog findings and possible differential pathways linking ADHD versus conduct problems to parental drinking.

The studies addressing links between ADHD and parental antisocial behavior have all been careful to account for the presence of conduct problems. Most of these studies suggest that parental antisocial behavior is more strongly associated with conduct problems than with ADHD (Biederman, Munir, & Knee, 1987; Frick, Kuper, Silverthorn, & Cotter, 1995). However, Cadoret and Stewart (1991) did find that criminality in biological parents predicted ADHD in adopted boys, while psychiatric problems in the adoptive parents predicted conduct problems. Thus, although most findings link parental antisocial behavior to child conduct problems more strongly than to child ADHD, some inconsistencies have emerged. And again, existing studies yield little insight into the developmental pathways underlying the associations.

Parental Attention-Deficit/Hyperactivity Disorder

Several studies have documented elevated rates of ADHD in families of children with the disorder (e.g. Biederman et al., 1995a; Faraone, Biederman, & Milberger, 1994), and as many as 40–60% of children of adults with ADHD also have the disorder (Minde et al., 2003). These rates of ADHD in the children are much higher than reported in other studies of first-degree relatives of ADHD probands, suggesting that the adult form of ADHD may have a particularly strong familial etiology.

The high rate of ADHD among parents of children with the disorder suggests several mechanisms of association. Although there is likely a shared genetic element to the association, mechanisms at the psychological and environmental level, such as psychological distress and parenting practices, may amplify or attenuate the relationships. Studies such as those of Rucklidge and Kaplan (1997) or Weinstein, Apfel, and Weinstein (1998) have found more psychiatric and personality problems among mothers who had ADHD compared to mothers without ADHD, even though both groups were parenting a child with ADHD. Exposure to parental ADHD also has been found to predict higher levels of family conflict and lower levels of family cohesion relative to families without parental ADHD, independent of other psychopathological conditions in parents (Biederman et al., 2002). In considering the links between parental ADHD and the comorbidity of child ADHD and conduct problems, despite minor inconsistencies, most studies show an elevated risk of adult ADHD in families of children with ADHD, independent of the presence of child conduct problems (Biederman et al., 1987; Faraone et al., 1995; Loney, Paternite, Schwartz, & Roberts, 1997; Schachar &Wachsmuth, 1990).

Arnold, O'Leary, and Edwards (1997) report an interesting set of findings outlining how adult ADHD may interact with parenting skills. Among couples with clinic-referred children with ADHD, they found that father involvement predicted more ineffective parenting only when the father had symptoms of ADHD. One obvious interpretation of these findings is that fathers' ADHD actively impairs their ability to be consistent and effective parents. Consistent with this, Harvey, Danforth, McKee, Ulaszek, and Friedman (2003) also found disturbances in parenting for fathers and mothers with symptoms of ADHD. However, the types of parenting disturbances (e.g. laxness, argumentativeness, overreactivity) were different for fathers and mothers, and varied with the type and degree of the parent's ADHD symptoms and the point in time at which parenting was assessed (before or after treatment). These findings suggest that the relations between parental ADHD, parenting behaviors, and child behaviors are complex and there is a need for further research to understand the processes by which these factors affect one another.

In sum, ADHD appears strongly associated in parents and children, and ADHD in parents appears to confer specific impairments in parental functioning above and beyond the influence of child ADHD. Since ADHD in adults has been related to elevated levels of problems such as substance abuse, depression, unemployment, and relationship disruption, the presence of parental ADHD may be linked to the greater stress, limited methods of coping, and fewer resources often associated with childhood ADHD. In addition, specific cognitive/emotional deficits associated with adult ADHD such as ineffective decision making, difficulties in filtering out and forgetting irrelevant information, or gaze instability (Ernst et al., 2003; White & Marks, 2004) may have a negative effect on parenting practices particularly in the context of challenging infant and child behaviors. Parents of children with ADHD are faced with complex care needs including coordinating with schools, identifying and using special medical services, learning about their child's disorder and its management, and providing direct in-home care for their children. Parental ADHD, especially if coupled with low income or other social disadvantages, will contribute to making these tasks more difficult (Litt, 2004).

Discussion of the Link between Parental Psychological Functioning and ADHD

In summary, across multiple aspects of parental psychological functioning the strongest associations typically are found between parental maladjustment and child conduct problems. Although ADHD that is not comorbid with conduct problems shows weaker associations, it does remain linked to parental psychological functioning. In particular, parent ADHD appears associated with child ADHD, rather than with conduct problems. However, existing studies offer only preliminary suggestions regarding the mechanisms that underlie these associations and their development over time. What little evidence does exist regarding the pathways of development is consistent with transactional models of influence, with the effects of parental psychological functioning at least partially mediated via parenting behaviors. Much remains to be done to test these and alternate models of development before conclusions can be drawn regarding the how and why of the links between dimensions of parental psychopathology and child ADHD and conduct problems.

The Role of the Family in the Treatment of ADHD

The many links between ADHD and family difficulties suggest that careful consideration be given to the role of families in treatments for the disorder. The primary approach to treatment of ADHD includes three main elements, typically used in combination: psychopharmacological intervention, educational intervention, and behavioral PMT (Pelham, Wheeler, & Chronis, 1998). Although medications and educational interventions both require family involvement and likely impact on the family, they do not target changes in family functioning as a primary goal. In contrast, PMT focuses specifically on providing parents with methods for effectively managing their child's ADHD symptoms, particularly accompanying oppositional behaviors (Anastopoulos & Farley, 2003). However, until recently (Chronis, Chacko, Fabiano, Wymbs, & Pelham, 2004), most treatments for ADHD have not systematically focused on many of the disturbances in family functioning noted above, for example, marital problems, sibling conflict, parenting stress, and parental ADHD or depression.

PMT for ADHD follows from procedures originally developed for parents of children with conduct and oppositional problems (McMahon & Forehand, 2003) with adaptations and enhancements to target-specific characteristics and concerns of children with ADHD and their families (Barkley, 1997b; Chronis et al., 2004). Although details vary depending on the age of the child and mode of treatment delivery (e.g. Carpenter, Frankel, Marina, Duan, & Smalley, 2004; Gordon, 2000), PMT typically includes: providing information to parents about ADHD; helping parents to understand the child, parent, situational, and other factors that contribute to oppositional behavior; helping parents learn effective strategies for managing their child's misbehavior (e.g. enhanced attention for appropriate behavior, giving effective commands, time-out procedures); using a home–school behavior daily report card; and problem-solving skills for managing future misconduct. Treatments often include booster sessions to review progress and to make adjustments to the treatment as needed.

Chronis et al. (2004) reviewed 28 studies of behavioral PMT for more than 1000 children with ADHD. This and other reviews have found substantial support for the effectiveness of PMT for school-age clinic-referred children with ADHD, with respect to parent-rated improvements in child behaviors, and observed reductions in parent's negative behavior and children's aggressive and defiant behaviors (e.g. Anastopoulos, Shelton, DuPaul, & Guevremont, 1993; Bor, Sanders, Markie-Dadds, 2002; Pisterman et al., 1989; Sonuga-Barke, Daley, Thompson, Laver-Bradbury, & Weeks, 2001; Strayhorn & Weidman, 1989). These interventions also have been associated with improvements in other areas of family functioning including increases in parenting self-esteem and reductions in parenting stress (e.g. Anastopolous et al., 1993; Pisterman et al., 1992).

Despite these successes, controlled outcome studies of PMT for children with ADHD are relatively few in number, and most have failed to examine long-term effects, effectiveness with low SES or ethnic minority families, generalization to non-treatment settings, or whether levels of improvement in child functioning are associated with a normalization of child behavior and family functioning (Smith et al., 2006). In addition, PMT programs appear to have limited success in altering symptoms of ADHD relative to oppositional or conduct problems, when carried out with preschool-age children in community samples (Barkley et al., 2000), or in primary care settings when delivered by service providers without specialized training in ADHD (Sonuga-Barke, Thompson, Daley, & Laver-Bradbury, 2004). For example, Sonuga-Barke et al. (2004) reported high rates of attrition and *decreases* in maternal well being following PMT for mothers of 3-year-old children, perhaps related to the increasing demands of child behavior at this age (regardless of ADHD symptoms) or to the additional burden of treatment. Since PMT specifically targets child and family functioning, the expectation has been that PMT might provide incremental advantages over and above gains associated with the use of stimulant medications. Research has generally not supported this expectation (Abikoff et al., 2004; Hechtman et al., 2004). Perhaps the strongest test of possible incremental advantages associated with combined forms of intervention was the multimodal treatment study of children with ADHD (MTA) (MTA Cooperative Group, 1999a, b). However, the behavioral interventions that were included in the MTA study combined PMT with both classroom interventions and an intensive summer treatment program making it impossible to assess specific incremental advantages that would be uniquely associated with PMT. On the other hand, even when incremental advantages for combined interventions were found in the MTA study, they were relatively small. In addition, results from the MTA suggest that SES and other family characteristics are likely to moderate the effects of interventions and that research to determine what types of children/families benefit from what types of treatment is an area deserving of further research (Rieppi et al., 2002). Most treatment studies of children with ADHD have failed to consider that many of the parents involved in these programs may themselves have ADHD or other forms of psychopathology, or may struggle with issues such as stress and marital discord. These are important omissions, since difficulties such as high levels of maternal ADHD symptoms may make it considerably more difficult for parents to follow through on treatment, sustain attention during PMT sessions, or remember to administer their child's medication (Chronis et al., 2004), and may significantly limit improvements achieved through PMT (Sonuga-Barke, Daley, & Thompson, 2002).

Conclusions and Future Directions

Our discussion of ADHD and the family leads us to three main conclusions. First, there is substantial research that implicates the importance of family factors in ADHD. Although the precise nature of the links between family characteristics and childhood ADHD is not yet known, the cumulative evidence to date would strongly support the need to consider family influences in the development, expression, outcome, and treatment of ADHD. Second, across existing studies there is inconsistency in findings that will need to be clarified in future research if the links between ADHD, conduct problems, and family characteristics are to be understood. Third, and perhaps most importantly from a DP perspective, there is a lack of research about the developmental progression of ADHD or the processes that underlie the interplay among family characteristics, childhood ADHD, and child conduct problems. In the sections that follow, we briefly discuss each of these main conclusions.

Importance of Family Factors in ADHD

Research suggests that ADHD in the family, whether present in the child, parent, or as is most often the case in both, can have a significant negative impact on family relationships. Apart from whether these disruptions are the result of shared genetic risk or due to disturbances in family processes important to the development of healthy family functioning, or, whether they are specific to ADHD versus other co-occurring risk factors, the extent and nature of these disruptions compels us to take family characteristics into account when studying or treating children with ADHD and their families.

From studies of parent–child interactions, adult alcohol abuse, and parental ADHD there is reasonable evidence that child ADHD can influence parent behavior and adjustment, and also that parenting behavior can impact on the presentation, and possibly the development, of ADHD symptoms and co-occurring conduct problems. From family studies, there is also reasonable evidence of specificity in families' histories for ADHD and conduct problems. That is, parent and child ADHD appear to be associated, as do parent and child conduct problems. Findings are less certain as to whether other family characteristics, such as life stress, marital disturbance, or parental psychological characteristics such as depression are specific to ADHD or even consistently linked to its appearance.

Across all research, a general impression is formed of a continuum of association, with family characteristics most strongly linked to child conduct problems, but also linked to child ADHD. However, the number of unsupportive or inconclusive studies seriously limits these conclusions. Preliminary findings from a small number of longitudinal studies suggest that disturbances in parenting during infancy may be related to later ADHD symptoms, and that this association may be stronger than those found between parenting and ADHD symptoms in older children. Although speculative at this time, it is possible that family influences may play a larger role during sensitive periods of early development, but less so after patterns of ADHD and conduct problems become more firmly established at both the behavioral and possibly the structural and functional neurobiological level of organization.

Inconsistencies in Findings

The research presented in this chapter indicates many inconsistencies and gaps in our knowledge of the families of children with ADHD. Some studies find no associations between family characteristics and either ADHD or conduct problems, others find ADHD and conduct problems are equally associated with family factors, and yet others show stronger associations between family factors and ADHD than conduct problems. Such inconsistencies are not easily explained and appear across multiple dimensions of family functioning. Caution needs to be exercised in drawing conclusions, and more research is needed before statements regarding which family factors are and are not associated with child ADHD, conduct problems, or both can be made with confidence. Methodological and theoretical conundrums might offer some explanation for the inconsistent findings that characterize this area. For example, measures of family functioning and measures of child symptomatology are often both based on parent reports, allowing for possible rater biases. Other methodological concerns arise in studies comparing ADHD and comorbid ADHD-conduct problem groups, including whether ADHD symptom severity is equivalent across groups and whether the comorbidity reflects one condition at different developmental stages, an additive combination of the two disorders, or a distinct condition associated with unique correlates not found in either condition alone (e.g. Biederman et al., 1987; Faraone, Biederman, Mennin, Russell, & Tsuang, 1998; Jensen, Martin, & Cantwell, 1997; Rutter & Sroufe, 2000; Schachar & Tannock, 1995).

A variety of sample differences also may contribute to the differences in findings across studies. Research on family factors and ADHD has seldom considered the influence of environment beyond the family, particularly the cultural or ethnic context (see work by Bussing, Schoenberg, & Perwien, 1998 for an exception). In line with the DP perspective that is advocated in this chapter, consideration of the broader social and cultural context of ADHD must be incorporated in studies of families of children with ADHD (Sameroff, 2000). Alongside culture, gender and ADHD subtype also stand as underrepresented variables in existing work. Future studies must focus careful attention on how the dynamics of family and child factors may differ across these child characteristics. For example, research into gender differences in ADHD has pointed to both similarities and differences in the manifestation of the disorder in boys and girls (Hinshaw & Blachman, in press), but as yet gender has received little attention in family studies. Similarly, work on the nature of the inattentive subtype of ADHD suggests that this may be a distinct disorder (Milich, Balentine, & Lynam, 2001) and, although some research suggests that subtype does not influence the familial transmission of ADHD (Faraone et al., 2000), more work is needed, and models linking family characteristics to child ADHD will need to be cognizant of possible similarities and differences across subtypes of the disorder. Finally, research is needed to expand what has been a focus primarily on mothers and sons to include fathers, other family subsystems (including sibling relationships), whole family variables, and the interplay among these subsystems. Knowledge of these domains will not only broaden our understanding, but the similarities and differences in associations between family factors and child ADHD across these multiple areas may inform us of the developmental pathways and associations operative in and across domains.

Lack of a Developmental Psychopathology Approach

In considering family factors and ADHD there is a general lack of research to inform a DP perspective on ADHD. Existing studies are predominantly correlational in nature and offer little understanding of how associations between family factors and child problems develop over time. Certainly, the heterogeneity of research findings is a strong indication of the existence of individual differences in how and when family factors are linked to the development of ADHD and conduct problems. As we have noted, family factors and child characteristics are likely to interact in a multiplicity of ways, yielding different developmental trajectories for the unfolding of ADHD symptomatology and conduct problems.

To understand these different pathways, both theoretical and empirical steps are needed. We believe that there is a need for greater development of theoretical models concerning family influences and ADHD. Much of the existing theoretical work in this area has focused either on the biological contributions of families (e.g. Faraone & Biederman, 2000) or on the contributions of family environment to the development of conduct problems secondary to ADHD (e.g. Patterson, DeGarmo, & Knutson, 2000). Despite the value of these models, other models that emphasize direct, indirect, and/or reciprocal contributions of family environment to ADHD also are needed. The ultimate value of these models will be found, not necessarily in their truth, but in their ability to guide research and advance our knowledge.

Empirically, there is a need for research to test the mechanisms and timing of influences and how these vary across children. We believe that such an approach, identifying different pathways for different children with ADHD, would enhance the regularity of findings and permit firmer, as well as richer, conclusions regarding the characteristics and functioning of families of children with ADHD. One approach to advancing research in this area is to use longitudinal, genetically informed research designs. Ideally, such studies would begin early in a child's life (perhaps even prenatally for families designated as being at risk for ADHD based on the presence of the disorder in one or both parents) and include repeated, developmentally sensitive measures of characteristics of the child and family and the larger environmental/cultural context. Although assessment of ADHD and conduct problems is obviously difficult in the first few years of life, recognition of important developmental processes such as emotion regulation, attachment, and language development offers a useful guide to the types of processes that are likely precursors to the patterns of "symptoms" identified in elementary school-aged children. Such designs would be maximally informative if they coupled extensive and multiple measures of neurological, psychological, and social characteristics with information regarding the genetic make-up of family members (e.g. DNA samples). As examples, such designs might yield information about children who are at risk for ADHD but fail to develop the disorder because of a protective family environment, or how family/environmental risk factors may alter the neurobiological functioning of children with or without vulnerabilities to ADHD. Similarly, longitudinal studies examining the course of parental ADHD (in one or both parents), parent–child interactions, and child development over time may shed light on contributions of genetic factors, parenting factors, or both that underlie the link between parental and child ADHD.

A second approach to research in this area, one that is complementary to the longitudinal bio-psychosocial approach outlined above, uses focused laboratory or cross-sectional studies to address specific questions regarding possible pathway influences. For example, studies using laboratory manipulations of child behavior (e.g. via medication) or parenting behavior (e.g. via stress induction, increased attention load, or medication) will continue to be informative regarding whether causal influence *can* flow from child to parent and *vice versa*. Similarly, focused studies of the parenting skills of adults with ADHD, particularly in relation to their interactions with infants and young children, will offer valuable information regarding the non-biological (and possibly biological) pathways through which the disorder may exert its familial influence. In sum, any number of studies of this type could be imagined and, if conducted carefully, each could contribute a valuable piece to the puzzle of multiple developmental pathways.

In summary, we argue that the primary challenge for future theory, research, and practice concerning families of children with ADHD is to clarify the nature and timing of the influences that operate in the associations between family and child characteristics. Although a few longitudinal and experimental studies have begun to address this need, much remains for future research development. In particular, greater sophistication is needed in exploring the ways in which genetic vulnerabilities, parenting, parental characteristics, and child experiences interact over time to produce or alter the pathway of development of ADHD. We believe that such research holds tremendous potential to inform intervention and, ultimately, prevention efforts for families and children who suffer from the impairments.

Acknowledgments

During the writing of the chapter Charlotte Johnston was supported by grants from the Canadian Institutes of Health Research and the Social Sciences and Humanities Research Council of Canada. The authors would like to acknowledge the library assistance of Olga Traczyk in the preparation of this chapter.

References

Abidin, R. R. (1986). *Parenting stress index: Test manual*. Charlottesville, VA: Pediatric Psychology Press.

Abikoff, H., Hechtman, L., Klein, R., Weiss, G., Fleiss, K., Etcovitch, J., Cousins, L., Greenfield, B., Martin, D., & Pollack, S. (2004). Symptomatic improvement in children with ADHD treated with long-term methylphenidate and multimodal psychosocial treatment. *Journal of the American Academy of Child and Adolescent Psychiatry*, *43*, 802–811.

American Psychiatric Association. (2000). *Diagnostic and statistical manual of mental disorders* (4th ed.-Text Revision). Washington, DC: Author.

Anastopoulos, A. D., & Farley, S. E. (2003). A cognitive-behavioral training program for parents of children with attention-deficit/hyperactivity disorder. In: A. E. Kazdin & J. R. Weisz (Eds), *Evidence-based psychotherapies for children and adolescents* (pp. 187–203). New York: Guilford.

Anastopoulos, A. D., Guevremont, D. C., Shelton, T. L., & DuPaul, G. J. (1992). Parenting stress among families of children with attention deficit hyperactivity disorder. *Journal of Abnormal Child Psychology, 20*, 503–520.

Anastopoulos, A. D., Shelton, T. L., DuPaul, G. J., & Guevremont, D. C. (1993). Parent training for attention-deficit hyperactivity disorder: Its impact on parent functioning. *Journal of Abnormal Child Psychology, 21*, 581–596.

Arnold, E. H., O'Leary, S. G., & Edwards, G. H. (1997). Father involvement and self reported parenting of children with attention deficit hyperactivity disorder. *Journal of Consulting and Clinical Psychology, 65*, 337–342.

August, G. J., MacDonald, A. W., Realmuto, G. M., & Skare, S. S. (1996). Hyperactive and aggressive pathways: Effects of demographic, family, and child characteristics on children's adaptive functioning. *Journal of Clinical Child Psychology, 25*, 341–351.

August, G. J., Realmuto, G. M., Joyce, R., & Hektner, J. M. (1999). Persistence and desistance of oppositional defiant disorder in a community sample of children with ADHD. *Journal of the American Academy of Child and Adolescent Psychiatry, 38*, 1262–1270.

Barkley, R. A. (1988). The effects of methylphenidate on the interactions of preschool ADHD children with their mothers. *Journal of the American Academy of Child and Adolescent Psychiatry, 27*, 336–341.

Barkley, R. A. (1989). Hyperactive girls and boys: Stimulant drug effects on mother–child interactions [published erratum appears in *Journal of Child Psychology and Psychiatry, 34*, 437]. *Journal of Child Psychology and Psychiatry, 30*, 379–390.

Barkley, R. A. (1997a). *ADHD and the nature of self-control*. New York: Guilford.

Barkley, R. A. (1997b). *Defiant children: A clinician's manual for assessment and parent training*. New York: Guilford.

Barkley, R. A. (in press). *Attention-deficit hyperactivity disorder: A handbook for diagnosis and treatment* (3rd ed.). New York: Guilford.

Barkley, R. A., Anastopoulos, A. D., Guevremont, D. C., & Fletcher, K. E. (1992). Adolescents with attention deficit hyperactivity disorder: Mother adolescent interactions, family beliefs and conflicts, and maternal psychopathology. *Journal of Abnormal Child Psychology, 20*, 263–288.

Barkley, R. A., & Cunningham, C. E. (1979). The effects of methylphenidate on the mother–child interactions of hyperactive children. *Archives of General Psychiatry, 36*, 201–208.

Barkley, R. A., Karlsson, J., & Pollard, S. (1985). Effects of age on the mother child interactions of ADD-H and normal boys. *Journal of Abnormal Child Psychology, 13*, 631–637.

Barkley, R. A., Karlsson, J., Pollard, S., & Murphy, J. V. (1985). Developmental changes in the mother child interactions of hyperactive boys: Effects of two dose levels of Ritalin. *Journal of Child Psychology and Psychiatry, 26*, 705–715.

Barkley, R. A., Karlsson, J., Strzelecki, E., & Murphy, J. V. (1984). Effects of age and Ritalin dosage on the mother–child interactions of hyperactive children. *Journal of Consulting and Clinical Psychology, 52*, 750–758.

Barkley, R. A., McMurray, M. B., Edelbrock, C. S., & Robbins, K. (1989). The response of aggressive and nonaggressive ADHD children to two doses of methylphenidate. *Journal of the American Academy of Child and Adolescent Psychiatry, 28*, 873–881.

Barkley, R. A., Shelton, T. L., Crosswait, C., Moorehouse, M., Fletcher, K., Barrett, S., Jenkins, L., & Metevia, L. (2000). Early psycho-educational intervention for children with disruptive behavior: Preliminary post-treatment outcome. *Journal of Child Psychology and Psychiatry, 41*, 319–332.

Battle, E. S., & Lacey, B. (1972). A context for hyperactivity in children, over time. *Child Development, 43*, 757–773.

Beck, S. J., Young, G. H., & Tarnowski, K. J. (1990). Maternal characteristics and perceptions of pervasive and situational hyperactives and normal controls. *Journal of the American Academy of Child and Adolescent Psychiatry, 29*, 558–565.

Becker, K., Holtmann, M., Laucht, M., & Schmidt, M. H. (2004). Are regulatory problems in infancy precursors of later hyperkinetic symptoms? *Acta Paediatrica, 93*, 1463–1469.

Befera, M. S., & Barkley, R. A. (1985). Hyperactive and normal girls and boys: Mother–child interaction, parent psychiatric status and child psychopathology. *Journal of Child Psychology and Psychiatry, 26*, 439–452.

Biederman, J., Faraone, S. V., Mick, E., Spencer, T., Wilens, T., Kiely, K., Guite, J., Ablon, J. S., Reed, E., & Warburton, R. (1995a). High risk for attention deficit hyperactivity disorder among children of parents with childhood onset of the disorder: A pilot study. *American Journal of Psychiatry, 152*, 431–435.

Biederman, J., Faraone, S. V., Mick, E., Williamson, S., Wilens, T. E., Spencer, T. H., Weber, W., Jetton, J., Kraus, I., Pert, J., & Zallen, B. (1999). Clinical correlates of ADHD in females: Findings from a large group of girls ascertained from pediatric and psychiatric referral sources. *Journal of the American Academy of Child and Adolescent Psychiatry, 38*, 966–975.

Biederman, J., Faraone, S. V., & Monuteaux, M. C. (2002). Impact of exposure to parental attention-deficit hyperactivity disorder on clinical features and dysfunction in the offspring. *Psychological Medicine, 32*, 817–827.

Biederman, J., Milberger, S., Faraone, S. V., Kiely, K., Guite, J., Mick, E., Ablon, S., Warburton, R., Reed, E., & Davis, S. G. (1995b). Impact of adversity on functioning and comorbidity in children with Attention-Deficit Hyperactivity Disorder. *Journal of the American Academy of Child and Adolescent Psychiatry, 34*, 1495–1503.

Biederman, J., Munir, K., & Knee, D. (1987). Conduct and oppositional disorder in clinically referred children with attention deficit disorder: A controlled family study. *Journal of the American Academy of Child and Adolescent Psychiatry, 26*, 724–727.

Bor, W., Sanders, M. R., & Markie-Dadds, C. (2002). The effects of the triple P-positive parenting program on preschool children with co-occurring disruptive behavior and attentional/hyperactive difficulties. *Journal of Abnormal Child Psychology, 30*, 571–587.

Brown, R. T., Borden, K. A., Clingerman, S. R., & Jenkins, P. (1988). Depression in attention deficit disordered and normal children and their parents. *Child Psychiatry and Human Development, 18*, 119–132.

Brown, R. T., & Pacini, J. N. (1989). Perceived family functioning, marital status, and depression in parents of boys with attention deficit disorder. *Journal of Learning Disabilities, 22*, 581–587.

Buhrmester, D., Camparo, L., Christensen, A., Gonzalez, L. S., & Hinshaw, S. P. (1992). Mothers and fathers interacting in dyads and triads with normal and hyperactive sons. *Developmental Psychology, 28*, 500–509.

Burt, S. A., Krueger, R. F., McGue, M., & Iacono, W. (2003). Parent–child conflict and the comorbidity among childhood externalizing disorders. *Archives of General Psychiatry, 60*, 505–513.

Bussing, R., Schoenberg, N. E., & Perwien, A. R. (1998). Knowledge and information about ADHD: Evidence of cultural differences among African American and white parents. *Social Science and Medicine, 46*, 919–928.

Byrne, J. M., DeWolfe, N. A., & Bawden, H. N. (1998). Assessment of attention deficit hyperactivity disorder in preschoolers. *Child Neuropsychology, 4*, 49–66.

Cadoret, R. J., & Stewart, M. A. (1991). An adoption study of attention deficit/hyperactivity/aggression and their relationship to adult antisocial personality. *Comprehensive Psychiatry, 32*, 73–82.

Camparo, L. B., Christensen, A., Buhrmester, D., & Hinshaw, S. P. (1994). System functioning in families with ADHD and non-ADHD sons. *Personal Relationships, 1*, 301–308.

Campbell, S. B. (1994). Hard-to-manage preschool boys: Externalizing behavior, social competence, and family context at two year follow-up. *Journal of Abnormal Child Psychology*, *22*, 147–166.

Campbell, S. B. (2000). Attention-Deficit/Hyperactivity Disorder: A developmental view. In: A. J. Sameroff, M. Lewis & S. M. Miller (Eds), *Handbook of developmental psychopathology* (2nd ed., pp. 383–401). New York: Kluwer Academic/Plenum.

Campbell, S. B., Breaux, A. M., Ewing, L. J., & Szumowski, E. K. (1986). Correlates and predictors of hyperactivity and aggression: A longitudinal study of parent referred problem preschoolers. *Journal of Abnormal Child Psychology*, *14*, 217–234.

Campbell, S. B., Breaux, A. M., Ewing, L. J., Szumowski, E. K., & Pierce, E. W. (1986). Parent identified problem preschoolers: Mother–child interaction during play at intake and 1 year follow up. *Journal of Abnormal Child Psychology*, *14*, 425–440.

Campbell, S. B., & Ewing, L. J. (1990). Follow up of hard to manage preschoolers: Adjustment at age 9 and predictors of continuing symptoms. *Journal of Child Psychology and Psychiatry*, *31*, 871–889.

Carbonneau, R., Tremblay, R. E., Vitaro, F., Dobkin, P. L., Saucier, J. F., & Pihl, R. O. (1998). Paternal alcoholism, paternal absence and the development of problem behaviors in boys from age six to twelve years. *Journal of Studies on Alcohol*, *59*, 387–398.

Carlson, E. A., Jacobvitz, D., & Sroufe, L. A. (1995). A developmental investigation of inattentiveness and hyperactivity. *Child Development*, *66*, 37–54.

Carpenter, E. M., Frankel, F., Marina, M., Duan, N., & Smalley, S. L. (2004). Internet treatment delivery of parent-adolescent conflict training for families with an ADHD teen: A feasibility study. *Child & Family Behavior Therapy*, *26*(3), 1–20.

Chronis, A. M., Chacko, A., Fabiano, G. A., Wymbs, B. T., & Pelham, W. E., Jr. (2004). Enhancements to the behavioral parent training paradigm for families of children with ADHD: Review and future directions. *Clinical Child and Family Psychology Review*, *7*, 1–27.

Chronis, A. M., Lahey, B. B., Pelham, W. E., Kipp, H., Baumann, B., & Lee, S. S. (2003). Psychopathology and substance abuse in parents of young children with Attention Deficit/Hyperactivity Disorder. *Journal of the American Academy of Child and Adolescent Psychiatry*, *42*, 1425–1432.

Clarke, L., Ungerer, J., Chahaud, K., Johnson, S., & Stiefel, I. (2002). Attention deficit hyperactivity disorder is associated with attachment insecurity. *Clinical Child Psychology and Psychiatry*, *7*, 179–198.

Colder, C. R., Lochman, J. E., & Wells, K. C. (1997). The moderating effects of children's fear and activity level of relations between parenting practices and childhood symptomatology. *Journal of Abnormal Child Psychology*, *25*, 251–263.

Cunningham, C. E., & Barkley, R. A. (1979). The interactions of hyperactive and normal children with their mothers in free play and structured task. *Child Development*, *50*, 217–224.

Cunningham, C. E., Benness, B. B., & Siegel, L. S. (1988). Family functioning, time allocation, and parental depression in the families of normal and ADHD children. *Journal of Clinical Child Psychology*, *17*, 169–177.

Cunningham, C. E., & Boyle, M. H. (2002). Preschoolers at risk for attention-deficit hyperactivity disorder and oppositional defiant disorder: Family, parenting, and behavioral correlates. *Journal of Abnormal Child Psychology*, *30*, 555–569.

Daley, D., Sonuga-Barke, E. J. S., & Thompson, M. (2003). Assessing expressed emotion in mothers of preschool AD/HD children: Psychometric properties of a modified speech sample. *British Journal of Clinical Psychology*, *42*, 53–67.

Davies, P. T., & Cicchetti, D. (Eds). (2004). Special issue: Family systems and developmental psychopathology. *Development and Psychopathology*, *16 (Whole No. 3)*, 477–797.

Dawson, G., Frey, K., Self, J., Panagiotides, H., Hessl, D., Yamada, E., & Rinaldi, J. (1999). Frontal brain electrical activity in infants of depressed and nondepressed mothers: Relations to variations in infant behavior. *Development and Psychopathology, 11*, 589–605.

DuPaul, G. J., McGoey, K. E., Eckert, T. L., & VanBrakle, J. (2001). Preschool children with Attention-Deficit/Hyperactivity Disorder: Impairments in behavioral, social, and school functioning. *Journal of the American Academy of Child and Adolescent Psychiatry, 40*, 508–515.

Edwards, G., Barkley, R. A., Laneri, M., Fletcher, K., & Metevia, L. (2001). Parent–adolescent conflict in teenagers with ADHD and ODD. *Journal of Abnormal Child Psychology, 29*, 557–572.

Emery, R. E. (1992). Family conflict and its developmental implications: A conceptual analysis of deep meanings and systemic processes. In: C. U. Shantz & W. W. Hartup (Eds), *Conflict in child and adolescent development* (pp. 270–298). New York: Cambridge University Press.

Epstein, J. N., Conners, C. K., Erhardt, D., Arnold, L. E., Hechtman, L., Hinshaw, S. P., Hoza, B., Newcorn, J. H., Swanson, J. M., & Vitiello, B. (2000). Familial aggregation of ADHD characteristics. *Journal of Abnormal Child Psychology, 28*, 585–594.

Ernst, M., Kimes, A. S., London, E. D., Matochik, J. A., Eldreth, D., Tata, S., Contoreggi, C., Leff, M., & Bolla, K. (2003). Neural substrates of decision making in adults with attention deficit hyperactivity disorder. *American Journal of Psychiatry, 160*, 1061–1070.

Faraone, S. V., & Biederman, J. (1997). Do attention deficit hyperactivity disorder and major depression share familial risk factors? *Journal of Nervous and Mental Disease, 185*, 533–541.

Faraone, S. V., & Biederman, J. (2000). Nature, nurture, and attention deficit hyperactivity disorder. *Developmental Review, 20*, 568–581.

Faraone, S. V., Biederman, J., Chen, W., Milberger, S., Warburton, R., & Tsuang, M. T. (1995). Genetic heterogeneity in attention deficit hyperactivity disorder (ADHD): Gender, psychiatric comorbidity, and maternal ADHD. *Journal of Abnormal Psychology, 104*, 334–345.

Faraone, S. V., Biederman, J., Keenan, K., & Tsuang, M. T. (1991). Separation of DSM-III attention deficit disorder and conduct disorder: Evidence from a family-genetic study of American child psychiatric patients. *Psychological Medicine, 21*, 109–121.

Faraone, S. V., Biederman, J., Mennin, D., Gershon, J., & Tsuang, M. (1996). A prospective four-year follow-up study of children at risk for ADHD: Psychiatric, neuropsychological and psychosocial outcome. *Journal of American Academy of Child and Adolescent Psychiatry, 35*, 1449–1459.

Faraone, S. V., Biederman, J., Mennin, D., Russell, R., & Tsuang, M. T. (1998). Familial subtypes of attention deficit hyperactivity disorder: A 4-year follow-up study of children from antisocial ADHD families. *Journal of Child Psychology and Psychiatry, 39*, 1045–1053.

Faraone, S. V., Biederman, J., Mick, E., Doyle, A. E., Wilens, T., Spencer, T., Frazier, E., & Mullen, K. (2001). A family study of psychiatric comorbidity in girls and boys with ADHD. *Biological Psychiatry, 50*, 586–592.

Faraone, S. V., Biederman, J., Mick, E., Williamson, S., Wilens, T., Spencer, T., Weber, W., Jetton, J., Kraus, I., Pert, J., & Zallen, B. (2000). Family study of girls with Attention Deficit Hyperactivity Disorder. *American Journal of Psychiatry, 157*, 1077–1083.

Faraone, S. V., Biederman, J., & Milberger, S. (1994). An exploratory study of ADHD among second degree relatives of ADHD children. *Biological Psychiatry, 35*, 398–402.

Fischer, M. (1990). Parenting stress and the child with attention deficit hyperactivity disorder. *Journal of Clinical Child Psychology, 19*, 337–346.

Frick, P. J., Kuper, K., Silverthorn, P., & Cotter, M. (1995). Antisocial behavior, somatization, and sensation-seeking behavior in mothers of clinic-referred children. *Journal of the American Academy of Child and Adolescent Psychiatry, 34*, 805–812.

Gadow, K. D., Nolan, E. E., Litcher, L., Carlson, B., Panina, N., Golovakha, E., Sprafkin, J., & Bromet, E. J. (2000). Comparison of Attention-Deficit/Hyperactivity Disorder symptoms syndromes in Ukrainian schoolchildren. *Journal of the American Academy of Child and Adolescent Psychiatry, 39,* 1520–1527.

Gillis, J. J., Gilger, J. W., Pennington, B. F., & DeFries, J. C. (1992). Attention deficit disorder in reading-disabled twins: Evidence for a genetic etiology. *Journal of Abnormal Child Psychology, 20,* 303–315.

Gomez, R., & Sanson, A. V. (1994). Mother–child interactions and noncompliance in hyperactive boys with and without conduct problems. *Journal of Child Psychology and Psychiatry, 35,* 477–490.

Gordon, D. A. (2000). Parent training via CD-ROM: Using technology to disseminate effective prevention practices. *The Journal of Primary Prevention, 21,* 227–251.

Greenberg, M. T., Speltz, M. L., & DeKlyen, M. (1993). The role of attachment in the early development of disruptive behavior problems. *Development and Psychopathology, 5,* 191–213.

Harrison, C., & Sofronoff, K. (2002). ADHD and parental psychological distress: Role of demographics, child behavioral characteristics, and parental cognitions. *Journal of the American Academy of Child and Adolescent Psychiatry, 41,* 703–711.

Hart, E. L., Lahey, B. B., Loeber, R., Applegate, B., & Frick, P. (1995). Developmental change in attention-deficit hyperactivity disorder in boys: A four-year longitudinal study. *Journal of Abnormal Child Psychology, 23,* 729–750.

Harvey, E. A. (2000). Parenting similarity and children with attention deficit/hyperactivity disorder. *Child and Family Behavior Therapy, 22,* 39–53.

Harvey, E., Danforth, J. S., McKee, T. E., Ulaszek, W. R., & Friedman, J. L. (2003). Parenting of children with attention-deficit/hyperactivity disorder: The role of parental ADHD symptomatology. *Journal of Attention Disorders, 7,* 31–42.

Hechtman, L., Abikoff, H., Klein, R., Greenfield, B., Etcovitch, J., Cousins, L., Fleiss, K., Weiss, M., & Pollack, S. (2004). Children with ADHD treated with long-term methylphenidate and multimodal psychosocial treatment: Implant on parental practices. *Journal of the American Academy of Child and Adolescent Psychiatry, 43,* 830–838.

Heiser, P., Friedel, S., Dempfle, A., Konrad, K., Smidt, J., Grabarkiewicz, J., Herpertz-Dahlmann, B., Remschmidt, H., & Hebebrand, J. (2004). Molecular genetic aspects of attention-deficit/hyperactivity disorder. *Neuroscience and Biobehavioral Reviews, 28,* 625–641.

Hinshaw, S. P., & Blachman, D. (in press). Attention-deficit/hyperactivity disorder in girls. In: D. J. Bell, S. L. Foster & E. J. Mash (Eds), *Handbook of behavioral and emotional problems in girls.* New York: Elsevier/Plenum Publishing.

Hinshaw, S. P., Zupan, B. A., Simmel, C., Nigg, J. T., & Melnick, S. (1997). Peer status in boys with and without attention deficit hyperactivity disorder: Predictions from overt and covert antisocial behavior, social isolation, and authoritative parenting beliefs. *Child Development, 68,* 880–896.

Jacobvitz, D., Hazan, N., Curran, M., & Hitchens, K. (2004). Observations of early triadic family interactions: Boundary disturbances in the family predict symptoms of depression, anxiety, and attention-deficit/hyperactivity disorder in middle childhood. *Development and Psychopathology, 16,* 577–592.

Jacobvitz, D., & Sroufe, L. A. (1987). The early caregiver child relationship and attention deficit disorder with hyperactivity in kindergarten: A prospective study. *Child Development, 58,* 1496–1504.

Jensen, P. S., Martin, B. A., & Cantwell, D. P. (1997). Comorbidity in ADHD: Implications for research, practice, and DSM-IV. *Journal of the American Academy of Child and Adolescent Psychiatry, 36,* 1065–1079.

Johnston, C. (1996). Parent characteristics and parent–child interactions in families of nonproblem children and ADHD children with higher and lower levels of oppositional-defiant behavior. *Journal of Abnormal Child Psychology, 24,* 85–104.

Johnston, C., & Freeman, W. (1998). Parent training interventions for sibling conflict. In: James M. Briesmeister & C. E. Schaefer (Eds). *Handbook of parent training: Parents as co-therapists for children's behavior problems* (2nd ed., pp. 153–176). New York: John Wiley.

Johnston, C., & Mash, E. J. (2001). Families of children with attention-deficit hyperactivity disorder: A review and recommendations for future research. *Clinical Child and Family Psychology Review, 4*, 183–207.

Johnston, C., Murray, C., Hinshaw, S. P., Pelham,W. E., & Hoza, B. (2002). Responsiveness in interactions of mothers and sons with ADHD: Relations to maternal and child characteristics. *Journal of Abnormal Child Psychology, 30*, 77–88.

Johnston, C., Scoular, D. J., & Ohan, J. L. (2004). Mothers' reports of parenting in families of children with symptoms of Attention-Deficit/Hyperactivity Disorder: Relations to impression management. *Child & Family Behavior Therapy, 26*, 45–61.

Kendall, J. (1999). Sibling accounts of ADHD. *Family Process, 38*, 117–136.

Kochanska, G. (1993). Toward a synthesis of parental socialization and child temperament in early development of conscience. *Child Development, 64*, 325–347.

Kotimaa, A. J., Moilanen, I., Taanila, A., Ebeling, H., Smalley, S. L., McGough, J. J., Hartikainen, A. L., & Jarvelin, M. R. (2003). Maternal smoking and hyperactivity in 8-year-old children. *Journal of the American Academy of Child and Adolescent Psychiatry, 42*, 826–833.

Kreppner, J. M., O'Connor, T.G., Rutter, M., & the English and Romanian Adoptees Study Team. (2001). Can inattention/overactivity be an institutional deprivation syndrome? *Journal of Abnormal Child Psychology, 29*, 513–528.

Kuntsi, J., & Stevenson, J. (2000). Hyperactivity in children: A focus on genetic research and psychological theories. *Clinical Child and Family Psychology Review, 3*, 1–24.

Kuperman, S., Schlosser, S. S., Lidral, J., & Reich, W. (1999). Relationship of child psychopathology to parental alcoholism and antisocial personality disorder. *Journal of the American Academy of Child and Adolescent Psychiatry, 38*, 686–692.

Lang, A. R., Pelham, W. E., Atkeson, B. M., & Murphy, D. A. (1999). Effects of alcohol intoxication on parenting behavior in interactions with child confederates exhibiting normal or deviant behaviors. *Journal of Abnormal Child Psychology, 27*, 177–189.

Leung, P. W. L., Ho, T. P., Luk, S. L., Taylor, E., Back-Shone, J., & Mak, F. L. (1996). Separation and comorbidity of hyperactivity and conduct disturbance in Chinese schoolboys. *Journal of Child Psychology and Psychiatry, 37*, 841–853.

Levy, F., & Hay, D. (2001). *Attention, genes, and ADHD*. Philadelphia, PA: Brunner-Routledge.

Levy, F., Hay, D., McLaughlin, M., Wood, C., & Waldman, I. (1996). Twin sibling differences in parental reports of ADHD, speech, reading and behaviour problems. *Journal of Child Psychology and Psychiatry, 37*, 569–578.

Lindahl, K. M. (1998). Family process variables and children's disruptive behavior problems. *Journal of Family Psychology, 12*, 420–436.

Linnet, K. M., Dalsgaard, S., Obel, C., Wisborg, K., Henriksen, T. B., Rodriguez, A., Kotimaa, A., Moilanen, I., Thomsen, P. H., Olsen, J., & Jarvelin, M. (2003). Maternal lifestyle factors in pregnancy risk of attention deficit hyperactivity disorder and associated behaviors: Review of the current evidence. *American Journal of Psychiatry, 160*, 1028–1040.

Litt, J. (2004). Women's carework in low-income households: The special case of children with attention deficit hyperactivity disorder. *Gender and Society, 18*, 625–644.

Loeber, R., Green, S. M., Lahey, B. B., Frick, P. J., & McBurnett, K. (2000). Findings on disruptive behavior disorders from the first decade of the developmental trends study. *Clinical Child and Family Psychology Review, 3*, 37–60.

Loney, J., Paternite, C. E., Schwartz, J. E., & Roberts, M. A. (1997). Associations between clinic referred boys and their fathers on childhood inattention overactivity and aggression dimensions. *Journal of Abnormal Child Psychology, 25*, 499–509.

Martin, C. S., Earleywine, M., Blackson, T. C., Vanyukov, M. M., Moss, H. B., & Tarter, R. E. (1994). Aggressivity, inattention, hyperactivity, and impulsivity in boys at high and low risk for substance abuse. *Journal of Abnormal Child Psychology, 22*, 177–203.

Mash, E. J., & Johnston, C. (1982). A comparison of the mother–child interactions of younger and older hyperactive and normal children. *Child Development, 53*, 1371–1381.

Mash, E. J., & Johnston, C. (1983a). Parental perceptions of child behavior problems, parenting self-esteem, and mothers' reported stress in younger and older hyperactive and normal children. *Journal of Consulting and Clinical Psychology, 51*, 86–99.

Mash, E. J., & Johnston, C. (1983b). Sibling interactions of hyperactive and normal children and their relationship to reports of maternal stress and self-esteem. *Journal of Clinical Child Psychology, 12*, 91–99.

Mash, E. J., & Johnston, C. (1983c). The prediction of mothers' behavior with their hyperactive children during play and task situations. *Child and Family Behavior Therapy, 5*, 1–14.

Mash, E. J., & Johnston, C. (1990). Determinants of parenting stress: Illustrations from families of hyperactive children and families of physically abused children. *Journal of Clinical Child Psychology, 19*, 313–328.

Mash, E. J., & Johnston, C. (1996). Family relational problems: Their place in the study of psychopathology. *Journal of Emotional and Behavioral Disorders, 4*, 240–254.

McMahon, R. J., & Forehand, R. L. (2003). *Helping the noncompliant child: Family based treatment for oppositional behavior* (2nd ed.). New York: Guilford.

Mick, E., Biederman, J., Faraone, S. V., Sayer, J., & Kleinman, S. (2002). Case-control study of attention-deficit hyperactivity disorder and maternal smoking, alcohol use, and drug use during pregnancy. *Journal of the American Academy of Child and Adolescent Psychiatry, 41*, 378–385.

Milberger, S., Biederman, J., Faraone, S. V., Guite, J., & Tsuang, M. T. (1997). Pregnancy, delivery and infancy complications and attention deficit hyperactivity disorder: Issues of gene environment interaction. *Biological Psychiatry, 41*, 65–75.

Milich, R., Balentine, A. C., & Lynam, D. R. (2001). ADHD combined type and ADHD predominantly inattentive type are distinct and unrelated disorders. *Clinical Psychology: Science and Practice, 8*, 463–488.

Minde, K., Eakin, L., Hechtman, L., Ochs, E., Bouffard, R., Greenfield, B., & Looper, K. (2003). The psychosocial functioning of children and spouses of adults with ADHD. *Journal of Child Psychology and Psychiatry, 44*, 637–646.

Moffitt, T. E. (1990). Juvenile delinquency and attention deficit disorder: Boys' developmental trajectories from age 3 to age 15. *Child Development, 61*, 893–910.

Molina, B. S., Pelham, W. E., & Lang, A. R. (1997). Alcohol expectancies and drinking characteristics in parents of children with attention deficit hyperactivity disorder. *Alcohol Clinical and Experimental Research, 21*, 557–566.

Morrell, J., & Murray, L. (2003). Parenting and the development of conduct disorder and hyperactive symptoms in childhood: A prospective longitudinal study from 2 months to 8 years. *Journal of Child Psychology and Psychiatry, 44*, 489–508.

MTA Cooperative Group. (1999a). A 14-month randomized clinical trial of treatment strategies for attention-deficit/hyperactivity disorder. *Archives of General Psychiatry, 56*, 1073–1086.

MTA Cooperative Group. (1999b). Moderators and mediators of treatment response for children with ADHD: The MTA Study. *Archives of General Psychiatry, 56*, 1088–1096.

Murphy, K. R., & Barkley, R. A. (1996). Parents of children with attention deficit/hyperactivity disorders: Psychological and attentional impairment. *American Journal of Orthopsychiatry, 66*, 93–102.

Nigg, J. T., Goldsmith, H. H., & Sachek, J. (2004). Temperament and attention deficit hyperactivity disorder: The development of a multiple pathway model. *Journal of Clinical Child and Adolescent Psychology, 33*, 42–53.

Nigg, J. T., & Hinshaw, S. P. (1998). Parent personality traits and psychopathology associated with antisocial behaviors in childhood attention deficit hyperactivity disorder. *Journal of Child Psychology and Psychiatry, 39*, 145–159.

O'Conner, T. G. (2003). Early experiences and psychological development: Conceptual questions, empirical illustrations, and implications for intervention. *Development and Psychopathology, 15,* 671–690.

Overmeyer, S., Taylor, E., Blanz, B., & Schmidt, M. H. (1999). Psychosocial adversities underestimated in hyperkinetic children. *Journal of Child Psychology and Psychiatry, 40,* 259–263.

Parke, R. D. (2004). Development in the family. *Annual Review of Psychology, 55,* 365–399.

Paternite, C. E., Loney, J., & Langhorne, J. E., Jr. (1976). Relationships between symptomatology and SES-related factors in hyperkinetic/MBD boys. *American Journal of Orthopsychiatry, 46,* 291–301.

Patterson, G. R., DeGarmo, D. S., & Knutson, N. (2000). Hyperactive and antisocial behaviors: Comorbid or two points in the same process. *Development and Psychopathology, 12,* 91–106.

Pelham, W. E., Lang, A. R., Atkeson, B., Murphy, D. A., Gnagy, E. M., Greiner, A. R., Vodde Hamilton, M., & Greenslade, K. E. (1997). Effects of deviant child behavior on parental distress and alcohol consumption in laboratory interactions. *Journal of Abnormal Child Psychology, 25,* 413–424.

Pelham, W. E., Lang, A. R., Atkeson, B., Murphy, D. A., Gnagy, E. M., Greiner, A. R., Hamilton, V. M., & Greenslade, K. E. (1998). Effects of deviant child behavior on parental alcohol consumption: Stress induced drinking in parents of ADHD children. *American Journal on Addictions, 7,* 103–114.

Pelham, W. E., Wheeler, T., & Chronis, A. (1998). Empirically supported psychosocial treatments for ADHD. *Journal of Clinical Child Psychology, 27,* 190–205.

Peris, T. S., & Hinshaw, S. P. (2003). Family dynamics and preadolescent girls with ADHD: The relationship with expressed emotion, ADHD symptomatology, and comorbid disruptive behavior. *Journal of Child Psychology and Psychiatry, 44,* 1177–1190.

Pierce, E. W., Ewing, L. J., & Campbell, S. B. (1999). Diagnostic status and symptomatic behavior of hard-to-manage preschool children in middle childhood and early adolescence. *Journal of Clinical Child Psychology, 28,* 44–57.

Pisterman, S., Firestone, P., McGrath, P., Goodman, J. T., Webster, I., Mallory, R., & Goffin, B. (1992). The effects of parent training on parenting stress and sense of competence. *Canadian Journal of Behavioural Science, 24,* 41–58.

Pisterman, S., McGrath, P., Firestone, P., Goodman, J. T., Webster, I., & Mallory, R. (1989). Outcome of parent-mediated treatment of preschoolers with attention deficit disorder with hyperactivity. *Journal of Consulting and Clinical Psychology, 57,* 628–635.

Podolski, C., & Nigg, J. T. (2001). Parent stress and coping in relation to child ADHD severity and associated child disruptive behavior problems. *Journal of Clinical Child Psychology, 30,* 503–513.

Pollard, S., Ward, E. M., & Barkley, R. A. (1983). The effects of parent training and Ritalin on the parent–child interactions of hyperactive boys. *Child and Family Behavior Therapy, 5,* 51–69.

Putnam, S. P., Sanson, A.V., & Rothbart, M. (2002). Child temperament and parenting. In: M. Bornstein (Ed.), *Handbook of parenting, Vol. 3* (2nd ed., pp. 1179–1197). Mahwah, NJ: Erlbaum.

Rieppi, R., Greenhill, L. L., Ford, R. E., Chuang, S., Wu, M., Davies, M., Abikoff, H. B., Arnold, L. E., Conners, C. K., Elliott, G. R., Hechtman, L., Hinshaw, S. P., Hoza, B., Jensen, P. S., Kraemer, H. C., March, J. S., Newcorn, J. H., Pelham, W. E., Severe, J. B., Swanson, J. M., Vitiello, B., Wells, K. C., & Wigal, T. (2002). Socioeconomic status as a moderator of ADHD treatment outcomes. *Journal of the American Academy of Child and Adolescent Psychiatry, 41,* 269–277.

Roy, P., Rutter, M., & Pickles, A. (2004). Institutional care: Associations between overactivity and lack of selectivity in social relationships. *Journal of Child Psychology and Psychiatry, 45,* 866–873.

Rucklidge, J. J., & Kaplan, B. J. (1997). Psychological functioning of women identified in adulthood with attention deficit/hyperactivity disorder. *Journal of Attention Disorders, 2,* 167–176.

Rutter, M., & Sroufe, L. A. (2000). Developmental psychopathology: Concepts and challenges. *Development and Psychopathology, 12*, 265–296.

Sameroff, A. J. (2000). Developmental systems and psychopathology. *Development and Psychopathology, 12*, 297–312.

Schachar, R., & Tannock, R. (1995). Test of four hypotheses for the comorbidity of attention deficit hyperactivity disorder and conduct disorder. *Journal of the American Association of Child and Adolescent Psychiatry, 34*, 636–648.

Schachar, R., & Wachsmuth, R. (1990). Hyperactivity and parental psychopathology. *Journal of Child Psychology and Psychiatry, 31*, 381–392.

Schachar, R., & Wachsmuth, R. (1991). Family dysfunction and psychosocial adversity: Comparison of attention deficit disorder, conduct disorder, normal and clinical controls. *Canadian Journal of Behavioural Science, 23*, 332–348.

Seipp, C. M., & Johnston, C. (2005). Mother-son interactions in families of boys with Attention-Deficit/Hyperactivity Disorder with and without oppositional behavior. *Journal of Abnormal Child Psychology, 33*, 87–98.

Sergeant, J. (2000). The cognitive-energetic model: An empirical approach to attention-deficit hyperactivity disorder. *Neuroscience and Biobehavioral Reviews, 24*, 7–12.

Shaw, D. S., Owens, E. B., Giovannelli, J., & Winslow, E. B. (2001). Infant and toddler pathways leading to early externalizing disorders. *Journal of the American Academy of Child and Adolescent Psychiatry, 40*, 36–43.

Shelton, T. L., Barkley, R. A., Crosswait, C., Moorehouse, M., Fletcher, K., Barrett, S., Jenkins, L., & Metevia, L. (1998). Psychiatric and psychological morbidity as a function of adaptive disability in preschool children with aggressive and hyperactive impulsive inattentive behavior. *Journal of Abnormal Child Psychology, 26*, 475–494.

Smith, B. H., Barkley, R. A., & Shapiro, C. J. (2006). Attention-deficit/hyperactivity disorder. In: E. J. Mash & R. A. Barkley (Eds), *Treatment of childhood disorders* (3rd ed.). New York: Guilford.

Sonuga-Barke, E. J. S. (2002). Psychological heterogeneity in AD/HD – A dual pathway model of behavior and cognition. *Behavioural Brain Research, 130*, 29–36.

Sonuga-Barke, E. J. S., Daley, D., & Thompson, M. (2002). Does maternal ADHD reduce the effectiveness of parent training for preschool children's ADHD? *Journal of the American Academy of Child and Adolescent Psychiatry, 41*, 696–702.

Sonuga-Barke, E. J. S., Daley, D., Thompson, M., Laver-Bradbury, C., & Weeks, A. (2001). Parent-based therapies for preschool attention deficit/hyperactivity disorder: A randomized, controlled trial with a community sample. *Journal of the American Academy of Child and Adolescent Psychiatry, 40*, 402–408.

Sonuga-Barke, E. J. S., Thompson, M., Daley, D., & Laver-Bradbury, C. (2004). Parent training for attention deficit/hyperactivity disorder: Is it as effective when delivered as routine rather than as specialist care? *British Journal of Clinical Psychology, 43*, 449–457.

Sroufe, L. A., & Jacobvitz, D. (1989). Diverging pathways, developmental transformations, multiple etiologies and the problem of continuity in development. *Human Development, 32*, 196–204.

St. Sauver, J. L., Barbaresi, W. J., Katusic, S. K., Colligan, R. C., Weaver, A. L., & Jacobson, S. J. (2004). Early life risk factors for attention-deficit/hyperactivity disorder: A population-based cohort study. *Mayo Clinic Proceedings, 79*, 1124–1131.

Stormont-Spurgin, M., & Zentall, S. (1996). Child rearing practices associated with aggression in youth with and without ADHD: An exploratory study. *International Journal of Disability, Development and Education, 43*, 135–146.

Strayhorn, J. M., & Weidman, C. S. (1989). Reduction of attention deficit and internalizing symptoms in preschoolers through parent–child interaction training. *Journal of the American Academy of Child and Adolescent Psychiatry, 28*, 888–896.

Swanson, J. M., Sunohara, G. A., Kennedy, J. L., Regino, R., Fineberg, E., Wigal, T., Lerner, M.,Williams, L., LaHoste, G. J., & Wigal, S. (1998). Association of the dopamine receptor D4 (DRD4) gene with a refined phenotype of attention deficit hyperactivity disorder (ADHD): A family-based approach. *Molecular Psychiatry, 3*, 38–41.

Szatmari, P., Offord, D. R., & Boyle, M. H. (1989). Correlates, associated impairments and patterns of service utilization of children with attention deficit disorder: Findings from the Ontario Child Health Study. *Journal of Child Psychology and Psychiatry, 30*, 205–217.

Tallmadge, J., & Barkley, R. A. (1983). The interactions of hyperactive and normal boys with their mothers and fathers. *Journal of Abnormal Child Psychology, 11*, 565–579.

Taylor, E. (1999). Developmental neuropsychopathology of attention deficit and impulsiveness. *Development and Psychopathology, 11*, 607–628.

Taylor, E., Chadwick, O., Heptinstall, E., & Danckaerts, M. (1996). Hyperactivity and conduct problems as risk factors for adolescent development. *Journal of the American Academy of Child and Adolescent Psychiatry, 35*, 1213–1226.

Taylor, E., Schachar, R., Thorley, G., & Wieselberg, M. (1986). Conduct disorder and hyperactivity: I. Separation of hyperactivity and antisocial conduct in British child psychiatric patients. *British Journal of Psychiatry, 149*, 760–767.

Teicher, M. H., Anderson, S. L., Polcari, A., Anderson, C. M., & Navalta, C. P. (2002). Developmental neurobiology of childhood stress and trauma. *Psychiatric Clinics of North America, 25*, 397–426.

Thapar, A. J. (2003). Attention deficit hyperactivity disorder: New genetic findings, new directions. In: R. Plomin & J. C. DeFries (Eds), *Behavioral genetics in the postgenomic era* (pp. 445–462). Washington, DC: American Psychological Association.

Tiet, Q. Q., Bird, H. R., Hoven, C.W., Moore, R., Wu, P., Wicks, J., Jensen, P. S., Goodman, S., & Cohen, P. (2001). Relationship between specific adverse life events and psychiatric disorders. *Journal of Abnormal Child Psychology, 29*, 153–164.

Tully, L. A., Arseneault, L., Caspi, A., Moffitt, T. E., & Morgan, J. (2004). Does maternal warmth moderate the effects of birth weight on twins' attention-deficit/hyperactivity disorder (ADHD) symptoms and low IQ? *Journal of Consulting and Clinical Psychology, 72*, 218–226.

Wakschlag, L. S., & Hans, S. L. (1999). Relation of maternal responsiveness during infancy to the development of behavior problems in high risk youths. *Developmental Psychology, 35*, 569–579.

Weinstein, C. S., Apfel, R. J., & Weinstein, S. R. (1998). Description of mothers with ADHD with children with ADHD. *Psychiatry: Interpersonal and Biological Processes, 61*, 12–19.

Wells, K. C., Epstein, J. N., Hinshaw, S. P., Conners, C. K., Klaric, J., Abikoff, H. B., Abramowitz, A., Arnold, L. E., Elliott, G., Greenhill, L. L., Hechtman, L., Hoza, B., Jensen, P. S., March, J. S., Pelham,W., Pfiffner, L., Severe, J., Swanson, J. M., Vitiello, B., & Wigal, T. (2000). Parenting and family stress treatment outcomes in Attention Deficit Hyperactivity Disorder (ADHD): An empirical analysis in the MTA study. *Journal of Abnormal Child Psychology, 28*, 543–553.

White, H. A., & Marks, W. (2004). Updating memory in list-method directed forgetting: Individual differences related to Adult Attention Deficit/Hyperactivity Disorder. *Personality and Individual Differences, 37*, 1453–1462.

Winsler, A. (1998). Parent child interaction and private speech in boys with ADHD. *Applied Developmental Science, 2*, 17–39.

Chapter 7

Family Factors and the Development of Anxiety Disorders

Natalie S. Gar, Jennifer L. Hudson and Ronald M. Rapee

Family Factors and the Development of Anxiety Disorders

Over the past 10–15 years, an accumulation of evidence has led to important advances in the understanding of the aetiology of internalizing disorders. Most theoretical models of childhood anxiety stress the interaction between genetic and environmental factors in the origin and maintenance of anxiety disorders (Chorpita & Barlow, 1998; Ginsburg, Siqueland, Masia-Warner, & Hedtke, 2004; Hudson & Rapee, 2004; Manassis & Bradley, 1994; Rubin & Mills, 1991). One main area of research involves the investigation of child-rearing patterns and family environment as important contributors to the development of childhood anxiety (for reviews see Ginsburg et al., 2004; Masia & Morris, 1998; Rapee, 1997; Wood, McLeod, Sigman, Hwang, & Chu, 2003). The purpose of this chapter is to provide a review of aspects of family influences with potential importance for the aetiology and maintenance of anxiety disorders. This chapter covers current research on the genetic transmission of anxiety and familial environmental influences including attachment, parenting dimensions, parent psychopathology, in addition to other aspects of the family environment such as cohesion and family climate. The chapter discusses these findings within the context of current models of anxiety development and examines limitations extant in the current literature.

Anxiety Runs in Families

A great deal of literature supports the familial transmission of anxiety disorders showing evidence of an increased prevalence of anxiety disorders among first-degree relatives of individuals with an anxiety disorder compared with relatives of individuals with no psychiatric illness (Last, Hersen, Kazdin, Orvaschel, & Perrin, 1991). Clearly, anxiety runs in

Psychopathology and the Family
Edited by J. L. Hudson and R. M. Rapee
Copyright © 2005 by Elsevier Ltd.
All rights of reproduction in any form reserved
ISBN: 0-08-044449-0

families. Evidence from twin studies suggests that genes account for approximately 30–50% of the variance in anxiety symptomatology (Andrews, Stewart, Allen, & Henderson, 1990; Barlow, 2002; Eley, 1997; Kendler, Neale, Kessler, Heath, & Eaves, 1992; Kendler et al., 1995; Thapar & McGuffin, 1995; Torgersen, 1983; Tyrer, Alexander, Remington, & Riley, 1987). Most researchers agree that genetic factors act as a general influence, and that specific disorders are accounted for by environmental factors (Barlow, 2002; Eley, 1997, 2001; Kendler, Heath, Martin, & Evans, 1987). In other words, a person may inherit a general predisposition toward anxiety or neurosis, rather than any specific genetic factor (Andrews et al., 1990). This propensity might then interact with adverse environmental events and cause the specific manifestation of an anxiety disorder (Eley, 2001).

A small number of studies have shown specific genetic contributions to certain anxiety disorders. In a twin study conducted by Torgerson (1983), genetic factors appeared to influence the development of Panic Disorder and Agoraphobia, while for Generalized Anxiety Disorder, specific genetic factors were not apparent. Kendler et al. (1995) adopted a slightly different hypothesis suggesting the possibility of two separate genetic pathways leading to the disorders. In this study, 1,030 female–female twin pairs were examined showing that Generalized Anxiety Disorder and Major Depression were greatly influenced by the same genetic factor, whereas Phobia, Panic Disorder, Alcoholism and Bulimia Nervosa were influenced by a second factor. Further research understanding the specific heritability of anxiety disorders is warranted.

One area of research that has received increasing attention as an early inherited sign of internalizing problems later in life is temperament. Early temperament, in part, represents the behavioural manifestations of the genetic transmission. One temperamental construct, termed "behavioural inhibition", has been explored by a number of researchers and identified as a possible precursor to future anxiety disorders (Biederman et al., 2001, 1993, 1990; Hirshfeld et al., 1992; Rosenbaum et al., 1992). Behaviourally inhibited infants tend to exhibit quiet fear and withdrawal in uncertain situations, wariness to interact with unfamiliar objects or people, shyness in novel situations, and clinging to the mother, as opposed to spontaneity, approach and interactions with new and uncertain surroundings and people (Biederman et al., 1990; Kagan, Reznick, & Snidman, 1988; Rosenbaum et al., 1991). Kagan (1989) suggests that roughly 10–15% of infants in the general population are behaviourally inhibited and that it is moderately stable over time (Biederman et al., 1993; Garcia Coll, Kagan, & Reznick, 1984; Hirshfeld et al., 1992; Kagan, 1989; Kagan & Garcia-Coll, 1984; Kagan et al., 1988; Reznick et al., 1986).

Kagan and colleagues (1989) have argued for the heritability of temperament and its physiological basis. They demonstrated that inhibited children showed evidence of chronically high sympathetic arousal, and hypothesized that inhibition occurs when there is reduced threshold to arousal in the amygdala. Similarly, extremely inhibited children were found to have significantly higher and more stable heart rates while processing information that is relatively difficult to assimilate (Garcia Coll et al., 1984).

A longitudinal design is an important method employed to investigate the relationship between inhibited temperament in childhood and solitude/socially reticent behaviour or anxiety problems later in life. One such study conducted by Prior, Smart, Sanson, and Oberklaid (2000), assessed 2,443 infants at 4–8 months and then at approximately 18-month intervals until the subjects were aged 13- or 14-years old. These results revealed a modest relationship between shyness in the infancy and toddlerhood period and later inhibition and anxiety, yet a substantial relationship between persistent shyness and later anxiety problems. When looking back to determine whether temperamental shyness was characteristic of children with anxiety problems in adolescence, almost half had never been reported as having a shy-inhibited temperament. These modest results suggested to the researchers that extremes of shy-inhibited behaviour may be a risk factor for later vulnerability to an anxiety disorders, but that this vulnerability is moderated by a combination of other child and family factors. Another longitudinal study found a relationship between toddler inhibition and non-social behaviours at age 4. When observed during a free-play situation, the preschool children who stood aside and watched their unfamiliar peers from afar were those 2-year olds who refrained from interacting and approaching unfamiliar toddler peers, adults, and objects (Rubin, Burgess, & Hastings, 2002). These results support the hypothesis that behavioural inhibition is moderately stable from toddlerhood to preschool, as well as the research concerning toddler interaction as a predictor of shy/wary behaviour among preschoolers.

Although there is accumulating evidence to indicate the influence of genetic and biological factors (Plomin & Rowe, 1979), many inhibited children do not remain inhibited throughout their childhood (Kagan et al., 1988), and not all temperamentally vulnerable children develop an anxiety disorder (Reznick et al., 1986). Genetics and temperamental disposition are key components contributing to the development of neurosis, but the origin of anxiety is best conceptualized as resulting from a combination of genetic and environmental factors (Rosenbaum, Biederman, Hirshfeld, Bolduc, & Chaloff, 1991). It is most likely that the development of anxiety disorders involves many environmental factors, one of which is a reciprocal relationship between a child's genetic vulnerability to exhibit high levels of arousal and emotionality and parental response to their sensitive child (Hudson & Rapee, 2004). We will now turn to a review of familial environmental influences on the development of anxiety disorders, all of which interact and influence the developing child and his ability to cope within different contexts.

Familial Environmental Influences

Attachment

Attachment refers to the establishment of early intimate relationships with caregivers, who serve an evolutionary function as a protective and secure base from which a child can explore the world (see Ungerer & McMahon, 2005 this volume). A healthy attachment style develops, when an infant is confident in the availability and predictability of the caregiver to respond in a reassuring way to relieve the infant's distress (Bowlby, 1969). These relationships are then internalized as internal working models of the relation of the self to intimates throughout the lifespan (Main, 1995; Sroufe, 1990). If this relationship is disrupted through repeated separation, a child may protest in an attempt to elicit reunion, becoming more dependent and apprehensive (Bowlby, 1969).

Most studies demonstrate that adolescents with insecure attachment styles are more likely to develop anxiety and depression problems than those who are securely attached

(Ginsburg et al., 2004; Main, 1995; Myhr, Sookman, & Pinard, 2004; Rosenstein & Horowitz, 1996; Stevenson-Hinde & Shouldice, 1990). In addition, clinic referred samples of children and adults show relatively low rates of secure attachment compared to non-clinic samples (Main, 1996). To investigate the relationship between attachment styles and psychopathology, Warren and colleagues (1997) conducted a longitudinal study which involved Ainsworth's 'strange situation' procedure when infants were 1-year old. Infant temperament and maternal anxiety were also assessed near birth. The schedule for Affective Disorders and Schizophrenia for School-Age Children was administered when the subjects were 17.5-years old. Results showed that an ambivalent attachment style significantly predicted adolescent anxiety disorders to a greater degree than maternal anxiety and temperament.

Similar results have been found in retrospective studies of attachment styles (Cowan, Cohn, Pape-Cowan, & Pearson, 1996; Papini & Roggman, 1992; Papini, Roggman, & Anderson, 1991). Children who classified themselves as having an avoidant or ambivalent attachment displayed higher levels of worry than children who classified themselves as securely attached (Muris, Mesters, Merckelback, & Hulsenbeck, 2000). Other studies have found slightly inconsistent results (Bates & Bayles, 1988; Deklyen, 1996; Lewis, Feiring, McGuffog, & Jaskir, 1984), possibly as a result of the questionable validity of self classification of attachment styles (Solomon & George, 1999; Van Dam & Van Ijzendoorn, 1988; van Ijzendoorn, Vereijken, Bakermans-Kranenburg, & Riksen-Walraven, 2004), as well as the psychometric problems typical of attachment style measures that are categorical in nature (Buelow, McClain, & McIntosh, 1996; Scharfe, 2002).

Two recent innovative studies conducted by Shamir-Essakow and colleagues (Shamir-Essakow et al., 2005) in the area of attachment have examined the relationship between behavioural inhibition, attachment style, and anxiety. One study (Shamir-Essakow et al., 2005) examined 104 children aged (3–4-year-old) classified as behaviourally inhibited versus uninhibited, and securely versus insecurely attached. After controlling for the effect of maternal anxiety, the researchers found that insecure attachment and behavioural inhibition individually operated as risk factors for anxiety, yet no interactive relationship was supported between the two factors. Anxiety symptoms were highest in the behaviourally inhibited and insecurely attached children whose mothers were also anxious. Within the insecure attachment groups, anxiety was highest in the insecure-disorganized and insecure-avoidant attached children, yet anxiety was present in the context of any of the insecure attachment classifications. A second study (Shamir-Essakow et al., 2004) examined similar groups of children and found that within the behaviourally inhibited group, mothers of both secure and insecure children incorporated cognitions about their child's difficult temperament. Mother's caregiving representations were assessed using the parent development interview (PDI) (Pianta, O'Connor, & Marvin, 1993), which focuses on parenting domains such as sensitivity and encouragement of exploration, as well as assessments of broader parenting aspects including scales of compliance, perspective-taking, enmeshment, emotional pain, worry and guilt. Inhibited mothers were more likely to describe their children as shy and anxious about separations, while the mothers of uninhibited children denied any difficulties associated with separation from their children. The mothers of inhibited children also showed high levels of perceived pain, difficulty and burden in their relationship with their children, and described their relationship as emotionally intense. These mothers perceived their children as more vulnerable and needy of comfort than mothers of uninhibited children. However, within the behaviourally inhibited group, mothers of children with secure attachment styles attempted to understand their child from the child's perspective, as well as identified with their child's internal state. In contrast, mothers of insecure inhibited children were less capable of interpreting their children's emotional cues and perceived their children more negatively. These mothers were more likely to view their children's emotions as invalid and to employ defence mechanisms against negative affect. The mothers with insecure-ambivalent attachments showed higher levels of boundary violation and tended not to distinguish their own experience from their children's experiences (enmeshment). One mother, for example, said: "He (son) is my life, I hold onto him too much, I guess. He stayed right next to me and the other preschoolers went off and played together. I thought that he was missing out on something, but at the same side of it I thought it was nice that he was with me. So, I did not push him to go". In addition, overprotection/overinvolvement with the child was common among these mothers. They often projected their own anxieties onto their children and were unable to mitigate the children's anxiety. One mother expressed about her son: "I am terrified of something happening to him, like car accident or, you know, something like that, I need to watch him all the time". Shamir-Essakow et al. suggested that these children may be less likely to develop the ability to self-regulate and to manage their own anxiety and emotional states in times of challenge or threat, thus increasing the risk of anxiety in the child. In addition, they hypothesized that mother's caregiving representations of their inhibited child could be a risk factor for the development of anxiety in their children, if not balanced by the perspective-taking behaviour of mothers of securely attached children.

In general, most studies indicate that the quality of early attachment has a significant effect on the development of later anxiety disorders. Inconsistent results in a small number of studies is likely due to the interplay of attachment style with other variables such as biological factors, environmental stressors, and demographic variables which influence whether a child will develop subsequent anxiety disorders (Lewis et al., 1984).

Parent Psychopathology

The research investigating the role of parental psychopathology in the development of childhood anxiety disorders, emphasizes the importance of considering the cyclic relationship between maternal behaviour and child contributions to the parent–child interaction (Hirshfeld, Biederman, Brody, Faraone, & Rosenbaum, 1997b; Hudson & Rapee, 2002; Mertesacker, Bade, Haverkock, & Pauli-Pott, 2004; Moore, Whaley, & Sigman, 2004; Whaley, Pinto, & Sigman, 1999).

A number of studies have indicated that maternal anxiety is an important factor that may contribute to the development of child anxiety symptoms (Hayward, Wilson, Lagle, Killen, & Taylor, 2004; Hudson & Rapee, 2002; Lieb et al., 2000; Mertesacker et al., 2004; Moore et al., 2004; Parker, 1981; Pauli-Pott, Mertesacker, & Beckmann, 2004; Shamir-Essakow et al., 2005; Whaley et al., 1999). Whaley et al. (1999) found that clinically anxious mothers were less warm and positive (showed less affection and smiled less), and more critical and catastrophizing during interactions with their children than non-clinically anxious mothers. These behaviours were more predictive of the development of child anxiety than were maternal diagnostic status and ongoing stressors (e.g. marital conflict, physical health of family members, financial strain). Clinically referred mothers were also less likely to encourage psychological autonomy in their child (e.g. solicit the child's opinion, acknowledge the child's view, encourage the child to think independently). While Whaley's study identified parenting behaviours that differed between anxious and non-anxious mothers, a more recent study expanded on this by including a larger sample of anxious children and examining whether parenting behaviours were more closely related to parent diagnosis, child diagnosis, or a combination of the two (Moore et al., 2004). Moore et al. added a group in which the child was anxious, but the mother was not. Results showed that mothers of anxious children, regardless of their own anxiety status, were less warm, and less granting of autonomy towards their children. In addition, anxious as well as non-anxious mothers of anxious children expected negative outcomes in conversational tasks to a greater degree than mothers with non-anxious children. Moore et al. hypothesized that these data suggest that overcontrolling, catastrophizing parental behaviour may develop partially as a reaction to characteristics of the anxious child, indicating mutual dyadic influences.

In another study, Hudson and Rapee (2002) investigated parental overinvolvement in anxious children and their siblings. Contrary to their hypothesis, parents of anxious children showed the same overinvolvement with the non-anxious siblings as they did with the anxious child. Hudson and Rapee suggested that it is possible that overinvolvement is a stable parenting trait and that other variables such as parental anxiety may play a crucial role in determining the degree of overinvolvement. Other studies have shown that anxiety disorders are elevated in children of parents with social phobia (Mancini, Van Ameringen, Szatmari, Fugere, & Boyle, 1996), agoraphobia (Capps, Sigman, Sena, Henker, & Whalen, 1996), and various other anxiety disorders or mixed anxiety depression (Beidel & Turner, 1997).

Despite some persuasive evidence showing a link between maternal anxiety status and childhood anxiety disorders, some studies have failed to find significant differences. In a recent study, Turner et al. (2003) developed observational play tasks, which used routine, non-conflictual and anxiety producing tasks, as opposed to previous studies which only used tasks specifically designed to be antagonistic. Contrary to their original hypothesis, Turner et al. found that anxious parents did not show increased levels of protectiveness (i.e. they did not attempt to actively inhibit their children from engaging in normal age appropriate activities or 'risky' play situations). These parents did not caution their children to be more careful nor did they make a greater number of critical comments. Yet, anxious parents did report higher levels of distress and apprehension, when their children were engaged in these activities. Turner et al. concluded that it is possible that anxious parents are not uniformly critical or overprotective, but that they may only respond in such a way when the situation is controversial or anxiety provoking. Surprising results were also found in a study, which showed no differences between anxious and non-anxious parents on the dimension of control, but rather that anxious parents were significantly less productively engaged, more withdrawn, and ignored their children to a greater extent than non-anxious parents (Woodruff-Borden, Morrow, Bourland, & Cambron, 2002). Anxious parents were also shown to agree less with their children and praised them less. In contrast to previous findings showing that anxious parents are more overinvolved with their children, these results suggest that children of anxious parents are left to cope and struggle through situations on their own to a greater extent than children of normal controls. These conflicting results suggest that maternal anxiety may influence child psychopathology in various ways and that there may be factors other than maternal anxiety that influence the parent–child dyad and contribute to the development of psychopathology.

As discussed above, behavioural inhibition was found to be a possible risk factor for future anxiety disorders. Research investigating the association between behavioural inhibition and parent psychopathology has indicated that maternal anxiety, criticism, overprotectiveness, control and self-sacrificing behaviours may influence the development of behavioural inhibition or social reticence in children (Hirshfeld, Biederman, Brody, Faraone, & Rosenbaum, 1997a; Hirshfeld et al., 1997b; Hirshfeld et al., 1992; Rubin et al., 2002). Hirshfeld et al. (1997b) examined the role of maternal psychopathology in influencing child behavioural inhibition and found that maternal criticism in mothers with anxiety disorders was significantly associated with child behavioural inhibition, independently of the child's number of disorders. The study also showed that in mothers with anxiety disorders only, maternal criticism was significantly associated with a high number of child disorders. Yet, in families with non-anxious mothers, maternal criticism did not influence the children's number of disorders. In a second study, Hirshfeld et al. (1997a) assessed an at-risk sample of 4–10-year-old children selected at 21 months ($n = 30$) as behavioural inhibited or not behaviourally inhibited. Using the Five-Minute-speech-sample (FMSS), a construct used to measure emotional overinvolvement (EOI) and criticism in parents, their findings demonstrated that mothers expressed significantly higher rates of criticism and dissatisfaction toward behaviourally inhibited children. In addition, EOI, specifically, self-sacrificing and overprotective behaviour was significantly associated with child separation anxiety disorder in the at-risk sample. Similar studies have shown that high maternal emotional overinvolvement in relatives is a risk factor for poor prognosis in the developmental course of a number of psychiatric disorders (Dadds & Roth, 2001).

Maternal behaviours also revealed meaningful connections to child behaviour in a study, which showed that when mothers were overinvolved, controlling and derisive, toddler inhibition predicted social reticence in preschoolers (Rubin et al., 2002). Rubin et al. suggested that mothers, who are overcontrolling and do not allow their child to develop and gain independence or improve their skills, as well as mothers, who are derisive and tell their children that they are incompetent, undermine the child's sense of self and contribute to socially wary behaviour in their children.

Slightly different results were found in a retrospective study by Merikangas, Avenevoli, Dierker, and Grillon (1999). Their results showed no differences in children of anxious parents and non-anxious parents on self-report questionnaire measures of temperament, however, differences were found on psychophysiological measures of arousal (e.g. startle reflex, autonomic reactivity, stress reactivity). In a more recent study, Warren et al. (2003), demonstrated that infants with mothers diagnosed with panic disorder did not show higher reactivity, behavioural inhibition, or ambivalent/resistant attachment. Yet, these infants did show different neurophysiological arousability to controls by displaying higher salivary cortisol levels and more disturbed sleep.

It is difficult to draw firm conclusions from studies investigating the associations between maternal anxiety and child temperament, as many are characterized by small sample sizes, absence of normal control groups and retrospective report, which may not truly reflect child temperament. Yet, the initial evidence suggests that an overcontrolling/over-protective and critical parenting style, as well as maternal anxiety, may be associated with anxiety in children. Whether these relationships are causal awaits further research.

Parenting and Anxiety

Offspring studies   Retrospective self-report measures have been used to assess various forms of family functioning and are the most widely used means of assessing childrearing patterns in anxiety. This is due in part to the time and cost efficiency of this method, as well as its ease of administration and scoring. Self-reports are also advantageous given that it is possible to assess subtle parenting behaviours and subjective cognitive and emotional experiences such as guilt induction and love withdrawal, which would be hard to measure through direct observation (Mattanah, 2001; Spence, Barrett, & Turner, 2003). Some studies have shown that there is little bias associated with these questionnaire scores and that self-report measures may reflect actual childrearing practices (Mackinnon, Henderson, & Andrews, 1991; Parker, 1990). Despite these advantages, self-report measures are limited in that they provide information on perceived childrearing and may not reflect actual parenting practices (Rapee, 1997). Various other limitations of self-report methodology will be discussed later in the chapter. Overall, studies have focused on the parenting dimensions of control/overprotection versus granting of autonomy and rejection versus acceptance. In general, most studies indicate that anxious children and adults perceive their parents as being high on the dimensions of control and rejection.

Several studies have measured children's perceptions of parental rearing styles. With regards to the dimension of control, results have been somewhat conflicting, and no definitive conclusions can be drawn. In some studies, there were significant and positive correlations between parental control and internalizing behaviours (Grüner, Muris, & Merckelbach, 1999; Mattanah, 2001; Pedersen, 1994), whereas in other studies no significant differences, and some cases, opposite effects were found (Muris, Meesters, Schouten, & Hoge, 2004; Perry & Millimet, 1977; Siqueland, Kendall, & Steinberg, 1996). Similarly, studies investigating the dimension of parental acceptance have been inconsistent (Grüner et al., 1999; Hernandez-Guzman & Sanchez-Sosa, 1996; Kliewer & Kung, 1998; Mattanah, 2001; Muris, Bogels, Meesters, van der Kamp, & van Oosten, 1996; Muris et al., 2000; Papini & Roggman, 1992; Papini et al., 1991; Pedersen, 1994; Siqueland et al., 1996; Tesser & Forehand, 1991). One recent study examined 159 primary school children in the Netherlands using the EMBU-C. This questionnaire measures perceptions of parental rearing behaviours and specifically asks questions regarding child perceptions of anxious rearing (e.g. 'Your parents are scared when you do something on your own'). This study found that rejection and anxious rearing behaviours were significantly and positively related to worry in the children (Muris et al., 2000).

Adult reports of perceptions of childrearing have yielded somewhat more consistent results than child-reports. In general, these studies show that anxious adults view their parents as having been more controlling, rejecting, overprotective, low in socialization and less caring than do non-anxious individuals (Alnaes & Torgersen, 1990; Arrindell et al., 1989; Capps et al., 1996; de Man, 1986; Ehiobuche, 1988; Frost, Steketee, Cohn, & Griess, 1994; Laraia, Stuart, Frye, Lydiard, & Ballenger, 1994; Lieb et al., 2000; Parker, 1979, 1981; Rapee & Melville, 1997; Siegelman, 1965; Silove, 1986).

Parent studies   Studies assessing direct reports from parents are considerably less common than those assessing reports from offspring. Research of this kind, investigating a controlling parenting style, have not yielded sufficient evidence to implicate this dimension in the development of anxiety (Rubin, Nelson, Hastings, & Asendorpf, 1999; Siqueland et al., 1996), although one study did show that mothers of withdrawn children reported the use of directive, high-powered, coercive strategies when educating their children (Rubin & Mills, 1990). A slightly larger number of studies have investigated the role of parental acceptance, but few have yielded statistically significant results (Hibbs et al., 1991; MacEwn & Barling, 1991; Muris et al., 1996; Scott, Scott, & McCabe, 1991).

Observational studies   Although they are time-consuming, costly and require complicated data analysis, observational ratings are considered more objective and provide a more comprehensive view of parent–child interactions than child or parent ratings alone. Family functioning involves complex interactions that are not necessarily available via self-report instruments (Ginsburg et al., 2004). In general, consistent findings have suggested that parents of anxious children are more overcontrolling/overinvolved, less accepting, and more likely to model anxious behaviours than parents of non-anxious children.

The majority of studies using observational ratings of overinvolvement and control have yielded significant effects in the expected direction; namely, that overprotective parenting is associated with child and adolescent anxiety (Dumas, LaFreniere, & Serketich, 1995; Hibbs et al., 1991; Hirshfeld et al., 1997a; Hudson & Rapee, 2001, 2002; Krohne & Hock, 1991; Mills & Rubin, 1998; Rubin, Cheah, & Fox, 2001; Siqueland et al., 1996; Stubbe, Zahner, Goldstein, & Leckman, 1993; Whaley et al., 1999). In a study of 43 clinically anxious, 20 oppositionally defiant, and 32 non-anxious 7–15-year-old children, Hudson and Rapee (2001) observed mother–child interactions while the child completed two difficult cognitive tasks. Mothers of anxious children and mothers of oppositional children gave more help and were more intrusive during the task than mothers of non-clinical children. Yet, no differences were found between mothers of anxious children and mothers of oppositionally defiant children on measures of overinvolvement or negativity, questioning the specificity of this relationship. In another study, Rubin and colleagues (2001) found that maternal oversolicitous behaviour and intrusive control during an unstructured free-play situation was significantly and positively predictive of children's reticent/shy/fearful behaviours, known to be associated with later anxiety. They suggested that this overprotective parenting style prevents such children from developing self-initiated coping techniques. Similar results were found in a study of 17 clinically anxious and 27 normal, 9–12-year old children. When discussing conflictual situations, parents of children with anxiety disorders were more controlling and less granting of autonomy than parents of non-anxious children (Siqueland et al., 1996). Several studies utilizing the FMSS (Hibbs et al., 1991; Hirshfeld et al., 1997a; Stubbe et al., 1993), found that emotional overinvolvement was associated with higher rates of anxiety disorders.

Findings have been slightly less consistent with regard to the dimension of parental acceptance, yet, a number of studies do suggest that children who have parents who are rejecting tend to have more anxiety disorders than those whose parents are accepting and warm. A number of studies showed that mothers of anxious children are more negative, less warm, and listen to their children less than mothers of non-anxious children (Dadds, Barrett, & Rapee, 1996; Dumas et al., 1995; Hudson & Rapee, 2001; Hummel & Gross,

2001). In contrast to these findings, studies by Siqueland (1996) and Stevenson-Hinde (1996) failed to find significant differences on the dimensions of warmth and positivity. As in the case of maternal overinvolvment and control, it is possible that other factors including maternal psychopathology could influence the degree of acceptance, positivity and warmth exhibited by the mothers in these tasks (Whaley et al., 1999).

A number of observational studies have been conducted examining the role of parental modelling of anxious behaviour and the transmission of cognitive biases to children (Barrett, Rapee, Dadds, & Ryan, 1996; Chorpita & Albano, 1996; Cobham, Dadds, & Spence, 1999; Dadds et al., 1996; Hummel & Gross, 2001; Shortt, Barrett, Dadds, & Fox, 2001; Whaley et al., 1999). Some of these studies have used an ambiguous situations task, which examines what has been termed the family enhancement of avoidant response (FEAR) effect. This task involves children being presented with ambiguous scenarios in which they are required to interpret the situation and plan how they would deal with each scenario. The child is then told to discuss the plan with their parents after which the child is asked a second time how they plan to act. Barrett et al. (1996) and Dadds et al. (1996) found that for anxious children only, the likelihood that the child would devise an avoidant strategy to deal with perceived threat increased significantly after the family discussion. The non-clinical children expressed prosocial solutions before and after the family discussions. Later studies yielded similar results (Chorpita & Albano, 1996; Shortt et al., 2001). Interestingly, one study examined the influence of context on the ambiguous situation task (Shortt et al., 2001). Contrary to predictions, this study showed that anxious children whose families completed the discussion task after the children had been offered treatment were more likely to show the FEAR effect than anxious families who completed the task as part of the assessment. As well, for physical ambiguous situations, anxious children changed to more prosocial responses after a discussion with their parent, while non-clinical children retained the same response before and after the family discussion. Surprising results were also found in a study by Cobham et al. (1999), which used a real threat task instead of the ambiguous situations used by Barrett et al. Cobham et al. found that parent–child discussions did not increase the child's anxiety or avoidance of the task. Parental anxiety status was also found to influence cognitive biases, avoidant responses and threat interpretation in studies by Whaley et al. (1999) and Shortt et al. (2001). These studies emphasize the importance of interpreting results with caution and examining other influences such as context, the nature of the experimental task, timing or parent psychopathology, which may affect study outcome.

Parenting behaviours and family interactions are complex and examination requires careful methodological consideration and planning. Advantages and disadvantages exist regarding each method of measurement and, therefore, combining sources from retrospective measures, parent reports, as well as observational methods likely provides the most comprehensive view of family functioning.

Other Aspects of the Family Environment

The study of various dimensions of the family environment related to childhood anxiety has yielded surprising results. In general, few consistent differences have been found between anxious and non-anxious families regarding family environmental variables such as maternal age, demographics, family conflict, SES, family size, enmeshment, cohesion, marital conflict and single parenting (Papini et al., 1991; Rapee & Melville, 1997; Siqueland et al., 1996; Stark, Humphrey, Crook, & Lewis, 1990; Whaley et al., 1999). One recent study found that parents with anxiety disorders, spouses of parents with anxiety disorders, and children of parents with anxiety disorders, endorse family environments that are significantly lower on expressiveness, a dimension that measures the extent to which family members are encouraged to openly express their feelings. Parents with anxiety disorders and their spouses also reported family environments that were lower in cohesion, a measurement of commitment, help, and support for one another (Turner et al., 2003). Another study examined 80 female patients diagnosed with panic disorder with agoraphobia compared to a control group of 100 female volunteers with no history of psychiatric illness. Results demonstrated that parental death, divorce or sexual mistreatment constituted risk factors for the development of anxiety (Laraia et al., 1994). Laraia et al. suggested that a conflicted family environment characterized by threats, coercion, violence, divorce, low parental warmth, lack of reasoning used in resolving family conflicts, the presence of chronic physical illness and substance abuse in the home may constitute risk factors for the development of future anxiety. An additional study showed that the main feature differentiating patients with avoidant personality disorder from normal controls were the perceptions of an unencouraging home climate and fewer demonstrations of love and pride in the child exhibited by the parent (Arbel & Stravynski, 1991; Shaw, Keenan, Vondra, Delliquadri, & Giovannelli, 1997). In a 4-year longitudinal study, Shaw et al. (1997) found that negative emotionality, disorganized attachment classification, negative life events, exposure to childrearing disagreements and parenting hassles were related to pre-school age internalizing problems. Mixed findings for family environmental variables prevent any firm conclusions on these dimensions at this point in time.

Limitations

Despite the recent increase of literature in the area of internalizing disorders, many studies suffer methodological limitations. Thus clear conclusions remain elusive and studies frequently show inconsistent results. In this section, we will review several of the main limitations extant in the current literature, which will hopefully aid the researcher in designing studies to refine and extend models of the relationship between family factors and anxiety disorders.

Assessment of Actual Child Behaviour

An important limitation of observational methodology, just like questionnaire methods, is that it is possible that these accounts and exchanges do not reflect actual childrearing behaviours or parent–child interactions. One factor that may influence how people act in a clinical setting is the context in which the experiment occurs. The differences found in the study described earlier by Shortt et al. (2001) suggested that families who thought that the results of the observational task were relevant to whether or not they would receive treatment may have been more inclined to 'fake good', as discussed by Kendall and Chansky (1991), in order to make a good impression on the experimenter. Similarly, Siqueland (1996) discusses the tendency of parents and children to present well in a clinical setting, as it is often hard for families to admit to difficulties within the home. It is thus questionable whether observational tasks are realistic, relevant to the anxiety disorder of interest, and developmentally appropriate for preschoolers or adolescents (Ginsburg et al., 2004). Discomfort with a clinical, novel setting may not elicit the same behaviours that a comfortable home environment would. These concerns alert researchers to exhibit caution when interpreting self-report measures or when assessing behaviours in an observational setting.

Retrospective Measurement

The reliability and validity of self-report methodology has often been questioned due to factors such as memory impairment and mood-congruent memory biases. Although there is some evidence to suggest that recall of significant past events is not affected by mood states (Brewin, Andrews, & Gotlib, 1993), most researchers agree that retrospective data are affected by reporting bias from the offspring's perspective (Rapee, 1997). Self-report questionnaires reflect perceptions of actual family functioning, which may be unintentionally distorted by participants, who may reframe their early lives in terms of current psychological status (Laraia et al., 1994). Furthermore, self-report ratings are often inconsistent with therapist or observational ratings of family functioning (Ginsburg et al., 2004; Muris et al., 1996; Rapee, 1997), suggesting that self-report instruments perhaps measure something different to that assessed by an observer.

Absence of Long-Term Prospective Studies

The literature thus far has suggested correlational rather than causal relationships. It cannot be concluded that a parenting dimension causes anxiety problems in children simply because the two are found to be associated in cross-sectional studies (Dadds & Roth, 2001). No studies have ruled out the influence of shared genes and in fact, a few have supported that notion that children's dispositional characteristics predict subsequent maternal behaviours (Fish & Crockenberg, 1986; Lee & Bates, 1985; Pelham et al., 1998; Rubin et al., 1999; Whaley et al., 1999). In other words, it is possible that overprotection is a result of anxiety rather than a cause. Child psychopathology is likely characterized by a cyclic relationship involving temperamental factors, parenting styles, and childrearing patterns, all of which need to be taken into account, when examining family influences on anxiety (Dadds & Roth, 2001; Rapee, 1997; Rubin & Mills, 1991). More longitudinal studies need to be performed at theoretically meaningful time-intervals in order to understand the direction of effects linking parenting behaviour and child anxiety (Rapee & Melville, 1997; Wood et al., 2003).

Other Limitations

Numerous other limitations have been discussed in the literature. These include the use of diverse methodologies, definitions and theories used across studies, as well as small sample sizes, non-representative samples and the lack of investigation of paternal influence

(Ginsburg et al., 2004; Rapee, 1997). Most studies have not used appropriate comparison groups, which prevents researchers from drawing conclusions regarding parental rearing styles that are specific to anxiety versus styles that lead to general psychopathology (Ginsburg et al., 2004; Rapee, 1997; Wood et al., 2003).

Theoretical Models

An in-depth examination of the models conceptualizing the development of anxiety is beyond the scope of this work. Yet, it is important to understand two concepts that guide many models of anxiety: *multifinality* and *equifinality*. Multifinality proposes that one risk factor can have a variety of outcomes, depending on the context in which it occurs (Dadds & Roth, 2001; Wood et al., 2003). For example, a child with a genetic predisposition towards behavioural inhibition may be at a higher risk for developing an anxiety disorder, yet, depending on the parental reaction to this predisposition the child may or may not become anxious. Equifinality proposes that there is more than one pathway to the same anxiety disorder, and that one risk factor cannot account solely for the development of a specific disorder (Wood et al., 2003). A child may develop a phobia of dogs due to a traumatic experience by having been bitten by a dog, or perhaps, due to parental modelling of anxious behaviour with dogs. These concepts guide the development of the majority of anxiety models, which suggest a bidirectional relationship between a variety of variables, which interact and contribute to the outcome of child anxiety.

Some models of anxiety focus on parental overinvolvment and control as a key factor in the development of childhood anxiety (Chorpita & Barlow, 1998; Krohne, 1990, 1992). One such model suggests that early experiences with uncontrollable and unpredictable circumstances may encourage an individual to interpret situations as out of one's control. This cognitive style may represent a psychological vulnerability for anxiety (Chorpita & Barlow, 1998). Another model suggests that restricting parental styles lead children to develop negative expectancies, which may then lead to higher trait anxiety. Conversely, a supporting parenting style promotes child competence and expectation of favourable outcomes (Krohne & Hock, 1991).

The model proposed by Hudson and Rapee (2004) suggests that a reciprocal relationship between child temperament and parental behaviour is partially responsible for the development of anxiety. Parents of children with a predisposition towards an anxious temperament may become more involved with their child in an effort to reduce the child's distress. This overinvolvement may reduce the child's perception of control and teach the child that the world is a dangerous place from which they have no control and need protection. This pattern may reinforce the child's vulnerability to anxiety by increasing the child's avoidance of threat. The model also posits that parental anxiety is important in determining the degree of parental overinvolvement. Anxious parents may be more likely to overprotect their children due to an increased perception of danger, while non-anxious parents may be more likely to encourage approach and independent behaviour.

Integrative models of anxiety suggest that the interactions between external (e.g. family) and internal (e.g. genetics) risk and protective factors contribute to the development of anxiety. One such model suggests that the transactions among temperamental dispositions in the child, socialization experiences with the parents and setting conditions contribute to the socioemotional adjustment of a child (Rubin & Mills, 1991). A similar model suggests that the interaction between temperament, attachment and the larger social system contribute to the development of internalizing difficulties (Manassis, Hudson, Webb, & Albano, 2004). Both of these models posit that an internal working model of felt security from the attachment relationship with the primary caregiver determines each child's approach to coping with arousal and social interactions.

The above models are useful for understanding the multiple pathways through which interacting variables such as parenting styles, child temperament and attachment may contribute to childhood anxiety disorders.

Conclusion

On the basis of the studies reviewed, there is clearly an important genetic influence on the development and maintenance of anxiety. There is evidence for increased physiological arousal, as well as temperamental tendencies towards or away from behavioural inhibition. Most researchers agree that the genetic effects are generalized, although there may be some predisposition for particular specific syndromes.

Since not all predisposed individuals develop an overt disorder, attention has been focused on the family environment to account for the development of symptoms. There is wide-spread consensus that the quality of the parent–child attachment is of primary importance to an individual's life-long sense of security or anxiety. The dimensions of parental sensitivity, consistency and contingency, parental encouragement of autonomy, lack of intrusion and excessive control are considered crucial variables. The attachment style on the parental side is greatly determined by the mental well-being, personality style and psychopathology of the parent. It has been demonstrated that maternal anxiety can be directly correlated with an anxiety disorder in the child. Similarly, patterns of overcontrol, overprotection or critical negativity also create the same tendencies and problems in the offspring. Although not all studies are conclusive as to this relationship, and variables are so numerous and complex making accuracy and specificity nearly impossible, the above generalizations hold true in most studies. There is a specific relationship between particular childrearing patterns and specific emotional traits - that is, between excessive parental control and anxiety, between parent's messages of potential threat or danger, and the level of anxious stress in the child and his resultant inability to learn realistic coping strategies.

While some other aspects of the family environment (e.g. demographics, maternal age, and socioeconomic status) show minimally consistent results relating to anxiety in children, certain other factors do seem to influence children's anxiety. Risk factors include parental death, divorce or conflict, violence or sexual mistreatment, chronic physical illness or substance abuse and a family environment of chaos, unpredictability, poor cohesion, poor expression of affect and lack of emotional support. This chapter has not explored the protective factors, which exist to mitigate against the development of anxiety in offspring, and this is a most crucial aspect to be investigated.

There is an ever-increasing body of literature examining the mutuality of the mother–child interaction. Given that there may be a genetically predisposed anxious child, this has an effect on the mother to shape her behaviour towards becoming more controlling, which in turn, might influence the child's reaction. Thus, the interplay of mothers' psychopathology and anxiety in the child may compound the situation. Cyclical relationships must be more thoroughly and systematically investigated in future research on the origins and maintenance of anxiety.

Offspring studies assess child-rearing patterns and family functioning by means of retrospective self-reports, which may reflect either actual or perceived reality. These studies show that subjective cognitive or emotional experiences of control/overprotection versus autonomy, and rejection versus acceptance do relate to anxiety in children. Child reports and parental studies are less conclusive; but adult reports show more consistent results — anxious patients view their parents as having been controlling, rejecting, overprotective, low on socializing, and less caring. Observational studies support this to be true: parental behaviour that is overinvolved, less accepting, and overprotective, may prevent children from developing confidence and self-initiating coping techniques. In addition, parental anxiety status may provide a model for the transmission of cognitive biases and less adaptive ways to handle emotional distress, like avoidant responses for perceived threats. And finally, when observations reveal poor emotional expression, poor family cohesion and poor emotional support of the child in the form of lack of encouragement and less displays of pride or love, the child shows more anxious behaviour and insecurity.

Methodological limitations have been described. Besides variability of reliability and validity in self reports and retrospective studies, the influence of the clinical setting itself may alter the information being gathered. Because human behaviour and interaction, as well as child-rearing and development is so very complex with a multitude of variables, only persistent, careful, systematic and sophisticated future research will begin to tease out the role of each ingredient in the multi-factorial puzzle of the influence of family factors in the creation or perpetuation of anxiety disorders.

References

Alnaes, R., & Torgersen, S. (1990). Parental representation in patients with major depression, anxiety disorder and mixed conditions. *Acta Psychiatrica Scandinavica, 81*, 518–522.

Andrews, G., Stewart, G., Allen, R., & Henderson, A. S. (1990). The genetics of six neurotic disorders: A twin study. *Journal of Affective Disorders, 19*, 23–29.

Arbel, N., & Stravynski, A. (1991). A retrospective study of separation in the development of adult avoidant personality disorder. *Acta Psychiatrica Scandinavica, 83*, 174–178.

Arrindell, W. A., Kwee, M. G. T., Methorst, G. J., van der Ende, J., Pol, E., & Moritz, B. J. M. (1989). Perceived parental rearing styles of agoraphobic and socially phobic in-patients. *The British Journal of Psychiatry, 155*, 526–535.

Barlow, D. H. (2002). *Anxiety and its disorders: The nature and treatment of anxiety and panic* (2nd ed.). New York: Guilford Press.

Barrett, P. M., Rapee, R. M., Dadds, M. M., & Ryan, S. M. (1996). Family enhancement of cognitive style in anxious and aggressive children. *Journal of Abnormal Child Psychology, 24*, 187–203.

Bates, J. E., & Bayles, K. (1988). Attachment and the development of behavior problems. In: J. Belsky & T. Nezworski (Eds), *Clinical implications of early attachment* (pp. 253–259). Hillsdale, NJ: Erlbaum.

Beidel, D. C., & Turner, S. M. (1997). At risk for anxiety: I. Psychopathology in the offspring of anxious parents. *Journal of the American Academy of Child and Adolescent Psychiatry, 36*, 918–924.

Biederman, J., Hirshfeld-Becker, D. R., Rosenbaum, J. F., Herot, C., Friedman, D., Snidman, N., Kagan, J., & Faraone, S. V. (2001). Further evidence of association between behavioral inhibition and social anxiety in children. *American Journal of Psychiatry, 158,* 1673–1679.

Biederman, J., Rosenbaum, J. F., Bolduc-Murphy, E. A., Faraone, S. V., Chaloff, J., Hirshfeld, D. R., et al. (1993). A 3-year follow-up of children with and without behavioral inhibition. *Journal of the American Academy of Child and Adolescent Psychiatry, 32,* 814–821.

Biederman, J., Rosenbaum, J. F., Hirshfeld, D. R., Faraone, S. V., Bolduc, E. A., Gersten, M., & Kagan, J. (1990). Psychiatric correlates of behavioral inhibition in young children of parents with and without psychiatric disorders. *Archives of General Psychiatry, 47,* 21–26.

Bowlby, J. (1969). *Attachment and loss: Attachment* (Vol. 1). England: Penguin Books.

Brewin, C. R., Andrews, B., & Gotlib, I. H. (1993). Psychopathology and early experience: A reappraisal of retrospective reports. *Psychological Bulletin, 113,* 82–98.

Buelow, G., McClain, M., & McIntosh, I. (1996). A new measure for an important construct: The attachment and object relations inventory. *Journal of Personality Assessment, 66,* 604–623.

Capps, L., Sigman, M., Sena, R., Henker, B., & Whalen, C. (1996). Fear, anxiety and perceived control in children of agoraphobic parents. *Journal of Child Psychology and Psychiatry and Allied Disciplines, 37,* 445–452.

Chorpita, B. F., & Albano, A. M. (1996). Cognitive processing in children: Relation to anxiety and family influences. *Journal of Clinical Child Psychology, 25,* 170–176.

Chorpita, B. F., & Barlow, D. H. (1998). The development of anxiety: The role of control in the early environment. *Psychological Bulletin, 124,* 3–21.

Cobham, V. E., Dadds, M. R., & Spence, S. H. (1999). Anxious children and their parents: What do they expect? *Journal of Clinical Child Psychology, 28,* 220–231.

Cowan, P. A., Cohn, D. A., Pape-Cowan, C. P., & Pearson, J. L. (1996). Parents' attachment histories and children's externalizing and internalizing behaviors: Exploring family systems models of linkage. *Journal of Consulting and Clinical Psychology, 64,* 53–63.

Dadds, M. R., Barrett, P. M., & Rapee, R. M. (1996). Family process and child anxiety and aggression: An observational analysis. *Journal of Abnormal Child Psychology, 24,* 715–734.

Dadds, M. R., & Roth, J. H. (2001). Family processes in the development of anxiety problems. In: M. W. Vasey & M. R. Dadds (Eds), *The developmental psychopathology of anxiety* (pp. 278–303). New York: Oxford University Press.

de Man, A. F. (1986). Parental control in child rearing and trait anxiety in young adults. *Psychological Reports, 59,* 477–478.

Deklyen, M. (1996). Disruptive behavior disorder and intergenerational attachment patterns. *Journal of Consulting and Clinical Psychology, 64,* 357–365.

Dumas, J. E., LaFreniere, P. J., & Serketich, W. J. (1995). "Balance of power": A transactional analysis of control in mother-child dyads involving socially competent, aggressive, and anxious children. *Journal of Abnormal Psychology, 104,* 104–113.

Ehiobuche, I. (1988). Obsessive-compulsive neurosis in relation to parental child-rearing patterns amongst the Greek, Italian, and Anglo-Australian subjects. *Acta Psychiatrica Scandinavica, 78,* 115–120.

Eley, T. C. (1997). General genes: A new theme in developmental psychopathology. *Journal of Child Psychology and Psychiatry, 6,* 90–95.

Eley, T. C. (2001). Contributions of behavioral genetics research: Quantifying genetic, shared environmental, and nonshared environmental influences. In: M. W. Vaseys & M. R. Dadds (Eds), *The developmental psychopathology of anxiety* (pp. 45–59). New York: Oxford Univerisity Press.

Fish, M., & Crockenberg, S. (1986). Correlates and antecedents of nine-month infant behavior and mother-infant interaction. *Infant Behavior and Development, 4,* 69–81.

Frost, R. O., Steketee, G., Cohn, L., & Griess, K. (1994). Personality traits in subclinical and non-obsessive-compulsive volunteers and their parents. *Behaviour Research and Therapy, 32,* 47–56.

Garcia Coll, C., Kagan, J., & Reznick, J. (1984). Behavioral inhibition in young children. *Child Development, 55*, 1005–1019.

Ginsburg, G. S., Siqueland, L., Masia-Warner, C., & Hedtke, K. A. (2004). Anxiety disorders in children: Family matters. *Cognitive and Behavioral Practice, 11*, 28–43.

Grüner, K., Muris, P., & Merckelbach, H. (1999). The relationship between anxious rearing behaviours and anxiety disorders symptomatology in normal children. *Journal of Behavior Therapy and Experimental Psychiatry, 30*, 27–35.

Hayward, C., Wilson, K. A., Lagle, K., Killen, J. D., & Taylor, C. (2004). Parent-reported predictors of adolescent panic attacks. *Journal of the American Academy of Child and Adolescent Psychiatry, 43*, 613–620.

Hernandez-Guzman, L., & Sanchez-Sosa, J. J. (1996). Parent-child interactions predict anxiety in Mexican adolescents. *Adolescence, 31*, 955–963.

Hibbs, E. D., Hamburger, S. D., Lenane, M., Rapoport, J. L., Kruesi, M. J., Keysor, C. S., et al. (1991). Determinants of expressed emotion in families of disturbed and normal children. *Journal of Child Psychology and Psychiatry and Allied Disciplines, 32*, 757–770.

Hirshfeld, D. R., Biederman, J., Brody, L., Faraone, S. V., & Rosenbaum, J. F. (1997a). Associations between expressed emotion and child behavioral inihibition and psychopathology: A pilot study. *Journal of the American Academy of Child and Adolescent Psychiatry, 36*, 205–213.

Hirshfeld, D. R., Biederman, J., Brody, L., Faraone, S. V., & Rosenbaum, J. F. (1997b). Expressed emotion toward children with behavioral inhibition: Associations with maternal anxiety disorder. *Journal of the American Academy of Child and Adolescent Psychiatry, 36*, 910–917.

Hirshfeld, D. R., Rosenbaum, J. F., Biederman, J., Bolduc, E. A., Faraone, S. V., Reznick, S. J., et al. (1992). Stable behavioral inhibition and its association with anxiety disorder. *Journal of the American Academy of Child and Adolescent Psychiatry, 31*, 103–111.

Hudson, J. L., & Rapee, R. M. (2001). Parent-child interactions and anxiety disorders: An observational study. *Behaviour Research and Therapy, 39*, 1411–1427.

Hudson, J. L., & Rapee, R. M. (2002). Parent-child interactions in clinically anxious children and their siblings. *Journal of Clinical Child and Adolescent Psychology, 31*, 548.

Hudson, J. L., & Rapee, R. M. (2004). From anxious temperament to disorder: An etiological model. In: R. G. Heimberg, C. L. Turk & D. S. Mennin (Eds), *Generalized anxiety disorder: Advances in research and practice* (pp. 51–76). New York: The Guildford Press.

Hummel, R. M., & Gross, A. M. (2001). Socially anxious children: An observational study of parent-child interaction. *Child and Family Behavior Therapy, 23*, 19–41.

Kagan, J. (1989). Temperamental contributions to social behavior. *American Psychologist, 44*, 668–674.

Kagan, J., & Garcia-Coll, C. (1984). Behavioral inhibition to the unfamiliar. *Child Development, 55*, 2212–2225.

Kagan, J., Reznick, J., & Snidman, N. (1988). Biological bases of childhood shyness. *Science, 240*, 167–171.

Kendall, P. C., & Chansky, T. E. (1991). Considering cognition in anxiety-disordered children. *Journal of Anxiety Disorders, 5*, 167–185.

Kendler, K. S., Heath, A. C., Martin, N. G., & Evans, L. J. (1987). Symptoms of anxiety and symptoms of depression: Same genes, different environments? *Archives of General Psychiatry, 44*, 451–457.

Kendler, K. S., Neale, M. C., Kessler, R. C., Heath, A. C., & Eaves, L. J. (1992). Major depression and generalized anxiety disorder. Same genes, (partly) different environments? *Archives of General Psychiatry, 49*, 716–722.

Kendler, K. S., Walters, E. E., Neale, M. C., Kessler, R. C., Heath, A. C., & Eaves, L. J. (1995). The structure of the genetic and environmental risk factors for six major psychiatric disorders in women: Phobia, generalized anxiety disorder, panic disorder, bulimia, major depression, and alcoholism. *Archives of General Psychiatry, 52,* 374–383.

Kliewer, W., & Kung, E. (1998). Family moderators of the relation between hassles and behavior problems in inner-city youth. *Journal of Clinical Child Psychology, 27,* 278–292.

Krohne, H. W. (1990). Parental childrearing and anxiety development. In: K. Hurrelmann & F. Loesel (Eds), *Health hazards in adolescence prevention and intervention in childhood and adolescence* (Vol. 8, pp. 115–130). Oxford, England: Walter De Gruyter.

Krohne, H. W. (1992). Developmental conditions of anxiety and coping: A two-process model of child-rearing effects. In: K. A. Hagtvet & T. B. Johnsen (Eds), *Advances in test anxiety research* (Vol. 7, pp. 143–155). Lisse, Netherlands: Swets & Zeitlinger Publishers.

Krohne, H. W., & Hock, M. (1991). Relationships between restrictive mother child interactions and anxiety of the child. *Anxiety Research, 4,* 109–124.

Laraia, M. T., Stuart, G. W., Frye, L. H., Lydiard, B. R., & Ballenger, J. C. (1994). Childhood environment of women having panic disorder with agoraphobia. *Journal of Anxiety Disorders, 8,* 1–17.

Last, C. G., Hersen, M., Kazdin, A., Orvaschel, H., & Perrin, S. (1991). Anxiety disorders in children and their families. *Archives of General Psychiatry, 48,* 928–934.

Lee, C. L., & Bates, J. E. (1985). Mother-child interaction at age two years and perveived difficult temperament. *Child Development, 56,* 1314–1325.

Lewis, M., Feiring, C., McGuffog, C., & Jaskir, J. (1984). Predicting psychopathology in six-year-olds from early social relations. *Child Development, 55,* 123–136.

Lieb, R., Wittchen, H.-U., Hofler, M., Fuetsch, M., Stein, M. B., & Merikangas, K. R. (2000). Parental psychopathology, parenting styles, and the risk of social phobia in offspring: A prospective-longitudinal community study. *Archives of General Psychiatry, 57,* 859–866.

MacEwn, K. E., & Barling, J. (1991). Effects of maternal employment experiences on children's behavior via mood, cognitive difficulties, and parenting behavior. *Journal of Marriage and the Family, 53,* 635–644.

Mackinnon, A., Henderson, A., & Andrews, G. (1991). The Parental Bonding Instrument: A measure of perceived or actual parental behavior? *Acta Psychiatrica Scandinavica, 83,* 153–159.

Main, M. (1995). Discourse, prediction, and recent studies in attachment: Implications for psychoanalysis. In: T. Shapiro & R. N. Emde (Eds), *Research in psychoanalysis: Process, development, outcome* (pp. 209–244). Madison, CT: International Universities Press, Inc.

Main, M. (1996). Introduction to the special section on attachment and psychopathology: 2. Overview of the field of attachment. *Journal of Consulting and Clinical Psychology, 64,* 237–243.

Manassis, K., & Bradley, S. J. (1994). The development of childhood anxiety disorders: Toward an integrated model. *Journal of Applied Developmental Psychology, 15,* 345–366.

Manassis, K., Hudson, J. L., Webb, A., & Albano, A. M. (2004). Beyond behavioral inhibition: Etiological factors in childhood anxiety. *Cognitive and Behavioral Practice, 11,* 3–12.

Mancini, C., Van Ameringen, M., Szatmari, P., Fugere, C., & Boyle, M. H. (1996). A high-risk pilot study of the children of adults with social phobia. *Journal of the American Academy of Child and Adolescent Psychiatry, 35,* 1511–1517.

Masia, C. L., & Morris, T. L. (1998). Parental factors associated with social anxiety: Methodological limitations and suggestions for integrated behavioral research. *Clinical Psychology: Science and Practice, 5,* 211–228.

Mattanah, J. F. (2001). Parental psychological autonomy and children's academic competence and behavioral adjustment in late childhood: More than just limit-setting and warmth. *Merrill-Palmer Quarterly, 47,* 355–376.

Merikangas, K. R., Avenevoli, S., Dierker, L., & Grillon, C. (1999). Vulnerability factors among children at risk for anxiety disorders. *Biological Psychiatry, 46,* 1523–1535.

Mertesacker, B., Bade, U., Haverkock, A., & Pauli-Pott, U. (2004). Predicting maternal reactivity/sensitivity: The role of infant emotionality, maternal depressiveness/anxiety, and social support. *Infant Mental Health Journal, 25*, 47–61.

Mills, R. S. L., & Rubin, K. H. (1998). Are behavioural and psychological control both differentially associated with childhood aggression and social withdrawal? *Canadian Journal of Behavioural Science, 30*, 132–136.

Moore, P. S., Whaley, S. E., & Sigman, M. (2004). Interactions between mothers and children: Impacts of maternal and child anxiety. *Journal of Abnormal Psychology, 113*, 471–476.

Muris, P., Bogels, S., Meesters, C., van der Kamp, N., & van Oosten, A. (1996). Parental rearing practices, fearfulness, and problem behaviour in clinically referred children. *Personality and Individual Differences, 21*, 813–818.

Muris, P., Meesters, C., Schouten, E., & Hoge, E. (2004). Effects of perceived control on the relationship between perceived parental rearing behaviors and symptoms of anxiety and depression in nonclinical preadolescents. *Journal of Youth and Adolescence, 33*, 51–58.

Muris, P., Mesters, C., Merckelback, H., & Hulsenbeck, P. (2000). Worry in children is related to perceived parental rearing and attachment. *Behaviour Research and Therapy, 38*, 487–497.

Myhr, G., Sookman, D., & Pinard, G. (2004). Attachment security and parental bonding in adults with obsessive-compulsive disorder: A comparison with depressed out-patients and healthy controls. *Acta Psychiatrica Scandinavica, 109*, 447–456.

Papini, D. R., & Roggman, L. A. (1992). Adolescent perceived attachment to parents in relation to competence, depression, and anxiety: A longitudinal study. *Journal of Early Adolescence, 12*, 420–440.

Papini, D. R., Roggman, L. A., & Anderson, J. (1991). Early-adolescent perceptions of attachment to mother and father: A test of emotional-distancing and buffering hypothesis. *Journal of Early Adolescence, 11*, 258–275.

Parker, G. (1979). Reported parental characteristics in relation to trait depression and anxiety levels in a non-clinical group. *Australian and New Zealand Journal of Psychiatry, 13*, 260–264.

Parker, G. (1981). Parental representations of patients with anxiety neurosis. *Acta Psychiatrica Scandinavica, 63*, 33–36.

Parker, G. (1990). The parental bonding instrument: A decade of research. *Social Psychiatry and Psychiatric Epidemiology, 25*, 281–282.

Pauli-Pott, U., Mertesacker, B., & Beckmann, D. (2004). Predicting the development of infant emotionality from maternal characteristics. *Development and Psychopathology, 16*, 19–42.

Pedersen, W. (1994). Parental relations, mental health, and delinquency in adolescents. *Adolescence, 29*, 975–990.

Pelham, W. E., Jr., Lang, A. R., Atkeson, B., Murphy, D. A., Gnagy, E. M., Greiner, A. R., et al. (1998). Effects of deviant child behavior on parental alcohol consumption: Stress-induced drinking in parents of ADHD children. *American Journal on Addictions, 7*, 103–114.

Perry, N. W., & Millimet, R. C. (1977). Child-rearing antecedents of low and high anxiety eighth-grade children. In: C. D. Speilberger & I. G. Sarason (Eds), *Stress and anxiety* (Vol. 4, pp. 189–204). New York: Wiley.

Pianta, R. C., O'Connor, T. G., & Marvin, R. S. (1993). *Measuring representations of parenting: An interview-based system*. Unpublished manuscript, University of Virginia, Charlottesville.

Plomin, R., & Rowe, D. C. (1979). Genetic and environmental etiology of social behavior in infancy. *Developmental Psychology, 15*, 62–72.

Prior, M., Smart, D., Sanson, A., & Oberklaid, F. (2000). Does shy-inhibited temperament in childhood lead to anxiety problems in adolescence? *Journal of the American Academy of Child and Adolescent Psychiatry, 39*, 461–468.

Rapee, R. M. (1997). Potential role of childrearing practices in the development of anxiety and depression. *Clinical Psychology Review, 17*, 47–67.

Rapee, R. M., & Melville, L. F. (1997). Recall of family factors in social phobia and panic disorder: Comparison of mother and offspring reports. *Depression and Anxiety, 5*, 7–11.

Reznick, J. S., Kagan, J., Snidman, N., Gersten, M., Baak, K., & Rosenberg, A. (1986). Inhibited and uninhibited children: A follow-up study. *Child Development, 57*, 660–680.

Rosenbaum, J. F., Biederman, J., Bolduc, E. A., Hirshfeld, D. R., Faraone, S. V., & Kagan, J. (1992). Comorbidity of parental anxiety disorders as risk for childhood-onset anxiety in inhibited children. *American Journal of Psychiatry, 149*, 475–481.

Rosenbaum, J. F., Biederman, J., Hirshfeld, D. R., Bolduc, E. A., & Chaloff, J. (1991). Behavioral inhibition in children: A possible precursor to panic disorder or social phobia. *Journal of Clinical Psychiatry, 52*, 5–9.

Rosenbaum, J. F., Biederman, J., Hirshfeld, D. R., Bolduc, E. A., Faraone, S. V., Kagan, J., et al. (1991). Further evidence of an association between behavioral inhibition and anxiety disorders: Results from a family study of children from a non-clinical sample. *Journal of Psychiatric Research, 25*, 49–65.

Rosenstein, D. S., & Horowitz, H. A. (1996). Adolescent attachment and psychopathology. *Journal of Consulting and Clinical Psychology, 64*, 244–253.

Rubin, K. H., Burgess, K. B., & Hastings, P. D. (2002). Stability and social-behavioral consequences of toddlers' inhibited temperament and parenting behaviors. *Child Development, 73*, 483–495.

Rubin, K. H., Cheah, C. S., & Fox, N. (2001). Emotion regulation, parenting and display of social reticence in preschoolers. *Early Education and Development, 12*, 97–115.

Rubin, K. H., & Mills, R. S. (1990). Maternal beliefs about adaptive and maladaptive social behaviors in normal, aggressive, and withdrawn preschoolers. *Journal of Abnormal Child Psychology, 18*, 419–435.

Rubin, K. H., & Mills, R. S. (1991). Conceptualizing developmental pathways to internalizing disorders in childhood. *Canadian Journal of Behavioural Science, 23*, 300–317.

Rubin, K. H., Nelson, L. J., Hastings, P., & Asendorpf, J. (1999). The transaction between parents' perceptions of their children's shyness and their parenting styles. *International Journal of Behavioral Development, 23*, 937–958.

Scharfe, E. (2002). Reliability and validity of an interview assessment of attachment representations in a clinical sample of adolescents. *Journal of Adolescent Research, 17*, 532–551.

Scott, W. A., Scott, R., & McCabe, M. (1991). Family relationships and children's personality: A cross-cultural, cross-source comparison. *British Journal of Social Psychology, 30*, 1–20.

Shamir-Essakow, G., Ungerer, J. A., & Rapee, R. M. (2005). Attachment, behavioral inhibition, and anxiety in preschool children. *Journal of Abnormal Child Psychology, 33*, 131–143.

Shamir-Essakow, G., Ungerer, J. A., Rapee, R. M., & Safier, R. (2004). Caregiving representations of mothers of behaviorally inhibited and uninhibited preschool children. *Developmental Psychology, 40*, 899–910.

Shaw, D. S., Keenan, K., Vondra, J. I., Delliquadri, E., & Giovannelli, J. (1997). Antecedents of preschool children's internalizing problems: A longitudinal study of low-income families. *Journal of the American Academy of Child and Adolescent Psychiatry, 36*, 1760–1767.

Shortt, A. L., Barrett, P. M., Dadds, M. R., & Fox, T. L. (2001). The influence of family and experimental context on cognition in anxious children. *Journal of Abnormal Child Psychology, 29*, 585–598.

Siegelman, M. (1965). College student personality correlates of early parent-child relationship. *Journal of Consulting Psychology, 29*, 558–564.

Silove, D. (1986). Perceived parental characteristics and reports of early parental deprivation in agoraphobic patients. *Australian and New Zealand Journal of Psychiatry, 20*, 365–369.

Siqueland, L., Kendall, P. C., & Steinberg, L. (1996). Anxiety in children: Perceived family environments and observed family interaction. *Journal of Clinical Child Psychology, 25*, 225–237.

Solomon, J., & George, C. (1999). The measurement of attachment security in infancy and childhood. In: J. Cassidy & P. R. Shaver (Eds), *Handbook of attachment: Theory, research, and clinical applications* (pp. 287–316). New York, NY: Guilford Press.

Spence, S. H., Barrett, P. M., & Turner, C. M. (2003). Psychometric properties of the Spence Children's Anxiety Scale with young adolescents. *Journal of Anxiety Disorders, 17,* 605–625.

Sroufe, A. L. (1990). Considering normal and abnormal together: The essence of developmental psychopathology. *Development and Psychopathology, 2,* 335–347.

Stark, K. D., Humphrey, L. L., Crook, K., & Lewis, K. (1990). Perceived family environments of depressed and anxious children: Child's and maternal figure's perspectives. *Journal of Abnormal Child Psychology, 18,* 527–547.

Stevenson-Hinde, J., & Glover, A. (1996). Shy girls and boys: A new look. *Journal of Child Psychology and Psychiatry and Allied Disciplines, 37,* 181–187.

Stevenson-Hinde, J., & Shouldice, A. (1990). Fear and attachment in 2.5-year-olds. *British Journal of Developmental Psychology, 8,* 319–333.

Stubbe, D. E., Zahner, G. E. P., Goldstein, M. J., & Leckman, J. F. (1993). Diagnostic specificity of a brief measure of expressed emotion: A community study of children. *Journal of Child Psychology and Psychiatry and Allied Disciplines, 34,* 139–154.

Tesser, A., & Forehand, R. (1991). Adolescent functioning: Communication and the buffering of parental anger. *Journal of Social and Clinical Psychology, 10,* 152–175.

Thapar, A., & McGuffin, P. (1995). Are anxiety symptoms in childhood heritable? *Journal of Child Psychology and Psychiatry and Allied Disciplines, 36,* 439–447.

Torgersen, S. (1983). Genetic factors in anxiety disorders. *Archives of General Psychiatry, 40,* 1085–1089.

Turner, S. M., Beidel, D. C., Roberson-Nay, R., & Tervo, K. (2003). Parenting behaviors in parents with anxiety disorders. *Behaviour Research and Therapy, 41,* 541–554.

Tyrer, P., Alexander, J., Remington, M., & Riley, P. (1987). Relationship between neurotic symptoms and neurotic diagnosis: A longitudinal study. *Journal of Affective Disorders, 13,* 13–21.

Ungerer, J., & McMahon, C. Attachment and psychopathology: A lifespan perspective. In: J. L. Hudson & R. M. Rapee (Eds), *Psychopathology and the family* (pp. 35–54). Oxford: Elsevier.

Van Dam, M., & Van Ijzendoorn, M. H. (1988). Measuring attachment security: Concurrent and predictive validity of the Parental Attachment Q-set. *Journal of Genetic Psychology, 149,* 447–457.

van Ijzendoorn, M. H., Vereijken, C. M. J. L., Bakermans-Kranenburg, M. J., & Riksen-Walraven, J. (2004). Assessing attachment security with the attachment Q sort: Meta-analytic evidence for the validity of the Observer AQS. *Child Development, 75,* 1188–1213.

Warren, S., Megan, R. G., Jerome, K., Anders, T. E., Simmens, S. J., Rones, M., Wease, S., Aron, E., Dahl, R., & Srouffe, L. A. (2003). Maternal panic disorder: Infant temperament, neurophysiology, and parenting behaviors. *Journal of the American Academy of Child and Adolescent Psychiatry, 42,* 814–825.

Warren, S. L., Huston, L., Egeland, B., & Sroufe, L. A. (1997). Child and adolescent anxiety disorders and early attachment. *Journal of the American Academy of Child and Adolescent Psychiatry, 36,* 637–644.

Whaley, S. E., Pinto, A., & Sigman, M. (1999). Characterizing interactions between anxious mothers and their children. *Journal of Consulting and Clinical Psychology, 67,* 826–836.

Wood, J. J., McLeod, B. D., Sigman, M., Hwang, W.-C., & Chu, B. C. (2003). Parenting and childhood anxiety: Theory, empirical findings, and future directions. *Journal of Child Psychology & Psychiatry & Allied Disciplines, 44,* 134–151.

Woodruff-Borden, J., Morrow, C., Bourland, S., & Cambron, S. (2002). The behavior of anxious parents: Examining mechanisms of transmission of anxiety from parent to child. *Journal of Clinical Child and Adolescent Psychology, 31,* 364.

Chapter 8

Eating Disorders

Tracey Wade

Eating Disorders Defined

The focus of the current chapter is on those eating disorders defined in the Diagnostic and Statistical Manual (DSM-IV; American Psychiatric Association (APA), 1994) — namely anorexia nervosa (AN), bulimia nervosa (BN) and eating disorders that do not meet strict diagnostic criteria, referred to as Eating Disorders Not Otherwise Specified (EDNOS) or atypical disorders. These latter disorders are virtually identical to either AN or BN, and account for at least half the cases seen in clinical referrals (Fairburn & Harrison, 2003). The evidence suggests that people with these atypical disorders display equivalent forms of associated psychopathology and disability to AN or BN (Garfinkel et al., 1996; Johnson, Spitzer, & Williams, 2001; McIntosh et al., 2004).

Aetiology of Eating Disorders: The Interplay between Heritability and the Environment

Evidence consistently indicates that eating disorders "run in families". There is a 7- to 12-fold increase in the prevalence of EDNOS in relatives of AN and BN probands compared to relatives of control families (Lilenfeld et al., 1998). However, such knowledge does not tell us *how* eating disorders are conveyed in the family. This may be due to genetic pathways or environmental influences within the family.

   Consistent with research in other areas of psychopathology (Rutter & Silberg, 2002), twin studies across different populations, using various measures of disordered eating, reliably find a substantial role for both genetic and non-shared (or unique) environmental factors to variation in liability to eating disorders, as well as behaviours and attitudes representative of such eating disorders (Bulik, Sullivan, Wade, & Kendler, 2000; Jacobi, Hayward, de Zwaan, Kraemer, & Agras, 2004). Environmental factors that are unique to individual family members are more important in influencing the development of

Psychopathology and the Family
Edited by J. L. Hudson and R. M. Rapee
Copyright © 2005 by Elsevier Ltd.
All rights of reproduction in any form reserved
ISBN: 0-08-044449-0

disordered eating than environments shared by family members. It is important to understand that non-shared environment can be either *objective*, an actual experience or event that is not shared by siblings, or *effective*, where the same event in a family can be experienced uniquely by each family member for reasons not attributable to their genotype (Turkheimer & Waldron, 2000). For example, siblings, due to differential environmental influences such as peer relationships and birth order, may experience a parental divorce differently. Thus a non-shared environment can include a family environment variable. Unusually, compared to most other psychopathologies, there also appears to be a contribution of the shared environment to the development of eating disorders. The shared environment is an important contributor to desired body size (Wade, Bulik, Heath, Martin, & Eaves, 2001a) and weight concern (Reichborn-Kjennerud et al., 2004; Wade, Martin, & Tiggemann, 1998). Weight concern occurs, where self-evaluation is unduly influenced by body weight to the extent that self-worth becomes mainly or solely evaluated with respect to body weight and is one of the diagnostic criterion for both AN and BN.

Thus the aetiology of eating disorders can be broadly conceptualised as involving two basic pathways. The first is through genetic pathways, which will include the heritability of various temperaments that can increase vulnerability for the development of an eating disorder. The second pathway is through specific types of environment. Complex traits like eating disorders are understood to be influenced by many genes and many specific (non-shared and shared) environmental factors. Hence, genetic factors are seen to operate in a probabilistic fashion, like risk factors rather then predetermined programming (Plomin, 2000). Two ways in which to understand the complex genotype-environment interplay are gene–environment correlations and genotype–environment interactions (Rutter & Silberg, 2002, see also Chapter 10). To date, neither of these interplays has been formally examined in the eating disorder literature.

Genotype–environment (g–e) correlations describe the extent to which individuals are exposed to certain environments as a function of their genetic propensities. Three types of g–e correlations have been hypothesised to exist (Scarr & McCartney, 1983) and previously discussed in terms of their relationships to eating disorders (Klump, McGue, & Iacono, 2000): passive, evocative and active. Passive g–e correlation occurs where parents provide their children with both genes and an environment that is conducive to the development of certain traits that occur independently of the offspring's characteristics or behaviours e.g. highly weight-conscious parents could transmit this characteristic to their children as well as providing a diet-conscious environment that is conducive to the trait's development. An evocative g–e correlation occurs when genetically influenced characteristics evoke an environmental response that reflects the genetic trait. For example, adopted children with genetic risk for antisocial behavioural problems can evoke a negative parenting style from their adoptive parents (O'Connor, Deater-Deckard, Fulker, Rutter, & Plomin, 1998). A postulated example of relevance to eating disorders is the child high in weight concern who evokes a controlling parental style as parents try to stop the child from dieting or seeing weight-conscious friends. Active g–e correlations refer to the situation where individuals actively select or create environments that are correlated with their genetic propensities e.g. the selection of weight conscious friends by an adolescent who also places importance on physical appearance.

Genotype–environment interactions (GxE) occur when the effect of the environment depends upon the genotype, such that individuals will be varyingly susceptible to the influence of high-risk environments proportional to their degree of genetic risk. One possible example of a GxE comes from the finding that proneness to anxiety (neuroticism) interacts with parental concern with physical appearance and attractiveness to increase weight preoccupation (Davis, Shuster, Blackmore, & Fox, 2004). In other words, low levels of neuroticism may protect a person from weight preoccupation in a family focused on appearance.

Within the context of understanding the complex gene–environment interplay, the purpose of this chapter is to review possible familial risk factors for eating disorders, including the types of heritable temperament that may predispose people to the development of an eating disorder, as well as the types of specific family environments (either non-shared or shared environment) that may correlate or interact with this temperament. The establishment of a variable as a risk factor requires precedence to the development of disordered eating to be established (Kraemer et al., 1997). It should be noted that familial temperament and psychopathology have been recognised as *potential risk factors*, as the studies in this area are of a cross-sectional nature (Jacobi et al., 2004). Specific family environments have been classified as *correlates*, as family environment variables have thus far largely failed to be identified as risk factors in longitudinal studies of eating disorder development (Jacobi et al., 2004; Polivy & Herman, 2002; Shisslak & Crago, 2001; Stice, 2002).

Heritable Temperaments and Psychopathologies that Increase Vulnerability to Developing an Eating Disorder

While a variety of psychopathologies are more likely to occur in people with eating disorders than people without eating disorders, such evidence is not sufficient to indicate the influence of a heritable temperament that produces vulnerability to eating disorders. The risk of other psychopathologies may be increased simply as a result of the eating disorder. Reports from relatives of the proband are more informative. The strongest design includes relatives of the eating disorder proband, as well as the proband themselves, where the influence of the proband's comorbid disorder of interest is controlled. In this context, if the eating disorder of the proband is then significantly associated with the comorbid disorder of interest in the relative, this indicates shared risk factors between the temperament and the eating disorder. For example, findings from a range of community-based studies suggest that BN and alcohol-related disorders do co-occur at a rate greater than chance, with presence of BN being associated with an approximately three-fold increase in the risk of alcoholism (Dansky, Brewerton, & Kilpatrick, 2000; Kendler et al., 1991; Welch & Fairburn, 1996). Furthermore, individuals with BN have been found to be more likely to have used illicit drugs than either non-eating disordered or psychiatric controls (Welch & Fairburn, 1996). However, there is consistent evidence across a range of family studies to suggest that there are no shared risk factors between alcohol abuse or dependence and BN (Bulik, 1991; Kaye et al., 1996; Kendler et al., 1995; Lilenfeld et al., 1998; von Ranson, McGue, & Iacono, 2003; Wade, Bulik, Prescott, & Kendler, 2004). In other words, when alcohol use in the eating disorder proband is controlled, there is no significant association between alcohol use in the relative and the eating disorder in the proband, indicating independent transmission of the two disorders. Similarly, when controlling for the proband's illicit psychoactive substance abuse, the eating disorder in the proband does not predict such abuse in the relative (Wade et al., 2004).

In recent years there have been several large family studies investigating reports of psychopathology from the family of the proband and the eating disorder proband, suggesting a variety of temperaments inherited from parents that may be risk factors for the development of eating disorders. Typically the profile for AN and BN are somewhat different, but also overlapping.

Obsessionality and AN

A family study incorporating both proband and family reports found that obsessive-compulsive personality disorder (OCPD), but not obsessive-compulsive disorder, may be a specific familial risk factor for AN. Rates of OCPD were found to be elevated among relatives of AN probands, irrespective of the presence of OCPD among the probands themselves (Lilenfeld et al., 1998). This finding was not replicated for the probands with BN. Similarly, an Italian study found that parents and siblings of eating disorder probands (84 with AN and 52 with BN) had significantly higher risk of obsessive-compulsive spectrum disorders than relatives of controls, even when controlling for these spectrum disorders in the proband (Bellodi et al., 2001). They found no differences in the morbidity risk for these spectrum disorders between the two eating disorder groups. It seems likely that these studies indicate that the underlying construct of obsessionality contributes to the development of AN, but as yet this continuous phenotype has not been examined in a family study design.

Other temperaments of interest that may be implicated in increasing risk for the development of AN are likely to be related to obsessionality. Trait anxiety, harm avoidance, perfectionism and diminished self-directedness are considered to represent parts of one underlying construct that includes obsessionality (The Price Foundation Collaborative Group, 2001). Less convincing evidence exists to implicate these temperaments in increasing risk of the development of AN. However, a comparison of the mothers and fathers of AN probands with control parents (Woodside et al., 2002) showed mothers of the AN probands to score significantly more highly on perfectionism as measured by the Frost Multi-dimensional Perfectionism Scale (Frost, Marten, Lahart, & Rosenblate, 1990), specifically on the concern over mistakes and parental criticism scales. Overall, these findings are consistent with a recent comprehensive review of eating disorder risk factors, where perfectionism was rated as a medium potency risk factor for AN (Jacobi et al., 2004).

Self-directedness is also considered to represent part of the underlying construct that is hypothesised to increase risk for the development of AN (The Price Foundation Collaborative Group, 2001). Self-directedness is a measure of autonomy or locus of control. Investigation of this construct has shown fathers of AN probands to have significantly higher scores on self-directedness than fathers of controls (Woodside et al., 2002). This latter finding is in direct contradiction with other studies of similar design where both fathers and mothers of AN probands were low in self-directedness (Fassino et al., 2002), as were mothers of BN probands (Fassino et al., 2003). These latter studies are more consistent with the idea that deficits in self-directedness may influence the development of AN.

Mothers of AN probands also score significantly higher on ineffectiveness and interoceptive awareness compared to control mothers (Woodside et al., 2002). People low on interoception are seen to have difficulty identifying emotion or dealing with strong feelings. Ineffectiveness and low interoception are seen to be risk factors for eating disorders (Jacobi et al., 2004). Ineffectiveness, also taken to indicate low self-esteem, has been posited to be a central contributor to the development of AN in the cognitive behavioural model of this disorder, where control over eating is used as a major index of self-worth (Fairburn, Shafran, & Cooper, 1999).

Anxiety, Neuroticism, Depression, Novelty Seeking and BN

A prospective longitudinal study of 2000 adolescents recruited from consecutive admissions to primary care settings in the USA found that problems with anxiety or depression tended to precede the onset of bulimic symptoms (Zaider, Johnson, & Cockell, 2002). Family studies of BN suggest that these heritable psychopathologies are important in increasing risk for BN. One twin study (Kendler et al., 1995) investigated the interplay of genetic and environmental causal factors simultaneously for six psychiatric disorders in women, including broadly defined bulimia, phobia, panic disorder, major depression, generalised anxiety disorder (GAD) and alcoholism. This study found evidence for shared genetic vulnerability between phobia, panic disorder and bulimia. A further study has supported the presence of shared vulnerability between BN and panic disorder, as well as BN and GAD, and BN and major depression (Hudson et al., 2003). A further study of male–female and female–female dizygotic (non-identical) twin pairs examined BN status in the sister as a predictor of a sibling's psychopathology while controlling for the corresponding psychopathology in the sister (Wade et al., 2004). This study showed that not only were GAD, panic disorder, neuroticism and major depression predicted by the sister's BN, but that shared risk factors between BN and GAD are only present in males. A 22-year longitudinal study identified higher levels of family depression in the parents whose children went on to develop an eating disorder compared to those who did not (Moorhead et al., 2003). Negative affectivity is seen to be a general risk factor for eating disorders, with childhood anxiety disorders being implicated in both the onset of AN and BN (Jacobi et al., 2004).

Cluster B personality disorders have been found to be elevated among BN probands, suggesting that affective instability and impulsivity may be important in the development of BN (Lilenfeld et al., 1998). Cluster B personality disorders are associated with high novelty seeking and low self-directedness in patients receiving treatment for major depression and BN (Mulder, Joyce, Sullivan, Bulik, & Carter, 1999). Wade et al. (2004) found that risk for BN in one sibling was translated to risk for higher levels of novelty seeking in the other sibling only if the other sibling was male. They also suggested use of psychoactive substances may be a behavioural marker for novelty seeking given that the use of psychoactive substances was significantly associated with novelty seeking in their male–female sample, with an odds ratio (OR) of 1.03 (95% CI: 1.00–1.06). Psychoactive substance use in one sibling was predicted by the sister's BN after controlling for her own substance use.

In summary, there is convincing evidence to suggest that an obsessional temperament in parents may be transmitted to their female offspring, thus increasing vulnerability to developing AN. With respect to BN, there is evidence to suggest various forms of anxiety (including neuroticism, panic disorder, phobias and GAD), depression and novelty seeking, may represent genetically transmitted temperaments that increase the likelihood of the development of BN.

Specific Family Environments that Increase Vulnerability to Developing an Eating Disorder

Casual observation of the eating disorder literature would suggest that family environment is a major contributor to the development of eating disorders. There is a long history of writing about clinical observations based on a small number of families presenting for treatment (e.g. Minuchin, Rosman, & Baker, 1978), and there is a myriad of cross-sectional studies showing probands with eating disorders reporting their families to be significantly more disturbed than children in control families. For example, women with AN referred to an eating disorder service most commonly reported the perceived causes of the eating problem as being dysfunctional families (Tozzi, Sullivan, Fear, McKenzie, & Bulik, 2003). In clinical populations, women with BN consistently report significantly more conflict, hostility and anger in their families of origin than control women (Johnson & Flach, 1985). As the severity of eating pathology increases, so too does proband reports of family dysfunction (Wisotsky et al., 2003).

However, these sorts of findings need to be interpreted carefully within the context of critical and substantive methodological problems and limitations. Reports of family dysfunction commonly differ between family members, with the affected member reporting a higher level of problems. Women with AN reported greater levels of enmeshment with mothers and fathers than controls (Rowa, Kerig, & Geller, 2001), but parents of these women did not endorse more boundary problems than control parents. Patients with acute AN also report significantly lower perceived autonomy with respect to their parents as well as greater exposure to high parental expectations than do their healthy sisters (Karwautz et al., 2003, 2001). In an interesting prospective study, Woodside and colleagues (1995a, 1995b) found that reports of family dysfunction were significantly worse from AN probands than from their respective family members, whose reports of family functioning were comparable to population norms. However, as treatment progressed and the influence of AN decreased, family reports of family dysfunction remained relatively unchanged but the reports of the AN probands became more favourable. Family members indicated that the main source of dysfunction was between the family and the woman with the eating disorder (Woodside et al., 1995a) and not other dimensions of family functioning.

Similarly, while women with BN perceive their families to be less cohesive, adaptable and supportive than controls, there was no difference between family reports for the two groups with respect to family functioning (Bonne et al., 2003). Women with a past history of BN retrospectively reported their parents to be less caring and more overprotective than did their unaffected identical twin (Wade et al., 2001a). However, a longitudinal study examining the direction of associations between parent-adolescent relationships and adolescent girls' unhealthy eating found a direct effect on parent-adolescent relationships (Archibald, Linver, Graber, & Brooks-Gunn, 2002). There was no direct effect in the opposite direction.

Overall, these findings suggest an effect of current eating disorder symptomatology on both the quality of family functioning and also the perceptions of family functioning by the person affected by disordered eating. Hence, substantial caution needs to be exercised in the interpretation of family studies of eating disorders. For this reason, only studies that incorporate multiple reports within the family or are longitudinal are examined in the following section. An additional issue is that, in a review of the 28 longitudinal studies of eating disorders that exist to date (Jacobi et al., 2004), 13 were considered to be not methodologically robust as they either contained too few cases, insufficient information on risk factors, broad outcome measures that did not reflect eating disorder symptomatology, or insufficient follow-up periods. Of the 15 studies that were methodologically robust, only five included family environment measures and only two of these found family variables to be risk factors for eating disorder development, specifically low levels of social support from families (Ghaderi, 2003), and abusive parental relationships (Johnson, Cohen, Kasen, & Brook, 2002). Hence, as few studies have been able to establish the precedence of family functioning in the development of disordered eating, the variables reviewed here must be seen at this stage to indicate correlates rather then true risk factors (Jacobi et al., 2004).

Early Feeding Difficulties and Parental Control

A number of studies from different perspectives report an association between feeding difficulties and eating disorders, and feeding difficulties and parental control. It should be noted that these studies focus primarily on mothers and that studies incorporating fathers are rare. Women with AN report higher levels of feeding difficulties in childhood than their non-affected sisters (Karwautz et al., 2001), and childhood digestive problems and picky eating have been found to predict anorexic symptoms (Marchi & Cohen, 1990). A community study that followed up three groups of 4-year old children (children with feeding problems, children with other disturbances such as fearfulness and children with no disturbances) found that while mothers of the children with feeding problems had no raised rate of any affective disorder, they did have a markedly raised rate of past or current eating disorder (OR = 11.1, 95% CI: 1.4–91.8) compared to the other two groups (Whelan & Cooper, 2000). Video-taped interactions show that mothers with eating disorders (primarily BN) use more verbal control in meal and play times than mothers with postnatal depression or controls (Stein et al., 2001). This maternal control was associated with maternal dietary restraint. Similarly, in mothers who do not have eating disorders, maternal attempts to control their child's eating by restricting access to foods is associated with maternal weight concern and dietary restraint (Francis, Hofer, & Birch, 2001; Tiggemann & Lowes, 2002) with the latter study finding this relationship to be independent of the child's actual or perceived weight.

Leann Birch and her colleagues have extensively examined the issue of control in early feeding (for a review, see Fisher & Birch, 2001). High levels of parental control in child feeding is negatively associated with the child's ability to regulate energy intake and to develop self-control in eating. Restricting access to foods turns these foods into "forbidden fruits" where children's preferences for those foods are enhanced. Additionally, such control is associated with children's responsiveness to internal cues of hunger and satiety. An extensive review of research in this area suggests that the association between maternal eating pathology and child-feeding problems may be mediated by maternal controlling behaviour and that food may become identified with control (Patel, Wheatcroft, Park, & Stein, 2002). It may be that, in children who have temperaments that put them at risk for anorexia nervosa, such control may lead to an overvaluation of food control in later life, whereas in individuals with temperaments that put them at risk of developing bulimia nervosa, such control may lead to a lack of control over eating and the development of binge eating behaviour. This can be potentially conceptualised as a passive genotype–environment correlation where the genetic inheritance of vulnerability to an eating disorder or weight concern is also associated with a controlling food environment that increases the probability of the child developing an eating disorder later in life. Alternatively, this could also be conceived of as a genotype–environment interaction.

Also implicated in these early feeding problems is the atmosphere at the meal table. Mothers with eating disorders are less likely to cook or eat with their children (Waugh & Bulik, 1999), and their households are more likely to be in conflict at mealtime (Stein, Woolley, Cooper, & Fairburn, 1994). Mothers who do not enjoy eating and fathers who experience difficulty maintaining an ideal weight (i.e. being overweight) longitudinally predict their 5-year old child's meagre eating (Saarilehto, Keskinen, Lapinleimu, Helenius, & Simell, 2001). Eating conflicts, struggles around meals and unpleasant meals in childhood also predict the development of AN (Marchi & Cohen, 1990).

Parental Eating Attitudes, Behaviours and Weight

A comparison of women with AN and their mothers with control women and their mothers showed no difference on levels of weight and shape concern between the two groups of mothers (Cooper, Galbraith, & Drinkwater, 2001). Interestingly, neither was there a correlation between shape and weight concern of the daughters and mothers in either group. Given that weight concern has been found to be affected only by environment (Wade et al., 1998), it suggests that the source of this influence is not in the family, and may reside in peer interactions or striving to emulate the bodies portrayed in the media, both found to be risk factors for the development of disordered eating in adolescents (McKnight Investigators, 2003). In a less extreme population and examining attitudes less proximally linked to the development of an eating disorder, a study of college girls and their mothers showed that while disturbed eating of the daughters was not associated with maternal dieting, disordered eating and concerns about body shape (called maternal modelling), there was an association between maternal modelling and daughters' concerns about shape (Kichler & Crowther, 2001). It has been suggested that the influence of maternal dieting on a daughter's drive for thinness or body dissatisfaction only exists for menstrual, not pre-menstrual girls (Wertheim, Martin, Prior, Sanson, & Smart, 2002). However, a follow-up study of 108 infants at 8 years of age showed that maternal restraint predicted worries about being too fat in girls but not boys (Jacobi, Agras, & Hammer, 2001). In this same study, higher maternal disinhibition scores also predicted weight control behaviours in the daughters, but paternal measures of disordered eating were not associated with the child's eating disturbance.

While negative familial communication (as reported by the daughter), including expressiveness, conflict, cohesion and disorganisation, has not been found to be associated with the daughter's disturbed eating or concerns about shape, the interaction between maternal modelling and negative communication was significantly associated with both variables (Kichler & Crowther, 2001). In other words, the influence of maternal modelling on daughters' disturbed eating and shape concern was significant at high levels of negative familial communication but not at low levels. Just as low levels of negative familial communication may protect against the influence of maternal modelling, so too may high levels of maternal identification (girls wishing to be like their mothers with respect to personality characteristics) protect against the influence of maternal body dissatisfaction with respect to girls' body esteem (Hahn-Smith & Smith, 2001).

While the majority of the literature in this area examines mothers and their daughters, there is also an increasing interest in the influence of fathers on their daughters' eating. A community survey of 50 father–daughter dyads in New Zealand, where the daughters were aged between 13 and 15 years, showed that the daughters of fathers who placed a high importance on female weight control and physical attractiveness, as opposed to fathers who placed medium or low importance on these issues, were significantly more likely to use self-induced vomiting for weight loss purposes than the daughters in the other two groups (Dixon, Gill, & Adair, 2003). In a longitudinal study following up over 10,000 girls and boys aged 9–14 years, both girls and boys who reported that their thinness or lack of fat was important to their fathers were more likely than their peers to become constant dieters (Field et al., 2001). It should be noted that another longitudinal study of around 1000 girls aged 11–14 years did not find that parental influences were significant predictors of eating disorder onset (McKnight Investigators, 2003). The study found that social pressure from peers and media was more influential.

Parental encouragement of their children to diet is a widespread phenomenon: 34% and 40% of mothers report respectively encouraging their sons and daughters to diet (Fulkerson et al., 2002). Of those boys and girls encouraged to diet, 43% of the boys and 46% of the girls were not classified as overweight. Encouragement to diet from either fathers or mothers was associated with daughters' drive for thinness and body dissatisfaction (Wertheim et al., 2002), though these associations were reduced when body mass index (BMI) was controlled. In a cross-sectional report from adolescent boys and girls and their mothers (Fulkerson et al., 2002), mothers' encouragement of daughters' dieting was associated with their daughters' weight-related concerns and behaviours but these associations were no longer significant when the girls' BMI was controlled. However, mothers' encouragement for sons to diet remained significantly associated with sons' weight-related concerns and behaviours even after controlling for the boys' BMI.

Higher BMI in the child or parent has not been convincingly demonstrated to be a risk factor for eating disorders (Jacobi et al., 2004). A 3-year follow-up of around 200 girls (10–15-year-old) suggested that body-related teasing or negative verbal commentary by family members mediated the relationship between BMI and body image disturbance (Thompson, Coovert, Richards, Johnson, & Cattarin, 1995). Conversely, longitudinal research also suggests that both perceived maternal and paternal acceptance is a significant protective factor for girls with respect to the development of body dissatisfaction (Barker & Glamabos, 2003).

In summary, it appears that parental eating attitudes and behaviours are typically not directly predictive of disordered eating in their offspring but are more likely to be implicated in interactional or mediational relationships. Such relationships have not been evaluated in longitudinal studies of eating disorder development (Stice, 2002) thus suggesting a valuable avenue for future investigation. Additionally, this seems an area that will be likely to yield an interaction between genetic and environmental influences or an evocative genotype–environment correlation (e.g. overweight children who are teased about appearance by their family may be at increased risk of developing an eating disorder).

Parenting Style

In common with most, if not all, forms of psychopathology, abusive parenting shows strong associations with the development of eating disorders. While a variety of studies show significant associations between eating pathology and retrospectively reported abuse, two longitudinal studies also clearly show this association. The first, from Australia, involved a 9-year follow-up of children on the records of the statutory child protection authority for notification of sexual abuse (Swanston et al., 2003). The children were followed-up at a mean of 19 years of age and compared to a non-abused group. The abused children were more likely to have a history of bingeing and self-induced vomiting, among a variety of other differences related to drug abuse, behaviour and mood. When simultaneously entering the variety of variables that differentiated between the two groups in a multi-variate regression, child sexual abuse was a significant predictor of self-esteem, disordered behaviour and bingeing. It has been suggested that behavioural impulsivity and drug use mediate the relationship between childhood sexual abuse and disordered eating (Wonderlich et al., 2001).

A large prospective study of 782 mothers and their offspring in the United States showed a wide range of childhood adversities to be associated with elevated risk for eating disorders and problems with weight or eating during adolescence or early adulthood (Johnson, et al., 2002), after controlling for the effects of age, childhood eating problems, difficult childhood temperament, parental psychopathology and co-occurring childhood adversities. Childhood adversities predictive of disordered eating included physical neglect, sexual abuse, low paternal affection, low paternal communication and low paternal time spent with the child. Interestingly, maladaptive paternal behaviour was uniquely associated with risk for eating disorders in offspring when controlling for maladaptive maternal behaviour, childhood maltreatment and other co-occurring childhood adversities.

A related focus on the impact of parental style on eating disorder development is the quality of social support from parents. The onset of eating disorder behaviour was predicted by four variables in a sample of 800 women (Ghaderi, 2003), including low self-esteem, low perceived social support from the family, high levels of body concern and high relative use of escape avoidance coping. These results are mirrored in a study of monozygotic (identical) twins, where women who had been affected by BN in their lifetime reported significantly lower self-esteem and maternal care than their unaffected co-twin (Wade, Treloar, & Martin, 2001c). However, the meaning of these findings is not clear. One possible interpretation is that environmental differences promote low self-esteem, a temperamental difference that then influences perceptions or functioning of the parental relationship. Further problems with interpretation of findings are suggested from a longitudinal study showing that adolescent reports of poor family relations and support were associated with onset of depression and not disordered eating (Graber & Brooks-Gunn, 2001). It may be that the co-occurrence of these two problems may cause some confounds in the research literature.

The Parental Relationship

One study (Wade, Bulik, & Kendler, 2001b) investigated the contribution of the quality of the parental marital relationship when the children were growing up (as reported by both the mother and the father) to the BN spectrum status of their offspring (766 complete twin pairs). BN status was ascertained from clinical interviews with the twins. The quality of the parental relationship was defined by perceptions of communication, care and conflict in the marital relationship and the reports of mother and father were positively correlated ($r = 0.52$, $p = 0.0001$). Sub-clinical BN was significantly associated with both the father's and mother's reports of the quality of the marital relationship, with greater perceived quality predicting lower prevalence of sub-clinical BN in offspring, even after controlling for the impact of parental psychopathology. The results of twin-model fitting showed that the full model (including additive genetic action, and both shared and non-shared environment) incorporating the quality of the marital relationship as a shared environment variable was significantly better fitting than the full model without this marital conflict variable, with 2% of the variance in liability to offspring sub-clinical BN accounted for by the quality of the parental relationship. This contribution is similar to that of parental loss in childhood to major depression (Kendler, Neale, Kessler, Heath, & Eaves, 1992). These estimations remind us that parental factors are one of a multitude of factors that contribute to the development of eating disorders symptoms. Again, this type of finding may be consistent with an interaction between genetic and environmental influences where anxious children may poorly tolerate parental conflict, thus having an enduring effect on the subsequent development of factors such as self-efficacy and regulation of negative emotion, increasing the likelihood of the development of BN.

Family Demographics

Traditionally, it has been held that disordered eating behaviour is associated with a higher socio-economic status (SES), especially in families where there is AN (McClelland & Crisp, 2001). However, this issue has been hotly debated over the last 10 years (Gard & Freeman, 1996). While "clinic cases" of AN (i.e. those referred for treatment) in the United Kingdom come from higher social classes (McClelland & Crisp, 2001), surveys of community cases consistently finds no such relationship. A British survey of 722 students found that more disturbed eating attitudes were significantly associated with having only one parent employed compared to two parents (Thomas, James, & Bachmann, 2002). A survey of over 17,000 adolescents in the USA found that parental SES was associated with adolescent body dissatisfaction but that there was no association between dieting and SES when BMI was controlled (Rogers, Resnick, Mitchell, & Blum, 1997). Further, SES was not significantly associated with eating disorder behaviours or low weight. A recent meta-analysis of the literature (Wildes, Emery, & Simons, 2001) indicated that associations with SES differences were greatest when examined with non-clinical or normative constructs such as dietary restraint and body dissatisfaction and weakest when clinical forms of eating disturbance were examined, such as binge eating.

Longitudinal research indicates that low parental education and poverty are predictive of obesity (Johnston et al., 2002) and that both obesity and weight dissatisfaction are associated with economic problems in the family (Mikkila, Lahti-Koski, Pietinen, Virtanen, & Rimpela, 2003). However, no longitudinal relationships exist between SES indicators and low body weight or bulimic behaviours (Johnston et al., 2002; Moorhead et al., 2003). A 22-year longitudinal study of American children found that, while SES was not associated with the development of an eating disorder, girls who developed eating disorders were significantly more likely at age 15 to have experienced stressful family events than their peers, including change in parental financial status, a job change requiring a father's absence from home and the loss of a job by a parent (Moorhead et al., 2003). In summary, it seems questionable that SES influences the development of eating pathology.

Role of the Family on Treatment Outcome

Given that the mean age of eating disorder development occurs in adolescence, families have typically been incorporated into the treatment of eating disorders, even if just at the level of psycho-education and support. However, little is known about the role of the family on treatment outcomes in eating disorders.

There are really only two strands of research that investigate this issue. The first examines the impact of expressed emotion (EE) on recovery from eating disorders in inpatient eating disorder programmes. A Dutch study by Eric van Furth et al. (1996) showed that the intake levels of family EE were low and decreased at the termination of treatment and at follow-up, 1-year later. The best predictor of outcome was the mother's critical comments, with a lower level of comments associated with better outcomes. High family EE at intake has also been shown to be associated with a trend to poorer outcomes in BN over a six-year follow-up, though no group × time interaction was found (Hedlund, Fichter, Quadflieg, & Brandl, 2003). It has been suggested that family psycho-education might help lower the distress and unhelpful EE interactions (Uehara, Kawashima, Goto, Tasaki, & Someya, 2001).

The second and more substantive strand of research into the role of the family in eating disorder treatment outcome is that examining the use of family therapy in children or young adolescents who have AN. To date, there is little research examining family therapy with BN, though studies are currently underway. Most researched is the family therapy known as the Maudsley model, a multi-factorial family therapy developed at the Maudsley Hospital in London (Dare & Eisler, 2002). Consistent with the lack of findings implicating the family in the development of eating disorders, this therapy views the eating disorder symptoms as a result of a complex interaction of a variety of aetiologic factors, where pathological family communications and patterns and relationships are seen to be a consequence of the illness. Thus, any covert blaming of the family by the helping professional is seen to unnecessarily increase the family distress. In this therapy, the family is considered to be a significant resource that must be used in the treatment of the patient (Lock, le Grange, Agras, & Dare, 2001). There are three stages of the therapy, the first borrowing heavily from structural family therapy. In this first stage, the family is encouraged to take control of their child's food intake. Assuming increased food intake and weight gain, the second stage deals with issues likely to cause tension in the family. Such issues typically focus on the needs for increased independence of the child and a reorganisation of the parental coalition to deal with the child's increasing independence of the family, allowing for more normalised psychosocial development. The final stage focuses on handing back responsibility for eating to the child.

To date there exist two randomised trials comparing the Maudsley style of family therapy with individual therapy (Robin, Siegel, Koepke, Moye, & Tice, 1994; Robin et al., 1999; Russell, Szmukler, Dare, & Eisler, 1987), and three studies comparing different types of family therapy (Eisler et al., 2000; Geist, Heinmaa, Stephens, Davis, & Katzman, 2000; le Grange, Eisler, Dare, & Russell, 1992). The two trials that compared family to individual therapy approaches found a favourable outcome for the family therapy approach, and family therapy has accordingly been recommended as the treatment of choice for adolescents with AN (National Institute for Clinical Excellence, 2004). Nonetheless, the methodology of these studies has been extensively criticised (Fairburn, 2005) as only one of the studies (Russell et al., 1987) has produced unambiguous results. In the second study (Robin et al., 1994; 1999), participants spent varying lengths of time in hospital programmes during the treatment period, thus making it difficult to attribute outcome to a specific intervention. Until we have a further understanding of whether this form of therapy is more effective than other types of widely acceptable individual therapies, we can make no conclusions about the importance of the family in recovery of the children and adolescents with AN. Hence, an area of need in future research is empirical studies that investigate the role of the family in the treatment of eating disorders.

Conclusions

While a variety of variables have been identified as risk factors for eating disorders (Jacobi et al., 2004; Stice, 2002), variables related to the family are only identified thus far as potential risk factors or correlates. While heritable variables such as obsessionality, anxiety and depression are considered to confer risk for the development of an eating disorder, there is poor evidence to date to suggest the role of specific family environment in increasing risk for eating disorders, apart from social support, and abuse and neglect. This may come as some surprise to many as there has been a widespread belief in the potency of family environments to cause eating disorders, despite a lack of longitudinal evidence (Stice, 2002). While it is certainly possible that family environments relating to controlling feeding styles by parents, parental eating attitudes and behaviour, and parental conflict may be found to be risk factors in future prospective and experimental studies, better designed research is urgently required (Stice, 2002). A design of particular relevance to this area, and the lack of which may partially account for the paucity of findings in this area, is the longitudinal study that examines interactions between family environment and other variables of interest. Also required are studies that compare family therapy approaches to individual therapy approaches so that conclusions about the role of family in treatment can be made.

References

American Psychiatric Association (APA). (1994). *Diagnostic and statistical manual of mental disorders* (4th ed.). Washington, DC: American Psychiatric Association.

Archibald, A. B., Linver, M. R., Graber, J. A., & Brooks-Gunn, J. (2002). Parent-adolescent relationships and girls' unhealthy eating: Testing reciprocal effects. *Journal of Research on Adolescence*, *12*, 451–461.

Barker, E. T., & Galambos, N. L. (2003). Body dissatisfaction of adolescent girls and boys: Risk and resource factors. *Journal of Early Adolescence*, *23*, 141–165.

Bellodi, L., Cavallini, M. C., Bertelli, S., Chiapparino, D., Roboldi, C., & Smeraldi, E. (2001). Morbidity risk for obsessive-compulsive spectrum disorders in first-degree relatives of patients with eating disorders. *American Journal of Psychiatry*, *158*, 563–569.

Bonne, O., Lahat, S., Kfir, R., Berry, E., Katz, M., & Bachar, E. (2003). Parent-daughter discrepancies in perception of family function in bulimia nervosa. *Psychiatry — Interpersonal and Biological Processes*, *66*, 244–254.

Bulik, C. M. (1991). Family histories of bulimic women with and without comorbid alcohol abuse or dependence. *American Journal of Psychiatry*, *148*, 1267–1268.

Bulik, C. M., Sullivan, P. F., Wade, T. D., & Kendler, K. S. (2000). Twin studies of eating disorders: A review. *International Journal of Eating Disorders*, *27*, 1–20.

Cooper, M., Galbraith, M., & Drinkwater, J. (2001). Assumptions and beliefs in adolescents with anorexia nervosa and their mothers. *Eating Disorders*, *9*, 217–223.

Dansky, B., Brewerton, T., & Kilpatrick, D. (2000). Comorbidity of bulimia nervosa and alcohol use disorders: Results from the national women's study. *International Journal of Eating Disorders*, *27*, 180–190.

Dare, C., & Eisler, I. (2002). Family therapy and eating disorders. In: C. G. Fairburn & K. D. Brownell (Eds), *Eating disorders and obesity: A comprehensive handbook* (2nd ed.), pp. 314–319. New York: Guilford Press.

Davis, C., Shuster, B., Blackmore, E., & Fox, J. (2004). Looking good — family focus on appearance and the risk for eating disorders. *International Journal of Eating Disorders*, *35*, 136–144.

Dixon, R. S., Gill, J. M. W., & Adair, V. A. (2003). Exploring paternal influences on the dieting behaviours of adolescent girls. *Eating Disorders*, *11*, 39–50.

Eisler, I., Dare, C., Hodes, M., Russell, G., Dodge, E., & le Grange, D. (2000). Family therapy for adolescent anorexia nervosa: The results of a controlled comparison of two family interventions. *Journal of Child Psychology and Psychiatry and Allied Disciplines, 41*, 727–736.

Fairburn, C. G. (2005). Evidence based treatment of anorexia nervosa. *International Journal of Eating Disorders, 37,* (supplement), S26–S30.

Fairburn, C. G. & Harrison, P. J. (2003). *Eating disorders*. Lancet, *361*, 407–416.

Fairburn, C. G., Shafran, R., & Cooper, Z. (1999). A cognitive behavioural theory of anorexia nervosa. *Behaviour Research and Therapy*, *37*, 1–13.

Fassino, S., Amianto, F., Daga, G. A., Leombruni, P., Garzaro, L., Levi, M., & Rovera, G. G. (2003). Bulimic family dynamics: Role of parents' personality — a controlled study with the temperament and character inventory. *Comprehensive Psychiatry, 44*, 70–77.

Fassino, S., Svrakic, D., Daga, G. A., Leombruni, P., Amianto, F., Stanic, S., & Rovera, G. G. (2002). Anorectic family dynamics: Temperament and character data. *Comprehensive Psychiatry, 43*, 114–120.

Field, A. E., Camargo, C. A., Taylor, C. B., Berkle, C. S., Roberts, S. B., & Colditz, G. A. (2001). Peer, parent, and media influences on the development of weight concerns and frequent dieting among preadolescent and adolescent girls and boys. *Pediatrics, 107*, 54–60.

Fisher, J. O., & Birch, L. L. (2001). Early experience with food and eating: Implications for the development of eating disorders. In: J. K. Thompson & L. Smolak (Eds), *Body image, eating disorders, and obesity in youth: Assessment, prevention, and treatment* (pp. 23–39). Washington, DC: American Psychological Association.

Francis, L. A., Hofer, S. M., & Birch, L. L. (2001). Predictors of maternal child-feeding style: Maternal and child characteristics. *Appetite, 37*, 231–243.

Frost, R. O., Marten, P., Lahart, C., & Rosenblate, R. (1990). The dimensions of perfectionism. *Cognitive Therapy and Research, 14*, 449–468.

Fulkerson, J. A., McGuire, M. T., Neumark-Sztainer, D., Story, M., French, S. A., & Perry, C. L. (2002). Weight-related attitudes and behaviours of adolescent boys and girls who are encouraged to diet by their mothers. *International Journal of Obesity, 26*, 1579–1587.

Gard, M. C., & Freeman, C. P. (1996). The dismantling of a myth: A review of eating disorders and socio-economic status. *International Journal of Eating Disorders, 20*, 1–12.

Garfinkel, P. E., Lin, E., Goering, P., Spegg, C., Goldbloom, D. S., Kennedy, S., Kaplan, A. S., & Woodside, D. B. (1996). Should amenorrhoea be necessary for the diagnosis of anorexia nervosa? Evidence from a Canadian community sample. *British Journal of Psychiatry, 168*, 500–506.

Geist, R., Heinmaa, M., Stephens, D., Davis, R., & Katzman, D. K. (2000). Comparison of family therapy and family group psychoeducation in adolescents with anorexia nervosa. *Canadian Journal of Psychiatry, 45*, 173–178.

Ghaderi, A. (2003). Structural modeling analysis of prospective risk factors for eating disorder. *Eating Behaviors, 3*, 387–396.

Graber, J. A., & Brooks-Gunn, J. (2001). Co-occurring eating and depressive problems: An 8-year study of adolescent girls. *International Journal of Eating Disorders, 30*, 37–47.

Hahn-Smith, A. M., & Smith, J. E. (2001). The positive influence of maternal identification on body image, eating attitudes, and self-esteem of Hispanic and Anglo girls. *International Journal of Eating Disorders, 29*, 429–440.

Hedlund, S., Fichter, M. M., Quadflieg, N., & Brandl, C. (2003). Expressed emotion, family environment, and parental bonding in bulimia nervosa: A 6-year investigation. *Eating and Weight Disorders, 8*, 26–35.

Hudson, J. I., Mangweth, B., Pope, H. G., De Col, C., Hausmann, A., Gutweniger, S., Laird, N. M., Biebl, W., & Tsuang, M. T. (2003). Family study of affective spectrum disorder. *Archives of General Psychiatry, 60*, 170–177.

Jacobi, C., Agras, W. S., & Hammer, L. (2001). Predicting children's reported eating disturbances at 8 years of age. *Journal of the Academy of Child and Adolescent Psychiatry, 40*, 364–372.

Jacobi, C., Hayward, C., de Zwaan, M., Kraemer, H. C., & Agras, W. S. (2004). Coming to terms with risk factors for eating disorders: Application of risk terminology and suggestions for a general taxonomy. *Psychological Bulletin, 130*, 19–65.

Johnson, C., & Flach, A. (1985). Family characteristics of 105 patients with bulimia. *American Journal of Psychiatry, 142*, 1321–1324.

Johnson, J. G., Spitzer, R. L., & Williams, J. B. W. (2001). Health problems, impairment and ill-nesses associated with bulimia nervosa and binge eating disorder among primary care and obstet-ric gynaecology patients. *Psychological Medicine, 31,* 1455–1466.

Johnson, J., Cohen, P., Kasen, S., & Brook, J. (2002). Childhood adversities associated with risk for eating disorders or weight problems during adolescence or early adulthood. *American Journal of Psychiatry, 159,* 394–400.

Karwautz, A., Nobis, G., Haidvogl, M., Wagner, G., Hafferl-Gattermayer, A., Wober-Bingol, C., & Friedrich, M. H. (2003). Perceptions of family relationships in adolescents with anorexia nervosa and their unaffected sisters. *European Child and Adolescent Psychiatry, 12,* 128–135.

Karwautz, A., Rabe-Hesketh, S., Hu, X., Zhao, J., Sham, P., Collier, D. A., & Treasure, J. L. (2001). Individual-specific risk factors for anorexia nervosa: A pilot study using a discordant sister-pair design. *Psychological Medicine, 31,* 317–329.

Kaye, W. H., Lilenfeld, L. R., Plotnicov, K., Merikangas, K. R., Nagy, L., Strober, M., Bulik, C. M., Moss, H., & Greeno, C. G. (1996). Bulimia nervosa and substance dependence: Association and family transmission. *Alcoholism: Clinical and Experimental Research, 20,* 878–881.

Kendler, K. S., MacLean, C., Neale, M. C., Kessler, R. C., Heath, A. C., & Eaves, L. J. (1991). The genetic epidemiology of bulimia nervosa. *American Journal of Psychiatry, 148,* 1627–1637.

Kendler, K. S., Neale, M. C., Kessler, R. C., Heath, A. C., & Eaves, L. J. (1992). Childhood parental loss and adult psychopathology in women. A twin study perspective. *Archives of General Psychiatry, 49,* 109–116.

Kendler, K. S., Walters, E. E., Neale, M. C., Kessler, R. C., Heath, A. C., & Eaves, L. J. (1995). The structure of the genetic and environmental risk factors for six major psychiatric disorders in women: Phobia, generalized anxiety disorder, panic disorder, bulimia, major depression and alco-holism. *Archives of General Psychiatry, 52,* 374–383.

Kichler, J. C., & Crowther, J. H. (2001). The effects of maternal modelling and negative familial communication on women's eating attitudes and body image. *Behavior Therapy, 32,* 443–457.

Klump, K. L., McGue, M., & Iacono, W. G. (2000). Age differences in genetic and environmental influences on eating attitudes and behaviors in preadolescent and adolescent twins. *Journal of Abnormal Psychology, 109,* 239–251.

Kraemer, H. C., Kazdin, A. E., Offord, D. R., Kessler, R. C., Jensen, P. S., & Kupfer, D. J. (1997). Coming to terms with the terms of risk. *Archives of General Psychiatry, 54,* 337–343.

le Grange, D., Eisler, I., Dare, C., & Russell, G. F. M. (1992). Evaluation of family treatments in ado-lescent anorexia nervosa — a pilot study. *International Journal of Eating Disorders, 12,* 347–357.

Lilenfeld, L. R., Kaye, W. H., Greeno, C. G., Merikangas, K. R., Plotnicov, K., Pollice, C., Rao, R., Strober, M., Bulik, C. M., & Nagy, L. (1998). A controlled family study of restricting anorexia and bulimia nervosa: Comorbidity in probands and disorders in first-degree relatives. *Archives of General Psychiatry, 55,* 603–610.

Lock, J., le Grange, D., Agras, W. S., & Dare, C. (2001). *Treatment manual for anorexia nervosa: A family based approach.* New York: Guilford Press.

Marchi, M., & Cohen, P. (1990). Early childhood eating behaviours and adolescent eating disorders. *Journal of the American Academy of Child and Adolescent Psychiatry, 29,* 112–117.

McClelland, L., & Crisp, A. (2001). Anorexia nervosa and social class. *International Journal of Eating Disorders, 29,* 150–156.

McIntosh, V. W., Jordan, J., Carter, F. A., McKenzie, J. M., Luty, S. E., Bulik, C. M., & Joyce, P. R. (2004). Strict versus lenient weight criterion in anorexia nervosa. *European Eating Disorders Review, 12,* 51–60.

McKnight Investigators. (2003). Risk factors for the onset of eating disorders in adolescent girls: Results of the McKnight longitudinal risk factor study. *American Journal of Psychiatry, 160,* 248–254.

Mikkila, V., Lahti-Koski, M., Pietinen, P., Virtanen, S. M., & Rimpela, M. (2003). TI associates of obesity and weight dissatisfaction among Finnish adolescents. *Public Health Nutrition, 6*, 49–56.

Minuchin, S., Rosman, B. L., & Baker, L. (1978). *Psychosomatic families: Anorexia nervosa in context*. Cambridge, MA: Harvard University Press.

Moorhead, D. J., Stashwick, C. K., Reinherz, H. Z., Giaconia, R. M., Streigel-Moore, R. M., & Paradis, A. D. (2003). Child and adolescent predictors for eating disorders in a community population of young adult women. *International Journal of Eating Disorders, 33*, 1–9.

Mulder, R. T., Joyce, P. R., Sullivan, P. F., Bulik, C. M., & Carter, F. A. (1999). The relationship among three models of personality and psychopathology: DSM-III-R personality disorder, TCI scores and DSQ defences. *Psychological Medicine, 29*, 943–951.

National Institute for Clinical Excellence. (2004). *Eating disorders. Core interventions in the treatment and management of eating disorders in primary and secondary care*. London: National Institute for Clinical Excellence.

O'Connor, T. G., Deater-Deckard, K., Fulker, D., Rutter, M., & Plomin, R. (1998). Genotype-environment correlations in late childhood and early adolescence: Antisocial behavior problems and coercive parenting. *Developmental Psychology, 34*, 970–981.

Patel, P., Wheatcroft, R., Park, R. J., & Stein, A. (2002). The children of mothers with eating disorders. *Clinical Child and Family Psychology Review, 5*, 1–19.

Plomin, R. (2000). Behavioural genetics in the 21st century. *International Journal of Behavioural Development, 24*, 30–34.

Polivy, J., & Herman, C. P. (2002). Causes of eating disorders. *Annual Review of Psychology, 53*, 187–213.

Reichborn-Kjennerud, R., Bulik, C. M., Kendler, K. S., Roysamb, E., Maes, H., Tambs, K., & Harris, J. R. (2004). Undue influence of weight on self-evaluation: A population-based twin study of gender differences. *International Journal of Eating Disorders, 35*, 123–132.

Robin, A. L., Siegel, P. T., Koepke, T., Moye, A. W., & Tice, S. (1994). Family therapy versus individual therapy for adolescent females with anorexia nervosa. *Journal of Developmental and Behavioral Pediatrics, 15*, 111–116.

Robin, A. L., Siegel, P. T., Moye, A. W., Gilroy, M., Dennis, A. B., & Sikand, A. (1999). A controlled comparison of family versus individual therapy for adolescents with anorexia nervosa. *Journal of the American Academy of Child and Adolescent Psychiatry, 38*, 1482–1489.

Rogers, L., Resnick, M. D., Mitchell, J. E., & Blum, R. W. (1997). The relationship between socioeconomic status and eating-disordered behaviours in a community sample of adolescent girls. *International Journal of Eating Disorders, 22*, 15–23.

Rowa, K., Kerig, P. K., & Geller, J. (2001). The family and anorexia nervosa: Examining parent-child boundary problems. *European Eating Disorders Review, 9*, 97–114.

Russell, G. F. M., Szmukler, G. I., Dare, C., & Eisler, I. (1987). An evaluation of family therapy in anorexia nervosa and bulimia nervosa. *Archives of General Psychiatry, 44*, 1047–1056.

Rutter, M., & Silberg, J. (2002). Gene-environment interplay in relation to emotional and behavioural disturbance. *Annual Review of Psychology, 53*, 463–490.

Saarilehto, S., Keskinen, S., Lapinleimu, H., Helenius, H., & Simell, O. (2001). Connections between parental eating attitudes and children's meagre eating: Questionnaire findings. *Acta Paediatrica, 90*, 333–338.

Scarr, S., & McCartney, K. (1983). How people make their own environments: A theory of genotype → environment effects. *Child Development, 54*, 424–435.

Shisslak, C. M., & Crago, M. (2001). Risk and protective factors in the development of eating disorders. In: J. K. Thompson & L. Smolak (Eds), *Body image, eating disorders, and obesity in youth: Assessment, prevention, and treatment* (pp. 103–125). Washington, DC: American Psychological Association.

Stein, A., Woolley, H., Murray, L., Cooper, P., Cooper, S., Noble, F., Affonso, N., & Fairburn, C. G. (2001). Influence of psychiatric disorder on the controlling behaviour of mothers with 1-year old infants: A study of women with maternal eating disorder, postnatal depression, and a healthy comparison group. *British Journal of Psychiatry, 179,* 157–162.

Stein, A., Woolley, H., Cooper, S. D., & Fairburn, C. G. (1994). An observational study of mothers with eating disorders and their infants. *Journal of Child Psychology & Psychiatry & Allied Disciplines, 35,* 733–748.

Stice, E. (2002). Risk and maintenance factors for eating pathology: A meta-analytic review. *Psychological Bulletin, 128,* 825–848.

Swanston, H. Y., Plunkett, A. M., O'Toole, B. I., Shrimpton, S., Parkinson, P. N., & Oates, R. K. (2003). Nine years after child sexual abuse. *Child Abuse and Neglect, 27,* 967–984.

The Price Foundation Collaborative Group. (2001). Deriving phenotypes in an international, multi-centre study of eating disorders. *Psychological Medicine, 31,* 635–645.

Thomas, C. L., James, A. C., & Bachmann, M. O. (2002). Eating attitudes in English secondary school students: Influences of ethnicity, gender, mood, and social class. *International Journal of Eating Disorders, 31,* 92–96.

Thompson, J. K., Coovert, M. D., Richards, K. J., Johnson, S., & Cattarin, J. (1995). Development of body image, eating disturbance, and general psychological functioning in female adolescents: Covariance structure modeling and longitudinal investigations. *International Journal of Eating Disorders, 18,* 221–236.

Tiggemann, M., & Lowes, J. (2002). Predictors of maternal control over children's eating behaviour. *Appetite, 39,* 1–7.

Tozzi, F., Sullivan, P. F., Fear, J. L., McKenzie, J., & Bulik, C. M. (2003). Causes and recovery in anorexia nervosa: The patient's perspective. *International Journal of Eating Disorders, 33,* 143–154.

Turkheimer, E., & Waldron, M. (2000). Nonshared environment: A theoretical, methodological, and quantitative review. *Psychological Bulletin, 126,* 78–108.

Uehara, T., Kawashima, Y., Goto, M., Tasaki, S., & Someya, T. (2001). Psychoeducation for the families of patients with eating disorders and changes in expressed emotion: A preliminary study. *Comprehensive Psychiatry, 42,* 132–138.

van Furth, E. F., van Strien, D. C., Martina, L. M. L., van Son, M. J. M., Hendrickx, J. J. P., & van Engeland, H. (1996). Expressed emotion and the prediction of outcome in adolescent eating disorders. *International Journal of Eating Disorders, 20,* 19–31.

von Ranson, K. M., McGue, M., & Iacono, W. G. (2003). Disordered eating and substance use in an epidemiological sample: II. Associations within families. *Psychology of Addictive Behaviours, 17,* 193–202.

Wade, T., Martin, N. G., & Tiggemann, M. (1998). Genetic and environmental risk factors for the weight and shape concerns characteristic of bulimia nervosa. *Psychological Medicine, 28,* 761–771.

Wade, T. D., Bulik, C. M., Heath, A. C., Martin, N. G., & Eaves, L. J. (2001a). The influence of genetic and environmental factors in estimations of current body size, desired body size, and body dissatisfaction. *Twin Research, 4,* 260–265.

Wade, T. D., Bulik, C. M., & Kendler, K. S. (2001b). Quality of the parental relationship: Investigation as a risk factor for sub-clinical bulimia nervosa. *International Journal of Eating Disorders, 30,* 389–400.

Wade, T. D., Bulik, C. M., Prescott, C., & Kendler, K. S. (2004). Gender influences on shared risk factors for bulimia nervosa and other psychiatric disorders. *Archives of General Psychiatry, 61,* 251–256.

Wade, T. D., Treloar, S. A., & Martin, N. G. (2001c). A comparison of family functioning, temperament and childhood conditions of monozygotic twin pairs discordant for lifetime bulimia nervosa. *American Journal of Psychiatry*, *158*, 1155–1157.

Waugh, E., & Bulik, C. M. (1999). Offspring of women with eating disorders. *International Journal of Eating Disorders*, *25*, 123–133.

Welch, S., & Fairburn, C. G. (1996). Impulsivity or comorbidity in bulimia nervosa: A controlled study of deliberate self-harm and alcohol and drug misuse in a community sample. *British Journal of Psychiatry*, *169*, 451–458.

Wertheim, E. H., Martin, G., Prior, M., Sanson, A., & Smart, D. (2002). Parent influences in the transmission of eating and weight related values and behaviours. *Eating Disorders*, *10*, 321–334.

Whelan, E., & Cooper, P. J. (2000). The association between childhood feeding problems and maternal eating disorder: A community study. *Psychological Medicine*, *30*, 69–77.

Wildes, J. E., Emery, R. E., & Simons, A. D. (2001). The roles of ethnicity and culture in the development of eating disturbance and body dissatisfaction: A meta-analytic review. *Clinical Psychology Review*, *21*, 521–551.

Wisotsky, W., Dancyger, I., Fornari, V., Katz, J., Wisotsky, W. L., & Swencionis, C. (2003). The relationship between eating pathology and perceived family functioning in eating disorder patients in a day treatment program. *Eating Disorders: The Journal of Treatment and Prevention*, *11*, 89–99.

Wonderlich, S., Crosby, R., Mitchell, J., Thompson, K., Redlin, J., Demuth, G., & Smyth, J. (2001). Pathways mediating sexual abuse and eating disturbance in children. *International Journal of Eating Disorders*, *29*, 270–279.

Woodside, D. B., Bulik, C. M., Halmi, K. A., Fichter, M. M., Kaplan, A., Berrettini, W. H., Strober, M., Treasure, J., Lilenfeld, L., Klump, K., & Kaye, W. H. (2002). Personality, perfectionism, and attitudes toward eating in parents of individuals with eating disorders. *International Journal of Eating Disorders*, *31*, 290–299.

Woodside, D. B., Shekter-Wolfson, L. F., Garfinkel, P. E., & Olmsted, M. P. (1995b). Family interactions in bulimia nervosa II: Complex intrafamily comparisons and clinical significance. *International Journal of Eating Disorders*, *17*, 116–126.

Woodside, D. B., Shekter-Wolson, L., Garfinkel, P. E., Olmsted, M. P., Kaplan, A. S., & Maddocks, S. E. (1995a). Family interactions in bulimia nervosa I: Study design, comparisons to established population norms, and changes over the course of an intensive day hospital treatment program. *International Journal of Eating Disorders*, *17*, 105–115.

Zaider, T. I., Johnson, J. G., & Cockell, S. J. (2002). Psychiatric disorders associated with the onset and persistence of bulimia nervosa and binge eating disorder during adolescence. *Journal of Youth and Adolescence*, *31*, 319–329.

Chapter 9

Familial Risk Factors for Substance Use Disorders

Shelli Avenevoli, Kevin P. Conway and
Kathleen Ries Merikangas

Introduction

Scope of the Problem

Substance use disorders (alcohol or drug abuse/dependence; SUDs) are among the most common psychiatric disorders. Nationwide surveys of adults have shown that nearly 27% of respondents met DSM-III-R criteria (American Psychiatric Association, 1987) for a lifetime SUD (Kessler et al., 1996) and 13% and 6.1% met DSM-IV criteria (APA, 1994) for a lifetime history of alcohol dependence and any drug use disorder, respectively (Grant, 1995), with estimates higher for men than for women. Systematic monitoring indicates that substance use in the United States typically begins during adolescence, increases into young adulthood, and gradually declines thereafter. Approximately 46% of adolescents have used alcohol by 8th grade, 66% by 10th grade, and 77% by 12th grade (Johnson, O'Malley, Bachman, & Schulenberg, 2003). The use of illicit drugs is also common during this period, as 23%, 41%, and 51% have tried an illicit drug by 8th, 10th, and 12th grades, respectively (Johnson et al., 2003). Estimates for SUDs among children and adolescents range from 1% to 15% for alcohol abuse or dependence and from 0.4% to 3.3% for drug abuse or dependence, depending on the age of the sample (see Weinberg, Rahdert, Colliver, & Glantz, 1998, for a review). Thus, although not all substance users develop SUDs, it is clear that most adolescents put themselves at risk by using drugs or alcohol. Once established, SUDs are chronic (Nestler & Malenka, 2004), are characterized by substantial comorbidity (Kessler et al., 1996, 1997; Merikangas et al., 1998b; Regier et al., 1990; Swendsen & Merikangas, 2000), and have considerable societal and personal costs (Goetzel, Hawkins, & Ozminkowski, 2003; Sanderson & Andrews, 2002).

Psychopathology and the Family
Edited by J. L. Hudson and R. M. Rapee
Copyright © 2005 by Elsevier Ltd.
All rights of reproduction in any form reserved
ISBN: 0-08-044449-0

Chapter Overview

Several decades of research have revealed that the etiology of SUDs comprises a complex network of interactive social, cultural, biological, and genetic factors. As the family unit is the primary source of transmission of these factors, much attention has been paid to the role of the family in the development and treatment of SUDs. A large proportion of the extant literature on family risk factors for SUDs focuses on adult and child offspring of alcoholics, with smaller bodies of research focusing on offspring of persons with drug disorders and on adolescents drawn from community or convenience samples.

This chapter presents a review of the literature on *family risk and protective factors* related to the etiology and progression of SUDs. The chapter focuses on SUDs, specifically alcohol and illicit drug abuse and dependence, compared to substance use that does not meet clinical criteria.[1] Data on substance use, problem use, or other behaviors (e.g. conduct problems) that are highly predictive of later SUDs are noted when findings on SUDs are limited. The chapter begins with a review of family studies that examine the role of family history of SUDs, followed by a review of research on the genetic risk believed to partially explain the strong familial associations. Substance-specific and non-specific family environmental factors are reviewed next. The chapter concludes with a brief overview of the role of the family in intervention efforts and suggestions for future research.

Family Alcohol and Drug Use Disorders

Family History of Substance Use Disorders

A positive family history of SUD (i.e. presence of a disorder in *any* first-degree relative: parents, siblings, or offspring) is a consistent and robust risk factor for substance use outcomes in first-degree relatives (for comprehensive reviews of alcoholism, see McGue, 1994 and Heath et al., 1997; and for drug abuse, see Gordon, 1994). Controlled family studies of alcohol use disorder reveal a threefold increased risk of alcoholism and twofold increased risk of drug abuse among the relatives of probands with alcoholism as compared to those of controls. Both alcohol abuse and dependence appear to be familial among females, whereas only dependence aggregates among the relatives of males with alcohol dependence (Merikangas et al., 1998c). Although there has been less systematic research on the familial aggregation of drug use disorders, numerous family history studies and uncontrolled and controlled family studies have demonstrated that rates of SUDs are elevated among relatives of drug abusers compared to that of controls and population expectations (Bierut et al., 1998; Croughan, 1985; Gfroerer, 1987; Hill, Cloninger, & Ayre, 1977; Meller, Rinehart, Cadoret, & Troughton, 1988; Merikangas et al., 1998d; Mirin, Weiss, & Michael, 1988; Mirin, Weiss, Griffin, & Michael, 1991; Rounsaville et al., 1991).

---

[1] Due to the brevity of this chapter, familial risk factors for tobacco dependence are not reviewed; the readers are referred to two recent review articles (Avenevoli & Merikangas, 2003; Darling & Cumsille, 2003).

One controlled family study of drug use disorders using contemporary family study data (Merikangas et al., 1998d) showed an eightfold increased risk of SUDs (opioids, cocaine, cannabis, and alcohol) among relatives of probands with drug disorders compared with relatives of psychiatric and normal controls.

Parental Substance Use Disorders

High-risk studies of offspring of parents with SUDs are a subset of family studies that provide information on premorbid risk factors for the development of SUDs. Because of the young age of the offspring in most of these samples, the studies tend to focus on outcomes of use or related psychopathology, as opposed to SUDs.

Aside from pre-existing emotional and behavior disorders, parental alcoholism has been shown to be the most consistent risk factor for the development of substance-related problems in vulnerable youth (Chassin, Rogosch, & Barrera, 1991; Hill & Hruska, 1992; Johnson, Leonard, & Jacob, 1989; Merikangas, Dierker, & Szatmari, 1998a; Reich, Earls, Frankel, & Shayka, 1993; Schuckit & Smith, 1996; Sher, Walitzer, Wood, & Brent, 1991). Parental alcohol use disorder has also been associated with (a) alcohol use disorder among young adult offspring in a prospective study (Chassin, Pitts, DeLucia, & Todd, 1999) and (b) the transition from use to hazardous use, abuse, dependence, and earlier onset of alcohol problems among young adults in a community study (Lieb et al., 2002). Studies have also suggested that offspring are at greater risk when parental alcoholism is current (e.g. Chassin et al., 1991). In a study using growth curve modeling, paternal alcoholism status was associated with boys' disruptive behaviors at concurrent time points (Loukas, Zucker, Fitzgerald, & Krull, 2003). Other studies suggest that parental substance abuse may contribute to greater risk during certain developmental periods. Moss, Clark and Kirisci (1997) reported that sons of fathers whose substance abuse ended before the child's sixth birthday had no more behavior problems than sons of non-substance abusing fathers; however, increases in behavior problems were found among sons whose fathers abused substances beyond this age.

Although most high-risk studies have focused on children of alcoholics, the few existing controlled studies of offspring of drug abusers have shown that parental drug use disorders are associated with (a) offspring substance use and SUDs, (b) the order of onset of the use of different substances, (c) patterns of transition from substance use to regular use and dependence, and (d) premorbid risk factors predictive of the development of substance abuse (Hopfer, Crowley, & Hewitt, 2003; Martin et al., 1994; Merikangas et al., 1998a; Moss, Majumder, & Vanyukov, 1994). For example, in a follow-up study over 8 years, offspring of parents with a SUD were at twofold increased risk for any SUD and a threefold risk for alcohol and marijuana abuse or dependence compared to offspring of parents without SUDs (Merikangas & Avenevoli, 2000). Some studies have reported specificity for substance use, such that adolescents are particularly likely to use the same illicit drug as their parents (Andrews, Hops, & Duncan, 1997; Merikangas & Avenevoli, 2000). The association between parent and adolescent substance use appears relevant across multiple sociodemographic contexts (e.g. Brook, Brook, Arencibia-Mireles, Richter, & Whiteman, 2001), and risk for SUD (Merikangas & Avenevoli, 2000), progression to regular use, and earlier onset of hazardous use (Lieb et al., 2002) increases with the number of parents affected. Although parental SUD is one of the most consistent and robust risk factors for offspring SUDs, it is important to note that most children of substance abusing parents never develop problems with drugs or alcohol.

Sibling Substance Use Disorders

In addition to parent–offspring associations for substance use and SUDs, research suggests strong sibling associations. Evidence from twin studies provides overwhelming support for the association between alcohol and drug use, abuse, and dependence among twins (e.g. Kendler, Karkowski, Neale, & Prescott, 2000; Pickens et al., 1991; Tsuang et al., 1998; Vanyukov & Tarter, 2000). Non-twin siblings have also shown associations. For example, siblings of adolescents in treatment for substance abuse and conduct problems had elevated rates of marijuana use, abuse, and dependence, compared to controls (Hopfer et al., 2003). In a longitudinal community study, sibling SUDs reported in early childhood predicted co-sibling drug disorders at age 21. Additionally, an adoption study found a significant association between non-biological siblings' alcohol use (McGue, Sharma, & Benson, 1996), suggesting the role of environmental factors. Evidence further suggests that sibling correlations for substance use are higher than parent–offspring correlations (Boyle, Sanford, Szatmari, Merikangas, & Offord, 2001; Hopfer et al., 2003), and that the influence of substance use among older siblings is greater than that of younger siblings (Boyle et al., 2001).

Genetic Factors

Evidence from Twin and Adoption Studies

Despite evidence indicating the association of SUDs among family members, the specific mechanisms through which family substance abuse exerts an influence are not clear. The twin and adoption study designs have traditionally been used to differentiate between genetic and environmental influences. In this section, we briefly review evidence that implicates genetic factors in the etiology of SUDs. In subsequent sections, we focus on broad and specific environmental factors that serve as direct risk factors for the onset and maintenance of SUDs and as factors that mediate or moderate the association between parent and offspring substance use.

There have been numerous twin studies that provide evidence that the strong degree of familial clustering of SUD can be attributed in part to genetic factors. Twin studies are useful because identical (monozygotic; MZ) twins share 100% of their genes whereas fraternal (dizygotic; DZ) twins share an average of 50% of their genes. If genetic factors play an important role in substance use and SUDs, then studies of twins should find greater similarity between MZ than DZ twins, assuming that the influence of familial environment on drug use outcomes is equal for MZ and DZ twins. Studies have examined substance use, abuse, and dependence in general (e.g. Grove et al., 1990; Jang, Livesley, & Vernon, 1995; Kendler et al., 2000; Pickens et al., 1991, Tsuang et al., 1998), as well as a diverse range of specific drugs including alcohol, tranquilizers, sedatives, cannabis, cocaine, stimulants, hallucinogens, and opiates (e.g. Claridge, Ross, & Hume, 1978; Gurling, Grant, & Dangl, 1985; Heath et al., 1997; Kendler, Karkowski, & Prescott, 1999; Kendler & Prescott, 1998a,b; McGue, Pickens, & Svikis, 1992; Pedersen, 1981; Pickens et al., 1991; Tsuang et al., 1998). The aggregate twin-study data suggest that genetic factors play a greater role in the etiology of more severe patterns of substance use, particularly abuse or dependence, than initial use or early stages of use, which appear to be strongly influenced by environmental factors (Kendler & Prescott, 1998b; Pickens et al., 1991; Rhee et al., 2003; Tsuang et al., 1996). Regarding sex differences, some studies report greater heritability estimates for males than for females (van den Bree, Johnson, Neale, & Pickens, 1998), whereas others show similarity in genetic risk for the sexes (Kendler, Prescott, Meyers, & Neale, 2003; Miles et al., 2001). A recent review (Hopfer et al., 2003), reporting on 19 twin and adoption studies that employed adolescent samples, suggests that genetic influence on substance use is modest and dependent upon measurement context, age, and regional differences. Heritability estimates have shown a developmental trend, with increasing heritability with age (Koopmans & Boomsma, 1996).

An optimal study paradigm for discriminating the role of genetic and environmental factors and their interaction in the development of a disorder is the cross-fostering study in which (a) adoptees with familial/biologic vulnerability are reared in homes of non-substance abusing adoptive parents, and (b) adoptees who lack a parental history of substance abuse are reared in homes of parents with substance abuse. The classic adoption studies of Cadoret and colleagues (Cadoret, 1992; Cadoret, Troughton, O'Gorman, & Heywood, 1986; Cadoret, Yates, Troughton, Woodworth, & Stewart, 1996) reveal that genetic factors play an important role in the risk for alcoholism and drug abuse. Additionally, their work identifies two major biologic/genetic pathways to the development of drug abuse in adoptees: one which is driven by substance abuse in the biologic parent and is limited to drug abuse and dependence in the adoptee; and another which appears to be an expression of underlying aggressivity and related to antisocial personality disorder (ASPD) in the biologic parent (Cadoret, Yates, Troughton, Woodworth, & Stewart, 1995; Cadoret et al., 1996). In another adoption study of 653 adopted adolescents (unreported genetic vulnerability), McGue et al. (1996) reported a small and non-significant association between adoptive parent problem drinking and adolescent alcohol use, suggesting that parent problem drinking has minimal environmental impact on adolescent drinking.

Finally, a growing list of studies indicates that the genetic risk associated with SUDs is more similar than different across the range of drug disorder classes (Kendler et al., 2003; Vanyukov & Tarter, 2000), thereby implicating a common underlying genetic system. Other findings suggest that a proportion of the heritability of substance abuse in adulthood can be attributed to a general vulnerability to externalizing disorders, including alcohol, drug, conduct, and antisocial personality disorders (Grove et al., 1990; Hicks, Krueger, Iacono, McGue, & Patrick, 2004; Kendler et al., 2003). Shared environmental influences have also been implicated (Rose, Dick, Viken, Pulkkinen, & Kaprio, 2001). Together, these findings underscore the complex nature by which genes may influence the development of SUD. Although abundant evidence implicates genetics as being involved in SUD etiology, the mechanisms by which genes express themselves are unknown and may vary by environmental context, age, and gender, and may also be mediated by behaviors that manifest themselves prior to the emergence of substance use problems.

Genes Implicated in Substance Use Disorders

Specific genes implicated for the clustering of SUDs among family members can be divided into two major classes: those involved in drug metabolism and those in brain reward systems. Reviews of candidate genes for substance use disorders are presented by Crabbe and Phillips (1998), Enoch and Goldman (1999), and Uhl (2004).

Environmental Factors

The literature on family environmental risk factors for SUD is vast and represents a range of theoretical perspectives, study designs, and specific environmental factors. For years, the field was characterized mainly by retrospective studies. Many recent and ongoing studies follow cohorts through childhood, adolescence, and in some cases young adulthood. Because the participants in these studies often have not passed through the period of risk for SUDs, findings generally focus on familial risk and protection for substance use and behavioral problems.

Evidence points to several environmental mechanisms through which families with and without a family history of SUD may enhance the risk of substance use and SUDs in their members. The family may influence risk through factors *specific* to substance use, such as through exposure to drugs in the prenatal phase of development or by providing negative role models of substance use. Additionally, family influences may represent more general features of the family environment, such as ineffective parenting, that increase the child's risk for a range of deviant behaviors, including SUDs. Both substance-specific and non-specific factors appear to contribute to the development of substance use problems.

Substance-Specific Family Influences

Prenatal Exposure   For several decades, the study of prenatal exposure to alcohol and illicit drugs has provided evidence of early physical, motor, cognitive, and social impairments among infants and young children exposed to these substances in utero (see Mayes & Truman, 2002, for a review). Studies that follow offspring who have been exposed prenatally to alcohol and opiates suggest difficulties in activity, concentration, and attention levels and behavioral problems in childhood and adolescence (Mayes & Truman, 2002). The few prospective studies that have examined links between fetal alcohol exposure and substance use outcomes report associations with adolescent and adult substance use and symptoms of nicotine, alcohol, and drug dependence, beyond the effects of maternal drug abuse (e.g. Baer, Sampson, Barr, Connor, & Streissguth, 2003). Many confounding factors, such as child behavioral problems (which can make children difficult to parent), the home environment, paternal SUD, and prenatal exposure to other substances may explain these associations. However, in a methodologically rigorous study, fetal exposure to alcohol (reported by mothers when pregnant) was associated with alcohol use and alcohol-related problems at age 14, after controlling for family history of alcoholism, fetal exposure to other substances, and other characteristics of the child and home (Baer, Barr, Bookstein, Sampson, & Streissguth, 1998). At the age 21 follow-up (Baer et al., 2003), prenatal alcohol exposure was a stronger predictor of alcohol-related problems (i.e. negative consequences of drinking and dependence symptoms; but not drinking rates once other factors were controlled) than a family history of alcoholism, and was not fully accounted for by postnatal exposure to parent drinking. Moreover, heavy episodic drinking during pregnancy was far more predictive of dependence symptoms among offspring than other non-episodic patterns of drinking. Interestingly, prenatal exposure was more likely to predict symptoms associated with the consequences of drinking, such as passing out, rather than the urge to drink.

Socialization Influences   A second category of substance-specific family factors refers to the socialization of substance use behaviors. Although it has been well established that parent and sibling substance use is associated with substance use among their relatives, there is a general paucity of literature examining the direct modeling of substance use behaviors among family members (Jacob & Johnson, 1997). Studies of parent modeling of substance use suggest an inconsistent or modest effect on offspring substance use across studies, although there is evidence that parental modeling is associated with change in offspring substance use over time, from no use to onset of use or from use to increased frequency of use (e.g. Ary, Tildesley, Hops, & Andrews, 1993). Other studies suggestive of modeling report that parents and children use the same substances and exhibit similar patterns of quantity/frequency of use. Parental modeling also may be linked to offspring substance use indirectly via offspring alcohol expectancies (i.e. beliefs about the effects of alcohol; Conway, Swendsen, & Merikangas, 2003; Jacob & Johnson, 1997; Sher, Wood, Wood, & Raskin, 1996). The use of drugs or alcohol as a coping strategy among parents may also serve as a model for the development of maladaptive coping skills among offspring (Patterson, 1986). A growing literature on sibling deviance (including substance use) suggests that adolescents are introduced to deviant behavior and deviant peer networks through shared activities with siblings (Brook, Brook, Gordon, Whiteman, & Cohen, 1990; Rowe & Gulley, 1992), supporting the role of modeling of substance behavior among siblings. The role of sibling modeling is further supported by findings that (a) substance use among older siblings is likely to influence alcohol and marijuana use and initiation among younger siblings, rather than the converse (Conger, Rutter, & Conger, 1994; Duncan, Duncan, & Hops, 1996), and (b) drinking patterns are more similar among same-sex, same-age siblings than opposite-sex, different-age siblings (McGue et al., 1996).

Other aspects of substance-specific socialization related to adolescent substance use include availability of substances, parental attitudes toward and rules against substance use, direct monitoring of substance use, and tolerance of substance use in the home (Hawkins, Catalano, & Miller, 1992). A recent prospective study reported that the risk for alcohol use in 7th grade was increased among children who perceived low parental monitoring of alcohol use in 5th grade and among those who had been allowed to have a drink of alcohol at home (Jackson, Henriksen, & Dickinson, 1999). On the other hand, rules against alcohol use and parental communication against alcohol use in the 5th grade were not related to drinking in 7th grade. The authors and others have suggested that children may perceive rules and communication against substance as a mixed message when delivered by parents who themselves misuse substances. Substance-specific socialization likely involves a complex interplay of factors, such that parents' own attitudes toward, use of, and access to drugs may influence their children's motivation for drug use and affiliation with drug-using peers (Duncan & Petosa, 1995; Garnier and Stein, 2002).

Non-Specific Family Influences

The direct modeling of parental substance use has been shown to have a smaller effect on substance use in offspring than other parent influences, chiefly those involving the quality of the parent–child relationship and parental monitoring of behavior (Molina, Chassin, & Curran, 1994). The literature on non-specific familial influences encompasses studies of parents with SUD as well as the broader literature on the association between family process and child developmental outcomes. Most studies linking parenting and family context factors to substance use focus on alcohol or marijuana use, with little research on the use, abuse, or dependence on more deviant illicit substances.

Parental Psychopathology   Parental depression, anxiety, and antisocial personality disorder (ASPD) are associated with offspring substance use and SUD, even when parental comorbid SUDs are controlled (Cadoret et al., 1995; Merikangas et al., 1998a). Aside from potential genetic risk for SUDs among offspring of parents with psychopathology, parental psychopathology may pose environmental risk through family interactions and parenting behaviors. The family environments of offspring of parents with depression are characterized by negative patterns of family interaction, lax monitoring, and inconsistent discipline and displays of affection. Depressive parents may also model maladaptive coping skills and cognitive styles to their offspring (Jacob & Johnson, 1997). Parents with anxiety are often overcontrolling and intrusive, and the family environments of offspring of parents with ASPD are characterized by poor supervision and harsh parenting (Laub & Sampson, 1988; West & Farrington, 1977). Parental SUDs comorbid with depression, anxiety, or ASPD further enhance risk for SUDs among offspring.

Parenting and the Parent–Child Relationship   The study of parenting has been a central theme in socialization research. Although much of the collective literature on the association between parenting and offspring substance use is based on small, clinical samples, indirect assessment of parenting behavior, or on retrospective reports of parenting by adults, most general statements concerning this association are now backed by longitudinal research studies employing adequately sized samples and either adolescent or observer reports of both maternal and paternal parenting behavior. The simplified and deterministic models of parental influence on child outcome that once dominated the field have also been replaced with the new generation of studies focused on interactive and mediational processes, "[revealing] a reality that is far more complex than … expected …" (Collins, Maccoby, Steinberg, Hetherington, & Bornstein, 2000, p. 11). In this section, we briefly review findings on main effects; more elaborate models representing pathways between parenting and child substance use problems are reviewed in the subsequent section.

Responsiveness   Parenting studies based on the seminal work of Diana Baumrind (1965, 1971, 1991a), Maccoby and Martin (1983), and others (Darling & Steinberg, 1993;

Steinberg, 2001) have focused on the core constructs of nurturance/responsiveness, and control/demandingness. Parental responsiveness may be loosely conceptualized as parental warmth, nurturance, support, involvement, availability, and attachment toward the child and as a bi-directional relationship that is loving, supportive, and accepting. Parental responsiveness is associated with positive developmental outcomes in children (Steinberg, 2001) and lower substance use (Brook et al., 1990; Brook, Kessler, & Cohen, 1999; Swadi, 1999; Wills & Cleary, 1996).

In contrast, parent–child relationships that lack closeness or parental involvement are associated with higher alcohol and marijuana use and with the initiation of drug use (Hawkins, Catalano, & Miller, 1992 for review; Wills, Resko, Ainette, & Mendoza, 2004). Furthermore, low attachment with parents is associated with the child's initiation of substance use at a young age (Bailey & Hubbard, 1990), a well-known risk factor for SUD (Grant & Dawson, 1998). In a prospective study, the quality of maternal interaction (i.e. coldness, unresponsiveness, and underprotectiveness) at age 5, as rated by two separate observers during mother–child interaction tasks, was associated with frequent marijuana use at age 18 (Shedler & Block, 1990). In a study of three large prospective samples representing Caucasian suburban, non-Caucasian urban, and Columbian adolescents, adolescent-reported identification (i.e. admiration, emulation, and similarity) with the mother and father decreased the odds of marijuana use. Maternal affection was associated with decreased risk in the two U.S. samples and paternal affection with decreased risk in the U.S. urban sample (Brook et al., 2001). The prospective association with parental warmth, however, is sometimes reduced or eliminated when other factors are considered (e.g. Kaplow, Curran, Dodge, & The Conduct Problems Prevention Research Group, 2002).

Behavioral Control   Parental control refers to the management of child behavior. Some researchers have emphasized the distinction between behavioral and psychological control and their differential association to child functioning; whereas increased behavioral control has been linked to positive child outcomes, psychological control has a negative impact on adjustment (Barber, 1996; Steinberg, 1990). Behavioral control or demandingness is characterized by parental monitoring and supervision, communication and enforcement of rules, and the use of consistent and inductive discipline. Low behavioral control has been consistently associated with behavioral and undercontrol problems among offspring (Kurdek & Fine, 1994; Loeber & Dishion, 1983; Patterson & Stouthamer-Loeber, 1984). A coercive interactional style between parents and offspring often maintains through childhood and adulthood and is characterized by low parental monitoring and ineffective discipline (Patterson, Reid, & Dishion, 1992). Such patterns have been associated with conduct problems in children and the eventual use and abuse of alcohol and drugs in longitudinal samples (e.g. Zucker, 1994).

The most widely studied aspect of behavioral control, monitoring or supervision, typically assessed as perceived supervision by adolescents, has shown direct and indirect (through contact with drug-using peers) influence on adolescent substance use in cross-sectional, retrospective, and prospective studies (Chilcoat & Anthony, 1996). Low parental monitoring predicts children's *initiation* of alcohol, marijuana, cocaine, and inhalant use at early ages (Chilcoat & Anthony, 1996; McCarthy & Anglin, 1990; Steinberg, Fletcher, & Darling, 1994) and the onset of regular drinking and heavy episodic drinking (Reifman,

Barnes, Dirtcheff, Farrel, & Uhteg, 1998). In contrast, high parental monitoring appears to be a protective factor; it has been associated with abstinence in a longitudinal sample of adolescents (Rose et al., 2001) and has been shown to delay the onset of use. Chilcoat and Anthony (1996), for example, found that adolescents in the top quartile of levels of parental monitoring in a large prospective sample delayed onset of substance use by 2 years compared to those in the lowest quartile.

Parental discipline has been linked to substance use cross-sectionally (Hawkins et al., 1992) and prospectively (Baumrind, 1991b). The review by Hawkins et al. (1992) suggest that "the risk of substance abuse appears to be increased by family management practices characterized by unclear expectations of behavior, few and inconsistent rewards for positive behavior, and excessively severe and inconsistent punishment for unwanted behavior". In a retrospective study of parental discipline, the perception of inconsistent and unfair discipline during childhood was associated with adult alcohol use disorders when controlling for child behavior problems (Holmes & Robins, 1987). Some studies, however, have failed to find an association between harsh discipline and alcoholism (Holmes & Robins, 1987; McCord, 1972, 1983). The role of discipline may vary by parent, by the specific substance of use, and the broader social context. For example, in her three-sample study mentioned above, Brook et al. (2001) reported that only adolescent-reported paternal punitive discipline was associated with marijuana use and only in the combined and Columbian samples. In a prospective study of early onset substance use, substance use assessed at ages 10, 11, and 12 was predicted by parental substance abuse and low levels of parental verbal reasoning (Kaplow et al., 2002). Parental warmth and physical punishment were not associated with substance use once other parent variables were controlled, suggesting that parental discipline may be indirectly associated with offspring substance use.

Psychological Control   Psychological control is characterized by intrusiveness, excessive criticism, love withdrawal, guilt induction, and overprotectiveness (Barber, 1996). Most research on the deleterious impact of psychological control focuses on internalizing problems among adolescents (see Chapters 6 and 7). Scant research has examined the association between psychological control or intrusiveness and substance use or SUDs among offspring. One study reported that maternal (but not paternal) use of guilt was associated with greater marijuana use (Brook et al., 1990). In a study that examined multiple dimensions of control, parental monitoring was the strongest and most robust predictor of alcohol and illicit drug use and conduct problems; coercive control was associated concurrently with greater substance use; and inductive control showed no association to substance use or any behavioral outcomes (Barnes & Farrell, 1992).

Parenting Style   Parenting style is distinct from specific parenting practices and represents the intersection of the two core domains of parenting to yield four main parenting types: authoritative, authoritarian, permissive, and neglectful (Darling & Steinberg, 1993). In general, authoritative parenting (i.e. high demandingness and responsiveness) is associated with lower substance use (Baumrind, 1991b; Lamborn, Mounts, Steinberg, & Dornbusch, 1991; Mounts & Steinberg, 1995) across family structures, race/ethnicities, and socioeconomic classes (Avenevoli, Sessa, & Steinberg, 1999). Excessively authoritarian (high demandingness, low responsiveness) or permissive parenting (the converse) styles are associated with increased drug use (Baumrind, 1983; Kandel & Andrews, 1987; Shedler & Block, 1990).

Neglect and Abuse   Child physical and sexual abuse and neglect have been linked to substance use and SUDs among offspring, particularly women, and to the cycle of substance abuse across generations (Dunn, Mezzich, Janiszewski, Kirisci, & Tarter, 2001; West & Prinz, 1987; Widom & Hiller-Sturmhofel, 2001). Clinical samples of adolescents and adults in treatment for SUDs often yield high rates of retrospectively reported physical and sexual abuse and neglect. Few studies have prospectively examined substance use outcomes among maltreated children. Widom, Weiler, and Cottler (1999) demonstrated that maltreated individuals were not at increased risk for drug abuse when followed prospectively, but when asked about their own maltreatment as adults were significantly more likely to report abuse or neglect. Child neglect has been more consistently linked to substance use. In a longitudinal study, child neglect at ages 10–12 predicted significant variance on a composite measure of substance use involvement and severity of substance use as well as increased risk for SUD at age 19 (Kirisci, Dunn, Mezzich, & Tarter, 2001).

Family Climate and other Dyadic Relationships   Exposure to marital discord is associated with increased risk for alcohol and illicit drug use among offspring (Baumrind, 1983; Simcha-Fagan, Gersten, & Langer, 1986). When comparing the importance of family structure versus family conflict, studies repeatedly suggest that family conflict is a stronger predictor of delinquent behavior, including substance use, among adolescents (Farrington, Gallagher, Morley, Ledger, & West, 1985; Hawkins et al., 1992; Porter & O'Leary, 1980). Research on sibling dyadic relationships is scant. However, theoretical positions postulate that a positive relationship with a sibling may reduce the risk of substance use via the promotion of conventional behavior and reduced family conflict (Brook et al., 1990; Lonczak et al., 2001).

Poor family cohesion has been linked with adolescent substance use (Kandel, 1990, 1996; Stoker & Swadi, 1990). In a 1-year prospective study of five age cohorts ages 11–15, family cohesion suppressed initial levels of alcohol consumption but was not associated with subsequent changes in use (Duncan, Duncan, & Hops, 1994). Family negative life events (e.g. parental unemployment, illness) have also been associated with adolescent substance use (Wills, Sandy, Yaeger, & Shinar, 2001). In a study of the Seattle Social Development Project encompassing multiple family context factors, high family conflict and low family bonding predicted illicit drug initiation from age 12 to 21 (Guo, Hill, Hawkins, Catalano, & Abbott, 2002), although the effect of family bonding declined after age 18. Finally, family religiosity has been consistently associated with lower substance use and has shown a buffering effect against life stress on initiation of tobacco, alcohol, and marijuana use as well as on the rate of growth in substance use from 7th to 10th grade (Wills, Yaeger, & Sandy, 2003).

Processes of Familial Risk

In their 1992 review, Hawkins and colleagues concluded that most studies focus on a small subset of risk factors, with little available evidence regarding the interaction among these factors, the specificity of effects to certain classes of drugs, and whether or not these factors are modifiable. A new generation of research studies has begun to chip away at these issues. Despite the increase in the number of studies, however, general conclusions are hampered by the inconsistency in definitions of substance use behavior (e.g. use, onset, quantity, dependence), the particular predictive variables studied, and the types of models (e.g. mediator) used to examine their interrelations.

Cumulative Factors   In addition to direct effects of specific family factors on substance use behaviors, there is evidence that underscores the significance of cumulative risk. The concept of multiple risk factors is illustrated in a longitudinal study of children who were assessed and followed from kindergarten to age 12 (Kaplow et al., 2002). Several factors were directly associated with early-onset drug use, including overactivity, thought problems, social problem-solving skills deficits, parental substance abuse, and lack of parental verbal reasoning. Yet when these factors were considered together, the risk of early-onset drug use increased linearly as the number of risk factors increased from zero to three. Children with no risk factors had less than a 10% chance of initiating substance use by age 12, children with one risk factor had approximately 33% chance of early-onset substance use, and children with two or more risk factors had greater than a 50% chance of early-onset substance use. In a second study, multiple adverse events in childhood increased risk for alcohol abuse (Dube, Anda, Felitti, Edwards, & Croft, 2002).

Multiple Factors   More studies are beginning to examine multiple family risk factors in the same models to elucidate the most powerful predictors and to account for correlation across factors. Although many specific findings are described above, some general statements are worth noting here. First, when multiple family factors are considered together, parental discipline and parental support are less effective than parental monitoring or parental bonding in predicting adolescence substance use. For example, in the New York longitudinal study, Brook et al. (1999) reported that in a grand model with many different predictors, identification with parent and church attendance by parent and child were associated with lower risk of onset of marijuana use; however, parental warmth, parent–child conflict and maternal consistency were not significant in the presence of these other factors. Second, studies of substance-specific versus non-specific factors have suggested that general parenting behaviors are more powerful in predicting substance use outcomes in adolescents.

Third, although family factors are important in predicting substance use and SUDs, sibling and peer factors are typically stronger main-effect predictors of substance *use* than parent factors. Sibling and peer alcohol and drug use are more consistently related to substance use among adolescents, and the effect of parental substance use often disappears when considered in the same model. However, parental SUD and parenting behaviors have a more powerful impact on *substance problems* among offspring than do peers. Most importantly, the impact of both parental substance use and parenting show indirect effects on offspring substance use via peer factors and offer protective effects against negative peer influences (see discussion below).

Mediators: Mechanisms of Risk and Protection   Most studies attempting to outline mechanisms of risk for SUDs have focused on children of alcoholics or other substance abusers. Parental SUD is associated with less effective parenting (see Mayes & Truman, 2002, for a review), including less responsiveness (Dube et al., 2001; Rutherford, Cacciola, Alterman, McKay, & Cook, 1997), greater parent–child conflict (Wills et al., 2001), more harsh and threatening discipline (DeLucia, Belz, & Chassin, 2001; Miller, Smyth, & Mudar, 1999; Mayes & Truman, 2002), lower monitoring of child behavior (Chilcoat, Breslau, & Anthony, 1996), and child maltreatment, particularly neglect (Dunn et al., 2002). Parental SUD also has an impact on the broader family environment via divorce, disrupted family structure, marital discord, domestic violence, low stability (e.g. more relocations), low family cohesion, stressful events, and family conflict (Chermack & Giancola, 1997; Collins & Messerschmidt, 1993). Mediational studies have suggested that the association between parent and offspring substance behaviors is explained in part by parenting behaviors. For example, parental alcoholism was associated with adolescent substance use and growth in substance use over time in part through decreased parental monitoring (Chassin, Pillow, Curran, Molina, & Barrera, 1993; Chassin, Curran, Hussong, & Colder, 1996). In samples of young adults, adolescent parental discipline has been shown to mediate the association between parental alcoholism and offspring drug use disorders (King & Chassin, 2004), and family violence has been shown to mediate the association between parental alcohol use disorder and offspring alcohol problems (Sher, Gershuny, Peterson, & Raskin, 1997).

The association between parental and offspring SUDs may be explained by other factors as well. Affiliation with deviant peers has been shown to mediate the association between parental alcohol use disorder and offspring substance use (Blanton, Gibbons, Gerrard, Conger, & Smith, 1997; Chassin et al., 1996; Garnier & Stein, 2002). Additionally, Sher et al. (1991) proposed that comorbidity was one of the key potential mediators of the development of alcoholism. Likewise, Chassin et al. (1991) revealed that the link between parental alcoholism and externalizing symptoms in children was mediated by co-occurring parental psychopathology and parental stress.

There is mixed support for the notion that child behavioral disinhibition, or undercontrol, is a mediator for family history of substance abuse. Some studies fail to show that behavior disinhibition transmits within families of drug abusers (Swendsen, Conway, Rounsaville, & Merikangas, 2002; Zaninelli, Porjesz, & Begleiter, 1992), suggesting that personality traits are individual (rather than familial) risk factors for drug abuse. In contrast, Elkins, McGue, Malone, and Iacono (2004) found that parental history of SUD is associated with decreased constraint among offspring. Sher et al. (1991) proposed separate pathways from parental history of alcoholism to alcohol use and abuse in offspring; one pathway reveals a direct link between parental alcoholism influencing alcohol expectancies which lead to increased consumption of alcohol; the other pathway comprises parental alcoholism associated with behavioral undercontrol, resulting in a broad array of risk-taking behaviors, particularly alcohol and drug use. In another study, Tarter, Kirisci, Habeych, Reynolds, & Vanyukov (2004) found that neurobehavioral disinhibition, drug use frequency, and social maladjustment mediated the association between parental and male offspring drug abuse.

In addition to examining mechanisms of the association between parent and offspring SUDs, parenting and family context factors and individual child factors have been examined together. For example, the association between poor parenting and substance abuse is mediated by factors in the child such as psychological dysregulation and poor social competence (Dawes, Clark, Moss, Kirisci, & Tarter, 1999; Murry & Brody, 1999; Taylor &

Machida, 1994). Family domain (family bonding, parental structure, and sibling drug use) was related to marijuana use 2 years later among Columbian adolescents via broad peer (drug use, deviance, and prosocial behavior) and personality (ego integration, unconventionality, and psychiatric symptoms) factors (Brook, Brook, Rosen, & Montoya, 2002). In the Seattle Social Development Project of youth interviewed annually from 10 to 16 years and at 18 years, Kosterman, Hawkins, Guo, Catalano, and Abbott (2000) reported that maternal bonding was indirectly associated with marijuana use initiation through peer use and norms for behavior. In the same study, parents' family management (e.g. monitoring, discipline) was indirectly associated with reduced likelihood of alcohol initiation, through parents' norms against teen alcohol use. In another study of substance-specific and non-specific parenting factors, Fletcher and Jefferies (1999) found that parental disciplinary consequences of engaging in substance use mediated the association between parental authoritativeness and lower substance use among girls, but not among boys.

Moderators: Interaction of Multiple Factors   A particularly understudied process of risk and protection is the *moderating* effects of family context factors, broader social factors, and individual factors on the association between parental and offspring substance abuse. Studies that have examined such effects suggest that the interaction between parental SUD and comorbid psychopathology yields greater risk and more severe substance use patterns among offspring. Moss, Lynch, Hardie, and Baron (2002), for example, have shown that offspring of fathers with both SUD and ASPD, compared to offspring of fathers with SUD only, had higher rates of internalizing and externalizing disorders. Chassin, Pitts, and Prost (2002) also found that children of alcoholics with comorbid ASPD, compared to children of alcoholics only, were more likely to be characterized by early and heavy drinking patterns during adolescence. In an analysis of Cadoret's adoption study, Langbehn, Cadoret, Caspers, Troughton and Yucuis (2003) showed that the presence of drug abuse and ASPD in the adoptee's biological father, compared to drug abuse without ASPD, posed greater risk for the development of drug use and disorder in the adoptee.

The effect of a family history of SUD may also vary by the number of parents with SUD. For example, analyses of the impact of parental concordance for substance use disorders revealed that families with two affected parents had higher proportions of unhealthy functioning and were more disengaged (i.e. less cohesion) regardless of the particular combination of parental diagnoses (Dierker, Merikangas, & Szatmari, 1999). Other studies have shown that family cohesion moderated the association between parental SUD and adolescent drug abuse (Hoffman & Cerbone, 2002).

Family factors have been shown to interact with peer influences on substance use problems (Gerrard, Gibbons, Zhao, Russell, & Reis-Bergan, 1999; Wills et al., 2004). Wood, Read, Roger, and Brand (2004) reported that parental influences (e.g. nurturance, modeling) moderated the association between peer influences and alcohol use and problems among late adolescents. Moss et al. (2002) also found that children of fathers with both SUD and ASPD, compared to children of fathers with SUD only, demonstrated greater affiliation with deviant peers, which, in turn, was associated with psychopathology. Results support a developmental model of antisocial problems that implicates a complex interaction between family processes and deviant peer associations as key factors in the development of antisocial problems.

Prevention and Treatment of Substance Use Disorders

Family-based interventions for the prevention and treatment of SUDs focus on the reduction of family risk factors and the enhancement of family protective factors (Dishion & Kavanagh, 2000; Kumpfer & Alder, 2003; Sanders, 2000; Weinberg et al., 1998). A recent review identified four types of family-based therapies — behavioral parent training, family skills training, family therapy, in-home family support — as highly effective in preventing substance abuse and/or improving child behavioral problems and family relations (Kumpfer & Adler, 2003). Specific prevention programs have focused on the parenting skills mentioned above, including parental monitoring and involvement, and the benefits of specific programs typically mirror the foci of the program (i.e. programs that attempt to enhance parental monitoring tend to improve monitoring) as well as yield negative associations with substance use (e.g. Dishion, Andrews, Kavanagh, & Soberman, 1996). A review of programs aimed at preventing alcohol misuse among youth suggested that the Strengthening the Families Program (a family-based program) showed the greatest promise in terms of preventing alcohol misuse over the long term (i.e. >3 years; Foxcroft, Ireland, Lister-Sharp, Lowe, & Breen, 2003). Successful programs are those that are research-based, involve multiple components (family, school, community), involve parent–child interaction, and are culturally and developmentally appropriate (Sloboda & David, 1997).

Family-based treatments for adolescent drug abuse, compared to other well-established treatments, have yielded higher engagement and retention rates, reduced drug use (up to 1 year later) and behavioral problems, and improved family functioning (see Rowe & Liddle, 2002, for a review; Weinberg et al., 1998). Studies evaluating treatment outcome among adult alcoholics and drug abusers highlight the potential of behavioral couples therapy and other family-based strategies for minimizing substance use, promoting abstinence, and improving individual and family functioning (O'Farrell & Fals-Stewart, 2002; Rowe & Liddle, 2002).

Conclusions

This chapter describes the many familial influences on the development of SUDs. The results of family, twin, adoption, and high-risk studies of SUDs reveal that both alcoholism and drug abuse/dependence is familial and that genetic factors explain a substantial proportion of the variance in their etiology, particularly substance use *disorders*. Factors associated with increased familial aggregation of these disorders include male gender, parental concordance, and comorbid psychopathology. Furthermore, a great deal of research supports direct links between specific family environmental factors — particularly parental monitoring and involvement and family cohesion — and child, adolescent and adult substance use and SUDs. Behavioral science studies that have examined processes of risk and protection highlight the complex interplay of multiple family, individual, and other factors in the prediction of substance use and related problems. A major challenge for developing successful models for understanding and treating SUDs is that there are *multiple pathways* to these disorders, with varying degrees of environmental and genetic contributions.

A focus on three important areas will further elucidate etiological processes and inform targets and strategies for prevention and treatment. First, more work is needed to outline specific factors and processes that predict initial use versus progression to SUD. One of the main issues of complexity surrounding the study of SUDs is that *initial exposure* to an exogenous mood-altering substance is a necessary, though not sufficient, condition for disorder expression. Thus, evaluating etiology of SUDs necessarily involves understanding factors associated with initial use as well as the progression from use to abuse or dependence. Second, much more research is needed to examine the processes of risk and protection with longitudinal cohorts in order to replicate, extend, and integrate extant findings. Models that reflect the complexity of and multiple pathways to the development of SUDs are particularly promising. Additionally, the identification of factors and processes that discriminate individuals at risk for SUDs who develop SUDs from their counterparts who do not develop SUDs are greatly needed to shed light on underlying protective mechanisms. Recognition of the dynamic nature of risk and protective factors, the trajectories of substance use, developmental status, and social context will further strengthen this research. Third, future research ought to pay greater attention to a number of understudied factors that may confound or strengthen models of SUD, particularly parental concordance for SUD, comorbid parental and child psychopathology, prenatal exposure to substances, and the bi-directional influences of parent and child behaviors.

A number of prospective studies currently underway incorporate many of these factors and methodological propositions. Additionally, recent trends in the field to combine different samples offer new opportunities to examine these potentially important processes with increased statistical power. Ultimately, the successful integration of the two lines of research that characterize the studies reviewed here — namely, genetic epidemiological studies, which seek to identify environmental and genetic contributions to SUDs, and psychosocial studies, which focus on complex models of etiology involving primarily environmental factors — holds the greatest promise for elucidating etiological processes and foci for intervention efforts (Avenevoli & Merikangas, 2003; Jacob et al., 2003).

References

American Psychiatric Association. (1987). *Diagnostic and statistical manual of mental disorders* (3rd ed., Revised). Washington, DC: American Psychiatric Association.

American Psychiatric Association. (1994). *Diagnostic and statistical manual of mental disorders* (4th ed.). Washington, DC: American Psychiatric Association.

Andrews, J. A., Hops, H., & Duncan, S. C. (1997). Adolescent modeling of parent substance use: The moderating effect of the relationship with the parent. *Journal of Family Psychology, 11,* 259–270.

Ary, D. V., Tildesley, E., Hops, H., & Andrews, J. (1993). The influence of parent, sibling, and peer modeling and attitudes on adolescent use of alcohol. *The International Journal of Addictions, 28,* 853–880.

Avenevoli, S., Sessa, F. M., & Steinberg, L. (1999). Family structure, parenting practices, and adolescent adjustment: An ecological examination. In: E. M. Hetherington (Ed.), *The impact of divorce, single parenthood, and remarriage on children and families.* Hillsdale, NJ: Lawrence Erlbaum.

Avenevoli, S., & Merikangas, K. R. (2003). Familial influences on adolescent smoking. *Addiction, 98*, 1–20.

Baer, J. S., Barr, H. M., Bookstein, F. L., Sampson, P. D., & Streissguth, A. P. (1998). Prenatal alcohol exposure and family history of alcoholism in the etiology of adolescent alcohol problems. *Journal of Studies on Alcohol, 59*, 533–543.

Baer, J. S., Sampson, P. D., Barr, H. M., Connor, P. D., & Streissguth, A. P. (2003). A 21-year longitudinal analysis of the effects of prenatal alcohol exposure on young adult drinking. *Archives of General Psychiatry, 60*, 377–385.

Bailey, S. L., & Hubbard, R. L. (1990). Developmental variation in the context of marijuana initiation among adolescents. *Journal of Health and Social Behavior, 31*, 58–70.

Barber, B. K. (1996). Parental psychological control: Revisiting a neglected construct. *Child Development, 67*, 3296–3319.

Barnes, G. M., & Farrell, M. P. (1992). Parental support and control as predictors of adolescent drinking, delinquency, and related problem behaviors. *Journal of Marriage and the Family, 54*, 763–776.

Baumrind, D. (1965). Parental control and parental love. *Children, 12*, 230–234.

Baumrind, D. (1971). Current patterns of parental authority. *Developmental Psychology Monograph, 4*(1, Pt. 2), 1–103.

Baumrind, D. (1983, October). Why adolescents take chances — And why they don't. Paper presented at the National Institute for Child Health and Human Development, Bethesda, MD.

Baumrind, D. (1991a). Parenting styles and adolescent development. In: J. Brooks-Gunn, R. Lerner & A. C. Petersen (Eds), *The Encyclopedia of Adolescence* (pp. 746–758). New York: Garland.

Baumrind, D. (1991b). The influence of parenting style on adolescent competence and substance use. *Journal of Early Adolescence, 11*, 56–95.

Bierut, L. J., Dinwiddie, S. H., Begleiter, H., Crowe, R. R., Hesselbrock, V., Nurnberger, J. I. Jr., Porjesz, B., Schuckit, M. A., & Reich, T. (1998). Familial transmission of substance dependence: Alcohol, marijuana, cocaine, and habitual smoking: A report from the Collaborative Study on the Genetics of Alcoholism. *Archives of General Psychiatry, 55*, 982–988.

Blanton, H., Gibbons, F. X., Gerrard, M., Conger, K. J., & Smith, G. E. (1997). Role of family and peers in the development of prototypes associated with substance use. *Journal of Family Psychology, 11*, 271–288.

Boyle, M. H., Sanford, M., Szatmari, P., Merikangas, K., & Offord, D. R. (2001). Familial influences on substance use by adolescents and young adults. *Canadian Journal of Public Health, 92*, 206–209.

Brook, J. S., Brook, D. W., Arencibia-Mireles, O., Richter, L., & Whiteman, M. (2001). Risk factors for adolescent marijuana use across cultures and across time. *Journal of Genetic Psychology, 162*, 357–374.

Brook, J. S., Brook, D. W., Gordon, H. S., Whiteman, M., & Cohen, P. (1990). The psychosocial etiology of adolescent drug use: A family interactional approach. *Genetics, Social, and General Psychology Monographs, 116*(2), 111–267.

Brook, D. W., Brook, J. S., Rosen, Z., & Montoya, I. (2002). Correlates of marijuana use in Colombian adolescents: A focus on the impact of the ecological/cultural domain. *Journal of Adolescent Health, 31*, 286–298.

Brook, J. S., Kessler, R. C., & Cohen, P. (1999). The onset of marijuana use from preadolescence and early adolescence to young adulthood. *Development and Psychopathology, 11*, 901–914.

Cadoret, R. J. (1992). Genetic and environmental factors in initiation of drug use and the transition to abuse. In: M. Glantz & R. Pickens (Eds), *Vulnerability to drug abuse* (pp. 99–113). Washington, DC: American Psychological Association.

Cadoret, R. J., Troughton, E., O'Gorman, T., & Heywood, E. (1986). An adoption study of genetic and environmental factors in drug abuse. *Archives of General Psychiatry, 43*, 1131–1136.

Cadoret, R. J., Yates, W. R., Troughton, E., Woodworth, G., & Stewart, M. A. (1995). Adoption study demonstrating two genetic pathways to drug abuse. *Archives of General Psychiatry, 52*, 42–52.

Cadoret, R. J., Yates, W. R., Troughton, E., Woodworth, G., & Stewart, M. A. (1996). An adoption study of drug abuse/dependence in females. *Comprehensive Psychiatry, 37*, 88–94.

Chassin, L., Curran, P., Hussong, A., & Colder, C. (1996). The relation of parent alcoholism to adolescent substance use: A longitudinal follow-up study. *Journal of Abnormal Psychology, 105*, 70–80.

Chassin, L., Pillow, D. R., Curran, P. J., Molina, B. S. G., & Barrera, M. Jr. (1993). Relation of parental alcoholism to early adolescent substance use: A test of three mediating mechanisms. *Journal of Abnormal Psychology, 102*, 3–19.

Chassin, L., Pitts, S. C., DeLucia, C., & Todd, M. (1999). A longitudinal study of children of alcoholics: Predicting young adult substance use disorders, anxiety, and depression. *Journal of Abnormal Psychology, 108*, 106–119.

Chassin, L., Pitts, S. C., & Prost, J. (2002). Binge drinking trajectories from adolescence to emerging adulthood in a high-risk sample: Predictors and substance abuse outcomes. *Journal of Consulting and Clinical Psychology, 70*, 67–78.

Chassin L., Rogosch, F., & Barrera, M. (1991). Substance use and symptomatology among adolescent children of alcoholics. *Journal of Abnormal Psychology, 100*, 449–463.

Chermack, S. T., & Giancola, P. R. (1997). The relation between alcohol and aggression: An integrated biopsychosocial conceptualization. *Clinical Psychology Review, 17*, 621–649.

Chilcoat, H. D., & Anthony, J. C. (1996). Impact of parent monitoring on initiation of drug use through late childhood. *Journal of the American Academy of Child and Adolescent Psychiatry, 35*, 91–100.

Chilcoat, H. D., Breslau, N., & Anthony, J. C. (1996). Potential barriers to parent monitoring: Social disadvantage, marital status, and maternal psychiatric disorder. *Journal of the American Academy of Child and Adolescent Psychiatry, 35*, 1673–1682.

Claridge, G., Ross, E., & Hume, W. I. (1978). *Sedative drug tolerance in twins*. Oxford, England: Pergamon Press.

Collins, W. A., Maccoby, E. E., Steinberg, L., Hetherington, E. M., & Bornstein, M. H. (2000). Contemporary research on parenting: The case for nature and nurture. *American Psychologist, 55*, 1–15.

Collins, J. J., & Messerschmidt, P. M. (1993). Epidemiology of alcohol related violence. *Alcohol Health Research World, 17*, 93–100.

Conger, R. D., Rutter, M. R., & Conger, K. J. (1994). The family context of adolescent vulnerability and resilience to alcohol use and abuse. *Sociological Studies of Children, 6*, 55–86.

Conway, K. P., Swendsen, J. D., & Merikangas, K. R. (2003). Expectancies, alcohol consumption, and problem drinking: The importance of family history. *Addictive Behaviors, 28*, 823–836.

Crabbe, J. C., & Phillips, T. J. (1998). Genetics of alcohol and other abused drugs. *Drug and Alcohol Dependence, 51*, 61–71.

Croughan, J. L. (1985). The contributions of family studies to understanding drug abuse. In: L. Robins (Ed.), *Studying drug abuse*. New Brunswick, NJ: Rutgers University Press.

Darling, N., & Cumsille, P. (2003). Theory, measurement, and methods in the study of family influences on adolescent smoking. *Addiction, 98*(Suppl. 1), 21–36.

Darling, N., & Steinberg, L. (1993). Parenting style as context: An integrative model. *Psychological Bulletin, 113*, 487–496.

Dawes, J., Clark, D., Moss, H., Kirisci, L., & Tarter, R. (1999). Family and peer correlates of behavioral self-regulation in boys at risk for substance abuse. *American Journal of Drug and Alcohol Abuse, 25*, 219–237.

DeLucia, C., Belz, A., & Chassin, L. (2001). Do adolescent symptomatology and family environment vary over time with fluctuations in paternal alcohol impairment? *Developmental Psychology*, *37*, 207–216.

Dierker, L. C., Merikangas, K. R., & Szatmari, P. (1999). Influences of parental concordance for psychiatric disorders on psychopathology in offspring. *Journal of the American Academy of Child and Adolescent Psychiatry*, *38*, 280–288.

Dishion, R. J., Andrews, D. W., Kavanagh, K., & Soberman, L. H. (1996). Preventive interventions for high-risk youth: The adolescent transitions program. In: R. D. Peters & R. J. McMahon (Eds), *Preventing childhood disorders, substance abuse, and delinquency* (pp. 184–214). Thousand Oaks, CA: Sage.

Dishion, T. J., & Kavanagh, K. (2000). A multilevel approach to family-centered prevention in schools: Process and outcome. *Addictive Behaviors*, *25*, 899–911.

Dube, S. R., Anda, R. F., Felitti, V. J., Edwards, V. J., & Croft, J. B. (2002). Adverse childhood experiences and personal alcohol abuse as an adult. *Addictive Behaviors*, *27*, 713–725.

Duncan, T. E., Duncan, S. C., & Hops, H. (1994). The effects of family cohesiveness and peer encouragement on the development of adolescent alcohol use: A cohort-sequential approach to the analysis of longitudinal data. *Journal of Studies on Alcohol*, *55*, 588–599.

Duncan, T. E., Duncan, S. C., & Hops, H. (1996). The role of parents and older siblings in predicting adolescent substance use: Modeling development via structural equation latent growth methodology. *Journal of Family Psychology*, *10*, 1353–1378.

Duncan, T. E., & Petosa, R. (1995). Social and community factors associated with drug use and abuse among adolescents. In: T. P. Gullotta, G. R. Adams & R. Montemayor (Eds), *Substance misuse in adolescence* (pp. 56–91). Thousand Oaks, CA: Sage.

Dunn, M. G., Mezzich, A., Janiszewski, S., Kirisci, L., & Tarter, R. E. (2001). Transmission of neglect in substance abuse families: The role of child dysregulation and parental SUD. *Journal of Child and Adolescent Substance Abuse*, *10*, 123–132.

Dunn, M. G., Tarter, R. E., Mezzich, A. C., Vanyukov, M., Kirisci, L., & Kirillova, G. (2002). Origins and consequences of child neglect in substance abuse families. *Clinical Psychology Review*, *22*, 1063–1090.

Elkins, I. J., McGue, M., Malone, S., & Iacono, W. G. (2004). The effect of parental alcohol and drug disorders on adolescent personality. *American Journal of Psychiatry*, *161*, 670–676.

Enoch, M. A., & Goldman, D. (1999). Genetics of alcoholism and substance abuse. *Psychiatric Clinics of North America*, *22*, 289–299.

Farrington, D. P., Gallagher, B., Morley, L., Ledger, R. J., & West, D. J. (1985). *Cambridge study in delinquent development: Long-term follow-up*. First annual report to the home office, August 31, 1985. Cambridge, England: Cambridge University.

Fletcher, A. C., & Jefferies, B. C. (1999). Parental mediators of associations between perceived authoritative parenting and early adolescent substance use. *Journal of Early Adolescence*, *19*, 465–487.

Foxcroft, D. R., Ireland, D., Lister-Sharp, D. J., Lowe, G., & Breen, R. (2003). Longer-term primary prevention for alcohol misuse in young people: A systematic review. *Addiction*, *98*, 397–411.

Garnier, H. E., & Stein, J. A. (2002). An 18-year model of family and peer effects on adolescent drug use and delinquency. *Journal of Youth and Adolescence*, *51*, 45–56.

Gerrard, M., Gibbons, F. X., Zhao, L., Russell, D. W., & Reis-Bergan, M. (1999). The effects of peers' alcohol consumption on parental influence: A cognitive mediational model. *Journal of Studies on Alcohol*, *13*, 32–44.

Goetzel, R. Z., Hawkins, K., & Ozminkowski, R. J. (2003). The health and productivity cost burden of the "top 10" physical and mental conditions affecting six large US employers in 1999. *Journal of Occupational and Environmental Medicine*, *45*, 5–14.

Gordon, H. W. (1994). Human neuroscience at National Institute on Drug Abuse: Implications for genetic research. *American Journal of Medical Genetics, 54*, 300–303.

Grant, B. F. (1995). Comorbidity between DSM-IV drug use disorders and major depression: results of a national survey of adults. *Journal of Substance Abuse, 7*, 481–497.

Grant, B. F., & Dawson, D. A. (1998). Age of onset of drug use and its association with DSM-IV drug abuse and dependence: Results from the National Longitudinal Alcohol Epidemiologic Survey. *Journal of Substance Abuse, 10*, 163–173.

Gfroerer, J. (1987). Correlation between drug use by teenagers and drug use by older family members. *American Journal of Drug and Alcohol Abuse, 13*, 95–108.

Grove, W., Eckert, E., Heston, L., Bouchard, T., Segal, N., & Lykken, D. (1990). Heritability of substance abuse and antisocial behavior: A study of monozygotic twins reared apart. *Biological Psychiatry, 27*, 1293–1304.

Guo, J., Hill, K. G., Hawkins, J. D., Catalano, R. F., & Abbott, R. D. (2002). A developmental analysis of sociodemographic, family, and peer effects on adolescent illicit drug initiation. *Journal of the American Academy of Child and Adolescent Psychiatry, 41*, 838–845.

Gurling, H., Grant, S., & Dangl, J. (1985). The genetic and cultural transmission of alcohol use, alcoholism, cigarette smoking and coffee drinking: A review and an example using a log linear cultural transmission model. *British Journal of Addiction, 80*, 269–279.

Hawkins, J. D., Catalano, R. F., & Miller, J. Y. (1992). Risk and protective factors for alcohol and other drug problems in adolescence and early adulthood: Implications for substance abuse prevention. *Psychological Bulletin, 112*, 64–105.

Heath, A. C., Bucholz, K. K., Madden, P., Dinwiddie, S. H., Slutske, W. S., Bierut, L. J., Statham, D. J., Dunne, M. P., Whitfield, J. B., & Martin, N. G. (1997). Genetic and environmental contributions to alcohol dependence risk in a national twin sample: Consistency of findings in women and men. *Psychological Medicine, 27*, 1381–1396.

Hicks, B. M., Krueger, R. F., Iacono, W. G., McGue, M., & Patrick, C. J. (2004). Family transmission and heritability of externalizing disorders: A twin-family study. *Archives of General Psychiatry, 61*, 922–928.

Hill, S. Y., Cloninger, C. R., & Ayre, A. B. (1977). Independent familial transmission of alcoholism and opiate abuse. *Alcoholism: Clinical and Experimental Research, 1*, 335–342.

Hill, S. Y., & Hruska, D. R. (1992). Childhood psychopathology in families with multigenerational alcoholism. *Journal of the American Academy of Child and Adolescent Psychiatry, 31*, 1024–1030.

Hoffmann, J. P., & Cerbone, F. G. (2002). Parental substance use disorder and the risk of adolescent drug abuse: An event history analysis. *Drug and Alcohol Dependency, 66*, 255–264.

Holmes, S. J., & Robins, L. N. (1987). The influence of childhood disciplinary experience on the development of alcoholism and depression. *Journal of Child Psychology and Psychiatry, 28*, 399–415.

Hopfer, C. J., Crowley, T. J., & Hewitt, J. K. (2003). Review of twin and adoption studies of adolescent substance use. *Journal of the American Academy of Child and Adolescent Psychiatry, 42*, 710–719.

Jackson, C., Henriksen, L., & Dickinson, D. (1999). Alcohol-specific socialization, parenting behaviors and alcohol use by children. *Journal of Studies on Alcohol, 60*, 362–367.

Jacob, T., & Johnson, S. (1997). Parenting influences on the development of alcohol abuse and dependence. *Alcohol, Health and Research World, 21*, 204–209.

Jacob, T., Waterman, B., Heath, A., True, W., Bucholz, K. K., Haber, R., Scherrer, J. & Fu, Q. (2003). Genetic and environmental effects on offspring alcoholism: New insights using an offspring-of-twins design. *Archives of General Psychiatry, 60*, 1265–1272.

Jang, K. L., Livesley, W. J., & Vernon, P. A. (1995). Alcohol and drug problems: A multivariate behavioral genetic analysis of co-morbidity. *Addiction, 90*, 1213–1221.

Johnson, S., Leonard, K. E., & Jacob, T. (1989). Drinking, drinking styles and drug use in children of alcoholics, depressives and controls. *Journal of Studies on Alcohol, 50*, 427–431.

Johnson, L. D., O'Malley, P. M., Bachman, J. G., & Schulenberg, J. E. (2003). Monitoring the Future National Survey Results on Drug Use, 1975–2003; Volume I, Secondary School Students (NIH publication no. 04-5507). Bethesda, MD: National Institute on Drug Abuse.

Kandel, D. B. (1990). Parenting styles, drug use, and children's adjustment in families of young adults. *Journal of Marriage and the Family, 52*, 183–196.

Kandel, D. B. (1996). The parental and peer contexts of adolescent deviance: An algebra of inter-personal influences. *Journal of Drug Issues, 26*, 289–315.

Kandel, D. B., & Andrews, K. (1987). Processes of adolescent socialization by parents and peers. *International Journal of the Addictions, 22*, 319–342.

Kaplow, J. B., Curran, P. J., Dodge, K. A., & The Conduct Problems Prevention Research Group. (2002). Child, parent, and peer predictors of early-onset substance use: A multisite longitudinal study. *Journal of Abnormal Child Psychology, 30*, 199–216.

Kendler, K. S., Karkowski, L. M., Neale, M. C., & Prescott, C. A. (2000). Illicit psychoactive substance use, heavy use, abuse and dependence in a US population-based sample of male twins. *Archives of General Psychiatry, 57*, 261–269.

Kendler, K. S., Karkowski, L., & Prescott, C. A. (1999). Hallucinogen, opiate, sedative and stimulant use and abuse in a population-based sample of female twins. *Acta Psychiatica Scandinavica, 99*, 368–376.

Kendler, K. S., & Prescott, C. A. (1998a). Cannabis use, abuse and dependence in a population-based sample of female twins. *American Journal of Psychiatry, 155*, 1016–1022.

Kendler, K. S., & Prescott, C. A. (1998b). Cocaine use, abuse and dependence in a population-based sample of female twins. *British Journal of Psychiatry, 173*, 345–350.

Kendler, K. S., Prescott, C. A., Meyers, J., & Neale, M. C. (2003). The structure of genetic and environmental risk factors for common psychiatric and substance use disorders in men and women. *Archives of General Psychiatry, 60*, 929–937.

Kessler, R. C., Crum, R. M., Warner, L. A., Nelson, C. B., Schulenberg, J., & Anthony, J. C. (1997). Lifetime co-occurrence of DSM-III-R alcohol abuse and dependence with other psychiatric disorders in the National Comorbidity Survey. *Archives of General Psychiatry, 54*, 313–321.

Kessler, R. C., Nelson, C. B., McGonagle, K. A., Edlund, M. J., Frank, R. G., & Leaf, P. J. (1996). The epidemiology of co-occurring addictive and mental disorders: Implications for prevention and service utilization. *American Journal of Orthopsychiatry, 66*, 17–31.

King, K. M., & Chassin, L. (2004). Mediating and moderated effects of adolescent behavioral undercontrol and parenting in the prediction of drug use disorders in emerging adulthood. *Psychology of Addictive Behaviors, 18*, 239–249.

Kirisci, L., Dunn, M. G., Mezzich, A. C., & Tarter, R. E. (2001). Impact of parental substance use disorder and child neglect severity on substance use involvement in male offspring. *Prevention Science, 2*, 241–255.

Koopmans, J. R., & Boomsma, D. I. (1996). Familial resemblances in alcohol use. *Journal of Studies on Alcohol, 57*, 19–28.

Kumpfer, K. L., & Alder, S. (2003). Dissemination of research-based family interventions for the prevention of substance abuse. In: Z. Sloboda & W. J. Bukoski (Eds), *Handbook of drug abuse prevention: Theory, science, and practice* (pp. 75–100). New York: Kluwer.

Kurdek, L. A., & Fine, M. A. (1994). Family acceptance and family control as predictors of adjustment in young adolescents: Linear, curvilinear, or interactive effects? *Child Development, 65*, 1137–1146.

Kosterman, R., Hawkins, J. D., Guo, J., Catalano, R. F., & Abbott, R. D. (2000). The dynamics of alcohol and marijuana initiation: Patterns and predictors of first use in adolescence. *American Journal of Public Health, 90*, 360–366.

Lamborn, S. D., Mounts, N. S., Steinberg, L., & Dornbusch, S. M. (1991). Patterns of competence and adjustment among adolescents from authoritative, authoritarian, indulgent, and neglectful families. *Child Development, 62,* 1049–1065.

Langbehn, D. R., Cadoret, R. J., Caspers, K., Troughton, E. P., & Yucuis, R. (2003). Genetic and environmental risk factors for the onset of drug use and problems in adoptees. *Drug and Alcohol Dependence, 69,* 151–167.

Laub, J. H., & Sampson, R. J. (1988). Unraveling families and delinquency: A reanalysis of the Gleucks' data. *Criminology, 26,* 355–380.

Lieb, R., Merikangas, K. R., Hofler, M., Pfister, H., Isensee, B., & Wittchen, H. -U. (2002). Parental alcohol use disorders and alcohol use and disorders in offspring: A community study. *Psychological Medicine, 32,* 63–78.

Loeber, R. T., & Dishion, T. (1983). Early predictors of male delinquency: A review. *Psychological Bulletin, 93,* 68–99.

Lonczak, H. S., Huang, B., Catalano, R. F., Hawkins, J. D., Hill, K. G., Abbott, R. D., Ryan, J. A. M., & Kosterman, R. (2001). The social predictors of adolescent alcohol misuse: A test of the social development model. *Journal of Studies on Alcohol, 62,* 179–189.

Loukas, A., Zucker, R. A., Fitzgerald, H. E., & Krull, J. L. (2003). Developmental trajectories of disruptive behavior problems among sons of alcoholics: Effects of parent psychopathology, family conflict, and child undercontrol. *Journal of Abnormal Psychology, 112,* 119–131.

Maccoby, E. E., & Martin, J. A. (1983). Socialization in the context of the family: Parent–child interaction. In: P. H. Mussen (Series Ed), & E. M. Hetherington (Vol. Ed), *Handbook of Child Psychology: Vol. 4. Socialization, personality, and social development* (4th ed., pp. 1–101). New York: Wiley.

Martin, C. S., Earleywine, M., Blackson, T. C., Vanyukov, M. M., Moss, H. B., & Tarter, R. E. (1994). Aggressivity, inattention, hyperactivity, and impulsivity in boys at high and low risk for substance abuse. *Journal of Abnormal Child Psychology, 22,* 177–203.

Mayes, L. C., & Truman, S. D. (2002). Substance abuse and parenting. In: M. Bornstein (Ed.), *Handbook of Parenting: Vol.4: Social conditions and applied parenting* (2nd ed.) (pp. 329–359). Mahwah, NJ: Lawrence Erlbaum.

McCarthy, W. J., & Anglin, M. D. (1990). Narcotics addicts: Effect of family and parental risk factors on timing of emancipation, drug use onset, pre-addiction incarcerations and educational achievement. *Journal of Drug Issues, 20,* 99–123.

McCord, J. (1972). Etiological factors in alcoholism: Family and personal characteristics. *Quarterly Journal of Studies on Alcohol,* 1027–1033.

McCord, J. (1983). A forty-year perspective on effects of child abuse and neglect. *Child Abuse & Neglect, 7,* 265–270.

McGue, M. (1994). Genes, environment, and the etiology of alcoholism. In: R. Zucker, G. Boyd & J. Howard (Eds), *The development of alcohol problems: Exploring the biopsychosocial matrix.* Rockville: U.S. Department of Health, Human Services Research Monograph no. 26.

McGue, M., Pickens, R. W., & Svikis, D. S. (1992). Sex and age effects on the inheritance of alcohol problems: A twin study. *Journal of Abnormal Psychology, 101,* 3–17.

McGue, M., Sharma, A., & Benson, P. (1996). Parent and sibling influences on adolescent alcohol use and misuse: Evidence from a U.S. adoption cohort. *Journal of Studies on Alcohol, 57,* 8–18.

Meller, W. H., Rinehart, R., Cadoret, R. J., & Troughton, E. (1988). Specific familial transmission in substance abuse. *International Journal of Addiction, 23,* 1029–1039.

Merikangas, K. R., & Avenevoli, S. (2000). Implications of genetic epidemiology for the prevention of substance use disorders. *Addictive Behaviors, 25,* 807–820.

Merikangas, K. R., Dierker, L. C., & Szatmari, P. (1998a). Psychopathology among offspring of parents with substance abuse and/or anxiety: A high-risk study. *Journal of the American Academy of Child Psychology and Psychiatry, 39,* 711–720.

Merikangas, K. R., Mehta, R. L., Molnar, B. E., Walters, E. E., Swendsen, J. D., Aguilar-Gaziola, S., Bijl, R. V., Borges, G., Caraveo-Anduaga, J. J., DeWit, D. J., Kolody, B., Vega, W. A., Wittchen, H. U., Kessler, R. C. (1998b). Comorbidity of substance use disorders with mood and anxiety disorders: Results of the international consortium in psychiatric epidemiology. *Addictive Behaviors*, *23*, 893–907.

Merikangas, K. R., Stevens, D. E., Fenton, B., Stolar, M., O'Malley, S., Woods, S. W., & Risch, N. (1998c). Comorbidity and familial aggregation of alcoholism and anxiety disorders. *Psychological Medicine*, *28*, 773–788.

Merikangas, K. R., Stolar, M., Steven, D. E., Goulet, J., Preisig, M. A., Fenton, B., Zhang, H., O'Malley, S., & Rounsaville, B. J. (1998d). Familial transmission of substance use disorders. *Archives of General Psychiatry*, *55*, 973–979.

Miles, D. R., van den Bree, M. B. M., Gupman, A. E., Newlin, D. B., Glantz, M. D., & Pickens, R. W. (2001). A twin study on sensation seeking, risk taking behavior and marijuana use. *Drug and Alcohol Dependence*, *62*, 57–68.

Miller, B. A., Smyth, N. J., & Mudar, P. I. (1999). Mothers' alcohol and other drug problems and their punitiveness toward their children. *Journal of Studies of Alcohol*, *60*, 632–642.

Mirin, S. M., Weiss, R. D., Griffin, M. L., & Michael, J. L. (1991). Psychopathology in drug abusers and their families. *Comprehensive Psychiatry*, *32*, 36–51.

Mirin, S. M., Weiss, R. D., & Michael, J. L. (1988). Psychopathology in substance abusers: Diagnosis and treatment. *American Journal of Drug and Alcohol Abuse*, *14*, 139–157.

Molina, B., Chassin, L., & Curran, P. J. (1994). A comparison of mechanisms underlying substance use for early adolescent children of alcoholics and controls. *Journal of Studies on Alcohol*, *55*, 269–275.

Moss, H., Clark, D., & Kirisci, L. (1997). Timing of parental substance use disorder cessation and effects of problem behaviors in sons. *American Journal of Addiction*, *6*, 30–37.

Moss, H. B., Lynch, K. G., Hardie, T. L., & Baron, D. A. (2002). Family functioning and peer affiliation in children of fathers with antisocial personality disorder and substance dependence: Associations with problem behaviors. *American Journal of Psychiatry*, *159*, 607–614.

Moss, H. B., Majumder, P. P., & Vanyukov, M. (1994). Familial resemblance for psychoactive substance use disorders: Behavioral profile of high-risk boys. *Addictive Behaviors*, *19*, 199–208.

Mounts, N., & Steinberg, L. (1995). An ecological analysis of peer influence on adolescent grade point average and drug use. *Developmental Psychology*, *31*, 915–922.

Murry, V., & Brody, G. H. (1999). Self-regulation and self-worth of Black children reared in economically stressed, rural, single mother-headed families: The contribution of risk and protective factors. *Journal of Family Issues*, *20*, 458–484.

Nestler, E. J., & Malenka, R. C. (2004). The addicted brain. *Scientific American*, March, *290*(3), 78–85.

O'Farrell, T. J., & Fals-Stewart, W. (2002). In: D. H. Sprenkle (Ed.), *Effectiveness research in marriage and family therapy* (pp. 123–161). Alexandria, VA: American Association for Marriage and Family Therapy.

Patterson, G. R. (1986). Performance models for antisocial boys. *American Psychologist*, *41*, 432–444.

Patterson, G. R., Reid, J. B., & Dishion, T. J. (1992). *Antisocial boys*. Eugene, Oregon: Castilia.

Patterson, G. R., & Stouthamer-Loeber, M. (1984). The correlation of family management practices and delinquency. *Child Development*, *55*, 1299–1307.

Pedersen, N. (1981). Twin similarity for usage of common drugs. *Progress in Clinical Biological Research*, *69*, 53–59.

Pickens, R., Svikis, D., McGue, M., Lykken, D., Heston, L., & Clayton, P. (1991). Heterogeneity in the inheritance of alcoholism: A study of male and female twins. *Archives of General Psychiatry*, *48*, 19–28.

Porter, B., & O'Leary, K. D. (1980). Marital discord and childhood problems. *Journal of Abnormal Child Psychology, 8*, 287–295.

Regier, D. A., Farmer, M. E., Rae, D. S., Locke, B. Z., Keith, S. J., & Judd, L. L. (1990). Comorbidity of mental disorders with alcohol and other drug abuse: Results from the epidemiologic catchment area (ECA) study. *Journal of the American Medical Association, 262*, 2511–2518.

Reich, W., Earls, F., Frankel, O., & Shayka, J. J. (1993). Psychopathology in children of alcoholics. *Journal of the American Academy of Child and Adolescent Psychiatry, 32*, 955–1002.

Reifman, A., Barnes, G. M., Dintcheff, B. A., Farrel, M. P., & Uhteg, L. (1998). Parental and peer influences on the onset of heavier drinking among adolescents. *Journal of Studies on Alcohol, 59*, 311–317.

Rhee, S. H., Hewitt, J. D., Young, S. E., Corley, R. P., Crowley, T. J., & Stallings, M. C. (2003). Genetic and environmental influences on substance initiation, use, and problem use in adolescents. *Archives of General Psychiatry, 60*, 1256–1264.

Rose, R. J., Dick, D. M., Viken, R. J., Pulkkinen, L., & Kaprio, J. (2001). Drinking or abstaining at age 14? A genetic epidemiological study. *Alcoholism: Clinical and Experimental Research, 25*, 1594–1604.

Rounsaville, B. J., Kosten, T. R., Weissman, M. M., Prosoff, B., Pauls, D., Anton, S. F., & Merikangas, K. R. (1991). Psychiatric disorders in relatives of probands with opiate addiction. *Archives of General Psychiatry, 48*, 33–42.

Rowe, C. L., & Liddle, H. A. (2002). Substance abuse. In: D. H. Sprenkle (Ed.), *Effectiveness research in marriage and family therapy* (pp. 53–87). Alexandria, VA: American Association for Marriage and Family Therapy.

Rowe, D. C., & Gulley, B. L. (1992). Sibling effects on substance use and delinquency. *Criminology, 30*, 217–233.

Rutherford, M. J., Cacciola, J. S., Alterman, A. I., McKay, J. R., & Cook, T. J. (1997). Young men's perceived quality of parenting based on family history of alcoholism. *Journal of Child and Adolescent Substance Abuse, 6*, 43–65.

Sanders, M. R. (2000). Community-based parenting and family support interventions and the prevention of drug abuse. *Addictive Behaviors, 25*, 929–942.

Sanderson, K., & Andrews, G. (2002). Prevalence and severity of mental health disability and relationship to diagnosis. *Psychiatric Services, 53*, 80–86.

Schuckit, M. A., & Smith, T. L. (1996). An 8-year follow-up of 450 sons of alcoholic and control subjects. *Archives of General Psychiatry, 53*, 202–210.

Shedler, J., & Block, J. (1990). Adolescent drug use and psychological health: A longitudinal inquiry. *American Psychologist, 45*, 612–630.

Sher, K. J., Walitzer, K. S., Wood, P. K., & Brent, E. E. (1991). Characteristics of children of alcoholics: Putative risk factors, substance use and abuse, and psychopathology. *Journal of Abnormal Child Psychology, 100*, 427–448.

Sher, K. J., Gershuny, B. S., Peterson, L., & Raskin, G. (1997). The role of childhood stressors in the intergenerational transmission of alcohol use disorders. *Journal of Studies on Alcohol, 58*, 414–427.

Sher, K. J., Wood, M. D., Wood, P. K., & Raskin, G. (1996). Alcohol outcome expectancies and alcohol use: A latent variable cross-lagged panel study. *Journal of Abnormal Psychology, 105*, 561–575.

Simcha-Fagan, O., Gersten, J. C., & Langer, T. (1986). Early precursors and concurrent correlates of illicit drug use in adolescents. *Journal of Drug Issues, 16*, 7–28.

Sloboda, Z., & David, S., National Institute on Drug Abuse. (1997). *Preventing drug use among children and adolescents*. NIH Publication No. 97-4212. Washington, DC: U.S. Government Printing Office.

Steinberg, L. (1990). Autonomy, conflict, and harmony in the family relationship. In: S. S. Feldmann & G. R. Elliott (Eds), *At the threshold: The developing adolescent* (pp. 255–276). Cambridge, MA: Harvard University Press.

Steinberg, L. (2001). We know some things: Parent-adolescent relationships in retrospect and prospect. *Journal of Research on Adolescence, 11,* 1–19.

Steinberg, L., Fletcher, A., & Darling, N. (1994). Parental monitoring and peer influences on adolescent substance use. *Pediatrics, 93,* 1060–1064.

Stoker, A., & Swadi, H. (1990). Perceived family relationships in drug abusing adolescents. *Drug and Alcohol Dependence, 25,* 293–297.

Swadi, H. (1999). Individual risk factors for adolescent substance use. *Drug and Alcohol Dependence, 55,* 209–224.

Swendsen, J. D., Conway, K. P., Rounsaville, B. J., & Merikangas, K. R. (2002). Are personality traits familial risk factors for substance abuse? Results of a controlled family study. *American Journal of Psychiatry, 159,* 1760–1766.

Swendsen, J. D., & Merikangas, K. R. (2000). The comorbidity of depression and substance use disorders. *Clinical Psychology Review, 20,* 173–189.

Tarter, R. E., Kirisci, L., Habeych, M., Reynolds, M., & Vanyukov, M. (2004). Neurobehavioral disinhibition in childhood predisposes boys to substance use disorder by young adulthood: Direct and mediated etiologic pathways. *Drug and Alcohol Dependence, 73,* 121–132.

Taylor, A. R., & Machida, S. (1994). The contribution of parent and peer support to Head Start children's early school adjustment. *Early Childhood Research Quarterly, 9,* 387–405.

Tsuang, M. T., Lyons, M. J., Eisen, S. A., Goldberg, J., True, W., Lin, N., Meyer, J. M., Toomey, R., Farone, S. V., & Eaves, L. (1996). Genetic influences on DSM-III-R drug abuse and dependence: A study of 3,372 twin pairs. *American Journal of Medical Genetics, 67,* 473–477.

Tsuang, M. T., Lyons, M. L., Meyer, J. M., Doyle, T., Eisen, S. A., Goldberg, J., True, W., Lin, N., Toomey, R., & Eaves, L. (1998). Co-occurrence of abuse of different drugs in men: The role of drug-specific and shared vulnerabilities. *Archives of General Psychiatry, 55,* 967–972.

Uhl, G. R. (2004). Molecular genetic underpinnings of human substance abuse vulnerability: Likely contributions to understanding addiction as a mnemonic process. *Neuropharmacology, 47,* 140–147.

Van den Bree, M. B. M., Johnson, E. O., Neale, M. C., & Pickens, R. W. (1998). Genetic and environmental influences on drug use and abuse/dependence in male and female twins. *Drug and Alcohol Dependence, 52,* 231–241.

Vanyukov, M. M., & Tarter, R. E. (2000). Genetic studies of substance abuse. *Drug and Alcohol Dependence, 39,* 101–123.

Weinberg, N. Z., Rahdert, E., Colliver, J. D., & Glantz, M. D. (1998). Adolescent substance abuse: A review of the past 10 years. *Journal of the American Academy of Child and Adolescent Psychiatry, 37,* 252–261.

West, D. J., & Farrington, D. P. (1977). *The delinquent way of life.* London: Heinemann.

West, M., & Prinz, R. J. (1987). Parental alcoholism and childhood psychopathology. *Psychological Bulletin, 102,* 204–218.

Widom, C. S., & Hiller-Sturmhofel, S. (2001). Alcohol abuse as a risk factor for and consequence of child abuse. *Alcohol Research & Health, 25,* 52–57.

Widom, C. S., Weiler, B. L., & Cottler, L. B. (1999). Childhood victimization and drug abuse: A comparison of prospective and retrospective findings. *Journal of Consulting and Clinical Psychology, 67,* 867–880.

Wills, T. A., & Cleary, S. D. (1996). How are social support effects mediated: A test with parental support and adolescent substance use. *Journal of Personality and Social Psychology, 71,* 937–952.

Wills, T. A., Sandy, J. M., Yaeger, A., & Shinar, O. (2001). Family risk factors and adolescent substance use: Moderation effects for temperament dimensions. *Developmental Psychology, 37,* 283–297.

Wills, T. A., Yaeger, A., & Sandy, J. (2003). Buffering effect of religiosity for adolescent substance use. *Psychology of Addictive Behaviors, 17,* 24–31.

Wills, T. A., Resko, J. A., Ainette, M. G., & Mendoza, D. (2004). Role of parent support and peer support in adolescent substance use: A test of mediated effects. *Psychology of Addictive Behaviors, 18,* 122–134.

Wood, M. D., Read, J. P., Roger, M. E., & Brand, N. H. (2004). Do parents still matter? Parent and peer influences on alcohol involvement among recent high school graduates. *Psychology of Addictive Behaviors, 18,* 19–30.

Zaninelli, R. M., Porjesz, B., & Begleiter, H. (1992). The Tridimensional Personality Questionnaire in males at high and low risk for alcoholism. *Alcoholism: Clinical and Experimental Research, 16,* 68–70.

Zucker, R. (1994). Pathways to alcohol problems and alcoholism: A developmental account of the evidence for multiple alcoholisms and for contextual contributions to risk. In: R. Zucker, G. Boyd & J. Howard (Eds), *The development of alcohol problems: Exploring the biopsychosocial matrix of risk.* National Institute on Alcohol Abuse and Alcoholism Research Monograph No. 26, NIH Pub. no. 94-3495 (pp. 244–290). Washington, DC: The Institute.

Chapter 10

Parenting and Personality Disorders

Joel Paris

Personality Disorders: Definitions and Assumptions

Personality disorders are defined in diagnostic and statistical manual of mental disorders (4th edition, text revision) (DSM-IV-TR) (American Psychiatric Association, 2000) as dysfunctional personality traits that lead to long-term problems in work and relationships, independent of context or current mental state. Beyond this overall definition, ten specific categories of disorder are described, grouped into three clusters based on common traits. cluster A, related to schizophrenic spectrum disorders, includes schizotypal, schizoid, and paranoid categories. cluster B, related to impulsive disorders, includes antisocial, borderline, narcissistic, and histrionic categories. cluster C, related to anxiety disorders, includes avoidant, dependent, and obsessive–compulsive categories. Since most of the research on personality disorders has focused on cluster B, the emphasis of this review will be on this group.

By definition, personality disorders have an early onset and a chronic course. Usually, personality pathology first becomes apparent in adolescence, and continues over the course of adult life. Some diagnoses, particularly the antisocial category, have established childhood precursors (Paris, 2003).

The course of personality disorders may provide clues to their etiology. It is well known in medicine that diseases with early symptoms followed by chronicity are associated with greater genetic vulnerability (Childs & Scriver, 1986). The course of personality disorders shows a similar pattern (Paris, 2003), suggesting that genetics and temperament must play a major role, even if these factors are unlikely to tell the whole story.

In the past, theorists made very different assumptions. It was generally agreed that the origins of personality disorders must lie in childhood. This concept, "the primacy of early experience" (Paris, 2000), assumed that the most important environmental factor in the lives of children is the quality of parenting they receive.

Psychoanalysis was an important source of the concept of primacy. Freud (1916) thought that adult psychopathology had origins in childhood, with symptoms determined by "fixation"

Psychopathology and the Family
Edited by J. L. Hudson and R. M. Rapee
Copyright © 2005 by Elsevier Ltd.
All rights of reproduction in any form reserved
ISBN: 0-08-044449-0

at a specific stage. Other psychoanalysts claimed that when pathology is unusually severe, the developmental period at which problems occurred must have "deeper" causes, even earlier in childhood. Thus, whereas Freud (1916) had considered age 3–5 to be crucial for neurotic symptoms, others (e.g. Klein, 1946; Erikson, 1950; Winnicott, 1958) proposed that problems in infancy could be responsible for disturbances in personality.

The problem with these concepts is that they were all based on reconstructions of childhood experience drawn from clinical data, not from empirical studies of child development. Moreover, all these theories failed to consider the possibility that temperamental factors might be as important for development as the quality of parenting, or that the quality of parenting might itself be influenced by the child's temperamental difficulties (Rutter, 1989). Finally, although there is evidence that environmental adversities can distort personality, early events may be no more important than later ones (Paris, 2000). The illusion of causality is created by the fact that adversities that start early are more likely to continue, leading to cumulative effects (Rutter & Maughan, 1997).

Later psychoanalytic theorists jettisoned the idea that severity of pathology is based on early adversity. Kohut (1977) suggested that the sense of self in children emerges from parental responses over time, using the metaphor of a barrel filling drop by drop. Thus, Kohut (1977) hypothesized that narcissistic personality disorder arises from a failure of empathic responses by parents to the needs of children over many years. The problem with this kind of formulation is that it attributes pathological outcomes to parental behaviors with a very high base rate. If children were that sensitive to failures in empathy, we should all be narcissistic.

Currently, the most influential developmental model derived from psychoanalysis is the attachment theory. Bowlby (1969–1980) had also proposed that psychopathology emerges from parental rejection and neglect over many stages of childhood. Modern psychoanalysts have embraced the attachment model (Fonagy & Target, 1999), since it is the first analytic theory to be linked to a large empirical literature (Cassidy & Shaver, 1999). Attachment theory has been applied specifically to borderline personality disorder (BPD), patients who show dramatically abnormal patterns of attachment, and it has been suggested that difficulties in attachment in early childhood could be a primary cause of the disorder (Fonagy & Target, 1999).

Like previous theories, all these ideas are also based more on hypothetical reconstruction than hard data. Moreover, the causal pathways proposed tend to be linear, while empirical evidence points to a much more complex and interactive relationship between adversity, attachment, and psychopathology (Rutter, 1995). Finally, it is important to note that early attachment problems, even when severe, are not necessarily irreversible; high-risk groups such as Romanian orphans (O'Connor & Rutter, 2000) show remarkable resilience. Moreover, prospective studies of attachment behavior (Cassidy & Shaver, 1999) do not show consistent continuity between patterns in early childhood and those established later in development. Finally, it is uncertain to what extent attachment styles are actually derived from parenting behaviors or whether they also reflect temperament (Thompson, Connell, & Bridges, 1988). Behavioral genetic research on attachment has had mixed results, with one study (Finkel & Matheny, 2000) finding a strong heritable component, while another (Bokhorst et al., 2003) found that shared environment influences infant behavior in the Strange Situation. It is also possible that temperamental effects on behavior increase rather than decrease with age (Plomin, Defries, McClearn, & Rutter, 2001).

Empirical Studies of Parenting and Personality

Empirical studies in developmental psychopathology (Cicchetti & Cohen, 1995) have generally supported the concept that adverse childhood experiences and family dysfunction are associated with mental disorders in adulthood. However, these conclusions must be moderated by methodological limitations. The main problem is that most studies linking childhood adversity with adult psychopathology are retrospective and therefore open to recall bias, particularly when data are obtained from seriously ill adults about childhood experiences (Paris, 2000). It is well established that people with serious problems in the present tend to remember more adversities in the past (Schacter, 1996). To address this problem one needs longitudinal data.

In fact, prospective community studies of children, such as the Albany–Saratoga study (Cohen, Brook, Cohen, Velez, & Garcia, 1990), have also supported an association between childhood adversity and psychopathology, with personality disorder symptoms being one negative outcome (Johnson, Cohen, Brown, Smailes, & Bernstein, 1999). But there are still problems: even with prospective data, an association between childhood adversity and personality disorders does not prove causation, since latent variables could account for the relationship.

Harris (1998) has argued that it is possible that relationships between childhood environment and adult outcome could be accounted for by genetic similarity between parents and children. Without genetic controls, it is difficult to conclude that family adversity, by itself, causes pathology. For that purpose, one would need to conduct twin studies using prospective designs. Unfortunately, this expensive research method has rarely been applied to the study of personality.

Research in behavior genetics, derived from large samples of twins, has examined the quantitative level of genetic and environmental contributions to personality traits. These findings present a challenge to the assumption that parenting plays a primary role in personality development. Using a variety of measures, research has consistently shown that half the variance in personality is genetic, and that the environmental component is almost entirely "unshared", i.e. not related to growing up in a particular family (Plomin et al., 2001). Twin studies of personality disorders show exactly the same pattern (Torgersen et al., 2000).

While these findings show that environment is just as important as heredity, large differences between siblings (as great as those between children growing up with different parents) do not support a simple relationship between parenting and personality. More generally, the relationship between family risk factors and psychopathological outcomes is rarely predictable. One reason is that environmental adversities have different effects on different individuals, depending on temperamental factors. Thus, psychological development arises from complex and interactive relationships between genes and environment. Moreover, many important factors affecting development come from outside the family (Rutter, 1989).

Another line of evidence derives from relationships between childhood adversity and adult personality disorder. Children with conduct disorder, the childhood precursor associated with an adult outcome of antisocial personality disorder, come from highly dysfunctional families, often associated with antisocial characteristics in the father (Robins, 1966). Notably, conduct disorder is unique in psychopathology, in that it has a large shared environmental component (Cadoret, Yates, Troughton, Woodworth, & Stewart, 1995), very possibly related to pathological parenting (Robins, 1966; Patterson & Yoerger, 1997). An adoption study (Cloninger, Sigvardsson, Bohman, & von Knorring, 1982) suggested that antisocial heredity is only pathogenic when it interacts with family dysfunction.

There is a particularly large literature showing an association between childhood adversities and borderline personality disorder (Paris, 1999, 2003). While all these data are retrospective, they are quite consistent; no studies have ever reported that patients with BPD fail to report childhood trauma. A wide variety of adverse events have been implicated, including sexual abuse, physical abuse from parents, and parental neglect (Zanarini, 2000).

However, this relationship between trauma and psychopathology is quite complex. The link between BPD and childhood sexual abuse has sometimes been interpreted simplistically, to suggest that these patients have a form of post-traumatic stress disorder (Herman & van der Kolk, 1987). A careful examination of the data, however, shows that most incidents are single molestations that rarely produce sequelae in community samples (Paris, 1994). Nonetheless, since about a third of borderline patients report serious childhood sexual abuse (Paris, 1994), it must be considered an important risk factor for the disorder. While only a minority of patients (about 25%) describe abuse from caretakers, those that do have more severe psychopathology (Soloff, Lynch, Kelly, Malone, & Mann, 2000). Moreover, even in cases when the perpetrator of abuse comes from outside the family, family dysfunction accounts for much of the outcome variance (Nash, Hulsely, Sexton, Harralson, & Lambert, 1993), suggesting that children who are abused by non-family members may not be properly protected by their parents.

What makes the interpretation of the relationship between adversity and personality disorder particularly complex is the evidence for resilience after traumatic events. Community surveys of the impact of childhood sexual abuse (Browne & Finkelhor, 1986; Rind & Tromofovitch, 1997), as well as of physical abuse (Malinovsky-Rummell & Hansen, 1993), have found that only a minority of children reporting abuse and trauma suffer measurable sequelae. In prospective longitudinal research, resilience is also the rule. In a high-risk sample from Hawaii exposed to poverty and severe family dysfunction, Werner and Smith (1992) found that the majority of children emerged as well-functioning adults (although many had first to weather a stormy adolescence). The gap between clinical and community studies might be accounted for if the patients clinicians see are more vulnerable to life events, probably based on their temperamental vulnerability, than more resilient populations who do not come for help.

One of the major large-scale prospective longitudinal research projects in the community, the Albany–Saratoga study (Cohen et al., 1990), found a significant relationship between childhood adversity and personality disorder symptoms. In a cohort of children followed into young adulthood, Johnson et al. (1999) reported that childhood adversities, including neglect, physical abuse, and sexual abuse were significantly associated with a higher number of the symptoms that define BPD. While this study is unique, the researchers had to use a continuous variable (number of symptoms) to measure outcome, since too few subjects actually had a diagnosable disorder. Another limitation was that the study lacked data on temperamental factors in early childhood that might have preceded these environmental adversities.

While most studies on the developmental precursors of personality disorders have focused on diagnoses with an impulsive picture, such as antisocial and borderline personality, there is also a need for research on disorders with a strong component of anxiety. Avoidant personality disorder is particularly common in the community (Grant et al., 2004), and its precursors may consist of early onset temperamental anxiety. A prospective study of high-risk children is being conducted by Kagan (1994), who has been following a cohort of highly shy ("behaviorally inhibited") children into adulthood. While many subjects were asymptomatic by adolescence, some continued to have anxiety symptoms, and Kagan (1994) has hypothesized that parental responses involving overprotection could make these outcomes more likely. Moreover, retrospective research has also suggested a relationship between family functioning and avoidant personality disorder (Head, Baker, & Williamson, 1991; Rettew et al., 2003). It is possible that future follow-ups will show that behavioral inhibition is a precursor of avoidant personality disorder.

Parenting in Context: A General Model of Personality Disorders

Neither chemical imbalances, psychological adversities, nor a troubled social environment fully account for the development of any mental disorder. Complex interactions between biological, psychological, and social factors are involved in the pathways leading to pathology. The stress-diathesis model (Monroe & Simons, 1991; Paris, 1999) is a general theory of psychopathology that understands mental disorders as arising from stressors (biological, psychological, and social adversities) with diatheses (genetic–temperamental factors leading to vulnerability).

Genetic variability influences the way individuals respond to their environment, while environmental factors determine whether genes are expressed. This principle helps to explain why adverse life events, by themselves, do not consistently lead to pathological sequelae. While most children are resilient to all but the most severe and consistent adversities (Rutter & Maughan, 1997), stressors will have greater effects on children who have temperamental diatheses creating vulnerability (Paris, 2000). Trait profiles, i.e. the predominance of specific personality dimensions reflecting temperamental vulnerability, would then determine what type of personality disorder develops in each individual.

Personality profiles can be measured through dimensional models (Livesley, 2003). One approach involves studying broad personality trait dimensions derived from studies of adult community populations (Costa & Widiger, 2001; Livesley et al., 1998). Another approach involves conceptualizing mental disorders, on both axis I and axis II, within four broad trait dimensions: cognitive, impulsive, anxious, and depressive (Siever & Davis, 1991). In both models, one would use underlying traits to classify personality disorders. The three clusters of disorder listed on axis II of DSM-IV-TR (American Psychiatric Association, 2000) provide one way of organizing the disorders, since cluster A is related to schizophrenia (Siever & Davis, 1991), while cluster B is related to other impulsive disorders (Zanarini, 1993; White, Gunderson, Zanarini, & Hudson, 2003), and cluster C is linked to disorders in the anxious spectrum (Kagan, 1994; Paris, 1997). Interestingly, factors parallel to the axis II clusters also emerge from studies of psychopathology, both in children (Achenbach & McConaughy, 1997) and in adults (Krueger, 1999), with cluster C corresponding to an internalizing dimension, and cluster B corresponding to an externalizing dimension.

Whatever dimensional schema one applies, adversities such as family pathology can increase the risk for the development of personality disorders, but need not have a specific relationship with any category. The form that personality disorders takes is more likely related to temperament (Paris, 2003). The heritability of personality traits is well established (Plomin et al., 2001). Behavioral genetic studies have shown that about half the variance affecting broad personality dimensions such as the Five Factor Model (Costa & Widiger, 2001) is genetic. Although these findings may not always apply to more specific facets of personality, Jang, Vernon, and Livesely (2001), studying 18 narrower dimensions, found all of them to have similar heritability to broader traits. The other half of the variance in personality traits is primarily environmental, although there is always some degree of measurement error associated with behavioral genetic methods (Plomin et al., 2001).

Since personality disorders are continuous with traits (Livesley et al., 1998), disorders should be expected to show similar heritability levels. This supposition was confirmed in a landmark study by Torgersen et al. (2000), who collected a large sample of twins in which one proband met criteria for categorical axis II diagnoses. Personality disorders had heritabilities resembling those observed for traits (i.e. close to half the variance). Even in disorders that have not traditionally been considered to be heritable (the borderline and narcissistic categories), genetic factors accounted for more than half of the variance. Although there were no antisocial patients in this cohort, other lines of research (Cloninger et al., 1982; Cadoret et al., 1995) point to heritable factors.

At the same time, half the variance in personality disorders is environmental in origin. The role of the environment can also be understood in the context of a stress-diathesis model. The risk factors associated with personality disorder need not be pathogenic by themselves. Trait profiles associated with genetic vulnerabilities would determine whether adverse life experiences lead to psychopathology. Moreover, even in the presence of temperamental vulnerability, environmental stressors need to be severe, continuous, and cumulative to generate psychopathology (Rutter, 1989).

Thus, while gene–environment interactions are crucial for outcome, family dysfunction would still play an important role as a risk factor. The crucial difference between this model and older theories is that abnormal parenting would only produce pathological sequelae in children who are temperamentally vulnerable. It should also be noted that family pathology, unlike specific traumatic events, is a continuous rather than a punctate factor in development. Finally, experiences that happen outside the family might be partly accounted for by co-occurring family dysfunction, so that well-functioning families can either make adversities less likely, or contain them when they do occur.

A final complication is that parenting itself can be, at least in part, an epiphenomenon of temperament (i.e. a gene–environment correlation; see Chapter 1 in this volume (Eley and Lau, 2005). In one large-scale study of families (Reiss, Hetherington, & Plomin, 2000), temperament of the child was observed to be the mediating variable determining the quality of interactions between parents and children. It is also well established that children with difficult and impulsive temperaments elicit negative reactions from family members, peers, and teachers (Rutter, 1989).

In this context, the observation of Robins (1966) that children with conduct disorder, when exposed to parental psychopathy (usually in the father), are more likely to develop adult antisocial personality disorder, can be interpreted in several ways. Parental antisociality may affect the child through common inheritance of traits, through modeling of pathological behavior, or through the direct effects of dysfunctional parenting (such as abuse and neglect). To separate these effects, one needs to control for temperamental factors in research designs.

Temperamental factors in children can be observed quite early on. By age three, those with unusually high levels of aggression and irritability have been identified as being at risk for antisocial personality disorder in early adulthood (Caspi, Moffitt, Newman, & Silva, 1996). When conduct symptoms begin earlier in childhood and are severe, antisocial personality is particularly likely to develop (Zoccolillo, Pickles, Quinton, & Rutter, 1992). Again, this early level of vulnerability may be due to genetic factors, to adverse events, or, as suggested in a recent prospective study (Kim-Cohen et al., 2003), to a combination of both.

Parenting in a Sociocultural Context

The impact of parenting on personality must also be placed in the context of culture and society. Family structures are not universal, but reflect the values of the larger culture. Thus, while traditional societies and families favor intergenerational continuity, modern societies and families prepare children for rapid social change (Lerner, 1958).

Personality disorders appear to be "socially sensitive", i.e. they vary in prevalence according to social context (Paris, 1996). While trait dimensions are similar in different societies (McCrae & Costa, 1999), disorders may not be. Antisocial personality has become more common in adolescents and young adults, both in North America and Europe, since the Second World War (Rutter & Smith, 1995). At the same time, cross-cultural studies show that antisocial personality disorder is relatively rare in traditional societies such as Taiwan (Hwu, Yeh, & Change, 1989) and Japan (Sato & Takeichi, 1993), while prevalence reaches North American and European levels in Korea (Lee et al., 1987).

An interface between parenting patterns and culture helps to explain these observations. The East Asian cultures that have a low prevalence of antisocial personality have cultural and family structures that are protective against antisocial behavior. Thus, families are a veritable mirror image of the risk factors for antisocial disorder described by Robins (1966), i.e. inconsistent discipline and parental absence. Instead, East Asian fathers are strong and authoritative, expectations of children are high, and family loyalty is prized. In addition, the wider community has high social cohesion, further containing those whose temperament makes them vulnerable to impulsive actions. In the same way, the less well-structured family and social structures in Western societies can be a risk factor for children with impulsive traits, making antisocial personality more prevalent.

Harris (1998) interprets the large role of unshared environment in personality as demonstrating the importance of peer groups and the broader social environment. On the other hand, the choice of peer groups is partly influenced by families, which remain the primary carriers of social and cultural values. It has been hypothesized that BPD is also increasing in prevalence, and that this change is due to the breakdown of traditional family and social structures guiding the development of adolescents and young adults (Millon, 2000). Linehan (1993) has suggested that patients with BPD are temperamentally vulnerable because of emotional dysregulation, and that recent decreases in social support have interfered with the buffering of affective intensity, effectively amplifying the trait. This failure of support could reflect failure of family members to validate emotional experiences and/or factors in the wider environment that promote individualism at the expense of social cohesion. These effects could be particularly relevant in Western societies.

Parallel conjectures can be made about other personality disorders. Although we have no good community studies of the prevalence of narcissistic personality, one might hypothesize that heritable traits are normally channeled into fruitful ambition by strong family and social structures, but that under conditions of rapid social change, they can become dysfunctional (Paris, 2003). Similarly, avoidant personality might be less likely to develop in a traditional society, where anxious traits are buffered by family and community structures, while in a modern individualistic society, the same traits could be disabling (Paris, 1997).

Family Factors Affecting Treatment Outcome

Clinicians treating patients with personality disorders have to decide whether to see families as allies or as perpetrators. Therapists certainly see cases in which parental dysfunction is dramatic: antisocial traits and substance abuse are likely to lead to abuse, and depression is likely to lead to neglect. Some of these risk factors may be associated with severity: for example, patients with borderline personality who have histories of child abuse are more likely to make suicide attempts (Soloff et al., 1998).

On the other hand, these patterns are by no means universal. Even in antisocial and BPDs for which these risks have been well documented, clinicians are just as likely to find themselves dealing with families who have good intentions but find themselves unable to deal with a troubled child.

There have been no clinical trials of family therapy for personality disorders. Also, in patients with BPD, the clinical picture may be too unstable to conduct formal courses of classical family therapy. However, psychoeducation for the families of patients with mental disorders has been developing rapidly (McFarlane, Dixon, Lukens, & Lucksted, 2003), and the method has now been applied to BPD (Gunderson, 2001). This clinical approach sees parents as being no less "victims" than identified patients, and is consistent with a stress-diathesis model of disorder. The goal is to reduce negative, conflictual interactions between patients and their families and to replace them with more supportive, problem-solving responses.

Conclusions

The evidence reviewed here is complex, but it generally supports the concept that abnormal parenting is a risk factor for developing personality disorders. However, a risk factor is not an explanation: one must consider how parenting interacts with other sources of vulnerability, whether biological, psychological, or social. In addition, the quality of family life reflects personality characteristics in parents themselves, which are also multidetermined. Finally, the quality of parenting and its impact on the child depends on the larger social environment.

References

Achenbach, T. M., & McConaughy, S. H. (1997). *Empirically based assessment of child and adolescent psychopathology: Practical applications* (2nd ed.). Thousand Oaks, CA: Sage.

American Psychiatric Association (2000). *Diagnostic and statistical manual of mental disorders* (4th ed., Text Revision). Washington, DC: American Psychiatric Press.

Bokhorst, C. L., Bakermans-Kranenburg, M. J., Pascofearon, R. M., Van ijzendoorn, M. H., Fonagy, P., & Schuengel, C. (2003). The importance of shared environment in mother–infant attachment security: A behavioral genetic study. *Child Development, 74,* 1769–1782.

Bowlby, J. (1969–1980). *Attachment and loss* (Vols. I, II and III). London: Hogarth Press.

Browne, A., & Finkelhor, D. (1986). Impact of child sexual abuse: A review of the literature. *Psychological Bulletin, 99,* 66–77.

Cadoret, R. J., Yates, W. R., Troughton, E., Woodworth, G., & Stewart, M. A. (1995). Genetic environmental interaction in the genesis of aggressivity and conduct disorders. *Archives of General Psychiatry, 52,* 916–924.

Caspi, A., Moffitt, T. E., Newman, D. L., & Silva, P. A. (1996). Behavioral observations at age three predict adult psychiatric disorders: Longitudinal evidence from a birth cohort. *Archives of General Psychiatry, 53,* 1033–1039.

Cassidy, J., & Shaver, P. R. (Eds) (1999). *Handbook of attachment: Theory, research and clinical aspects.* New York: Guilford.

Childs, B., & Scriver, C. R. (1986). Age at onset and causes of disease. *Perspectives in Biology and Medicine, 29,* 437–460.

Cicchetti, D., & Cohen, D. J. (1995). Perspectives on developmental psychopathology. In: D. Cicchetti & D. J. Cohen (Eds), *Developmental psychopathology, Vol. 1: Theory and methods* (pp. 3–20). Oxford, England: Wiley.

Cloninger, C. R., Sigvardsson, S., Bohman, M., & von Knorring, A. L. (1982). Predisposition to petty criminality in Swedish adoptees, II: Cross-fostering analysis of gene-environment interactions. *Archives of General Psychiatry, 39,* 1242–1247.

Cohen, P., Brook, J. S., Cohen, J., Velez, N., & Garcia, M. (1990). Common and uncommon pathways to adolescent psychopathology and problem behavior. In: L. Robins & M. Rutter (Eds), *Straight and devious pathways from childhood adulthood* (pp. 242–258). New York, Cambridge: University Press.

Costa, P. T., & Widiger, T. A. (Eds) (2001). *Personality disorders and the five-factor model of personality* (2nd ed.). Washington, DC: American Psychological Association.

Erikson, E. (1950). *Childhood and society.* New York: Norton.

Finkel, D., & Matheny, A. P. (2000). Genetic and environmental influences on a measure of infant attachment security. *Twin Research, 3,* 242–250.

Fonagy, P., Target, M. (1999). *Psychoanalytic theories of personality and its development.* London: Whurr Publications.

Freud, S. (1916). A general introduction to psychoanalysis. In: J. Strachey, *The standard edition of the psychological works of Sigmund Freud* (Vols. XV and XVI). London: Hogarth Press.

Grant, B. F., Hasin, D. S., Stinson, F. S., Dawson, D. A., Chou, S. P., Ruan, W. J., & Pickering, R. (2004). Prevalence, correlates, and disability of personality disorders in the United States. Results from the National Epidemiological Survey of Alcohol and Related Conditions. *Journal of Clinical Psychiatry*, *65*, 948–958.

Gunderson, J. G. (2001). Borderline personality Disorder: A clinical guide. Washington, DC: American Psychiatric Press.

Harris, J. R. (1998). *The nurture assumption*. New York: Free Press.

Head, S. B., Baker, J. D., & Williamson, D. A. (1991). Family environment characteristics and dependent personality disorder. *Journal of Personality Disorders*, *5*, 256–263.

Herman, J., & van der Kolk, B. (1987). Traumatic antecedents of borderline personality disorder. In: B. van der Kolk (Ed.), *Psychological trauma* (pp. 111–126). Washington, DC: American Psychiatric Press.

Hwu, H. G., Yeh, E. K., & Change, L. Y. (1989). Prevalence of psychiatric disorders in Taiwan defined by the Chinese Diagnostic Interview Schedule. *Acta Psychiatrica Scandinavia*, *79*, 136–147.

Jang, K., Vernon, P. A., & Livesley, W. J. (2001). Behavioural Genetic Perspectives on Personality Function. *Canadian Journal of Psychiatry*, *46*, 234–244.

Johnson, J. J., Cohen, P., Brown, J., Smailes, E. M., & Bernstein, D. P. (1999). Childhood maltreatment increases risk for personality disorders during early adulthood. *Archives of General Psychiatry*, *56*, 600–606.

Kagan, J. (1994). *Galen's prophecy*. New York: Basic.

Kim-Cohen, J., Caspi, A., Moffitt, T. E., Harrington, H., Milne, B. J., & Poulton, R. (2003). Prior juvenile diagnoses in adults with mental disorder: Developmental follow-back of a prospective-longitudinal cohort. *Archives of General Psychiatry*, *60*, 709–717.

Klein, M. (1946). *Envy and gratitude*. New York: International Universities Press.

Kohut, H. (1977). *The restoration of the self*. New York: International Universities Press.

Krueger, R. F. (1999). The structure of common mental disorders. *Archives of General Psychiatry*, *56*, 921–926.

Lee, K. C., Kovac, Y. S., & Rhee, H. (1987). The national epidemiological study of mental disorders in Korea. *Journal of Korean Medical Science*, *2*, 19–34.

Lerner, D. (1958). *The passing of traditional society*. New York: Free Press.

Linehan, M. M. (1993). *Cognitive behavioral therapy of borderline personality disorder*. New York: Guilford.

Livesley, W. J. (2003). *Personality disorders: A practical approach*. New York: Guilford.

Livesley, W. J., Jang, K. L., & Vernon, P. A. (1998). Phenotypic and genetic structure of traits delineating personality disorder. *Arch Gen Psychiatry*, *55*, 941–948.

Malinovsky-Rummell, R., & Hansen, D. J. (1993). Long-term consequences of physical abuse. *Psychological Bulletin*, *114*, 68–79.

McCrae, R. R., & Costa, P. T. (1999). A five-factor theory of personality. In: L. A. Pervin & O. P. John (Eds), *Handbook of personality: Theory and research* (2nd ed., pp. 139–153). New York: Guilford.

McFarlane, W. R., Dixon, L., Lukens, E., & Lucksted, A. (2003). Family psychoeducation and schizophrenia: A review of the literature. *Journal of Marital and Family Therapy*, *29*, 223–245.

Meehl, P. E. (1990). Toward an integrated theory of schizotaxa, schizotypy, and schizophrenia. *Journal of Personality Disorders*, *4*, 1–99.

Millon, T. (2000). Sociocultural conceptions of the borderline personality. *Psychiatric Clinics of North America*, *23*, 123–136.

Monroe, S. M., & Simons, A. D. (1991). Diathesis–stress theories in the context of life stress research. *Psychological Bulletin*, *110*, 406–425.

Nash, M. R., Hulsely, T. L., Sexton, M. C., Harralson, T. L., & Lambert, W. (1993). Long-term effects of childhood sexual abuse: Perceived family environment, psychopathology, and dissociation. *Journal of Consulting and Clinical Psychology, 61,* 276–283.

O'Connor, T. G., & Rutter, M. (2000). Attachment disorder behavior following early severe deprivation. Extension and longitudinal follow-up. *Journal of American Academy of Child and Adolescent Psychiatry, 39,* 703–712.

Paris, J. (1994). *Borderline personality disorder: A multidimensional approach.* Washington, DC: American Psychiatric Press.

Paris, J. (1996). *Social factors in the personality disorders.* Cambridge: Cambridge University Press.

Paris, J. (1997). Childhood trauma as an etiological factor in the personality disorders. *Journal of Personality Disorders, 11,* 34–49.

Paris, J. (1999). *Nature and nurture in psychiatry.* Washington, DC: American Psychiatric Press.

Paris, J. (2000). *Myths of childhood.* Philadelphia: Brunner/Mazel.

Paris, J. (2003). *Personality disorders over time.* Washington, DC: American Psychiatric Press.

Patterson, G. R., & Yoerger, K. (1997). A developmental model for late-onset delinquency. In: D.W. Osgood (Ed), *Motivation and delinquency Nebraska symposium on motivation* (Vol. 44, pp. 119–177). Lincoln, NE: University of Nebraska Press.

Plomin, R., DeFries, J. C., McClearn, G. E., & Rutter, M. (2001). *Behavioral genetics* (4th ed.). New York: Freeman.

Reiss, D., Hetherington, E. M., & Plomin, R. (2000). *The relationship code.* Cambridge, MA: Harvard University Press.

Rettew, D. C., Zanarini, M. C., Yen, S., Grilo, C. M., Skodol, A. E., Shea, M. T., McGlashan, T. H., Morey, L. C., Culhane, M. A., & Gunderson, J. G. (2003). Childhood antecedents of avoidant personality disorder: A retrospective study. *Journal of the American Academy of Child & Adolescent Psychiatry, 42,* 1122–1130.

Rind, B., & Tromofovitch, P. (1997). A meta-analytic review of findings from national samples on psychological correlates of child sexual abuse. *Journal of Sex Research, 34,* 237–255.

Robins, L. N. (1966). *Deviant children grown up.* Baltimore: Williams and Wilkins.

Rutter, M. (1989). Pathways from childhood to adult life. *Journal of Child Psychology and Psychiatry, 30,* 23–51.

Rutter, M. (1995). Clinical implications of attachment concepts, retrospect and prospect. *Journal of Child Psychology and Psychiatry, 36,* 549–571.

Rutter, M., & Maughan, B. (1997). Psychosocial adversities in psychopathology. *Journal of Personality Disorders, 11,* 19–33.

Rutter, M., & Smith, D. J. (1995) *Psychosocial problems in young people,* Cambridge: Cambridge University Press.

Sato, T., & Takeichi, M. (1993). Lifetime prevalence of specific psychiatric disorders in a general medicine clinic. *General Hospital Psychiatry, 15,* 224–233.

Schacter, D. L. (1996). *Searching for memory.* New York: Basic.

Siever, L. J., & Davis, K. L. (1991). A psychobiological perspective on the personality disorders. *American Journal of Psychiatry, 148,* 1647–1658.

Soloff, P. H., Lynch, K. G., Kelly, T. M., Malone, K. M., & Mann, J. J. (2000). Characteristics of suicide attempts of patients with major depressive episode and borderline personality disorder: A comparative study. *American Journal of Psychiatry, 157,* 601–608.

Thompson, R. A., Connell, J. P., & Bridges, L. J. (1988). Temperament, emotion, and social interactive behavior in the strange situation. *Child Development, 56,* 1106–1110.

Torgersen, S., Lygren, S., Oien, P. A., Skre, I., Onstad, S., Edvardsen, J., Tambs, K., & Kringlen, E. (2000). A twin study of personality disorders. *Comprehensive Psychiatry, 41,* 416–425.

Werner, E. E., & Smith, R. S. (1992). *Overcoming the Odds: High risk children from birth to adulthood.* New York: Cornell University Press.

White, C. N., Gunderson, J. G., Zanarini, M. C., & Hudson, J. I. (2003). Family studies of borderline personality disorder: A review. *Harvard Review of Psychiatry, 11,* 8–19.

Winnicott, D. W. (1958). Psychoses and child care. In: D.W. Winnicott (Ed.), *Collected papers* (pp. 219–228). London: Tavistock.

Zanarini, M. C. (1993). Borderline personality as an impulse spectrum disorder. In: J. Paris (Ed.), *Borderline personality disorder: Etiology and treatment* (pp. 67–86). Washington, DC: American Psychiatric Press.

Zanarini, M. C. (2000). Childhood experiences associated with the development of borderline personality disorder. *Psychiatric Clinics North America, 23,* 89–101.

Zoccolillo, M., Pickles, A., Quinton, D., & Rutter, M. (1992). The outcome of childhood conduct disorder: Implications for defining adult personality disorder and conduct disorder. *Psychological Medicine, 22,* 971–986.

Chapter 11

Family Factors in Schizophrenia and Bipolar Disorder

Jill M. Hooley, Kristen A. Woodberry and Caitlin Ferriter

Schizophrenia and bipolar disorder are severe forms of mental illness that result in serious impairment in day-to-day functioning. Characteristic symptoms of schizophrenia include hallucinations, delusions, and disorganized speech and behavior. Although patients with bipolar disorder may also experience many of these psychotic symptoms, their major problem is mood instability. Periods of abnormally elevated mood, increased energy, and decreased need for sleep alternate with episodes of depressed mood, decreased interest, and low energy.

There is little doubt that both schizophrenia and bipolar disorder have strong biological underpinnings. Genetic factors have been implicated in the etiology of both conditions and many abnormalities in neurochemistry and neuroanatomy have also been identified (Harrison & Weinberger, 2005). In light of this, consideration of the role of family factors in the development, course, and outcome of these forms of major mental disorder might, at first glance, seem rather unusual. However, despite their clear biological bases, both schizophrenia and bipolar disorder appear to be forms of pathology that are best understood within the context of a diathesis-stress (or vulnerability-stress) model (Zubin & Spring, 1977). The diathesis-stress model incorporates both biological and environmental factors into an integrated explanatory framework and is now the dominant heuristic for understanding psychopathology. By virtue of their placement on the vulnerability continuum, individuals are considered to be at greater or lesser risk of developing psychopathology when they are exposed to environmental stressors.

In this chapter, we review evidence for the role of family factors in the development and maintenance of schizophrenia and bipolar disorder. Implicit in our discussion is that patients with these disorders have biological vulnerabilities that render them more liable to develop pathology or to experience relapse in the face of stressful experiences. Schizophrenia research has been instrumental in recognizing the importance of families, not because they play a causal role in the etiology of major mental illness, but because what happens in the family environment has implications for whether and how an illness diathesis is expressed. As a result, there has been an important shift in viewing families,

Psychopathology and the Family
Edited by J. L. Hudson and R. M. Rapee
Copyright © 2005 by Elsevier Ltd.
All rights of reproduction in any form reserved
ISBN: 0-08-044449-0

not only as a factor in illness onset and maintenance, but also as a tremendous resource for prevention and recovery.

Schizophrenia

Family Variables and the Etiology of Schizophrenia

Social class and parental age   Research investigating the role of family factors in the development of schizophrenia has identified a small number of family-based demographic variables that are associated with elevated risk for the disorder. Low social class is one such example. It has long been known that people with schizophrenia are over-represented in more disadvantaged socio-economic groups — a fact that is explained in part by the downward social drift caused by having a disorder that makes it very difficult to work (Faris & Dunham, 1939). However, it is also the case that being born into a lower social class (rather than drifting there due to illness) does appear to elevate risk for the development of schizophrenia (Goldberg & Morrison, 1963). One possible explanation for this is that poverty increases exposure to life stress.

There is also evidence that having an older father may increase a child's risk of developing schizophrenia. Byrne and colleagues (Byrne, Agerbo, Ewald, Eaton, & Mortenson, 2003) identified an association between increased risk of schizophrenia and advanced paternal age, particularly for females whose fathers were over 50 years at the time of their birth. A similar pattern was revealed for males whose fathers were between 50 and 54 years old. Exactly why having an older father should confer increased risk for the development of schizophrenia is not yet clear. However, one possibility is that advanced parental age increases risk for genetic mutations.

Communication deviance   Despite evidence for the relationship between schizophrenia and family variables such as social class and parental age, the majority of research investigating the role of the family in the etiology of the disorder has focused on family behavior. More specifically, this research has highlighted the role of abnormal or compromised family communication patterns in the development of schizophrenia. A central variable in this regard is a measure of family communication called communication deviance.

Wynne and Singer (1963) developed the construct of communication deviance (CD) to characterize a pattern of unclear, fragmented, disruptive, or amorphous communication that they observed in relatives of patients with schizophrenia. Although it can be assessed from family conversations (Velligan et al., 1996) or using other tasks (e.g. Rund, Øie, Borchgrevink, & Fjell, 1995), CD (Table 1) is generally measured using transcripts from projective tests such as the Rorschach or the Thematic Apperception Test (TAT; Jones, 1977). These tests require the speaker — generally the parent of the patient — to describe what he or she sees in the projective stimulus to a member of the research team. An individual who is high in CD will offer a description that is difficult for the listener to follow and understand. In the context of these tests, then, CD has been defined as the degree to which a speaker has difficulty in sharing and maintaining a focus of attention with the listener (Wynne & Singer, 1963).

Table 1: Main family communication variables.

	Communication Deviance (CD)	Expressed Emotion (EE)	Affective Style (AS)
What it is:	Pattern of **unclear, fragmented, disruptive or amorphous** communication	The extent to which a relative speaks ***about*** a patient in a manner that is **critical, hostile,** or reflects **emotional overinvolvement (EOI)**	Measure of verbal behaviors ***between*** patients and relatives including ***both*** **positive (supportive) and negative (critical, intrusive)** statements
What it is believed to represent:	How well a speaker can share and maintain a focus of attention with the listener; Possible perceptual-cognitive disturbance and/or disturbance in linguistic-verbal reasoning	An important aspect of a patient's family social environment evident in the tone and affective content of the relative's speech about the patient	The degree to which EE attitudes are expressed during actual family interactions
What trained coders rate in measuring this construct:	Transcripts in which the speaker (usually parent of the patient) describes what s/he sees in the projective stimuli of either the Rorschach or the TAT; or observations of actual family interactions	(1) The Camberwell Family Interview (CFI): 1–2 h semistructured (audiotaped) interview conducted with the relative regarding the ill family member (2) The Five Minute Speech Sample (FMSS): 5 min of the relative (audiotaped) speaking about the patient	Verbatim transcripts of 10-min family interactions during a problem-solving task
Criteria for a rating of HIGH, or in the case of AS, NEG-ATIVE:	Descriptions that are **hard to follow or understand:** transcripts are rated according to multiple categories (e.g. unclear or unstable references, language anomalies, reasoning problems, and contradictions) and the frequency of CD scores is divided by the number of responses.	(1) **Any hostile comment** (2) **More than six critical comments** (or comments expressing dislike or resentment) OR (3) **A rating of 3 or more on EOI** (markedly protective or overconcerned attitudes toward the patient)	(1) **Critical statements** (benign or situation-specific, harsh or personal) (2) **Intrusive statements** (relative implies a knowledge of patient's internal feelings or motives beyond what the patient has stated)

Table 1: Continued.

	Communication Deviance (CD)	**Expressed Emotion (EE)**	**Affective Style (AS)**
Specific examples:	**Euphemisms, slips of the tongue, odd sentence construction**: "it's going to be up and downwards along the process all the while to go through something like this" **Ambiguous references:** "Kid stuff that's one thing but *something else* is different too"	**Critical:** "I don't like it when he goes out late at night" **Hostile:** "This kid is a con artist" **EOI:** "I quit my job and went into debt so I can be home in case he ever needs me"	**Critical:** "you have a bad attitude about school", "you are a lazy person", "you make life difficult for all of us" **Intrusive:** "you're not angry, you're depressed" **Supportive:** "you do that well"
How it is distinguished from other constructs:	Pertains to the **form, clarity or structure** of communication rather than its emotional content	Pertains to a **relative's emotional attitudes toward a patient**. Typically measured in speech *about* a patient and not necessarily reflective of actual patient–relative interactions	Pertains to *both* relative and patient emotional attitudes as **communicated directly to each other** and including *both* positive and negative statements

Empirical studies have consistently identified greater levels of CD in the parents of patients with schizophrenia compared with either the parents of healthy control children or the parents of children with non-psychotic disorders (Miklowitz et al., 1991 or Hooley & Hiller, 2001 for reviews). This suggests that these parents have difficulty in establishing and maintaining a common focus of attention. An important issue, however, is whether the unusual patterns of communication found in the parents of those with schizophrenia contribute to the development of schizophrenia, or whether such communication deficits simply represent a reaction to the child's developing disorder.

To explore this issue, Goldstein and his colleagues (Goldstein, 1987) conducted a 15-year prospective study to examine whether parental CD predicted the development of schizophrenia or schizophrenia spectrum disorders in adolescents at genetic risk. The results indicated that high baseline levels of parental CD predicted the development of later schizophrenia spectrum disorders in the at-risk children. This suggested that disturbed patterns of communication are not merely reactions to the presence of a severe psychotic disorder in the offspring but may instead play a causal role in the development of schizophrenia, broadly defined.

The notion that parental CD might interact with genetic risk to trigger the development of schizophrenia in vulnerable individuals received further support from an important study of Finnish adoptees conducted by Wahlberg, Tienari, and their colleagues (Wahlberg et al., 2000). These researchers looked at levels of thought disorder in adopted children who were at high (by virtue of having a biological relative with schizophrenia) and normal risk for developing schizophrenia and whose adoptive parents were rated as either being low or high in CD. For children at genetic risk, high levels of CD in the adoptive parents were predictive of later thought disorder. In contrast, parental CD was *not* related to later thought disorder in adopted children at normal risk. These results are consistent with the notion that unclear patterns of communication in the family may exacerbate a genetic predisposition for impairments in thought and attention.

Interestingly, parents of high-risk adopted children were not more likely than parents of normal risk adopted children to demonstrate elevated levels of CD. In other words, parental CD does not appear to be a reaction to living with a disturbed offspring. Importantly, it also appears that low levels of parental CD may function to protect individuals at genetic risk from developing the disorder. One of the most striking findings in the Wahlberg et al. (2000) study was that high-risk children who were raised in low CD homes were *less* likely to develop schizophrenia than children in any other group.

Family functioning   A recent follow-up of the same Finnish adoptee sample has provided further evidence implicating family variables in the etiology of schizophrenia (Tienari et al., 2004). Family functioning was rated from individual and joint family interviews using a 33-item rating scale (Tienari et al., 1994). Using techniques of factor analysis and principal components analysis, three new dimensions (critical/conflictual, constricted, and boundary problems) were then identified. The critical/conflictual dimension incorporated ratings of criticism and conflict (both parent–parent and parent–offspring), whereas the constricted dimension incorporated ratings of items such as flat affect and constricted communication. The dimension of boundary problems captured ratings of items such as chaotic structure as well as individual and generational enmeshment.

A methodological strength of the follow-up study was that clinical outcome was assessed in terms of diagnoses rather than the presence of thought disorder. Consistent with the earlier results on CD, adoptees at high genetic risk who were reared in families rated as high on any or all of these three family dysfunction dimensions had significantly more schizophrenia-spectrum diagnoses (including both affective and non-affective psychotic disorders as well as schizotypal personality disorder) than those reared in families with low ratings on the three family variables. Again, however, high-risk adoptees reared in families rated as low in family dysfunction had surprisingly low rates of schizophrenia-spectrum diagnoses at follow-up.

It warrants mention that neither high genetic risk nor dysfunctional family environment alone predicted later schizophrenia-spectrum diagnosis. Consistent with the diathesis-stress model, the development of schizophrenia-spectrum disorders appears to be related to an interaction between genes and environment. Moreover, as was the case for communication deviance, there were no overall differences in family dysfunction in the families of low versus high genetic risk adoptees. This suggests that, like CD, family dysfunction (at least as measured in this study) is not a direct result of exposure to the behavior of an at-risk offspring. Instead the results highlight the greater sensitivity of genetically liable individuals to family environmental variables that are both problematic and protective.

In summary, research investigating the role of families in the etiology of schizophrenia provides evidence that CD and a range of family dysfunction variables can contribute to the development of this disorder. The nature and magnitude of the influence of these variables remains unclear. However, the findings are consistent with a diathesis-stress formulation with family CD and family dysfunction being psychosocial risk factors for schizophrenia *only* in children who are already genetically vulnerable.

Family Variables and the Course of Schizophrenia

The severe and debilitating nature of schizophrenia creates an important role for families in the management of the illness. Not only are families usually the first to recognize and report symptoms of the disorder, but they are also often required to manage the treatment of patients after they have been released from the hospital. In light of this, much research has been conducted to determine how family attitudes toward the patient are linked to the course of the patient's disorder in a positive or negative way. The most well-studied variables in this regard are expressed emotion (EE) and affective style (AS).

Expressed emotion EE is a measure of the family environment that is typically assessed through a 1–2 h semi-structured interview conducted with the patient's relative (Vaughn & Leff, 1976). EE is rated based on how the relative speaks about the patient and is composed of three principal elements: Criticism, Hostility and Emotional Overinvolvement (EOI).

Criticism is the expression of dislike or resentment about some aspect of the patient's behavior, in either the content or negative voice tone of the relative's speech. Whereas criticism typically targets specific behaviors, hostility is a more extreme expression of negative feelings about the patient as a person. The third element of EE, EOI is characterized by an extremely dramatic or overprotective attitude toward the patient (Table 1 for examples).

One of the most consistent findings in the literature is that patients suffering from schizophrenia who return to homes containing high-EE relatives have relapse rates that are more than double those found in patients returning to families who are low in EE (Butzlaff & Hooley, 1998). Moreover, EE is not a relapse risk indicator that is specific only to schizophrenia. EE has also been found to predict relapse in unipolar depression (Vaughn & Leff, 1976; Hooley & Teasdale, 1989), bipolar disorder (Miklowitz, Goldstein, Nuechterlein, Synyder, & Mintz, 1988), and other disorders such as alcohol abuse (O'Farrell, Hooley, Fals-Stewart, & Cutter, 1998).

Why do relatives of psychiatric patients differ in their levels of EE? Current theoretical models (Barrowclough & Hooley, 2003; Hooley & Gotlib, 2000) suggest that critical attitudes in the family are formed through a complex interaction between relatives and patients that centers on issues of control. Relatives of patients with schizophrenia who score high on measures of EE are characterized by less flexibility and tolerance and tend to believe that patients have more control over the negative aspects of their illness than low EE relatives do. They also tend to behave in more controlling ways toward patients (Hooley & Campbell, 2002). Taken together, the available studies indicate that the expectations that relatives have and the causal attributions that they make regarding the ability of the patient to manage the illness may contribute to the presence of critical and hostile attitudes.

Research investigating the interactions between patients with schizophrenia and their relatives supports the idea that high-EE families present a more stressful environment for patients. There is good evidence that high EE is related to more negative behaviors on the part of relatives when actually interacting with patients (see Hooley, Rosen, & Richters, 1995, for review). Hahlweg et al. (1989) found that high-EE critical relatives were characterized by negative interaction styles, which included negative non-verbal affect, criticism, and negative solutions to problematic issues. Moreover, these families demonstrated long-lasting, negative *reciprocal* interaction patterns, suggesting that the patients also contributed to the negative nature of the interactions.

Wuerker (1994) looked at interactions between relatives and patients with schizophrenia and bipolar disorder during problem-solving tasks. Her results suggest that high-EE families engage in more competitions for control than families who are low in EE, regardless of diagnosis. Wuerker also found that patients with schizophrenia and bipolar disorder asserted control *more* than parents did during these interactions. Additionally, Cook, Strachen, Goldstein, and Miklowitz (1989) found similar reciprocal patterns in high-EE families of adolescents at-risk for developing schizophrenia, suggesting that such patterns of interaction may be relatively stable and enduring characteristics of these families. Considered together, these results suggest that EE may be best described as a transactional process that entails competition for control. Importantly, these studies also highlight the role that patients themselves play in generating and maintaining levels of conflict within these high-EE families.

Affective style   Affective style (AS; Doane, Falloon, Goldstein, & Mintz, 1985) was developed to assess, in a more direct fashion, how the attitudes of relatives are expressed during these interactions with patients. As illustrated in Table 1, AS measures levels of *both* positive (supportive) and negative (critical, intrusive) verbal behaviors between patients and relatives during a 10-min family problem-solving task that usually takes place after the patient has been discharged from the hospital. Although research suggests that EE and AS are overlapping but independent constructs (Miklowitz, Goldstein, & Nuechterlein, 1995) the use of AS as an indicator of family emotional environment has largely been eclipsed by EE.

Indeed, research examining the role of AS in schizophrenia reveals some striking continuities with the research on EE. Notably, Doane et al. (1985) found that levels of negative AS in relatives predicted the relapse of patients. Moreover, Rosenfarb, Nuechterlein, Goldstein, and Subotnik (2000) found that levels of interpersonal criticism in family members interacted with deficits in working memory to predict the presence of unusual thinking in patients with schizophrenia. Together, these studies suggest that the affective quality of family interactions may exacerbate cognitive deficits to contribute to the presence — or reemergence — of symptoms in patients with schizophrenia.

Research examining the role of AS in schizophrenia also supports relationships between AS, relapse, and family interactions that are distinct from those of EE. Whereas EE demonstrates a non-specific relationship between schizophrenia and relapse, there is evidence to suggest that levels of AS may distinguish families of patients with schizophrenia from families of patients with other mental illnesses. Miklowitz et al. (1995) found that relatives of patients with schizophrenia made twice as many negative AS statements as did relatives of patients with bipolar disorder. Importantly, these negative statements were characterized by higher levels of intrusiveness and corresponded to high levels of self-denigrating statements in the patients with schizophrenia. Although, as we shall discuss later, AS has also been found to predict relapse in patients with bipolar disorder (Miklowitz et al., 1988), this study revealed that levels of negative AS may be more pervasive in families of patients with schizophrenia. Moreover, the findings suggest that levels of AS in the relatives of patients with schizophrenia may elicit negative reactions in the patients.

The relative specificity of negative AS to schizophrenia reinforces the importance of patient–family interactions. Whereas families may have similar negative attitudes (EE) toward patients with different symptoms, the expression of these attitudes (AS) and the subsequent interactions appear to differ in the context of different disorders. In essence, patient symptoms may actually play a role in shaping the environmental factors that then determine their later risk.

Communication deviance, affective style and expressed emotion   To what extent do CD, EE, and AS measure overlapping aspects of the family environment and to what extent are they indicators of independent underlying constructs? In general, studies that have looked specifically at these relationships have failed to identify consistent associations between CD, EE, and AS. For example, although Miklowitz et al. (1986) reported that high-EE families demonstrated higher levels of CD than did low-EE families, this effect was largely due to the association between EOI (an element of EE) and CD. Moreover, in two other studies no relation between EE and CD was found (Docherty, 1995; Nugter, Dingemans, Linszen, Van der Does, & Gersons, 1997b). There is also no clear association between CD and AS (Doane, West, Goldstein, Rodnick, & Jones, 1981; Nugter et al., 1997b).

For the relatives of schizophrenia patients, empirical evidence does support a link between the constructs of EE and AS. High-EE relatives of schizophrenia patients have been shown to make more negative AS statements (Miklowitz, Goldstein, Falloon, & Doane, 1984; Nugter et al., 1997b, Strachan, Leff, Goldstein, Doane, & Burtt, 1986). Interestingly, however, this does not appear to be the case for the relatives of manic patients (Miklowitz, Goldstein, Nuechterlein, Snyder, & Doane, 1987, Miklowitz et al., 1988).

Taken together, the available evidence suggests that EE and AS may be more closely related to each other than they are to CD. This is perhaps not too surprising, insofar as EE and AS are both measures of the emotional environment of the family whereas CD measures the ability of a family member to create a focus of attention and meaning with another person.

Family burden   As noted earlier, the debilitating nature of schizophrenia requires significant involvement on the part of the families. The stress of caring for a chronically ill patient has been well documented (Abramowitz & Coursey, 1989, Dore & Romans, 2001,

Perlick et al., 1999) with levels of burden being especially high for families of individuals with schizophrenia and bipolar disorders (Chakrabati & Kulhara, 1999). Family members are often called upon to manage financial and legal matters, arrange treatment, and obtain medications. In addition, relatives also endure the emotional toll of caring for a loved one who has been debilitated by a serious disorder. Given this, studies that explore how family burden affects attitudes toward patients and the ability of relatives to be successful in a care-taking role are obviously important.

Empirical evidence suggests that relatives who feel burdened in their roles as care-takers also tend to be rated as being high in EE (Scazufca & Kuipers, 1996). Relatives of patients with schizophrenia who had more supportive social networks also reported less pessimism about the ability of patients to reach social and affective goals. (Magliano et al., 2003). These results suggest that decreasing the experience of burden may have important implications for the relatives' expectations about the patient, and for reducing levels of EE. Given the importance of expectations and family stress in relapse, as highlighted by the EE literature, it is clear that more research is needed to evaluate the effect of family burden on family environment and patient outcome.

The Role of the Family in the Treatment of Schizophrenia

Research implicating disturbed family communication patterns — both in form and content — in the development and maintenance of schizophrenia, along with research on the effects of family burden, suggests that, if we want to help patients, the family environment may be an important target of intervention. Indeed, although medications remain the first-line treatment for schizophrenia, family interventions have come to occupy a major role in the treatment process.

The most widely used and efficacious forms of family interventions for patients with schizophrenia involve a combination of neuroleptic treatment and family intervention (see Hahlweg & Wiedemann, 1999 or Kopelowicz, Liberman, & Zarate, 2002 for reviews). Such treatment programs have demonstrated convincing efficacy in terms of their ability to prevent relapse; 1 year relapse rates for patients receiving this multi-method treatment plan are nearly one-fifth that of patients receiving only medication (Hahlweg & Wiedemann, 1999). Numerous approaches to family interventions have been utilized, including support groups, psychoeducation, and behavioral family therapy (BFT; Falloon, Boyd, & McGill, 1984). Various combinations of these approaches have also been carried out in both single- and multi-family settings.

Despite this variety, there are several common elements in the treatments. These include education regarding the nature and etiology of schizophrenia, including factors that contribute to its development and maintenance, assistance in the utilization of resources, instruction in healthy communication and problem-solving skills, and support (Kopelwicz et al., 2002). Along with reducing relapse and improving patient social functioning, combinations of these elements have proven effective at reducing family burden (Hahlweg & Wiedemann, 1999), improving family atmosphere (Mueser et al., 2001; Berglund, Vahlne, & Edman, 2003), and generating a more positive attitude in the family regarding the patient (Berglund et al., 2003). Thus, family interventions appear to be a potentially important vehicle for creating positive change in both the patient and the family.

The effectiveness of family interventions in reducing the symptoms and relapse of patients not only highlights the importance of involving the family in the treatment of schizophrenia, but also underscores the role of the family variables in contributing to relapse. For example, by providing education regarding the nature of the symptoms of schizophrenia, family interventions may help correct misinformation about how much control the patient has over the illness. Additionally, by teaching families skills for healthy communication and problem solving, these interventions may help reduce stressful and negative interactions between patients and family members. Thus, the ability of family treatment to facilitate the rehabilitation of the patient reinforces the contribution of these family environmental variables to the illness.

To explore the mechanism behind the efficacy of family-based interventions, however, it is necessary to examine how levels of EE, AS, and CD change with family treatment. The majority of the family-based treatments are derived from research into the EE, (and to a lesser extent), the AS and CD constructs. From an empirical perspective, if these variables are causally implicated in the relapse process, treatments that result in lower levels of EE, AS, or CD should also result in better patient outcomes. Unfortunately, despite the wealth of literature supporting the predictive role of family variables such as EE and AS in the relapse of patients with schizophrenia, few studies have assessed how family interventions influence the affective quality of family communication over the course of treatment. In parents receiving BFT, Hahlweg and Wiedemann (1999) identified decreases in negative verbal and non-verbal behavior, as well as increases in positive communication that also corresponded to low rates of relapse. There is also some evidence that reducing levels of negative AS during treatment contributes to better clinical outcome in patients (Miklowitz, 1994). Even though levels of EE do seem to change following family interventions, levels of EE may rise again after the intervention ends (Lenior, Dingemans, Schene, Hart, & Linszen, 2002). In contrast, CD has been found to be quite resistant to change during family-based interventions (Nugter, Dingemans, Linszen, Van der Does, & Gersons, 1997a; Rund et al., 1995). Findings such as these underscore the need to develop interventions that target CD specifically. They also highlight the need to improve current family-based treatment approaches so that they produce more lasting reductions in EE.

Bipolar Disorder

Research on the etiology of bipolar disorder has lagged behind research on schizophrenia and has often been subsumed within research on broader categories of illness such as psychotic illnesses, "major mental illness", and affective disorders. Partly due to recent changes in subtype classifications of bipolar disorder, identification of risk factors is still fairly preliminary. As with schizophrenia, genetic factors play an important role in creating susceptibility to bipolar disorder (Angst, Gamma, & Endrass, 2003; Gershon, 1990; McGuffin et al., 2003). Again, however, the evidence also points to the importance of other factors. In this regard, stress appears to play a major role.

There is fairly consistent, albeit not yet conclusive evidence that stressful life events can precipitate mania, especially a first episode. Although much more research remains to be done, empirical studies suggest that individuals who develop bipolar disorder are likely to have been exposed to stressful life events within a short period just prior to onset (Tsuchiya, Byrne, & Mortensen, 2003).

Families may be implicated in stressful life events in many ways. Although they may function in a protective role (for example, buffering the impact of a stressor or helping an individual cope), they may also directly create stress for patients, indirectly increase the likelihood that an individual will experience stress, or shape and limit an individual's response to stress. Moreover, in the case of shared stressors, the family's own stress responses may actually compound stress for vulnerable individuals. In the sections below, we consider several family-based sources of stress that are associated with increased risk for the development of bipolar disorder. However, readers should keep in mind that strong prospective research designs are needed to verify which factors truly add risk and which simply co-occur with symptom onset.

Family Variables and Increased Risk for Bipolar Disorder

Family-based demographic variables   At the most fundamental level, simply starting a family appears to increase the risk of onset of bipolar disorder. Two studies show increased rates of onset of bipolar disorder in women in the first 3 and 12 months following childbirth (Terp & Mortensen, 1998; Videbech, & Gouliaev 1995).

Coming from a non-intact family is also associated with an elevated risk for developing bipolar disorder. In a large community sample of 4,547 individuals followed prospectively over 15 years, Angst et al. (2003) found that individuals who went on to develop bipolar disorder were 2–3 times more likely to come from a non-intact family. Of course, this could simply reflect the fact that problems may cluster in families with higher rates of mood disorders.

Family environment   In the Finnish adoption study described earlier, Tienari et al. (2004) described various forms of family dysfunction that were associated with the later development of psychotic disorders, including affective psychosis. Echoing this finding, Alnaes and Torgersen (1993) have reported that marital discord between an individual's parents can increase that individual's risk for developing bipolar disorder more specifically. Again, however, given that bipolar disorder tends to run in families, it is not clear if marital discord between the parents is linked to mood lability in the parents themselves or whether it is an independent risk factor. Certainly, the possibility that marital problems in the parents arise from the stress of dealing with a temperamentally challenging child who is in the early stages of susceptibility to mood instability also warrants consideration. Dysfunctional early relationships with parents have been associated with increased risk of developing bipolar disorder in some studies (Rosenfarb, Becker & Kahn, 1994; Alnaes & Torgersen, 1993). However, this association is not invariably found (Perris et al., 1986).

Family Factors and the Course of Bipolar Disorder

Communication deviance   Elevated levels of CD have been found in parents of patients with bipolar disorder. However, the potential role of CD in the development or course of this disorder remains unexplored. Interestingly, even though levels of CD are similar in relatives of both schizophrenia and bipolar patients, levels of CD differ across patients; individuals with bipolar disorder tend to show higher levels of CD when interacting with a relative than patients with schizophrenia do (Miklowitz et al., 1991).

Differences in the type of CD have also been found across bipolar and schizophrenia samples. Parents of manic patients seem to be more likely than those of schizophrenia patients to exhibit "contorted, peculiar language". This includes odd word order, leaving words out, or inclusion of many unnecessary words or details. Parents of manic patients also appear to be more likely to make tangential, inappropriate remarks than do parents of schizophrenia patients. During the interactions used to assess CD, manic patients, as well as their parents, demonstrated odd word usage and unusually constructed sentences more frequently than schizophrenia patients.

Expressed emotion   Bipolar patients who return to live with high-EE families relapse at almost twice the rate (90% vs. 54%) of those living in low-EE family environments (Miklowitz et al., 1988). The association between high EE and relapse has been replicated in at least three additional studies and is one of the most robust findings in the literature on family factors and outcome in bipolar disorder. One major difference concerning the link between EE and relapse in bipolar disorder and in schizophrenia is that, even when they live with low-EE families, bipolar patients are still at very high risk of relapse (Miklowitz et al., 1987). This suggests that although EE is an important variable with regard to predicting the clinical outcome of bipolar patients, other factors also warrant consideration. Perhaps because patients with bipolar disorder are especially stress sensitive, they are liable to break down in the face of stress from a greater variety of sources.

There is no evidence that EE is related to either symptom severity or specific clinical features of bipolar disorder (Heikkilä et al., 2002). Nonetheless, consistent with the diathesis-stress model, researchers such as Miklowitz and Goldstein (1997) believe that EE may have its greatest impact on those patients who are most biologically vulnerable. Furthermore, the occurrence of high EE does follow some patterns. It is more likely to be high in families of young and unmarried individuals and higher in parents than in spouses (Heikkilä et al., 2002). Again, as in schizophrenia, interactions between high EE relatives and patients reveal more interpersonal conflict than is found in low EE relative-patient pairs (Simoneau, Miklowitz, & Saleem, 1998).

Affective style   Consistent with the findings for schizophrenia, relatives' negative AS is associated with higher relapse rates in patients with bipolar disorder. Miklowitz et al. (1988) found that the best prediction of relapse over no relapse came from combined measures of EE assessed during an inpatient phase and measurements of AS assessed during an outpatient stabilization phase. Of those patients whose relatives scored high on both AS and EE, 94% had recurrences of mania or depression compared to only 17% of those whose relatives who scored low on both measures. Greater AS was also associated with poorer social-interpersonal functioning at follow-up and oppositional, "refusing" responses on the part of patients (Miklowitz et al., 1995).

Family conflict   Outside the EE literature, family conflict has been identified as a potential risk factor for relapse, especially for women. In a prospective study concerning negative life events, Christensen et al. (2003) found that family conflict preceded the emergence of a new depressive episode in females with bipolar disorder. Again however, the interplay between symptomatology and family issues warrants mention. It is highly plausible that family conflict might both result from and also trigger the symptoms of bipolar disorder.

Social support   Researchers studying mood disorders have had a greater interest in the role of social support than researchers studying schizophrenia, most likely due to the more prominent role of social support in theories of etiology, particularly for depressive episodes. Findings from this body of research are often hard to compare because definitions and measures of social support differ. In particular, perceptions of support may differ from external measures of support and can be influenced by factors such as mood and severity of symptoms.

Prospective studies obviously provide the best source of information. In one early investigation, a supportive social network was associated with fewer episodes, better social adjustment, and better global assessment in lithium-treated patients with bipolar disorder (O'Connell, Mayo, Eng, Jones, & Gabel, 1985). Johnson and her colleagues have also reported that patients with bipolar disorder who had low levels of social support took longer to recover and had more depressive (but not more manic) symptomatology (Johnson, Winett, Meyer, Greenhouse, & Miller, 1999). Patients with lower levels of social support were also more likely to relapse (Johnson, Lundstrom, Aberg–Wistedt, & Mathe, 2003). In a related vein, support for a person's self-esteem appeared to be the most important predictor of positive change in those with bipolar disorder followed up over a 6 month period (Johnson, Meyer, Winett, & Small, 2000).

Worthy of note is that patients who had a partner at the onset of their disorder did not consistently report more or less social support at the time of the study compared to those without partners (Johnson et al., 2003). They were, however, more likely to be in full remission. This suggests that, even in the absence of an increased perception of support, partners may serve a beneficial role. It is still not clear whether partners facilitate remission, possibly by helping patients find and comply with treatment, or whether patients able to find partners are simply more likely to recover.

The Role of the Family in the Treatment of Bipolar Disorder

Treatment for bipolar disorder has been slow to include families, possibly due to a different view of patient reliance on families and the family's role in recovery. However, for reasons quite similar to those with schizophrenia (levels of impairment, non-compliance with treatment, burden on family, and psychosocial factors influencing the course of bipolar disorder), treatments have recently been developed to include and even focus on the families of individuals with this disorder when they are available and willing to participate. Drawing directly from effective treatment models for schizophrenia, single and multiple family treatments are now being studied.

Family-focused therapy (FFT)   Family-Focused Therapy (FFT) is modeled after Falloon's single family psychoeducational treatment developed for schizophrenia. This treatment targets psychoeducation, communication skills training, and problem-solving skills training. The objectives are adapted for bipolar disorder. Often both patients and families need help in distinguishing whether behaviors (e.g. enthusiasm) represent personality traits or signs of illness. There is also a special focus on reestablishing functional relationships after mood episodes given the episodic nature of bipolar disorder. These modifications highlight the particular role of affect in bipolar disorder and the sometimes marked difference in functioning during an episode versus during recovery.

There have been two randomized controlled studies of FFT to date. One compared FFT and pharmacology to less intensive crisis management and pharmacotherapy and found that those in FFT had fewer relapses, longer survival intervals before relapse, greater reductions in mood disorder symptoms, and better medication adherence over 2 years (Miklowitz, George, Richards, Simoneau, & Succath, 2003). A related study compared FFT to individual therapy and found that the FFT group was less likely to be rehospitalized during a 2-year post-treatment follow-up period (12% vs. 60%). When hospitalizations that occurred during treatment were also considered, just over half of the FFT group was rehospitalized compared with almost 90% of the individual treatment group (Rea et al., 2003).

Further findings from these studies suggest that although the FFT and individual treatment groups did not differ on likelihood of a first relapse or relapse during treatment, the FFT group had fewer relapses over the 2 years. There was no evidence that this was merely due to differences in medication compliance. Differences were most dramatic for patients with poorer premorbid functioning for whom participation in FFT decreased the odds of relapse by a factor of 3. FFT may provide a protective role for these patients; those with better premorbid functioning seemed to do better regardless of the type of treatment. Another interesting finding from the larger of the two studies suggests that participation in FFT was associated with greater reductions in patients' depressive symptoms than in their manic symptoms. The authors suggest that FFT may complement medications that typically target manic symptoms.

Integrated family and individual therapy   Integrated family and individual therapy (IFIT) is a treatment model that is unique to bipolar disorder. As its name suggests, it reflects the integration of family psychoeducation with individual interpersonal and social rhythm therapy (IPSRT). IPSRT, developed by Ellen Frank, is designed to teach patients to maintain regular daily routines and sleep/wake cycles in an effort to reduce risk for relapse. The combined family and individual approach emphasizes the understanding of mutually reciprocal relationships between life stress, environmental context, and the onset of mood disorder symptoms. It also involves the family in helping patients maintain regular routines. Preliminary outcomes for IPSRT and standard pharmacotherapy indicate that it may be helpful in reducing subsyndromal symptoms and in the maintenance of a stable euthymic mood state (Frank, 1999).

One open treatment study comparing IFIT with family psychoeducation and crisis management found that those in IFIT took longer to relapse and had greater reductions in depressive symptoms over 1 year of treatment (Miklowitz et al., 2003). Combining individual and family treatment with medication may help to protect patients with bipolar disorder from early relapse and ongoing depression.

Concluding Comments

We are fortunate that the era of blaming families for the development of major mental disorders such as schizophrenia is now in the past. There is no convincing empirical evidence to support the idea that families cause the serious psychopathological conditions that we have described in this chapter. On the contrary, in these more enlightened (and research-oriented) times, family members are regarded as important resources in patient treatment.

Families also have a role to play with respect to the prevention of serious psychopathology, however. Consistent with the diathesis-stress paradigm, certain kinds of problematic family environments appear to be linked to the emergence of psychopathology in individuals who are at high genetic risk. In this regard such variables as CD and family conflict are attracting empirical attention. Going forward, we anticipate a growing partnership between behavior geneticists and family environment researchers, and an emphasis on exploring gene X environment interactions (e.g. Caspi et al., 2004). To the extent that family researchers have identified characteristics of families that may be protective or, conversely, may be capable of triggering the onset of psychopathology, work in this new area is already off to a good start. Much of what we have learned about how to measure and quantify key aspects of the family environment is now poised to be used in the context of a new and exciting research environment.

For example, the EE literature makes it clear that patients diagnosed with schizophrenia, mood disorders, and other psychopathological conditions are at significantly higher risk of relapse if they live with family members who are critical of them. However, the mechanisms by which an interpersonal event like criticism from a family member can culminate in a bio-behavioral outcome like symptom relapse are far from clear. In an effort to explore the neurobiological consequences of exposure to criticism, Hooley and her colleagues have developed an affective challenge paradigm designed to integrate EE research with neuroimaging. This approach is using functional magnetic resonance imaging (fMRI) to explore focal activation changes that occur in the brains of healthy controls and in people with a known vulnerability to major depression while they are hearing criticism from their own mothers (Hooley, Gruber, Scott, Hiller, & Yurgelun-Todd, 2005).

In conclusion, the time appears to be ripe for a resurgence of interest in families and psychopathology. Researchers who study psychosocial stress now have much to offer researchers interested in such topics as behavior genetics and affective neuroscience. Rather than considering genetic or biological variables in isolation of the social environment, there is now a growing trend toward integration. Efforts to explore the links between interpersonal experiences and biology are likely to shape the research agenda for the next several decades.

References

Abramowitz, I. A., & Coursey, R. D. (1989). Impact of an educational support group on family participants who take care of their schizophrenic relatives. *Journal of Consulting and Clinical Psychology, 57*(2), 232–236.

Alnaes, R., & Torgersen, S. (1993). Mood disorders: Developmental and precipitating events. *Canadian Journal of Psychiatry, 38*, 217–224.

Angst, J., Gamma, A., & Endrass, J. (2003). Risk factors for the bipolar and depression spectra. *Acta Psychiatrica Scandinavica, 108*(s418), 15–20.

Barrowclough, C. M., & Hooley, J. M. (2003). Attributions and expressed emotion: A review. *Clinical Psychology Review, 23*(6), 849–880.

Berglund, N., Vahlne, J. O., & Edman, A. (2003). Family intervention in schizophrenia: Impact on family burden and attitude. *Social Psychiatry and Psychiatric Epidemiology, 38*, 116–121.

Butzlaff, R. L., & Hooley, J. M. (1998). Expressed emotion and psychiatric relapse: A meta-analysis. *Archives of General Psychiatry, 55*, 547–552.

Byrne, M., Agerbo, E., Ewald, H., Eaton, W. W., & Mortenson, P. B. (2003). Parentel age and risk of schizophrenia: A case-control study. *Archives of General Psychiatry, 60*, 673–678.

Caspi, A., Moffitt, T. E., Morgan, J., Rutter, M., Taylor, A., Arseneault, L., Tully, L., Jacobs, C., Kim-Cohen, J., & Polo-Tomas, M. (2004). Maternal expressed emotion predicts children's anti-social behavior problems: Using monozygotic-twin differences to identify environmental effects on behavioral development. *Developmental Psychology, 40*(2), 149–161.

Chakrabarti, S., & Kulhara, P. (1999). Family burden of caring for people with mental illness. *The British Journal of Psychiatry, 174*(5), 463.

Christensen, E. M., Gjerris, A., Larsen, J. K., Bendtsen, B. B., Larsen, B. H., Rolff, H., Ring, G., & Schaumberg, E. (2003). Life events and onset of a new phase in bipolar affective disorder. *Bipolar Disorders, 5*, 356–361.

Cook, W. L., Strachan, A. M., Goldstein, M. J., & Miklowitz, D. J. (1989). Expressed emotion and reciprocal affective relationships in families of disturbed adolescents. *Family Process, 28*, 337–348.

Doane, J. A., West, K. L., Goldstein, M. J., Rodnick, E. H., & Jones, J. E. (1981). Parental communication deviance and affective style: Predictors of subsequent schizophrenia spectrum disorders in vulnerable adolescents. *Archives of General Psychiatry, 38*, 679–685.

Doane, J. A., Falloon, I. R. H., Goldstein, M. J., & Mintz, J. (1985). Parental affective style and the treatment of schizophrenia. *Archives of General Psychiatry, 42*, 34–42.

Docherty, N. M. (1995). Expressed emotion and language disturbances in parents of stable schizophrenia patients. *Schizophrenia Bulletin, 21*, 411–418.

Dore, G., & Romans, S. E. (2001). Impact of bipolar affective disorder on family and partners. *Journal of Affective Disorders, 67*, 147–158.

Falloon, I. R. H., Boyd, J. L., & McGill, C. W. (1984). *Family care of schizophrenia*. New York: Guilford.

Faris, R. E. L., & Dunham, H. W. (1939). *Mental disorders in urban areas*. Chicago: University of Chicago Press.

Frank, E. (1999). Interpersonal and social rhythm therapy prevents depressive symptomatology in bipolar I patients. *Bipolar Disorder, 1*(Suppl. 1), 13.

Gershon, E. S. (1990). Genetics. In: F.K. Goodwin & K. R. Jamison (Eds), *Manic-depressive illness* (pp. 373–401). New York: Oxford University Press.

Goldberg, E. M., & Morrison, S. L. (1963). Schizophrenia and social class. *British Journal of Psychiatry, 109*, 785–802.

Goldstein, M. J. (1987). The UCLA high-risk project. *Schizophrenia Bulletin, 13*(3), 505–514.

Hahlweg, K., Goldstein, M. J., Nuechterlein, K. H., Magaña, A. B., Mintz, J., Doane, J. A., Miklowitz, D. J., & Snyder, K. S. (1989). Expressed emotion and patient–relative interaction in families of recent-onset schizophrenics. *Journal of Consulting and Clinical Psychology, 57*(1), 11–18.

Hahlweg, K., & Wiedemann, G. (1999). Principles and results of family therapy in schizophrenia. *European Archives of Psychiatry and Clinical Neuroscience, 249*(Suppl. 4), IV/108–IV/115.

Harrison, P. J., & Weinberger, D. R. (2005). Schizophrenia genes, gene expression and neuropathology: On the matter of their convergence. *Molecular Psychiatry, 10*(1), 40–68.

Heikkilä, J., Karlsson, H., Taiminen, T., Lauerma, H., Ilonen, T., Leinonen, K.-M., Wallenius, E., Virtanen, H., Heinimaa, M., Koponen, S., Javo, P., Kaljonen, A., & Salakangas, R. K. R. (2002). Expressed emotion is not associated with disorder severity in first-episode mental disorder. *Psychiatry research, 111,* 155–165.

Hooley, J. M., & Campbell, C. (2002). Control and controllability: An examination of beliefs and behavior in high and low expressed emotion relatives. *Psychological Medicine, 32,* 1091–1099.

Hooley, J. M., & Gotlib, I. H. (2000). A diathesis-stress conceptualization of expressed emotion and clinical outcome. *Applied & Preventive Psychology, 9,* 135–151.

Hooley, J. M., Gruber, S. A., Scott, L. A., Hiller, J. B., & Yurgelun-Todd, D. A. (2005). Activation in Dorsolateral Prefrontal Cortex in Response to Maternal Criticism and Praise in Recovered Depressed and Healthy Control Participants. Biological Psychiatry, *57,* 809–812.

Hooley, J. M., & Hiller, J. B. (2001). Family relationships and major mental disorder: Risk factors and preventive strategies. In: B. Sarason & S. Duck (Eds), *Personal relationships: Implications for clinical and community psychology* (pp. 61–87). New York: Wiley.

Hooley, J. M., Rosen, L. R., & Richters, J. E. (1995). Expressed emotion: Toward a clarification of a critical construct. In: G. Miller (Ed.), *The behavioral high-risk paradigm in psychopathology* (pp 88–120). New York: Springer.

Hooley, J. M., & Teasedale, J. D. (1989). Predictors of relapse in unipolar depressives: Expressed emotion, marital distress, and perceived criticism. *Journal of Abnormal Psychology, 98,* 229–235.

Johnson, L., Lundström, O., Äberg-Wistedt, A., & Mathé, A. A. (2003). Social support in bipolar disorder: Its relevance to remission and relapse. *Bipolar Disorders, 5*(2), 129–138.

Johnson, S. L., Meyer, B., Winett, C. A., & Small, J. (2000). Social support and self-esteem predict changes in bipolar depression but not mania. *Journal of Affective Disorders, 58,* 79–86.

Johnson, S. L., Winett, C. A., Meyer, B., Greenhouse, W. J., & Miller, I. (1999). Social support and the course of bipolar disorder. *Journal of Abnormal Psychology, 108,* 558–566.

Jones, J. E. (1977). Patterns of transactional style deviance in the TATs of parents of schizophrenics. *Family Process, 16,* 327–337.

Kopelowicz, A., Liberman, R. P., & Zarate, R. (2002). Psychosocial treatments for schizophrenia. In: P. E. Nathan & J. M. Gorman (Eds), *A guide to treatments that work* (2nd ed., pp. 201–228). New York: Oxford University Press.

Lenior, M. E., Dingemans, P. M. A., Schene, A. H., Hart, A. A. M., & Linszen, D. H. (2002). The course of parental expressed emotion and psychotic episodes after family intervention in recent-onset schizophrenia: A longitudinal study. *Schizophrenia Research, 57,* 183–190.

Magliano, L., Fiorillo, A., Malangone, C., Marasco, C., Guarneri, M., & Maj, M. (2003). The effect of social network on burden and pessimism in relatives of patients with schizophrenia. *American Journal of Orthopsychiatry, 73*(3), 302–309.

McGuffin, P., Rijsdijk, F. V., Andrew, M., Sham, P., Katz, R., & Cardno, A. (2003). The heritability of bipolar affective disorder and the genetic relationship to unipolar depression. *Archives of General Psychiatry, 60,* 497–502.

Miklowitz, D. J. (1994). Family risk indicators in schizophrenia. *Schizophrenia Bulletin, 20*(1), 137–149.

Miklowitz, D. J., George, E. L., Richards, J. A., Simoneau, T. L., & Succath, R. L. (2003). A randomized study of family-focused psychoeducation and pharmacotherapy in the outpatient management of bipolar disorder. *Archives of General Psychiatry, 60,* 904–912.

Miklowitz, D. J., & Goldstein, M. J. (1997). *Bipolar disorder: A family-focused treatment approach.* New York: Guilford.

Miklowitz, D. J., Goldstein, M. J., Falloon, I. R. H., & Doane, J. A. (1984). Interactional correlates of expressed emotion in the families of schizophrenics. *British Journal of Psychiatry, 144,* 482–487.

Miklowitz, D. J., Goldstein, M. J., & Nuechterlein, K. H. (1995). Verbal interactions in the families of schizophrenic and bipolar affective patients. *Journal of Abnormal Psychology, 104*(2), 268–276.

Miklowitz, D. J., Goldstein, M. J., Nuechterlein, K. H., Snyder, K. S., & Doane, J. A. (1987). The family and the course of recent-onset mania. In: K. Hahlweg & M. J. Goldstein (Eds), *Understanding major mental disorder: The contribution of family interaction research* (pp. 195–211). New York: Family Process Press.

Miklowitz, D. J., Goldstein, M. J., Nuechterlein, K. H., Snyder, K. S., & Mintz, J. (1988). Family factors and the course of bipolar affective disorder. *Archives of General Psychiatry, 45,* 225–231.

Miklowitz, D. J., Richards, J. A., George, E. L., Frank, E., Suddath, R. L., Powell, K. B., & Sacher, J. A. (2003). Integrated family and individual therapy for bipolar disorder: Results of a treatment development study. *Journal of Clinical Psychiatry, 64*(2), 182–191.

Miklowitz, D. J., Strachan, A. M., Goldstein, M. J., Doane, J. A., Snyder, K. S., Hogarty, G. E., & Falloon, I. R. H. (1986). Expressed emotion and communication deviance in the families of schizophrenics. *Journal of Abnormal Psychology, 95*(1), 60–66.

Miklowitz, D. J., Velligan, D. I., Goldstein, M. J., Nuechterlein, K. H., Gitlin, M. J., Ranlett, G., & Doane, J. A. (1991). Communication deviance in families of schizophrenic and manic patients. *Journal of Abnormal Psychology, 100*(2), 161–173.

Mueser, K. T., Sengupta, A., Schooler, N. R., Bellack, A. S., Xie, H., Glick, I. D., Keith, S. J. (2001). Family treatment and medication dosage reduction in schizophrenia: Effects on patient social functioning, family attitudes, and burden. *Journal of Consulting and Clinical Psychology, 69*(1), 3–12.

Nugter, M. A., Dingemans, P. M. A. J., Linszen, D. H., Van der Does, A. J. W., & Gersons, B. P. R. (1997a). Parental communication deviance: Its stability and the effect of treatment on recent-onset schizophrenia. *Acta Psychiatrica Scandinavia, 95,* 199–204.

Nugter, M. A., Dingemans, P. M. A. J., Linszen, D. H., Van der Does, A. J. W., & Gersons, B. P. R. (1997b). The relationships between expressed emotion, affective style, and communication deviance in recent-onset schizophrenia. *Acta Psychiatrica Scandinavia, 96,* 445–451.

O'Connell, R., Mayo, J. A., Eng, L. K., Jones, J. S., & Gabel, R.H. (1985). Social support and long-term lithium outcome. *British Journal of Psychiatry, 147,* 272–275.

O'Farrell, T., Hooley, J. M., Fals-Stewart, W., & Cutter, H. S. G. (1998). Expressed emotion and relapse in alcoholic patients. *Journal of Consulting and Clinical Psychology, 66,* 744–752.

Perlick, D., Clarkin, J. F., Raue, P., Greenfield, S., Struening, E., & Rosenheck, R. (1999). Burden experienced by care-givers of persons with bipolar affective disorder. *British Journal of Psychiatry, 175,* 56–62.

Perris, C., Arrindell, W. A., Perris, H., Eisemann, M., van der Ende, J., & von Knorring, L. (1986). Perceived depriving parental rearing and depression. *British Journal of Psychiatry, 148,* 170–175.

Rea, M. M., Tompson, M. C., Miklowitz, D. J., Goldstein, M. J., Hwang, S., & Mintz, J. (2003). Family-focused treatment versus individual treatment for bipolar disorder: Results of a randomized clinical trial. *Journal of Consulting and Clinical Psychology, 71*(3), 482–492.

Rosenfarb, I. S., Becker, J., & Kahn, A. (1994). Perceptions of parental and peer attachments by women with mood disorders. *Journal of Abnormal Psychology, 103,* 637–644.

Rosenfarb, I. S., Nuechterlein, K. H., Goldstein, M. J., & Subotnik, K. L. (2000). Neurocognitive vulnerability, interpersonal criticism, and the emergence of unusual thinking by schizophrenic patients during family transactions. *Archives of General Psychiatry, 57*(12), 1174–1179.

Rund, B. R., Øie, M., Borchgrevink, T. S., & Fjell, A. (1995). Expressed emotion, communication deviance, and schizophrenia: An exploratory study of the relationship between two family variables and the course and outcome of a psychoeducational treatment programme. *Psychopathology, 28*, 220–228.

Scazufca, M., & Kuipers, E. (11996). Links between expressed emotion and burden of care in relatives of patients with schizophrenia. *British Journal of Psychiatry, 168*(5), 580–587.

Simoneau, T. L., Miklowitz, D. J., & Saleem, R. (1998). Expressed emotion and interactional patterns in the families of bipolar patients. *Journal of Abnormal Psychology, 107*, 497–507.

Strachan, A. M., Leff, J. P., Goldstein, M. J., Doane, J. A., & Burtt, C. (1986). Emotional attitudes and direct communication in the families of schizophrenics: A cross-national replication study. *British Journal of Psychiatry, 149*, 279–287.

Terp, I. M., & Mortensen, P. B. (1998). Post-partum psychoses. Clinical diagnoses and relative risk of admission after parturition. *British Journal of Psychiatry, 172*, 521–526.

Tienari, P., Wynne, L. C., Moring, J., Lahti, I., Naarala, M., Sorri, A., Wahlberg, K. -E., Saarento, O., Sietamaa, M., Kaleva, M., & Läksy, K. (1994). The Finnish adoptive family study of schizophrenia: Implications for family research. *British Journal of Psychiatry, 164*(Suppl. 23), 20–26.

Tienari, P., Wynne, L. C., Sorri, A., Lahti, I., Läksy, K., Moring, J., Naarala, M., Nieminen, P., Wahlberg, K. -E. (2004). Genotype-environment interaction in schizophrenia-spectrum disorder: Long-term follow-up study of Finnish adoptees. *British Journal of Psychiatry, 184*, 216–222.

Tsuchiya, K. J., Byrne, M., & Mortensen, P. B. (2003). Risk factors in relation to an emergence of bipolar disorder: A systematic review. *Bipolar Disorders, 5*, 231–242.

Vaughn, C., & Leff, J. (1976). The measurement of expressed emotion in the families of psychiatric patients. *The British Journal of Social and Clinical Psychology, 15*, 157–165.

Velligan, D. I., Miller, A. L., Eckert, S. L., Funderburg, L. G., True, J. E., Mahurin, R. K., Diamond, P., & Hazelton, B. C. (1996). The relationship between parental communication deviance and relapse in schizophrenic patients in the 1-year period after hospital discharge. *The Journal of Nervous and Mental Disease, 184*, 490–496.

Videbech, P., & Gouliaev, G. (1995). First admission with puerperal psychosis: 7–14 years of follow-up. *Acta Psychiatrica Scandinavica, 91*, 167–173.

Wahlberg, K. E., Wynne, L. C., Oja, H., Keskitalo, P., Anais-Tanner, H., Koistinen, P., Tarvainen, T., Hakko, H., Lahti, I., Moring, J., Naarala, M., Sorri, A., & Tienari, P. (2000). Thought disorder index of Finnish adoptees and communication deviance of their adoptive parents. *Psychological Medicine, 30*(1), 127–136.

Wuerker, A. M. (1994). Relational control patterns and expressed emotion in families of persons with schizophrenia and bipolar disorder. *Family Process, 33*, 389–407.

Wynne, L. C., & Singer, M. T. (1963). Thought disorder and family relations of schizophrenics: I. A research strategy. *Archives of General Psychiatry, 9*, 191–198.

Zubin, J. & Spring, B. J. (1977). Vulnerability: A new view of schizophrenia. *Journal of Abnormal Psychology, 86*, 103–126.

Chapter 12

Depression and the Family*

Judy Garber

Introduction

Depression is a complex, multi-faceted condition that involves the interplay among genetic, biological, cognitive, interpersonal, and contextual factors. The family contributes to the development and maintenance of depression across these multiple levels of analysis. Several excellent reviews have been published describing families of depressed adults (Brewin, Andrews, & Gotlib, 1993; Burbach & Borduin, 1986; Gerlsma, Emmelkamp, & Arrindell, 1990; Keitner & Miller, 1990), parenting and families of depressed children and adolescents (Blatt & Homann, 1992; Burbach & Borduin, 1986; Chiariello & Orvaschel, 1995; Kaslow, Deering, & Racusin, 1994; Marton & Maharaj, 1993; McCauley & Myers, 1992a; Rapee, 1997; Sheeber, Hops, & Davis, 2001), and offspring of depressed mothers (Beardslee, Versage, & Gladstone, 1998; Cummings & Davies, 1999; Downey & Coyne, 1990; Elgar, McGrath, Waschbusch, Stewart, & Curtis, 2004a; Gelfand & Teti, 1990; Goodman & Gotlib, 1999, 2002; Hammen, 1991; Lovejoy, Graczyk, O'Hare, & Neuman, 2000; Radke-Yarrow, 1998) and depressed fathers (Connell & Goodman, 2002; Kane & Garber, 2004). The present chapter highlights and extends these former reviews and presents an overall framework for understanding the link between the family and depression.

Epidemiology: The Scope of the Problem

Depression is one of the most prevalent of all psychiatric disorders, ranked as the single most burdensome disease in the world in terms of total disability-adjusted life years among people in the middle years of life (Murray & Lopez, 1996). Depression is rare in preschool age (Kashani & Carlson, 1987) and preadolescent children (Cohen et al., 1993; Costello

*Judy Garber was supported in part by grants (R01MH57822; R01MH64735) and a Research Scientist Development Award (K02 MH66249) from the National Institute of Mental Health and a grant from the William T. Grant Foundation (173096) during completion of this work.

Psychopathology and the Family
Edited by J. L. Hudson and R. M. Rapee
Copyright © 2005 by Elsevier Ltd.
All rights of reproduction in any form reserved
ISBN: 0-08-044449-0

et al., 1996), but increases during adolescence with an average 6-month prevalence rate of 3.6% (ranging from 0.4% to 9.8%) (Birmaher et al., 1996a; Fleming & Offord, 1990; Lewinsohn & Essau, 2002). Point prevalence for major depressive disorder (MDD) among adults in Western industrialized countries is about 4.9%: 2.3% to 3.2% for men and 4.5% to 9.3% for women (Blazer, Kessler, McGonagle, & Swartz, 1994).

Lifetime prevalence of MDD is 8.3% to 18.5% in adolescents (about 24% for females, 11.6% for males; Lewinsohn, Hops, Roberts, Seeley, & Andrews, 1993) and 17% in adults (21.3% for women, 12.7% for men; Blazer et al., 1994). In the National Comorbidity Survey (Kessler & Walters, 1998), lifetime prevalence of MDD among 15- to 18-year-olds was about 14%, and an additional 11% had a lifetime history of minor depression, with higher rates in females than males. Kessler, Avenevoli, and Merikangas (2001) found that risk of the first onset of MDD begins in the early teens and continues to rise through the mid-20s.

The 2:1 sex ratio commonly found in adults (Weissman & Olfson, 1995) begins in adolescence. In preadolescents, the rate of MDD is about equal in girls and boys (Angold & Rutter, 1992; Fleming, Offord, & Boyle, 1989) or higher among boys (Costello et al., 1996; Ryan et al., 1987). The prevalence of dysthymic disorder has been found to be greater in girls than boys aged 8–11 years old (Polaino-Lorente & Domenech, 1993). The gender ratio for depression changes after puberty, with the rates increasing among adolescent girls by about age 14 (Hankin et al., 1998; Wade, Cairney, & Pevalin, 2002). The highest prevalence of MDD is in women in their child-bearing years (Heneghan, Silver, Westbrook, Bauman, & Stein, 1998; Kessler, 2003), particularly economically disadvantaged, single mothers (Lanzi, Pascoe, Keltner, & Ramey, 1999).

Depression has a chronic, episodic course with frequent recurrences and considerable impairment that accounts for a substantial proportion of the health care costs incurred by adolescents (Birmaher et al., 1996a; Birmaher, Ryan, Williamson, Brent, & Kaufman, 1996b) and adults (Katon & Sullivan, 1990). Adolescent depression is associated with academic problems, substance abuse, cigarette smoking, high-risk sexual behavior, physical health problems, impaired social relationships, and a 30-fold increased risk of completed suicide (Birmaher et al., 1996a; Rohde, Lewinsohn, & Seeley, 1994; Stolberg, Clark, & Bongar, 2002). Moreover, episodes of depression during childhood or adolescence increase the risk of subsequent episodes; among children and adolescents, recurrence rates have ranged from 20% to 72% over 2 to 10 years (Emslie et al., 1997; Harrington, Fudge, Rutter, Pickles, & Hill, 1990; Kovacs et al., 1984b; Lewinsohn, Rohde, Klein, & Seeley, 1999). Early-onset mood disorders (i.e. prior to age 20) are associated with increased risk of relapse (Gonzales, Lewinsohn, & Clarke, 1985; Keller, Lavori, Lewis, & Klerman, 1983), a more severe course (Hammen, Davila, Brown, Ellicott, & Gitlin, 1992; Kovacs et al., 1984a), and increased familial loading of depression (e.g. Weissman, Warner, Wickramaratne, & Prusoff, 1988). Recurrent depressive episodes have more impairment in school, work, and interpersonal relationships (Lewinsohn, Rohde, Seeley, Klein, & Gotlib, 2003; Rao et al., 1995) and an increased risk of suicide (Kovacs, Goldston, & Gatsonis, 1993; Weissman et al., 1999a). Moreover, the longer depressive episodes last, the more difficult they are to treat (Judd et al., 1998; Thase & Howland, 1994). Thus, depression can be a serious, life-long condition with many associated impairments. Early identification of the processes that underlie the development of depression should facilitate the creation of prevention and treatment programs.

A Biopsychosocial Framework of the Relation between the Family and Depression

Depression runs in families (Hammen, 1991, Sullivan, Neale, & Kendler, 2000). Families contribute both direct and indirect genetic and environmental effects through gene-environment correlations and interactions. The question of genes *or* environment simply is not relevant. Rather, the more important question is *how* do genes and the family environment independently and together contribute to the development and maintenance of depression. Based on his transgenerational study of parenting among monozygotic and dizygotic adult twins, their parents, and their children, Kendler (1996) suggested that parenting is influenced by attitudes derived from the parent's own family of origin, genetic-temperamental characteristics of the parent affecting their parenting behaviors, and genetic-temperamental characteristics of their children influencing the elicitation and provision of parenting.

Figure 1 shows a general framework for describing the relation between the family and depression. Although several pathways are possible, the primary pathway is a-f-b-g-c-d, which indicates that genes (a) as well as parenting behaviors (f) contribute to children's temperament; children's temperament (b) and parenting (g) then influence how the child appraises and responds to stress (c), which interacts with stress (d) to produce depression. That is, individuals who have certain kinds of temperament (e.g. neurotic, stress reactive), which is the result of both genes and environment (e.g. parenting), are more likely to perceive stressful life events as threatening, and engage in maladaptive responses when stressors occur; such perceptions and responses likely are the result of both temperament and parenting. Additional pathways of note are that genes as well as parents' own learning history can influence their behaviors toward their children (e); on the other hand, children's temperament (f) likely will affect how parents respond to them. Moreover, the family environment itself may be a source of stress (h) through such things as marital discord, financial strain, and parental psychopathology. Parents' behaviors can be another source of stress through abuse, maltreatment, neglect, and hostility (i). Finally, depression itself then can feedback into the family by increasing negative interpersonal interactions (j) as well as through generating higher levels of stress (k).

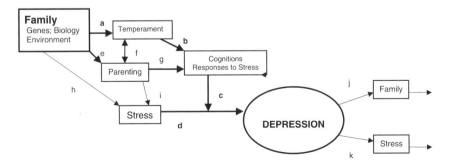

Figure 1: A biopsychosocial framework of the relation between the family and depression.

Genes and Biology

Genes Family, twin, and adoption studies have yielded varying results regarding the extent of the genetic contributions to individual differences in depression (Wallace, Schneider, & McGuffin, 2002). Family studies have shown that children of depressed parents are about three times more likely to experience an episode of depression than are children of normal controls (Klein, Lewinsohn, Seeley, & Rohde, 2001; Weissman, Warner, Wickramaratne, Moreau, & Olfson, 1997), and the risk of having a depressive episode is higher in relatives of depressed children than in relatives of psychiatric and normal controls (e.g. Harrington et al.,1993; Neuman, Geller, Rice, & Todd, 1997; Williamson et al., 1995). However, family studies confound genetic and shared environmental effects. Familiality of depression also could be due to psychosocial factors such as maladaptive parenting styles, marital dysfunction, and stress, which also are associated with parental psychopathology (Goodman & Gotlib, 1999).

Twin studies with children have yielded heritability estimates comparable to those found in adults. A meta-analysis (Sullivan et al., 2000) obtained heritability estimates between 30% and 40% for the liability to MDD; the remaining variance in liability then could be attributed to unique environment. In a study of 41 twin pairs aged 6–16, Wierzbicki (1987) reported heritability estimates of 0.32 for child-reported depression, and 0.93 for parent report of children's symptoms. The Virginia Twin Study of Adolescent Behavioral Development (Eaves et al., 1997) consists of 1412 twin pairs aged 8–16 years old. Based on child self-report, heritability estimates were small (0.15 for girls, 0.16 for boys) and shared environmental effects were small to moderate (0.26 for girls, 0.14 for boys), whereas parent report yielded much larger heritability estimates (0.60 for mothers, 0.65 for fathers) and shared environment effects were negligible. Non-shared environmental factors also played a moderate role in both child report (0.59 for girls, 0.70 for boys) and parent report (0.35 for mothers, 0.40 for fathers) of children's depression (Eaves et al., 1997). The higher parent-report heritabilities may be partially due to parents seeing MZ twins as more phenotypically similar than DZ twins across constructs, thereby elevating heritability estimates based on parent report.

Thapar and McGuffin (1994) also reported large genetic contributions to individual differences in parent-reported depression ($h^2 = 0.79$) in a sample of 411 twin pairs aged 8–16, and shared environment effects were non-significant. When only the 8–11 years old pairs were examined, however, shared environmental effects for parent-reported depression accounted for 77% of the variance and heritability effects were negligible. Child self-report measures were not available. In adolescents, the heritability estimate for self-reported depression was also high ($h^2 = 0.70$). Finally, in a sample of 395 twin pairs, 8–16 years old, Eley, Deater-Deckard, Fombonne, Fulker, and Plomin (1998) found similar heritability estimates for both child-reported depression ($h^2 = 0.48$) and parent-reported depression ($h^2 = 0.49$). Shared environment effects were greater in adolescents (0.28) than children (0.08), and heritability estimates were moderate in both groups; $h^2 = 0.34$ for children and $h^2 = 0.28$ for adolescents. These results also suggest age differences, but in the opposite direction. In this case, shared environmental effects were stronger in adolescents.

Thus, twin studies indicate that genes account for approximately 30–50% of the variance in child-reported depression. The evidence for environmental effects is mixed. In addition, genetic and environmental influences differ by informant (Eaves et al., 1997; Wierzbicki, 1987) and age (Eley et al., 1998; Thaper & McGuffin, 1994). Early onset (< 20 years old) depressions are associated with greater risk for depression in family members (Weissman et al., 1986, 1988), although the evidence for this is inconsistent (Sullivan et al., 2000). Alternatively, childhood depression has been associated with greater environmental contributions (Thaper & McGuffin, 1994). It is unclear whether earlier onset depression is due to greater genetic influences or factors within the shared environment of families with a depressed proband (Rutter et al., 1990).

Adoption designs generally can disentangle shared and non-shared environmental effects. Eley et al. (1998) used a sibling adoption design and an offspring design to assess the variance accounted for by genetic and environmental factors in child- and parent-reported depression. Neither the sibling nor the parent-offspring correlations showed a significant genetic effect. There was evidence of some shared environmental effects, although these were greater for parents' reports indicating inflation possibly due to method bias in the relation between mothers' report of their own and their children's symptoms. The results also suggested a substantial role for non-shared environmental effects.

Thus, findings from twin and adoption studies of child and adolescent depression differ. Whereas twin studies suggest a moderate role for genetic influences on individual differences in depression, adoption studies typically have reported negligible genetic effects. Twin studies report non-significant effects of shared environment, whereas adoption studies suggest a small but significant shared environment effect. Both designs provide evidence of moderate to large non-shared environmental influences.

In summary, behavioral genetic designs provide evidence of both genetic and environmental effects (Plomin, DeFries, McClearn, & McGuffin, 2001; Sullivan et al., 2000). Estimates of heritability tend to be moderate and shared environment effects tend to be small. Both tend to vary as a function of informant, age, and severity of depressive symptoms. Small shared environmental effects, however, do not mean that parent and other family influences are unimportant. The most parsimonious explanation may be that "it is not the general qualities of some facet of the environment (e.g. a parent's rearing style, neighborhood, poverty) but rather how these qualities influence an individual and how he or she interacts with this part of the environment across developmental stages" (Sullivan et al., 2000, p. 1559).

Support for a diathesis-stress model of depression has been provided by the recent finding by Caspi and colleagues (Caspi et al., 2003) that individuals' responses to adversity were moderated by their genetic makeup. Caspi et al. (2003) found that a functional polymorphism in the promoter region of the serotonin transporter (5-HTT) gene moderated the effect of stressful life events on depression. Individuals with one or two copies of the short allele of the 5-HTT promoter polymorphism were more stress-sensitive and exhibited more depressive symptoms, disorders, and suicidality in response to negative life events than did those who were homozygous for the long allele. Although these results are promising, recent meta-analyses (Anguelova, Benkelfat, & Turecki, 2003; Munafo et al., 2003) indicate that the association between variation in the polymorphism in the 5-HTT gene and risk for MDD or associated personality traits is small to modest. In a replication of the Caspi et al. (2003) study, Kendler, Kuhn, Vittum, Prescott, and Riley (2005) concluded that "the 5-HTT may be an example of a gene that influences liability to MD not by a main effect on risk but rather by control of sensitivity to the pathogenic effects of the environment" (p. 534).

Although vulnerability to depression clearly has a genetic component, it is not yet clear what is inherited that places individuals at greater risk. Genetic factors may contribute to neurobiological, personality, and/or cognitive vulnerabilities, which then interact with the environment to produce depressive symptoms. Non-shared environmental effects, that is, experiences that are unique to individuals within a family, emerge as the largest environmental influence on individual differences in childhood depression (Plomin et al., 2001; Sullivan et al., 2000). The latter has been found to be true for most forms of psychopathology, as well as for certain personality traits and cognitive abilities (Plomin et al., 2001). The mechanisms through which genes influence individual differences in depression as well as their potentially complex interactions with environmental factors still need to be identified.

Neurobiological Vulnerability   One mechanism by which genes influence behavior is through neurobiology. Psychobiological studies of depression in children generally have attempted to replicate results of studies with adults (Kaufman, Martin, King, & Charney, 2001). This research has focused on dysregulation in neuroendocrine and neurochemical systems (Ryan, 1998), disturbances in sleep architecture (Dahl & Ryan, 1996; Emslie, Weinberg, Kennard, & Kowatch, 1994), and functional and anatomical brain differences in depressed and high-risk children (Dawson, Klinger, Panagiotides, Hill, & Spieker, 1992; Field, Fox, Pickens, & Nawrocki, 1995).

Depressed children and adolescents as well as never-depressed youth with a high family loading of depressive disorders (i.e. high risk) show both neuroendocrine and neurochemical dysregulation (Birmaher et al., 1997; Ryan & Dahl, 1993). Abnormalities in the hypothalamic-pituitary-adrenal (HPA) axis, in particular, have been implicated in depressive disorder, particularly HPA axis response to stress (Dahl & Ryan, 1996). When pharmacologically challenged by artificial stimulation of the growth hormone system, currently depressed and high-risk children typically show blunted GH secretion compared to normal controls (Birmaher et al., 1997; Ryan et al., 1994) and low GH response following clinical remission (Dahl et al., 2000). In addition, depressed and high-risk children have neurochemical dysregulation, particularly in the serotonergic system, as demonstrated by a blunted cortisol response and an increased prolactin response after administration of L-5-hydroxytryptophan compared to normal controls (Birmaher et al., 1997; Ryan et al., 1992). Thus, GH system dysregulation and serotonergic system dysregulation may be vulnerability markers for depression and may run in families (Dinan, 1998).

Evidence also exists of functional and anatomical brain differences in currently depressed and high-risk children compared to normal controls. Resting frontal brain asymmetry has been linked with depression in adults and appears to persist into remission (Tomarken & Keener, 1998). Studies of brain asymmetry in children have found left frontal hypoactivation in the infant (Dawson et al., 1992; Field et al., 1995) and adolescent (Tomarken, Dichter, Garber, & Simien, 2004) offspring of depressed compared to nondepressed mothers. Davidson, Pizzagalli, Nitschke, and Putnam (2002) have proposed that such decreased left frontal activation reflects an under-activation of the approach system and reduced positive emotionality. The extent to which this brain asymmetry is a marker of vulnerability transmitted across generations, which predicts depression in youth is not yet known.

Thus, the neurobiological literature in children and adolescents is generally consistent with adult findings, although more variable due to maturational differences (Kaufman et al., 2001). Several potential biological vulnerability markers have been identified that not only differentiate currently depressed and non-depressed youth, but also have been found among never-depressed children with high familial loading of depression. Such cross-generational findings may begin to address the question of what is transmitted genetically. One behavioral manifestation of genetic/biological vulnerability is through temperament and personality.

Temperament and Personality

Temperament generally is defined as "the constitutionally based individual differences in emotional, motor and attentional reactivity and self-regulation" (Rothbart & Bates, 1998, p. 109), and a relatively stable and consistent behavioral, emotional, and/or cognitive pattern (Rothbart, Posner, & Hershey, 1995; Shiner, 1998). Similarly, the construct of personality refers to "individual differences in the tendency to behave, think, and feel in certain consistent ways" (Caspi, 1998, p. 312). Temperament is thought to emerge early in life and to have a genetic/biological basis (e.g. Eisenberg, Fabes, Guthrie, & Reiser, 2000), although experience, particularly within the social context, can affect its development and expression (Caspi, Henry, McGee, Moffitt, & Silva, 1995; Hartup & van Lieshout, 1995). The correlations between early temperamental characteristics and later adjustment have been found to be only modest, however (Rothbart & Bates, 1998), leading to the suggestion that these associations are likely moderated by environmental factors (e.g. Bates, Pettit, & Dodge, 1995).

Several researchers have suggested that a certain type of personality or temperament increases risk for developing major depression (e.g. Boyce, Parker, Bernett, Cooney, & Smith, 1991; Hirschfeld et al., 1989; Kendler, Neale, Kessler, Heath, & Eaves, 1993). For example, Kendler et al. (1993) reported a significant correlation between neuroticism and the liability to major depression, and suggested that this relation was due to genetic factors that influenced both. Traits that have been particularly linked with depression are negative and positive emotionality and to a lesser extent constraint and attentional control (Clark, Watson, & Mineka, 1994; Compas, Connor Smith, & Jaser, 2004; Derryberry & Rothbart, 1988). Negative emotionality (NE) reflects a sensitivity to negative stimuli, increased wariness, vigilance, physiological arousal, and emotional distress. Emotional distress can be divided further into fear and anger, with each having different action tendencies (Buss & Plomin, 1984; Rothbart & Bates, 1998). Other constructs related to NE include negative affectivity (Clark & Watson, 1991), neuroticism (Eysenck, 1952), the Behavioral Inhibition System (BIS) (Gray, 1987), stress reactivity (Boyce et al., 2001), "difficult temperament" (Thomas & Chess, 1977), behavioral inhibition (Kagan & Snidman, 1991), and harm avoidance (Cloninger, 1987).

Positive emotionality (PE) is characterized by sensitivity to reward cues, approach, energy, involvement, sociability, and adventurousness. PE is related to such constructs as positive affectivity (Clark & Watson, 1991), extraversion (Eysenck & Eysenck, 1985), the

Behavioral Activation System (BAS) (Gray, 1987), activity and approach (Thomas & Chess, 1977), and novelty seeking (Cloninger, 1987). According to the tripartite model (Clark & Watson, 1991; Watson & Clark, 1995), high levels of negative affectivity (NA) are associated with both depression and anxiety, whereas low levels of positive affectivity (PA) are uniquely related to depression, particularly anhedonia.

Significantly higher levels of neuroticism (N) are reported by individuals in an episode of MDD compared to when they are not depressed (Boyce et al., 1991; Kendler et al., 1993), whereas the levels of extraversion/positive emotionality (E/PE) tend to remain low even after recovery from an MDE (e.g. Hirschfeld, Klerman, Clayton, & Keller, 1983; Kendler et al., 1993). Some studies, however, have found that the level of N in remitted depressed patients is still higher than in nondepressed controls (Hirschfeld & Klerman, 1979; Reich, Noyes, Hirschfeld, Coryell, & O'Gorman, 1987), although others have not found such a difference (Kendler et al., 1993; Liebowitz, Stallone, Dunner, & Fieve, 1979). Taken together, these results indicate that in relation to depression, PE is a relatively stable trait, whereas N has both a state and trait component (Klein, Durbin, Shankman, & Santiago, 2002).

Longitudinal studies have shown that neuroticism predicts later negative affect and symptoms of emotional distress (Costa & McCrae, 1980; Levenson, Aldwin, Bosse, & Spiro, 1988) over and above initial symptom levels (Gershuny & Sher, 1998). Moreover, neuroticism is a significant risk for the onset, recurrence, and chronicity of MDD (Clark et al., 1994; Kendler et al., 1993; Kendler, Gardner, & Prescott, 2002; Wilhelm et al., 1999). In a large adult female twin sample, Kendler et al. (1993) showed that neuroticism predicted the onset of MDD over a 1-year period, and using a multi-factorial model, Kendler et al. (2002) reported that beyond stressful life events, neuroticism was the strongest predictor of the onset of major depression.

Studies of neurotic-like traits in children also have found evidence of a link with depression. Elevated levels of behavioral inhibition have been observed in laboratory tasks with young offspring of depressed parents (Kochanska, 1991; Rosenbaum et al., 2000). Caspi, Moffit, Newman, and Silva (1996) reported that children who had been rated as inhibited, socially reticent, and easily upset at age 3 had elevated rates of depressive disorders at age 21. Similarly, physicians' ratings of children's behavioral apathy at ages 6, 7, and 11 predicted adolescent mood disorders and chronic depression in middle adulthood (van Os, Jones, Lewis, Wadsworth, & Murray, 1997). A related trait of "difficult temperament", characterized by inflexibility, low positive mood, and withdrawal was found to correlate with depressive symptoms concurrently and prospectively in adolescents (Davies & Windle, 2001).

The relation between temperament and mood disorders may be moderated by gender and family environment. Gjerde (1995) found that chronic depression during adulthood was predicted by shy and withdrawn behavior in girls, and higher levels of under-controlled behaviors in boys at ages 3 and 4. In a study of families undergoing a divorce, Lengua, Wolchik, Sandler, and West (2000) showed that the relation between PE and depression in children was moderated by parental rejection such that low PE predicted higher levels of depressive symptoms among children with high levels of parental rejection, and high levels of impulsivity and depression were significantly associated among children receiving inconsistent parental discipline. Thus, some evidence exists of an association between NE and PE during childhood and subsequent depression, although this relation may vary as a function of other factors such as age, gender, context, and how the traits are measured.

In addition, temperament has been examined as a potential moderator of the relation between parenting and depression because the magnitude of the bivariate relation tends to be only mild or moderate (Gerlsma et al., 1990; Maccoby & Martin, 1983). Despite claims that children with different predispositions react differently to the same family environment (e.g. Barber, 1992; Collins, Maccoby, Steinberg, Hetherington, & Bornstein, 2000), few studies have actually investigated the moderating effects of temperament on the links between parenting and later adjustment (Rothbart & Bates, 1998), and most of the evidence of interactions between temperament and parenting has been found with regard to externalizing (e.g. Bates, Petti, Dodge, & Ridge, 1998; O'Connor & Dvorak, 2001) rather than internalizing problems. In general, child personality and parenting have tended to show primarily additive effects with regard to internalizing symptoms. Moderate bivariate relations have been found between parent behaviors (e.g. support, control, harshness) and depression, and between personality, particularly neuroticism, and depression (O'Connor & Dvorek, 2001). Likewise, children scoring low on traits such as extraversion and emotional stability (i.e. overcontrolled) exhibit higher levels of internalizing behaviors than resilient children (Van Leeuwen, Mervielde, Braet, & Bosmans, 2004).

One interaction that has been replicated with regard to internalizing symptoms is between overcontrolled personality and high negative parental control (Van Leeuwen et al., 2004). Highly ego resilient children with highly controlling parents (O'Connor & Dvorek, 2001), and overcontrollers with highly restrictive parents have higher levels of depressive symptoms than their counterparts with less restrictive parents (Dubas, Gerris, Janssens, & Vermulst, 2002). Of course, without prospective studies that control for prior levels of depression, it is possible that parental restrictiveness and control are a reaction to children's depression rather than depression being an outcome.

According to the goodness-of-fit-theory (Thomas & Chess, 1977), what is most important in determining child outcomes is the fit between the child's personality and parents' behaviors. When there is a mismatch, behavioral and emotional problems may develop. It also is possible that the interaction effect is not the result of restrictive parenting *per se*, but rather is due to individual characteristics of the parents that co-occur with restrictive control, such as parental depression or neuroticism. Such environmental influences (i.e. parenting) may partly reflect genetic effects through genotype-environment covariation (Lahey, Waldman, & McBurnett, 1999). Caspi (1998) suggested that interactions of child temperament and parenting may reflect "evocative person-environment transactions . . . On the basis of their unique personality characteristics, individuals act, and the environment reacts, resulting in mutually interlocking evocative transactions" (p. 357).

Thus, certain stable personality characteristics (e.g. neuroticism) can increase the likelihood of depression, although parents' behaviors certainly can affect children's outcomes. Parents sometimes are blamed for certain child outcomes, without also considering the contribution of the child's characteristics. The most probable model is that contextual factors (e.g. parent behaviors) combined either additively or interactively with certain child temperaments can either increase or decrease the likelihood children developing emotional and behavior problems.

Finally, potential mediators of the relation between personality and depression, particularly under condition of stress, have included appraisals, expectations, and coping (Beevers & Meyer, 2002; Compas, Connor-Smith, Saltzman, Thomsen, & Wadsworth, 2001; Lengua et al., 1999). Negative affectivity leads to greater emotional arousal, more difficulty modulating emotional reactivity to stress, and a greater likelihood of using avoidance coping (Compas et al., 2004). In contrast, high levels of the temperamental characteristic of attentional control can facilitate the use of secondary control coping strategies such as distraction and cognitive restructuring and thereby reduce the likelihood of depression, whereas poor attentional control has been found to be associated with higher levels of depressive symptoms (Thomsen et al., 2002).

Parenting has been found to be a mediator between temperament and depression. In a 9-year longitudinal study of 389 Finnish children, hostile maternal child rearing attitudes, measured at age 9, were found to mediate the relation between children's difficult temperament, reported by mothers when children were age 6, and adolescent-reported depressive symptoms at age 15 (Katainen, Räikkönen, Keskivaara, & Keltikangas-Järvinen, 1999). These tempermental difficulties may be sustained through dynamic social interchanges, sometimes referred to as evocative or reactive genotype-environment interactions (Scarr, 1992; Scarr & McCartney, 1983). That is, child characteristics and behaviors evoke reciprocal sustaining responses from others, which then potentially increase the likelihood of depression (Caspi, Bern, & Elder, 1994). Moreover, children's characteristics that evoke negative reactions from their mothers may themselves be under some genetic control, such that both child difficultness and maternal hostility may stem from the same genetic origin (Plomin, Reiss, Hetherington, & Howe, 1994).

In summary, the importance of temperament with regard to depression and the family is that (a) temperament is transmitted in part genetically, although experience also can affect its development; (b) children's temperament likely influences others' reactions to them, particularly parenting behaviors; and (c) temperament may moderate the effects of the family environment on children's outcomes. That is, temperament and parenting can both be viewed as "risk factors" (Kazdin, Kraemer, Kessler, Kupfer, & Offord, 1997) with influences that often are conditional upon each other.

The Family Environment and Depression

Various aspects of the family environment have been examined in relation to depression including parental psychopathology, particularly mood disorders, attachment, child-rearing practices, and communication and interaction patterns among family members. The present chapter reviews concurrent, predictive, and reciprocal relations between the family environment and depression. Potential mechanisms linking parenting and depression, and between parent and child depressions are discussed. Finally, implications for intervention are suggested.

Methodological Considerations   Much of the early literature was based on the recollections of adult depressed patients about their childhood (e.g. Gerlsma et al., 1990), but was limited by the problems of retrospective recall such as the influence of the current affective state of the reporter and a tendency to alter past characteristics to match present perceptions. Although retrospective recall can make some contribution (Brewin et al., 1993), convergent evidence from other methods strengthens the conclusions that can be drawn.

The field then advanced to studies comparing the current reports of depressed versus non-depressed children about their families (McCauley & Myers, 1992). Perceptions of the family environment may be as predictive of children's symptoms as are the actual behaviors of family members. Indeed, such perceptions may mediate the link between parenting and child depression (e.g. Jacquez, Cole, & Searle, 2004). Studies using self-report questionnaires also have the advantage of providing information about the proximal family environment across relatively long periods of time. Nevertheless, cross-sectional, self-report accounts are limited because they could be influenced by the reporter's mood state. That is, the extent to which children's responses on questionnaires accurately reflect their family environments rather than their negative response style cannot be determined from these studies. Indeed, depressed children have been found to misinterpret parental affect and discount supportive behavior (Downey & Walker, 1992; Sanders, Dadds, Johnston, & Cash 1992; Shirk, Van Horn, & Leber, 1997). Studies that controlled for current mood (e.g. Zemore & Rinholm, 1989) or compared current versus remitted depressed persons (e.g. Lewinsohn & Rosenbaum, 1987; Perris et al., 1986) have been used to reduce concerns about mood state dependence, although findings of such studies have been less consistent.

An important advance in this literature has been the increasing use of observational studies of behaviors of depressed and nondepressed individuals interacting with members of their family (e.g. Lovejoy et al., 2000; Sheeber et al., 2001). Such studies have provided rich insights into how depressed individuals' behavior affects their family members, and vice versa. This information might be especially useful for developing interventions. One limitation, however, is that observational studies typically have not disentangled the direction of the relation between the behaviors of each person in the interaction. Studies examining the sequential patterns of interactions (e.g. Sheeber, Hops, Andrews, Alpert, & Davis, 1998) have found evidence that parents' behaviors actually may reinforce and thereby perpetuate depressed adolescent's expressions of dysphoria. More studies using these kinds of analyses are needed.

Another limitation of observational studies concerns ecological validity; that is, how representative are laboratory interaction tasks of real interaction patterns? In addition, these lab studies present only a brief snapshot in time, and do not provide information about the developmental history and stability of the observed behaviors during periods when the depressed family member is not symptomatic. Finally, an increasing number of prospective studies have been examining the relation between prior family and parenting characteristics and subsequent depression, although some of these studies (e.g. Burge & Hammen, 1991) have failed to control for prior levels of depressive symptoms, making it impossible to draw conclusions about the temporal links between the variables of interest.

One other limitation in this literature has been the relatively few studies that have examined mechanisms. When associations are found between certain family characteristics and depression, what processes account for these relations? An increasing number of studies have attempted to address two important mediation questions: (a) Is the relation between parental and child depression mediated by parenting behaviors? (b) Is the relation between parenting behaviors and depression mediated by negative cognitions? Although several studies have used more sophisticated statistical techniques such as structural equation modeling to test these mediation questions, unfortunately many of these studies have been based on cross-sectional data, and have not tested the alternative, reverse direction model. Few, if any, studies have conducted an adequate longitudinal test of mediation across multiple time points controlling for all auto-correlations as recommended by Cole and Maxwell (2003). With these methodological concerns in mind, the remainder of this chapter reviews the literature on families and depression. Although individual studies might have different kinds of methodological flaws, it is still possible to summarize the general trends that have emerged.

Family Environment   Exposure to adverse family environments characterized by the absence of supportive and facilitative interactions and, elevated levels of conflict, critical, and/or angry interactions is associated with depression in children and adolescents. Evidence that depression is inversely related to level of family support, attachment, and approval has been found in community (e.g. Hops, Lewinsohn, Andrews, & Roberts, 1990; McFarlane, Bellissimo, Norman, & Lange, 1994), clinical (e.g. Armsden, McCauley, Greenberg, Burke, & Mitchell, 1990; Barrera & Garrison-Jones, 1992), and at-risk samples (Garber, Robinson, & Valentiner, 1997). Similarly, the association between depression and family conflict has been reported in clinical (Fendrich, Warner, & Weissman, 1990; Stark, Humphrey, Crook, & Lewis, 1990), community (Cole & McPherson, 1993; Hops et al., 1990), and at-risk (Garber & Little, 1999; Rueter, Scaramella, Wallace, & Conger, 1999) samples.

The family environment can be grouped into two broad dimensions of positive and negative relationships, which are comprised of dimensions of family adaptability, cohesion, emotional expressiveness, support, organization, control, and conflict. Adaptability reflects flexibility versus rigidity in response to challenge. Cohesion involves the emotional bonds that family members have toward each other and can range from enmeshment/over involvement to disengaged. Child-rearing behaviors also have been divided into two key dimensions of warmth/affection/praise versus hostility/rejection/criticism and control/intrusiveness versus autonomy granting (Darling & Steinberg, 1993; Gerlsma et al., 1990; Maccoby & Martin, 1983). Control has been further divided into psychological control (e.g. guilt-inducing versus autonomy granting), and behavioral control (monitoring, limit-setting, supervision) ranging from firm to lax (Barber, 1996; Schwarz, Barton-Henry, & Pruzinsky, 1985).

Measures often used to assess the family environment include the Family Environment Scale (FES) (Moos & Moos, 1981; Hammen et al., 1992), the Family Assessment Device (FAD) (Miller, Epstein, Bishop, & Keitner, 1985), and Family Adaptability and Cohesion Evaluation Scales (FACES) (Olsen, 1986). Commonly used measures of parenting include the Children's Report of Parent's Behavior Inventory (CRPBI) (Schaefer, 1965; Schludermann & Schludermann, 1970) and the Parent Bonding Inventory (PBI) (Parker, Tupling, & Brown, 1979). The FES is one of the most widely used family questionnaires and measures the degree to which family members support each other and are committed to the family (cohesion), the extent to which family members express their feelings openly (expressiveness), the degree to which autonomy and self-sufficiency is encouraged (independence), the amount of order versus chaos in the family (organization), rigidity of family rules (control), and conflict among family members.

Most studies using these various measures have been cross-sectional and correlational, group comparisons of currently depressed and non-depressed individuals, or retrospective reports of currently depressed adults about their childhood. Blatt and Homann (1992) summarized this literature by stating that "comparisons of depressed and nondepressed individuals in both nonclinical and clinical samples indicate that depressed individuals report more negative experiences with their parents" (p. 68). Depressed adults describe their parents as having been less positively involved, more controlling, intrusive, guilt inducing, critical, rejecting, inconsistently affectionate, and generally less supportive than do non-depressed controls (McCranie & Bass, 1984; Oliver & Berger, 1992; Parker, 1983; Whisman & Kwon, 1992). In their meta-analysis of studies of retrospective reports of perceived parenting style, Gerlsma et al. (1990) concluded that depressed adults generally recall their parents as having been less affectionate and more psychologically controlling, in particular.

Findings from studies of currently depressed children are consistent with these earlier retrospective studies. Parents of currently depressed children have been found to be often angry, critical, and emotionally neglectful (Poznanski & Zrull, 1970). Depressed children have described their parents as authoritarian and controlling (Amanat & Butler, 1984; Stark et al., 1990), and their families as being less cohesive and supportive and more autocratic than have non-psychiatric controls (Stark et al., 1990; Walker, Garber, & Greene, 1993). In addition, currently depressed children report more family conflict, a more negative affective family tone, and poorer relationships with their parents, who they characterize as rejecting, psychologically unavailable, and controlling (Burbach, Kashani, & Rosenberg, 1989; Stein et al., 2000). Studies of community youth with diagnosed depression also have reported disturbed family relationships prior to, during, and subsequent to major depressive episodes (Garrison et al., 1997; Lewinsohn et al., 1994; Reinherz, Paradis, Giaconia, Stashwick, & Fitzmaurice, 2003).

The parenting dimensions of rejection/criticism versus acceptance/warmth and control/intrusiveness versus autonomy granting have been specifically linked with depression and anxiety, respectively (Rapee, 1997). Rapee concluded that despite different methods and limitations, the literature on the relation between childrearing and depression indicates that perceived parental rejection is significantly associated with depressive symptoms. Although the relation is strongest when the same informant reports about both parenting and child symptoms, studies using other methods to assess parental rejection such as others' report and observation also have shown a significant link with depression. Mothers of depressed children describe themselves as more rejecting, less communicative, and less affectionate than do mothers of both normal and psychiatric controls (Lefkowitz & Tesiny, 1984; Puig-Antich et al., 1985a). Utilizing multiple reporters, Puig-Antich et al. (1993) found that depressed adolescents and their parents reported significantly poorer family relationships than did non-depressed controls. Relationships with their mothers and fathers were characterized by less communication, more tension, and more frequent corporal punishment. Interestingly, Puig-Antich et al. (1993) found an unusually high level of agreement between children and their parents about their relationship (r = 0.67 to 0.81), whereas other studies have found low concordance between depressed individuals' and their relatives' ratings of their families (e.g. Oliver, Handal, Finn, & Herdy, 1987; Stark et al., 1990). Studies that have combined multiple informants have shown that parental hostility, harsh discipline, and family conflict are associated with internalizing symptoms (Conger, Ge, Elder, Lorenz, & Simons, 1994; Ge, Conger, Lorenz, & Simons, 1994; Sheeber, Hops, Alpert, Davis, & Andrews, 1997).

As an alternative to questionnaires, some researchers have used the Five-Minute Speech Sample (FMSS) (Magana et al., 1986) to assess parental attitudes about their depressed child. Parents are asked to describe their child and their relationship for five, uninterrupted minutes. Their monologue then is coded for "expressed emotion", which is comprised of criticism and emotional over-involvement (Hooley, 1986). Using this method, Asarnow, Tompson, Hamilton, Goldstein, and Guthrie (1994), Asarnow, Tompson, Woo, and Cantwell (2001) have found that depressed children are more likely than normal controls to belong to families rated high on the criticism dimension of expressed emotion.

Finally, observations of child and parent behavior during laboratory interaction tasks also have found greater dysfunction in families of depressed children. Parents of depressed children display less positive, rewarding, and responsive behaviors than do parents in comparison families (Cole & Rehm, 1986; Messer & Gross, 1995). Cole and Rehm (1986) showed that parents of depressed children set comparable standards to parents of children without any psychiatric diagnoses but they were less positive and rewarding. In a community sample of adolescents, a latent construct of parental acceptance, composed of parent and adolescent reports and global observational ratings, was found to be inversely associated with internalizing symptoms (Fauber, Forehand, Thomas, & Wierson, 1990). In addition, mothers of depressed adolescents have been found to display less facilitative behavior during problem-solving discussions than do mothers of healthy adolescents (Sheeber & Sorensen, 1998).

In contrast, studies of observed conflictual behavior of parents during interactions with their depressed children have not yielded as compelling results. Observational studies in which elevations in family members' negative behaviors were associated with depression in youth (e.g. Kobak, Sudler, & Gamble, 1991; Messer & Gross, 1995) included both aggressive/angry behaviors and depressive/withdrawn behaviors as their index of "negativity". Moreover, observers in the Kobak et al. (1991) study rated the overall dyad, rather than the parent and adolescent separately. Thus it is not clear if parents' aggressive behaviors, in particular, or elevations in adolescents' depressive behaviors simply were associated with their depressive symptoms. Other studies have not found differences between depressed and normal controls in rates of parents' critical or aggressive behaviors (Hamilton, Asarnow, & Tompson 1999; Sheeber & Sorensen, 1998), or in rates of father-aversive behavior, and only limited differences in rates of mother-aversive behavior (Dadds, Sanders, Morrison, & Rebgetz, 1992; Sanders et al., 1992). Thus, the overall evidence from cross-sectional studies using self-rated perceptions, parents' and observers' ratings indicates that parents of depressed youth appear to be less positive and generally more negative than parents of non-depressed children.

Cross-sectional designs, however, do not allow us to determine the extent to which such adverse family relationships are antecedents, concomitants, or consequences of depressive symptoms. Are these family characteristics stable, and do they elicit depression in children and adolescents? Regarding the stability question, adolescents' negative perceptions of their family environment have been found to be a stable characteristic of those prone to higher levels of depressive symptoms (Hops et al., 1990). In clinical samples, mothers' perceptions of adverse family relations were found to continue after their children's depressive episodes had remitted (Puig-Antich et al., 1985b), and adult patients' perceptions of negative parenting were stable even 3 years past their depressive episode (Gotlib, Mount, Cordy, & Whiffen, 1988). Such reported stability, however, does not clarify whether formerly depressed individuals' perceptions about or their actual family environment remain stable even when they are no longer depressed, or whether they predict subsequent depression.

Is there prospective evidence that family factors temporally precede increases in depressive symptoms or disorders? Table 1 describes several longitudinal studies that have examined this question. Only studies that had at least two time points and controlled for prior levels of depressive symptoms were included here. The general conclusion is that perceptions of the family environment (Barber, 1996; Burt, Cohen, & Bjorck, 1988; Garrison, Jackson, Marsteller, McKeown, & Addy, 1990; Jacquez et al., 2004; McFarlane, Bellissimo, & Norman, 1995; McKeown et al., 1997; Miller, Warner, Wickramaratne, & Weissman, 1999; Reinherz et al., 2003; Rueter et al., 1999; Sheeber et al., 1997; Windle, 1992), parental expressed emotion (Asarnow, Goldstein, Tompson, & Guthrie 1993; Jacquez et al., 2004), and observed parental behaviors (Ge, Best, Conger, & Simons 1996; Sheeber et al., 1997) significantly predict increases in depressive symptoms, controlling for prior levels of symptoms, across times ranging from 2 weeks to 10 years. Two studies predicted diagnoses of depressive disorders from prior measures of family functioning. Rueter et al. (1999) found that escalating conflict between parents and adolescents predicted increases in adolescent internalizing symptoms, which in turn increased the risk of onset of an internalizing disorder (including mood and anxiety disorders). Reinherz et al. (2003) showed that low levels of family cohesion reported at age 15 doubled the odds of having a major depressive episode between ages 18 and 26.

Two studies (Garrison et al., 1990; McKeown et al., 1997) found that adolescents' reports of family adaptability and cohesion on the FACES II made significant prospective contributions to the prediction of adolescent depressive symptoms, controlling for prior symptom levels. Two other studies (Burt et al., 1988; Sheeber et al., 1997) used the FES to measure the family environment. Burt et al. (1988) found significant cross-sectional relations between the family environment and later adolescent depressive symptoms, but in only one instance was the longitudinal relation significant; girls' concurrent ratings of family expressiveness predicted depression after controlling prior depressive symptoms. Sheeber et al. (1997) combined the cohesion scale from the FES with adolescents' reports of maternal support and conflict behavior and observations of mother and child interactions to create maternal support and conflict composites. Using these multi-method assessments to build structural equation models, Sheeber et al. (1997) showed that lower family support and greater conflict predicted adolescent depression at a 1-year follow-up, controlling for Time 1 depression.

Also using observational data, Ge et al. (1996) examined the relation of parenting to adolescent internalizing (depression and anxiety) symptoms. Observations of family discussions yielded three dimensions of parenting behavior: warmth, hostility, and disciplinary skill. Parental warmth predicted lower levels and maternal hostility predicted higher

Table 1: Prospective studies predicting change in depressive symptoms and/or a depressive episode.

Authors/ year	Sample	Age @ T1	N	Assessments/ Interval	Predictors	Outcome measures	Results	Predict Sx change	Predict disorder
Asarnow et al. (1993)	Clinical (inpatient MDD or DD)	7–14 years	26	2 assessments/ 1–5 years apart	Maternal expressed emotion (FMSS-EE); diagnoses (K-SADS-E)	K-SADS-E (dx during 1st year after discharge)	Low maternal EE predicted recovery not accounted for by treatment.	Y	N
Barber (1996)	Comm.	Grades 5 & 8	774	2 assessments/ 1 year apart	Child report of parent psychological and behavioral. control (PCS-YSR); Dep. sxs. (CDI)	CDI	Parent psychological but not behavioral control at T2 predicted dep. sxs at T2, controlling T1 dep. sxs	Y	N
Burt et al. (1988)	Comm.	Grades 7 & 8	302	2 assessments/ 5 months apart	Child-report of family cohesion, control, expressiveness, in-dependence, organization, (FES); Dep. sxs (CDI)	CDI	T2 family expressiveness predicted girls' T2 dep. sxs, controlling T1 dep. sxs	Y (limited)	N
Garrison et al. (1990)	Comm.	Grade 7	550	3 assessments/ 1 year apart	Self-report family adaptability	CES-D	Family adaptability at T1 predicted	Y	N

Study	Sample	Age/Grade	N	Design	Measures	Dep. measure	Findings		
					and cohesion (FACES-II); Dep. sxs. (CES-D)		T3 dep. sxs., controlling T1 dep. sxs.		N
Ge et al. (1996)	Comm.	Grade 7; 12–14 years	388	2 assessments/ 4 years apart	Observed parental warmth, hostility, discipline, Dep sxs (SCL–90)	CES-D; TRF; NEO-PI	Lower parental warmth and higher maternal hostility predicted increases in dep sxs	Y	N
Jacquez et al. (2004)	Comm.	14–18 years	72	2 assessments/ 2–8 weeks apart	Maternal criticism (FMSS-EE; FEICS; DOCS Dep. Sxs (CDI; IDS)	CDI, IDS	Maternal criticism predicted T2 dep sxs, controlling T1 dep sxs	Y	N
McFarlane et al. (1995)	Comm. at risk for academic failure	Grade 10	682	2 assessments/ 6 months apart	Self-report social support — family (SSQ); self-report symptom count and diagnoses (IDD)	IDD	T2 family support predicted T2 dep. sxs. & diagnoses, controlling T1 dep.	Y	N
McKeown et al. (1997)	Comm.	Grades 7 & 8	1939	2 assessments/ 1 year apart	Family cohesion (FACES-II); Dep. sxs. (CES-D)	CES-D	T1 family cohesion predicted T2 dep. sxs., controlling T1 dep. sxs	Y	N

Table 1: Continued.

Authors/ year	Sample	Age @ T1	N	Assessments/ Interval	Predictors	Outcome measures	Results	Predict Sx change	Predict disorder
Miller et al. (1999)	High-risk offspring of dep. mothers	7–26 years	137	2 assessments/ 10 years later	Parental Bonding Inventory (PBI); Self-esteem (CSEI); K-SADS diagnoses	K-SADS diagnoses	Among female offspring of depressed mothers, T1 maternal affectionless-control was associated with T1 low self-esteem which predicted MDD 10 yrs later	N	N
Reinherz et al. (2003)	Comm.	15 years	354	3 assessments/ 3–9 years later	Hx of family violence, abuse; cohesion (FACES)	DIS	Those exposed to family violence before age 15 were 4 X more likely to have MDD between 18 & 26. Those scoring 1 SD above the mean on Cohesion were 2 X as likely to have MDD	N	Y
Rueter et al. (1999)	Comm.	12–13 years	303	5 assessments/ 7 years later	Parent–child conflict measured with the Issues	CIDI (Dep dxs)	Conflict & int sxs predicted onset of Dep or Anx	Y	Y

Study	Sample	Age	N	Design	Measures	Dep measure	Findings	Mediated
					Checklist (IC); Dep sxs (SCL-90)		Int sxs mediated the relation bt disagreements and disorder	N
Sheeber et al. (1997)	Comm.	14–20 years	242	2 assessments/ 1 year apart	Family support, conflict, cohesion (FES); Child report of maternal support (PARI, CBQ, conflict (IC), Parent-child interaction coded w/ LIFE for support & conflict (PSI); Dep. sxs composite created from CES-D, BDI, 4 suicide items	Dep. sxs composite (CES-D, BDI, 4 suicide items)	Greater family support at T1 predicted fewer dep. sxs; at T2, controlling T1 dep. sxs; Greater family conflict at T1 predicted greater dep. sxs at T2, controlling T1 dep. sxs	Y
Windle (1992)	Comm.	Grades 10 and 11	277	2 assessments/ 6 months apart	Perceived Family Support (PSS-Fam) Dep. sxs (CES-D)	CES-D	For girls, lower perceived family support predicted T2 dep sxs, controlling T1 dep sxs	Y

Note: **Notation key:** anx = anxiety; bt = between; comm. = community; DD = Dysthymic Disorder; dep. = depression; dx = diagnosis; grp = group; hx = history; int = internalizing; MDD = Major Depressive Disorder; MDE = Major Depressive Episode; pts = points; rel. = relationship; sxs = symptoms; T = time. **Measures key:** BDI = Beck Depression Inventory; CBQ = Conflict Behavior Questionnaire; CDI = Child Depression Inventory; CES-D = Center for Epidemiological Studies-Depression Scale; CIDI = Composite International Diagnostic Interview; DIS = Diagnostic Interview Schedule; DOCS = Domains of Criticism Scale; FACES-II = Family Adaptability and Cohesion Evaluation Scales; FEICS = Family Emotional Involvement and Criticism Scale; FES = Family Environment Scale; FMSS-EE = Five-Minute Speech Sample – Expressed Emotion; IC = Issues Checklist; IDS = Interview of Depressive Symptoms; K-SADS = Schedule for Affective Disorders & Schizophrenia for School-Age Children; K-SADS-E = K-SADS Epidemiological version; LIFE = Living in Familial Environments; PARI = Parent Attitude Research Instrument; PCS-YSR = Psychological Control Scale – Youth Self-Report; PRS = Parent Rating Scale; PSS-Fam = Perceived Social Support from Family; SCL–90-R = Symptom Checklist–90-R; SSQ = Social Support Questionnaire.

levels of internalizing symptoms in adolescents, controlling for prior adolescent internalizing symptoms. Finally, high levels of maternal criticism have been associated with relapse of depression in children and adolescents (Asarnow et al., 1993).

In sum, a concurrent relation between family factors and depression in youth has been well established. Evidence from longitudinal studies has been more mixed. Although controlling for earlier depression, two prospective studies reported results from family measures concurrent with the outcome (Barber, 1996; Burt et al., 1988), one study found that adolescent depression also predicted later ratings of parental behavior (Barber, 1996), and one study reported a single significant finding for girls (Burt et al., 1988). In addition, a few studies have reported only cross-sectional analyses despite having longitudinal data available (Ohannessian, Lerner, Lerner, & von Eye, 1994; Papini & Roggman, 1992), and others have reported null findings (Burge & Hammen, 1991; Burge et al., 1997). Burge and Hammen (1991) showed that maternal communication style predicted depressive symptoms 6 months later but not when controlling for prior child symptom levels. They commented that maternal communication may function to maintain children's symptoms and that "investigations of temporal precedence of the mother's affect on children's outcomes would need to be done from birth" (p. 179). Parental hostility and parent–child conflict have been prospectively linked to internalizing symptoms (Ge et al., 1996) and the onset of internalizing disorders (Rueter et al., 1999), although these studies focused on internalizing symptoms and disorders rather than depression in particular.

Despite these largely consistent findings, conclusions regarding the etiological significance of the family climate must be considered tentative at this point. This is because of the relatively limited number of prospective investigations, and even within such studies, few researchers have directly tested the possibility that negative family relationships may develop consequent to depressive symptoms. More longitudinal studies are needed to further address questions about the causal relations between the family environment and subsequent depression. How strong is this relation, and over what period of time? What aspects of the family environment and parenting are particularly likely to predict depression in children and adolescents? Does the absence of positive or the presence of negative parenting or both predict depression? What is the relation between perceptions about parents and their actual behaviors, and what is the relative strength of each to depression? Do family characteristics predict the onset of depressive disorders as well as increases in depressive symptoms? What is the specificity of these family characteristics to depression, *per se*? In addition to naturalistic, prospective studies, some of these questions can be best addressed in the context of intervention studies designed to prevent the onset of depression. Because it is not possible to randomly assign children to different families or different parenting styles, we must rely on studies that attempt to alter family patterns and then observe their effects on children's outcomes.

Family Effects on the Course of Depression   Although different factors likely influence the onset, persistence, and recurrence of depressive disorders in youth, it also is possible that some of the same familial processes that contribute to onset will affect its course and maintenance. Aspects of the parent–child relationship, such as maternal discipline, quality of the relationship with the father, levels of emotional expressiveness of parents toward their children (Asarnow et al., 1993; Sanford et al., 1995), and the overall quality of the family environment (Goodyer, Germany, Gowrusankur, & Altham, 1991; McCauley et al., 1993) have been found to predict the course of depressive episodes in clinically depressed children. McCauley et al. (1993) showed that higher levels of family stress were associated with a longer initial episode and lower social competence 3 years later. Persistence also has been found to be associated with being less involved with fathers, and less responsive to mother's discipline compared with those who remit (Sanford et al., 1995). High expressed emotion (EE) (i.e. criticism, emotional over involvement) in families of depressed children is associated with a more insidious onset of MDD (Asarnow, Ben-Meir, & Goldstein, 1987) and significantly lower recovery rates at the end of the first year after hospitalization compared to children from low EE homes (Asarnow et al., 1993). In a longitudinal community study of preadolescents, Cohen, Brook, Cohen, Velez, and Garcia (1990) reported that power-assertive punishment and inconsistent parenting predicted persistence of depressive symptoms. On a more positive side, Goodyer, Germany, Gowrusankur, and Altham (1991), in a 1-year follow-up study of depressed children aged 7–17 years, found that remission was predicted by improvements in the maternal confiding relationship. Thus increasing positive interactions as well as reducing or eliminating negative parenting may help to produce a better outcome.

The more disturbed course for some depressed children may be because the adverse family relationships persist or even worsen during and after the child's depressive episode has remitted (Lewinsohn et al., 1994; Puig-Antich et al., 1985b; Shiner & Marmorstein, 1998). The child's own behaviors also may contribute to the continuation or exacerbation of a problematic family environment and therefore should be a focus of any intervention aimed at enhancing the parent–child relationship. Programs that educate both the adolescent and parent about depressive disorders, combined with specific strategies to foster positive parent-adolescent emotional involvement, improved discipline practices, and decreased conflict could shorten the length of the episode as well as decrease the likelihood of recurrence. Parents and children need to learn more positive ways of interacting that can become a stable part of their repertoire across time.

Do Negative Cognitions Mediate the Relation between Dysfunctional Parenting and Depression?

If dysfunctional parenting and depression are significantly related, what accounts for this? That is, what are the mechanisms by which problematic parenting leads to depression? Interventions aimed at more proximal mediators might be as important as changing the parenting behaviors that cause them.

Several theories, including attachment (Ainsworth, 1979; Bowlby, 1980), object relations (Baldwin, 1992; Westin, 1991), cognitive (Beck, 1967; Ingram, Miranda, & Segal, 1998), and cognitive-interpersonal (e.g. Gotlib & Hammen, 1992; Haines, Metalsky, Cardamone, & Joiner, 1999), have suggested that harsh, critical, punitive, rejecting, and/or neglectful parenting will lead to the development of depressive "working models" or "cognitive schema" about the self and others. Bowlby asserted that early insecure attachments contribute to children's developing inferences about their acceptability and "lovableness". The nature and quality of children's experiences with attachment figures are internalized into cognitive working models, which are later used to appraise new situations and guide behavior. Cognitive models of depression similarly assert that an important consequence of early adverse life experiences is the formulation of negative cognitive schema (Abramson, Metalsky, & Alloy, 1989; Beck, 1967; Ingram et al., 1998). Thus, consensus across these theories is that early adverse experiences and insecure attachments to primary caregivers can create psychological vulnerability in the form of negative self-schema and mistrust of others, which then increase risk of developing depression (Beck, 1987; Blatt & Homann, 1992; Segal, 1988).

Parent socialization styles characterized by warmth, autonomy granting, and contingency communicate to children a sense of mastery and control (Carton & Nowicki, 1994; Grolnick & Ryan, 1989; Skinner, Zimmer-Gembeck, & Connell, 1998). In contrast, parenting behaviors such as rejection, low caring and warmth, and negative control, also referred to as "affectionless control" (Parker, 1983), may be key to the development of negative views of the self and a sense of noncontingency in the world leading to subsequent depression (Garber & Flynn, 1998; Ingram et al., 1998; Rose & Abramson, 1992). Maternal criticism and rejection are particularly likely to foster a negative self-image in children, which in turn will increase their risk for depression (Garber et al., 1997; Goodman, Adamson, Riniti, & Cole, 1994). Indeed, significant associations have been found between low parental acceptance/warmth and high parental control and the children's negative cognitive styles (e.g. Randolph & Dykman, 1998; Rudolph, Kurlakowsky, & Conley, 2001; Stark, Schmidt, & Joiner 1996; Whisman & Kwon, 1992; Whisman & McGarvey, 1995), and between poor parenting or abuse and excessive self-blame or -criticism (Brewin, Firth-Cozens, Furnham, & McManus, 1992; Gibb, 2002). In an early prospective study, Koestner, Zuroff, and Powers (1991) found that parental rejection and restrictive control assessed during childhood predicted subsequent self-criticism during adolescence.

A special section of *Cognitive Therapy and Research* in 2001 was devoted to longitudinal studies specifically designed to examine the link between parenting and children's negative cognitions. Garber and Flynn (2001) showed that low maternal acceptance predicted children's subsequent low self-worth, and high maternal psychological control predicted children's depressive attributional style, even after controlling for maternal depression history. Rudolph et al. (2001) reported that higher levels of perceived parental rejection predicted lower self-perceptions of control in adolescents as well as teachers' ratings of adolescents' helpless behavior. Interestingly, Alloy et al. (2001) found an association between low perceived emotional warmth from fathers, but not mothers, and college students' negative cognitive styles. In a companion study of the same sample, Gibb et al. (2001) reported an association, even when controlling for current depressive symptoms, between cognitive vulnerability status and childhood experiences of emotional maltreatment including humiliation, rejection, and teasing. These investigators (Alloy et al., 2001; Gibb et al., 2001) suggested a potential continuum of emotional rejection, ranging from mild negative parenting practices and feedback to more severe emotional abuse as possible precursors to the development of the cognitive vulnerability to depression and to depression itself. Thus, both cross-sectional and longitudinal studies consistently demonstrate that low parental acceptance and high parental control are associated with negative cognitions in offspring.

There also is a growing body of evidence showing a significant relation between negative cognitive style and depression, particularly in the context of stress (for reviews, see Abramson et al., 2002; Joiner & Wagner, 1995; Kaslow, Adamson, & Collins, 2000).

Prospective studies of children and adolescents have shown that global self-worth (Allgood-Merton, Lewinsohn, & Hops, 1990; Vitaro, Pelletier, Gagnon, & Baron, 1995), negative attributions (Hankin, Abramson, & Siler, 2001; Hilsman & Garber, 1995; Lewinsohn, Joiner, & Rohde, 2001; Nolen-Hoeksema, Girgus, & Seligman, 1992; Panak & Garber, 1992; Robinson, Garber, & Hilsman, 1995), inferential style (Abela, 2001), and perceived self-competence in specific domains (Hoffman, Cole, Martin, Tram, & Seroczynski, 2000; Vitaro et al., 1995) significantly predict increases in depressive symptoms (e.g. Allgood-Merton et al., 1990; Vitaro et al., 1995) and diagnoses (e.g. Hammen, 1988), controlling for prior levels of depression, and often in interaction with negative life events. Other studies, however, have not found these cognitions to predict depressive symptoms (Bennett & Bates, 1995; DuBois, Felner, Brand, & George, 1999; Robertson & Simons, 1989) or onset of new episodes (Goodyer, Herbert, Tamplin, & Altham, 2000). Possible reasons for these failures have included small samples, not testing cognitions in the context of stress, not priming negative cognitions with mood or stress inductions, and the use of samples that were receiving treatment.

Overall, then, support exists for components of the mediation model as outlined by Baron and Kenny (1986). That is, the predictor A (dysfunctional parenting) predicts the outcome C (depression); A also predicts the mediator B (negative cognitions); and negative cognitions predict depression. Is there evidence that the inclusion of the mediator significantly reduces the relation between A and C, thereby supporting the mediation model? Both cross-sectional (Carnelley, Pietromonaco, & Jaffe, 1994, Garber et al., 1997; McGinn, Cukor, & Sanderson, 2005; Muris, Schmidt, Lambrichs, & Meesters, 2001), and prospective (e.g. Alloy et al., 2001; Hankin, Kassel, & Abela, 2005; Jacquez et al., 2004; Roberts, Gotlib, & Kassel, 1996) studies have found that negative cognitions (i.e. low self-worth, dysfunctional attitudes, self-efficacy) partially mediate the relation between dysfunctional parenting (i.e. insecure attachment, rejection, neglect) and depressive symptoms. For example, Jacquez et al. (2004) found that adolescents' self-perceived competence mediated the relation between negative maternal feedback and adolescent depressive symptoms, even after controlling for prior levels of depression. In a study of college students, Hankin et al. (2005) showed that insecure attachment consistently predicted prospective increases in depressive symptoms across three studies. Moreover, this relation was mediated by both dysfunctional attitudes and low self-esteem. In particular, avoidant and anxious attachment dimensions were associated with higher levels of dysfunctional attitudes; greater dysfunctional attitudes, in turn, were associated with lower self-esteem, which in turn predicted increases in depressive symptoms 8 weeks later. These findings are consistent with Bowlby's (1980) suggestion that insecurely attached individuals develop negative internal working models about the self and others based on interactions with important individuals, and such cognitive models subsequently confer vulnerability to depression. Interestingly, the cognitive risk factors pathway in Hankin et al. (2005) only mediated the relations between insecure attachment and increases in depressive but not anxious symptoms, thus showing some specificity to the model.

Muris, Meesters, Schouten, and Hoge (2004) also found a different pattern of relations among parenting, cognitions, and depression versus anxiety. In a community sample of 11–14-year olds, Muris et al. (2004) showed that negative parental rearing practices were associated with higher levels of both depression and anxiety, which at the same time were related to lower levels of perceived control. They found no evidence, however, of mediational effects of perceived control on the link between perceived parenting and either depression or anxiety, but there was evidence that perceived control moderated the relation between anxious parenting and child anxiety symptoms.

Thus, the relation between some forms of dysfunctional parenting and depression appears to be at least in part mediated through the cognitive schema children develop about themselves, their world, and others. Future studies in this area need to address more specific questions regarding differential effects of fathers versus mothers, are particular kinds of parenting associated with particular kinds of cognitions or does a more general pattern of "bad" parenting lead to negative cognitions. Is there a "global parenting style" that creates an overall emotional climate that guides parents' behaviors? Identifying how particular dimensions of parenting are linked with specific child outcomes may be difficult. Finally, what factors moderate the effects of poor parenting on the development of negative cognitions and subsequent depression (e.g. other supportive adults, age, gender, temperament), and what are the implications of these findings for intervention? Should prevention programs aim to improve parenting, cognitive restructuring, or both?

Effects of Depression on the Family

Relatively few studies have specifically examined the effects of children's depression on their family environment (path g in Fig. 1), and much of the available information comes from cross-sectional studies. Longitudinal studies generally have focused more on how the family affects children's depression, rather than the reverse. The relevant question is not what is the direction of the relation between families and depression, but rather how does the family contribute to depression, and then how does depression impact the family?

Depressed youth have deficits in social behaviors that interfere with their developing and maintaining satisfying interpersonal relationships (e.g. Bell-Dolan, Reaven, & Peterson, 1993; Rubin & Mills, 1988); such problem behaviors can affect relationships in the family as well. For example, in a community sample of adolescent girls, Slavin and Rainer (1990) found that depressive symptoms predicted decrements in family support. Barber (1996) showed that not only do children's reports of their parents' psychologically controlling behavior predict increases in children's depressive symptoms, but children's prior symptoms also predicted their ratings of their parents' subsequent behaviors. In contrast, two other longitudinal studies (Sheeber et al., 1997; Stice, Ragan, & Randall, 2004) did not find that children's depression predicted decreases in perceived family support over time. The failure to find an effect could have been due to stability in family support, or the timing of measurement of symptoms and support, given that other studies (Barber, 1996; Sim, 2000; Zimmerman, Ramirez-Valles, Zapert, & Maton, 2000) have shown depression to be linked to lower levels of perceived parental support.

Observational studies have been particularly informative about parent–child relationships in families of depressed youth. During family interaction tasks, depressed children have been rated as showing more negative and guilt-inducing behavior compared to non-depressed psychiatric and control participants (Hamilton et al., 1999). Consistent with Coyne's (Coyne, 1976; Coyne, Burchill, & Stiles, 1991) interpersonal cycle model, observational studies also have shown that depressed youth elicit distress reactions from their mothers (Sheeber et al.,

1998) as well as from unfamiliar adults (Mullins, Peterson, Wonderlich, & Reaven, 1986). Sheeber et al. (1998) found that parents of depressed adolescents responded positively to their adolescent's depressive behaviors such as whining, sadness, anxiety, and self-critical statements, whereas parents of non-depressed adolescents responded less positively to such statements in their children. When depressed adolescents displayed depressive behaviors, their mothers were more likely to try to solve their problems or reassure them that things would be okay compared to mothers of non-depressed adolescents. Fathers also were less likely to respond with anger and aggression to depressive behavior in their depressed children. Thus, parents react differently to their adolescent's expressions of depressive symptoms, depending on its frequency and intensity. Such parent responses to children's depressive symptoms may inadvertently serve to reinforce and sustain them.

In another observational study, parents of depressed children also were found to make *fewer* negative comments in response to their children's depressive statements than did parents of non-depressed children (Slesnick & Waldron, 1997). In this study, depressed children made more depressed statements, but did not differ from non-depressed children in their hostile statements and depressive behavior. These observational studies indicate that depressed youth may be differentially reinforced for their expressions of depressive behaviors, and this might be one mechanism by which such behaviors are maintained.

Long-term effects of depression on social functioning also have been found. For example, individuals who experience high levels of depressed mood in adolescence have difficulties in maintaining intimate relationships with their spouses in young adulthood, thereby repeating their experiences of distance from their parents in adolescence (Kandel & Davies, 1986). Thus, it seems that depression during childhood and adolescence can alter how others respond to them immediately and across time. Several important questions remain. What direct and indirect causal mechanisms influence the relation between the family environment and depression in youth, and how do these change with development? What other yet unmeasured variables affect this association? How do we best demonstrate the reciprocal and transactional nature of parent–child relationships in association with depression?

Mutual Influences

Parents and children mutually influence each other; their relationship is dynamic, transactional, and reciprocal. Children's temperament and related affect and behaviors can impact their parents' attitudes and responses to them, which in turn can affect children's subsequent emotional and behavioral development (e.g. Katainen et al., 1999). Such evocative person–environment correlations can sustain and exacerbate difficulties in the parent–child relationship (Caspi et al., 1994). These exchanges are even more complicated when personality characteristics (e.g. neuroticism) shared by parents and children yield a particularly poor "fit" (Thomas & Chess, 1977).

Mutual influences between parental depression and child functioning are particularly noteworthy. Parental depression may have dysfunctional effects on the quality of the mother–child relationship, elicit various forms of child maladjustment, and over time, such child behaviors in turn likely provoke and maintain negative maternal attitudes and behaviors toward the child (e.g. Cummings & Davies, 1994; Goodman & Gotlib, 1999; Kaslow et al., 1994). Child maladjustment can influence maternal functioning and increase the risk of or exacerbate her depression. Mothers of clinically disturbed children have been found to have higher rates of depression (e.g. Civic & Holt, 2000; Elgar, Waschbusch, McGrath, Stewart, & Curtis, 2004b; Harrison & Sofronoff, 2002; Pelham et al., 1997). For example, Harrison and Sofronoff (2002) found that child hyperactivity accounted for 21% of the variance in maternal depression. In a study examining daily-reported maternal mood and child disruptive behaviors in 30 mother–child dyads over 8 weeks, Elgar et al. (2004b) used pooled time series analyses and found that temporal relations between maternal and child outcomes changed according to the type of maternal mood and child behavior being studied. Controlling for cross-sectional relations, prior child inattentive/impulsive/overactive (IO) was related to maternal anger and fatigue, and previous child oppositional/defiant behavior (OD) was related to maternal confusion. In contrast, maternal depression, low energy, anger, and anxiety each predicted subsequent child IO, and maternal confusion and anxiety each predicted subsequent child OD.

Observational studies also have nicely demonstrated the mutual effects children's depressive behaviors have on their parents' responses to them and how such responses then serve to reinforce and maintain children's depressive symptoms (e.g. Sheeber et al., 1998). A few longitudinal studies have attempted to disentangle temporal relations between maternal and child functioning. In a study assessing maternal depression and child behavior problems on two occasions separated by a year, Forehand and McCombs (1988) found stronger relations between Time 1 maternal depression and Time 2 child problems than the reverse. Elgar et al. (2004a) noted, however, that these results are difficult to interpret because there were just two assessments and the test-retest reliability of their measures was discrepant.

Elgar, Curtis, McGrath, Waschbusch, and Stewart (2003) conducted a 4-year cross-lagged panel study of maternal depression and child problems (i.e. hyperactivity, aggression, emotional problems). They found that whereas maternal depressive symptoms tended to coincide with or precede child emotional problems, they tended to change as a consequence of child aggression and hyperactivity. Also using a cross-lagged effect model, with three waves of panel data Ge, Conger, Lorenz, Shanahan, and Elder (1995) examined mutual influences in parent and adolescent psychological distress reported independently by dyads of mothers–sons, mothers–daughters, fathers–sons, and fathers–daughters. Controlling for earlier emotional status, parent and adolescent distress were reciprocally related across time, although these mutual influences were moderated by gender. The strongest cross-lagged associations occurred between mothers and sons and between fathers and daughters at different points in development. Sons' and mothers' symptoms of distress were most strongly associated during early adolescence, whereas daughters and fathers showed a similar pattern during mid-adolescence. Thus, both short- and long-term mutual influences appear to operate on parental and child functioning, although the nature of these temporal relations depends on the type of child behavior and dimension of parental mood. The significant cross-lagged associations across time found between parent and adolescent distress are consistent with the general notion of bidirectional influences in individual development (Bell & Chapman, 1986) as well as more specific models of depression that emphasize interpersonal vicious cycles (e.g. Coyne, 1976; Gotlib & Hammen, 1992).

Family Environment as a Stressor

In addition to parenting behaviors and the overall emotional climate in the family, other aspects of the family environment can be a stressor that increases the likelihood of depression. Some sources of family stress that have been especially linked with the development of depression include parental psychopathology, particularly depression as well as other disorders such as substance abuse and anti-social personality disorder (Beardslee et al., 1998; Goodman & Gotlib, 1999), parental loss (e.g. Crook & Eliot, 1980; Tennant, Bebbington, & Hurry, 1980) marital discord, separation and divorce (e.g. Grych & Fincham, 1993; Kim, Capaldi, & Stoolmiller, 2003; See Chapter 4 in this Volume), family violence, abuse, neglect (e.g. Kilpatrick et al., 2003), and economic hardship, social adversity, and poverty (e.g. Boyle & Pickles, 1997; Fergusson, Horwood, & Lynskey, 1995). Moreover, these stressors are not independent. For example, marital problems can be both an antecedent and a consequence of parental psychopathology (e.g. Davies, Dumenci, & Windle, 1999; Downey & Coyne, 1990); divorce and accompanying economic strain then often follow. Children facing multiple stressors are especially likely to be at risk. For example, in a study of inner city, low-income African-American families, high rates of both neglect and conflict were found, and both were associated with depression in those children (Sagrestano, Paikoff, Holmbeck, & Fendrich, 2003).

Family discord, which is prominent in families with a depressed parent (Hops et al., 1987), exposes children to stressful conditions and to poor models for handling interpersonal conflict (Hammen, Brennan, & Shih, 2004; See Chapter 4 in this Volume). Marital discord also may compromise children's sense of mastery by exposing them to stressful interpersonal circumstances over which they have little control, yet still feel responsible (Grych & Fincham, 1993; Haines et al., 1999). This then undermines children's sense of social competence and expectations of the world as being contingent and responsive, and contributes to difficulties in coping with stressful situations that trigger depression (Rudolph et al., 2001).

Early parental loss through death, separation, or abandonment has been linked with later depression, although reviews of this literature indicate that studies of this relation have yielded inconsistent results (e.g. Crook & Eliot, 1980; Tennant, Bebbington, & Hurry, 1980). One factor hypothesized to moderate this relation is the quality of care received by the child following the loss of a parent (Bowlby, 1980). Indeed, studies have shown that an increased likelihood of depression occurred not by early maternal loss *per se*, but by the inadequate care that frequently followed the loss (Bifulco, Brown, & Harris, 1987; Harris, Brown, & Bifulco, 1986).

Poverty has been linked with an early onset of depression. Epidemiological (e.g. Robins, Locke, & Regier, 1991) and longitudinal studies (Johnson, Cohen, Dohrenwend, Link, & Brook, 1999; Gilman, Kawachi, Fitzmaurice, & Buka, 2002) have shown a relation between lower family socioeconomic status (SES) and depression, and this vulnerability is particularly strong for single mothers living in poverty (Bruce, Takeuchi, & Leaf, 1991). Possible mediators between SES disadvantage and depression include lack of access to adequate health care and educational opportunities, fewer social resources, and greater exposure to violence. Indeed, children living in lower SES conditions are most likely to witness violence and to be the victims of abuse (Buka, Stichick, Birdthistle, &

Earls, 2001). Reviews of the literature on the consequences of poverty, particularly with regard to depression (Aber, Bennett, Conley, & Li, 1997; Leventhal & Brooks-Gunn, 2000; Turner & Lloyd, 1999) have highlighted the need to address the large public health risk factors that increase the likelihood of adolescent depression, particularly exposure to violence.

Individuals who experience physical and/or sexual abuse have high rates of depression during both childhood and adulthood (Boudewyn & Liem,1995; Kaufman, 1991; Silverman, Reinherz, & Giaconia, 1996; Toth, Manly, & Cicchetti, 1992). For example, in a longitudinal study of a representative community sample of 375 participants, Silverman et al. (1996) showed that individuals who had been abused prior to age 18, by age 21 had significant impairment in functioning and higher rates of depressive and anxious symptoms, psychiatric diagnoses, and suicidality than their non-abused peers. In addition, biological correlates of depression, such as HPA axis dysregulation, have been increasingly correlated with histories of childhood abuse (e.g. Heim et al., 2000). Neurobiological and neuroendocrine studies of depressed women have shown that violence-related trauma experienced during childhood has profound and lasting effects on brain structure and function (Heim, Newport, Bonsall, Miller, & Nemeroff, 2001). Thus, multiple aspects of the family environment in addition to parenting behaviors increase stress and subsequent mood disorders during both childhood and adulthood.

Offspring of Depressed Parents

Depression in parents has been particularly associated with problems in the family environment and children's maladjustment (e.g. Beardslee et al., 1998; Elgar et al., 2004a; Goodman & Gotlib, 1999, 2002). Many of the same basic processes described earlier regarding family influences on the development of depression are relevant to explaining the transmission of psychopathology from depressed parents to their offspring. These include: (a) depressed parents and their children share common genes, which result in similar biological sensitivity and reactivity to stress; (b) depressed parents' attitudes and behaviors contribute to child psychopathology through various social learning processes including modeling and reinforcement, which contribute to the development of negative cognitions and maladaptive responses to stress; (c) parents' depression and associated symptoms increase the stressors encountered by the family, which then can affect children's functioning; and (d) children's temperament and associated behaviors affect parenting attitudes and behaviors in a series of reciprocal transactions, which then can perpetuate parents' depression and its consequences.

With regard to the psychosocial transmission of risk for depression in families with a depressed parent, at least three important questions are relevant: (a) What is the evidence that the parenting of depressed parents is impaired? (b) Does negative parenting behavior mediate the relation between parent and child depression? (c) Are the processes linking parenting and depression different for offspring of depressed versus non-depressed parents?

Parenting of Depressed Parents   Depressed parents have more dysfunctional relationships with their children than do non-depressed parents (Goodman & Gotlib, 1999, 2002; Radke-Yarrow, 1998). Compared to non-depressed parents, depressed parents report more conflict and less cohesion in their families (Billings & Moos, 1983; Warner, Mufson, & Weissman, 1995), and their spouses tend to agree with these perceptions (Billings & Moos, 1983). Depressed mothers also report being less involved and affectionate and have poorer communication with their children (Weissman, Paykel, & Klerman, 1972). These mothers tend to feel more hostile toward their children and less positive and competent about their parenting than do well mothers (Webster-Stratton & Hammond, 1988; Weissman & Paykel, 1974).

Using measures of EE, several studies have found that, compared to non-depressed mothers, depressed mothers exhibit higher levels of EE, particularly criticism, when talking about their children (Frye & Garber, 2005; Goodman et al., 1994; Nelson, Hammen, Brennan, & Ullman, 2003; Schwartz, Dorer, Beardslee, Lavori, & Keller, 1990). Moreover, higher levels of criticism have been found to be associated with an increased levels of depression, and both internalizing and externalizing problems (Frye & Garber, 2005; Nelson et al., 2003; Schwartz et al., 1990) in offspring of depressed mothers, over and above the contribution of maternal depression alone.

Finally, observational studies also have shown that depressed parents exhibit more negative behaviors and criticism and fewer positive behaviors when interacting with their children than do non-depressed parents (e.g. Gordon et al., 1989; Webster-Stratton & Hammond, 1988). In a meta-analytic review, Lovejoy et al. (2000) analyzed the results of 46 observational studies comparing depressed and non-depressed mothers interacting with their children, and found a moderate effect size for measures of negative maternal behaviors ($d = 0.40$) and disengaged maternal behaviors ($d = 0.29$), and a small effect size ($d = 0.16$) for measures of positive maternal behavior. The general conclusion is that depressed mothers exhibit significantly more negative behaviors (e.g. criticism, negative remarks directed at or about the child, guilt-induction, negative affect) (Hamilton et al., 1993; Jacob & Johnson, 1997; Nolen-Hoeksema, Wolfson, Mumme, & Guskin, 1995; Webster-Stratton & Hammond, 1988), more disengaged, withdrawn, and off-task behaviors (e.g. Gordon et al., 1989; Hart, Jones, Field, & Lundy, 1999; Tarullo, DeMulder, Martinez, & Radke-Yarrow, 1994), and fewer positive behaviors (e.g. happy or caring affect, warmth) (Hamilton, Jones, & Hammen, 1993; Hops et al., 1987) than non-depressed mothers.

Negative Parenting as a Mediator   Does negative parenting actually mediate the relation between parental depression and psychopathology in their offspring? Evidence required to support this mediation hypothesis would be that parental depression predicts depression in offspring, which it does (e.g. Beardslee et al., 1998); parental depression predicts dysfunctional parenting, and it does, as just reviewed here; dysfunctional parenting predicts depression in children, and it does (see Table 1); and the relation between parent and child depression is at least partly accounted for by parenting behaviors. The evidence for this last part has been mixed.

Elgar et al. (2004a) provided a nice conceptualization of how depression could affect parents' ability to show firm and consistent discipline with children, leading to a worsening of the children's behavior. Depressed parents then grow more dysphoric, weary, and withdrawn resulting in increasingly ineffective discipline. The cycle persists in part due to the parent's low perceived self-efficacy (Teti & Gelfand, 1991) and increasing behavior problems in the child.

Some studies have found support for this mediation hypothesis (e.g. Andrews, Brown, & Creasey, 1990; Bifulco et al., 2002; Leinonen, Solantaus, & Punamaki, 2003), although others have not (e.g. Fendrich et al., 1990; Frye & Garber, 2005; Jones, Forehand, & Neary, 2001; Kim et al., 2003). Bifulco et al. (2002) showed that the relation between maternal history of depression and depression in their children was almost entirely mediated by child-rated neglect and abuse. Leinonen et al. (2003) reported that fathers' punitiveness mediated the relation between paternal depressive symptoms and internalizing symptoms in daughters and depressive symptoms in sons. In contrast, in a sample of boys at risk for behavior problems, Kim et al. (2003) found that observed parenting practices did not mediate the effects of either maternal or paternal depressive symptoms on the development of depressive symptoms in young men 10 years later, controlling for their earlier anti-social behavior.

The role of parenting as a mediator between parental depression and child outcomes has been more evident with regard to children's disruptive behaviors (e.g. Fendrich et al., 1990; Leinonen et al., 2003). Leinonen et al. (2003) showed that the relation between maternal depressive symptoms and their sons' substance use and poor school performance was mediated by non-involved mothering. Parental expressed emotion, an index of criticism, also has been found to mediate the link between maternal depression and children's problem behaviors (e.g. Bolton et al., 2003; Nelson et al., 2003). In a cross-sectional study, Nelson et al. (2003) showed that high EE criticism served as a significant intervening variable between maternal depression history and child externalizing symptoms. Nelson et al. (2003) noted, however, that it also is quite possible that the direction of the relation between maternal criticism and child behavior problems could be the reverse. Indeed, Frye and Garber (2005) showed that children's externalizing symptoms partially mediated the link between maternal depression and maternal criticism.

Thus, although theorists (e.g. Garber & Martin, 2002; Goodman & Gotlib, 1999) have suggested that the high rates of psychopathology found among offspring of depressed parents are partially the result of dysfunctional parenting, empirical evidence supporting this mediation model has been inconsistent. More prospective studies are needed that address factors that could affect the role of parenting in the cross-generational transmission of depression such as the heterogeneity of parental depression with regard to severity, chronicity, recurrence, comorbidity, timing, extent of psychopathology in the other parent, heterogeneity of parenting behaviors and characteristics, the contribution of children's temperament and behaviors to their interactions with parents, children's age and gender, parents' gender and marital status, social resources, different methods of assessing the constructs of interest, and the time lag between assessments.

Are the Effects of Negative Parenting Different for Offspring of Depressed Parents?
Are the processes that link the family environment and children's depression different for offspring of depressed versus non-depressed parents? Do certain types of parenting behaviors increase children's risk for depression regardless of their parents' history of depression themselves, or are the effects different for high-risk offspring? To address these questions, studies have examined the relation between the family environment and child depression in families with and without a depressed parent (Hammen et al., 2004; Miller et al., 1999; Shiner & Marmorstein, 1998). In a cross-sectional study of 816 mothers and

their 15-year-old children, Hammen et al. (2004) found an interesting interaction between maternal depression and family discord/stress in relation to offspring depression. At low levels of family discord, offspring of depressed and non-depressed mothers did not differ in rates of mood disorders, but among children exposed to high levels of family conflict, those with a depressed mother were significantly more likely to have depressive disorders themselves than were children of non-depressed women. Hammen et al. (2004) concluded that maternal depression potentiated the effects of family adversity. That is, exposure to stress was associated with depression among offspring of depressed but not non-depressed mothers.

In another study of the relations between the family environment and depression in high- and low-risk offspring, Miller et al. (1999) found that among daughters of mothers with a history of depression, maternal affectionless-control was cross-sectionally associated with daughters' low self-esteem, which then was associated with increased rates of depression at a 10-year follow-up. In contrast, among daughters of mothers without a history of depression, maternal affectionless control was not associated with either concurrent low self-esteem or depression 10 years later. None of these associations were significant in sons. Miller et al. (1999) speculated that high-risk girls may be particularly sensitive to parenting behaviors, or more inclined to internalize maternal rejection, which then contributes to low self-esteem. Thus, again it was the combination of maternal depression and dysfunctional parenting (i.e. maternal affectionless control) that was associated with low self-esteem during childhood and subsequent depression, rather than either alone.

Finally, Shiner and Marmorstein (1998) showed that among adolescents with lifetime depression, only those whose mothers also had ever been depressed reported disturbed family relationships, relative to the controls. It is possible that the ever-depressed adolescents with ever-depressed mothers experienced a more generally disturbed family environment than did the other adolescents. Such a disturbed environment could be created by the parents, by the adolescents themselves, or by a reciprocal interaction between them. Another possibility, however, is that that these adolescents have a greater genetic predisposition toward depression than do the ever-depressed adolescents with never-depressed mothers; this stronger genetic predisposition potentially could manifest itself as a cognitive bias or as an oversensitivity toward appraising and experiencing interpersonal relationships in a negative fashion. Thus, the familial aggregation of depression across generations increases the chances of dysfunctional family relationships likely due to a combination of greater genetic risk and negative interaction patterns.

Overall, the results of these studies are consistent with a multiple risk factor model of the intergenerational transmission of depression, and suggest a pattern of sensitivity and reactivity to adverse conditions among high-risk offspring. Family adversity (e.g. poor parenting, discord) in homes with a depressed parent may be particularly depressogenic in children with "sensitive predispositions", resulting from a genetically transmitted temperament. Although maternal depression is frequently associated with adverse family environments, when family conditions are not stressful, children's risk of disorder may not differ greatly from that of children of never-depressed women. Thus, the particular combination of maternal depression, family adversity, and child sensitivity to stress is especially perilous with regard to the development of mood disorders, due to the complex relation of heredity and environment.

Families and the Treatment of Child and Adolescent Depression

The research reviewed here has shown that the family environment and parent–child inter-actions are disrupted in families of depressed youth, suggesting a possible role for the fam-ily in interventions for treating and preventing mood disorders. Given that family factors have been found to predict outcome and treatment response among depressed youth (Asarnow et al., 1993; Birmaher et al., 2000; Emslie et al., 1997), and given the high rates of psychopathology in parents and other family members of depressed children and ado-lescents (e.g. Klein et al., 2001; Neuman et al., 1997), intervention for the whole family may be warranted. Kazdin and Weisz (1998) noted that, "Child and adolescent therapy is often de facto 'family context' therapy". The transactional relations between the maladap-tive family environment of depressed children and the subsequent impact of their symp-toms on the family, which further fuels family dysfunction suggests a role for the family in treatment.

Family interventions have several potential advantages. First, other members of the family including siblings as well as parents likely can benefit from intervention, thereby possibly changing the overall family context in which the depressed child lives. Second, given that depression tends to be highly comorbid, particularly with anxiety and disruptive disorders (Angold, Costello, & Erkanli, 1999), which themselves are associated with fam-ily dysfunction (e.g. Rapee, 1997; Patterson, 1982), interventions that focus on parenting and communication within the family system likely can reduce the negative effects of these comorbid disorders as well. Despite these reasonable theoretical and empirical reasons to expect that family-based treatments for depression in youth would be successful, there have been relatively few randomized controlled trials of family therapy for depression, or interventions that involve parents, and the few studies that have been conducted have yielded mixed findings.

Outcome of Family Interventions with Depressed Children and Adolescents   Brief psycho-educational family interventions may offer some benefits to families of depressed youth. In a 2-hour program presented to 62 parents of depressed adolescents, information was provided about the diagnosis, course, and treatment of affective illness, and methods of coping with a depressed family member (Brent, Poling, McKain, & Baugher, 1993). Although the program emphasized the chronic and recurrent course of depression, Brent et al. (1993) suggested that future interventions should focus on the typical course of depressive illness, its relation to normal adolescent development, and how family members should respond to a depressed adolescent. Regarding outcome, parents showed improve-ment in knowledge about affective illness, change in their inaccurate beliefs about depres-sion and its treatment, and almost uniformly reported the program to be both useful and interesting.

In a large controlled clinical trial comparing systemic-behavioral family therapy (SBFT), individual cognitive-behavioral therapy (CBT), and individual non-directive supportive therapy with depressed adolescents, Brent et al. (1997) provided a similar brief family psy-choeducation component to all treatment conditions based on their earlier program (Brent et al., 1993) in order to improve compliance and reduce attrition. The SBFT emphasized reframing, communication, and problem-solving skills training aimed at altering family interaction patterns. Results indicated that CBT was significantly more effective than SBFT, which was comparable in efficacy to the nondirective supportive therapy. Thus, the family intervention in this well-executed clinical trial was not as effective as CBT. It is not clear, however, if SBFT would have been more effective than a no intervention group.

Another study compared a combined cognitive-behavioral and family education intervention to a waitlist control condition for children in grades 4 through 6 who reported depressive symptoms (Asarnow, Scott, & Mintz, 2002). The children first received nine sessions of group CBT followed by the family education (Fam Ed) session, which aimed to promote generalization of skills learned in CBT to key environmental contexts (home, school, community). The parent-only segment of the Fam Ed session emphasized helping children to generalize the skills to real problems and to feel positively about the CBT skills they had learned. Parents and children then came together for a multiple family meeting during which videos of the children illustrating the treatment model were presented, and children were given awards for their accomplishments during CBT. Parents and their children then engaged in structured game-like exercises that taught parents CBT skills and promoted generalization. Finally, children presented their parents with an award for their participation in the family session.

Children in the intervention group had a significantly greater reduction in depressive symptoms compared to the wait list control group. Almost all children and parents rated the intervention to be enjoyable. All parents rated the family component as useful, although only 40% thought that additional family sessions would be helpful. Thus, parents might recognize the benefits of participating in an intervention to treat their children's depression, but may be reluctant to devote much time to it. Developing a program that imparts information to parents in a brief but comprehensive way is an important challenge for future studies. Although the results of the Asarnow et al. (2002) study highlight a potential role for families in interventions with depressed children, without a comparison group of CBT without the family component, it is not possible to determine whether the family education session actually added anything.

A study by Wood, Harrington, and Moore (1996) testing a depression-specific treatment had a similar limitation. That is, without a CBT group that did not have a parent component, it is not possible to evaluate the incremental contribution of the family involvement *per se*. In this study, parents were encouraged to help in the CBT with their children. Results showed that this CBT intervention was significantly better than relaxation training in reducing depression, but the added benefit of the family component cannot be determined with this design.

Other studies (Clarke, Rohde, Lewinsohn, Hops, & Seeley, 1999; Lewinsohn, Clarke, Hops, & Andrews, 1990) have more systematically examined whether adding a parent group to a CBT group intervention for depressed adolescents was more effective than a CBT group only, and a waitlist control. Neither of these studies found the addition of the parent group provided any benefit over and above the CBT group alone. One difficulty with these studies, however, was that the parent attendance rates were very low. Thus, the effects of a group that parents actually receive cannot be evaluated.

Fristad et al. (Fristad, Gavazzi, Centolella, & Soldano, 1996; Fristad, Gavazzi, & Soldano, 1998; Fristad, Goldberg-Arnold, & Gavazzi, 2003) developed a multi-family psychoeducation group (MFPG) intervention designed to serve as an adjunct to typical treatments for mood disorders (e.g. medication management and individual/family psy-chotherapy). Each of the six psychoeducational group sessions begins and ends with both the parents and children together. Most of the didactic information and practice, however, occurs in the "breakout sessions", which are conducted separately for parents and children. Information is provided to parents about mood symptoms and disorders, treatment, and healthy/unhealthy family responses to the disorder. Parents also are presented with infor-mation about the educational and mental health systems to help them become more active consumers and effective advocates for their children. The goals of the child groups are to provide an opportunity for children to meet others who cope with similar difficulties, learn about depressive symptoms and their management, build anger management and social skills, and discuss common developmental issues they confront.

Fristad et al. (2003) examined the impact of MFPG on mood-disordered children aged 8–11 and their families. Families were randomly assigned to either immediate MFPG plus treatment as usual (n = 18) or a 6-month waitlist condition plus treatment as usual (n = 17). At the 6-month follow-up, immediate MFPG families reported increased parental knowl-edge about childhood mood symptoms, parent-reported increases in positive family inter-actions, child-reported increases in parental support, and increased utilization of appropriate services by families. However, no impact on decreasing negative family inter-actions was found, nor were any improvements in depressive symptoms reported. Given that the precise role of parental support and positivity in the onset and maintenance of depression has not yet been established, it is not known whether improvements in these domains will reduce depression in children.

Several other family-based programs are in various stages of development and evalua-tion. Diamond, Reis, Diamond, Siqueland, and Isaacs (2002) developed attachment-based family therapy (ABFT) for depressed adolescents. ABFT is based on attachment theory, which asserts that poor attachment bonds, high conflict, harsh criticism, and low affective attunement can lead to negative family environments (e.g. neglect, abuse, abandonment) that inhibit the development of internal and interpersonal coping skills needed to buffer against stressors that can cause or exacerbate depression (Cummings & Cicchetti, 1990; Rudolph et al., 2000). ABFT further assumes that attachment failures can be resolved, parents can become better caregivers, and adolescents can rebuild trust and communication with their parents. Therapy focuses on rebuilding the bond between adolescents and parents so that the family can serve as a secure base from which the adolescent develops increasing autonomy. The therapeutic strategies involve reframing the goals of treatment from focusing on the adolescent's symptoms to improving the quality of the parent–adolescent relationship, build-ing alliances between the therapist and both the parent and adolescent, and expanding adolescents' competencies.

Results thus far indicate that at post-treatment, 81% of adolescents treated with ABFT no longer met criteria for MDD, in contrast with 47% of patients in the waitlist group. Compared with the waitlist group, those treated with ABFT showed a significantly greater reduction in depressive and family conflict. At the 6-month follow-up, of the 15 treated cases assessed, 13 (87%) continued to not meet criteria for MDD. Thus, ABFT appears to be a promising treatment for adolescent depression.

Kaslow et al. (Schwartz, Kaslow, Racusin, & Carton, 1998; Sexson, Glanville, & Kaslow, 2001) have written a great deal about the role of attachment in depression and have developed a related intervention known as Interpersonal Family Therapy (IFT). IFT integrates theory and techniques from family systems perspectives, cognitive behavioral approaches, attachment theory, interpersonal therapy, and developmental psychopathology. The treatment aims to decrease depressive symptoms, change maladaptive cognitive patterns, improve family affective communication, increase adaptive behavior, and improve both interpersonal and family functioning. The treatment attempts to identify and intervene in areas of specific concern within each family, thus providing a more tailored approach. Although this program has not yet been tested in a controlled clinical trial, it seems to have great potential.

Finally, Asarnow, Jaycox, and Tompson (2001) reported that they were developing a family-focused intervention for depressed children (aged 8–14) based on both family systems and cognitive-behavioral models. This program presents family psychoeducation and skills and aims to educate families about the interpersonal nature of depression, teach communication and problem-solving skills, improve positive support, and address specific family problems. The efficacy of this program has not yet been tested.

Thus, family education interventions are feasible and acceptable to parents and children. A few studies have found that psychoeducation improved outcome and course of unipolar depression in adults (Jacobson, Dobson, Fruzzetti, & Schmaling, 1991; O'Leary & Beach, 1990). Although studies of psychoeducation with families of depressed children have found that parents become more knowledgeable about depression, improvement on children's depression, *per se*, has not yet been demonstrated. Interestingly, although most of the family programs included a psychoeducation component, there is no evidence in the literature that an absence of such knowledge contributes to the onset or maintenance of the disorder. Studies first need to demonstrate that improving the family's understanding about mood disorders actually affects children's depression, and if so, then how does such knowledge improve children's symptoms. Does knowledge increase the likelihood that parents will be more tolerant and patient with their depressed children? If so, then should family interventions not target these parent characteristics directly?

It also is interesting that despite the fact that most of the families that participated in the family interventions rated them positively, a large number of families drop out after they have been randomized to the family treatment. Brent et al. (1997) reported that 60% (9 of 15) of those refusing treatment had been randomized to the family treatment condition. This is consistent with the finding of Asarnow et al. (2002) that parents were not interested in participating in a more extended course of family therapy.

What Should be the Focus of Family Interventions?   Given the relatively modest success of family-based interventions thus far, questions remain regarding what should be the focus of interventions for depressed children and adolescents. What are the implications of the literature reviewed here for treatment? Should the family even be part of treatment? Probably the more appropriate questions are "For whom should the family be part of treatment?" and "What should be the nature of such treatment?"

First, there is clear evidence that depressed individuals perceive their parents to manifest a range of undesirable behaviors toward them including rejection, criticism, over control, and intrusiveness, as well as a lack of positive behaviors such as support, warmth, and involvement. The extent to which these perceptions of and/or actual parenting characteristics contribute to the onset and maintenance of depressive symptoms and disorders in children and adolescents is not precisely known, although the consistent correlational evidence suggests that reducing these negative parenting behaviors and increasing positive parenting could help and probably would not hurt. The questions for intervention researchers are how to best change these parenting characteristics, and does doing so actually reduce the likelihood of onset and maintenance of mood disorders?

Second, interpersonal relationships are dynamic and transactional. Thus, children's contribution to problems in their relationship with their parents also should be addressed. Blame should be de-emphasized, whereas realistic evaluation of each person's behaviors should be the focus. How are these behaviors being perceived by others and how can their behaviors as well as their perceptions be changed?

Third, given that family members typically do not perceive the family environment in quite the same way (Katz, 2004), clinicians working with depressed adolescents should be prepared to address these differences directly during treatment. Emphasis should not be on who is "correct", but rather on the validity of each of their perspectives, and possible reasons for their differences.

Fourth, what do parents and children specifically do during their interactions that inadvertently reinforces the other's depressive behaviors? Sheeber et al. (1998) showed using sequential analysis of laboratory interactions that mothers of depressed adolescents increased facilitative behaviors (i.e. approving and affirming statements) and fathers of depressed adolescents decreased their aggressive behaviors (i.e. irritable tone, disapproving) in response to their adolescent's depressive behaviors more than did the parents of non-depressed teens. A greater awareness of this dynamic, and guidance about how to change the contingencies could help to reduce these behaviors.

Fifth, given the high rate of depression in offspring of depressed parents, and depression in parents of depressed children, collateral treatment for depressed parents may be necessary, although probably not sufficient. The extent to which the benefits of treating depressed parents "trickle down" to their children is currently being studied (Garber et al., 2003; Pilowsky et al., 2004; Riley, Broitman, Coiro, & Keefer, 2003) but is not yet known. Even more important than decreasing or eliminating the parent's depression is to target the processes that mediate between parents' and children's psychopathology. Some of these mechanisms were identified here including dysfunctional parenting, increased stress, and negative cognitions, but studies of interventions that directly reduce these mediating processes are needed.

Finally, Asarnow et al. (2001) noted an important observation regarding possible developmental differences in the role of the family in treatment. In a study of treatment of anxiety, Barrett, Dadds, and Rapee (1996) compared CBT, CBT plus family treatment, and a wait list control group. They found that the combined CBT plus family treatment showed the most improvement (84%), then the CBT-only group (57%), and only 26% in the wait-list control group recovered. Barrett et al. also found an interesting age effect such that younger children (ages 7–10) had a significantly better outcome in the combined intervention, whereas for older children (aged 11–14), both active treatments were effective, suggesting that the family component did not add anything over and above CBT for adolescents. Thus, as the role of the family changes with development, so will the efficacy of including parents in treatment likely change as children mature.

Because the causes of depression involve multiple interrelated factors, it is not likely that any single intervention approach will successfully treat all cases of depression. Comprehensive interventions that target multiple domains including interpersonal relationships, family environment, parenting behaviors, stress, coping, and negative cognitions, as well as biology, likely will have the greatest effect. However, not all depressed individuals need or will respond favorably to all types of treatments. Therefore, careful assessments should identify individual patient's particular area(s) of concern, and interventions should be selected from empirically validated treatment approaches, and then tailored to the patient's specific needs.

References

Abela, J. R. Z. (2001). The hopelessness theory of depression: A test of the diathesis-stress and causal mediation components in third and seventh grade children. *Journal of Abnormal Child Psychology, 29*, 241–254.

Aber, J. L., Bennett, N. G., Conley, D. C., & Li, J. (1997). The effects of poverty on child health and development. *Annual Review of Public Health, 18*, 463–483.

Abramson, L. Y., Alloy, L. B., Hankin, B. L., Haeffel, G. J., MacCoon, D. G., & Gibb, B. E. (2002). Cognitive vulnerability-stress models of depression in a self-regulatory and psychobiological context. In: C.L. Hammen, & I.H. Gotlib (Eds), *Handbook of depression* (pp. 268–294). New York: Guilford Press.

Abramson, L. Y., Metalsky, G. I., & Alloy, L. B. (1989). Hopelessness depression: A theory-based subtype of depression. *Psychological Review, 96*, 358–372.

Ainsworth, M. D. S. (1979). Attachment related to mother — infant interaction. In: L. S. Rosenblatt, R. A. Hinde, C. Beer & M. Busnel (Eds), *Advances in the study of behavior* (Vol. 9, pp. 1–51). New York: Academic Press.

Allgood-Merton, B., Lewinsohn, P., & Hops, H. (1990). Sex differences and adolescent depression. *Journal of Abnormal Psychology, 99*, 55–63.

Alloy, L. B., Abramson, L. Y., Tashman, N. A., Berrebbi, D. S., Hogan, M. E., Whitehouse, W. G., Crossfield, A. G., & Morocco, A. (2001). Developmental origins of cognitive vulnerability to depression: Parenting, cognitive, and inferential feedback styles of the parents of individuals at high and low cognitive risk for depression. *Cognitive Therapy and Research, 25*, 397–423.

Amanat, E., & Butler, C. (1984). Oppressive behaviors in the families of depressed children. *Family Therapy, 11*, 65–75.

Andrews, B., Brown, G.W., & Creasey, L. (1990). Intergenerational links between psychiatric disorder in mothers and daughters: The role of parenting experiences. *Journal of Child Psychology and Psychiatry, 31*, 1115–1129.

Angold, A., Costello, E. J., & Erkanli, A. (1999). Comorbidity. *Journal of Child Psychology and Psychiatry, 40*, 57–87.

Angold, A., & Rutter, M. (1992). Effects of age and pubertal status on depression in a large clinical sample. *Development and Psychopathology, 4*, 5–28.

Anguelova, M., Benkelfat, C., & Turecki, G. (2003). A systematic review of association studies investigating genes coding for serotonin receptors and the serotonin transporter, I: Affective disorders. *Molecular Psychiatry, 8*, 574–591.

Armsden, G. C., McCauley, E., Greenberg, M. T., Burke, P. M., & Mitchell, J. (1990). Parent and peer attachment in early adolescent depression. *Journal of Abnormal Child Psychology, 18*, 683–697.

Asarnow, J. R., Ben-Meir, S. L., & Goldstein, M. J. (1987). Family factors in childhood depressive and schizophrenia-spectrum disorders: A preliminary report. In: M. J. Goldstein & K. Hahlweg (Eds), *Understanding major mental disorder: The contribution of family interaction research* (pp. 123–138). New York: Family Process Press.

Asarnow, J. R., Goldstein, M. J., Tompson, M., & Guthrie, D. (1993). One-year outcomes of depressive disorders in child psychiatric in-patients: Evaluation of the prognostic power of a brief measure of expressed emotion. *Journal of Child Psychology and Psychiatry, 34*, 129–137.

Asarnow, J. R., Jaycox, L. H., & Tompson, M. C. (2001). Depression in youth: Psychosocial interventions. *Journal of Clinical Child Psychology, 30*, 33–47.

Asarnow, J. R., Scott, C. V., & Mintz, J. (2002). A combined cognitive-behavioral family education intervention for depression in children: A treatment development study. *Cognitive Therapy and Research, 26*, 221–229.

Asarnow, J. R., Tompson, M., Hamilton, E. B., Goldstein, M. J., & Guthrie, D. (1994). Family expressed emotion, childhood-onset depression, and childhood-onset schizophrenia spectrum disorders: Is expressed emotion a nonspecific correlate of child psychopathology or a specific risk factor for depression? *Journal of Abnormal Child Psychology, 22*, 129–146.

Asarnow, J. R., Tompson, M., Woo, S., & Cantwell, D. P. (2001). Is expressed emotion a specific risk factor for depression or a nonspecific correlate of psychopathology. *Journal of Abnormal Child Psychology, 29,* 573–583.

Baldwin, M. W. (1992). Relational schemas and the processing of social information. *Psychological Bulletin, 112*, 461–484.

Barber, B. K. (1992). Family, personality, and adolescent problem behaviors. *Journal of Marriage and the Family, 54*, 69–79.

Barber, B. K. (1996). Parental psychological control: Revisiting a neglected construct. *Child Development, 67*, 3296–3319.

Baron, R. M., & Kenny, D. A. (1986). The moderator-mediator variable distinction in social psychological research: Conceptual, strategic, and statistical considerations. *Journal of Personality and Social Psychology, 51*, 1173–1182.

Barrett, P. M., Dadds, M. R., & Rapee, R. M. (1996). Family treatment of childhood anxiety: A controlled trial. *Journal of Consulting and Clinical Psychology, 64*, 333–342.

Barrera, M. Jr.,& Garrison-Jones, C. (1992). Family and peer social support as specific correlates of adolescent depressive symptoms. *Journal of Abnormal Child Psychology, 20*, 1–16.

Bates, J. E., Pettit, G. S., & Dodge, K. A. (1995). Family and child factors in stability and change in children's aggressiveness in elementary school. In: J. McCord (Ed.), *Coercion and punishment in long-term perspectives* (pp. 124–138). New York: Cambridge University Press.

Bates, J. E., Pettit, G. S., Dodge, K. A., & Ridge, B. (1998). Interaction of temperamental resistance to control and restrictive parenting in the development of externalizing behavior. *Developmental Psychology, 34*, 982–995.

Beardslee, W. R., Versage, E. M., & Gladstone, T. R. G. (1998). Children of affectively ill parents: A review of the past 10 years. *Journal of the American Academy of Child and Adolescent Psychiatry, 37*, 1134–1141.

Beck, A. T. (1967). *Depression: Causes and treatment*. Philadelphia: University of Pennsylvania Press.

Beck, A. T. (1987). Cognitive models of depression. *Journal of Cognitive Psychotherapy: An International Quarterly, 1*, 5–37.

Beevers, C. G., & Meyer, B. (2002). Lack of positive experiences and positive expectancies mediate the relationship between BAS responsiveness and depression. *Cognition and Emotion, 16*, 549–564.

Bell, R. Q., & Chapman, M. (1986). Child effects in studies using experimental or brief longitudinal approaches to socialization. *Developmental Psychology, 22*, 595–603.

Bell-Dolan, D. J., Reaven, N. M., & Peterson, L. (1993). Depression and social functioning: A multidimensional study of the linkages. *Journal of Clinical Child Psychology, 22*, 306–315.

Bennett, D. S., & Bates, J. E. (1995). Prospective models of depressive symptoms in early adolescence: Attributional style, stress, and support. *Journal of Early Adolescence, 15*, 299–315.

Bifulco, A. T., Brown, G. W., & Harris, T. O. (1987). Childhood loss of parent, lack of adequate parental care and adult depression: A replication. *Journal of Affective Disorders, 12*, 115–128.

Bifulco, A. T., Moran, P. M., Ball, C., Jacobs, C., Bains, R., Bunn, A., & Cavagin, J. (2002). Child adversity, parental vulnerability and disorder: Examination of inter-generational transmission of risk. *Journal of Child Psychology and Psychiatry and Allied Disciplines, 43*, 1075–1086.

Billings, A. G., & Moos, R. H. (1983). Comparisons of children of depressed and non-depressed parents: A social-environmental perspective. *Journal of Abnormal Child Psychology, 11*, 483–486.

Birmaher, B., Brent, D. A., Kolko, D., Baugher, M., Bridge, J., Holder, D., Iyengar, S., & Ulloa, R. E. (2000). Clinical outcome after short-term psychotherapy for adolescents with major depressive disorder. *Archives of General Psychiatry, 57*, 29–36.

Birmaher, B., Kaufman, J., Brent, D. A., Dahl, R. E., Perel, J. M., Al-Shabbout, M., Nelson, B., Stull, S., Rao, U., Waterman, G. S., Williamson, D. E., & Ryan, N. D. (1997). Neuroendocrine response to 5-hydroxy-l-tryptophan in prepubertal children at high risk of major depressive disorder. *Archives of General Psychiatry, 54*, 1113–1119.

Birmaher, B., Ryan, N. D., Williamson, D. E., Brent, D. A., & Kaufman, J. (1996b). Childhood and adolescent depression: A review of the past 10 years, Part II. *Journal of the American Academy of Child and Adolescent Psychiatry, 35*, 1575–1583.

Birmaher, B., Ryan, N. D., Williamson, D. E., Brent, D. A., Kaufman, J., Dahl, R. E., Perel, J., & Nelson, B. (1996a). Childhood and adolescent depression: A review of the past ten years. Part I. *Journal of the American Academy of Child & Adolescent Psychiatry, 35*, 1427–1439.

Blatt, S. J., & Homann, E. (1992). Parent–child interaction in the etiology of dependent and self-critical depression. *Clinical Psychology Review, 12*, 47–91.

Blazer, D. G., Kessler, R. C., McGonagle, K. A., & Swartz, M. S. (1994). The prevalence and distribution of major depression in a national community sample: The national comorbidity survey. *American Journal of Psychiatry, 151*, 979–986.

Bolton, C., Calam, R., Barrowclough, C., Peters, S., Roberts, J., Wearden, A., & Morris, J. (2003). Expressed emotion, attributions and depression in mothers of children with problem behavior. *Journal of Child Psychology and Psychiatry, 44*, 242–254.

Boudewyn, A. R., & Liem, J. H. (1995). Childhood sexual abuse as a precursor to depression and self-destructive behavior in adulthood. *Journal of Traumatic Stress, 8*, 445–459.

Bowlby, J. (1980). *Attachment and loss: Vol. 3. Loss: Sadness and depression*. New York: Basic Books.

Boyce, P., Parker, G., Bernett, B., Cooney, M., & Smith, F. (1991). Personality as a vulnerability factor to depression. *British Journal of Psychiatry, 159*, 106–114.

Boyce, W. T., Quas, J., Alkon, A., Smider, N. A., Essex, M. J., Kupfer, D. J., & MacArthur Assessment Battery Working Group. (2001). Autonomic reactivity and psychopathology in middle childhood. *British Journal of Psychiatry, 179*, 144–150.

Boyle, M. H., & Pickles, A. (1997). Maternal depressive symptoms and ratings of emotional disorder symptoms in children and adolescents. *Journal of Child Psychology and Psychiatry, 38*, 981–992.

Brent, D. A., Holder, D., Kolko, D., Birmaher, B., Baugher, M., Roth, C., Iyengar, S., & Johnson, B. A. (1997). A clinical psychotherapy trial for adolescent depression comparing cognitive, family, and supportive treatments. *Archives of General Psychiatry, 54*, 877–885.

Brent, D. A., Poling, K., McKain, B., & Baugher, M. (1993). A psychoeducational program for families of affectively ill children and adolescents. *The Journal of American Academy of Child and Adolescent Psychiatry, 32*, 770–774.

Brewin, C. R., Andrews, B., & Gotlib, I. H. (1993). Psychopathology and early experience: A reappraisal of retrospective reports. *Psychological Bulletin, 113*, 82–98.

Brewin, C. R., Firth-Cozens, J., Furnham, A., & McManus, I. C. (1992). Self-criticism in adulthood and recalled childhood experience. *Journal of Abnormal Psychology, 101*, 561–566.

Bruce, M. L., Takeuchi, D. T., & Leaf, P. J. (1991). Poverty and psychiatric status: Longitudinal evidence from the New Haven Epidemiologic Catchment Area Study. *Archives of General Psychiatry, 48*, 470–474.

Buka, S. L., Stichick, T. L., Birdthistle, I., & Earls, F. J. (2001). Youth exposure toviolence: Prevalence, risks, and consequences. *American Journal of Orthopsychiatry, 71*, 298–310.

Burbach, D. J., & Borduin, C. M. (1986). Parent–child relations and the etiology of depression: A review of methods and findings. *Clinical Psychology Review, 6*, 133–153.

Burbach, D. J., Kashani, J. H., & Rosenberg, T. K. (1989). Parental bonding and depressive disorders in adolescents. *Journal of Child Psychology and Psychiatry, 30*, 417–429.

Burge, D., & Hammen, C. (1991). Maternal communication: Predictions of outcome at follow-up in a sample of children at high and low risk for depression. *Journal of Abnormal Psychology, 100*, 174–180.

Burge, D., Hammen, C., Davila, J., Daley, S., Paley, B., Lindberg, N., Herzberg, D., & Rudolph, K. (1997). The relationship between attachment cognitions and psychological adjustment in late adolescent women. *Development and Psychopathology, 9*, 151–168.

Burt, C. E., Cohen, L. H., Bjorck, J. P. (1988). Perceived family environment as a moderator of young adolescents' life stress adjustment. *American Journal of Community Psychology, 16*, 101–122.

Buss, A. H., & Plomin, R. (1984). *Temperament: Early developing personality traits.* Hillsdale, NJ: Erlbaum.

Carnelley, K. B., Pietromonaco, P. R., & Jaffe, K. (1994). Depression, working models of others, and relationship functioning. *Journal of Personality & Social Psychology, 66*, 127–140.

Carton, J. S., & Nowicki, S. (1994). Antecedents of individual differences in locus of control of reinforcement: A critical review. *Genetic, Social, and General Psychology Monographs, 120*, 31–81.

Caspi, A. (1998). Personality development across the life course. In: W. Damon (Series Ed.) & N. Eisenberg (Vol. Ed.), *Handbook of child psychology: Vol. 3. Social, emotional, and personality development* (pp. 311–388). New York, NY: John Wiley & Sons, Inc.

Caspi, A., Bern, D. J., & Elder, G. H. Jr. (1994). Continuities and consequences of interactional styles across the life course. *Journal of Personality, 62*, 375–406.

Caspi, A., Henry, B., McGee, R. O., Moffitt, T. E., & Silva, P. A. (1995). Temperamental origins of child and adolescent behavior problems: From age three to age fifteen. *Child Development, 66*, 55–68.

Caspi, A., Moffitt, T. E., Newman, D. L., & Silva, P. A. (1996). Behavioral observations at age 3 years predict adult psychiatric disorders: Longitudinal evidence from a birth cohort. *Archives of General Psychiatry, 53*, 1033–1039.

Caspi, A., Sugden, K., Moffitt, T. E., Taylor, A., Craig, I. W., Harrington, H., McClay, J., Mill, J., Martin, J., Braithwaite, A., & Poulton, R. (2003). Influence of life stress on depression: Moderation by a polymorphism in the 5-HTT gene. *Science, 301*, 386–389.

Chiariello, M. A., & Orvaschel, H. (1995). Patterns of parent–child communication: Relationship to depression. *Clinical Psychology Review, 15,* 395–407.

Civic, D., & Holt, V. L. (2000). Maternal depressive symptoms and child behavior problems in a nationally representative normal birthweight sample. *Maternal and Child Health Journal, 4*, 215–221.

Clark, L. A., & Watson, D. (1991). Tripartite model of anxiety and depression: Psychometric evidence and taxonomic implications. *Journal of Abnormal Psychology, 100*, 316–336.

Clark, L. A., Watson, D., & Mineka, S. (1994). Temperament, personality, and the mood and anxiety disorders. *Journal of Abnormal Psychology, 103*, 103–116.

Clarke, G. N., Rohde, P., Lewinsohn, P. M., Hops, H., & Seeley, J. R. (1999). Cognitive–behavioral treatment of adolescent depression: Efficacy of acute group treatment and booster sessions. *Journal of the American Academy of Child and Adolescent Psychiatry*, *38*, 272–279.

Cloninger, C. R. (1987). A systematic method for clinical description and classification of personality variants: A proposal. *Archives of General Psychiatry*, *44*, 573–588.

Cohen, P., Brook, J. S., Cohen, J., Velez, N., & Garcia, M. (1990). Common and uncommon pathways to adolescent psychopathology and problem behavior. In: L. Robins & M. Rutter (Eds), *Straight and devious pathways childhood to adulthood*. London: Cambridge University Press.

Cohen, P., Cohen, J., Kasen, S., Velez, C. N., Hartmark, C., Johnson, J., Rojas, M., Brook, J., & Streuning, E. L. (1993). An epidemiological study of disorders in late childhood and adolescence: I. Age- and gender-specific prevalence. *Journal of Child Psychology and Psychiatry*, *34*, 851–867.

Cole, D. A., & Rehm, L. P. (1986). Family interaction patterns and childhood depression. *Journal of Abnormal Child Psychology*, *14*, 297–314.

Cole, D. A., & Maxwell, S. E. (2003). Testing mediational models with longitudinal data: Questions and tips in the use of structural equation modeling. *Journal of Abnormal Psychology*, *112*, 558–577.

Cole, D. A., & McPherson, A. E. (1993). Relation of family subsystems to adolescent depression: Implementing a new family assessment strategy. *Journal of Family Psychology*, *7*, 119–133.

Collins, W. A., Maccoby, E. E., Steinberg, L., Hetherington, E. M., & Bornstein, M. H. (2000). Contemporary research on parenting. The case for nature and nurture. *American Psychologist*, *55*, 218–232.

Compas, B. E., Connor Smith, J., & Jaser, S. S. (2004). Temperament, stress reactivity, and coping: Implications for depression in childhood and adolescence. *Journal of Clinical Child and Adolescent Psychology*, *33*, 21–31.

Compas, B. E., Connor-Smith, J. K., Saltzman, H., Thomsen, A. H., & Wadsworth, M. E. (2001). Coping with stress during childhood and adolescence: Problems, progress, and potential in theory and research. *Psychological Bulletin*, *127*, 87–127.

Connell, A. M., & Goodman, S. H. (2002). The association between psychopathology in fathers versus mothers and children's internalizing and externalizing behavior problems. *Psychological Bulletin*, *128*, 746–773.

Conger, R. D., Ge, X., Elder, G. H. Jr., Lorenz, F. O., & Simons, R. L. (1994). Economic stress, coercive family process, and developmental problems of adolescents. *Child Development*, *65*, 541–561.

Costa, P. T., & McCrae, R. R. (1980). Influence of extraversion and neuroticism on subjective well being: Happy and unhappy people. *Journal of Personality and Social Psychology*, *38*, 668–678.

Costello, E. J., Angold, A., Burns, B. J., Stangl, D. K., Tweed, D. L., Erkanli, A., & Worthman, C. M. (1996). The Great Smoky Mountains Study of youth: Goals, design, methods, and the prevalence of DSM-III-R disorders. *Archives of General Psychiatry*, *53*, 1129–1136.

Coyne, J. C. (1976). Depression and the response of others. *Journal of Abnormal Psychology*, *85*, 186–193.

Coyne, J. C., Burchill, S. A. L., & Stiles, W. B. (1991). An interactional perspective on depression. In: D. R. Forsyth & C. R. Snyder (Eds), *Handbook of social and clinical psychology: The health perspective* (pp.327–349). Elmsford, NY: Pergamon Press, Inc

Crook, T., & Eliot, J. (1980). Parental death during childhood and adult depression: A critical review of the literature. *Psychological Bulletin*, *87*, 252–259.

Cummings, E. M., & Cicchetti, D. (1990). Toward a transactional model of relations between attachment and depression. In: M. T. Greenberg, D. Cicchetti, & E. M. Cummings (Eds), *Attachment in the preschool years: Theory, research, and intervention* (pp. 339–372). Chicago: University of Chicago Press.

Cummings, E. M., & Davies, P. T. (1994). Maternal depression and child development. *Journal of Child Psychology and Psychiatry, 35*, 73–112.

Cummings, E. M., & Davies, P. T. (1999). Depressed parents and family functioning: Interpersonal effects and children's functioning and development. In: T. Joiner & J. C. Coyne (Eds), *The interactional nature of depression* (pp. 299–327). Washington, DC: American Psychological Association.

Dadds, M. R., Sanders, M. R., Morrison, M., & Rebgetz, M. (1992). Childhood depression and conduct disorder: II. An analysis of family interaction patterns in the home. *Journal of Abnormal Psychology, 101*, 505–513.

Dahl, R. E., Birmaher, B., Williamson, D. E., Dorn, L., Perel, J., Kaufman, J., Brent, D. A., Axelson, D. A., & Ryan, N. D. (2000). Low growth hormone response to growth hormone-releasing hormone in child depression. *Biological Psychiatry, 48*, 981–988.

Dahl, R. E., & Ryan, N. D. (1996). The psychobiology of adolescent depression. In: D. Cicchetti & S. L. Toth (Eds), *Rochester symposium on developmental psychopathology, Vol. 7: Adolescence: Opportunities and challenges* (pp. 197–232). Rochester, NY: Rochester University Press.

Darling, N., & Steinberg, L. (1993). Parenting style as context: An integrative model. *Psychological Bulletin, 113*, 487–496.

Davidson, R. J., Pizzagalli, D., Nitschke, J. B., & Putnam, K. (2002). Depression: Perspectives from affective neuroscience. *Annual Review of Psychology, 53*, 545–574.

Davies, P. T., Dumenci, L., & Windle, M. (1999). The interplay between maternal depressive symptoms and marital distress in the prediction of adolescent adjustment. *Journal of Marriage and the Family, 61*, 238–254.

Davies, P. T., & Windle, M. (2001). Interparental discord and adolescent adjustment trajectories: The potentiating and protective role of intrapersonal attributes. *Child Development, 72*, 1163–1178.

Dawson, G., Klinger, L. G., Panagiotides, H., Hill, D., & Spieker, S. (1992). Frontal lobe activity and affective behavior of infants of mothers with depressive symptoms. *Child Development, 63*, 725–737.

Derryberry, D., & Rothbart, M. K. (1988). Arousal, affect, and attention as components of temperament. *Journal of Personality and Social Psychology, 55*, 958–966.

Diamond, G. S., Reis, B. F., Diamond, G. M., Siqueland, L., & Isaacs, L. (2002). Attachment-based family therapy for depressed adolescents: A treatment development study. *Journal of the American Academy of Child and Adolescent Psychiatry, 41*, 1190–1196.

Dinan. T. G. (1998). Neuroendicrine markers: Role in the development of antidepressants. *CNS Drugs, 10*, 145–157.

Downey, G., & Coyne, J. C. (1990). Children of depressed parents: An integrative review. *Psychological Bulletin, 108*, 50–76.

Downey, G., & Walker, E. (1992). Distinguishing family-level and child-level influences on the development of depression and aggression in children at risk. *Development and Psychopathology, 4*, 81–95.

Dubas, J. S., Gerris, J. R. M., Janssens, J., & Vermulst, A. A. (2002). Personality types of adolescents: Concurrent correlates, antecedents and type X parenting interactions. *Journal of Adolescence, 25*, 79–92.

DuBois, D. L., Felner, R. D., Brand, S., & George, G. R. (1999). Profiles of self-esteem in early adolescence: Identification and investigation of adaptive correlates. *American Journal of Community Psychology, 27*, 899–932.

Eaves, L. J., Silberg, J. L., Meyer, J. M., Maes, H. H., Simonoff, E., Pickles, A., Rutter, M., Neale, M. C., Reynolds, C. A., Erikson, M. T., Heath, A. C., Loeber, R., Truett, K. R., & Hewitt, J. K. (1997). Genetics and developmental psychopathology: 2. The main effects of genes and environment on behavioral problems in the Virginia twin study of adolescent behavioral development. *Journal of Child Psychology and Psychiatry, 38*, 965–980.

Eisenberg, N., Fabes, R. A., Guthrie, I. K., & Reiser, M. (2000). Dispositional emotionality and reg-ulation: Their role in predicting quality of social functioning. *Journal of Personality and Social Psychology, 78*, 136–157.

Eley, T. C., Deater-Deckard, K., Fombonne, E., Fulker, D. W., & Plomin, R. (1998). An adoption study of depressive symptoms in middle childhood. *Journal of Child Psychology and Psychiatry, 39*, 337–345.

Elgar, F. J., Curtis, L. J., McGrath, P. J., Waschbusch, D. A., & Stewart, S. H. (2003). Antecedent–consequence conditions in maternal mood and child adjustment: A four-year cross-lagged study. *Journal of Clinical Child and Adolescent Psychology, 32*, 362–374.

Elgar, F. J., McGrath, P. J., Waschbusch, D. A., Stewart, S. H., & Curtis, L. J. (2004a). Mutual influ-ences on maternal depression and child adjustment problems. *Clinical Psychology Review, 24*, 441–459.

Elgar, F. J., Waschbusch, D. A., McGrath, P. J., Stewart, S. H., & Curtis, L. J. (2004b). Temporal rela-tions in daily-reported maternal mood and disruptive child behavior. *Journal of Abnormal Child Psychology, 32*, 237–247.

Emslie, G. J., Rush, A. J., Weinberg, W. A., Gullion, C. M., Rintelmann, J., & Hughes, C. W. (1997). Recurrence of major depressive disorder in hospitalized children and adolescents. *Journal of the American Academy of Child and Adolescent Psychiatry, 36*, 785–792.

Emslie, G. J., Weinberg, W. A., Kennard, B. D., & Kowatch, R. A. (1994). Neurobiological aspects of depression in children and adolescents. In: W.M. Reynolds & H.E. Johnston (Eds), *Handbook of depression in children and adolescents* (pp. 143–165). New York: Plenum.

Eysenck, H. J. (1952). *The scientific study of personality* (Vol. xiii, p. 320). Oxford, England: Macmillan.

Eysenck, H. J., & Eysenck, M. W. (1985). *Personality and individual differences: A natural science approach.* New York: Plenum Press.

Fauber, R., Forehand, R., Thomas, A. M., & Wierson, M. (1990). A mediational model of the impact of marital conflict on adolescent adjustment in intact and divorced families: The role of disrupted parenting. *Child Development, 61*, 1112–1123.

Fendrich, M., Warner, V., & Weissman, M. M. (1990). Family risk factors, parental depression, and psychopathology in offspring. *Developmental Psychology, 26*, 40–50.

Fergusson, D. M., Horwood, L. J., & Lynskey, M. T. (1995). Maternal depressive symptoms and depressive symptoms in adolescents. *Journal of Child Psychology and Psychiatry and Allied Disciplines, 36*, 1161–1178.

Field, T., Fox, N. A., Pickens, J., & Nawrocki, T. (1995). Relative frontal EEG activation in 3- to 6 month-old infants of "depressed" mothers. *Developmental Psychology, 31*, 358–363.

Fleming, J. E., & Offord, D. R. (1990). Epidemiology of childhood depressive disorders: A critical review. *Journal of the American Academy of Child and Adolescent Psychiatry, 29*, 571–580.

Fleming, J. E., Offord, D. R., & Boyle, M. H. (1989). Prevalence of childhood and adolescent depres-sion in the community: Ontario child health study. *British Journal of Psychiatry, 155*, 647–654.

Forehand, R., & McCombs, A. (1988). Unraveling the antecedent–consequence conditions in mater-nal depression and adolescent functioning. *Behavior Research and Therapy, 26*, 399–405.

Fristad, M. A., Gavazzi, S. M., Centolella, D. M., & Soldano, K. W. (1996). Psychoeducation: A promising intervention strategy for families of children and adolescents with mood disorders. *Contemporary Family Therapy, 18*, 371–384.

Fristad, M. A., Gavazzi, S. M., & Soldano, K. W. (1998). Multi-family psychoeducation groups for childhood mood disorders: A program description and preliminary efficacy data. *Contemporary Family Therapy, 20*, 385–402.

Fristad, M. A., Goldberg-Arnold, J. S., & Gavazzi, S. M. (2003). Multi-family psychoeducation groups in the treatment of children with mood disorders. *Journal of Marital and Family Therapy, 29*, 491–504.

Frye, A. A., & Garber, J. (2005). The relations among maternal depression, maternal criticism, and adolescents' externalizing and internalizing symptoms. *Journal of Abnormal Child Psychology, 33*, 1–11.

Garber, J., & Flynn, C. (1998). Origins of the depressive cognitive style. In: D. Routh & R. J. DeRubeis (Eds), *The science of clinical psychology: Evidence of a century's progress* (pp. 53–93). Washington, DC: American Psychological Association.

Garber, J., & Flynn, C. (2001). Predictors of depressive cognitions in young adolescents. *Cognitive Therapy and Research, 25*, 353–376.

Garber, J., & Little, S. (1999). Predictors of competence among offspring of depressed mothers. *Journal of Adolescent Research, 14*, 44–71.

Garber, J., & Martin, N. C. (2002). Negative cognitions in offspring of depressed parents: Mechanisms of risk. In: S.H. Goodman, & I.H. Gotlib (Eds), *Children of depressed parents: Mechanisms of risk and implications for treatment* (pp. 121–153). Washington, DC: American Psychological Association.

Garber, J., McCauley, E., Diamond, G., Burks, V. S., Schloredt, K., & Flynn, C. A. (2003). The effect of parents' treatment for depression on offspring. Presented at the biennial meeting of the Society for Research on Child Development, Tampa, FL, April 7–10.

Garber, J., Robinson, N. S., & Valentiner, D. (1997). The relation between parenting and adolescent depression: Self-worth as a mediator. *Journal of Adolescent Research, 12*, 12–33.

Garrison, C., Jackson, K., Marsteller, F., McKeown, R., & Addy, C. (1990). A longitudinal study of depressive symptomatology in young adolescents. *Journal of Child and Adolescent Psychiatry, 29*, 581–585.

Garrison, C. Z., Waller, J. L., Cuffe, S., McKeown, R., Addy, C., & Jackson, K. (1997). Incidence of major depressive disorder and dysthymia in young adolescents. *Journal of the American Academy of Child and Adolescent Psychiatry, 36*, 458–465.

Ge, X., Best, K. M., Conger, R. D., & Simons, R. L. (1996). Parenting behaviors and the occurrence and co-occurrence of adolescent depressive symptoms and conduct problems. *Developmental Psychology, 32*, 717–731.

Ge, X., Conger, R. D., Lorenz, F. O., Shanahan, M., & Elder, G. H. Jr. (1995). Mutual influences in parent and adolescent psychological distress. *Developmental Psychology, 31*, 406–419.

Ge, X., Conger, R. D., Lorenz, F. O., & Simons, R. L. (1994). Parents' stressful life events and adolescent depressed mood. *Journal of Health and Social Behavior, 35*, 28–44.

Gelfand, D. M., & Teti, D. M. (1990). The effects of maternal depression on children. *Clinical Psychology Review, 10*, 329–353.

Gerlsma, C., Emmelkamp, P. M. G., & Arrindell, W. A. (1990). Anxiety, depression and perception of early parenting: A meta-analysis. *Clinical Psychology Review, 10*, 251–277.

Gershuny, B. S., & Sher, K. J. (1998). The relation between personality and anxiety: Findings from a 3 year prospective study. *Journal of Abnormal Psychology, 107*, 252–262.

Gjerde, P. F. (1995). Alternative pathways to chronic depressive symptoms in young adults: Gender differences in developmental trajectories. *Child Development, 66*, 1277–1300.

Gibb, B. E. (2002). Childhood maltreatment and negative cognitive styles: A quantitative and qualitative review. *Clinical Psychology Review, 22*, 223–246.

Gibb, B. E., Alloy, L. B., Abramson, L. Y., Rose, D. T., Whitehouse, W. G., Donovan, P., Hogan, M. E., Cronholm, J., & Tierney, S. (2001). History of childhood maltreatment, negative cognitive styles, and episodes of depression in adulthood. *Cognitive Therapy and Research, 25*, 425–446.

Gilman, S. E., Kawachi, I., Fitzmaurice, G. M., & Buka, S. L. (2002). Socioeconomic status in childhood and the lifetime risk of major depression. *International Journal of Epidemiology, 31*, 359–367.

Gonzales, L. R., Lewinsohn, P. M., & Clarke, G. N. (1985). Longitudinal follow up of unipolar depressives: An investigation of predictors of relapse. *Journal of Consulting and Clinical Psychology, 53*, 461–469.

Goodman, S. H., Adamson, L. B., Riniti, J., & Cole, S. (1994). Mothers' expressed attitudes: Associations with maternal depression and children's self esteem and psychopathology. *Journal of the American Academy of Child and Adolescent Psychiatry, 33*, 1265–1274.

Goodman, S. H., & Gotlib, I. H. (1999). Risk for psychopathology in the children of depressed mothers: A developmental model for understanding mechanisms of transmission. *Psychological Review, 106*, 458–490.

Goodman, S. H. & Gotlib, I. H. (Eds). (2002). *Children of depressed parents: Mechanisms of risk and implications for treatment.* Washington, DC: American Psychological Association.

Goodyer, I. M., Germany, E., Gowrusankur, J., & Altham, P. (1991), Social influences on the course of anxious and depressive disorders in school-age children. *British Journal of Psychiatry, 158*, 676–684.

Goodyer, I. M., Herbert, J., Tamplin, A., & Altham, P. M. E. (2000). Recent life events, cortisol, dehydroepiandrosterone and the onset of major depression in high-risk adolescents. *British Journal of Psychiatry, 177*, 499–504.

Gordon, D., Burge, D., Hammen, C., Adrian, C., Jachicke, C., & Hiroto, D. (1989). Observations of interactions of depressed women with their children. *American Journal of Psychiatry, 146*, 50–55.

Gotlib, I. H., & Hammen, C. L. (1992). *Psychological aspects of depression :Toward a cognitive-interpersonal integration.* Chichester, UK: Wiley.

Gotlib, I. H., Mount, J. H., Cordy, N. I., & Whiffen, V. E. (1988). Depression and perceptions of early parenting: A longitudinal investigation. *British Journal of Psychiatry, 152*, 24–27.

Gray, J.A. (1987). The neuropsychology of emotion and personality. In: S.D. Iversen & S.M. Stahl (Eds), *Cognitive neurochemistry* (pp.171–190). London: Oxford University Press.

Grolnick, W. S., & Ryan, R. M. (1989). Parent styles associated with children's self-regulation and competence in school. *Journal of Educational Psychology, 81*, 143–154.

Grych, J. H., & Fincham, F. D. (1993). Children's appraisals of marital conflict: Initial investigations of the cognitive–contextual framework. *Child Development, 64*, 215–230.

Haines, B. A., Metalsky, G. I., Cardamone, A. L., & Joiner, T. (1999). Interpersonal and cognitive pathways into the origins of attributional style: A developmental perspective. In: T. Joiner & J. C. Coyne (Eds), *The interactional nature of depression: Advances in interpersonal approaches* (pp. 65–92). Washington, DC: American Psychological Association.

Hamilton, E. B., Asarnow, J. R., & Tompson, M. C. (1999). Family interaction styles of children with depressive disorders, schizophrenia-spectrum disorders, and normal controls. *Family Process, 38*, 463–476.

Hamilton, E. B., Jones, M., & Hammen, C. (1993). Maternal interaction style in affective disordered, physically ill, and normal women. *Family Process, 32*, 329–340.

Hammen, C. (1988). Self cognitions, stressful events, and the prediction of depression in children of depressed mothers. *Journal of Abnormal Child Psychology, 16*, 347–360.

Hammen, C. (1991). *Depression runs in families: The social context of risk and resilience in children of depressed mothers.* New York: Springer.

Hammen, C., Brennan, P. A., & Shih, J. H. (2004). Family discord and stress predictors of depression and other disorders in adolescent children of depressed and nondepressed women. *Journal of the American Academy of Child and Adolescent Psychiatry, 43*, 994–1002.

Hammen, C., Davila, J., Brown, G., Ellicott, A., & Gitlin, M. (1992). Psychiatric history and stress: Predictors of severity of unipolar depression. *Journal of Abnormal Psychology, 101*, 45–52.

Hankin, B. L., Abramson, L. Y., Moffitt, T. E., Silva, P. A., McGee, R., & Angell, K. E. (1998). Development of depression from preadolescence to young adulthood: Emerging gender differences in a 10-year longitudinal study. *Journal of Abnormal Psychology, 107*, 128–140.

Hankin, B. L., Abramson, L. Y., & Siler, M. (2001). A prospective test of the hopelessness theory of depression in adolescence. *Cognitive Therapy and Research, 25*, 607–632.

Hankin, B. L., Kassel, J. D., & Abela, J. R. Z. (2005). Adult attachment dimensions and specificity of emotional distress symptoms: Prospective investigations of cognitive risk and interpersonal stress generation as mediating mechanisms. *Personality and Social Psychology Bulletin, 31,* 136–151.

Harrington, R. C., Fudge, H., Rutter, M., Bredenkamp, D., Groothues, C., & Pridham, J. (1993). Child and adult depression: A test of continuities with data from a family study. *British Journal of Psychiatry, 162,* 627–633.

Harrington, R., Fudge, H., Rutter, M., Pickles, A., & Hill, J. (1990). Adult outcomes of childhood and adolescent depression. *Archives of General Psychiatry, 47,* 465–473.

Harris, T., Brown, G. W., & Bifulco, A. T. (1986). Loss of parent in childhood and adult psychiatric disorder: The role of lack of adequate parental care. *Psychological Medicine, 16,* 641–659.

Harrison, C., & Sofronoff, K. (2002). ADHD and parental psychological distress: Role of demographics, child behavioral characteristics, and parental cognitions. *Journal of the American Academy of Child and Adolescent Psychiatry, 41,* 703–711.

Hart, S., Jones, N. A., Field, T., & Lundy, B. (1999). One-year-old infants of intrusive and withdrawn depressed mothers. *Child Psychiatry and Human Development, 30,* 111–120.

Hartup, W. W., & van Lieshout, C. F. M. (1995). Personality development in social context. *Annual Review of Psychology, 46,* 655–687.

Heim, C., Newport, J. D., Bonsall, R., Miller, A. H., & Nemeroff, C. B. (2001). Altered pituitary-adrenal axis responses to provocative challenge tests in adult survivors of childhood abuse. *American Journal of Psychiatry, 158,* 575–581.

Heim, C., Newport, J. D., Heit, S., Graham, Y. P., Wilcox, M., Bonsall, R., Miller, A. H., & Nemeroff, C. B. (2000). Pituitary-adrenal and autonomic responses to stress in women after sexual and physical abuse in childhood. *Journal of the American Medical Association, 284,* 592–597.

Heneghan, A. M., Silver, E. J., Westbrook, L., Bauman, L. J., & Stein, R. E. K. (1998). Depressive symptoms in mothers with young children: Who is at risk? *Pediatrics, 102,* 1394–1400.

Hilsman, R., & Garber, J. (1995). A test of the cognitive diathesis-stress model of depression in children: Academic stressors, attributional style, perceived competence, and control. *Journal of Personality and Social Psychology, 69,* 370–380.

Hirschfeld, R. M. A., & Klerman, G. L. (1979). Personality attributes and affective disorders. *American Journal of Psychiatry, 136,* 67–70.

Hirschfeld, R. M. A., Klerman, G. L., Clayton, P. J., & Keller, M. B. (1983). Personality and depression: Empirical findings. *Archives of General Psychiatry, 40,* 993–998.

Hirschfeld, R. M. A., Klerman, G. L., Lavori, P., Keller, M. B., Griffith, P., & Coryell, W. (1989). Premorbid personality assessments of first onset of major depression. *Archives of General Psychiatry, 46,* 345–350.

Hoffman, K. B., Cole, D. A., Martin, J. M., Tram, J., & Serocynski, A. D. (2000). Are the discrepancies between self- and others' appraisals of competence predictive or reflective of depressive symptoms in children and adolescents: A longitudinal study, Part II. *Journal of Abnormal Psychology, 109,* 651–662.

Hooley, J. M. (1986). An introduction to EE measurement and research. In: M. J. Goldstein, I. Hand & K. Hahlweg (Eds), *Treatment of schizophrenia: Family assessment and intervention* (pp. 25-34). New York: Springer-Verlag.

Hops, H., Biglan, A., Sherman, L., Arthur, J., Friedman, L., & Osteen, V. (1987). Home observations of family interactions of depressed women. *Journal of Consulting and Clinical Psychology, 55,* 341–346.

Hops, H., Lewinsohn, P. M., Andrews, J. A., & Roberts, R. E. (1990). Psychosocial correlates of depressive symptomatology among high school students. *Journal of Clinical Child Psychology, 19,* 211–220.

Ingram, R. E., Miranda, J., & Segal, Z. V. (1998). *Cognitive vulnerability to depression.* New York: Guilford Press.

Jacob, T., & Johnson, S. L. (1997). Parent–child interaction among depressed fathers and mothers: Impact on child functioning. *Journal of Family Psychology, 11*, 391–409.

Jacobson, N. S., Dobson, K., Fruzzetti, A. E., & Schmaling, K. B. (1991). Marital therapy as a treatment for depression. *Journal of Consulting and Clinical Psychology, 59*, 547–557.

Jacquez, F., Cole, D. A., & Searle, B. (2004). Self-perceived competence as a mediator between maternal feedback and depressive symptoms in adolescents. *Journal of Abnormal Child Psychology, 32*, 355–367.

Johnson, J. G., Cohen, P., Dohrenwend, B. P., Link, B. G., & Brook, J. S. (1999). A longitudinal investigation of social causation and social selection processes involved in the association between socioeconomic status and psychiatric disorders. *Journal of Abnormal Psychology, 108*, 490–499.

Joiner, T. E., & Wagner, K. D. (1995). Attribution style and depression in children and adolescents: A meta-analytic review. *Clinical Psychology Review, 5*, 777–798.

Jones, D. J., Forehand, R., & Neary, E. M. (2001). Family transmission of depressive symptoms: Replication across Caucasian and African American mother-child dyads. *Behavior Therapy, 32*, 123–138.

Judd, L. L., Akiskal, H. S., Maser, J. D., Zeller, P. J., Endicott, J., Coryell., W., Paulus, M. P., Kunovac, J. L., Leon, A. C., Mueller, T. I., Rice, J. A., & Keller, M. B. (1998). A prospective 12-year study of subsyndromal and syndromal depressive symptoms in unipolar major depressive disorders. *Archives of General Psychiatry, 55*, 694–700.

Kagan, J., & Snidman, N. (1991). Temperamental factors in human development. *American Psychologist, 46*, 856–862.

Kandel, D. B., & Davies, M. (1986), Adult sequelae of adolescent depressive symptoms. *Archives of General Psychiatry, 43*, 255–262.

Kane, P. P., & Garber, J. (2004). The relation between fathers' depression and children's externalizing and internalizing symptoms and conflict: A meta-analysis. *Clinical Psychology Review, 24*, 339–360.

Kashani, J. H., & Carlson, G. A. (1987). Seriously depressed preschoolers. *American Journal of Psychiatry, 144*, 348–350.

Kaslow, N. J., Adamson, L. B., & Collins, M. H. (2000). A developmental psychopathology perspective on the cognitive components of child and adolescent depression. In: A. J. Sameroff, M. Lewis & S. M. Miller (Eds), *Handbook of developmental psychopathology* (2nd ed., pp. 491–510). New York: Kluwer/Plenum.

Kaslow, N. J., Deering, C. G., & Racusin, G. R. (1994). Depressed children and their families. *Clinical Psychology Review, 14*, 39–59.

Katainen, S., Räikkönen, K., Keskivaara, P., & Keltikangas-Järvinen, L. (1999). Maternal child-rearing attitudes and role satisfaction and children's temperament as antecedents of adolescent depressive tendencies: Follow-up study of 6- to 15-year-olds. *Journal of Youth and Adolescence, 28*, 139–163.

Katon, W., & Sullivan, M. D. (1990). Depression and chronic mental illness. *Journal of Clinical Psychiatry, 51*, 3–14.

Katz, S. H. (2004). The role of family interactions in adolescent depression: A review of research findings. *Adolescent Psychiatry, 23*, 41–58.

Kaufman, J. (1991). Depressive disorders in maltreated children. *Journal of the American Academy of Child and Adolescent Psychiatry, 30*, 257–265.

Kaufman, J., Martin, A., King, R. A., & Charney, D. (2001). Are child- , adolescent-, and adult-onset depression one and the same disorder? *Biological Psychiatry, 49*, 980–1001.

Kazdin, A. E., Kraemer, H. C., Kessler, R. C., Kupfer, D. J., & Offord, D. R. (1997). Contributions of risk-factor research to developmental psychopathology. *Clinical Psychology Review, 17*, 375–406.

Kazdin, A. E., & Weisz, J. R. (1998). Identifying and developing empirically supported child and adolescent treatments. *Journal of Consulting and Clinical Psychology, 66*, 19–36.

Keitner, G. I., & Miller, I. W. (1990). Family functioning and major depression: An overview. *American Journal of Psychiatry, 147*, 1128–1137.

Keller, M. B., Lavori, P. W., Lewis, C. E., & Klerman, G. L. (1983). Predictors of relapse in major depressive disorder. *Journal of the American Medical Association, 250*, 3299–3304.

Kendler, K. S. (1996). Parenting: A genetic-epidemiological study. *American Journal of Psychiatry, 153,* 11–20.

Kendler, K. S., Gardner, C. O., & Prescott, C. A. (2002). Toward a comprehensive developmental model for major depression in women. *American Journal of Psychiatry, 159*, 1133–1145.

Kendler, K. S., Kuhn, J. W., Vittum, J., Prescott, C. A., & Riley, B.(2005).The interaction of stressful life events and a serotonin transporter polymorphism in the prediction of episodes of major depression: A replication. *Archives of General Psychiatry, 62*, 529–535.

Kendler, K. S., Neale, M., Kessler, R. C., Heath, A. C., & Eaves, L. I. (1993). A longitudinal twin study of personality and major depression in women. *Archives of General Psychiatry, 50*, 853–862.

Kessler, R. C. (2003). Epidemiology of women and depression. *Journal of Affective Disorders, 74*, 5–13.

Kessler, R. C., Avenevoli, S., & Merikangas, K. R. (2001). Mood disorders in children and adolescents: An epidemiologic perspective. *Biological Psychiatry, 49*, 1002–1014.

Kessler R. C., & Walters, E. E. (1998), Epidemiology of DSM-III-R major depression and minor depression among adolescents and young adults in the national comorbidity survey. *Depression and Anxiety, 7*, 3–14.

Kim, H. K., Capaldi, D. M., & Stoolmiller, M. (2003). Depressive symptoms across adolescence and young adulthood in men: Predictions from parental and contextual risk factors. *Development and Psychopathology, 15*, 469–495.

Kilpatrick, D. G., Ruggiero, K. J., Acierno, R., Saunders, B. E., Resnick, H. S., & Best, C. L. (2003). Violence and risk of PTSD, major depression, substance abuse/dependence, and comorbidity: Results from the National Survey of Adolescents. *Journal of Consulting and Clinical Psychology, 71*, 692–700.

Klein, D. N., Durbin, C. E., Shankman, S. A., & Santiago, N. J. (2002). Depression and personality. In: C. L. Hammen, & I. H. Gotlib (Eds), *Handbook of depression* (pp. 115–140). New York, NY: Guilford Press.

Klein, D. N., Lewinsohn, P. M., Seeley, J. R., & Rohde, P. (2001). A family study of major depressive disorder in a community sample of adolescents. *Archives of General Psychiatry, 58*, 13–20.

Kobak, R. R., Sudler, N., & Gamble, W. (1991). Attachment and depressive symptoms during adolescence: A developmental pathways analysis. *Development and Psychopathology, 3*, 461–474.

Kochanska, G. (1991). Patterns of inhibition to the unfamiliar in children of normal and affectively ill mothers. *Child Development, 62,*250–263.

Koestner, R., Zuroff, D. C., & Powers, T. A. (1991). Family origins of adolescent self-criticism and its continuity into adulthood. *Journal of Abnormal Psychology, 100*, 191–197.

Kovacs, M., Feinberg, T. L., Crouse-Novak, M. A., Paulauskas, S. L., & Finkelstein, R. (1984a). Depressive disorders in childhood. I. A longitudinal prospective study of characteristics and recovery. *Archives of General Psychiatry, 41*, 229–237.

Kovacs, M., Feinberg, T. L., Crouse-Novak, M., Paulauskas, S. L., Pollock, M., & Finkelstein, R. (1984b). Depressive disorders in childhood. II. A longitudinal study of the risk for a subsequent major depression. *Archives of General Psychiatry, 41*, 653–659.

Kovacs, M., Goldston, D., & Gatsonis, C. (1993). Suicidal behaviors and childhood onset depressive disorders: A longitudinal investigation. *Journal of the American Academy of Child and Adolescent Psychiatry, 32*, 8–20.

Lahey, B. B., Waldman, I. D., & McBurnett, K. (1999). The development of antisocial behavior: An integrative causal model. *Journal of Child Psychology and Psychiatry, 40*, 669–682.

Lanzi, R. G., Pascoe, J. M., Keltner, B., & Ramey, S. L. (1999). Correlates of maternal depressive symptoms in a national Head Start program sample. *Archives of Pediatric and Adolescent Medicine, 153*, 801–807.

Lefkowitz, M. M., & Tesiny, E. P. (1984). Rejection and depression: Prospective and contemporaneous analyses. *Developmental Psychology, 20*, 776–785.

Lengua, L. J., Sandler, I. N., West, S. G., Wolchik, S. A., & Curran, P. J. (1999). Emotionality and self-regulation, threat appraisal, and coping in children of divorce. *Development and Psychopathology, 11*, 15–37.

Lengua, L. J., Wolchik, S. A., Sandler, I. N., & West, S. G. (2000). The additive and interactive effects of parenting and temperament in predicting problems of children of divorce. *Journal of Clinical Child Psychology, 29*, 232–244.

Leinonen, J. A., Solantaus, T. S., & Punamaki, R. L. (2003). Parental mental health and children's adjustment: The quality of marital interaction and parenting as mediating factors. *Journal of Child Psychology and Psychiatry, 44*, 227–241.

Levenson, M. R., Aldwin, C. M., Bosse, R., & Spiro, A. (1988). Emotionality and mental health: Longitudinal findings from the normative aging study. *Journal of Abnormal Psychology, 97*, 94–96.

Leventhal, T., & Brooks-Gunn, J. (2000). The neighborhoods they live in: The effects of neighborhood residence on child and adolescent outcomes. *Psychological Bulletin, 126*, 309–337.

Lewinsohn, P. M., Clarke, F. N., Hops, H., & Andrews, J. (1990). Cognitive–behavioral treatment for depressed adolescents. *Behavior Therapy, 21*, 385–401.

Lewinsohn, P. M., & Essau, C. A. (2002). Depression in adolescents. In: C. L. Hammen & I. H. Gotlib (Ed.), *Handbook of depression* (pp.541–559). New York: Guilford Press.

Lewinsohn, P. M., Hops, H., Roberts, R. E., Seeley, J. R., & Andrews, J. A. (1993). Adolescent psychopathology: I. Prevalence and incidence of depression and other DSM-III-R disorders in high school students. *Journal of Abnormal Psychology, 102*, 133–144.

Lewinsohn, P. M., Joiner, T. E., & Rohde, P. (2001). Evaluation of cognitive diathesis-stress models in predicting major depressive disorder in adolescents. *Journal of Abnormal Psychology, 110*, 203–215.

Lewinsohn, P. M., Roberts, R. E., Seeley, J. R., Rohde, P., Gotlib, I. H., & Hops, H. (1994). Adolescent psychopathology: II. Psychosocial risk factors for depression. *Journal of Abnormal Psychology, 103*, 302–315.

Lewinsohn, P. M., Rohde, P., Klein, D. N., & Seeley, J. R. (1999). Natural course of adolescent major depressive disorder: I. Continuity into young adulthood. *Journal of the American Academy of Child and Adolescent Psychiatry, 38*, 56–63.

Lewinsohn, P. M., Rohde, P., Seeley, J. R., Klein, D. N., & Gotlib, I. H. (2003). Psychosocial functioning of young adults who have experienced and recovered from major depressive disorder during adolescence. *Journal of Abnormal Psychology, 112*, 353–363.

Lewinsohn, P. M., & Rosenbaum, M. (1987). Recall of parental behavior by acute depressives, remitted depressives, and nondepressives. *Journal of Personality and Social Psychology, 52*, 611–619.

Liebowitz, M. R., Stallone, F., Dunner, D. L., & Fieve, R. R. (1979). Personality features of patients with primary affective disorder. *Acta Psychiatrica Scandinavica, 60*, 214–224.

Lovejoy, M. C., Graczyk, P. A., O'Hare, E., & Neuman, G. (2000). Maternal depression and parenting: A meta-analytic review. *Clinical Psychology Review, 20*, 561–592.

Maccoby, E., & Martin, J. (1983) Socialization in the context of the family: Parent–child interactions. In: E. M. Hetherington (Ed.), & P. H. Mussen (Series Ed.), *Handbook of child psychology: Vol. 4. Socialization, personality, and social development* (p. 1101). New York: Wiley.

Magana, A. B., Goldstein, M. J., Karno, M., Miklowitz, D. J., Jenkins, J., & Falloon, I. R. H. (1986). A brief method for assessing expressed emotion in relatives of psychiatric patients. *Psychiatry Research, 17*, 203–212.

Marton, P., & Maharaj, S. (1993). Family factors in adolescent unipolar depression. *Canadian Journal of Psychiatry, 38*, 373–382.

McCauley, E., & Myers, K. (1992b). The longitudinal clinical course of depression in children and adolescents. *Child and Adolescent Psychiatric Clinics of North America, 1*, 183–196.

McCauley, E., Myers, K., Mitchell, J., Calderon, R., Schloredt, K., & Treder, R. (1993). Depression in young people: initial presentation and clinical course. *Journal of the American Academy of Child Adolescent Psychiatry, 32*, 714–722.

McCranie, E. W., & Bass, J. D. (1984). Childhood family antecedents of dependency and self-criticism: Implications for depression, *Journal of Abnormal Psychology, 93*, 3–8.

McFarlane, A. H., Bellissimo, A., & Norman, G. R. (1995). The role of family and peers in social self-efficacy: Links to depression in adolescence. *American Journal of Orthopsychiatry, 65*, 402–410.

McFarlane, A. H., Bellissimo, A., Norman, G. R., & Lange, P. (1994). Adolescent depression in a school-based community sample: Preliminary findings on contributing social factors. *Journal of Youth and Adolescence, 23*, 601–620.

McGinn, L. K., Cukor, D., Sanderson, W. C. (2005). The relationship between parenting style, cognitive style, and anxiety and depression: Does increased early adversity influence symptom severity through the mediating role of cognitive style? *Cognitive Therapy and Research, 29*, 219–242.

McKeown, R. E., Garrison, C. Z., Jackson, K. L., Cuffe, S. P., Addy, C. L., & Waller, J. L. (1997). Family structure and cohesion, and depressive symptoms in adolescents. *Journal of Research on Adolescence, 7*, 267–281.

Messer, S. C., & Gross, A. M. (1995). Childhood depression and family interaction: A naturalistic observation study. *Journal of Clinical Child Psychology, 24,* 77–88.

Miller, I. W., Epstein, N. B., Bishop, D. S., & Keitner, G. I. (1985). The McMaster Family Assessment Device: Reliability and validity. *Journal of Marital and Family Therapy, 11*, 345–356.

Miller, L., Warner, V., Wickramaratne, P., & Weissman, M. M. (1999). Self-esteem and depression: Ten year follow-up of mothers and offspring. *Journal of Affective Disorders, 52*, 41–49.

Moos, R., & Moos, B. (1981). *Family environment scale manual*. Palo Alto: Consulting Psychologists Press.

Mullins, L. L., Peterson, L., Wonderlich, S. A., & Reaven, N. M. (1986). The influence of depressive symptomatology in children on the social responses and perceptions of adults. *Journal of Clinical Child Psychology, 15*, 233–240.

Munafo, M. R., Clark, T. G., Moore, L. R., Payne, E., Walton, R., & Flint, J. (2003). Genetic polymorphisms and personality in healthy adults: A systematic review and meta-analysis. *Molecular Psychiatry, 8*, 471–484.

Muris, P., Meesters, C., Schouten, E., & Hoge, E. (2004). Effects of perceived control on the relationship between perceived parental rearing behaviors and symptoms of anxiety and depression in nonclinical preadolescents. *Journal of Youth and Adolescence, 33*, 51–58.

Muris, P., Schmidt, H., Lambrichs, R., & Meesters, C. (2001). Protective and vulnerability factors of depression in normal adolescents. *Behavior Research and Therapy, 39*, 555–565.

Murray, C. J. L., & Lopez, A. D. (Eds). (1996). *The global burden of disease*. Cambridge, MA: Harvard University.

Nelson, D. R., Hammen, C., Brennan, P. A., & Ullman, J. B. (2003). The impact of maternal depression on adolescent adjustment: The role of expressed emotion. *Journal of Consulting and Clinical Psychology, 71*, 935–944.

Neuman, R. J., Geller, B., Rice, J. P., & Todd, R. D. (1997) Increased prevalence and earlier onset of mood disorders among relatives of prepubertal versus adult probands. *Journal of the American Academy of Child and Adolescent Psychiatry, 36*, 466–473.

Nolen-Hoeksema, S., Girgus, J. S., & Seligman, M. E. P. (1992). Predictors and consequences of childhood depressive symptoms: A 5-year longitudinal study. *Journal of Abnormal Psychology, 101*, 405–422.

Nolen-Hoeksema, S., Wolfson, A., Mumme, D., & Guskin, K. (1995). Helplessness in children of depressed and nondepressed mothers. *Developmental Psychology, 31*, 377–387.

O'Connor, B. P., & Dvorak, T. (2001). Conditional associations between parental behavior and adolescent problems: A search for personality–environment interactions. *Journal of Research in Personality, 35*, 1–26.

Ohannessian, C. M., Lerner, R. M., Lerner, J. V., & von Eye, A. (1994). A longitudinal study of perceived family adjustment and emotional adjustment in early adolescence. *Journal of Early Adolescence, 14*, 371–390.

O'Leary, K., & Beach, S. R. (1990). Marital therapy: A viable treatment for depression and marital discord. *American Journal of Psychiatry, 147*, 183–186.

Oliver, J. M., & Berger, L. S. (1992). Depression, parent-offspring relationships, and cognitive vulnerability. *Journal of Social Behavior and Personality, 7*, 415–429.

Oliver, J. M., Handal, P. J., Finn, T., & Herdy, S. (1987). Depressed and nondepressed students and their siblings in frequent contact with their families: Depression and perceptions of the family. *Cognitive Therapy and Research, 11*, 501–515.

Olsen, D. H. (1986). Circumplex model VII: Validation studies and FACES III. *Family Process, 26*, 337–351.

Panak, W. F., & Garber, J. (1992). Role of aggression, rejection, and attributions in the prediction of depression in children. *Development and Psychopathology, 4*, 145–165.

Papini, D. R., & Roggman, L. A. (1992). Adolescent perceived attachment to parents in relation to competence, depression, and anxiety: A longitudinal study. *Journal of Early Adolescence, 12*, 420–440.

Parker, G. (1983). Parental 'affectionless control' as an antecedent to adult depression: A risk factor delineated. *Archives of General Psychiatry, 40*, 956–960.

Parker, G., Tupling, H., & Brown, L. B. (1979). A parental bonding instrument. *British Journal of Medical Psychology, 52*, 1–10.

Patterson, G. R. (1982). *A social learning approach to family intervention: Vol. 3. Coercive family process.* Eugene, OR: Castalia.

Pelham, W. E., Lang, A. R., Atkeson, B., Murphy, D. A., Gnagy, E. M., Greiner, A. R., Vodde-Hamilton, M., & Greenslade, K. E. (1997). Effects of deviant child behavior on parental distress and alcohol consumption in laboratory interactions. *Journal of Abnormal Child Psychology, 25*, 413–424.

Perris, C., Arrindell, W. A., Perris, H., Eisemann, M., van der Ende, J., & von Rnorring, L. (1986). Perceived depriving parental rearing and depression. *British Journal of Psychology, 148*, 170–175.

Pilowsky, D. J., Wickramaratne, P., Rush, A. J., Hughes, C., Garber, J., Malloy, E., King, C., Cerda, G., Sood, A. B., Alpert, J. E., Wisniewski, S., Trivedi, M. H., Talati, A., Carlson, M., Liu, H. H., Fava, M., & Weissman, M. M. (2004). *STAR-D-child study: Rationale, design and methods.* Presented at the annual meeting of the American Psychiatric Association, New York.

Plomin, R., DeFries, J. C., McClearn, G. E., & McGuffin, P. (2001). *Behavior genetics* (4th ed.). New York: Worth.

Plomin, R., Reiss, D., Hetherington, E. M., & Howe, G. (1994). Nature and nurture: Genetic contributions to measures of the family environment. *Developmental Psychopathology, 30*, 32–43.

Polaino-Lorente, A., & Domenech, E. (1993). Prevalence of childhood depression: Results of the first study in Spain. *Journal of Child Psychology and Psychiatry, 34,* 1007–1017.

Poznanski, E., & Zrull, J. P. (1970). Childhood depression: Clinical characteristics of overtly depressed children. *Archives of General Psychiatry, 23,* 8–15.

Puig-Antich, J., Kaufman, J., Ryan, N. D., Williamson, D. E., Dahl, R. E., Lukens, E., Todak, G., Ambrosini, P., Rabinovich, H., & Nelson, B. (1993). The psychosocial functioning and family environment of depressed adolescents. *Journal of the American Academy of Child and Adolescent Psychiatry, 32,* 244–253.

Puig-Antich, J., Lukens, E., Davies, M., Goetz, D., Brennan-Quattrock, J., & Todak, G. (1985a). Psychosocial functioning in prepubertal major depressive disorders: I. Interpersonal relationships during the depressive episode. *Archives of General Psychiatry, 42,* 500–507.

Puig-Antich, J., Lukens, E., Davies, M., Goetz, D., BrennanQuattrock, J., & Todak, G. (1985b). Psychosocial functioning in prepubertal major depressive disorders: II. Interpersonal relationships after sustained recovery from affective episode. *Archives of General Psychiatry, 42,* 511–517.

Radke-Yarrow, M. (1998). *Children of depressed mothers.* Cambridge: Cambridge University Press.

Randolph, J. J., & Dykman, B. M. (1998). Perceptions of parenting and depression-proneness in the offspring: Dysfunctional attitudes as a mediating mechanism. *Cognitive Therapy and Research, 22,* 377–400.

Rapee, R. M. (1997). Potential role of childrearing practices in the development of anxiety and depression. *Clinical Psychology Review, 17,* 47–67.

Rao, U., Ryan, N. D., Birmaher, B., Dahl, R. E., Williamson, D. E., Kaufman, J., Rao, R., & Nelson, B. (1995). Unipolar depression in adolescents: Clinical outcomes in adulthood. *Journal of the American Academy of Child and Adolescent Psychiatry, 34,* 566–578.

Reich, J., Noyes, R., Hirschfeld, R., Coryell, W., & O'Gorman, M. (1987). State and personality in depressed and panic patients. *American Journal of Psychiatry, 144,* 181–187.

Reinherz, H. Z., Paradis, A. D., Giaconia, R. M., Stashwick, C. K., & Fitzmaurice, G. (2003). Childhood and adolescent predictors of major depression in the transition to adulthood. *American Journal of Psychiatry, 160,* 2141–2147.

Riley, A. W., Broitman, M., Coiro, M. J., & Keefer M (2003). Treating maternal depression: Effects on parenting and on children's behavior. Paper presented at the annual meeting of the Society for Research in Child Development, Tampa, Florida, April 26.

Roberts, J. E., Gotlib, I. H., & Kassel, J. D. (1996). Adult attachment security and symptoms of depression: The mediating roles of dysfunctional attitudes and low self-esteem. *Journal of Personality and Social Psychology, 70,* 310–320.

Robertson, J. N., & Simons, R. L. (1989). Family factors, self-esteem, and adolescent depression. *Journal of Marriage & Family, 51,* 125–138.

Robins, L. N., Locke, B. Z., & Regier, D. A. (1991). An overview of psychiatric disorders in America. In: L. N. Robins & D. A. Regier (Eds), *Psychiatric disorders in America: The epidemiologic catchment area project* (pp. 328–366). New York: The Free Press.

Robinson, N. S., Garber, J., & Hilsman, R. (1995). Cognitions and stress: Direct and moderating effects on depressive versus externalizing symptoms during the junior high school transition. *Journal of Abnormal Psychology, 104,* 453–463.

Rohde, P., Lewinsohn, P. M., & Seeley, J. R. (1994). Are adolescents changed by an episode of major depression? *Journal of the American Academy of Child and Adolescent Psychiatry, 33,* 1289–1298.

Rose, D. T., & Abramson, L. Y. (1992). Developmental predictors of depressive cognitive style: Research and theory. In: D. Cicchetti & S.L. Toth (Eds), *Rochester symposium on developmental psychopathology* (Vol. 4, pp. 323–349). Hillsdale, NJ: Erlbaum.

Rosenbaum, J., Biederman, J., Hirshfeld Becker, D. R., Kagan, J., Snidman, N., Friedman, D., Nineberg, A., Gallery, D. J., & Faraone, S. V. (2000). A controlled study of behavioral inhibition in children of parents with panic disorder and depression. *American Journal of Psychiatry, 157,* 2002–2010.

Rothbart, M. K., & Bates, J. (1998). Temperament. In: W. Damon & N. Eisenberg (Eds), *Handbook of child psychology: Social, emotional, and personality development* (Vol. 3, pp. 105–176). New York: Wiley.

Rothbart, M. K, Posner, M. I., & Hershey, K. L. (1995). Temperament, attention, and developmental psychopathology. In: D. Cicchetti & D. Cohen (Eds), *Developmental psychopathology: Vol. 1. Theory and methods* (pp. 315–340). New York: Wiley.

Rubin, K. H., & Mills, R. S. L. (1988). The many faces of social isolation in childhood. *Journal of Consulting and Clinical Psychology, 56*, 916–924.

Rudolph, K. D., Hammen, C., Burge, D., Lindbert, N., Herzberg, D., & Dalie, S. E. (2000). Toward an interpersonal life-stress model of depression: the developmental context of stress generation. *Development and Psychopathology, 12*, 215–234.

Rudolph, K. D., Kurlakowsky, K. D., & Conley, C. S. (2001). Developmental and social-contextual origins of depressive control-related beliefs and behavior. *Cognitive Therapy and Research, 25*, 447–475.

Rueter, M. A., Scaramella, L., Wallace, L. E., & Conger, R. D. (1999). First-onset of depressive or anxiety disorders predicted by the longitudinal course of internalizing symptoms and parent-adolescent disagreements. *Archives of General Psychiatry, 56*, 726–732.

Rutter, M., Macdonald, H., Le Couteur, A., Harrington, R., Bolton, P., & Bailey, A. (1990). Genetic factors in child psychiatric disorders — II. Empirical findings. *Journal of Child Psychology and Psychiatry, 31*, 39–83.

Ryan, N. D. (1998). Psychoneuroendocrinology of children and adolescents. *The Psychiatric Clinics of North America, 21*, 435–441.

Ryan, N. D., Birmaher, B., Perel, J. M., Dahl, R. E., Meyer, V., Al-Shabbout, M., Iyengar, S., & Puig-Antich, J. (1992). Neuroendocrine response to L-5-hydroxytryptophan challenge in prepubertal major depression. *Archives of General Psychiatry, 49*, 843–851.

Ryan, N. D., & Dahl, R. (1993). The biology of depression in children and adolescents. In: J. J. Mann & D. J. Kupfer (Eds), *Biology of depressive disorders, Part B: Subtypes of depression and comorbid disorders* (pp. 37–58). New York: Plenum.

Ryan, N. D., Dahl, R. E., Birmaher, B., Williamson, D. E., Iyengar, S., Nelson, B., Puig-Antich, J., & Perel, J. M. (1994). Stimulatory tests of growth hormone secretion in prepubertal major depression: Depressed versus normal children. *Journal of the American Academy of Child and Adolescent Psychiatry, 33*, 824–833.

Ryan, N. D., Puig-Antich, J., Ambrosini, P., Rabinovich, H., Robinson, D., Nelson, B., Iyengar, S., & Twomley, J. (1987). The clinical picture of major depression in children and adolescents. *Archives of General Psychiatry, 44*, 854–861.

Sagrestano, L. M., Paikoff, R. L., Holmbeck, G. N., & Fendrich, M. (2003). A longitudinal examination of familial risk factors for depression among inner-city African American adolescents. *Journal of Family Psychology, 17*, 108–120.

Sanders, M. R., Dadds, M. R., Johnston, B. M., & Cash, R. (1992). Childhood depression and conduct disorder: I. Behavioral, affective, and cognitive aspects of family problem-solving interactions. *Journal of Abnormal Psychology, 101*, 495–504.

Sanford, M., Szatmari, P., Spinner, M., Munroe-Blum, H., Ellen Jamieson, E., Walsh, C., & Jones, D. (1995). Predicting the one-year course of adolescent major depression. *Journal of the American Academy of Child and Adolescent Psychiatry, 34*, 1618–1628.

Scarr, S. (1992). Developmental theories for the 1990s: Development and individual differences. *Child Development, 63*, 1–19.

Scarr, S., & McCartney, K. (1983). How people make up their own environments: A theory of genotype-environment effects. *Child Development, 54*, 424–435.

Schaefer, E. S. (1965). A configural analysis of children's reports of parent behavior. *Journal of Consulting Psychology, 27*, 552–557.

Schludermann, E., & Schludermann, S. (1970). Replicability of factors in children's report of parent behavior (CRPBI). *Journal of Psychology, 76*, 239–249.

Schwartz, C. E., Dorer, D. J., Beardslee, W. R., Lavori, P. W., & Keller, M. B. (1990). Maternal expressed emotion and parental affective disorder: Risk for childhood depressive disorder, substance abuse, or conduct disorder. *Journal of Psychiatry Research, 24*, 231–250.

Schwartz, J. A. J., Kaslow, N. J., Racusin, G. R., & Carton, E. R. (1998). Interpersonal family therapy for childhood depression. In: V. B. Van Hasselt & M. Hersen (Eds), *Handbook of psychological treatment protocols for children and adolescents* (pp. 109–151). Mahwah, NJ: Erlbaum.

Schwarz, J. C., Barton-Henry, M. L., & Pruzinsky, T. (1985). Assessing child-rearing behaviors: A comparison of ratings made by mother, father, child, and sibling on the CRPBI. *Child Development, 56*, 462–479.

Segal, Z. V. (1988). Appraisal of the self-schema construct in cognitive models of depression. *Psychological Bulletin, 103*, 147–162.

Sexson, S. B., Glanville, D. N., & Kaslow, N. J. (2001). Attachment and depression: Implications for family therapy. *Child and Adolescent Psychiatric Clinics of North America, 10*, 465–471.

Sheeber, L., Hops, H., Alpert, A., Davis, B., & Andrews, J. (1997). Family support and conflict: Prospective relations to adolescent depression. *Journal of Abnormal Child Psychology, 25*, 333–344.

Sheeber, L., Hops, H., Andrews, J., Alpert, T., & Davis, B. (1998). Interactional processes in families with depressed and non-depressed adolescents: Reinforcement of depressive behavior. *Behavior Research and Therapy, 36*, 417–427.

Sheeber, L., Hops, H., & Davis, B. (2001). Family processes in adolescent depression. *Clinical Child and Family Psychology Review, 4*, 19–35.

Sheeber, L., & Sorensen, E. (1998). Family relationships of depressed adolescents: A multi-method assessment. *Journal of Clinical Child Psychology, 27*, 268–277.

Shiner, R. L. (1998). How shall we speak of children's personalities in middle childhood? A preliminary taxonomy. *Psychological Bulletin, 124*, 308–332.

Shiner, R. L., & Marmorstein, N. (1998). Family environments of adolescents with lifetime depression: Associations with maternal depression history. *Journal of the American Academy of Child and Adolescent Psychiatry, 37*, 1152–1160.

Shirk, S. R., Van Horn, M.,& Leber, K. (1997). Dysphoria and children's processing of supportive interactions. *Journal of Abnormal Child Psychology, 25*, 239–249.

Silverman, A. B., Reinherz, H. Z., & Giaconia, R. M. (1996). The long-term sequelae of child and adolescent abuse: a longitudinal community study. *Child Abuse and Neglect, 20*, 709–723.

Sim, H. (2000). Relationship of daily hassles and social support to depression and antisocial behavior among early adolescents. *Journal of Youth and Adolescence, 29*, 647–659.

Skinner, E. A., Zimmer-Gembeck, M. J., & Connell, J. P. (1998). Individual differences and the development of perceived control. *Monographs of the Society for Research in Child Development, 63* (2–3), v-220.

Slavin, L. A., & Rainer, K. L. (1990). Gender differences in emotional support and depressive symptoms among adolescents: A prospective analysis. *American Journal of Community Psychology, 18*, 407–421.

Slesnick, N., & Waldron, H. B. (1997). Interpersonal problem-solving interactions of depressed adolescents and their parents. *Journal of Family Psychology, 11*, 234–245.

Stark, K. D., Humphrey, L. L., Crook, K., & Lewis, K. (1990). Perceived family environments of depressed and anxious children: Child's and maternal figure's perspectives. *Journal of Abnormal Child Psychology, 18,* 527–547.

Stark, K. D., Schmidt. K. L., & Joiner. T. E., Jr. (1996). Cognitive triad: Relationship to depressive symptoms, parents' cognitive triad, and perceived parental messages. *Journal of Abnormal Child Psychology, 24*, 615–631.

Stein, D., Williamson, D. E., Birmaher, B., Brent, D. A., Kaufman, J., Dahl, R. E., Perel, J. M., & Ryan, N. D. (2000). Parent-child bonding and family functioning in depressed children and children at high risk for future depression. *Journal of the American Academy of Child and Adolescent Psychiatry, 39,* 1387–1395.

Stice, E., Ragan, J., & Randall, P. (2004). Prospective relations between social support and depression: Differential direction of effects for parent and peer support? *Journal of Abnormal Psychology, 113,* 155–159.

Stolberg, R. A., Clark, D. C., & Bongar, B. (2002). Epidemiology, assessment, and management of suicide in depressed patients. In: I. H. Gotlib & C. L. Hammen (Eds), *Handbook of depression* (pp. 581–601). New York: Guilford Press.

Sullivan, P. F., Neale, M. C., & Kendler, K. S. (2000). Genetic epidemiology of major depression: Review and meta-analysis. *American Journal of Psychiatry, 157,* 1552–1562.

Tarullo, L. B., DeMulder, E. K., Martinez, P. E., & Radke-Yarrow, M. (1994). Dialogues with preadolescents and adolescents: Mother–child interaction patterns in affectively ill and well dyads. *Journal of Abnormal Child Psychology, 22,* 33–51.

Tennant, C., Bebbington, P., & Hurry, J. (1980). Parental death in childhood and risk of adult depressive disorders: A review. *Psychological Medicine, 10,* 289–299.

Teti, D. M., & Gelfand, D. M. (1991). Behavioral competence among mothers of infants in the first year: The mediational role of maternal self-efficacy. *Child Development, 62,* 918–929.

Thapar, A., & McGuffin, P. (1994). A twin study of depressive symptoms in childhood. *British Journal of Psychiatry, 165,* 259–265.

Thase, M. E., & Howland, R. H. (1994). Refractory depression: Relevance of psychosocial factors and therapies. *Psychiatric Annals, 24,* 232–240.

Thomas, A., & Chess, S. (1977). *Temperament and development.* Oxford, England: Brunner/Mazel.

Thomsen, A. H., Compas, B. E., Colletti, R. B., Stanger, C., Boyer, M. C., & Konik, B. S. (2002). Parent reports of coping and stress responses in children with recurrent abdominal pain. *Journal of Pediatric Psychology, 27,* 215–226.

Tomarken, A. J., Dichter, G. S., Garber, J., & Simien, C. (2004). Relative left frontal hypo-activation in adolescents at risk for depression. *Biological Psychology, 67,* 77–102.

Tomarken, A. J., & Keener, A. D. (1998). Frontal brain asymmetry and depression: A self-regulatory perspective. *Cognition and Emotion, 12,* 387–420.

Toth, S. L., Manly, J. T., & Cicchetti, D. (1992). Child maltreatment and vulnerability to depression. *Development and Psychopathology, 4,* 97–112.

Turner, R. J., & Lloyd, D. A. (1999). The stress process and the social distribution of depression. *Journal of Health and Social Behavior, 40,* 374–404.

Van Leeuwen, K. G., Mervielde, I., Braet, C., & Bosmans, G. (2004). Child personality and parental behavior as moderators of problem behavior: Variable- and person-centered approaches. *Developmental Psychology, 40,* 1028–1046.

van Os, J., Jones, P., Lewis, G., Wadsworth, M., & Murray, R. (1997). Developmental precursors of affective illness in a general population birth cohort. *Archives of General Psychiatry, 54,* 625–631.

Vitaro, F., Pelletier, D., Gagnon, C., & Baron, P. (1995). Correlates of depressive symptoms in early adolescence. *Journal of Emotional and Behavioral Disorders, 3,* 241–251.

Wade, T. J., Cairney, J., & Pevalin, D. J. (2002). Emergence of gender differences in depression during adolescence: National panel results from three countries. *Journal of the American Academy of Child and Adolescent Psychiatry, 41,* 190–198.

Walker, L. S., Garber, J., & Greene, J. (1993). Psychosocial correlates of recurrent childhood pain: A comparison of pediatric patients with recurrent abdominal pain, organic illness, and psychiatric disorders. *Journal of Abnormal Psychology, 102,* 248–258.

Wallace, J., Schneider, T., & McGuffin, P. (2002). Genetics of depression. In: I. H. Gotlib & C. L. Hammen (Eds), *Handbook of depression* (pp. 169–191). New York: Guilford.

Warner, V., Mufson, L., & Weissman, M. M. (1995). Offspring at high and low risk for depression and anxiety: Mechanisms of psychiatric disorder. *Journal of the American Academy of Child and Adolescent Psychiatry, 34*, 786–797.

Watson, D., & Clark, L. A. (1995). Depression and the melancholic temperament. *European Journal of Personality, 9*, 351–366.

Webster-Stratton, C., & Hammond, M. (1988). Maternal depression and its relationship to life stress, perceptions of child behavior problems, parenting behaviors, and child conduct problems. *Journal of Abnormal Child Psychology, 16*, 299–315.

Weissman, M. M., Merikangas, K. R., Wickramaratne, P., Kidd, K. K., Prusoff, B. A., Leckman, J. F., & Pauls, D. L. (1986). Understanding the clinical heterogeneity of major depression using family data. *Archives of General Psychiatry, 43*, 430–434.

Weissman, M. M., & Olfson, M. (1995). Depression in women: Implications for health care research. *Science, 269*, 799–801.

Weissman, M. M., & Paykel, E. S. (1974). *The depressed woman: A study of social relationships.* Chicago, IL: University of Chicago Press.

Weissman, M. M., Paykel, E. S., & Klerman, G. L. (1972). The depressed woman as a mother. *Social Psychiatry, 7*, 98–108.

Weissman, M. M., Warner, V., Wickramaratne, P., Moreau, D., & Olfson, M. (1997). Offspring of depressed parents. 10 Years later. *Archives of General Psychiatry, 54*, 932–940.

Weissman, M. M., Warner, V., Wickramaratne, P., & Prusoff, B. A. (1988). Early-onset major depression in parents and their children. *Journal of Affective Disorders, 15*, 269–277.

Weissman, M. M., Wolk, S., Goldstein, R. B, Moreau, D., Adams, P., Greenwald, S., Klier, C. M., Ryan, N. D., Dahl, R. E., & Wickramaratne, P. (1999a). Depressed adolescents grown up. *Journal of the American Medical Association, 281*, 1707–1713.

Westin, D. (1991). Social cognition and object relations. *Psychological Bulletin, 109*, 429–455.

Whisman, M. A., & Kwon, P. (1992). Parental representations, cognitive distortions, and mild depression. *Cognitive Therapy and Research, 16,* 557–568.

Whisman, M. A., & McGarvey, A. L. (1995). Attachment, depressotypic cognitions, and dysphoria. *Cognitive Therapy & Research, 19*, 633–650.

Wierzbicki, M. (1987). Similarity of monozygotic and dizygotic child twins in level and lability of subclinically depressed mood. *American Journal of Orthopsychiatry, 57*, 33–40.

Wilhelm, K., Parker, G., Dewhurst-Savellis, J., & Asghari, A. (1999). Psychological predictors of sigle and recurrent major depressive episodes. *Journal of Affective Disorders, 54*, 139–147.

Williamson, D. E., Ryan, N. D., Birmaher, B., Dahl, R. E., Kaufman, J., Rao, U., & Puig-Antich, J. (1995). A case-control family history study of depression in adolescents. *Journal of the American Academy of Child and Adolescent Psychiatry, 34*, 1596–1607.

Windle, M. (1992). A longitudinal study of stress buffering for adolescent problem behaviors. *Developmental Psychology, 28*, 522–530.

Wood, A., Harrington, R., & Moore, A. (1996). Controlled trial of a brief cognitive–behavioural intervention in adolescent patients with depressive disorders. *Journal of Child Psychology and Psychiatry and Allied Disciplines, 37*, 737–746.

Zemore, R., & Rinholm, J. (1989). Vulnerability to depression as a function of parental rejection and control. *Canadian Journal of Behavioural Science, 21*, 364–376.

Zimmerman, M. A., Ramirez-Valles, J., Zapert, K. M., & Maton, K. I. (2000). A longitudinal study of stress-buffering effects for urban African-American male adolescent problem behaviors and mental health. *Journal of Community Psychology, 28*, 17–33.

SECTION III

Chapter 13

Family Involvement in Psychotherapy: What's the Evidence?

Katharina Manassis

Involving the family in psychotherapy, especially psychotherapy involving children, is intuitively appealing to clinicians. Families have increasingly been seen as not only maintaining or exacerbating maladaptive symptoms, but also as agents of therapeutic change that can help reduce symptoms and relapse of illness.

It is often assumed that there is substantial evidence to support family participation in psychotherapy. As this chapter will review, however, evidence for the benefits of family participation varies greatly by disorder. Moreover, the family's involvement in therapy is sometimes not the main focus of study, but is examined as a correlate or moderator of treatment outcome after testing the 'main' hypotheses of a clinical trial. In addition, because the nature and amount of family participation varies from one study to the next, there has been little replication of significant findings that have emerged. Approaches to family participation vary from educating families about disorder, to providing behavioral advice to parents or other family members, to viewing the family as a dynamic system that facilitates or hinders recovery in the affected family member. For many disorders, it is not clear which of these approaches is optimal, and combined approaches (for example, behavioral family systems therapy; Robin et al., 2000) have recently emerged.

Mindful of these limitations of the literature, one can still examine the role of family participation in treatment in relation to a number of common mental health conditions. In this chapter, interventions that include the family will be examined in relation to: internalizing disorders, externalizing disorders (including attention deficit hyperactivity disorder), autism spectrum disorders, eating problems/disorders, substance abuse, schizophrenia, and adolescent risk behaviors. There is a separate chapter in this volume addressing prevention. To conclude the chapter, limitations of the literature and opportunities for research will be further discussed.

Studies included were gleaned from a systematic search of medical and psychology databases, but in the interest of brevity and coherence only key findings are reported with emphasis on randomized controlled trials. Substantial literature has also examined the role of the family in the treatment of various childhood medical conditions, in child maltreatment and

Psychopathology and the Family
Edited by J. L. Hudson and R. M. Rapee
Copyright © 2005 by Elsevier Ltd.
All rights of reproduction in any form reserved
ISBN: 0-08-044449-0

its prevention, in addressing parental psychopathology, and in general family therapies (not focused on any particular disorder), but these topics are beyond the scope of the present chapter.

Internalizing Disorders

Anxiety Disorders

Several randomized controlled trials have examined the role of parental involvement in cognitive behavioral therapy (CBT) for childhood anxiety disorders, the best-studied treatment for these conditions. For example, Mendlowitz et al. (1999) studied group CBT, randomizing families to child group only, parent group only, combined treatment with child group and parent group, or a waiting list control condition. Child and parent groups were each 12 sessions long, with the parent group teaching strategies for child anxiety management and encouraging parents to apply these. While all active treatments showed reduced anxiety symptoms post-treatment, combined treatment showed additional benefits in fostering children's use of more adaptive coping strategies. The sample was physician-referred, and concurrent medication was permitted at constant dose, suggesting greater severity of illness than in some trials. In a separate trial in the same research center, Crawford and Manassis (2001) found family functioning and levels of frustration in families highly predictive of CBT outcomes in anxious children.

The importance of parental involvement in CBT has been examined more extensively by Barrett, Dadds, and Rapee (1996). They developed a behavioral family intervention to reduce families' tendency to encourage avoidant responses in their anxious children. In their first trial, combined treatment appeared superior to CBT alone (84% versus 57% remission), with further gains evident at 6- and 12-month follow-up in the combined condition (Barrett et al., 1996). Female and younger children appeared to do best in the combined condition. In a second trial, the same group found no further benefit from adding family management to child CBT immediately post-treatment, but a significantly greater remission from anxiety disorders at 1 year post-treatment when families had received the combined treatment (Barrett, 1998). Interestingly, this research team then related parental anxiety level to treatment differences (Cobham, Dadds, & Spence, 1998). Remission from anxiety disorder in the child was greater for the combined treatment only if the parent reported a high level of anxiety him/herself, suggesting that anxious parents have particular difficulty helping their children cope with anxiety and treatment participation may therefore be especially important in this group.

By contrast, Nauta, Scholing, Emmelkamp, and Minderaa (2003) did not find any added benefit for parent training when added to 12 sessions of child CBT. They randomized 79 children and teens aged 7–18 to either active treatment or waitlist control, and then further randomized the active treatment cell to either CBT only, or CBT with 7 sessions of parent training. Both active treatment groups showed greater symptomatic gains than waitlist control, post-treatment and at 3-month follow-up. The study's wide age range, brief parent training, and short follow-up period may, however, account for these discrepant findings.

Spence, Donovan, and Brechman-Toussaint (2000) studied cognitive behavioral therapy for childhood social phobia, with or without parental involvement. Both treatment groups improved compared to waitlist control, post-treatment and at 12-month follow-up. There was a trend towards superior results with parental involvement, but this effect was not statistically significant. Treatment for the specific disorder chosen (social phobia), however, requires children to change in contexts that do not necessarily involve their parents. This factor might account for the limited benefits of parental involvement.

Rather than adding parent training to an existing CBT model, Toren et al. (2000) developed an integrated, 10-session parent–child CBT group therapy program for children with anxiety disorders. They did an open trial of 24 children, but evaluated them at multiple time points, clearly showing symptomatic decreases during the treatment and follow-up periods, but not prior to treatment. Replicating the study by Cobham et al. (1998), they also found children with mothers with an anxiety disorder improved more than children of non-anxious mothers.

Finally, Barrett, Healy-Farrell, and March (2003) studied a 14-session cognitive-behavioral family treatment (CBFT) for obsessive compulsive disorder (OCD), delivered in either group or individual format, in relation to waitlist control. OCD diagnostic status and severity changed significantly for both active treatment conditions, immediately and at 6-month follow-up. There were no outcome differences between the individual or group format. In this study, there was no comparison with an active treatment that did not include families.

Summarizing the above, most studies found either added benefit when a parent component was added to CBT for childhood anxiety, or anxiety remission with integrated parent–child CBT treatment programs. There was variability, however, in the degree of parental involvement, length of time samples were followed, sample characteristics, and outcome measures. These factors make the studies difficult to compare. Two studies found an association between the benefits of parental involvement and high parental anxiety. One study found female gender and young age predictive of response to family intervention.

Depression

Brent, Holder, and Kolko (1997) developed and studied a family intervention for depressed youth (aged 13–18), based on a behavioral family systems approach. They combined an examination of dysfunctional patterns of interaction and communication (characteristic of a family systems approach) with a behavioral approach using problem-solving strategies. The family intervention was, however, not manualized. This family intervention was compared with individual cognitive behavioral therapy and with individual non-directive supportive therapy of equal duration (12–16 weeks) in a large randomized controlled trial ($n = 107$). Cognitive behavioral therapy resulted in the highest rate of remission (64.7%) of the three modalities and the most rapid symptom relief as rated by interviewers. The family intervention and the non-directive supportive therapy showed about equal efficacy (37.9 and 39.4% remission, respectively). Furthermore, family functioning measures did not appear to predict initial treatment outcomes. Interestingly, they did predict recurrence of depression 1 and 2 years after treatment, and additional treatment use (Birmaher, Brent, & Kolko, 2000). Thus, supporting impaired families beyond the acute treatment phase may be important in long-term outcomes for depressed teens. Also, given the moderate efficacy of the CBT treatment, this study suggested a further question: could the combination of CBT with family intervention produce even better outcomes?

Clarke, Rhode, Lewinsohn, Hops, and Seeley (1999) attempted to answer this question. They randomized 123 adolescents to a 16-session CBT program, to CBT plus a separate skill-teaching parents' group (8 sessions), or to a waitlist control group. Recovery rates for the active treatment groups (65 and 69%, respectively) differed significantly from that of the waitlist control group (48%), but not from each other. In other words, the addition of the parents' group did not appear to confer added benefit beyond the benefits of CBT. It is possible, of course, that 8 sessions is too little for parent treatment to be efficacious. Also, while parent groups have been shown efficacious when focused on behavioral or problem-solving approaches (for example, Mendlowitz et al., 1999), they may not provide the same opportunity to address individual family systems issues as the intervention offered by Brent and co-workers. Given the high rates of family dysfunction reported in relation to adolescent depression, the addition of family systems therapy to CBT would be worth exploring.

A recent study by Diamond, Reis, Diamond, Siqueland, and Isaacs (2002) found promising results for a 12-week attachment-based family therapy (ABFT) relative to waitlist control. They studied 32 predominantly African-American and inner-city adolescents meeting criteria for major depressive disorder in a randomized controlled trial. ABFT focused on improving parent–child relationships by enhancing empathic (versus dismissive or critical) interpersonal responses. Remission rates were 81% for the intervention condition and 47% for the control condition, with ABFT also showing greater reduction in depressive symptoms, anxiety symptoms, and family conflict. Although the number of participants was modest, findings are particularly noteworthy given the disadvantaged nature of the sample. Recruitment and retention of depressed adolescents in treatment has been problematic in CBT trials, even in more privileged samples. Comparisons of this treatment with CBT or with the combination of CBT and ABFT appear warranted.

In summary, the few existing trials of family intervention with depressed teens suggest that family intervention is likely superior to waitlist control, but not clearly superior to CBT. Studies of treatments that combine CBT with the most successful family interventions appear worthwhile. Given the high rates of relapse in adolescent depression, the role of family intervention in relapse prevention merits further study as well.

Externalizing Disorders

Conduct Disorder and Oppositional Behavior

By contrast to other diagnostic categories, parent-focused intervention in behavior disorders has been studied extensively. Several models of family-focused intervention have been applied with externalizing disorders. Patterson and colleagues developed and tested Parent Management Training (PMT), aimed to alter specific parenting practices (Patterson,

1982). This approach has been studied in numerous centres and populations, and shown to have both short- and long-term benefits for behavioral control (McMahon, 1994). Beyond behavioral improvements, improvements in school performance, sibling behavior, and maternal stress and depression have been associated with PMT (Patterson & Fleischman, 1979). Adding PMT to cognitive behavioral intervention for antisocial behavior has also been found to produce better outcomes than cognitive behavioral intervention alone (Kazdin, Bass, & Siegel, 1989).

Other parent-focused approaches include Carol Webster-Stratton's parent training program, evaluated in numerous clinical and at-risk samples (Webster-Stratton, 1998). In this program, parent groups are focused around video vignettes that demonstrate positive parenting skills. Eisenstadt and colleagues developed parent–child interaction therapy (Eisenstadt, Eyberg, & McNeil, 1993). This model is focused on improving parent–child attachment and has shown efficacy in at least five clinical trials.

Henggeler and Bourduin's "multisystemic family therapy" offers more intensive intervention for seriously disturbed youth (Henggeler & Bourduin, 1990). Intervention occurs in the home and community, and is individualized to address various social and family systems factors thought to contribute to youth behavior problems in each case. Therapists are available to families 24 h per day over a 4 to 6 month period. Several trials have shown reduced delinquency, drug use, and incarceration in youth from participating families.

Given the success of family intervention in this population, a number of reviews and meta-analyses of this work have emerged in the literature. Barlow and Stewart-Brown (2001), for example, systematically reviewed group parent education programs targeting behavior problems in 3 to 10-year-old children. They included published studies that used a control group and at least one standardized measure of child behavior. Sixteen such studies were identified, among 255 relevant publications. They concluded that despite considerable heterogeneity of interventions, populations, and outcome measures, positive change in both parental perceptions and objective measures of children's behavior was evident in the majority of studies. The small proportion of controlled studies (16 of 255) was cited as the major limitation of this literature, and reviews of other clinically relevant outcomes in this population, and other age groups were advocated.

Subsequently, Barlow and Parsons (2003) published a similar review of randomized controlled trials with at least one standardized behavioral outcome measure for 0 to 3-year-old children. Only five such studies were found, and these were subjected to separate meta-analyses of parent reports of child behavior, independent assessments of child behavior, and follow-up data. All three meta-analyses showed greater gains for intervention than control groups, but only independent assessments of child behavior differed significantly between the two. Given the paucity of studies and mixed results, the benefits of parent-based intervention in this age group are less clear, and further research is needed. Nixon (2002) reached similar conclusions in a review of parent training to address behavioral problems in preschoolers. Lack of accessibility and delivery of interventions was also identified as a problem, and studies of telephone or videotape-based interventions were advocated.

Mabe, Turner, and Josephson (2001) systematically reviewed PMT for child conduct disorder. They found limited support for improved parent–child relationships, mood, social competence, and school competence with intervention, in addition to definite behavioral gains. If confirmed by more rigorous trials, these would constitute substantial additional clinical benefits. Although acknowledging limitations of the cited studies, these authors advocate greater accessibility of this treatment and greater inclusion in mental health training programs.

Woolfenden, Williams, and Peat (2002) conducted a meta-analysis of trials of family intervention for conduct disorder and/or delinquency in youth aged 10–17 years. Although only 8 randomized controlled trials were found among 749 studies, data from these 8 trials found decreased time in institutions and decreased risk of re-arrest in treated subjects. Interventions varied, but included mainly PMT and multisystemic therapy.

Thus, although the small number of randomized controlled trials is disappointing, there is definite support for the efficacy of parent management training for child behavioral problems, at least in the school aged population. Greater dissemination of these interventions has been advocated. Greater study of long-term benefits is also warranted. Also, because there are several models of intervention (see above), comparisons of different models and further studies examining predictors of success for each model are indicated. These studies would allow better matching of child and family characteristics with the intervention model most likely to be effective in each case.

Attention Deficit Hyperactivity Disorder (ADHD)

Parental involvement in the treatment of ADHD deserves separate discussion, as ADHD is one of the few childhood conditions where the majority of treated children take medication. Combining patients from 26 randomized controlled trials (999 total), Klassen, Miller, Raina, Lee, and Olsen (2000) found that behavioral therapies, which regularly included parents, were not successful in ameliorating ADHD symptoms in the absence of medication. Also, combination treatment using both medication and behavioral intervention was not significantly better than medication alone.

Since then, the large, randomized Multimodal Treatment Study of ADHD (MTA study) reached substantially the same conclusion (The MTA Cooperative Group, 1999). Children aged 7–10 with ADHD were provided either treatment as usual in the community, medication management alone, psychosocial treatment alone, or a combination of medication and psychosocial treatment. The psychosocial treatment was intensive, and included: 30 parent-training sessions, 20 school visits and teacher-training sessions, a summer treatment program for the children, and a part-time classroom aide. Most children showed the greatest symptom remission when administered medication with or without the psychosocial treatment. Only in children with ADHD and comorbid anxiety disorder(s) did the efficacy of the psychosocial treatment approach that of medication. Additional, smaller trials have also found that parent training does not result in further symptom reduction in ADHD children in the presence of medication (Montiel et al., 2002; Weinberg, 2000). Some gains have been reported in parent–child relationships (decreased conflict) and in non-ADHD classroom behavior, but not in core ADHD symptoms (Anastopoulos, Shelton, & DuPaul, 1993). The strong neuropsychological basis of ADHD may account for its lack of response to parent-based intervention alone.

Nevertheless, interest in parent training persists due in large part to concerns about adverse effects of stimulants, particularly in younger children. Many parents and clinicians are uncomfortable using stimulant medications in preschoolers, and diagnostic specificity for ADHD is also lower in this age group. Some authors have also advocated using parent training to allow for a reduction in stimulant dose, in children sensitive to stimulant side effects (Horn et al., 1991).

Sonuga-Barke, Daley, Thompson, Laver-Bradbury, and Weeks (2001) compared parent training, parent support, and waitlist control in the treatment of ADHD-like symptoms in 3-year olds. They found reduced ADHD symptoms and increased maternal well-being in the parent training group relative to the other two. They concluded that psychostimulants may not be a necessary component of effective treatment in this age group. They then examined the effect of maternal ADHD on the intervention's success using regression analysis (Sonuga-Barke, Daley, & Thompson, 2002). High levels of maternal ADHD limited improvements, suggesting that parental ADHD may have to be treated for this intervention to succeed. Long-term outcomes have not been studied, and it is unclear whether treating these very early symptoms of ADHD truly prevents disorder at school age, or whether maturation of the central nervous system would improve symptoms in some of these children anyway.

Autism Spectrum Disorders

Intensive behavioral interventions administered by professionals have shown promising results in outcomes for autistic children, when begun at a very early age (usually, prior to age 3) (Lovaas & Smith, 1989). Due to their intensity (40 h of intervention per week is recommended), however, such interventions can be extremely costly and are not always covered by medical insurance plans. Moreover, many autistic children are diagnosed after age 3, and are treated even later. For both reasons, parent-mediated interventions in autism are now receiving increased attention.

Unfortunately, a recent systematic review of this area (Diggle, McConachie, & Randle, 2003), was only able to locate two randomized controlled trials of such interventions that included at least one, objective child-related outcome measure. Differences in type of intervention, comparison groups, and outcome measures were too great to compare the two studies. In one study ($n = 24$), child language (by parent report) and maternal knowledge of autism were significantly greater in the parent training intervention than in a 'local services only' comparison group (Drew et al., 2003). Lack of checking regarding implementation of the parent training intervention, non-matching of groups on initial IQ, and intensive behavioral intervention (by professionals) provided to some children in the 'local resources' group were cited as limitations. In the other study (Lovaas & Smith, 1989), intensive intervention by professionals was associated with better, measurable child outcomes than parent-mediated intervention, but there was no difference on parent and teacher reports of skills and behaviors.

Less rigorous studies have included several open trials, and one randomized controlled trial that used only parent-report outcomes. In the latter study (Sofronoff & Farbotko, 2002), parents of children with Asperger syndrome were provided with 6 h of training, either in 1-hour sessions or in a single intensive workshop. Regardless of format of training, they reported fewer problem behaviors in their children and increased self-efficacy compared to a non-intervention control group at 4 weeks and 3 months follow-up. In a fairly large open trial in Britain (*n* = 66), Bibby, Eikeseth, Martin, Mudford, and Reeves (2001) implemented parent-managed behavioral interventions by providing regular professional consultation. Progress in mental age, language, and adaptive behavior was evident in 60 children after 1 year. A longer follow-up (mean = 31.6 months), however, revealed that mean IQ had not changed. Significant behavioral gains had persisted, but none of the participants that had reached school age were in an unassisted mainstream placement. In a smaller open trial (*n* = 6), Smith, Groen, and Wynn (2000) taught parents how to implement Lovaas' intensive behavioral program at home in six full-day workshops with follow-up consultations over 2 to 3 years. They found five children acquired skills initially, but only two clearly improved on standardized tests at 2 to 3-year follow-up. The authors advocated further, multimodal assessment of parent-directed treatment, in view of their mixed results.

It is difficult to draw conclusions, given the early stage of research in this field. Several studies suggest that parent-mediated intervention may be beneficial to the child, at least in the short term (1 year or less) relative to non-intervention. Parental self-efficacy may also result in more harmonious family relationships and other benefits that are not easily captured on standardized measures. Ongoing professional involvement appears to be needed to improve longer term developmental outcomes in this population, but further randomized controlled trials are sorely needed.

Eating Problems

Eating problems are not a diagnostic category in DSM-IV (American Psychiatric Association, 1994), yet several studies have examined the role of parental involvement in addressing unhealthy dietary habits in children. Two studies examined parent-mediated exposure to either fruit or vegetables. Wardle et al. (2003) randomized 156 parent of 2 to 6-year-old children to either a 2-week exposure program, an information condition involving provision of nutritional advice, and a non-intervention control condition. Children in the exposure condition showed greater increases in liking, ranking, and consumption of the 'target vegetable' they had been exposed to versus children in the other two conditions. Gribble, Falciglia, Davis, and Couch (2003) developed a curriculum based on social learning theory for fifth and sixth grade students and their parents, with the goal of increasing fruit consumption. They compared completers of the program (*n* = 9) with participants who did not attend more than one session (*n* = 17) and showed increased knowledge and fruit intake in the children, with decreased use of controlling feeding strategies in their parents in the experimental group relative to the non-participant 'controls'. The high non-participation rate and non-random nature of the study, however, suggests caution in interpreting these findings.

Interventions targeting obesity in children are being increasingly studied, as this problem has dramatically increased in North America in recent decades (Gortmaker, Must, & Perrin, 1993). Epstein, Wing, and Koeske (1981), for example, randomized 6–12 year old obese children to individual behavior modification, concurrent behavior modification for parent and child, and a non-behavioral control condition (14 sessions per treatment). All three groups showed a decrease in percent overweight, but when parents were included the children maintained their weight loss at 5-year follow-up whereas other groups did not. Beech et al. (2003) provided nutritional information and behavioral advice in a 12-week interactive group program targeting obesity in African-American girls aged 8–10. They randomized the girls ($n = 60$) to child group, parent group, or a self-esteem group control condition. Participants in both experimental conditions showed a trend toward reduced body mass index and waist circumference, and reduced consumption of sweetened beverages. Recruitment, retention, and participation rates were reported, and found to be excellent. Sample size was small (about 20 per cell), likely accounting for the lack of significant differences.

Although the diversity of interventions makes it difficult to compare the above studies directly, the findings suggest that behavioral interventions involving parents merit consideration in children with eating problems, especially if they can be presented in a manner that minimizes treatment drop-out. Parental modeling may also facilitate maintenance of treatment gains.

Eating Disorders

In a detailed review of psychological treatments for anorexia nervosa, Kaplan (2002) found fewer than 20 controlled trials. He concluded that family therapy for younger patients with shorter duration of illness was the only intervention with some evidence base, but studies are not extensive. Only one of these family-based interventions has been manualized (Lock & Le Grange, 2001). For bulimia nervosa, family-based treatment has only been described in case reports (Le Grange, Lock, & Dymek, 2003).

Examining the controlled trials for anorexia more closely, one finds some inconsistency among the results for various trials. Russell, Szmukler, Dare, and Eisler (1987) found clear advantages for family therapy in comparison to individual supportive therapy in weight-restored anorexic girls under age 18 who had been ill for less than 3 years, but patients over 18 improved more with individual therapy. Robin et al. (2000) compared behavioral family systems therapy (BFST; emphasis on parent in control of eating, cognitive restructuring, and strategic-behavioral interventions to change family interactions) with ego-oriented individual therapy (emphasis on individual treatment of adolescent with parents seen collaterally). Thirty-seven adolescents with anorexia nervosa were randomized to one or the other condition. BFST was associated with greater weight gain and resumption of menstruation than the other condition, though both resulted in improvements.

By contrast, Crisp et al. (1991) ($n = 90$) found that female adolescents with anorexia did equally well in behavior therapy, behavior therapy plus supportive individual counseling, and behavior therapy plus family counseling. All three conditions were superior to a no treatment control condition when examining weight gain and return of menstruation, and improvements were maintained at 1-year follow-up.

Comparing different types of family intervention, Geist, Heinmaa, Stephens, Davis, and Katzman (2000) found that 4 months of family therapy and family psychoeducation both resulted in significant restoration of body weight in female adolescent anorexics. Similarly, Le Grange, Eisler, Dare, and Russell (1992) found comparable improvements occurred with conjoint family therapy (i.e. all family members treated together in the same room) as with separate counseling for parents and affected child in a small group of anorexic teens.

Thus, with the exception of Crisp's study, there appears to be support for family involvement in the treatment of adolescent anorexics. The best type of family intervention, however, remains to be determined.

Substance Abuse

Family intervention in the treatment of drug abuse has included, primarily, family psychoeducation and family therapy. Individual therapy, peer group therapy, and medical interventions (for example, methadone maintenance) are other common interventions. A recent meta-analysis by Stanton and Shadish (1997) compared these modalities in 1571 individuals with substance abuse disorders of varying ages (adolescent to adult). They concluded that, when treatment drop-outs were considered 'failures', family therapy was superior to other psychological modalities and was a useful adjunct to medical intervention. Interestingly, when only treatment completers were analyzed, the benefits of family therapy appeared less robust. The authors concluded that a greater proportion of poor prognosis cases were retained in family therapy than in the other modalities, and future studies must correct for this differential attrition between various psychological interventions. It appears that one of the key benefits of family therapy is families' ability to keep the patient participating in treatment.

Over a dozen randomized, controlled clinical trials have now shown greater efficacy (usually measured as drug-free days per year) for family therapy than other modalities (Waldron, 1997). One of the best known is Liddle and Dakof's (1995) multidimensional family therapy. This is an intensive 12–15 session family therapy delivered in the context of a multisystemic, multicomponent treatment program for adolescent drug abusers. In their research program, Liddle's group has examined treatment efficacy, the importance of adapting treatment themes to race and gender (to engage certain populations in treatment), the role of the therapist–adolescent alliance, the role of parenting, and in-session patterns of relationship change.

Recent studies are dismantling family treatments to determine which components contribute most to therapeutic change, and comparing outpatient family treatments to residential care in terms of both efficacy and cost effectiveness (Dennis, Titus, & Diamond, 2002). While results appear promising, especially in the adolescent population, these treatments may be difficult to implement in the substantial number of individuals affected by substance abuse who have distant or very strained relationships with their families (e.g. street youth, long-term substance abusers).

Schizophrenia

In schizophrenia, family intervention has been studied as an adjunct to pharmacotherapy. Given the strong biological basis of the disorder, few would advocate family intervention on its own. Nevertheless, an impressive body of research has focused on family treatment as an important aspect of preventing relapse in this devastating illness. Moreover, there is a clear theoretical model underlying family intervention in this disorder. When family members harbor negative attributions about schizophrenia or the family member affected by it, and particularly when they show high levels of "expressed emotion", onset of the illness is earlier and relapse is more frequent (Vaughn & Leff, 1981). Expressed emotion consists of the frequent expression of negative, critical thoughts and feelings within the family.

Based on this understanding of the relationship between family processes and illness, a number of family-based therapies have been developed and evaluated. A detailed review is provided in Goldstein (1991). Family therapy, when combined with medication, has consistently been shown superior in preventing relapse relative to other psychological interventions (e.g. supportive therapy, social skills training). In addition, Goldstein, Rodnick, and Evans (1978) did a unique, interesting examination of the relationship between family therapy and medication. They found comparable rates of relapse for moderate doses of medication versus low-dose medication and family therapy. In other words, the need for medication may be reduced when family therapy is included in the treatment program. Given that many unpleasant and potentially debilitating side effects of neuroleptic medication are dose-related, including family therapy may have a substantial positive impact on the patient's quality of life.

Recent studies have attempted to dismantle family intervention to determine the most essential components (for example, education, support, communication training), to compare different types of intervention, to examine subgroups who benefit more from certain types of intervention, and to examine cost-effectiveness. For example, Tarrier, Barrowclough, and Vaughn (1988) found that high expressed emotion families benefited more from longer intervention (9 months versus two sessions), regardless of the type of family intervention (educational versus experiential). By contrast, other investigators found no difference between using monthly family education sessions as an adjunct to medication and using more frequent home visits (Schooler, 1997). These investigators, however, did not subdivide families according to expressed emotion or other characteristics. As concerns about health care costs increase, less intensive interventions are becoming more popular, but the above studies suggest that they may not be suitable for all families.

Early Intervention with Adolescent Risk Behaviors

Parents of adolescents have often been engaged in interventions designed to reduce or prevent adolescent risk behaviors. Because the literature in this area has focused increasingly on 'harm reduction' rather than primary prevention (White & Pitts, 1999), this topic is included in the present chapter. Examples include parent-based interventions to prevent or reduce adolescents' alcohol consumption, alcohol-impaired driving, early onset of sexual intercourse, exposure to HIV, substance abuse, delinquency, self-harm behavior, and suicide risk (for example, Blake, Simkin, Ledsky, Perkins, & Calabrese, 2001; Mason, Kosterman, Hawkins, Haggerty, & Spoth, 2003; Toumbourou & Gregg, 2002; Turrisi, Jaccard, Taki, Dunnam, & Grimes, 2001). Many are open or non-random trials. This lengthy list also highlights one of the difficulties with research in this area: because few studies target the same risk behaviors, little replication or comparison of interventions has occurred. Furthermore, given limitations of time and resources, it is not feasible to provide large numbers of teens multiple interventions to prevent multiple risk behaviors. Interventions must either be behavior-specific and administered only to groups at high risk for that particular behavior, or be administered broadly and address multiple risk behaviors.

Universal interventions that promote responsible choices in the face of a variety of potential risks and temptations would seem ideal. Toumbourou and Gregg (2002) described such an intervention that targeted multiple risk factors. They studied professionally led, school-based groups aimed to empower parents to assist one another to improve communication skills and relationships with their adolescents. Fourteen intervention high schools were closely matched to fourteen comparison schools. They found increased maternal care, reduced parent–child conflict, reduced substance abuse, and less delinquency in intervention schools, with the largest impacts associated with directly participating parents. Interestingly, where best-friend dyads were identified, the best friend's positive family relationships reduced substance abuse among respondents. This and other social factors were thought to account for benefits to non-participating families at intervention schools.

Parent-related interventions that target single risk behaviors and have been studied in a randomized, controlled fashion include: the Preparing for the Drug Free Years Program (Mason et al., 2003), an intervention to reduce college student binge-drinking (Turrisi et al., 2001), and an intervention to reduce early onset sexual intercourse (Blake et al., 2001). Mason et al. (2003) randomized 429 rural adolescents to either a universal, family-focused intervention to reduce substance abuse and delinquency, or a control condition. Using latent growth curve modeling, they showed a slower rate of linear increase over time in substance abuse and delinquency in the experimental condition than the control condition. Turrisi et al. (2001) educated parents of recent high school graduates about binge drinking and how to discuss this subject with their teens just before they started college. Teens whose parents implemented the intervention were compared to a control sample during the first college semester. Significantly lower drinking tendencies and consequences related to drinking were found in the experimental group. It would be interesting to determine whether this effect persisted beyond the first semester. Blake et al. (2001) studied an abstinence-based curriculum for reducing early onset sexual intercourse. They randomized 351 middle school students to receive either classroom instruction alone or classroom instruction plus five homework assignments to be completed by students together with their parents. Relative to the classroom only group, they found that the group who were given the homework assignments reported greater self-efficacy for refusing high-risk behaviors, less intention to have sex before finishing high school, and more frequent discussions with their parents about sexual consequences. Unfortunately, follow-up data have not yet been reported to determine whether behavior actually differed between groups.

Interestingly, all the above interventions emphasized improved communication between parents and their adolescents. Further studies are therefore indicated to examine whether parent–teen communication is a key mediator of change. Apart from the longitudinal study by Mason et al. (2003), all studies cited are limited by short follow-up intervals.

Summary of the Literature

The first striking aspect of the literature regarding family-based interventions is its variability. Some disorders have an established theoretical basis for family intervention, and numerous randomized controlled trials to support interventions based on the theory. Research on family intervention for some other disorders is still in its infancy. In some disorders, family interventions are the mainstay of treatment, while in others they are adjunctive to medication at best.

Among the best-studied interventions are those for conduct and oppositional disorders of childhood. Here, there is definite evidence for efficacy but further work is needed on issues of dissemination, generalizability, and comparisons of types of family intervention. Family interventions to reduce relapse in schizophrenia are also well-established, and (unlike most interventions) are grounded in a clear theoretical model (the 'expressed emotion' model). The potential for reducing medication doses with successful family therapy is appealing in this population as well. Optimizing the amount and type of intervention for each case remains a research challenge. Numerous randomized controlled trials have shown efficacy for family therapy in the treatment of substance abuse, with the added benefit of higher patient participation in treatment when the family is involved. This treatment is not feasible for all substance abusers, however, as many have distant relationships with family members.

Evidence is beginning to accumulate for the efficacy of family interventions in internalizing disorders, anorexia nervosa, and adolescent risk behaviors. When done in the context of various CBT treatment programs, most trials found family interventions beneficial in the treatment of childhood anxiety disorders. Variability in the nature of the samples and interventions studied, however, makes it difficult to compare studies directly. Children whose parents were also anxious benefited more in some trials. Results appear less promising for family intervention in adolescent depression, but too few studies have been done to draw firm conclusions and manualized treatments are sorely needed. Similar to the situation in anxiety disorders, most studies support family intervention in anorexia nervosa, but interventions have been heterogenous. It is unclear which type of intervention is best. No randomized controlled trials have examined family intervention for bulimia nervosa, though some of the anorexia trials included bulimic subjects. Several randomized controlled trials have also examined diverse family interventions to address adolescent risk behaviors. Emphasis on improving parent–child communication is emerging as a common feature of many interventions. More study is clearly needed, especially of interventions that address multiple risk behaviors.

A small number of randomized trials have examined parent interventions to help children with autism and children with unhealthy eating behaviors. Only two rigorous randomized controlled trials have examined parent-implemented behavior modification in young autistic children. Initial findings suggest that impressive gains may be achieved in the short term, but ongoing professional involvement is likely needed to ensure long-term benefits for child development. Parent-implemented behavior modification has also been studied in a few trials examining unhealthy eating and obesity. While results appear promising, retention of patients in treatment and facilitating parental modeling of healthy eating have been identified as challenges.

Family intervention in ADHD has been studied in a number of trials and found not to confer added benefit to children on stimulant medication, with the possible exception of children with comorbid internalizing disorders. It may still be worth pursuing, however, in subgroups where the use of stimulant medication is less desirable (for example, very young children or children with adverse reactions to stimulants).

Further Research

To substantially advance studies of family-based intervention, future research must address gaps in the existing literature more systematically. First, therapies must be grounded in theories of family processes or mechanisms that can trigger or maintain disorder, or have the potential to ameliorate impairment in individuals affected by the disorder. Using this theoretical base, interventions must be developed that both educate families on the nature of the disorder and address the most salient family dynamics related to that disorder. Ideally, these interventions should be manualized with clear criteria for training and adherence to the therapy proposed.

Samples for study must reflect a broad range of sociodemographic characteristics, with samples large enough to draw meaningful conclusions. Sample attrition in various treatments must be accounted for, to allow for fair comparisons. The dose, duration, and type of treatment must be clearly described. Further randomized comparisons between different treatments and control groups are indicated for many disorders. Outcome measures must be well-described and standardized. Relapse prevention is clearly an important outcome for many, more chronic disorders.

The influence of subject age, developmental stage, gender, and parental characteristics (including parental psychopathology) on outcomes must be examined. Studies examining interactions between family interventions and medical or other psychological interventions for the disorder in question must be pursued. Long-term follow-ups are indicated to evaluate maintenance of treatment effects and the effects of the treatment on subsequent developmental stages. Replication of findings is indicated for many disorders.

If efficacy is established for an intervention, component analyses to develop more potent and cost-effective treatment are warranted. Subgroup analyses are also indicated, to better tailor treatment to individual and family characteristics. Finally, optimal methods of dissemination of evidence-based treatments, and studies of their generalizability to populations outside academic centres are needed to make these interventions relevant to the broader community.

References

American Psychiatric Association (1994). *Diagnostic and statistical manual of mental disorders, Fourth Edition (DSM-IV)*. Washington, DC: American Psychiatric Association.
Anastopoulos, A. D., Shelton, T. L., & DuPaul, G. T. (1993). Parent training for attention deficit hyperactivity disorder: Its impact on parent functioning. *Journal of Abnormal Child Psychology*, 21, 581–596.

Barlow, J., & Parsons, J. (2003). Group-based parent-training programmes for improving emotional and behavioral adjustment in 0–3 year old children. *Cochrane Database Systematic Reviews, 1,* CD003680.

Barlow, J., & Stewart-Brown, S. (2001). Behavior problems and group-based parent education programs. *Journal of Developmental and Behavioral Pediatrics, 21,* 356–370.

Barrett, P. M. (1998). Evaluation of cognitive-behavioral group treatments for childhood anxiety disorders. *Journal of Clinical Child Psychology, 27,* 459–468.

Barrett, P. M., Dadds, M. R., & Rapee, R. M. (1996). Family treatment of childhood anxiety: A controlled trial. *Journal of Consulting and Clinical Psychology, 64,* 333–342.

Barrett, P. M., Healy-Farrell, L., & March, J. S. (2003). Cognitive-behavioral family treatment of childhood obsessive compulsive disorder: A controlled trial. *Journal of the American Academy of Child and Adolescent Psychiatry, 43,* 46–62.

Beech, B. M., Klesges, R. C., Kumanyika, S. K., Murray, D. M., Klesges, L., McClanahan, B., Slwason, D., Nunnally, C., Rochon, J., McLain-Allen, B., & Pree-Cary, J. (2003). Child- and parent-targeted interventions: The Memphis GEMS pilot study. *Ethnicity and Disease, 13*(1 Suppl. 1), S40–S53.

Bibby, P., Eikeseth, S., Martin, N. T., Mudford, O. C., & Reeves, D. (2001). Progress and outcomes for children with autism receiving parent-managed intensive interventions. *Research in Developmental Disabilities, 22,* 425–447.

Birmaher, B., Brent, D. A., & Kolko, D. (2000). Clinical outcome after short-term psychotherapy for adolescents with major depressive disorder. *Archives of General Psychiatry, 57,* 29–36.

Blake, S. M., Simkin, L., Ledsky, R., Perkins, C., & Calabrese, J. M. (2001). Effects of a parent-child communications intervention on young adolescents' risk fore early onset of sexual intercourse. *Family Planning Perspectives, 33,* 52–61.

Brent, D. A., Holder, D., & Kolko, D. (1997). A clinical psychotherapy trial for adolescent depression comparing cognitive, family, and supportive therapy. *Archives of General Psychiatry, 54,* 77–88.

Clarke, G. N., Rhode, P., Lewinsohn, P. M., Hops, H., & Seeley, J. (1999). Cognitive-behavioral treatment of adolescent depression: Efficacy of acute group treatment and booster sessions. *Journal of the American Academy of Child and Adolescent Psychiatry, 38,* 272–279.

Cobham, V. E., Dadds, M. R., & Spence, S. H. (1998). The role of parental anxiety in the treatment of childhood anxiety. *Journal of Consulting and Clinical Psychology, 66,* 893–905.

Crawford, A. M., & Manassis, K. (2001). Familial predictors of treatment outcome in childhood anxiety disorders. *Journal of the American Academy of Child and Adolescent Psychiatry, 40,* 1182–1189.

Crisp, A. H., Norton, K., Gowers, S., Halek, C., Bowyer, C., & Yeldham, D. (1991). A controlled study of the effect of therapies aimed at adolescent and family psychopathology in anorexia nervosa. *British Journal of Psychiatry, 159,* 325–333.

Dennis, M., Titus, J. C., & Diamond, G. (2002). The cannabis youth treatment (CYT) experiment: Rationale, study design and analysis plans. *Addiction, 97*(Suppl. 1), 16–34.

Diamond, G. S., Reis, B. F., Diamond, G. M., Siqueland, L., & Isaacs, L. (2002). Attachment-based family therapy for depressed adolescents: A treatment development study. *Journal of the American Academy of Child and Adolescent Psychiatry, 41,* 1190–1196.

Diggle, T., McConachie, H. R., & Randle, V. R. (2003). Parent-mediated early intervention for young children with autism spectrum disorder. *Cochrane Database Systematic Reviews, 1,* CD003496.

Drew, A., Baird, G., Baron-Cohen, S., Cox, A., Slonims, V., Wheelwright, S., Swettenham, J., Berry, B., & Charman, T. (2003). A pilot randomized controlled trial of a parent training intervention for preschool children with autism. *European Child and Adolescent Psychiatry, 11,* 266–272.

Eisenstadt, T. H., Eyberg, S., & McNeil, C. B. (1993). Parent–child interaction therapy with behavior problem children: Relative effectiveness of two stages and overall treatment outcome. *Journal of Clinical Child Psychology, 22,* 42–51.

Epstein, L., Wing, R., & Koeske, R. (1981). Child and parent weight loss in family-based behavior modification programs. *Journal of Consulting and Clinical Psychology, 49,* 674–685.

Geist, R., Heinmaa, M., Stephens, D., Davis, R., & Katzman, D. (2000). Comparison of family therapy and family group psychoeducation adolescents with anorexia nervosa. *Canadian Journal of Psychiatry, 45,* 173–178.

Goldstein, M. J. (1991). Psychosocial (non-pharmacological) treatments for schizophrenia. In: A. Tazman & S. M. Goldfinger (Eds), *Review of psychiatry* (pp. 116–135). Washington, DC: American Psychiatric Association.

Goldstein, M. J., Rodnick, E. H., & Evans, J. R. (1978). Drug and family therapy in the aftercare of acute schizophrenics. *Archives of General Psychiatry, 35,* 1169–1177.

Gortmaker, S. L., Must, A., & Perrin, J. M. (1993). Social and economic consequences of overweight in adolescents and young adults. *New England Journal of Medicine, 329,* 1008–1012.

Gribble, L. S., Falciglia, G., Davis, A. M., & Couch, S. C. (2003). A curriculum based on social learning theory emphasizing fruit exposure and positive parent-child feeding strategies: A pilot study. *Journal of the American Dietetic Association, 103,* 100–103.

Henggeler, S. W., & Bourduin, C. M. (1990). *Family therapy and beyond: A multisystemic approach to treating the behavior problems of children and adolescents.* Pacific Grove, CA: Brooks/Cole.

Horn, W. F., Ialongo, N. S., Pascoe, J. M., Greenberg, G., Packard, T., Lopez, M., Wagner, A., & Puttler, L. (1991). Additive effects of psychostimulants, parent training, and self-control therapy with ADHD children. *Journal of the American Academy of Child and Adolescent Psychiatry, 30,* 233–240.

Kaplan, A. S. (2002). Psychological treatments for anorexia nervosa: A review of published studies and promising new directions. *Canadian Journal of Psychiatry, 47,* 235–242.

Kazdin, A. E., Bass, D., & Siegel, T. (1989). Cognitive-behavioral therapy and relationship therapy in the treatment of children referred for antisocial behavior. *Journal of Consulting and Clinical Psychology, 57,* 522–535.

Klassen, A., Miller, A., Raina, P., Lee, S. K., & Olsen, L. (2000). Attention-deficit hyperactivity disorder in children and youth: A quantitative systematic review of the efficacy of different management strategies. *Canadian Journal of Psychiatry, 44,* 1007–1016.

LeGrange, D., Eisler, I., Dare, C., & Russell, G. (1992). Evaluation of family treatment in adolescent anorexia nervosa: A pilot study. *International Journal of Eating Disorders, 12,* 347–357.

LeGrange, D., Lock, J., & Dymek, M. (2003). Family-based therapy for adolescents with bulimia nervosa. *American Journal of Psychotherapy, 57,* 237–251.

Liddle, H. L., & Dakof, G. (1995). Family-based treatment for adolescent drug use: State of the science. In: E. Rahdert (Ed.), *Adolescent drug abuse: Assessment and treatment* (pp. 218–254). Rockville, MD: NIDA.

Lock, J., & LeGrange, D. (2001). Can family-based treatment of anorexia nervosa be manualized? *Journal of Psychotherapy Practice and Research, 10,* 253–261.

Lovaas, O. I., & Smith, T. (1989). A comprehensive behavioral theory of autistic children: Paradigm for research and treatment. *Journal of Behavioral Therapy and Experimental Psychiatry, 20,* 17–29.

Mabe, P. A., Turner, M. K., & Josephson, A. M. (2001). Parent management training. *Child and Adolescent Psychiatric Clinics of North America, 10,* 451–464.

Mason, W. A., Kosterman, R., Hawkins, J. D., Haggerty, K. P., & Spoth, R. L. (2003). Reducing adolescents' growth in substance use and delinquency: Randomized trial effects of a parent-training prevention intervention. *Prevention Science, 4,* 203–212.

McMahon, R. (1994). Diagnosis, assessment and treatment of externalizing problems in children: The role of longitudinal data. *Journal of Consulting and Clinical Psychology, 62,* 901–917.

Mendlowitz, S., Manassis, K., Bradley, S., Scapillato, D., Miezitis, S., & Shaw, B. (1999). Cognitive behavioral group treatments in childhood anxiety disorders: The role of parental involvement. *Journal of the American Academy of Child and Adolescent Psychiatry, 38,* 1223–1229.

Montiel, N. C., Peata, J. A., Espina, M. G., Ferrer-Hernandez, M. E., Lapez-Rubio, A., Puetas-Sanchez, S., & Cardozo-Durain, J. J. (2002). A pilot study of methylphenidate and parent training in the treatment of children with attention-deficit hyperactivity disorder. *Reviews in Neurology, 35,* 201–205.

Nauta, M. H., Scholing, A., Emmelkamp, P. M., & Minderaa, R. B. (2003). Cognitive-behavioral therapy for children with anxiety disorders in a clinical setting: No additional effect of a cognitive parent training. *Journal of the American Academy of Child and Adolescent Psychiatry, 42,* 1270–1278.

Nixon, R. D. (2002). Treatment of behavior problems in preschoolers: A review of parent training programs. *Clinical Psychology Review, 22,* 525–546.

Patterson, G. R. (1982). *A social learning approach to family interventions: Coercive family process,* Eugene, OR: Castalia.

Patterson, G. R., & Fleischman, M. J. (1979). Maintenance of treatment effects: Some considerations concerning family systems and follow-up data. *Behavior Therapy, 10,* 168–185.

Robin, A. L., Siegel, P. T., Moye, A. W., Gilroy, M., Dennis, A. B., & Sikand, A. (2000). A controlled comparison of family versus individual therapy for adolescents with anorexia nervosa. *Journal of the American Academy of Child and Adolescent Psychiatry, 38,* 1482–1489.

Russell, G., Szmukler, G. I., Dare, C., & Eisler, I. (1987). An evaluation of family therapy in anorexia and bulimia nervosa. *Archives of General Psychiatry, 44,* 1047–1056.

Schooler, N. R. (1997). Relapse and rehospitalization during maintenance treatment of schizophrenia. *Archives of General Psychiatry, 54,* 453–463.

Smith, T., Groen, A. D., & Wynn, J. W. (2000). Randomized trial of intensive early intervention for children with pervasive developmental disorder. *American Journal of Mental Retardation, 105,* 269–285.

Sofronoff, K., & Farbotko, M. (2002). The effectiveness of parent management training to increase self-efficacy in parents of children with Asperger syndrome. *Autism, 6,* 271–286.

Sonuga-Barke, E. J., Daley, D., & Thompson, M. (2002). Does maternal ADHD reduce the effectiveness of parent training for preschool children's ADHD? *Journal of the American Academy of Child and Adolescent Psychiatry, 41,* 696–702.

Sonuga-Barke, E. J., Daley, D., Thompson, M., Laver-Bradbury, C., & Weeks, A. (2001). Parent-based therapies for preschool attention-deficit/hyperactivity disorder: A randomized controlled trial with a community sample. *Journal of the American Academy of Child and Adolescent Psychiatry, 40,* 402–408.

Spence, S. H., Donovan, C., & Brechman-Toussaint, M. (2000). The treatment of childhood social phobia: The effectiveness of a social skills training-based, cognitive behavioral intervention, with and without parental involvement. *Journal of Child Psychology and Psychiatry, 41,* 713–726.

Stanton, M. D., & Shadish, W. R. (1997). Outcome, attrition, and family-couples treatment for drug abuse: A meta-analysis and review of the controlled, comparative studies. *Psychology Bulletin, 122,* 170–191.

Tarrier, N., Barrowclough, C., & Vaughn, C. (1988). The community management of schizophrenia: A controlled trial of a behavioral intervention with families to reduce relapse. *British Journal of Psychiatry, 153,* 532–542.

The MTA Cooperative Group (1999). A 14-month randomized clinical trial of treatment strategies for attention-deficit/hyperactivity disorder. *Archives of General Psychiatry, 56,* 1073–1086.

Toren, P., Wolmer, L., Rosental, B., Eldar, S., Koren, S., Lask, M., Weizman, R., & Laor, N. (2000). Case series: Brief parent-child group therapy for childhood anxiety disorders using a manual-based cognitive-behavioral technique. *Journal of the American Academy of Child and Adolescent Psychiatry, 39*, 1309–1312.

Toumbourou, J. W., & Gregg, M. E. (2002). Impact of an empowerment-based parent education program on the reduction of youth suicide risk factors. *Journal of Adolescent Health, 31*, 277–285.

Turrisi, R., Jaccard, J., Taki, R., Dunnam, H., & Grimes, J. (2001). Examination of the short-term efficacy of a parent intervention to reduce college student drinking tendencies. *Psychology of Addictive Behavior, 15*, 366–372.

Vaughn, C. E., & Leff, J. P. (1981). Patterns of emotional response in relatives of schizophrenic patients. *Schizophrenia Bulletin, 7*, 43–44.

Waldron, H. B. (1997). Adolescent substance abuse and family therapy outcome. In: T.H. Ollendick & R.J. Prinz (Eds), *Advances in clinical child psychology* (pp. 199–234). New York: Plenum.

Wardle, J., Cooke, L.J., Gibson, E. L., Sapochnik, M., Sheiham, A., & Lawson, M. (2003). Increasing children's acceptance of vegetables: A randomized trial of parent-led exposure. *Appetite, 40*, 155–162,

Webster-Stratton, C. (1998). Prevention of conduct problems in Head Start children: Strengthening parent competencies. *Journal of Consulting and Clinical Psychology, 66*, 715–730.

Weinberg, H. A. (2000). Parent training for attention-deficit hyperactivity disorder: Parental and child outcome. *Journal of Clinical Psychology, 55*, 907–913.

White, D., & Pitts, M. (1999). Educating young people about drugs: A systematic review. *Addiction, 93*, 1475–1487.

Woolfenden, S. R., Williams, K., & Peat, J. K. (2002). Family and parenting interventions for conduct disorder and delinquency: A meta-analysis of randomized controlled trials. *Archives of Diseases of the Child, 86*, 251–256.

Chapter 14

Clinical Perspectives on Involving the Family in Treatment

Frank M. Dattilio

Family Impact on the Etiology of Psychopathology: Chicken or the Egg

The professional literature is quite stealth in its presentation of research on family dynamics and their effect on psychopathology. However, there is a decided lack of emphasis in the professional literature on the actual interventions available involving the family, be it the family-of-origin or the immediate family, as a change agent in the course of treatment. Specifically, how and when to use family members in treatment is an important topic, depending on the etiology of the disorder and whether or not the psychopathology is clearly rooted in family dynamics.

A distinction should be made at this point between family-of-origin and the immediate family. Family-of-origin pertains to the body of individuals from which one hails; namely, parents, siblings, etc. In some cases, this might also include an adopted family as well. The immediate family, on the other hand, involves the downward descent, which includes the individual's spouse and offspring (from the union with their spouse), in which they are involved on a day-to-day basis.

The conceptualization of how the family impacts on psychopathology in individuals is nicely outlined elsewhere in this volume (see Section II). Thus, it is the aim of this particular chapter to address the practical applications of methods that include families in treatment for a specific problem. This chapter highlights specific methods and strategies to use with families and when not to include family members in treatment. Some of the pitfalls in dealing with the challenges encountered with difficult families is also addressed.

Because there is some controversy in the field with regard to whether to involve family members in treatment, the plan was to structure this chapter from a dual perspective, focusing on both pros and cons of involving family members in the treatment regime. In one respect, if a therapist chooses to involve family members in treatment, he/she needs to consider how and when family members should be used and in what medium. In some instances, a therapist or clinician may decide not to involve family members in treatment,

Psychopathology and the Family
Edited by J. L. Hudson and R. M. Rapee
ISBN: 0-08-044449-0

or actually preclude their involvement, and simply work with an individual on a solo basis. When this is the case, then the specific rationale should be underlined as to why, along with directives on how clinicians should manage a family who may desire to interfere or disrupt the course of individual treatment. The goal is that by taking a two-pronged approach, one can provide a broad perspective in the best interest of educating clinicians comprehensively about family impact on psychopathology and treatment.

Mental disorders impose a great burden, not only on those diagnosed with them, but also on patient's families, employers, friends, and affiliates peripherally involved in their life. Such disorders take their toll by causing serious emotional stress and by reducing the patient's ability to function effectively in the routine of daily life. Since most mental disorders involve significant distress or impairment, those that involve a more serious disorder such as psychosis, severe personality disorders, or major mood disorders and substance abuse, can have such a profound impact on family life that they often handicap the affected individuals and their families from interacting in a salubrious fashion (Falloon, 2002).

Family vs. Individual Psychotherapy

Individual and family psychotherapy each offer two things; an approach to treatment and a way of understanding human behavior. As approaches to treatment, both individual and family therapies have several assets. Individual therapy can provide the concentrated focus to aid an individual in facing their problems with the goal of reducing symptomatology and learning to become more fully actualized. Clinicians also recognize the importance of family life in shaping personality, but assume that these influences are internalized and that intrapsychic dynamics become the dominant force that controls behavior. On the other hand, a family therapy perspective assumes the position that dominant forces in an individual's life is located external to oneself. This first external experience involves one's family-of-origin. An individual may base his or her framework and perceptions of life on the changing organization of the family. When family organization is transformed through therapy, the lives of every family member are altered accordingly. Consequently, changing the family dynamics or a part of their interaction, changes the life of each of its members. This is an important aspect, particularly in a systems theory — the effects that the individual parts have on the whole. By introducing change to the family structure, improvement can be lasting because each family member is changed and continues to exert synchronized change on each other. For the individual who is diagnosed with a mental illness, such change is in essence a means of restructuring their environment in addition to making the needed changes with their individual psyche as well, which would also be fortified by individual therapy.

Family therapy has proven to be efficacious as a modality of treatment for individual psychopathology. While family therapy is relatively a neophyte in the armamentaria of psychotherapeutic approaches, it does show promise with regard to effectiveness regarding the outcome literature. Literature reviews have concluded that sufficient data do exist to support the efficacy of family therapy with no evidence or indication that families are harmed as a result of undergoing conjoint treatment (Pinsof, Wynne, & Hambright, 1996; Pinsof & Wynne, 1995). Further comprehensive reviews have demonstrated that family therapy treatment is significantly better than no treatment control (Baucom, Shoham,

Mueser, Daiuto, & Stickle, 1998; Dunn & Schwebel, 1995). Further meta-analysis of 163 randomized clinical trials indicate that the effect size for couple and family therapy is comparable to those of other psychotherapeutic modalities (Shadish, Ragsdale, Glaser, & Montgomery, 1995). The authors of this analysis found that for the 71 studies in which family therapy was compared with no treatment control group, an effect size substantially greater than those reported in pharmaceutical, medical, and surgical studies was obtained. For 23 studies in which family therapy was compared with individual therapy, the meta-analytic results yielded no substantial differences, though there were several studies in which individual child therapy was found to be superior to family therapy. Some of these modalities included behavior therapy, cognitive-behavior therapy, and insight-oriented psychotherapy.

As for serious mental disorders, many of the early systems theorists predicated their research on family therapy with families with disturbed young adults including psychotic and depressive disorders (Nichols & Schwartz, 2001). Currently, there exists strong outcome evidence for treating adults with bipolar disorders (Clarkin et al., 1990; Clarkin, Carpenter, Hill, Wilner, & Glick, 1998) along with schizophrenic disorders (Goldstein & Miklowitz, 1995) and psychoeducational family context that includes training and coping skills, improving communication, and crisis intervention. In fact, the aspect of family psychoeducational training has proven in many cases to be more effective than individual therapy for those diagnosed with psychotic disorders (Falloon, Boyd, & McGill, 1982).

Family-of-Origin

While the term family-of-origin is associated with a number of names in family therapy (Bowen, 1978; Haley, 1980), probably one of the most prolific authors of family-of-origin therapy is the late James Framo, a clinical psychologist, who was a pioneer in family therapy. Early in his career, it became apparent to Framo that some of the more severe types of problems that many people struggled with themselves were in their intimate relationships and had much to do with what they had not yet worked through from their original family. Framo had the idea that instead of having people talk about their families and their experiences, which is customary in traditional psychotherapy, he took the bold step of actually including family members from his family-of-origin in the therapy sessions. At the time that Framo first started doing this, there were no particular guidelines or rules or regulations for conducting such sessions (Framo, 1976). Framo would eventually go on to conduct over 500 family-of-origin sessions before writing his book on the topic, "Family-Of-Origin Therapy" (Framo, 1992).

While these family-of-origin sessions vary considerably in focus, style, pace, content, and issues, Framo did espouse to a guideline that he used with each family-of-origin session. The first stage involved dealing with resistance that individuals show in bringing the family-of-origin together for a therapy session. This led to the preparation phase, which involved strategies for bringing the family together to work through possible issues in an individual's life. Techniques that were used during the course of the sessions involved procedures such as reducing anxiety and getting to know one another, getting past anger issues and possible family members who were justified in anger, siblings' relationships, and most importantly family relations and their affect on the identified patient's behaviors. A major part of therapy involved weaving together the themes and facilitating healing interventions, particularly as it related to the individual's difficulties.

Sometimes it is important for an adult patient to understand that parents can only love the way they can love, not necessarily the way the children need them to love. Consequently, relinquishing the fantasy of what the parent should give and settle for what the parents are capable of giving is very important. Another example involves those clients who had been overly attached to their original family, either consciously or unconsciously, usually loosen their ties and are more committed to their nuclear family. In fact, attachment theory is used to explain a significant degree of psychopathology that exists with many who are deemed mentally ill. Consequently, family-of-origin sessions can help heal early wounds incurred during the parent–child relationship and create a more viable and realistic relationship with immediate family members, such as a spouse. It may also help them to better orient themselves with others in their life. Later in this chapter, a case example underlies this intervention with a young woman who engaged in compulsive hair pulling. Much of her behavior disorder stemmed from the dynamics that existed with her immediate family. Her disorder tied in with the parents' family-of-origin and their own dysfunctional dynamics. The case is an illustration of how a combination of individual and family therapy can have a profound affect on an individual's disposition.

Assessment

The determination of etiology of any psychopathological disorder is paramount to the development of the treatment plan. That is, constructing a road map in treatment is contingent on the topographical information that is obtained. Consequently, a road map or guideline that is based on erroneous or faulty information will, no doubt, lead the unsuspecting travelers astray.

In the same respect, deciding on a plan of treatment when working with individuals, particularly in the context of family, is also contingent on an accurate assessment. This includes individual assessments of the family members as well as the family in its entirety.

Several areas of assessment involve the history and outline of family-of-origin, knowing about any history of mental illness with one's ancestors, understanding family dynamics, development of family schema, basic standards, and history of mental illness with members of immediate family and/or family-of-origin. Reducing the various elements of specific illness and attributing it to the family's functioning is also a crucial aspect of treatment. Also, tracing the elements of psychopathology in the family-of-origin is important, particularly with such conditions as bipolar and psychotic disorders due to their higher susceptibility to pathogenesis.

There are various techniques that may be used in family assessment to root out the etiology of psychopathology and determine the best method of treatment. Understanding the dynamics of psychopathology within the family is a core element in being able to tailor a treatment plan for an individual as well as the adjoining family's optimal results. There are several methods in addition to clinical interviews, which will be addressed specifically in this section.

Clinical Interview

Often, clinical interviews vary depending on the style of the clinician conducting the interview. The family-of-origin inventory developed by Stuart (1995), is very comprehensive in collecting background information and often sets the premise for which individuals can expand questions regarding mental illness within the family and family dynamics. This is described in detail below.

Inventories and Questionnaires

There are a host of couple and family inventories and questionnaires that may provide additional information with respect to family dynamics, schemas, rules and regulations, standards, etc. Some of the more popular inventories and assessment techniques are listed below with a description of their use. In any particular therapeutic modality, these inventories may vary, but essentially many of them are used when attempting to derive a clinical picture of family dynamics.

The *Family Beliefs Inventory* (Vincent-Roehling & Robin, 1986) assesses 10 potentially unrealistic beliefs that parents and adolescents maintain about their relationships, and that are likely to contribute to parent–adolescent conflict. Respondents read vignettes describing areas of conflict (e.g. choice of friends, spending time away from home) and then indicate their degree of agreement or disagreement with each other on several beliefs. This measure is excellent because it cuts right to the heart of the belief system that family members hold and provides insight into the family schema. The validity and reliability of the measure is fairly high and it is easy to score.

Several attribution scales have been developed for use in clinical research, and these can be applied in clinical practice as well. Pretzer, Epstein, and Fleming's (1991) *Marital Attitude Survey* (MAS) includes subscales assessing attributions for relationship problems to one's own behavior, one's own personality, the partner's behavior, the partner's personality, the partner's lack of love, and the partner's malicious intent. Fincham and Bradbury's (1992) Relationship Attribution Measure asks the respondent to rate his or her agreement with statements reflecting attributions about 10 hypothetical negative partner behaviors (e.g. "Your husband/wife criticizes something you say"). Baucom et al. (1996) developed the Relationship Attribution Questionnaire, with which the respondent rates causal and responsibility attributions for real problems in his or her relationship, as well as the degrees to which the problems are attributed to boundary, control, and investment factors similar to those assessed in relationship standards by the ISRS.

Concerning the assessment of expectancies, Pretzer et al.'s (1991) MAS also includes subscales assessing partners' generalized expectancies for overcoming relationship problems, including the perceived ability of the partners to change their relationship and the expectancy that they actually will improve the relationship. At present there are no measures of partners' or family members' expectancies concerning more specific positive and negative events that may occur in their relationships.

There are no parallel forms of these attribution and expectancy measures designed to assess cognitions in parent–child relationships. However, in clinical practice one could adapt the couple-oriented items for family assessment.

Numerous other self-report questionnaires have been developed to assess aspects of parent–child relationships and general family functioning. Excellent reviews of these measures can be found in the texts by Grotevant and Carlson (1989), Touliatos, Perlmutter, and Strauss (1990), and Jacob and Tennenbaum (1988). Some instruments, such as the Family Environment Scale (Moos & Moos, 1986), and the Family Adaptability and Cohesion Evaluation Scales III (Olson, Portner & Lavee, 1985), assess family members' global perceptions of such family characteristics as cohesion, problem solving, communication quality, role clarity, emotional expression, and values. Other scales, such as the Family Inventory of Life Events and Changes (McCubbin, Patterson, & Wilson, 1985), and the Family Crisis-Oriented Personal Evaluation Scales (McCubbin, Larsen, & Olsen, 1985), provide more specialized assessment of family functioning (e.g. members' perceptions of particular stressors and family coping strategies). As mentioned previously, because the family-of-origin is also an important factor in treatment, the Family-of-Origin Scale (Hovestadt, Anderson, Piercy, Cochran, & Fine, 1985) is an excellent tool to measure the self-perceived levels of health in one's family-of-origin. In general, these scales do not provide data about specific cognitive, behavioral, and affective variables central to assessment, but they do tap into a variety of important components of family functioning likely to be of interest to all family therapists. A few instruments tap family members' attitudes about parenting roles and thus are more directly relevant to cognitive assessment.

The basic concept behind using these inventories in the early stages of the family assessment is to draw on the family members' ability to express themselves nonverbally. Sometimes they are more willing to answer items on inventories rather than revealing themselves verbally in the family context. In addition, it allows clinicians to highlight specific areas to focus on and address during individual or family sessions. For example, if several members of the family respond to an issue with regard to trusting other family members on the *Family Belief Inventory*, this is certainly an area to pinpoint. An affirmative response to the statement, "Our family doesn't know how to communicate with each other", is also an area to pinpoint.

While these inventories focus on cognitions and beliefs, they are not always enough to reveal more serious psychopathology, which can indeed cause turbulence in the course of family therapy.

Depending on the extent of the psychopathology, additional psychodiagnostic testing may be required if the treating clinician is not necessarily trained in clinical psychology, then referrals should be made for psychodiagnostic assessment to narrow or clarify a specific mental disorder. This is particularly the case when the clinical picture becomes mixed and the need to rule out certain disorders becomes critical. For example, differentiating between schizoaffective disorders and bipolar disorders with regard to treatment often times presents as a challenge. Determining whether or not a psychotic process does exist or a delusional system is intact may make a difference in terms of the course and outline of treatment. To illustrate this point, consider the young child who is referred for treatment because of acting-out behaviors. Attempting to understand the etiology of this problem is clearly delineated when looking at the immediate family, the family-of-origin, and the trickle down effect that previous experiences may have on the behavior of offspring. In the case vignette described below, three generations of a Czech-American family were seen in treatment because of the 10-year-old son's deviant oppositional behaviors in school. Upon the initial assessment, it was surmised that the child's acting-out behaviors, as with most cases, were related to some issue involving his immediate family. In this particular case, the therapist asked the parents to come in for a family session and constructed a genogram. The results revealed that both of the children's parents were first generation Czech-Americans. The parents of both the mother and father (the child's maternal and paternal grandparents) had been born in what is now the Czech Republic. Both sets of grandparents were Holocaust survivors and two of the grandparents had witnessed the direct execution of their own parents, as well as other relatives by the Nazis during the German occupation in Europe during World War II.

The grandparents had eventually been released from German labor camps and had migrated to the United States, but after witnessing so many atrocities, they had experienced severe depression. This condition affected them for the remainder of their lives. This depressive condition inadvertently affected their offspring who had grown up struggling with their parents' chronic condition of withdrawal and despair. The parents of the 10-year-old boy informed the therapist that when they were children they had often become depressed and withdrawn due to the general emotional atmosphere of their household. They also said that they had difficulty trusting others and had experienced a generalized sense of oppression by authority, particularly those of German descent.

This emotional affect had been passed down in an indirect form to the 10-year-old child who had initially been designated in therapy as the identified patient. Instead of responding with typical depressive symptoms, however, the child, due to his own personality dynamics, denied his depression and expressed his conflicts in an oppositional manner by acting-out behaviors in school, particularly with the headmaster, who happened to be of German descent. In one sense, this may be viewed as a representation of his family's issues with authority. This is not to say that some physiological component was not at work here, however, that was not easily determined. It appeared more so that the young boy was attempting to avoid becoming depressed.

Treatment involved family therapy and also some family-of-origin sessions in order to address the lineage of depression, which was estimated to be handed down subtly from one generation to the next. In this case, much of the therapist's work involved helping the boy's parents become aware of how an almost 60-year-old trauma had affected several generations of the family, and that this young man's acting-out behaviors were, in part, very likely his own means of surviving in a circumstance that he sensed with authority. Specific attention was also drawn to how the parents were subtly reinforcing the child's behaviors by expressing their disdain for authority figures in the household. This is a classic example of how generations are affected by significant collective traumas. In other countries, other forms of collective trauma can have similar effects. British pioneers in family therapy, namely Mr. John Byng-Hall (1973, 1982), believe that often family myths and generational patterns of depression may originate from unresolved crisis such as failed mourning, abandonment, or abortion and may become dominant forces in family's psychic lives over the course of generations.

Furthermore, the concept of "trauma organized systems" suggests that some families organize in certain ways to cope with crisis in trauma and do not change their way of reacting and functioning even when the trauma has long passed. This concept has proven quite helpful in understanding the behavior of the family subjected to the traumas such as political oppression or physical and sexual abuse (Dattilio, 2001). Consequently, in the above case, a detailed assessment was extremely important in gathering information from families-of-origins of several generations, as well as the experience of the individual suffering from the mental illness. Had the therapist not included the family during the initial assessment and had not investigated into the dynamics of each parent's family-of-origin, this issue may never have been uncovered and could have possibly affected the success of the treatment.

Genograms

Genograms are a written symbolic diagram of a family's system. Unlike the family tree, a genogram is used both diagnostically and therapeutically in order to uncover important information about one's history and one's family-of-origin. Genogramming has been a significant aspect in family therapy and a frequently used technique. For several decades, its many advantages have contributed to its continued use. Genogramming has been written about extensively in certain texts (McGoldrick & Gerson, 1985; Kaslow, 1995) and relies on the use of symbols to depict family members across generations. This is particularly important when dealing with mental illness and psychopathology in tracing the reconnecting links to one's family-of-origin. This process also helps individuals to depict those relatives who comprise their historic past and present and who may have contributed to a specific mental illness. Individuals are asked to draw a family tree as far back as they can remember. The family tree descends from the top of the page from the senior progenitors to the youngest children in the group. A chronological diagram emerges of how people are related to one another and may contain such information as dates of birth, marriage, divorce, and death. One area of particular interest is to attempt to trace whether or not any emotional or behavioral problems or clarified mental illness existed with any of the ancestors. Typically, this involves having a patient or a family embark on visiting members of one's family-of-origin, who may still be alive and jog their memories for missing information. The therapist's role is to coach the individual on the specific questions to ask in order to obtain information that is most helpful. Interestingly, in many cases, individuals have unearthed long-buried family secrets that may clearly have affected the course of treatment. The idea of having individuals produce genograms is also to put them in touch with the intergenerational transmission process, as Bowen referred to it (1978). Such information shows clear reasons for the way things were done, or how one's pathology has evolved through the generations of family members. This is not an excuse for them to blame their problems on ancestors, but more so to understand how links occur.

Genogramming has also been a very useful process in aiding many to become aware of the family's tendency to triangulate relationships, which is believed by theorists often to be a source of mental illness. Triangulation is a reactive process whereby a third person who is sensitized to the anxiety in a couple or family moves in to offer reassurance or calm things down. A classic example is the teenage daughter who attempts to reduce her parents' intense marital conflict by talking individually to each parent or to the parent whom she has the most influence with. In this respect, her intervention serves to pull the parents together. As her parents grow to be dependent on her intervening, she becomes triangulated, which can often be a very uncomfortable or burdensome role for her (Guerin, Fay, Burden, & Kautto, 1987). Consequently, such information may help individuals learn how to detriangulate and ultimately develop more healthy and satisfying interpersonal relationships with their own immediate family.

Interviewing and Assessment

Family therapists vary widely in the extent to which they conduct formal assessments. Typically, when an individual is interviewed, a structured interviewing schedule, such as the Structured Clinical Interview Schedule for DSM-IV (SCID) (Spitzer, Williams, & Gibbon, 1994), may be used in order to render a differential diagnosis. Various psychological tests, including projective tests and personality inventories, may also be ordered. One thing that seems to be in universal agreement is that regardless of the approach on assessment, most therapists probably spend too little time making careful evaluations of individuals and their families before embarking on treatment.

Typically, background information is gathered through the use of an intake schedule, such as chief complaint and the demographic information, as well as presenting problem. Also, listing symptoms that fall within the affective physiological, cognitive, and behavioral domain, length of problems, and similar problems in the past. Also, specific thoughts and feelings that center around problems are addressed, along with the primary ways in which it interferes with their functioning in life.

When involving the family in treatment, an important step is to identify problems that become entrenched because they are embedded in powerful, but often invisible structures. Thus, becoming aware and developing a clear understanding about the family structure is extremely important in understanding the development of one's psychopathology and also how the family perpetuates such problems. Ways in which the problem impacts on the family and affects that dynamic is also important for a therapist to focus. Therapists may then ask about actual functioning subsystems and nature of the boundaries between them. Also, the nature of boundaries in couple or family systems is important, along with identifying triangles that exist. Triangles are described as a stable relationship structure that involves a third person (Guerin & Guerin, 2002). Identifying triangles is also very important. Further understanding of who plays what roles in the family is essential, particularly with matters of power and control. From a cognitive-behavioral standpoint, understanding schemas and interrelationships that contribute to family dysfunction are key to developing a solid treatment plan.

Behavioral Observation and Change

As a result of the limitations of the self-report inventories mentioned above, it is extremely important for a clinician to observe samples of family members' interactions directly. Careful and detailed observation of behavior and its consequences are really important when understanding family dynamics. Opportunities for behavioral observations exist from the first moment that a family enters a therapist's office. An experienced couple and family therapist becomes adept at noticing the process of verbal and nonverbal behaviors that occur between family members as they talk to one another and the therapist. Although the topic or the content of the discussions are important, the goal of systematic behavioral observation is to identify specific acts by each individual, and the sequence of acts among family members that are constructive and pleasing or destructive and aversive. In particular, those behaviors that may be destructive, aversive, and manipulative are aspects that need to be noted and documented. The observation of family interaction can vary according to the amount of structure that the clinician imposes on the interaction, as well as the amount of structure in the clinician's observation criteria or coding system.

Obviously, family members' interactions are going to differ in the therapist's office from what typically transpires at home, but, through interactions, family members can reveal significant patterns that do provide insight into issues in the relationship. With disorders such as depression and schizophrenia, often times there are dominant themes in the family interaction between parent and child where they may cut off or devalue each other in subtle ways. These are clearly areas of note for clinicians. Determining which family members tend to be more spontaneous as opposed to others that fade in the background is often very telling. One of the benefits of imposing very little structure in family therapy is to sample a family's communication in a naturalistic way within the office setting. In this manner, the therapist can pinpoint where a significant amount of dysfunction occurs.

In contrast to a relatively unstructured interaction, clinicians provide a family with specific topics for discussion that may be even more revealing with regard to how they function together. The goal, such as trying to understand one another's thinking patterns and feelings, or to resolve particular relationship issues may be pertinent. What family members do with each other's emotions is extremely important and we see this, particularly in areas of severe psychopathology. For example, in using some of the inventories mentioned previously, such as Spanier's (1976) *Dyadic Adjustment Scale*, this may allow individuals to rate the degree of conflict in which their interaction affects one another. Areas of demonstration of affection, amount of time spent together, and so on, helps the clinician to select areas to focus on in treatment. Obviously, as a skilled clinician begins to observe behavior, areas of weakness and disturbance will surface. This is particularly so when heated issues arise. A skilled clinician is able to look for coalitions or alliances that are formed among family members and illustrate how they contribute to polarization within a family unit.

One of the areas that is very helpful to observe is the exercise of instructing a family to engage in problem-solving discussions during the course of a session. In this respect, the clinician is able to identify a specific difficulty with this specialized form of communication. This is similar to the enactment that Minuchin and other family therapists have used in family therapy in the past (Minuchin, 1974). Depending on the modality of treatment that the clinician is using, he or she may choose to become more directive in the process and focus on certain interventions. For example, family members who fail to define a problem in specific behavioral terms may handicap themselves and preclude them from generating a feasible solution. Others fail to evaluate advantages and disadvantages of proposed solutions and subsequently become discouraged when they try to carry out the solution and encounter unanticipated obstacles or drawbacks. How family members deal with frustrations in themselves and others often provide therapists with clues as to what may contribute to anxiety and depression in the family system. By observing family members' discussions during the therapy session, the clinician can identify the specific problematic behaviors and can plan interventions to improve their problem-solving skills, and can also help address issues of dysfunction. A clinician's observation for repetitive patterns that may contribute to depression or anxiety, or even disordered thinking, is tantamount in uncovering dysfunctional patterns among family members. Using basic principles of functional analysis, a clinician can observe antecedent events and consequences that may be controlling the negative interaction between family members. For example, two parents may complain repeatedly that their child rarely reveals his feelings, but, interestingly, the clinician observes that whenever the child does express his feelings, his parents either turn away suddenly or sometimes more overtly cut him off and deny his feelings by saying, "Oh, well, you shouldn't feel this way" or "No, you can't feel that way, it's foolish", etc. Such circular causal processes in family interactions can be observed when a clinician identifies how one individual's behavior prompts the other's withdrawal and vice versa, and the effect that this has on one's psychodynamics. This can be highlighted in terms of acknowledging destructive patterns that may be contributing to depression and low self-esteem or any one number of elements of psychopathology.

Assessment of Cognitions

Clinical interviews with family members together, or individually, provide an opportunity for clinicians to elicit idiosyncratic cognitions and to track influential processes that cannot be assessed by standardized questionnaires. Socratic questioning is one method that involves a series of systematic questions that are used to chip away at defenses during both the exploration and/or assessment phase, as well as the beginning of treatment, in order to uncover thoughts and underlying beliefs (Dattilio, 2000; Beck, 1995). Using techniques such as *Socratic Questioning* may enable a clinician to piece together a chain of thoughts that mediate between events and relationships and each individual's emotional and behavioral responses. For example, one method of questioning that involves a technique known as, *Downward Arrow*, was developed by Aaron Beck and Associates (1979). This technique was developed to uncover the underlying schema or assumptions that an individual has that generate dysfunctional or distorted thoughts. This may be done by identifying the initial thought and then following it downward by saying, "If so, then what"? For example, in a particular family in which the adult son was reluctant to move out because he felt the need to remain attached to his family for "safety", he had become very avoidant and withdrew socially, requiring excessive reassurance from his family constantly. When using *Downward Arrow* with respect to what the true belief was that underlied his avoidance and lack of movement, the technique yielded the following (Figure 1).

As one can view in this segment of *Downward Arrow*, the core belief is the fear of failure and even death. Therefore, it is clear to see that this individual believes he is nothing without his family. Interestingly, in reviewing family dynamics, despite the fact that the parents wanted very much to see their son go out and be successful, they also had their own doubts about his ability to survive and would subtly reinforce him remaining at home. Using the same technique when examining the parents' cognitions uncovered some of their fears that perhaps their son was not capable of functioning on his own, despite the fact that he was an adult. So, many of the parents' behaviors were subtly reinforcing his dependency and staying at home, when, overtly, they were making statements that they wanted him to move out and be independent. This type of subtle double-bind seems to create a lot of confusion and dysfunction and caused stuck movement for the son, as well as the family.

I need to stay with my family where it's safe.

If I venture out into the world, life's too dangerous and I'll never be as good as others anyway.

I'm not as good as others because people don't care and won't care about me.

If people don't care, something bad will happen to me.

If something bad happens to me, life won't be worth living

and I won't be able to manage on my own.

Therefore, I need to stay with my family so I can feel secure.

One should not take risks because life may let them down and I will likely die.

Figure 1: Downward arrow of avoidant son.

Addressing these types of cognitions is very important in family treatment. Restructuring the parents' thinking so that they would become more optimistic, and actually follow-through and take the risk of promoting their son's independence, would then embolden them to support their son's independence. Any work done with their son in terms of him taking steps to begin to move outward, take risks, and see that maybe he is not as destined to fail as he anticipates himself to be, would be of great benefit. The use of the *Downward Arrow* technique serves to uncover an underlying schema of vulnerability and helplessness, along with the fear of failure in all family members. The technique allows the individuals to become aware of their chain of thoughts, see how it can lead to erroneous conclusions, and reinforce longstanding assumptions that may not necessarily carry much weight.

The above examples illustrate how clinicians attempt to gather information about family members' cognitions as they occur during the family interactions rather than relying on only the client's retrospective accounts of the situation. The difference here is that we can gather more adjoining evidence that supports the behaviors, which in this case is very strong because it is part of the family unit and deals with it directly to expedite the healing process.

Including Family in Treatment

Depending on the modality of treatment, both individual or family psychotherapy may be utilized from a variety of different modalities. These modalities are obviously voluminous and are outlined in basic introductory texts to family therapy (Nichols & Schwartz, 2001; Goldenberg & Goldenberg, 2003). Despite the particular modality of family therapy used, two of the most effective techniques in working with families centers around communications training and structured problem-solving training.

Communications Training

Many family therapy approaches involve the goal of communications training to facilitate the ability of the family unit to conduct its own problem-solving discussions. Communication training enhances the ability to define problems or goals in a highly specific fashion, to positively reinforce progress toward objectives, to prompt behavior change without coercion, and to listen with empathy to assist each other to express their needs in terms of specific everyday problems and goals. Lack of effective communication skills is one of the leading problems in families and may contribute to misunderstandings and arguments that can be very destructive. The ultimate, of course, is that family members may avoid any discussion which can severely handicap them. The majority of families are capable of improving interpersonal communications substantially and derive benefits from specific training. There are structured communication training packages that facilitate didactic instruction, coaching, and reinforcement of progress among family members (Markman, Stanley, & Blumberg, 1994; Miller & Miller, 1997). Homework practice is a key component to ensure that skills are not restricted to practice within the therapy session, but generalized in everyday interaction (Bevilacqua & Dattilio, 2001). The focus on family communication should be oriented toward the specific mental disorder in the family since many have specific deficits in their interpersonal communication, such as individuals with schizophrenia, severe personality disorders, or severe depression and anxiety. Consequently, each communications training program is tailored to address the specific needs of the family.

A perfect example of this is the case in which a schizoid female would speak cryptically for fear that she would be too vulnerable to the other family members' criticisms if she were to speak directly. In addition, this individual had significant paranoia along with her schizoid personality, but did have more control over her ability to speak in cryptic terms. Part of the treatment involved reducing her anxiety and helping her take a step-by-step method toward being more direct in her expression, which eventually drew a more favorable response from her family members. This was a very tedious process, however, and required a great deal of time. It also involved skills on the part of the therapist to work with the family members to develop a language that was less threatening to the young girl so that she would not feel as intimidated. In a sense, the clinician had to teach this family how to learn to communicate with each other in a way that was not threatening.

Communications training may also be conducted over the course of time in therapy as opposed to just in one period and may be intertwined with other therapeutic techniques and interventions as well.

Structured Problem-Solving Training

The lack of problem-solving abilities is often a critical element found within families of individuals with mental disorders, as well as family dysfunction in general. The fact that poor decision making can contribute to excess tension and alienation among family members underscores this clearly. In structured problem-solving training, a clinician's aim is to teach a family to convene its own structured problem-solving sessions rather than merely to assist in the problem-solving process during therapy sessions. The idea is to provide them with a paradigm that they can follow in mediating their thoughts and impulsive behaviors and to help them think through options in order to weigh the likelihood of what they choose as being the best option available. Helping family members learn skills that they can use in every day problem solving is most essential. Only when stress is threatening to overwhelm a family's problem-solving capacity, or when there are early signs of an impending major episode of mental disorder, does a therapist consider becoming an active participant in the family problem-solving effort.

Typically, structured problem-solving programs involve teaching a number of steps, which include the following:

1. *Defining the problem and achieving a goal.* This involves pinpointing the exact issue that needs to be addressed and defining it clearly. Often times individuals are unclear as to what the problem is and may have different perceptions. Working on these perceptions and unifying them onto one global consensus that allows them to agree on the definition of the problem, is essential;
2. *Listing alternative solutions.* This involves brainstorming lists of possible solutions no matter how far out or unrealistic they may seem to be. This is somewhat of a cathartic method, but allows individuals to throw everything out on the table for exploration and review them altogether in order to make a comparison;
3. *Evaluating the consequence of proposed solutions.* This involves a brief review of the proposed solutions, highlighting the main strengths and weaknesses of each, and through a process of elimination deciding which solutions would be the more viable. Once again, emphasis is placed on agreement and solution and talking through, using communication skills in order to best assess what would be the most effective solution;
4. *Choosing the optimal solution.* Family members each choose what they think would be a good solution then poll their thoughts together and vote on a common solution that may address the problem;
5. *Planning.* A detailed plan drawn up to define the specific steps to ensure efficient implementation of the optimal solution and measures for what to do in the event that those solutions cannot be used. Helping the family to select an alternative plan B and plan C also aids in dealing with unforeseen circumstances;
6. *Review and implement the specific solution.* The efforts of family members' attempt to implement the agreed upon plan are reviewed in a constructive manner that facilitates continued efforts until a solution has been achieved;
7. *Acknowledging that resolution has been achieved and reinforcing the process.*

Often times a clinician can assist families to establish regular structured family meetings on a weekly basis and, during those discussions, run through any problems that arise.

Sometimes a therapist can have family members videotape their problem-solving strategies so that they can be reviewed in the therapy session and discussions can be held to evaluate the pros and cons of their process.

Main Principles to Consider for Including Families in Treatment

Deciding to include a family in treatment is a very difficult decision — often one that may need careful consideration. In fact, clinicians may sometimes find that it was a mistake to involve the family only after they have embarked on the course of family therapy. Even though such incidents can occur, every effort should be made to try to avoid such mistakes if possible. A number of steps are suggested to determine when to include the family in treatment.

1. Families of patients with mental disorders should be included in treatment specifically when it is determined that a significant part of the mental illness has been derived from, or is being fueled by, the family dynamics. Research indicates that any type of mental illness can have its origin in the roots of family dynamics, including those that involve chemical disorders, such as bipolar illnesses, and determining when family dynamics exacerbate conditions of mental disorder, such as depression, anxiety, or thought disorder (Pennington, 2002);
2. When it is determined that restructuring the family dynamics can be beneficial in the treatment and amelioration of dysfunction, then it is usually beneficial to include other family members in session. An example might be the power of rearranging family interaction to facilitate an offspring going out on his own and emancipating himself as in the earlier example. Another example may be where a family needs to forgive or release an individual or support them in a different way;
3. When pressure is needed to get a patient to take a step toward change, family support may be a tremendous aid. Often times, in individual therapy, a clinician does not have enough power in the relationship to elicit movement in a desirable direction. In this respect, family members can be used to do this in ways that individual therapy would never facilitate.

When Not to Involve Family in Individual Treatment

A number of years ago, there was a book that appeared in the popular sector entitled, "Toxic Parents" (Forward, 1989). This book highlighted a case situation in which the parents and family members were actually toxic or poisonous to individuals with no redeeming quality for change. Unfortunately, sometimes this is the case and involving such family members in treatment should be avoided. Below is a list of possible guidelines or steps to follow:

1. In conducting an initial assessment and determining the volatility that may resonate from a family or rampant psychopathology that may exist which would be overwhelming to a clinician, this may be a time to avoid working with the family and working more with the individual;

2. Not everyone is amenable to participating in family therapy and, depending on the circumstance, a patient may lose trust in the clinician if family members are brought in. This is a time when the use of other family members in treatment should be avoided;

3. Extremely sensitive or personal areas, such as sexuality or certain types of odd or unusual behaviors, that can be easily treated without the need for family support, might be better addressed without the inclusion of family members;

4. When an assessment is conducted with the family and it is determined by the clinician that because of factors such as low level of intellectual functioning, or other handicaps, it may preclude them from being used effectively, this is also when family members might be avoided;

5. At times when the therapeutic relationship that exists alone between a clinician and client is powerful and may be contaminated by including family members, this should also be avoided.

Case Example

Lillian was a 17-year-old, Caucasian female who was referred by a local hospital's psychiatric unit subsequent to a voluntary admission due to suicidal ideation of disturbing frequency, duration, and intensity. It was reported that Lillian had a long history of dysthymic disorder and had recently become suicidal. On admission to the hospital, she was depressed and anxious, but cooperative and congenial with the healthcare professionals and the inpatient treatment team. There were also reports that she had begun pulling hair out of her head, as well as her eyebrows, and, as a result, she was placed on Fluovaxitine, 20 mg, 1 tablet every morning. She was also prescribed Trazodone, 50 mg, 1 tablet at bedtime, for sleep, because of reported difficulties with insomnia. Lillian remained in the hospital for only 1 week and was able to recover rather quickly. She reported a cessation of suicidal ideation. She engaged in individual, group, and milieu therapy. Upon further improvement, she was discharged to her parents and was followed by a psychiatrist and a therapist for counseling. Unfortunately, Lillian and her parents did not feel that the therapist had been very effective, particularly with the family problems and her compulsive hair pulling. The family was consequently referred to another therapist for consultation by her family physician.

Upon the initial visit with Lillian and her parents, it was reported that Lillian was pulling the hair out of her head and eyebrows and was also cutting herself with a razorblade on the tops of her forearms. She apparently broke up with her boyfriend and was very distressed over the loss.

It was also reported that Lillian had made an earlier suicide attempt at age 14 over family problems. She was diagnosed with Major Depressive Disorder and Obsessive-Compulsive Disorder. Lillian's mother claimed that she was particularly aggravated with her daughter's previous treatment because she did not feel that she, herself, was included enough in the process of treatment. I was informed that Lillian had received a full medical work-up, including a blood profile, CAT Scan, and additional diagnostic tests, all of which yielded negative results.

Upon the initial family session, Lillian informed me that she started pulling her hair out approximately one and a half years prior in an attempt to alleviate guilt. This behavior was a self-punitive reaction to her guilt, which she readily admitted. Lillian felt that everything that happened in her life with her parents and her relationship with her boyfriend was her fault. She also experienced anxiety dealing with her relationship with her boyfriend.

Background information indicated that Lillian was an only child and always felt that she was very independent. She first began pulling out selective hairs from her head at age 14, due to feelings of frustration and anger. She tried to stop her hair pulling, but her anxiety and depression would increase each time she would attempt to refrain. She felt tormented by it. She also experienced thoughts in her head such as, "I'm a loser", and "I'm stupid". There was also a perfectionistic mode to her thinking. Lillian would only pull the dark hair out of her head. When I mentioned to her that it was ironic that her mother had very dark hair as opposed to Lillian, whose hair was strawberry-blond, she became very quiet and made no comment.

The family therapy session involved mother, father, and Lillian, at which point we began to explore some of Lillian's family dynamics. Lillian began to explain to me that she experienced a considerable amount of guilt and that the hair pulling was really more of an expression of her anger and resentment for her mother, who she always felt was intrusive in her life. She was also partially angry with her father, who Lillian felt was too passive and readily complied in response to his wife's commands. Lillian always felt that her father should have stood up more for her against her mother, but failed to do so. In some ways, Lillian considered this an abandonment.

The initial phase of treatment focused on the tension that existed in the family and moved away from Lillian's particular self-abuse behaviors. Lillian's specific symptoms were dealt with separately in individual sessions with Lillian using a cognitive-behavioral approach.

The dynamics of the family were interesting in that Lillian's mother came across as an extremely overbearing and intrusive individual. She would always push Lillian very hard to succeed in life, which is why Lillian believed that she developed a perfectionistic belief system. In some sense, Lillian wanted to comply with her mother's request, but at the same time, resented her mother's intrusiveness and did not feel as though she could live up to her mother's expectations. This feeling of being "stuck" fueled her into literally pulling her out of her head. Lillian's father, unfortunately, maintained the homeostasis in the family by simply going along and trying to keep peace with both his wife and Lillian, but, at the same time, he tried to avoid any confrontation with either individual. It would have been very easy to allow this situation to evolve into therapy between Lillian and her mother, since father maintained such a passive stance. I repeatedly encouraged the father to join the situation and called him on his passiveness, slowly integrating him more into the therapy process. This met with quite a bit of resistance from the mother who, at times, vied for power and control over her husband until she was informed repeatedly that one of the problems in the family was that there was an insufficient balance with the control and power between her and her husband. Interestingly, during this phase of treatment, Lillian reported that her hair pulling increased, almost as a way of trying to symbolically intervene in her parents' dispute.

Surprisingly, despite their resistance, Lillian's parents were very open to my suggestions. Much of my individual work with Lillian involved using *in vivo* exposure and response prevention, which is the technique of choice in cognitive-behavior therapy with trichotillamania (compulsive hair pulling). Lillian was repeatedly exposed to hair that she felt tempted to pull out and asked to refrain from pulling, allowing her anxiety to escalate to the point where it would peak. She was then instructed to wait-it-out until her anxiety level decreased. Any kind of motivations toward self-mutilating behaviors, such as cutting or scratching herself, was addressed in the same fashion, based on a graded hierarchy. When Lillian would become agitated and depressed, cognitive restructuring techniques were utilized in order to help her process her thoughts and emotions and balance them. Lillian's father was also requested to assist her more as a coach and request that mother not become directly involved, but support her husband's work with Lillian. Lillian also bought into the symbolic notion that her pulling of only the dark hairs from her head was a way of pulling her mother out of her life. Consequently, a part of our work involved Lillian becoming more assertive with her mother and confronting her and also accepting the fact that she was not perfect and would never meet up to all of her mother's expectations.

Interestingly, a large part of the treatment involved dealing with some of the family-of-origin of both parents in order to better understand the family dynamics. The individual treatment for this young lady was similar to the type of 14-week cognitive-behavioral intervention programs that utilize the structured parent-skills-training component for adolescents with obsessive-compulsive disorder. The following modules are included in the component, which involve: (1) forming a supportive team, (2) psychoeducation, (3) differential reinforcement of behavior, (4) parental participation in relaxation and anxiety mediation techniques, (5) reduction of family accommodation and/or tensions and conflict, (6) parental anxiety management, (7) encouragement of family supportive exposure and response prevention, and (8) problem-solving skills training (Waters, Barrett, & March, 2001).

In order to employ some of these techniques, both of Lillian's parents shared some of their specific experiences from their respective families-of-origin.

Lillian's father spoke about the fact that his own biological father had passed away when he was 9 years of age and he was left to be raised in a home with two older sisters and a mother. He reported that the home was a female-dominated environment where the mother ruled with an iron fist. Lillian's father claims that he learned to follow the lead of his mother and sisters very early in his life and never rebelled against them. He found that life was more peaceful when things seemed to work this way. He also had no male role model during his upbringing, so he had no clue as to how a male might act in harmony with the family. He stated that, consequently, he also married someone who he felt was similar to the role model that he was exposed to during his upbringing. Interestingly, Lillian's father also stated that both of his sisters married into families in which the male assumed the more passive role.

With regard to Lillian's mother's upbringing, she recalls having a two-parent family, but her father was an alcoholic and was very abusive verbally when intoxicated. She grew up with a lot of resentment toward men and felt, in many respects, that unless one kept on top of a relationship, "men will control them and overwhelm them". Surprisingly, Lillian's maternal grandmother was a relatively passive individual, which created a disdain on Lillian's mother's part for her own mother. She had always wished that her mother would stand up more to her father and that, in some respects, she herself as a young girl would stand up against her father and say what she felt. She claims that this is where she learned to be dominant and also developed the notion that the mother is the more appropriate individual to rule the household. Lillian's mother also alluded to the fact that she struggled with a lot of insecurities herself because of her upbringing. She wanted only the best for her daughter and did not want her daughter to struggle with the same issues that she had struggled with during her upbringing. Hence, she believed that it was best to set high expectations for her so that her daughter would do well in life.

By obtaining this information from the parents' respective families-of-origins, the therapist was able to clearly piece together how the specific family dynamics developed and contributed to the dissension that existed in the present family system. Educating the family to these principles of the system was the initial step. The concept of introducing change was the next step, obtaining collaboration from all family members under the guise that the present system was not working effectively, and making suggestions for alterations/modifications as seen in the example above.

The total course of treatment lasted more than 1 year. Lillian stopped pulling her hair and reported no urge to do so. Lillian's parents also entered into marital therapy and began to vigorously address their relationship problems. A 1-year follow-up indicated that Lillian's hair pulling and depressive behaviors had not returned.

Conclusion

Involving the family in treatment is something that should be evaluated on a case-by-case basis. As stated previously, in some cases, involving family members in treatment can be unproductive and possibly even destructive. When used at the right time, in the most effective manner, family treatment can be extremely effective in facilitating behavioral and emotional change for those with psychological disorders. The more severely mentally ill can be helped, but with a longer term course of treatment and additional treatment regimes (i.e. adjunct therapy and medication).

The reader is urged to proceed with caution whenever choosing to include family members in treatment. A thorough assessment and treatment plan should be designed in advance and, most importantly, the client should never feel pressured to include family members in the course of therapy. With this said, involving family members in treatment can often be extremely beneficial.

References

Baucom, D., Shoham, V., Mueser, K. T., Daiuto, A. D., & Stickle, T. R. (1998). Empirically supported couple and family interventions for marital distress and adult mental health problems. *Journal of Consulting and Clinical Psychology, 66*, 53–88.

Baucom, D. H., Epstein, N., Daiuto, A. D., Carels, R. A., Rankin, L. A., & Burntee, C. K. (1996). Cognitions in marriage: The relationship between standards and attributions. *Journal of Family Psychology, 10*, 209–222.

Beck, J. S. (1995). *Cognitive therapy: Basics and beyond.* New York: Guilford Press.

Bevilacqua, L. J., & Dattilio, F. M. (2001). *Brief family therapy homework planner.* New York: Wiley.

Bowen, M. (1978). *Family therapy in clinical practice*. New York: Jason Aronson.

Byng-Hall, J. (1973). Family myths used as defence in conjoint family therapy. *British Journal of Medical Psychology*, *46*, 239–250.

Byng-Hall, J. (1982). Dysfunctions of feeling: Experiential life of a family. In: A. Bentovim, G. G. Barnes & A. Cooklin (Eds), *Family therapy: Complimentary frameworks of theory and practice*. London: Academic Press.

Clarkin, J. F., Carpenter, D., Hill, J., Wilner, P., & Glick, I. (1998). Effects of psychoeducational intervention for married patients with bipolar disorder and their spouses. *Psychiatric Services*, *49*, 531–533.

Clarkin, J. F., Glick, I. D., Haas, G. L., Spencer, J. H., Lewis, A. B., Peyser, J., DeMane, N., Good-Ellis, M., Harris, E., & Lestelle, V. (1990). A randomized clinical trial of inpatient family intervention V: Results for affective disorders. *Journal of Affective Disorders*, *18*, 17–28.

Dattilio, F. M. (Ed.). (1998). *Case studies in couple and family therapy: Systemic and cognitive perspectives*. New York: Guilford.

Dattilio, F. M. (2000). Cognitive-behavioral strategies. In: J. Carlson & L. Sperry (Eds), *Brief therapy with individuals and couples* (pp. 33–70). Phoenix, AZ: Zeig, Tucker & Thiesen.

Dattilio, F. M. (2001). Letter to the Editor: The ripple effects of depressive schemas on psychiatric patients. *Archives in Psychiatry and Psychotherapy*, *3(2)*, 50–91.

Dattilio, F. M. (2002). Letter to the editor: The ripple effects of depressive schemas on psychiatric patients. *Archives in Psychiatry and Psychotherapy*, *3*, 90–91.

Dattilio, F. M. & Jongsma, A. E. (2000). *The family therapy treatment planner*. New York: Wiley.

Dunn, R. L., & Schwebel, A. I. (1995). Meta-analytic review of marital therapy outcome research. *Journal of Family Psychology*, *21*, 475–510.

Falloon, I. (2002). Cognitive-behavioral family and educational interventions for schizophrenic disorders (3–17). In: S. G. Hofmann & M. C. Tompson (Eds), *Treating chronic and severe mental disorders: A handbook of empirically supported interventions*. New York: Guilford.

Falloon, I. R. H., Boyd, J. L., & McGill, C. W. (1982). Family management in the prevention of exacerbations of schizophrenia: A controlled study. *New England Journal of Medicine*, *306*, 1437–1440.

Fincham, F. D., & Bradbury, T. N. (1992). Assessing attributions in marriage: The relationship attribution measure. *Journal of Personality and Social Psychology*, *62*, 457–468.

Forward, S. (1989). *Toxic parents*. New York: Bantam Books.

Framo, J. L. (1976). Family-of origin as a therapeutic resource for adults in marital and family therapy: You can and should go home again. *Family Process*, *15*, 193–210.

Framo, J. L. (1992). *Family-of-origin: An integrative approach*. New York: Brunner/Mazel, Inc.

Goldenberg, I., & Goldenberg, H. (2003). Family therapy. An overview (6th ed.). Belmont, CA: Brooks/Cole.

Goldstein, M. J., & Miklowitz, D. J. (1995). The effectiveness of psychoeducational family therapy in the treatment of schizophrenic disorders. *Journal of Marital and Family Therapy*, *21*, 361–376.

Grotevant, H. D., & Carlson, C. I. (1989). *Family assessment: A guide to methods and measures*. New York: Guilford Press.

Guerin, K., & Guerin, P. (2002). Bowenian family therapy. In: J. Carlson & D. Djos (Eds), *Theories and strategies of family therapy*. Boston: Allyn & Bacon.

Guerin, P. G., Fay, L., Burden, S., & Kautto, J. (1987). *The evaluation and treatment of marital conflict: A four stage approach*. New York: Basic Books.

Haley, J. (1980). *Leaving home*. New York: McGraw Hill.

Hovestadt, A. J., Anderson, W. T., Piercy, F. A., Cochran, S. W., & Fine, M. (1985). Family-of-origin scale. *Journal of Marital and Family Therapy*, *11*, 287–297.

Jacob, T., & Tennenbaum, D. L. (1988). *Family assessment: Rationale, methods, and future directions*. New York: Plenum Press.

Kaslow, F. (1995). *Projective genogramming*. Sarasota, FL: Professional Resource Press.

Markman, H. J. S., Stanley, S., & Blumberg, S. L. (1994). *Fighting for your Marriage*. San Francisco: Jossey Bass.

McCubbin, H. I., Larsen, A., & Olsen, D. H. (1985). F-COPES: Family crisis oriented personal evaluation scales. In: D. H. Olsen, H. I. McCubbin, H. Barnes, A. Larsen, M. Muxen & M. Wilson (Eds), *Family Inventories* (rev. ed., pp. 215–218). St. Paul: Family Social Science, University of Minnesota.

McCubbin, H. I., Patterson, J. M., & Wilson, L. R. (1985). FILE: Family inventory of life events and changes. In: D. H. Olson, H. I. McCubbin, H. Barnes, A. Larsen, M. Muxen & M. Wilson (Eds), *Family inventories* (rev. ed., pp. 272–275). St. Paul: Family Social Science, University of Minnesota.

McGoldrick, M., & Gerson, R. (1985). *Genograms in Family Assessment*. New York: W. W. Norton.

Miller, S., & Miller, P. A. (1997). *Core communications, skills, and processes*. Littleton, Co: Interpersonal Communications Programs.

Minuchin, S. (1974). *Families and family therapy*. Cambridge, MA: Harvard University Press.

Moos, R. H., & Moos, B. S. (1986). *Family environment scale manual* (2nd ed.). Palo Alto, CA: Consulting Psychologists Press.

Nichols, M. P., & Schwartz, R. C. (2001). *Family Therapy: Concepts and methods*. Boston, MA: Allyn & Bacon.

Olson, D. H., Portner, J., & Lavee, Y. (1985). *FACES-III manual*. St. Paul: Family Social Science, University of Minnesota.

Pennington, B. F. (2002). *The development of psychopathology: Nature and nurture*. New York: Guilford.

Pinsof, W. M., & Wynne, L. C. (1995). The efficacy of marital and family therapy: An empirical overview, conclusions, and recommendations. *Journal of Marital and Family Therapy, 21*, 585–614.

Pinsof, W. M., Wynne, L. C., & Hambright, A. B. (1996). The outcomes of couple and family therapy: Findings, conclusions, and recommendation. *Psychotherapy, 33*, 3321–3331.

Pretzer, J. L, Epstein, N., & Fleming, B. (1991). The marital attitude survey: A measure of dysfunctional attributions and expectancies. *Journal of Cognitive Psychotherapy, 5*, 131–148.

Shadish, W. R., Ragsdale, K., Glaser, R. R., & Montgomery, L. M. (1995). The efficacy and effectiveness of marital and family therapy: A perspective from meta-analysis. *Journal of Marital and Family Therapy, 21*, 345–360.

Spanier, G. B. (1976). Measuring dyadic adjustment: New scales for assessing the quality of marriage and similar dyads. *Journal of Marriage and the Family, 38*, 15–28.

Spitzer, R. L., Williams, J. B. W., & Gibbon, M. (1994). *Instruction manual for the structural clinical Interview for DSM-IV* (SCID). Washington, DC: American Psychiatric Press.

Stuart, R. B. (1995). *Family-of-origin inventory*. New York: Guilford.

Touliatos, J., Perlmutter, B. F., & Strauss, M. A. (Eds). (1990). *Handbook of family measurement techniques*. Newbury Park, CA: Sage.

Vincent-Roehling, P. V., & Robin, A. L. (1986). Development and validation of the family beliefs inventory: A measure of unrealistic beliefs among parents and adolescents. *Journal of Consulting and Clinical Psychology, 54*, 693–697.

Waters, T. L., Barrett, P. M., & March, J. S. (2001). Cognitive-behavioral family treatment of childhood obsessive-compulsive disorder: Preliminary findings. *American Journal of Psychotherapy, 55*, 372–387.

Chapter 15

Family Intervention and Prevention of Behavioural and Emotional Disorders in Childhood and Adolescence

Matthew R. Sanders and Alan Ralph

This chapter outlines the conceptual and empirical basis for the development of a comprehensive parenting and family intervention program as part of a multi-component strategy to prevent behavioural and emotional problems in children and adolescents. The family provides the first and most important, social, emotional, interpersonal, economic, and cultural context for human development and, as a result, family relationships have a pervasive influence on the wellbeing of children. Disturbed family relationships are generic risk factors, and positive family relationships are protective factors that are related to a wide variety of mental health problems that occur from infancy to old age (Sanders, 1995). Many significant mental health, social, and economic problems are linked to disturbances in family functioning and the breakdown of family relationships (Chamberlain & Patterson, 1995; Patterson, 1982; Sanders & Duncan, 1995). Epidemiological studies indicate that family risk factors such as poor parenting, family conflict, and marriage breakdown strongly influence children's development (e.g. Cummings & Davies, 1994; Dryfoos, 1990; Robins, 1991). Specifically, the lack of a warm positive relationship with parents; insecure attachment; harsh, inflexible, rigid, or inconsistent discipline practices; inadequate supervision of and involvement with children; marital conflict and breakdown; and parental psychopathology (particularly maternal depression) increase the risk that children develop major behavioural and emotional problems, including substance abuse, antisocial behaviour, and juvenile crime (e.g. Coie, 1996; Loeber & Farrington, 1998).

Rationale for a Family-Based Population Approach to Prevention

There have been several recent comprehensive reviews that have documented the efficacy of behavioural family intervention (BFI) as an approach to treating children and their families (Lochman, 1990; McMahon, 1999; Sanders, 1996, 1998; Taylor & Biglan, 1998).

Psychopathology and the Family
Edited by J. L. Hudson and R. M. Rapee
Copyright © 2005 by Elsevier Ltd.
All rights of reproduction in any form reserved
ISBN: 0-08-044449-0

This literature will not be revisited here in detail. There is clear evidence that BFI can benefit children with disruptive behaviour disorders, particularly children with oppositional defiant disorders (ODD) and their parents (Forehand & Long, 1988; McMahon & Wells, 1998; Webster-Stratton, 1994). The empirical basis of BFI is strengthened by evidence that the approach can be successfully applied to many other clinical problems and disorders, including attention deficit hyperactivity disorder (Barkley, Guevremont, Anastopoulos, & Fletcher, 1992), persistent feeding difficulties (Turner, Sanders, & Wall, 1994), pain syndromes (Sanders, Shepherd, Cleghorn, & Woolford, 1994), anxiety disorders (Barrett, Dadds, & Rapee, 1996), autism and developmental disabilities (Schreibman, Kaneko, & Koegel, 1991), achievement problems, and habit disorders, as well as everyday problems of normal children (see Sanders, 1996; Taylor & Biglan, 1998, for reviews of this literature). Parenting and family-oriented interventions have also been increasingly used with parents of adolescents at risk of drug abuse, conduct problems and delinquency, attention deficit disorder, eating disorders, depression, and chronic illness (Dishion & Andrews, 1995; Irvine, Biglan, Smolkowski, Metzler, & Ary, 1999; Spoth, Redmond, & Shin, 2001).

Meta-analyses of treatment outcome studies of family focused interventions often report large effect sizes (Serketich & Dumas, 1996), with good maintenance of treatment gains (Forehand & Long, 1988). Treatment effects have been shown to generalize to school settings (McNeil, Eyberg, Eisenstadt, Newcomb, & Funderbunk, 1991) and to various community settings outside the home (Sanders & Glynn, 1981). Parents participating in these programs are generally satisfied consumers (Webster-Stratton, 1989).

It is also becoming increasingly evident that the benefits of BFI are not restricted to children, with several studies now reporting effects in other areas of family functioning, including reduced maternal depression and stress, increases in parental satisfaction and efficacy, and reduced marital conflict over parenting issues (e.g. Nicholson & Sanders, 1999; Sanders, Markie-Dadds, Tully, & Bor, 2000; Sanders & McFarland, 2000; Webster-Stratton, 1998).

BFI's have met a number of important scientific and clinical criteria, which strengthen confidence in the intervention approach:

1. Replicated findings: Primary treatment effects, which have shown that decreases in parental negative disciplinary behaviour and increases in parents' use of a variety of positive attending and other relationship enhancing skills lead to improved child behaviour, have been replicated many times in different studies, involving different investigators, in several different countries, with a diverse variety of client populations (Sanders, 1999);
2. Demonstrations of clinically meaningful outcomes for families: Clinically meaningful outcomes have been demonstrated by applying rigorous criteria for clinical improvement such as the clinical reliable change index (Jacobson & Truax, 1991) for child outcomes. These have shown that as many as 75% of children display evidence of clinically reliable change. Furthermore there is little evidence that parenting interventions produce negative side effects, symptom substitution, or other adverse family outcomes;
3. Effectiveness of different delivery modalities: There is increasing evidence showing that a variety of delivery modalities can produce similar positive outcomes for children and adolescents including individual, group, telephone assisted, and self-directed variants of parenting programs (e.g. Connell, Sanders, & Markie-Dadds, 1997; O'Dell, 1974; Ralph & Sanders, 2003, 2004; Stallman, Ralph, & Sanders, submitted);

4. High levels of consumer acceptability: High levels of consumer satisfaction have been repeatedly demonstrated in different controlled evaluations of BFI and for specific advocated parenting techniques (McMahon, 1999; Webster-Stratton, 1989);

5. Effectiveness with a range of family types: In the area where the strongest support for BFI is evident, namely for disruptive behaviour problems in preadolescent children, interventions have been successfully used with two biological parent families, step parents, and single parents. Until relatively recently there were few well-controlled studies examining family intervention with adolescents. This situation has changed and it is reasonable to conclude that family intervention is potentially effective with a variety of adolescent problems, including substance abuse (Liddle & Dakof, 1995; Alexander, Holtzworth-Munroe, & Jameson, 1994), anti social behaviour (Henggeler, Borduin, & Mann, 1993), and eating disorders (Le Grange, Eisler, Dare, & Russell, 1992).

In sum, these findings confirm that BFI is a powerful clinical resource for effecting change in family relationships for a wide range of behavioural and emotional problems in children.

A Population Perspective on Prevention and Family Intervention

Perhaps the most important challenge facing the field of family intervention is to reorient our focus from treatment outcome studies to the development and evaluation of a population perspective on family problems, including the effective dissemination of what is known to work in promoting effective parenting and positive family relationships. A comprehensive population based strategy is required. This strategy needs to be designed to enhance parental competence, prevent dysfunctional parenting practices, promote better teamwork between partners and thereby reduce an important set of family risk factors associated with behavioural and emotional problems in children and adolescents. In order for such a population approach to be effective several scientific and clinical criteria need to be met (Taylor, 1999).

Knowledge of the Prevalence and Incidence of Child Outcomes Being Targeted

A number of studies in the US, Canada, United Kingdom, New Zealand, Germany, and Australia have established the prevalence rates of behavioural and emotional problems in children, showing that about 18% of children experience behavioural or emotional problems (e.g. Zubrick et al., 1995). Parents themselves report a high level of concern about their child's behaviour and adjustment. For example, in a recent epidemiological survey of Queensland, when asked, "Do you consider your child to have a behavioural or emotional problem?", 28% of parents said 'yes' (Sanders et al., 1999), reflecting the high degree of parental concern about children.

Knowledge of the Prevalence and Incidence of Family Risk Factors

Some studies that have established the incidence and prevalence of child behaviour problems have also examined parenting practices, disciplinary styles, psychological adjustment, and marital conflict. For example, Sanders et al. (1999) found that 70% of parents of children under the age of 12 years report they smack their children at least occasionally, 3% reported hitting their child with an object other than their hand, and 25% of parents reported significant disagreements with partners over parenting issues. Ralph et al. (2003) found that between 14% and 21% of parents of young adolescents aged between 12 and 14 reported feeling nervous, down in the dumps, or downhearted and blue much of the time, with between 30% and 40% reporting high levels of emotional dependence on their adolescents' well-being.

Knowledge that Changing Specific Family Risk and Protective Factors Leads to a Reduction in the Incidence and Prevalence of the Target Problem

An effective population level parenting strategy must make explicit the kinds of parenting practices that are considered harmful to children. The core constructs believed to underpin competent parenting need to be articulated so that targets for intervention can be specified. The validity of the family intervention model would be greatly strengthened if improvements in child functioning were shown to be directly related to specific decreases in dysfunctional parenting and increases in competent parenting variables specified by the model. For example, there is now considerable evidence to support the proposition that teaching parents positive parenting and consistent disciplinary skills results in significant improvements in behaviour for the majority of oppositional and disruptive children, particularly young children, attesting to the importance of reducing patterns of coercive parent–child interaction (Patterson, 1982).

Having Effective Family Interventions

A population perspective requires a range of effective family interventions to be available. The approach to family intervention must also be subjected to comprehensive and systematic evaluation with rigorous scientific controls using either intrasubject replication designs or traditional randomized controlled clinical trials with sufficient statistical power to detect meaningful differences between intervention and control conditions. An effective family intervention strategy should seek to demonstrate that short-term intervention gains maintain over time, are cost effective relative to no-intervention alternatives or usual community care, and are associated with high levels of consumer satisfaction and community acceptance. It is not sufficient just to demonstrate that a strategy results in improvements in family interaction based exclusively on parental reports, although this is a necessary first step. The mechanisms purported to underlie the improvements in family interaction must also be demonstrated to change and be responsible for the observed improvements.

Family Interventions must be Culturally Appropriate

An effective population strategy should be tailored in such a way that it is accessible, relevant and respectful of the cultural values, beliefs, aspirations, traditions, and identified needs of different ethnic groups. Factors such as family structure, roles and responsibilities, predominant cultural beliefs and values, child raising practices and developmental issues, sexuality and gender roles may be culturally specific and need to be addressed. While there is much to learn about how to achieve this objective in a multicultural context, it is likely that sensitively tailored parenting programs can be effective with a variety of cultural groups. It is important that the multicultural context within which assessment, intervention, and research programs operate is made clear in evaluations. There is an ethical imperative to ensure that interventions designed to enskill parents and children in the dominant culture are not at the expense of language and other competencies or values in the child's own culture.

Interventions Need to be Widely Available

A key assumption of a population-based approach is that parenting and other family intervention strategies should be widely accessible in the community. It is important that barriers to accessing parenting and other family intervention programs are reduced. Inflexible clinic hours may prevent working parents from participating in parenting programs. Families most in need of help with emotional and behavioural problems often do not seek or gain access to support services. Families which are socially and economically disadvantaged are less likely to refer themselves for help. In addition, the family intervention services may be viewed as coercive and intrusive, rather than helpful. Use of the internet, CD-ROM-based applications, and media interventions, all have the potential to increase the reach of interventions to hard-to-access groups, although such approaches require systematic evaluation.

A Population Approach to Prevention — The Triple P-Positive Parenting Program

Approaches to prevention are now typically conceptualized as falling into one of three categories: universal, selective, or indicated (Mrazek & Haggerty, 1994). A universal prevention strategy targets an entire population (e.g. national, local community, neighbourhood or school); selective prevention programs refer to strategies that target specific subgroups of the general population that are believed to be at greater risk that others for developing a problem (e.g. low income families, young single mothers); and indicated preventive interventions target high risk individuals, who are identified as having detectable problems, but who do not yet meet diagnostic criteria for a behavioural disorder (e.g. disruptive and aggressive children). The Triple P-Positive Parenting Program is a multi-level, parenting and family support strategy developed by the first author and his colleagues at the University of Queensland in Brisbane, Australia. The program aims to prevent severe behavioural, emotional, and developmental problems in children by enhancing the knowledge, skills, and confidence of parents. It incorporates universal, selective, and indicated interventions organized across five levels on a tiered continuum of increasing strength (see Table 1) for parents of children from birth to age 12. Recently the program has been extended in collaboration with the second author to provide the same levels of support for parents of teenagers aged 12–16.

Level 1, a universal parent information strategy, provides all interested parents with access to useful information about parenting through a coordinated media and promotional

Table 1: The Triple P Model of parenting and family support.

Level of Intervention	Target population	Intervention methods	Program resources	Possible target areas
1. *Universal Triple P* Media-based parenting information campaign	All parents interested in information about parenting and promoting their child's development	A coordinated information campaign using print and electronic media and other health promotion strategies to promote awareness of parenting issues and normalize participation in parenting programs such as Triple P. May include some contact with professional staff (e.g., telephone information line)	• *Guide to Triple P* • Triple P media and promotions kit (including promotional poster, brochure, radio announcements, newspaper columns)	General parenting issues; common every day behavioural and developmental issues
2. *Selected Triple P* Information and advice for a specific parenting concern	Parents with specific concerns about their child's behaviour or development	Provision of specific advice on how to solve common child developmental issues and minor child behaviour problems. May involve face-to-face or telephone contact with a practitioner (about 20 min over two sessions) or (60–90 min) seminars	• *Guide to Triple P* • *Positive Parenting* booklet • *Positive Parenting for Parents with Teenagers* booklet • *Triple P Tip Sheet Series* • *Every Parent Video Series* • Developmental wall charts	Common behaviour difficulties or developmental transitions, such as toilet training, bedtime or sleep problems, diet and nutrition, puberty
3. *Primary Care Triple P* Narrow focus parenting skills training	Parents with specific concerns about their child's behaviour or development who require consultations or active skills training	A brief program (about 80 min over four sessions) combining advice with rehearsal and self-evaluation as required to teach parents to manage discrete child problem behaviour. May involve face-to-face or telephone contact with a practitioner	• Level 2 materials • *Practitioner's Manual for Primary Care Triple P* • *Practitioner's Manual for Primary Care Teen Triple P* • Consultation flip charts	Discrete child behaviour problems, such as tantrums, whining, fighting with siblings; aggressive or oppositional behaviour; home-school problems

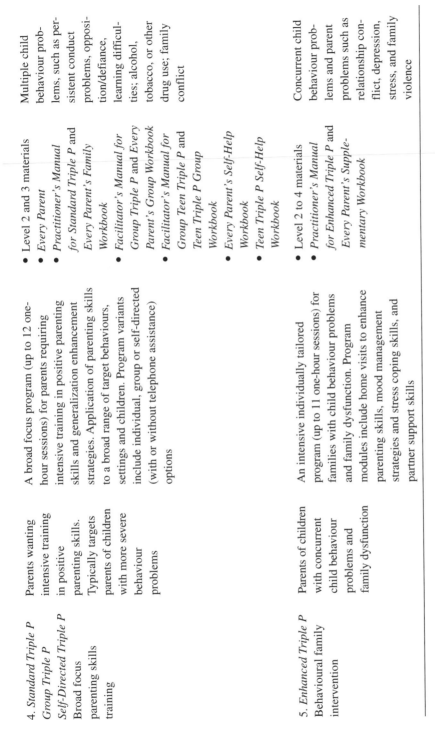

4. *Standard Triple P* / *Group Triple P* / *Self-Directed Triple P* — Broad focus parenting skills training	Parents wanting intensive training in positive parenting skills. Typically targets parents of children with more severe behaviour problems	A broad focus program (up to 12 one-hour sessions) for parents requiring intensive training in positive parenting skills and generalization enhancement strategies. Application of parenting skills to a broad range of target behaviours, settings and children. Program variants include individual, group or self-directed (with or without telephone assistance) options	• Level 2 and 3 materials • *Every Parent* • *Practitioner's Manual for Standard Triple P and Every Parent's Family Workbook* • *Facilitator's Manual for Group Triple P and Every Parent's Group Workbook* • *Facilitator's Manual for Group Teen Triple P and Teen Triple P Group Workbook* • *Every Parent's Self-Help Workbook* • *Teen Triple P Self-Help Workbook*	Multiple child behaviour problems, such as persistent conduct problems, opposition/defiance, learning difficulties; alcohol, tobacco, or other drug use; family conflict
5. *Enhanced Triple P* — Behavioural family intervention	Parents of children with concurrent child behaviour problems and family dysfunction	An intensive individually tailored program (up to 11 one-hour sessions) for families with child behaviour problems and family dysfunction. Program modules include home visits to enhance parenting skills, mood management strategies and stress coping skills, and partner support skills	• Level 2 to 4 materials • *Practitioner's Manual for Enhanced Triple P and Every Parent's Supplementary Workbook*	Concurrent child behaviour problems and parent problems such as relationship conflict, depression, stress, and family violence

campaign using print and electronic media, as well as user-friendly parenting tip sheets and videotapes, which demonstrate specific parenting strategies. This level of intervention aims to increase community awareness of parenting resources, receptivity of parents to participating in programs, and to create a sense of optimism by depicting solutions to common behavioural and developmental concerns. Level 2 is a brief primary health care selective intervention providing anticipatory developmental guidance to parents of children with mild behaviour difficulties. This level of intervention can be delivered individually (one to two sessions), or to large groups of parents as three 90-min seminars. Level 3, a four-session more intensive selective intervention, targets children with mild to moderate behaviour difficulties and includes active skills training for parents. Level 4 is an indicated intensive 8- to 10-session individual or group training program for parents of children with more severe behavioural difficulties, and Level 5 is an enhanced behavioural family intervention program for families, where parenting difficulties are complicated by other sources of family distress (e.g. marital conflict, parental depression, high levels of stress, or teenage relationship problems).

In summary, this tiered multilevel strategy recognizes that there are differing levels of dysfunction and behavioural disturbance in children and adolescents, and parents have differing needs and desires regarding the type, intensity, and mode of assistance they may require. The multilevel strategy is designed to maximize efficiency, contain costs, avoid waste and over-servicing, and ensure the program has wide reach in the community. The program targets five different developmental periods from infancy to adolescence, and within each developmental period the reach of the intervention can vary from being very broad (targeting an entire population) or quite narrow (targeting only high-risk children). Also the multidisciplinary nature of the program involves the better utilization of the existing professional workforce in the task of promoting competent parenting.

Theoretical Basis

Triple P is a form of behavioural family intervention based on social learning principles (e.g. Patterson, 1982). Triple P aims to enhance family protective factors and reduce risk factors associated with severe behavioural and emotional problems in children and adolescents. Specifically the program aims to (1) enhance the knowledge, skills, confidence, self sufficiency, and resourcefulness of parents; (2) promote nurturing, safe, engaging, non-violent, and low conflict environments for children; and (3) promote children's social, emotional, language, intellectual, and behavioural competencies through positive parenting practices.

The program content draws on research from the following six domains:

1. Social learning models of parent–child interaction highlight the reciprocal and bi-directional nature of parent–child interactions (e.g. Patterson, 1982). This model identifies learning mechanisms, which maintain coercive and dysfunctional patterns of family interaction and predict future antisocial behaviour in children (Patterson, Reid, & Dishion, 1992). As a consequence the program specifically teaches parents positive child management skills as an alternative to coercive parenting practices;
2. Research in child and family behaviour therapy and applied behaviour analysis has developed many useful behaviour change strategies, particularly research which

focuses on rearranging antecedents of problem behaviour through designing more positive engaging environments for children (Risley, Clarke, & Cataldo, 1976; Sanders, 1992, 1996);

3. Developmental research on parenting in everyday contexts has identified children's competencies in naturally occurring everyday contexts, drawing heavily on work, which traces the origins of social and intellectual competence to early parent–child relationships (e.g. Hart & Risley, 1995; White, 1990). Children's risk of developing severe behavioural and emotional problems is reduced by teaching parents to use naturally occurring daily interactions to teach children language, social skills, and developmental competencies; and problem solving skills in an emotionally supportive context. Children are at greater risk for adverse developmental outcomes, including behavioural problems, if they fail to acquire core language competencies and impulse control during early childhood (Hart & Risley, 1995). Particular emphasis is placed on using child-initiated interactions as a context for the use of incidental teaching (Hart & Risley, 1975);

4. Social information processing models highlight the important role of parental cognitions such as attributions, expectancies, and beliefs as factors, which contribute to parental self-efficacy, decision-making, and behavioural intentions (e.g. Bandura, 1977, 1995). Parents' attributions are specifically targeted in the intervention by encouraging parents to identify alternative social interactional explanations for their child's behaviour;

5. Research from the field of developmental psychopathology has identified specific risk and protective factors that are linked to adverse developmental outcomes in children and adolescents (e.g. Bongers, Koot, van der Ende, & Verhulst, 2003; Grych & Fincham, 1990; Hart & Risley, 1995; Rutter, 1995). Specifically the risk factors of poor parent management practices, marital family conflict, and parental distress are targeted risk factors. As parental discord is a specific risk factor for many forms of child and adolescent psychopathology (Grych & Fincham, 1990; Rutter, 1995; Sanders, Nicholson, & Floyd, 1997), the program fosters collaboration and teamwork between carers in raising children. Improved couples' and family communication is an important vehicle to reduce marital conflict over child rearing issues, and to reduce personal distress of parents and children in conflictual relationships (Sanders, Markie-Dadds, & Turner, 1998). Triple P also targets distressing emotional reactions of parents including depression, anger, anxiety, and high levels of stress especially with the parenting role (Sanders et al., 1998). Distress can be alleviated through parents developing better parenting skills, which reduces feelings of helplessness, depression, and stress. Enhanced levels of the intervention use cognitive-behaviour therapy techniques of mood monitoring, challenging dysfunctional cognitions and attributions, and by teaching parents specific coping skills for high-risk parenting situations;

6. A public health perspective on family intervention involves the explicit recognition of the role of the broader ecological context for human development (e.g. Biglan, 1995; Mrazek & Haggerty, 1994; National Institute of Mental Health, 1998). As pointed out by Biglan (1995) the reduction of antisocial behaviour in children requires the community context for parenting to change. Triple P's media and promotional strategy as part of a larger system of intervention aims to change this broader ecological context of parenting. It does this by normalizing parenting experiences (particularly the process of participating in parent education), by breaking

down parents' sense of social isolation, increasing social and emotional support from others in the community, and validating and acknowledging publicly the importance and difficulties of parenting. It also involves actively seeking community involvement and support in the program by the engagement of key community stakeholders (e.g. community leaders, businesses, schools, and voluntary organizations);

Empirical Basis of Program

Research into a system of behavioural family intervention that eventually became known as Triple P began in 1977 with the first findings published in the early 1980s (e.g. Sanders & Glynn, 1981). Since that time the intervention methods used in Triple P have been subjected to a series of controlled evaluations using both intrasubject replication designs and traditional randomized control group designs (see Sanders, 1999, for a review).

Randomized Efficacy Trials

Following this initial research a series of controlled outcome studies sought to improve the outcomes of standard parent training by systematically targeting other family risk factors, such as marital discord and parental depression. Marital conflict has been shown to be a risk factor for the development of antisocial behaviour in children, particularly boys (Emery, 1982). Dadds, Schwartz, and Sanders (1987) evaluated a brief, four-session marital communication (partner support training) intervention to complement parenting skills training. This intervention involved teaching couples to support rather than to undermine or criticize each other. It also taught couples problem solving skills to resolve disagreements about parenting. In a controlled evaluation of this combined intervention, the provision of partner support training significantly improved outcome on both child and parent observational measures for families with marital discord, but not for parents without marital discord. This finding suggested that when child management problems are complicated by marital conflict, better longer term (i.e. 6 months) outcomes for both child and parent are likely when marital communication is specifically targeted.

Another study sought to assess the effects of parent training with clinically depressed parents of oppositional children. Sanders and McFarland (2000) randomly assigned 47 mothers, who met diagnostic criteria for either major depression or dysthymia to either a standard BFI condition or to an enhanced BFI condition. The enhanced condition provided additional treatment components that specifically targeted the mothers' depression, including mood monitoring, cognitive restructuring, and cognitive coping skills. Both the standard and the enhanced condition produced significant reductions in children's aversive behaviour and in mothers' mood at post intervention. However, at 6-month follow-up more families in the enhanced condition (53%) compared to standard BFI (13%) experienced concurrent clinically reliable reductions in both maternal depression and child disruptive behaviour. These findings suggest that Triple P can be a viable treatment option for clinically depressed mothers.

A recent large-scale randomized control trial compared the efficacy of three different variants of the Triple P intervention for a large sample of disruptive 3-year olds (Sanders et al., 2000a). The parents of 305 preschoolers, who were considered to be high risk for conduct problems on the basis of elevated rates of disruptive behaviour, high levels of parenting conflict, maternal depression, single parenthood status, or low socioeconomic status, were recruited. Parents were randomly assigned to either standard (Level 4) behavioural family intervention (SBFI), self directed (Level 4) behavioural family intervention using a self-help manual (SDBFI), enhanced (Level 5) behavioural family intervention (EBFI), or to a waitlist control (WL) condition. The enhanced condition combined the partner support and coping skills interventions described previously to form a comprehensive adjunctive intervention for high risk families. At post intervention, the two therapist assisted conditions (EBFI and SBFI) produced similar improvements and were associated with significantly lower levels of observed and parent-reported disruptive child behaviour, lower levels of dysfunctional parenting, greater parental competence, and higher consumer satisfaction than self directed (SDBFI) or WL conditions. However, at 1 year follow-up, children in all three Triple P variants had achieved similar levels of clinically reliable change in their disruptive behaviour but with parents in the therapist-assisted conditions being more satisfied in their parenting roles than parents in the self-directed condition.

This study showed with a large sample of parents that more is not always better than less. The provision of a generic enhanced family intervention should be reserved for those families, who fail to make adequate improvement after standard BFI and who still have elevated scores on measures of adult psychosocial adjustment. It also raised the interesting possibility that self-directed program variants could be effective for some families. This issue was examined more closely in a series of studies on self-directed interventions.

Effects of Self-Directed Variants

Not all parents are able to attend regular consultation sessions and this is a particular issue for parents living in rural and remote areas that are typically not well served with mental health facilities. An enhanced self-directed intervention was therefore developed and evaluated, based on the intervention that showed promise in the trial described above, but adding weekly telephone contact. Connell et al. (1997) randomly allocated 24 families living in rural areas to either the enhanced self-directed program or a waitlist control group. All families had a child aged between 2 and 5 years, who scored in the clinical range for disruptive behaviour problems. Telephone calls occurred once weekly for 10 weeks and ranged from 5 to 30 min, with an average of 20 min. The calls prompted parents to use the self-help materials, which included a copy of every parent: A positive approach to children's behaviour (Sanders, 1992) and Every Parent's Workbook (Sanders, Lynch, & Markie-Dadds, 1994). Following intervention, families in the enhanced self-directed condition showed significantly lower levels of disruptive child behaviour, lower levels of coercive parent behaviour, greater parenting competence, and reduced levels of depression and stress when compared to families in the waitlist condition. At post-intervention, 100% of children in the waitlist group and 33% of children in the intervention condition were in the clinical range for disruptive behaviour. There was a high level of parent satisfaction with the intervention for both mothers and fathers (Connell et al., 1997). These finding showed that a brief, largely self-directed version of Triple P can be effective with families that traditionally have had little access to mental health services.

Two other studies examined the effectiveness of self-directed variants of Triple P for parents of preschool-aged children with oppositional behaviour problems. Markie-Dadds and Sanders (2004) randomly assigned 64 parents with a child aged between 2 and 5 years to either the original standard self-directed program (no telephone contact) or to a waitlist control group. All parents were concerned about their child's behaviour. Parents in the self-directed condition received a copy of the same parenting materials as used in Connell et al. (1997), and completed the program at home over a 10-week period. At post-intervention, parents in the self-directed program used less coercive parenting practices than parents in the waitlist group. Children in the self-directed condition were rated by their parents as having a significantly lower level of disruptive behaviour than children in the control group at post-intervention with these differences being maintained at 6-month follow-up.

Markie-Dadds, Sanders, and Smith (1997) compared the effects of three intervention conditions: written information alone (standard self-directed), written information plus telephone counselling (enhanced self-directed) and waitlist control group. Forty-five families with a child aged between 2 and 5 years, who were at risk for the development of behavioural problems participated in the program. Results indicated that the enhanced self-directed and telephone backup condition produced more positive outcomes for parents and children in comparison with both the standard self-directed program and waitlist group, on measures of child disruptive behaviour.

Two variants of self-directed Teen Triple P were compared to a waitlist control group in a randomized controlled trial with 51 families, who reported high levels of parent-adolescent conflict with early adolescent children aged between 11 and 13 (Stallman et al., submitted). Families were randomly assigned to a 10-module workbook program supplemented by a video, or to an enhanced program with the addition of 10, 15-min weekly telephone consultations. At post-intervention, using parent report measures of adolescent behaviour and parenting practices, parents in the enhanced condition reported significantly fewer adolescent behavioural problems and less use of dysfunctional parenting strategies than parents in either the standard or waitlist conditions. Improvements were maintained at 3-month follow-up.

These findings show that while the standard self-directed programs were effective with some families, effects could be enhanced by the provision of brief telephone calls using a self-regulatory framework, which encouraged parents to take control of the learning process.

Evaluation of Group Triple P

Continuing concern about mental health costs has led to the search for more cost efficient ways of delivering family interventions within a population level prevention framework. Several studies have shown that parent training administered in groups could be successful (e.g. Cunningham, 1996). The group version of Triple P (Turner, Markie-Dadds, & Sanders, 1997) was first trialled in a large-scale population trial involving 1673 families in East Perth, in Western Australia. Preliminary data from this trial showed that parents in the geographical catchment area which received the intervention, reported significantly greater reductions on measures of child disruptive behaviour than parents in the non-intervention comparison group (Zubrick et al., in press). Prior to intervention, 42% of children had levels of disruptive behaviour in the clinical range. Following participation in Group Triple P, the level of children's disruptive behaviour had reduced by half to 20%. Participation in the group program also resulted in significant reductions in dysfunctional parenting practices, marital conflict, parental stress and depression, as well as significant improvements in marital satisfaction.

Group Teen Triple P has also demonstrated improvements for parents of children aged 12–14 years in two preliminary studies. In the first pilot study, after participating in the 8-week program 27 parents reported significant reductions in conflict with their teenager, and on measures of laxness, over-reactivity, and disagreements with their partner over parenting issues. In addition, parents reported significant improvements on measures of self-regulation, including self-efficacy, self-sufficiency, and self-management, and reductions on measures of depression, anxiety, and stress (Ralph & Sanders, 2003).

In a larger second trial, 303 parents of first-year students attending 15 high schools in metropolitan Brisbane participated in 30 Group Teen Triple P parenting groups conducted by school-based facilitators. Results again showed that parents reported significant reductions in conflict with their teenager, and on measures of laxness, over-reactivity, and disagreements with their partner over parenting issues, and reductions on measures of depression and stress (Ralph, Stallman, & Sanders, submitted).

Effects of Using the Media to Deliver Triple P

Evidence that parents can benefit from self-help variants of Triple P raised the further possibility that the mass media could be used to teach parenting skills. Prior research by Webster-Stratton (1994) had previously shown that videomodelling could be effective in teaching parenting skills to parents of conduct problem children. Although no studies have specifically examined the impact on parent–child interaction of a universal regular television series as a medium for parent training, we have completed a study evaluating the "Families" television series as an intervention for parents of young children. This 13-episode series included a weekly segment on Triple P. Fifty six parents of preschool aged children were randomly assigned either to a TV viewing condition or to a no intervention control group (Sanders, Montgomery, & Brechman-Toussaint, 2000). All 13 episodes were viewed through the medium of videotapes over a 6-week period rather than live to air, as the program was not shown in Australia when it originally went to air in New Zealand. Hence, the outcome data from this study reflect the effects of a media intervention under relatively "ideal" conditions of viewing (i.e. parents watched all episodes, and back up Triple P facts sheets were provided for each episode). Only parents in the TV viewing condition reported a significant reduction in disruptive behaviours, an increase in parenting confidence, a decrease in dysfunctional parenting practices, and high overall levels of consumer satisfaction with the program. These findings showed that a media intervention could effect changes in parenting practices and therefore children's behaviour. Such findings are consistent with other research by Webster-Stratton (1994), which has demonstrated the benefits of showing parents videotape models of parenting skills as an intervention with oppositional children.

Effects of Brief Primary Care Interventions

Although, there have been no controlled evaluations of level 3 interventions there have been several brief intervention studies targeting discrete problems such as sleep disturbance, feeding difficulties, and habit disorders, which have used similar interventions in a brief consultation format (Christensen & Sanders, 1987; Dadds, Sanders, & Bor, 1984; Sanders, Bor, & Dadds, 1984). Two randomized controlled trials are in progress involving primary care nurses in the implementation of either level 2 or level 3 interventions, plus one study evaluating the effectiveness of training general medical practitioners to provide Triple P Level 2 and 3 consultation advice to parents.

Other Related Research

Although the BFI methods used in Triple P have been applied primarily with children with conduct problems, several other projects have used similar family intervention methods with other problems. For example, Lawton and Sanders (1994) described the adaptation of BFI for parents living in stepfamilies. Nicholson and Sanders (1999) randomly assigned 42 stepfamilies to either therapist-directed BFI, self-directed BFI, or to a waitlist condition. Compared to control families, families receiving BFI reported significantly greater reductions from pre- to post-intervention in couple conflict over parenting, and were more likely to show clinically significant and statistically reliable change on a range of family and child measures. There were no differences between the therapist and the self directed BFI conditions on measures of child problem behaviour.

Another series of studies has focused on the application of BFI methods to children with recurrent abdominal pain (Sanders et al., 1994), and persistent feeding difficulties (Turner et al., 1994). It is beyond the scope of this chapter to review this work, other than to highlight the versatility of a family intervention model that can be applied to a diverse range of clinical problems.

Current Issues in Family-Based Prevention of Child and Adolescent Behavioural and Emotional Disorders

While considerable progress has been made in developing effective prevention programs, there are several significant obstacles to the implementation of effective community-wide prevention programs. These include problems that relate to the nature of child and adolescent behavioural problems themselves, structural obstacles relating to the organization of health care and educational services for children, dissemination to practitioners, and sociopolitical considerations, which affect children and their families.

Relationship between Child and Parent Problems

Children's behaviour problems and parental adjustment difficulties tend to covary. Even though a child may not be showing significant overt signs of maladjustment, the environmental conditions, which give rise to subsequent problems may be operative within the family (Kazdin, 1987; Patterson, 1982, 1986). A child may not display significantly disordered behaviour, although the parent does. This is no more apparent than in a household, where the mother is depressed and there is significant marital conflict. Effective prevention programs may need to concurrently address adult personal and marital adjustment issues as well as child issues, when these factors remain unchanged during the parenting intervention.

Changing Nature of Developmental Advice Required by Parents

Another challenge for prevention programs is the changing nature of the developmental and parenting advice required by parents to manage children's behaviour over time (Sanders, 1992; Sanders & Dadds, 1982). A current Australian longitudinal study that has followed ~ 1600 children from infancy to 17–18 years of age identified two pathways associated with the development of antisocial behaviour in children and adolescents (Vassallo et al., 2002). The authors describe one group of children, whose problem behaviour becomes entrenched in the preschool years, and another with problems only emerging around the age of 12–13 years. Prevention programs targeted at each developmental phase therefore need to be designed accordingly. As children move towards adolescence, greater involvement by the child in family problem solving becomes possible. While specific compliance training, which teaches parents to issue clear, specific, and enforceable instructions, and to back them up with effective consequences (e.g. time-out), can be effective with young children, the same tactics used with teenagers are not appropriate and are less likely to be effective. Appropriate goals for achieving increases in adolescent independence and autonomy may become compromised if parents fail to recognize the need for a less intrusive parenting style while still attempting to maintain some level of control over age-appropriate rules and limits (Barber, 2002). The extent to which parents receiving early child management training make age appropriate adjustments as their child matures is not known. Interventions may need to prepare parents for future, yet to be encountered circumstances (e.g. preparing a child to start school or go on their first date), the importance and salience of which may not be immediately apparent to parents when their children are toddlers or preschoolers.

Interrelationships between Different Risk Factors

The various family factors related to increased risk of behavioural problems rarely occur in isolation from each other. While some families experience specific difficulties, it is more common for families to experience several difficulties simultaneously (Rutter & Quinton, 1984). Problems of unemployment, lack of social support, and depression often co-occur, as do marital difficulties and depression (Dadds, 1987; Rutter, Cox, Tupling, Berger, & Yule, 1975). Family breakdown and social adversity are closely linked. Families most at risk for psychopathology have lower levels of participation in preschool programs for children, have more chronic health problems, have lower levels of appropriate utilization of health care services, and are less interpersonally skilled at negotiating with authorities regarding their families' needs (Fergusson, Dimond, Horwood, & Shannon, 1984).

Socially disadvantaged families may be more difficult to reach with preventive programs. This may be an unavoidable reality in preventive programming in which families at the greatest risk of severe long term adjustment problems are the most difficult to recruit.

Recruiting and Engaging Multidistressed Families

Children at greatest risk for the development of conduct disorders are those from multi-distressed families (Offord, 1989; Robins, 1991), who traditionally have not fared well in psychological interventions designed to treat conduct problems (Kazdin, 1987). High-risk families are difficult to recruit, engage, and retain in prevention programs. A variety of strategies may be employed to recruit families including: the use of media outreach; direct mail; and, using settings where parents with children in the eligible age group meet regularly or at least have some contact, such as day-care centres, playgroups, preschools, schools, community centres, or contacts through family doctors. Possible strategies for promoting engagement include increasing the accessibility of the program while minimizing the response cost to the participants through the provision of: training in the home or at local community venues; prompts and reminder calls for forthcoming appointments, and; incentives for clinic attendance and participation (e.g. free child care and transport, lottery tickets, or even cash payments). In a review of developmental and clinical research findings, Morrisey-Kane and Prinz (1999) conclude that there are strategies that can be used to increase the likelihood of engagement. These include letter writing, intensive phone contact, and parent information sessions. However, they recommend an approach that integrates child, parent, social network, school, agency, and community involvement in an ecological, multi-level approach. The recent development of two series of Triple P seminars for parents of young children and parents of teenagers has been undertaken in part to increase engagement at a low level of commitment that may then increase parents' willingness to consider engagement at a higher level, such as a group program. Research into the effectiveness of this strategy is currently underway with both age groups.

Family Breakdown

Parenting difficulties can contribute to marital conflict, which in turn can contribute to the development of behavioural problems in children (Emery, 1982; Grych & Fincham, 1990). With between 1/3 and 1/2 of Western marriages ending in divorce (Glick & Lin, 1986), there is potential merit in considering programs dealing with the prevention of marital distress in premarried couples as a possible means for decreasing the risk of subsequent behavioural disturbance in offspring (Markman, Floyd, Stanley, & Lewis, 1987).

Social Adversity

A major challenge for prevention programs is determining how to deal with parenting problems and child rearing difficulties that are related to the family's socioeconomic status. Families surviving on reduced incomes due to unemployment frequently experience problems of depression, alcohol abuse, and domestic violence (e.g. Warr, 1982). These parents may benefit from a variety of survival skills, which, while not solving their financial worries, may enable the family to cope more effectively with their circumstances (Sanders, 1999). Targets for intervention may include learning to ask the right questions of welfare or social security personnel; coping with frustration and delays when dealing with bureaucracy; and handling problems with landlords, significant others, parents, in-laws, ex-spouses, schools, and police. Families caught in the poverty trap, living in inadequate housing conditions in high crime areas may also be extremely difficult to engage in any prevention program. The need to intervene at a political level is apparent. However, political level interventions designed to reduce poverty and social disadvantage, while laudable, may not have a significant impact on the prevalence of children's antisocial behaviour because the majority of children, who develop behavioural and emotional problems are not in the bottom quintile of the income distribution.

Childcare and Female Participation in the Workforce

Many developed nations have witnessed a steady increase in the number of mothers with young children participating in the work force. For example, in 1998, of Australian two-parent families with dependent children, 61% of females were employed, while among sole parents, 41% of females were employed (National Council of Women of Australia, 1999). Many young children are now looked after by multiple caregivers. Some early problem behaviours like aggression occur in multiple settings and may complicate the implementation of parenting programs. Preventive efforts may be difficult to deliver to families because both caregivers are likely to be outside the home. Preventive programs need to target multiple caregivers and children in settings such as day-care and kindergarten. Some excellent examples of high-quality day-care environments which incorporate behavioural strategies such as planned activities, incidental teaching, and behaviour management routines have been reported (e.g. Herbert-Jackson, O'Brien, Porterfield, & Risley, 1977).

Costs of Prevention

One argument used to promote prevention is that preventive programs are likely to be cost effective and reduce the costs of treating antisocial behaviour, drug abuse, and other mental health problems. Although effective preventive efforts offer better mental health, they are likely to be expensive to implement. A meaningful cost-benefit analysis of prevention must distinguish between direct and indirect costs, that is the costs borne by the health budget, and those costs, emotional or other, borne by the families and children with significant psychopathology (Eisenberg, 1989).

Preventive Efforts must not have Deleterious Effects

Some preventive efforts have had negative effects on their participants (e.g. Fo & O'Donnell, 1975; Davidson & Wolfred, 1977) such that children, who were not generally at risk for antisocial behaviour before a program, were at increased risk after their participation. This is a more common problem when preventive efforts are directed at the community en masse (Kazdin, 1987). Careful evaluation and monitoring of prevention programs must be maintained at all times to ensure that deleterious effects are avoided or counteracted if present. For example, encouraging parents to discuss the risks associated with alcohol use with their teenagers might seem to be a useful strategy. However, one study has shown that teenagers, who are aware of such risks have increased alcohol consumption (Yarnold, 1998).

Length of Intervention

It is unclear whether prevention programs should be intensive programs, conducted when children are at a particular developmental level (e.g. toddlers), or protracted over time so families receive periodic assistance as their child approaches a developmental task or transition (e.g. starting school, moving to high school). Advantages of a time-limited program are that it is easier to keep families engaged, there are fewer changes in program personnel so continuity of care is maintained, and it is easier to secure funding support. In a protracted program, parents can receive active guidance and support over a longer time span and at a time when they are confronting parenting tasks addressed by the program (e.g. preparing a child to start school).

Strength of Intervention for Different Groups

An important yet unresolved issue is the strength of intervention necessary to prevent the development of disorder in groups at differing levels of risk. Kazdin (1987) argued that it is fruitless offering low strength interventions to families where the child had already developed conduct disorder. When dealing with high-risk families whose children have yet to develop the disorder, the number of risk variables, which need to be addressed for a prevention program to be effective, is not known. It may be necessary to provide more than the child-focused parent training interventions, especially when a parent is depressed or when there are marital difficulties or high levels of parental stress. Techniques such as cognitive therapy, problem solving training, and stress management procedures may effectively complement parent-training strategies. However, there is conflicting evidence concerning the necessity of adjunctive interventions. For example, in a randomized trial of a parenting intervention combined with a school-based program to reduce substance initiation in middle-school children, Spoth, Redmond, Trudeau, and Shin (2002) reported relative reduction rates for alcohol initiation of 30% for the combined intervention, but only 4% for the school-based program. This raises the question about the relative efficacy of delivering the parenting intervention alone. Ultimately, the strength of intervention issue can only be resolved empirically. The ultimate question posed by Paul (1969) in relation to treatment evaluation is also pertinent to the prevention area. "What treatment, by whom, is most effective with this problem, under this set of circumstances, in this setting, and how does the treatment effect come about?" (p. 44).

Who Should Deliver Parenting Programs?

Evidence-based parenting interventions have primarily been developed by psychologists trained in the value of scientist practitioner frameworks. However, a range of other disciplines provide counsel and advice to parents about parenting and behaviour management issues, but have had little exposure to evidence-based programs. There is a need to develop appropriate training courses and methods of instruction to enable multiple disciplines to support parenting. For example, Sanders, Tully, Turner, Maher, and McAuliffe (2003) developed and evaluated the effects of a brief 3-day primary-care training course on parent consultation skills for general practitioners. After training GPs were significantly more confident in their parenting skills, and on an observational measure showed improvements in their consultation skills compared to a waitlist control group of general practitioners.

Practitioner Resistance to Evidence-Based Programs

Although there is evidence that many practitioners welcome and positively evaluate training in evidence based parenting programs, it would be naive to assume that training programs that require changes in work practices would necessarily be embraced with open arms. Sources of practitioner resistance can include concerns about manualized interventions being too rigid and prescriptive, concerns about the ethics of certain procedures such as time out in managing children's behaviour, and concerns about prevention programs taking away needed resources for treatment of severe end cases. The task of a professional trainer involved in dissemination although rewarding is not always easy. Figure 1 captures a conceptual model that articulates the hypothesized origins of trainee resistance. This is an adaptation of the model of parental resistance during parent training developed by Patterson and Chamberlain (1994). It should be noted that practitioner resistance is conceptualized as being related to both historical events and the practitioner's experiences in dealing with resistive people and also the trainer's behaviour in reinforcing resistive behaviour.

Turner, Nicholson, and Sanders (in press) found in a recent follow-up study of 1,078 primary-care practitioners that practitioner self-efficacy and line management support were the best predictors of subsequent program implementation by staff 8 months

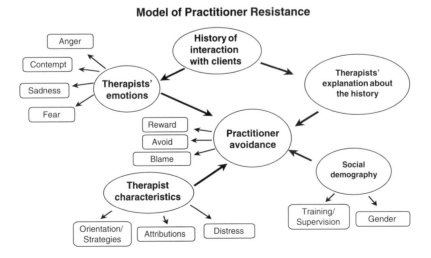

Figure 1: Model of practitioner resistance.

post-training. This finding highlights the importance of the post-training environment including supervision of trained practitioners.

Funding of Parenting Programs

Decisions about which parenting programs should be publicly funded are controversial. Although various lists of evidence-based programs have appeared from time to time, consistent evaluation criteria need to be applied and these lists need frequent updating to remain contemporary.

Cultural Diversity

Culturally and linguistically diverse communities are increasingly seeking parenting programs that are effective with different ethnic groups and communities. Every parent raises their children within a broader cultural context that involve values, traditions, rituals, mores and belief systems concerning parenting practices that are considered acceptable. What is sometimes not recognized is that parenting programs that are effective with one group can, with relatively minor adaptation, be effective with others. For example, the Group version of Triple P has been successfully used in several different countries including Hong Kong, Japan, Singapore, Germany, and Switzerland. In this context it is important to differentiate between culturally specific beliefs (e.g. some Chinese parents report they believe praising children is bad for them) and beliefs that may be held by parents in any community. In order to be optimally effective, trainers need to develop process management strategies for addressing both types of issues. These include checking with parents in a group situation whether these are widely held beliefs; reframing concepts using local words and phrases that are culturally acceptable; and ensuring that parents' developmental goals for their children and their families are identified and acknowledged, while at the same time offering a range of strategies shown to be effective across diverse cultural settings for parents to choose from.

Dissemination to Professionals

Clinical researchers often lament the lack of uptake of empirically supported interventions by practitioners (Backer, Liberman, & Kuehnel, 1986; Biglan, 1995; Fixsen & Blasé, 1993). The effective dissemination of empirically supported interventions is of major importance to all prevention researchers, policy advisers, and organizations involved in the provision of mental health and family intervention services. Obstacles to the utilization of empirically supported interventions include the lack of reinforcement for clinical researchers to engage in dissemination activities when academic promotion depends on grants and publication rates. There are also significant practical obstacles to conducting controlled research into dissemination itself, including lack of reliable and valid measures of practitioner uptake or resistance, and concerns about randomization of practitioners or services to different conditions of dissemination. Some practitioners have also been critical of randomized clinical trial methodology, which is portrayed as having little relevance, because of the highly restrictive selection criteria which are typically used in trials, the elimination of comorbidity, the use of student therapists, and the reliance on manualized treatments which necessarily limit the extent of flexible tailoring that many practitioners value.

Active strategies must be in place, as in Triple P, to promote program use and fidelity, and to support practitioners' use of the program through access to consultation support, research updates on the scientific basis of the program, newsletters, data management and scoring software, media promotional kits to support the use of the program, web sites, program consultation, and evaluation advice.

Harnessing Public Support for Increasing the Availability of Parenting Programs

A population health approach to parenthood preparation needs public support for it to be accepted by parents. Some parents still view the suggestion that they should undertake a parenting program as casting aspersions on their competence as a parent. However, the idea that completion of a parenting programs is a health-positive step parents can take to give their children opportunities is likely to be enhanced by having a range of evidence-based options with flexible delivery modalities that can cater for individual preference. To ensure proper tailoring of programs to the needs of parents there is a need for more consumer-focused research examining parental preferences for the design of parenting programs.

Strengthening Use of the Media

The media has a powerful influence in the lives of the community. Many professionals view the influence of the media of parents and families as largely negative. Furthermore, some professionals actively avoid having anything to do with the media. However, harnessing the support of the media to increase public awareness and support for parenting programs is a very useful way of normalizing and destigmatizing parenthood preparation. For example, the Every Family Initiative funded by *beyondblue*: The National Depression Initiative in Australia uses a comprehensive cross media strategy that has incorporated television advertising, current affairs stories, newspaper and radio spots on positive parenting as the first of five levels of intervention in a current population-level trial.

Conclusion

Family-based interventions have the potential to meaningfully contribute to the management and prevention of a range of different forms of child and adolescent behaviour disorders, including substance abuse, conduct disorder, eating disorder, and depression for adolescents. With respect to conduct disorder and substance abuse, there is increasing evidence that family interventions that engage parents of adolescents can be effective. Numerous studies show that adolescents with conduct problems are particularly resistant to treatment, and considerable effort and expertise are needed to make any impact on this problem, underlining the need to intervene much earlier.

This chapter documents the critical importance of family relationships, and how families can be meaningfully involved in both the prevention and treatment of mental health problems. There is clear evidence that family intervention is a powerful intervention technology for a wide range of child and adolescent mental health problems. Although there is also evidence to support the efficacy of some prevention programs delivered in schools, a failure to change the child's family environment may lead to an erosion of any gains that might be made while a child attends an enriched school environment, as illustrated by Honig, Lally, and Mathieson (1982). Developing quality day-care and educational environments for children, and attempts to assist the family, should be seen as complementary rather than as mutually exclusive aims. Other researchers have argued that multilevel, multicomponent prevention programs conducted in collaboration with families, schools, and communities are necessary to promote competence in children (Weissberg, Caplan, & Harwood, 1991). Ultimately, rigorous longitudinal research will identify those components of a prevention program that are both necessary and sufficient for reducing the incidence of conduct-disordered behaviour in the community.

However, there are many unresolved problems that must be addressed before the field makes a significant impact on the mental health of broad communities. First, research is clearly needed to examine the dissemination process. Too few practitioners have had adequate training in the delivery of family intervention programs. This knowledge domain should be an integral part of the training of all mental health practitioners. Second, despite the repeated calls for empirical research into other forms of family therapy, the weight of the evidence clearly shows that cognitive behavioural and social learning approaches to working with families have the most empirical support. Training programs should give priority to training practitioners in empirically validated forms of family intervention. Finally, much more research is required to examine how treatment strength can be better tailored to family characteristics, preferences, and needs. Empirically based decision rules are needed to guide practitioners in determining which type of approach (e.g. self-directed, group, brief, telephone assisted) is needed, at different points of the developmental trajectory for different constellations of problems.

The task of supporting parents is best viewed as a process that begins with pregnancy and continues until children leave home and become fully independent adults. Parenting support needs to be viewed on a continuum whereby the informational needs of parents change as a function of the parent's experience and the child's developmental level. The strength or intensity of the intervention families require may also change as a function of life transitions (separation, divorce, repartnering, illness, loss, trauma, and financial hardship). A universal parenthood program requires greater flexibility in how parenting programs are offered to parents. As the next generation of parenting programs evolve, a strong commitment to the promotion of empirically supported parenting practices is required. Little progress is likely until parenthood preparation is seen as a shared community responsibility.

The future development of Triple P will rest in part on the program's capacity to evolve in the light of new evidence concerning the strengths and limitations of the model. The prospect of developing a comprehensive, high-quality, empirically supported, multi-level, preventively oriented, universal, freely accessible parenting support strategy remains the fundamental goal of Triple P. To achieve this ideal, research is required to identify responders to different delivery modalities, and resolve how to engage and maintain in intervention, families which traditionally have been less likely to participate in parenting skills programs (e.g. fathers, indigenous parents). Parenting programs that are truly universal must also examine the parenting and family support needs of children with special needs such as disabilities, chronic or terminal illness, or who have suffered neurological damage as a result of injuries.

References

Alexander, J. F., Holtzworth-Munroe, A., & Jameson, P. B. (1994). The process and outcome of marital and family therapy: Research review and evaluation. In: A. E. Bergin & S. L. Garfield (Eds), *Handbook of Psychotherapy and Behaviour Change* (4th ed.) (pp. 595–630). New York: Wiley.

Backer, T. E., Liberman, R. P., & Kuehnel, T. G. (1986). Dissemination and adoption of innovative psychosocial interventions. *Journal of Consulting and Clinical Psychology, 54*, 111–118.

Bandura, A. (1977). Self-efficacy: Toward a unifying theory of behavioural change. *Psychological Review, 84*, 191–215.

Bandura, A. (1995). *Self-efficacy in changing societies.* New York: Cambridge University Press.

Barber, B. K. (Ed.) (2002). *Intrusive parenting: How psychological control affects children and adolescents.* Washington, DC: American Psychological Association.

Barkley, R. A., Guevremont, D. C., Anastopoulos, A. D., & Fletcher, K. E. (1992). A comparison of three family therapy programs for treating family conflicts in adolescents with attention-deficit hyperactivity disorder. *Journal of Consulting and Clinical Psychology, 60*, 450–462.

Barrett, P. M., Dadds, M. R., & Rapee, R. M. (1996). Family treatment of childhood anxiety: A controlled trial. *Journal of Consulting and Clinical Psychology, 65*, 627–635.

Biglan, A. (1995). Translating what we know about the context of antisocial behaviour into a lower prevalence of such behaviour. *Journal of Applied Behaviour Analysis, 28*, 479–492.

Bongers, I. L., Koot, H. M., van der Ende, J., & Verhulst, F. C. (2003). The normative development of child and adolescent problem behaviour. *Journal of Abnormal Psychology, 112*, 179–192.

Chamberlain, P., & Patterson, G. R. (1995). Discipline and child compliance in parenting. In: M. H. Bornstein (Ed.), *Handbook of parenting, Vol. 4: Applied and practical parenting* (pp. 205–225). Mahwah, NJ, USA: Lawrence Erlbaum.

Christensen, A. P., & Sanders, M. R. (1987). Habit reversal and DRO in the treatment of thumbsucking: An analysis of generalization and side effects. *Journal of Child Psychology and Psychiatry, 28*, 281–295.

Coie, J. D. (1996). Prevention of violence and antisocial behaviour. In: R. D. Peters & R. J. McMahon (Eds), *Preventing childhood disorders, substance abuse, and delinquency* (pp. 1–18). Thousand Oaks, CA: Sage.

Connell, S., Sanders, M. R., & Markie Dadds, C. (1997). Self-directed behavioural family intervention for parents of oppositional children in rural and remote areas. *Behaviour Modification, 21*, 379–408.

Cummings, E. M., & Davies, P. (1994). *Children and marital conflict: The impact of family dispute and resolution.* New York: Guildford Press.

Cunningham, C. E. (1996). Improving availability, utilization, and cost efficacy of parent training programs for children with disruptive behaviour disorders. In: R. D. Peters & R. J. McMahon (Eds), *Preventing childhood disorders, substance abuse, and delinquency* (pp. 144–160). Thousand Oaks, Sage.

Dadds, M. R. (1987). Families and the origins of child behaviour problems. *Family-Process, 26*, 341–357.

Dadds, M. R., Sanders, M. R., & Bor, W. (1984). Training children to eat independently: Evaluation of mealtime management training for parents. *Behavioural Psychotherapy, 12*, 356–366.

Dadds, M. R., Schwartz, S., & Sanders, M. R. (1987). Marital discord and treatment outcome in the treatment of childhood conduct disorders. *Journal of Consulting & Clinical Psychology, 55,* 396–403.

Davidson, W. S., & Wolfred, T. R. (1977). Evaluation of a community-based behaviour modification program for prevention of delinquency. *Community Mental Health Journal, 13,* 296–306.

Dishion, T. J., & Andrews, D. W. (1995). Preventing escalation in problem behaviours with high-risk young adolescents: Immediate and 1-year outcomes. *Journal of Consulting and Clinical Psychology, 63,* 538–548.

Dryfoos, J. G. (1990). *Adolescents at risk: Prevalence and prevention.* New York: Oxford University Press.

Eisenberg, L. (1989). Public policy: Risk factor or remedy. In: D. Shaffer, I. Philips & N. B. Enzer (Eds), *Prevention of mental disorders, alcohol and other drug use in children and adolescents* (pp. 125–155), (DHHS Publication No. ADM 89-1646). Washington, DC: Alcohol and Drug Use and Mental Health Administration.

Emery, R. E. (1982). Interparental conflict and the children of discord and divorce. *Psychological Bulletin, 92,* 310–330.

Fergusson, D. M., Dimond, M. E., Horwood, L. J., & Shannon, F. T. (1984). The utilisation of pre-school health and education services. *Social Science and Medicine, 19,* 1173–1180.

Fixsen, D. L., & Blasé, K. A. (1993). Creating new realities: Program development and dissemination. *Journal of Applied Behaviour Analysis, 26,* 597–615.

Fo, W. S. O., & O'Donnell, C. R. (1975). The buddy system: Effect of community intervention on delinquent offences. *Behaviour Therapy, 6,* 522–524.

Forehand, R. L., & Long, N. (1988). Outpatient treatment of the acting out child: Procedures, long term follow-up data, and clinical problems. *Advances in Behaviour Research and Therapy, 10,* 129–177.

Glick, P. C., & Lin, S. L. (1986). Recent changes in divorce and remarriage. *Journal of Marriage and the Family, 48,* 737–747.

Grych, J. H., & Fincham, F. D. (1990). Marital conflict and children's adjustment: A cognitive-contextual framework. *Psychological Bulletin, 108,* 267–290.

Hart, B., & Risley, T. R. (1975). Incidental teaching of language in the preschool. *Journal of Applied Behaviour Analysis, 8,* 411–420.

Hart, B., & Risley, T. R. (1995). *Meaningful differences in the everyday experience of young American children.* Baltimore: Paul H. Brookes Publishing.

Henggeler, S. W., Bourdin, C. M., & Mann, B. J. (1993). Advances in family therapy: Empirical foundations. *Advances in Clinical Child Psychology, 15,* 207–241.

Herbert-Jackson, E., O'Brien, M., Porterfield, J., & Risley, T. R. (1977). *The Infant Center: A complete guide to organizing and managing infant day care.* Baltimore, MD: University Park Press.

Honig, A. S., Lally, J. R., & Mathieson, P. H. (1982). Personal and social adjustment of school children after 5 years in the Family Development Program. *Child Care Quarterly, 11,* 136–146.

Irvine, A. B., Biglan, A., Smolowski, K., Metzler, C. W., & Ary, D. V. (1999). The effectiveness of a parenting skills program for parents of middle-school students in small communities. *Journal of Consulting and Clinical Psychology, 67,* 811–825.

Jacobson, N. S., & Truax, P. (1991). Clinical significance: A statistical approach to defining meaningful change in psychotherapy research. *Journal of Consulting and Clinical Psychology, 59,* 12–19.

Kazdin, A. E. (1987). Treatment of antisocial behaviour in children: Current status and future directions. *Psychological Bulletin, 102,* 187–203.

Lawton, J. M., & Sanders, M. R. (1994). Designing effective behavioural family interventions for stepfamilies. *Clinical Psychology Review, 14,* 463–496.

Le Grange, D., Eisler, I., Dare, C., & Russell, G. F. (1992). Evaluation of family treatments in adolescent anorexia nervosa: A pilot study. *International Journal of Eating Disorders, 12,* 347–357.

Liddle, H. A., & Dakof, G. A. (1995). Therapy for drug abuse: Promising but not definitive. Special issue: The effectiveness of marital and family therapy. *Journal of Marital and Family Therapy, 21,* 511–543.

Lochman, J. E. (1990). Modification of childhood aggression. In: M. Hersen, R. M. Eisler & P. M. Miller (Eds), *Progress in behaviour modification* (Vol. 25, pp. 47–85). New York: Academic Press.

Loeber, R., & Farrington, D. P. (1998). Never too early, never too late: Risk factors and successful interventions for serious and violent juvenile offenders. *Studies on Crime and Crime Prevention, 7,* 7–30.

Markie-Dadds, C., & Sanders, M. R. (submitted). Self-directed Triple P (positive parenting program) for mothers with children at-risk of developing conduct problems.

Markie-Dadds, C., Sanders, M. R., & Smith, J. (1997). *Self-directed behavioural family intervention for parents of oppositional children in rural and remote areas.* Paper presented at the 20th national conference of the Australian Association for cognitive and behaviour therapy, Brisbane, Qld.

Markman, H. J., Floyd, F.J., Stanley, S. M., & Lewis, H. C. (1987). Prevention. In: N. S. Jacobson & A. S. Gurman (Eds), *Clinical handbook of marital therapy* (pp. 173–195). New York: Guildford.

McMahon, R. J. (1999). Parent training. In: S. W. Russ & T. Ollendick (Eds), *Handbook of psychotherapies with children and families.* New York: Plenum Press.

McMahon, R. J., & Wells, K. C. (1998). Conduct problems. In: E. J. Mash & R. A. Barkley (Eds), *Treatment of childhood disorders* (2nd ed.) (pp. 111–207). New York: Guilford Press.

McNeil, C. B., Eyberg, S., Eisenstadt, T. H., Newcomb, K., & Funderbunk, B. (1991). Parent child interaction therapy with behaviour problem children: Generalization of treatment effects to the school setting. *Journal of Clinical Child Psychology, 20,* 140–151.

Morrisey-Kane, E., & Prinz, R. J. (1999). Engagement in child and adolescent treatment: The role of parental cognitions and attributions. *Clinical Child and Family Psychology Review, 2,* 183–198.

Mrazek, P., & Haggerty, R. J. (1994). *Reducing the risks for mental disorders.* Washington, DC: National Academy Press.

National Council of Women of Australia. (1999). *Balancing life and work.* National Council of Women of Australia, Melbourne, VIC.

National Institute of Mental Health. (1998). *Priorities for prevention research at NIMH: A report by the national advisory mental health council workgroup on mental disorders prevention research* (NIH Publication No. 98-4321). Washinton, DC: U.S. Government Printing Office.

Nicholson, J. M., & Sanders, M. R. (1999). Randomized controlled trial of behavioural family intervention for the treatment of child behaviour problems in stepfamilies. *Journal of Divorce and Remarriage, 30,* 1–23.

O'Dell, S. (1974). Training parents in behaviour modification: A review. *Psychological Bulletin, 81,* 418–433.

Offord, D. R. (1989). Conduct disorder: Risk factors and prevention. In: D. Shaffer, I. Philips & N. B. Enzer (Eds), *Prevention of mental disorders, alcohol and other drug use in children and adolescents* (pp. 273–307, DHHS Publication No. ADM 89-1646) Washington, DC: Alcohol, Drug Use and Mental health Administration.

Patterson, G. R. (1982). *Coercive family process.* Eugene, OR: Castalia Press.

Patterson, G. R. (1986). Performance models for antisocial boys. *American Psychologist, 41,* 432–444.

Patterson, G. R., & Chamberlain, P. (1994). A functional analysis of resistance during parent training therapy. *Clinical Psychology: Science and Practice, 1,* 53–70.

Patterson, G. R., Reid, J. B., & Dishion, T. J. (1992). *Antisocial Boys.* Eugene, OR: Castalia.

Paul, G. L. (1969). Behaviour modification research. In: C. M. Franks (Ed.). *Behaviour therapy: Appraisal and status* (pp. 29–62). New York: McGraw-Hill.

Ralph, A., & Sanders, M. R. (2003). Preliminary evaluation of the Group Teen Triple P program for parents of teenagers making the transition to high school. *Australian e-Journal for the Advancement of Mental Health, 2*(3). www.auseinet.com/journal/vol2iss3/ralphsanders.pdf.

Ralph, A., & Sanders, M. R. (2004). Community-based parenting program for the prevention of adolescent antisocial behaviour. *Trends and issues*, Australian Institute of Criminology, No. 282, August.

Ralph, A., Stallman, H. M., & Sanders, M. R. (submitted). School-based delivery of a brief group parenting program for parents of early adolescents: Group Teen Triple P.

Ralph, A., Toumbourou, J. W., Grigg, M. Mulcahy, R., Carr-Gregg, M., & Sanders, M. R. (2003). Early intervention to help parents manage behavioural and emotional problems in early adolescents: What parents want. *Australian e-Journal for the Advancement of Mental Health*, 2(3). www.auseinet.com/journal/vol2iss3/ralph.pdf.

Risley, T. R., Clark, H. B., & Cataldo, M. F. (1976). Behavioural technology for the normal middle class family. In: E. J. Mash, L. A. Hamerlynck & L. C. Handy (Eds), *Behaviour modification and families* (pp. 34–60). New York: Brunner/Mazel.

Robins, L. N. (1991). Conduct disorder. *Journal of Child Psychology and Psychiatry and Allied Disciplines*, *32*, 193–212.

Rutter, M. (1995). *Psychosocial disorder in young people: Time trends and their causes*. London: Wiley.

Rutter, M., Cox, A., Tupling, C., Berger, M., & Yule, W. (1975). Attainment in two geographical areas: 1. The prevalence of psychiatric disorder. *British Journal of Psychiatry*, *126*, 493–509.

Rutter, M., & Quinton, D. (1984). Parental psychiatric disorder: Effects on children. *Psychological-Medicine*, *14*, 853–880.

Sanders, M. R. (1992). Enhancing the impact of behavioural family intervention with children: Emerging perspectives. *Behaviour Change*, *9*, 115–119.

Sanders, M. R. (Ed.) (1995). *Healthy families, healthy nation: Strategies for promoting family mental health in Australia*. Queensland, Australia: Australian Academic Press.

Sanders, M. R. (1996). New directions in behavioural family intervention with children. In: T. H. Ollendick & R. J. Prinz (Eds), *Advances in clinical child psychology* (Vol. 18, pp. 283–330). New York: Plenum Press.

Sanders, M. R. (1998). The empirical status of psychological interventions with families of children and adolescents. In: L. L'Abate (Ed.). *Family psychopathology: The relational roots of dysfunctional behaviour*. New York: Guildford Press.

Sanders, M. R. (1999). Triple P-positive parenting program: Towards an empirically validated multilevel parenting and family support strategy for the prevention of behaviour and emotional problems in children. *Clinical Child and Family Psychology*, *2*, 71–90.

Sanders, M. R., Bor, B., & Dadds, M. R. (1984). Modifying bedtime disruptions in children using stimulus control and contingency management procedures. *Behavioural Psychotherapy*, *12*, 130–141.

Sanders, M. R., & Dadds, M. R. (1982). The effects of planned activities and child management training: An analysis of setting generality. *Behaviour Therapy*, *13*, 1–11.

Sanders, M. R., & Duncan, S. B. (1995). Empowering families: Policy, training, and research issues in promoting family mental health in Australia. *Behaviour Change*, *12*, 109–121.

Sanders, M. R. & Glynn, E. L. (1981). Training parents in behavioural self-management: An analysis of generalization and maintenance effects. *Journal of Applied Behaviour Analysis*, *14*, 223–237.

Sanders, M. R., & McFarland, M. L. (2000). The treatment of depressed mothers with disruptive children: A controlled evaluation of cognitive behavioural family intervention. *Behaviour Therapy*, *31*, 89–112.

Sanders, M. R., Lynch, M., & Markie-Dadds, C. (1994). *Every parent's workbook: A guide to positive parenting*. Brisbane, Australia: Australian Academic Press.

Sanders, M. R., Markie-Dadds, C., & Turner, K. M. T. (1998). *Practitioner's manual for enhanced Triple P*. Brisbane, Australia: Families International Publishing.

Sanders, M. R., Markie-Dadds, C., Tully, L., & Bor, B. (2000a). The Triple P – Positive Parenting Program: A comparison of enhanced, standard and self-directed behavioural family intervention for parents of children with early onset conduct problems. *Journal of Consulting and Clinical Psychology, 68*, 624–640.

Sanders, M. R., Montgomery, D. T., & Brechman-Toussaint, M. L. (2000b). The mass media and prevention of child behaviour problems: The evaluation of a television series to promote positive outcomes for parents and their children. *Journal of Child Psychology and Psychiatry, 41*, 939–948.

Sanders, M. R., Nicholson, J. M., & Floyd, F. J. (1997). Couples' relationships and children. In: W. K. Halford & H. J. Markman (Eds), *Clinical handbook of marriage and couples interventions* (pp. 225–253). Chichester, England UK: Wiley.

Sanders, M. R., Shepherd, R. W., Cleghorn, G., & Woolford, H. (1994). The treatment of recurrent abdominal pain in children. A controlled comparison of cognitive-behavioural family intervention and standard pediatric care. *Journal of Consulting and Clinical Psychology, 62*, 306–314.

Sanders, M. R., Tully, L. A., Baade, P., Lynch, M. E., Heywood, A., Pollard, G., & Youlden, D. (1999). A survey of parenting practices in Queensland: Implications for Mental Health Promotion. *Health Promotion Journal of Australia, 9*, 105–114.

Sanders, M. R., Tully, L. A., Turner, K. M. T., Maher, C., & McAuliffe, C. (2003). Training GPs in parent consultation skills: An evaluation of training for Triple P – Positive Parenting Program. *Australian Family Physician, 32*, 1–6.

Schreibman, L., Kaneko, W. M., & Koegel, R. L. (1991). Positive affect of parents of autistic children: A comparison across two teaching techniques. *Behaviour Therapy, 22*, 479–490.

Serketich, W. J., & Dumas, J. E. (1996). The effectiveness of behavioural parent training to modify antisocial behaviour in children: A meta-analysis. *Behaviour Therapy, 27*, 171–186.

Spoth, R. L., Redmond, C., & Shin, C. (2001). Randomised trial of brief family interventions for general populations: Adolescent substance use outcomes 4 years following baseline. *Journal of Consulting and Clinical Psychology, 67*, 619–630.

Spoth, R. L., Redmond, C., Trudeau, L., & Shin, C. (2002). Longitudinal substance initiation outcomes for a universal preventive intervention combining family and school programs. *Psychology of Addictive Behaviors, 16*, 129–134.

Stallman, H. M., Ralph, A., & Sanders, M. R. (submitted). Evaluation of self-directed teen Triple P: A behavioural family intervention to reduce risk factors for adolescent behavioural and emotional problems.

Taylor, C. B. (1999). *Population-based psychotherapy: Issues related to combining risk factor reduction and clinical treatment in defined populations.* Paper presented at the 29th annual congress of the European Association of behavioural and cognitive therapies, Dresden, Germany.

Taylor, T. K., & Biglan, A. (1998). Behavioural family interventions for improving child-rearing: A review of the literature for clinicians and policy makers. *Clinical Child and Family Psychology, 1*, 41–60.

Turner, K. M. T., Sanders, M. R., & Wall, C. R. (1994). Behavioural parent training versus dietary education in the treatment of children with persistent feeding difficulties. *Behaviour Change, 11*, 242–258.

Turner, K. M. T., Nicholson, J. M., & Sanders, M. R. (submitted). The influence of self-efficacy and training, program and work-place factors on the implementation of behavioural family intervention and primary care.

Turner, K. M. T., Markie-Dadds, C., & Sanders, M. R. (1997). *Facilitator's manual for group Triple P.* Brisbane, Australia: Families International Publishing.

Vassallo, S., Smart, D., Sanson, A., Dussuyer, I., McKendry, B., Toumbourou, J., Prior, M., & Oberklaid, F. (2002). *Patterns and precursors of adolescent antisocial behaviour: The first report December 2002.* Melbourne: Crime Prevention Victoria.

Warr, P. (1982). Psychological aspects of employment and unemployment. *Psychological Medicine*, *12*, 7–11.

Webster-Stratton, C. (1989). Systematic comparison of consumer satisfaction of three cost effective parent training programs for conduct problem children. *Behaviour Therapy*, *20*, 103–115.

Webster-Stratton, C. (1998). Preventing conduct problems in head start children: Strengthening parenting competencies. *Journal of Consulting and Clinical Psychology*, *66*, 715–730.

Webster-Stratton, C. (1994). Advancing videotape parent training: A comparison study. *Journal of Consulting and Clinical Psychology*, *62*, 583–593.

Weissberg, R. P., Caplan, M., & Harwood, R. L. (1991). Promoting competent young people in competence-enhancing environments: A systems-based perspective on primary prevention. *Journal of Consulting and Clinical Psychology*, *59*, 830–841.

White, B. L. (1990). *The first three years of life*. New York: Prentice Hall Press.

Yarnold, B. M. (1998). The use of alcohol by Miami's adolescent public school students 1992: Peers, risk taking, and availability as central forces. *Journal of Drug Education*, *28*, 211–233.

Zubrick, S. R., Silburn, S. R., Garton, A., Burton, Dalby, R., Carlton, J., Shepherd, C., & Lawrence, D. (1995). *Western Australian child health survey: Developing health and well-being in the nineties*. Perth, Western Australia: Australian Bureaus of Statistics and the Institute for Child Health Research. (ISNNO 642 20754 2).

Zubrick, S. R., Northey, K., Silburn, S. R., Lawrence, D., Williams, A. A., Blair, E., Robertson, D., & Sanders, M. (in press). Prevention of child behavior problems through universal implementation of a group behavioral family intervention. *Prevention Science.*

Author Index

Subject Index